DISCARD
CADL

The Practical Handbook of Library Architecture

ALA Editions purchases fund advocacy, awareness, and accreditation programs for library professionals worldwide.

The Practical Handbook of Library Architecture

Creating Building Spaces that Work

FRED SCHLIPF
+ JOHN A. MOORMAN

CHICAGO 2018

FRED SCHLIPF has been hanging out in library buildings since the early 1940s (at about the age of four, he turned out all the lights in the Detroit Lakes (Minnesota) Public Library one evening—a happy moment that is still both bright and dark in his memory), and has been working for libraries and teaching about libraries and consulting on library buildings since he was 17. He's been a library school faculty member for over 50 years, and he spent nearly 33 years as director of The Urbana Free Library, the public library of Urbana, Illinois (just down the street from the University of Illinois). He's done formal building consulting for between 150 and 200 libraries and quick consulting for many more, and he visits library buildings everywhere he goes. He has a BA from Carleton College and an MA and PhD from the Graduate Library School of the University of Chicago. He has served on dozens of committees and task forces of the American Library Association, Illinois State Library, Illinois Library Association, local library groups in Illinois, and the Illuminating Engineering Society of North America. He was Illinois Librarian of the Year in 2000.

JOHN A. MOORMAN has worked as director of five public libraries and a multi-type library system, most recently the Decatur (Illinois) Public Library and the Williamsburg (Virginia) Regional Library. He has a PhD from the University of Illinois library school. He has been active in state and national library associations. When not working with buildings, he developed a specialty in legislative matters, served as a registered lobbyist, and chaired legislative-related committees for the Illinois and Virginia Library Associations. He is a past president of the Virginia Library Association and a lifelong elected honorary member of that association. Within the American Library Association (ALA) he served on the Public Library Association's Board of Directors, the ALA Council, and the ALA Executive Board, as well as serving on, and chairing, many committees and task forces.

© 2018 by the American Library Association

Extensive effort has gone into ensuring the reliability of the information in this book; however, the publisher makes no warranty, express or implied, with respect to the material contained herein.

ISBN: 978-0-8389-1553-0 (paper)

Library of Congress Cataloging-in-Publication Data
Names: Schlipf, Frederick A., author. | Moorman, John A., author.
Title: The practical handbook of library architecture : creating building spaces that work / Frederick A. Schlipf, John Moorman.
Description: Chicago : ALA Editions, an imprint of the American Library Association, 2017. | Includes bibliographical references and index.
Identifiers: LCCN 2017007498 | ISBN 9780838915530 (pbk. : alk. paper)
Subjects: LCSH: Library architecture—Handbooks, manuals, etc. | Library buildings—Design and construction—Handbooks, manuals, etc. | Library fittings and supplies—Handbooks, manuals, etc. | Library architecture—United States—Handbooks, manuals, etc. | Library buildings—United States—Handbooks, manuals, etc.
Classification: LCC Z679 .S33 2017 | DDC 727/.8—dc23 LC record available at https://lccn.loc.gov/2017007498

Cover design by Kimberly Thornton. Book design by Alejandra Diaz in the Minion Pro and Ropa Soft Pro typefaces.

♾ This paper meets the requirements of ANSI/NISO Z39.48-1992 (Permanence of Paper).

Printed in the United States of America
22 21 20 19 18   5 4 3 2 1

Contents

Preface   xxxi

PART I | INTRODUCTION

Ch 1   Introduction   3

Ch 2   More Than Two Hundred Snappy Rules for Good and Evil in Library Architecture   9

PART II | ABOUT LIBRARY BUILDINGS

Ch 3   The Library Construction Process   23

     I. Introduction   23

     II. Motivations   23

     III. Building Programs   24

     IV. Building Consultants   26

     V. Architects and Design   28

     VI. Construction Options and Site Selection   33

     VII. Dysfunctional Design Concepts   37

     VIII. Schematic Designs   39

     IX. Renderings and Models   41

     X. Money   42

     XI. Design Development   44

     XII. Bid Documents, aka Construction Documents   44

XIII. Bidding **45**

XIV. Construction Management **47**

XV. Design-Build Projects **47**

XVI. Groundbreaking **48**

XVII. The Construction Process **49**

XVIII. Moving **53**

XIX. Ribbon Cutting **53**

XX. Ten-Month Post-Occupancy Evaluation **55**

XXI. Rewards for the Stressed-Out Librarian **55**

Ch 4 **Basic Configuration of Library Spaces** **57**

I. Introduction **57**

II. External Configuration **61**
- A. Structural Shapes, *61*
- B. Compass Orientation of Entrances, *61*
- C. Where to Put the Entrance, *62*
- D. Number of Entrances, *62*

III. Internal Layout and Room Shapes **63**
- A. Avoid Labyrinths, *63*
- B. Maintain Sight Lines, *64*
- C. Avoid Strangely Shaped Spaces, *65*
- D. When Possible, Use "Main Streets", *65*
- E. Avoid "Beads-on-a-String" Designs, *66*
- F. The Wonderful T-Shaped Space, *66*
- G. Let Functional Needs Drive Structural Spaces, *66*

IV. Traffic Flow **67**

V. Window Placement **71**

VI. Artistic Ceiling Shapes **73**

VII. Curved Walls **74**

VIII. Basements **74**

IX. Snappy Rules on the Basic Configuration of Library Spaces **76**

| Ch 5 | **Evaluating Library Buildings by Walking Around** | 79 |

    I. Reasons for Evaluating Buildings on Your Own   79

    II. The Problems with Asking the Staff   80

    III. Appearance   80

    IV. Sense of Welcome   81

    V. Staff Service Points   82

    VI. Natural Light   82

    VII. Artificial Light   83

    VIII. Acoustics   84

    IX. Electrical Wiring   85

    X. HVAC (Heating, Ventilating, and Air Conditioning)   85

    XI. Furnishings   86

    XII. Storage   87

    XIII. Fragile Construction Materials   88

    XIV. Flexibility   88

    XV. Functional Arrangement of Rooms   89

    XVI. Ceilings   89

    XVII. Acrophobia   89

    XVIII. Floor Coverings   90

    XIX. Ornamental Spaces   90

    XX. Protection from the Elements   90

    XXI. Security   91

    XXII. Expandability   92

    XXIII. Water Features   92

    XXIV. Omissions   92

Ch 6   Dysfunctional Designs   93

    I. Introduction   **93**

    II. Common Dysfunctional Architectural Design Concepts   **96**
- A. Skylights, *96*
- B. Atriums, *99*
- C. Designer Staircases, *103*
- D. Courtyards, *111*
- E. Indoor Water Features, *112*
- F. Non-Rectangular Interior Spaces, *113*
- G. Bad Lighting, *115*
- H. Multiple Public Entrances, *120*
- I. Architectural Solutions to Furniture Problems, *122*
- J. Non-Acoustic Ceilings, *123*
- K. Inflexibility, *125*
- L. Bad Sight Lines, *126*
- M. Excessive Use of Soffits, *128*
- N. Balconies, *129*
- O. Features That Panic People with Acrophobia, *130*
- P. Features That Lead to Particular Maintenance Problems, *132*
- Q. Buildings That Can't Be Expanded, *139*
- R. Screen Porches, *140*
- S. Monitor Windows, *141*
- T. Use of Esoteric Glass, *142*
- U. Dysfunctional Service Desks, *144*
- V. Reading Terraces, *146*
- W. Problem Features Yet to Be Invented, *147*

    III. In Defense of Designers   **148**

    IV. The Good News   **150**

    V. Snappy Rules on Dysfunctional Design   **150**

Ch 7   Converting Non-Library Spaces to Public Libraries   153

    I. Introduction   **153**

    II. Planning Conversions of Non-Library Spaces   **154**

    III. Rationales for Conversions   **155**
- A. Good Reasons for Conversions, *155*
- B. And (of Course) Bad Reasons for Conversions, *156*

IV. **Common Problems in Conversions** 157
- A. Poor Natural Light and Insufficient Windows, 157
- B. Unwanted Partitions and Floors, 157
- C. Bad Locations, 157
- D. Obsolete or Nonexistent Air Conditioning, 158
- E. Insufficient Floor Strength, 158
- F. Lack of Utilities, 159
- G. Lack of Expansion Space, 159
- H. Accessibility Problems, 159
- I. Parking Problems, 160
- J. Bearing Walls, 160
- K. Basements, 161
- L. Cheap Construction, 161
- M. Code Compliance Problems, 162
- N. Asbestos, Lead Paint, and Other Pollutants, 162
- O. Converting Historic Structures, 162
- P. Buildings "Designed for Adding an Extra Floor", 163
- Q. Insufficient Electrical Wiring and Outlets, 164
- R. Unworkable Lighting, 164
- S. Low Ceilings, 164
- T. The High Cost of Conversions, 165

V. **Types of Buildings That Might Be Converted to Libraries** 165
- A. Schools, 165
- B. Banks, 167
- C. Department Stores, 167
- D. Strip Malls, 168
- E. Big Box Stores, 169
- F. Historic Stores on Courthouse Squares, 170
- G. Churches, 172
- H. Houses, 173
- I. Automobile Salesrooms, 174
- J. Abandoned Government Buildings, 174

VI. **Summary** 175

VII. **Snappy Rules for Converting Non-Library Spaces to Public Libraries** 177

PART III | BASIC STEPS

Ch 8 Programming 181

    I. Introduction **181**

    II. Purpose of Building Programs **184**
- A. Cookbooks for Library Design, *184*
- B. Presentations to Your Community, *185*
- C. Proactive Statements of Needs, *186*
- D. Required Documentation for Grant Applications, *187*
- E. Sorting out Differences of Opinion, *187*
- F. Providing an Opportunity for User Input before Design, *187*

    III. Input on Programs **188**
- A. Observations by Consultants, *188*
- B. Interviews with Staff and Management, *188*
- C. Focus Groups, *190*
- D. Surveys, *197*

    IV. Typical Contents of Programs **198**
- A. Table of Contents, *198*
- B. Description of the Agency the Library Will Serve, *201*
- C. Long-Range Plans as They Relate to Space Needs, *202*
- D. Review of Applicable Service Standards and Restrictions, *202*
- E. Functional Evaluations of Current Facilities, *204*
- F. Structural Evaluations of Current Facilities, *204*
- G. Enumeration of Required Spaces and Contents, *205*
- H. Things That Don't Belong in Programs, *207*

    V. Methods of Space Estimating **208**
- A. Sources of Planning Numbers, *208*
- B. Planning Space for Collections, *209*
- C. Additional Space, *211*
- D. Putting Numbers Together, *212*

    VI. Who Should Write Your Building Program? **214**
- A. Programs by Building Consultants, *214*
- B. Programs by Architects, *215*
- C. Programs by Owners, *216*

    VII. How to Hire Building Consultants **216**

VIII. Program-Writing Methods **218**
   A. Successive Program Drafts, *218*
   B. Cutting Building Programs, *219*
   C. Final Review with Architects and Library Building Consultants, *220*

IX. Two-Phase Building Programs **221**

X. What to Do When Your Architects Ignore Your Programs **222**

XI. Quick Space Estimates Using Formulas **223**

XII. Conclusions **224**

XIII. Snappy Rules on Programming **224**

Ch 9 Design **227**

I. Introduction **227**

II. The Role of the Architect in the Building Process **228**
   A. Program Review or Verification, *230*
   B. Evaluation of Existing Structures. *232*
   C. Feasibility Studies, *234*
   D. Schematic Design, *234*
   E. Estimating, *239*
   F. Assistance with Fundraising, *240*
   G. Design Development, *243*
   H. Construction Documents, *244*

III. Hiring an Architect **247**
   A. Locating Architectural Firms, *248*
   B. Investigating the Prior Work of Architectural Firms, *249*
   C. Requests for Qualifications, *252*
   D. Proposals from Architectural Firms, *260*
   E. Special Problems with Teams, *261*
   F. Evaluating Proposals, *262*
   G. Interviews, *263*
   H. Possible Questions for Architect Interviews, *268*
   I. Final Selection, *272*
   J. Contracting with Architects, *274*
   K. Understanding Architects, *278*

IV. Design Competitions **279**

V. Planning Groups **280**

VI. What Can Go Wrong When You Work with Architects? **281**
   A. Loss of Control to Architects, *281*
   B. Architects Who Ignore Building Programs, *282*
   C. Architectural Firms That Substitute Personnel, *282*
   D. Architects Who Refuse to Listen to Owners, *283*
   E. Owners Who Refuse to Pay Attention to the Process, *284*
   F. Owners with No Practical Experience with Buildings, *284*
   G. Owners Who Are Painfully Indecisive, *285*
   H. Owners Who Want to Do Illegal Things, *286*
   I. Architects Who Do Sloppy Work, *286*
   J. Owners Who Refuse to Be Realistic about Costs, *287*
   K. Owners Who Think They Know It All (but Don't), *287*
   L. Architects Who Cut Corners to Save Their Own Time or to Increase Profits, *287*
   M. Architects Who Are Bullies and Raging Egomaniacs, *288*

VII. Snappy Rules on Design **289**

Ch 10 Site Selection **293**

I. Introduction **293**

II. Evaluating Potential Sites **294**
   A. Always Employ Professionals, *295*
   B. Soil Conditions, *297*
   C. Utilities, *298*
   D. Surface Water Runoff Detention and Retention, *300*
   E. Subsurface Water, *301*
   F. Floodplains, *301*
   G. Site Configuration, *302*
   H. Site Topography, *302*
   I. Brownfield Sites, *303*
   J. Good and Bad Neighbors, *305*
   K. Size, *306*
   L. Historic Buildings and Neighborhoods, *315*
   M. Archaeology, *318*
   N. Orientation to the Compass, *319*
   O. Easements, *320*
   P. Land Ownership, *320*

III. Special Site Needs of Various Types of Libraries 321
    A. Public Libraries, *321*
    B. Academic Libraries, *329*
    C. School Libraries, *330*
    D. Special Libraries, *331*

IV. Summary 332

V. Snappy Rules on Library Site Selection 333

Ch 11   Zoning, Covenants, and Codes   337

I. Introduction 337

II. Zoning 338

III. Covenants 340

IV. Codes 341
    A. Building and Life-Safety Codes, *341*
    B. Energy Codes, *341*
    C. Accessibility Codes, *342*

V. LEED 344

VI. Snappy Rules on Zoning, Covenants, and Codes 345

Ch 12   Construction   347

I. Introduction 347

II. Standard Steps in the Construction Process 348
    A. Construction Documents and Specifications, *348*
    B. Bidding, *349*
    C. Awarding Contracts, *356*
    D. Construction Administration, *357*
    E. Design-Bid-Build Projects, *358*

III. Construction Management Firms 366
    A. Traditional Construction Management, *367*
    B. Construction Management at Risk, *367*
    C. Value Engineering, *368*
    D. Hiring Construction Managers, *368*

xiv Contents

    IV. Design-Build Projects   **370**

    V. Move-Out vs. Phased Construction   **371**

    VI. The Librarian's Role in Construction   **373**

    VII. Public Ceremonies   **374**
- A. Introduction, *374*
- B. Groundbreakings, *375*
- C. Laying Cornerstones, *377*
- D. Signing Beams, *377*
- E. Topping Out, *378*
- F. Phase I Completion Events, *379*
- G. Tours of the Work in Progress, *379*
- H. Construction Plaques, *380*
- I. Donor Recognition Plaques, *382*
- J. Donor Receptions, *382*
- K. Ribbon Cuttings, *382*

    VIII. Punch Lists   **384**

    IX. Post-Occupancy Inspection   **388**

    X. Snappy Rules on Construction   **388**

Ch 13   Remodeling and Expanding Library Buildings   **391**

    I. Introduction   **391**

    II. Comparative Costs   **392**

    III. Problems with the Reuse and Expansion of Old Library Buildings   **393**
- A. Changed Building Codes, *393*
- B. New Code Categories Resulting from Expansion, *394*
- C. Asbestos and Other Pollutants, *394*
- D. Bearing Walls, *395*
- E. HVAC, *396*
- F. Electrical Wiring, *397*
- G. Windows, *399*
- H. Cheap or Fragile Construction Materials, *400*
- I. Poor Functional Locations, *400*
- J. Matching Historic Exteriors, *401*
- K. Adjacent Land, *403*
- L. Accessibility, *405*
- M. Basements in Expanded Historic Buildings, *406*

IV. Phasing Expansion Projects   407
   A. Advantages of Phased Construction, *407*
   B. Problems with Phasing, *407*
   C. So Why Phase Your Project?, *409*

V. Snappy Rules on Remodeling and Expanding Libraries   410

PART IV | MONEY

Ch 14   Building Costs   415

I. Introduction   415

II. Capital Costs   416
   A. Projecting Building Costs Prior to Design, *416*
   B. Estimating, *416*
   C. Components of Building Costs, *418*

III. Anticipating Operating Costs   423

IV. Snappy Rules on Building Costs   425

Ch 15   Funding   427

I. Introduction   427

II. Sources of Money   428
   A. Money on Hand, *428*
   B. Savings Set Aside from Operating Funds, *429*
   C. Referendums and Bond Issues, *429*
   D. Bequests, *430*
   E. Mortgages, *432*
   F. Fundraising, *432*
   G. 501(c)(3) Foundations, *438*
   H. Grants, *439*
   I. Special Appropriations, *442*

III. Snappy Rules on Funding   442

IV. Bibliography   443

PART V | LIBRARY SPACES

Ch 16   User Seating   447

    I. Introduction **447**

    II. How Much User Seating? **450**

    III. How Library Furniture Is Ordered **452**
        A. Inventories of Existing Furniture, *452*
        B. Selecting New Furniture, *452*

    IV. Tables **453**
        A. Configurations, *453*
        B. Requirements, *455*
        C. Options, *458*
        D. Adaptations Based on Age of Users, *458*

    V. Chairs **460**
        A. Soft Seating, *460*
        B. Chairs for Seating at Tables, *464*
        C. Padded Benches, *466*
        D. Booths, *466*
        E. Window Seats, *466*
        F. Novelty Seating for Children, *467*

    VI. Placement of User Seating in Library Buildings **468**
        A. Adequate Clearances, *468*
        B. Seating Next to Shelving, *469*
        C. Seating by Windows, *469*
        D. Movable Seating, *470*
        E. Seating without Users' Backs to the Room, *470*

    VII. Snappy Rules on User Seating **471**

Ch 17   Collection Storage   475

    I. Introduction **475**

    II. Steel Cantilever Shelving **477**
        A. Advantages of Steel Cantilever Shelving, *478*
        B. Specifying Steel Cantilever Shelving, *478*
        C. Compact Shelving, *485*

III. Alternatives to Steel Cantilever Shelving **487**
    A. Shelving with End-Supported Shelves, *487*
    B. Wood Shelving, *488*
    C. Non-Library Shelving, *489*

IV. Shelving Placement **489**
    A. All Library Floors Need to Be Strong Enough for Books, *489*
    B. Be Careful with Perimeter Shelving, *490*
    C. Ranges of Shelves Belong in Parallel Rows, *490*
    D. Absolutely No Dead-End Stack Aisles, *491*
    E. Aisles Oriented for Best Practical Staff Oversight, *491*
    F. Electrical Outlets Everywhere, *492*
    G. Unbroken Call Number Ranges, *492*
    H. Lighting Stack Aisles, *493*
    I. Stack Aisle Widths, *497*
    J. Cross Aisles, *498*
    K. Seismic Issues, *498*
    L. Multi-Deck Shelving Supported by Shelving Columns, *499*
    M. Marking the Contents of Shelving Ranges, *499*
    N. Shelving on Casters, *500*

V. Other Types of Storage **501**
    A. Flip Bins, *501*
    B. Spinners, *501*
    C. Atlas Cases, *502*
    D. Map Cases, *503*
    E. Dictionary Stands, *503*
    F. Microfilm and Microfiche Cabinets, *503*
    G. Pamphlet Files, *504*
    H. Tubs for Board Books, *505*
    I. Display Shelves, *505*

VI. High-Density Storage **506**

VII. Estimating Required Space for Collection Storage **506**

VIII. Snappy Rules on Collection Storage **506**

Ch 18   **Public Service Desks**   **509**

    I. Introduction **509**

    II. Typical Functions of Public Service Desks **510**

III. Placement of Public Service Desks 512

IV. Essential Features of Public Service Desks 514

V. Testing Proposed Public Service Desks 518
    A. Evaluating Schematic Designs, *518*
    B. Using Trial Models of Desks, *519*

VI. Types of Public Service Desks 520
    A. Lending Desks, *520*
    B. Reference and Reader Guidance Desks, *540*
    C. Desks for Entrance and Exit Control, *544*
    D. Concierge Desks, *544*
    E. Desks for Special Collections, *545*
    F. Multifunction Desks, *545*

VII. Public Service Desks and Security 546
    A. Exit Control, *546*
    B. Oversight of Library Spaces, *547*
    C. Security for Library Staff, *548*

VIII. Common Problems in the Design of Public Service Desks 548
    A. Monumentality, *548*
    B. Inflexibility, *550*
    C. Fragile Top Surfaces, *553*
    D. Persistence of Obsolete Desks Due to Sentiment, *554*
    E. Bad Color Choices, *554*
    F. Fortress Desks, *555*
    G. Obsolete Features Still Found in Lending Desks, *556*
    H. Bad Lighting, *559*
    I. Bad Acoustics, *559*

IX. Library Supply Company Service Desks 560

X. Encouraging Valedictory Remarks 560

XI. Snappy Rules on Public Service Desks 561

Ch 19 Program and Study Rooms 563

I. Introduction 563

II. General Features of Typical Meeting Rooms 564
    A. Room Configuration, *564*
    B. Determining Meeting Room Capacities, *565*
    C. Calculating Required Space, *565*
    D. Locating Program Rooms in Buildings, *569*

E. Furnishings, *570*

F. Lighting, *572*

G. Acoustics, *574*

H. HVAC, *577*

I. Coat Storage, *578*

J. Wiring, *579*

K. Audiovisual Equipment, *581*

L. Storage Closets, *582*

M. Kitchenettes, *586*

N. Floor Coverings, *588*

O. Ceiling Height, *589*

P. Accessibility, *590*

Q. Security, *591*

III. **Types of Program and Study Rooms 592**

A. Auditoriums, *592*

B. Classrooms, *593*

C. Multipurpose Rooms and Community Rooms, *595*

D. Conference and Seminar Rooms, *597*

E. Quiet Reading Rooms, *599*

F. Study Rooms, *601*

G. Children's Craft and Story Rooms, *603*

H. Multilevel Children's Reading Rooms, *608*

I. Maker Spaces, *610*

J. Faculty Studies, *610*

IV. **Special Problems and Opportunities with Program and Study Rooms 611**

A. Loss of Control to Parent Institutions, *611*

B. Donor Recognition Opportunities, *611*

C. Meeting Room Issues, *612*

V. **Common Errors in the Design of Program and Study Rooms 614**

A. Undersized Meeting Rooms, *614*

B. Inadequate Storage Space, *614*

C. Study Rooms with Opaque Walls, *615*

D. Inadequate Wiring, *615*

E. Inadequate Kitchenettes, *615*

F. No After-Hours Access, *616*

G. Inadequate Acoustics, *616*

H. Tricky Lighting Control Devices, *616*

I. Movable Room Dividers, *617*

J. Folding Chairs, *617*

VI. **Snappy Rules on Program and Study Rooms 617**

Ch 20 Display and Exhibit Areas   619

    I. Introduction **619**

    II. Open Exhibit Areas **621**

    III. Display Cases **621**

    IV. Wall Spaces for Hanging Artworks **623**

    V. Pinnable Surfaces **623**

    VI. Security Issues **624**

    VII. Permanent Works of Art **625**

    VIII. Exterior Displays **625**

    IX. Combined Libraries and Museums **626**

    X. Policies on Displays and Exhibits **626**

    XI. Snappy Rules on Display and Exhibit Areas **627**

Ch 21 Restrooms   629

    I. Introduction **629**

    II. Building Codes **631**

    III. Fixtures and Equipment **632**

        A. Toilets, *632*

        B. Stall Enclosures, *634*

        C. Urinals, *635*

        D. Washbasins, *636*

        E. Soap Dispensers, *636*

        F. Hand Drying, *638*

        G. Mirrors, *639*

        H. Shelves, *640*

        I. Feminine Hygiene Products, *640*

        J. Hypodermic Needles, *640*

        K. Ventilation, *640*

        L. Mop Basins, *641*

    IV. Accommodations for Children and Infants **641**

        A. Children's Restrooms, *641*

        B. Changing Tables, *642*

        C. Infant Seats, *642*

D. Restrooms for Story and Craft Rooms, *643*

E. Restrooms for Users Needing Assistance by People of the Opposite Sex, *643*

V. **Size and Location of Restrooms** **643**

A. Number of Fixtures, *643*

B. Locations, *644*

C. Staff Restrooms, *645*

D. Implications for Expansion, *645*

E. Accommodations for Transgender Users, *646*

VI. **Security** **646**

A. Staff Oversight, *646*

B. Single-User Restrooms, *647*

C. Doorless Restrooms, *648*

D. Video Surveillance, *648*

E. Restrooms as Tornado Shelters, *648*

VII. **Lighting** **649**

A. Motion Sensors, *649*

B. Manually Switched Lighting, *650*

C. Light Distribution, *650*

VIII. **Planning for Maintenance** **650**

A. Floor Coverings, *650*

B. Floor Drains, *651*

C. Wall Coverings, *651*

D. Graffiti, *651*

IX. **Snappy Rules on Library Restrooms** **652**

Ch 22 **Staff Workrooms** **655**

I. **Introduction** **655**

II. **General Considerations for Staff Workrooms** **655**

III. **Individual Workrooms** **657**

IV. **Architectural Features of Workrooms** **659**

A. Wiring, *659*

B. Natural and Artificial Light, *659*

C. Windows to the Rest of the Library, *660*

D. Running Water, *660*

E. Temperature Control, *661*

F. Ventilation, *661*

G. Restrooms, *661*

H. Clothes Washers and Dryers, *661*

I. Built-In Furnishings, *662*

V. **Workroom Furnishings** **662**

A. Desks, *662*

B. Modular Office System Workstations, *663*

C. Workroom Chairs, *663*

D. Space for Visitors, *664*

E. Worktables, *664*

F. Storage Cabinets, *665*

G. Coat and Purse Storage, *665*

H. Shelving, *665*

I. File Storage, *666*

J. Wall Space, *666*

K. Open Floor Space, *667*

L. Printers, *667*

M. Telephones, *667*

N. Paper Shredders, *667*

O. Refrigerators, *667*

P. Bulletin Boards, *668*

Q. Built-In Cabinetry, *668*

R. Ventilation, *668*

S. Secure Storage, *668*

T. Flexibility, *669*

VI. **Spaces with Shared Equipment** **669**

VII. **Staff Conference Rooms** **669**

VIII. **Specialized Workrooms** **670**

A. Graphic Arts, *670*

B. Technical Services, *672*

C. Children's Departments, *674*

IX. **Workspaces in Otherwise Public Areas** **676**

X. **Required Workroom Sizes** **677**

XI. **Snappy Rules on Staff Workrooms** **677**

| Ch 23 | **Staff Facilities** | **681** |

    I. Introduction   **681**

    II. Staff Lunchrooms   **682**

        A. Functions, *682*

        B. Location, *682*

        C. Food Preparation and Serving, *683*

        D. Seating, *687*

        E. Vending Machines, *687*

        F. Computer Workstations, *688*

        G. Staff Picture Boards, *688*

        H. Bulletin Boards, *688*

        I. Secluded Spaces, *689*

        J. Decor, *689*

        K. Entertainment, *689*

        L. Estimating Staff Lunchroom Space Needs, *689*

    III. Staff Restrooms   **690**

    IV. Staff Coat and Purse Storage   **692**

        A. Coat Storage, *692*

        B. Purse Storage, *693*

    V. Staff Mailboxes   **694**

    VI. Staff Bike Storage and Showers   **695**

    VII. Snappy Rules on Staff Facilities   **696**

| Ch 24 | **Storerooms** | **699** |

    I. Introduction   **699**

    II. Locations of Storage Spaces   **701**

    III. Assigned Storage Spaces   **702**

    IV. Shared Storage Spaces   **705**

    V. Meeting and Program Room Storage Spaces   **705**

    VI. Mechanical Equipment Storage Spaces   **707**

        A. Outdoor Equipment, *707*

        B. Ladders, *708*

        C. HVAC Equipment, *709*

        D. Vehicle Storage, *709*

VII. Describing Storage Spaces in Building Programs **709**

VIII. Protecting Storage Spaces from Looters Who Covet Your Space **711**

IX. Snappy Rules on Storerooms **712**

PART VI | TECHNICAL ISSUES

Ch 25 Lighting **717**

I. Introduction **717**

II. General Lighting Concepts **718**
   A. A Few Common Lighting Terms, *718*
   B. Illumination Levels, *720*
   C. Glare, *722*
   D. Color Rendering, *724*
   E. Color Temperature, *725*

III. Types of Light Sources **725**
   A. Incandescent, *725*
   B. Fluorescent, *728*
   C. High-Intensity Discharge (HID), *729*
   D. Light-Emitting Diodes (LEDs), *731*
   E. Selecting Light Sources, *732*

IV. Lighting Strategies **733**
   A. Uplighting, *733*
   B. Downlighting, *735*
   C. Task Lighting, *738*

V. Energy-Saving Ideas **741**
   A. Efficient Lighting, *741*
   B. Motion Sensor Switches, *742*
   C. Daylight Sensors, *743*
   D. Reduced Illumination Levels and Library Security, *744*
   E. Limits on Efficacy, *744*

VI. Common Lighting Problems and How to Avoid Them **744**
   A. Lack of Flexibility, *745*
   B. Glare, *745*
   C. Gloom, *747*
   D. Dark Perimeters, *747*

E. Architectural Features That Complicate Lighting, *748*

F. Lighting That Is Hard to Maintain, *749*

G. Buying Lighting, *754*

H. Pendant Globe Lights and Other Gimmicks, *755*

I. Troublesome Security Lighting, *755*

J. Historic Lighting Fixtures, *756*

VII. An Easy Formula for Multifunction Library Lighting **756**

VIII. Coping with Natural Light **757**

A. Compass Points Matter, *758*

B. Controlling Daylight, *761*

C. Skylights, *765*

D. Effects of Unwanted Daylight, *766*

E. Views of the Outside World, *766*

IX. A Final Word on Lighting **767**

X. Snappy Rules on Library Lighting **767**

Ch 26 Elevators, Staircases, Railings, and Ramps **771**

I. Introduction **771**

II. Elevators **772**

A. Real Elevators, *772*

B. Elevator Maintenance and Problems, *773*

C. Unfortunate Substitutes for Real Elevators, *775*

D. Dumbwaiters, *776*

III. Staircases **777**

A. Strangely Configured Staircases, *778*

B. Oddly Shaped Treads, *779*

C. Floating Staircases, *781*

D. Open Risers, *782*

E. Staircases in Atriums, *783*

F. Staircases with Central Openings, *784*

G. Glass Walls Adjacent to Staircases, *785*

H. Staircase-Like Structures, *785*

I. Unnecessary Staircases, *786*

J. Staircases and Fires, *786*

IV. Railings **787**

A. Railings That Can Be Climbed, *787*

B. Glass Railings, *788*

C. Painted Handrails, *790*
D. Railings on Narrow Walkways, *790*
E. Railings That Cannot Be Comfortably Grabbed, *791*
F. Railings That People Can Fall Through, *792*
G. Low Railings for Children, *792*

V. Ramps **792**

VI. Snappy Rules on Elevators, Staircases, Railings, and Ramps **793**

Ch 27 Electrical Systems 797

I. Introduction **797**

II. Nomenclature **798**

III. Electrical Circuits **799**

IV. Electrical Outlets **801**

V. Electrical Switches **804**

VI. Emergencies **805**

VII. Snappy Rules on Electrical Systems **806**

Ch 28 Heating, Ventilating, and Air Conditioning Systems 807

I. Introduction **807**

II. General Complexity **808**

III. Temperature Control and Zoning **810**

IV. Humidity Control **811**

V. Ductwork **812**

VI. Energy Conservation **813**

VII. Special HVAC Problems **814**

VIII. Snappy Rules on HVAC Systems **815**

Ch 29 Plumbing Systems 817

    I. Introduction **817**

    II. Food Preparation and Service Areas **818**

    III. Staff Workroom Plumbing **819**
        A. Washbasins, *819*
        B. Washers and Dryers, *819*

    IV. Custodial Workrooms **820**

    V. Hose Bibs **820**

    VI. Water "Features" **821**
        A. Indoor Water Features, *821*
        B. Outdoor Water Features, *822*

    VII. Storm Drains **823**

    VIII. Detention and Retention Basins **824**

    IX. Snappy Rules on Plumbing Systems **825**

Ch 30 Security 827

    I. Introduction **827**

    II. Security through Building Design **828**
        A. Fire-Resistant Construction, *828*
        B. Flood-Resistant Construction, *830*
        C. Single Public Entrances, *832*
        D. Good Sight Lines, *833*
        E. No Places Where People Can Be Trapped, *835*
        F. Windstorm Shelters, *836*
        G. Earthquake Preparedness, *837*
        H. Providing Security by Avoiding Shared Buildings, *838*
        I. Windows, *838*
        J. Terraces, *839*
        K. Dangerous Architectural Features, *839*

    III. Theft Control Systems **840**
        A. Typical High-Risk Materials, *840*
        B. Economic Models, *841*
        C. Improved Oversight, *842*
        D. Sequestering Theft-Prone Materials, *844*
        E. Keeping Unauthorized People out of the Library, *845*
        F. Electronic Theft-Prevention Systems, *845*

IV. Theft of Library Equipment and of Personal Possessions   **851**

V. Entrance and Exit Control Equipment   **853**
  A. Building Codes, *853*
  B. Modern Panic Hardware, *854*
  C. Key Systems, *855*
  D. Proximity and Swipe Cards, *856*

VI. Intrusion Alarms   **857**

VII. Fire Protection Systems   **859**
  A. Fire Alarm Systems, *859*
  B. Sprinkler Systems, *860*
  C. Escape Routes, *864*
  D. Portable Fire Extinguishers, *864*

VIII. Humidity Control   **865**

IX. Video Surveillance Systems   **866**
  A. Equipment Specifications, *867*
  B. Common Camera Locations, *869*

X. Miscellaneous Issues in Patron and Staff Security   **870**
  A. Panic Buttons, *870*
  B. Portable Alarm Devices, *870*
  C. Public Library Children's Departments, *871*

XI. Public Relations Implications   **872**

XII. Insurance   **872**
  A. Basic Insurance Concepts, *873*
  B. Fire and Windstorm, *877*
  C. Automotive Insurance, *880*
  D. Flood Insurance, *880*
  E. Liability Insurance, *881*
  F. Builder's Risk Insurance, *882*
  G. Insurance Not Relevant to Buildings, *882*

XIII. Snappy Rules on Library Security   **883**

| Ch 31 | Walls, Floors, and Ceilings | 885 |

    I. Introduction   **885**

    II. Health Problems   **886**

    III. Walls   **888**
        A. Controlling Sound Transmission, *888*
        B. Preventing Damage to Drywall and Paint, *888*

    IV. Floors   **891**
        A. Bearing Strength, *891*
        B. Floor Surfaces, *892*

    V. Ceilings   **900**
        A. Acoustic Tile, *901*
        B. Drywall, *902*
        C. Wood, *902*
        D. Summary, *902*

    VI. Snappy Rules on Walls, Floors, and Ceilings   **902**

Appendix: Vocabulary   905
Index   963

Preface

A large number of people have helped us with this book.

Many librarians gave us advice over the years, taking time to show us through their libraries, pointing out both the wonderful and the not-so-wonderful features.

Many others took time to read portions of this book and tell us where we were either dead wrong or omitting vital facts or were difficult to understand. Without their help, we could never have finished the book, and we would be terrified that we got things seriously wrong.

Here, in alphabetical order, are some of the people who helped us by reading chapters.

- *Celeste Choate*, Executive Director of The Urbana (Illinois) Free Library (Fred's old library), who read many of the chapters in the book and suggested points that had been omitted.
- *Jim Derden* of State Farm of Bloomington, Illinois, and a retired contractor, who read and commented on the chapters on design, construction, and security.
- *Julie Derden*, librarian at Illinois State University at Normal, and professional editor, who read and commented on the chapters on programming and staff workrooms.
- *Jack Hayes*, president, Frederick Quinn Corporation, Addison, Illinois, construction management, who read and commented on the chapters on design and construction.
- *Diane Hillard*, a biologist and Fred's wife, who read chapters of the book and told us (in the very friendliest sort of way) where we were clear as mud.
- *Bill Hobbs*, Brown, Hobbs, McMurray (insurance), Urbana, Illinois, who read and improved the chapter on security.

- *Brad Hoff*, Thompson Electronics, who reviewed and corrected the chapter on security.
- *John Howard*, director, Farmington Area Public Library District, Illinois, and professional fundraiser, who expanded and improved the section on money.
- *Joe Huberty*, partner, Engberg-Anderson architects, Milwaukee, Wisconsin, and extraordinary expert on library building design, who answered endless technical questions for Fred, and who read and commented on the chapters on design and construction.
- *Mark Misselhorn*, apaceDesign, Peoria, Illinois, and architect on many library construction projects, who read and commented on the chapters on design and construction.
- *Bev Obert*, retired director of an Illinois multi-type library system and of Illinois public libraries, who read and commented on almost all of the chapters in the book.
- *Karl Schlipf*, a computer expert for the University of Illinois and Fred's son, who rescued Fred on a number of (often very late-night) occasions when Fred embroiled himself and his computer in electronic messes, some merely stupid but several others genuinely serious and manuscript-threatening.

We also want to thank our editors at ALA Editions, Jamie Santoro and Angela Gwizdala, who provided support and help and exhibited extraordinary patience as we struggled to finish writing.

Since we occasionally ignored really good advice from people who read sections of the book, it's important to point out that any errors are due exclusively to our stubborn attitudes and behavior.

Part I
Introduction

Introduction

THIS IS A HOW-TO-DO-IT book on library buildings. It's intended primarily for use by professional librarians, and it's written by professional librarians who have spent their lives working in and coping with library buildings. We obviously hope that library owners, managing boards, and architects will read it as well, but we are particularly interested in working with librarians, who we feel are too often nearly ignored when it comes to planning the spaces they know best and work in constantly.

Our main reason for writing this book was our continual unhappiness with aspects of new and remodeled library buildings. No matter how handsome new buildings were, functional things went wrong too often. Starting in 1998, we gave a number of programs at Public Library Association conferences on good and bad ideas in library architecture, including "The Seven Deadly Sins of Library Architecture" (1998), "(Un)desiderata: 27 Snappy Rules for Good and Evil in Library Architecture" (2000), "Let There Be at Least Halfway Decent Light: How Library Illumination Systems Work—And Don't Work" (2002), and "The Curse of Carnegie: Can Modern Public Libraries Find True Happiness in Historic Buildings: 21 Useful Aphorisms" (2006).

We had so much fun writing "snappy rules" for library architecture that we've included a couple dozen of them at the end of each chapter in this book.

One question we always ask ourselves is how so many dysfunctional ideas have managed to permeate library buildings. We're convinced that part of the problem is the nature of librarians. By and large, librarians are friendly and helpful people, who are probably given far too little to complaining. (We know that describes us ... Or maybe not.) When we ask directors of new buildings about dysfunctional features, what we hear is almost never a rueful, "Yes, we know," but rather an appreciative, "But it's so much better than our old building." Unfortunately, "better than our old building" doesn't always make it good enough.

Fred's students have reviewed drafts of the chapters in this book. The students tell him that they always start by reading the "snappy rules" and then get on with the full text. You may find that a good approach as well, but a lot of good stuff is not covered by any of the snappy rules, just as some good points appear only as snappy rules.

In writing this book we've assumed that very few people will read the entire thing straight through. As a result, some chapters repeat important points that appear in other chapters. However, we've tried to remove excessive repetition from individual chapters (not always successfully), and we've tried to tell favorite war stories only once.

This book is far longer than we imagined it would be when we started out. Much of the problem appears to be due to the fact that there are very few sweeping rules of functional library design, but rather a nearly endless number of useful details. The sweeping rules are repeated endlessly in the book, but just in case people feel that there should be rules in the introduction, here are some of the basics:

- Keep space flexible. Use all-purpose, low-glare lighting. Keep ceilings high enough. Make all floors strong enough for books. Don't build stuff in when movable furniture works just as well. Beware of ornamental soffits. Have electrical outlets everywhere. Tell your architects that libraries move stuff around all the time, and they'll have to plan for that.
- Design for security. One public entrance is almost always enough. Pay attention to sight lines. Provide glass walls for study rooms. Avoid places where users or staff can be cornered. Control humidity at all times. Don't build "reading terraces." Don't force people to grope their way into dark rooms to activate automatic lights. Have exterior book return slots lead to fireproof receiving areas. Beware of basements. Keep floors wide and open.
- Provide bright but low-glare lighting. All exterior pieces of glass that face any direction except straight north require movable blinds. (Cute little windows need cute little blinds.) Avoid harsh, direct lights, such as recessed downlights

and direct LED lights. Bounce almost all light off ceilings. Saving energy by making lights too dim involves missing the entire point of libraries.
- Make library users comfortable. Provide pleasant places to sit. Don't frighten people who have acrophobia. Don't create places where people can be cornered. Avoid atriums and floating staircases passionately. Keep indoor air fresh and comfortable. Always try chairs out before buying them. Use round tables only for coffee. Provide elbowroom.
- Keep things simple. The sequence of call numbers in shelving needs to be easy to figure out. Service desks need to be easy to find. Build no more partitions than necessary. Don't create labyrinths. Provide directional signs. Beware of courtyards, which tend to lead to beads-on-a-string room arrangements.
- Plan for growth. Despite digital enthusiasms, book collections continue to grow and libraries continue to run out of space for books. Sooner or later, all libraries need extra workspaces for extra staff. And they need new spaces for users. Don't let political pressures lead you to construct a building that is full the day it opens. (We were tempted to say "fiscal or political pressures," but most fiscal pressures are actually political pressures.) Never construct a building that can't be expanded.
- Never lose control. Do preemptive building programming. Make sure that someone who knows a lot about how libraries occupy space plays a central role in your library's planning team. Never give your designers any rights to your building after the ribbon is cut. Avoid design competitions and other building beauty contests. And never let aesthetics trump function.

We wrote this book over a number of years.

The oldest chapter is "The Library Construction Process" which we first wrote as a handout to accompany our talk at a Public Library Association symposium on library buildings in 1999 and have revised more or less annually since then.

Fred wrote the chapter on "Evaluating Library Buildings by Walking Around" for use by his clients for whom he was writing building programs.

The vocabulary list at the end of this book began as a handout for Fred's how-to-do-it course on library buildings at the University of Illinois library school in Urbana-Champaign. The main change for this book is the removal of references to a number of local buildings in Urbana and Champaign.

Two of the chapters have appeared in somewhat similar form in articles Fred wrote for *Library Trends:* "The Dark Side of Library Architecture: The Persistence of Dysfunctional Designs" (2011) and "Remodeling and Expanding Carnegie-Era Library Buildings" (2014).

Much of John's article on "Library Buildings: Planning and Programming" (*Library Trends*, 2011) is incorporated in the chapter on "Programming."

This book has been underway for more years than we ever intended. We finally finished a full draft in 2016 by hiding from the world, by both being retired at last (from our day jobs, at least), and by Fred's backing off from consulting on building projects.

Because we have extremely different writing styles, we were unable to assign chapters to one or the other of us. Fred tends to be wordy and given to smart remarks. He wrote the first draft of the text. John tends to be sober and professional and well-organized. He added missing things, clarified Fred's hasty diction, and removed some of Fred's more seriously ill-considered remarks.

We could not have written this book without the help of many friends and colleagues who read drafts of chapters and told us gently where we had wandered off the track.

Most of the book is based on the authors' personal experiences during two lifetimes of working in library buildings, consulting on library building design, and teaching how-to-do-it courses on library buildings, rather than on the published library literature, and you won't find a lot of citations to the library literature.

A note on pronouns. First person is us. Second person is our librarian friends and colleagues. And third person is everyone else.

This is a very personal document. We wrote like crazy for years and finally decided we had to quit. The book's coverage is somewhat uneven, depending on the degree to which we think librarians need to focus on things and the frequency with which things seem to go wrong in library buildings.

We've put a lot of emphasis on things to avoid, particularly things that owners and architects *and* architectural critics tend to love, but that librarians and library users tend to hate. Our experience has been that the relationship between architects and owners (city fathers, university trustees, school boards, and the rest) is sometimes similar to the relationship between Svengali and Trilby, with the Innocent Owners sometimes Led Down the Garden Path.

The problem with library buildings is that bad decisions can last a century. Poorly selected books can be dumped into the next book sale, and uncomfortable furniture wears out or can be transferred to the library staff lunchroom, but buildings last for generations. If we get only one chance to do it right, we need to make sure that we really do get it right the very first time we do it.

But often we get it wrong. As a library director told us: "Once a week we tell ourselves how great it is to work in a library designed by a world-famous architect. The rest of the time we hate the place."

We hope that this book reduces your chance of hating the place.

We've tried hard to make this book helpful, friendly, and usable. Please call or e-mail us if you have questions. Tell us what we've left out. Tell us (particularly if you are a practicing librarian) what you think we got wrong and should change. If we live long enough to write a second edition of the book, we'll try to incorporate all sorts of ideas that people send us. Although we're connected to social media, we almost never look at it, so the way to get in touch with us is by telephone, U.S. mail, and e-mail.

We also tend to have a lot of strong opinions. So, on the advice of all sorts of people, we hereby expressly disclaim liability to any and all persons and entities for personal injury, property damage, and any other damage of any kind or nature (whether or not such damages are direct, indirect, consequential, or compensational) resulting from or in any way related to the information and opinions in this book.

FRED SCHLIPF
PO Box 816
Urbana, IL 61803–0816
217–898–1393 | fschlipf@illinois.edu

JOHN A. MOORMAN
7275 Monon Court
Indianapolis, IN 46256–1984
757–561–1024 | moorman.consult@att.net

2

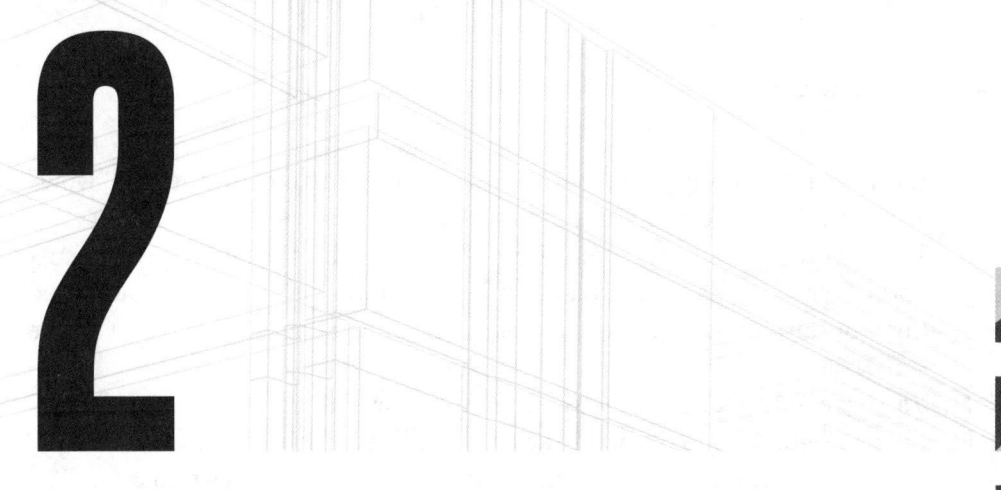

More than Two Hundred Snappy Rules for Good and Evil in Library Architecture

SINCE WRITING SNAPPY RULES is always fun, here are some of them. Most of them can be found in the various chapters of the book, but others are here alone.

1. Don't be led astray by winsome but dysfunctional designs. As P. J. O'Rourke said, "It's always tempting to impute unlikely virtues to the cute."
2. A badly designed and constructed building is a pain forever. Or until it falls down, whichever comes first. Never cut planning time short.
3. Select your architect with care. There are some amazingly competent designers around.
4. Having the same firm write your building program and design your library is always a seriously bad idea.
5. You will have a far better-balanced project if your consultant is a librarian with a knowledge of buildings rather than an architect with a knowledge of libraries.
6. Never have an architect write your building program. With a tiny number of exceptions, architects don't know enough about libraries, even if they've designed a few. And few architects can divorce themselves from design issues that should come later.
7. If you hire a world-famous architect, you'll probably get a lot less library than you pay for and have a lot higher operating costs than you hope for.
8. The single most important construction material is money.
9. In addition to being functional disasters, atriums with dramatic staircases are one of the most overworked clichés in unoriginal library architecture.

If one is inflicted on your library, you'll be gaining five minutes of "wow" and suffering 50 to 100 years of problems.
10. When you are planning a building, always think in terms of project cost and never in terms of construction cost. And make sure all of your hired help (building consultants, architects, and construction managers) do the same.
11. You have only one chance with naming opportunities. Plan first and negotiate second. All too often, libraries initially give things away too cheaply and find themselves short of money but fresh out of places to name.
12. Donors would rather pay for a new college library (think shining city on the hill) than for a new dormitory (think restrooms on Friday night). This is probably why dormitories are often named after early college presidents.
13. Never begin with a project cost and design a building that fits. Start with needs, estimate costs, ask whether you can afford them, and *only if and only when you decide it's too expensive,* compromise on needs.
14. Skylights are too bright by day, too dark by night, and noisy, but they make up for all that by leaking.
15. Unless you have a particularly nasty turn of mind, there's no real need to terrify all your users who have a fear of heights.
16. Reading terraces accessible from inside libraries are golden doors to the theft of library materials. The term *secure reading terrace* is a total oxymoron.
17. Saying that a new library "meets all applicable codes" is a little like saying that it's right on the edge of being illegal.
18. Even if it's stupid, as long as it's legal you can have anything you want.
19. Creating excitement with light in a library is like creating excitement with steps in a nursing home.
20. The best entrances to libraries face south. The worst face north and west.
21. Regardless of initial intent, *all library floors need to be strong enough to bear the weight of books.* Flimsy floors are never a good investment.
22. When the time comes to replace sections of your carpet, it will no longer be in production. That's why people invented attic stock.
23. There's no such thing as too many electrical outlets in a library. Or too many electrical circuits in a library kitchenette.
24. When your architects ask you where you want to put computers, the correct answer always is, "Anywhere we want."
25. Preparing building programs and selecting architects can take a surprising amount of time and cost surprisingly little. It's a lot easier to have a program completed and an architect waiting in the wings than to suddenly have to rush madly about.
26. *NEVER build a library on land to which you do not hold completely clear title.*

27. For financing public library buildings, know the spirit of your community. Some angrily antitax people can be amazingly generous when asked for voluntary donations.
28. Any project larger than a woodshed will be called a Taj Mahal and a monument to the inflated egos of managing boards. It's good to have people handy (usually consultants and architects) who can point out the actual modesty of your plans.
29. Unless your name is "Library of Congress" or "British Museum," you don't need a round reading room or a dome.
30. ALL windows that don't face directly north need blinds, including especially little tiny windows high up that look innocent on the plans. "Modern glass" is not a substitute. (You can often expect a fight from your architects on the unshaded windows issue. They will be wrong, but they will be impressively determined.)
31. Most departmental libraries benefit from a "T"-shaped interior furniture layout. Enter from the center of the broad side of the department, facing the service desk. Walk to the desk and then turn left or right for the rest of the department.
32. A "monitor" is a four-sided structure that rises above the roof and has glass on all four sides. Since monitors do not have adjustable blinds, this is glass on three sides too many. Stop monitors the first time you hear them mentioned.
33. A schematic design without furniture placement is *totally useless*. Reject it.
34. Beware of designing buildings that are just small enough to slither under code requirements. Sooner or later, you'll need to expand, and the cost of upgrading the existing building can be painfully high.
35. Trying to weasel out of building codes is not a good idea, as the choice of verb suggests.
36. In addition to spreading Legionnaires' disease, indoor "water features" have many other nasty aspects. For example, mayors tend to fall into them.
37. Anyone who has dealt with children in a library knows that "infectious" does not apply just to lilting laughter. All staff workrooms need sinks.
38. If you have an open exterior staircase leading down to a basement door, sooner or later the drain at the bottom of the steps will plug up and rainwater will flow into your basement.
39. The most important place for childproof (tamper-resistant) electrical outlets is in public library *adult* departments, because that's where parents hand their keys to their children to play with while the parents are otherwise occupied.
40. There's no such thing as too many electrical circuits in kitchenettes.

41. If your library has balconies a dozen stories above the main level, you will terrify your users with acrophobia, and sooner or later someone will jump off. "Splat" is not an encouraging sound to hear while you're at the reference desk.
42. Study rooms need individual thermostats. If two rooms share one thermostat, the people in the room without the thermostat are likely to be seriously unhappy.
43. High-quality cantilever steel shelving can last a century, but it's extremely difficult to repaint. This tells us why bright orange and vivid magenta are seriously bad color choices.
44. If you arrange shelving around the walls of a room, know how you will prevent people sitting at tables from blocking access to those bookshelves.
45. It's hard to shelve books on spinner racks because there are so many small pockets. Spinners also tend to tip over in the presence of enthusiastic teenagers.
46. When as a library user you're trotting along a range of shelves and they end at 327.8, it should be extremely clear where to find 327.9.
47. Libraries are inherently flat rather than vertical. A twelve-story library on a small piece of land is Not a Good Thing.
48. If anyone who does not work for a library is authorized to have a key to the building, there will be trouble.
49. Dead-end aisles in shelving areas are a particularly nasty threat to the personal safety of both library users and staff. And they're seriously rude to people in wheelchairs.
50. If you've never worked in a library, you have no right to object to plans to include a staff restroom.
51. Outside of study rooms, program rooms, and restrooms, libraries don't benefit from small spaces for public use. *Wide, flat, and open makes a happy library.*
52. Study tables should be rectangular with chairs on two sides only. Round tables are for conversation only. Pleasant libraries need a few round tables, but only a few.
53. If your windows are custom-made on a different continent, you'll have an interesting time after the Big Hailstorm.
54. A reading table without electrical outlets on top is just about as modern as a reading room with kerosene lighting.
55. A building project can absorb the full attention of a library administrator for years. Don't expect staff to add it to their other duties.
56. One of the truly fine places for a special library is next door to the cafeteria.
57. Programming is inexpensive, and proactive programming is invaluable.
58. Thank all of your donors. For some donors, $100 was a greater stretch than $100,000 for other donors.

59. The planning process begins with enumerating needs. Then estimate costs, ask whether you can afford them, and, finally, *if and only if it's too expensive*, compromise on needs.
60. Protect your library building's expansion space with the fierceness of a mother grizzly bear with cubs. You'll need the fierceness, for many people cast covetous eyes on open spaces, often displaying glib self-justification.
61. Starting your project by asking how much money you have to spend is often totally backwards planning.
62. If you know you'll be expanding your library, have your library building consultant write a two-phase building program and have your architects prepare schematic designs for both phases. If you don't do this, you may find that you've painted yourself into a corner, and that your Phase I design makes it impossible to construct Phase II.
63. No sane library wants anything to do with screen porches.
64. Don't ever buy cheap shelving. If it isn't steel cantilever shelving, the right price to pay is free.
65. Outside of counters with sinks, none of the furniture in library workrooms should be built in.
66. A toilet stall without two sturdy hooks for coats, purses, book bags, jackets, coats, and so on is an abomination.
67. "Design first, program second" is an easy recipe for a seriously bad building.
68. Forcing a contractor to honor a mistakenly low bid may lead to nothing but trouble.
69. If your contractor messes up, be extraordinarily careful about accepting cash in lieu of corrected work. If your architects encourage you to accept a cash settlement, always talk to your owner's rep and the consulting librarian. You have a right to a building that works the way it is supposed to, and it's easy to bargain away proper performance for far too little money.
70. When it comes to groundbreaking and ribbon cutting, short public ceremonies followed by extensive eating and drinking make everyone happy.
71. Most soffits (lowered sections of ceilings) are a seriously bad idea, including in particular all perimeter soffits and all soffits over service desks. Recessed downlights in soffits just make things a lot worse.
72. Buy strong furniture. There is no theoretical upper limit to the number of teenagers that can occupy a single armchair.
73. All library glass surfaces that do not face straight north need blinds. Your architects will almost certainly argue with you on this point, but they will be amazingly (not to mention spectacularly and extraordinarily) wrong.
74. Sofas in public libraries have two uses—sleeping and necking. Unless you are eager to create opportunities for sleeping and necking, never buy sofas.
75. The number of architects who understand libraries is exceeded by several thousand percent by the number of architects who don't understand libraries but are confident that they do.

76. The least expensive source of good library security is good sight lines.
77. The right number of entrances into a library is anything up to one.
78. Staircases with open risers are a tribute to everyone who loves to terrify people who suffer from fear of heights. But very few people like looking down to the floor below between their feet. Don't go there.
79. If you don't want to climb the stairs, the elevator should be immediately next door. (Sometimes designers hide the elevator down the hall and around the corner, apparently hoping to encourage people to climb the cute stairs.)
80. If you put your reading room light switches where kids can play with them, kids will turn off your reading room lights.
81. Light switches that require user training are a bad idea in meeting rooms shared with the general public. Keep things simple.
82. If the lights in a room are controlled by sensors, they should turn on BEFORE people enter the room, rather than forcing people to grope their way into a dark space.
83. The fact that people occasionally walk to the public library on perfectly lovely spring days does not mean you don't need a parking lot.
84. Angry historical preservationists should come accompanied by checkbooks.
85. The rights of people with disabilities overrule the rights of designers to be cute.
86. Before you start remodeling an old building, always ask your architects what it would cost to simply start over and erect a new building. Sometimes starting over is cheaper, and with lower long-term operating costs to boot.
87. Legitimate fundraising consultants always work for agreed fees or hourly salaries and never (as in NEVER) for a percentage of fees raised.
88. Unless your library is so far south that you worry about Burmese pythons lurking in the parking lot, you need an entrance that faces south. Under duress, settle for east.
89. Curved exterior walls lead to all sorts of problems with shelving placement, light fixture location, workroom shapes, acoustics, and other good things. On the other hand, they cost a lot more than straight walls.
90. Clarify contractually that your architects have no rights to your building once it's completed. This is a building, not fine art. You must have the right to alter anything you want at any time you want, whether your architects like it or not.
91. If your restroom washbasins aren't strong enough to bear the weight of adults, sooner or later someone will break one off the wall.
92. Owners who can't unload vacant buildings often have special epiphanies about what wonderful libraries they'll make.
93. Unfortunately, there's often no such thing as a "free" building, and lots of "free" buildings can end up costing more than starting over from scratch.

94. When a building is standing vacant, there is likely to be a very good reason. Or many very good reasons.
95. Converting a building that has no expansion space and no off-street parking space into a library involves making two impressively major errors at the same time.
96. Punch listing tries the previously warm social relationships between owners and contractors.
97. At groundbreaking and ribbon-cutting events, what people want to hear is probably more important than what you want to tell them.
98. One of the first and most vital decisions in library planning is stack aisle width, because it determines structural column spacing.
99. No matter how short your library is of space, never have book aisles with dead ends.
100. To the intense chagrin of some designers, end panel indicators you can actually read are far more important that indicators that provide aesthetic gratification.
101. Shelving does best in long, continuous ranges. Dividing it up into lots of separate chunks in lots of separate spaces is A Very Seriously Bad Thing.
102. Shelving needs to be in parallel rows. Always.
103. Shelves supported by clips on the end panels, or slipped into slots in the end panels, have a tendency to fall, dumping books on the place (or persons) beneath.
104. Triangular and round interior spaces cost a lot more to construct, but they compensate for it by not holding much.
105. You need a good excuse for internal partitions. "Functional necessity" is often a good excuse. "Architectural concept" is almost never a good excuse.
106. Funny-shaped buildings may be architecturally interesting, but they're usually expensive and dysfunctional. Curved walls are funny-shaped.
107. Basements in new libraries cost about the same amount as extra floors, but they have many fewer advantages. *As in no advantages whatsoever.*
108. An Illinois public library has a young adult study room with one tiny window. The library staff call it "the sex room."
109. If you have to install dark gray film on a window to block the glare, you should be asking yourself why you allowed someone to install that window in the first place.
110. You always need more storage space than your board of trustees, university administration, school principal, or hospital administrator think you need.
111. If you have study rooms that can't be supervised by your staff from service desks, they'll spend a lot of time running back and forth, peeking into study room windows.
112. High-density storage next to your library is infinitely better than high-density storage two counties off.

113. Always have your consulting librarian check your schematic design for functionality.
114. For any library construction project larger than a bicycle shed, you need an architect.
115. If your architects have little or no library experience, decide how you will fill the gap.
116. Of all architectural words of tongue or pen, "We will reinvent the library" are among the most terrifying.
117. Good librarians can be seriously annoying to architects who start off with little intention of listening to them.
118. Be particularly wary and aggressive when your library is a small element in a large building. Do proactive programming. Insist on being heard.
119. Sometimes the word *concept* should bring terror to your heart.
120. Clarify contractually what will happen if your lowest bid is significantly higher than your architects' estimate.
121. Complete honesty in architectural renderings is of mixed value. Sometimes it's better to leave off the HVAC penthouse.
122. One way to design a library building is to lay out all the needed spaces and then wrap an attractive exterior around them. Another way is to design an attractive exterior and then cram all the library spaces into it. The latter approach was invented by Procrustes, and you will not enjoy the results.
123. Soaring spaces with monumental staircases provide a few moments of "wow," followed by endless years of problems with heating, lighting, maintenance, acoustics, getting from point A to point B, unusable but expensive space, and (for many users) paralyzing fear of heights. Say "no" early and often.
124. Make sure that your library staff have enough time to work on your building project.
125. Don't pressure architects to do something illegal.
126. If your architects have to labor mightily to talk you into their design concept, it may be because it's a crummy concept.
127. Design competitions for less than truly major libraries may simply drive off good architects. (They may also be a sign of excess owner pomposity.)
128. Working with your architects to list words that will define your project is fun, but don't engrave them on the front of your building.
129. If users have to shield their eyes from the glare anywhere in your library, something is wrong.
130. If you stand at the top of a staircase, looking down, and start fantasizing about tumbling down head over heels, this is Not a Good Thing.
131. Water features may be exciting and desirable, but only in someone else's library. If you're stuck with one, convert it to a planter.

132. "How will we change the light bulbs?" is an important question. If your designer says, "Use a lift," that is about as helpful as being told to "Use a screwdriver" when you ask how to rebuild the carburetor on your XKE.
133. If a railing has horizontal bars that can be climbed like a ladder, someone's child will climb them. And fall off.
134. Never allow anyone to put perimeter soffits in your library.
135. Your architects and engineers are your experts on codes of all sorts.
136. Screen porches sound romantic, but they're not. Always say "No."
137. Book stacks don't fit into non-rectangular spaces.
138. Sight lines are vital, whether they're cute or not.
139. *Ars longa, technologia brevis est.* (Fake Latin for "technology is fleeting, but art—as in architecture, for example—endures.")
140. Rooms with dark ceilings are hard to light. Historic dark ceilings probably need to be preserved, but we don't need to create any new ones.
141. There are no cheap substitutes for elevators.
142. As with other building codes, the requirements of the Americans with Disabilities Act are legal minimums, not ideals. Don't feel seriously smug about things if your building just squeaks through.
143. The undersides of floating staircases are wonderful places to bump one's head.
144. Steps that serve no necessary purpose whatsoever serve no purpose whatsoever.
145. Staircases should not terrify library users, who are nice people and deserve better treatment.
146. A member of a governing board envisions a balcony overlooking a library atrium as an inspirational vantage point. A library manager wonders how long it will be before someone falls off.
147. There is no excuse for staircases with funny-shaped treads.
148. For people with a serious fear of heights, a glass-walled elevator is not a kindly alternative to a vertiginous staircase.
149. Beware of providing eternal exhibit space for things you don't own.
150. Never compromise with color rendering index (CRI). There's no need to accept anything less than 85.
151. And never compromise with color temperature. Anything higher than 3500K is too cold.
152. Be sure your lighting is bright enough. Anything less than 50 foot-candles of soft, even light is unacceptable, and 60 foot-candles is a lot better.
153. Entryways need to be brightly lit and welcoming, even though all most people do is just move on through them.
154. No motion detectors should force people to grope their way into dark rooms.

155. With the exception of study rooms and program rooms, put light switches where library users can't play around with them.
156. When it comes to a bond referendum, making sure your friends all vote works a lot better than trying to convert your enemies.
157. Remodeling is almost always more expensive than either your critics or supporters expect.
158. Construction costs tend to increase faster than the value of money in the bank.
159. Some donors come equipped not only with money (good) but also with weird structural ideas they want to inflict on you (bad). Some want to pay only part of the cost of the building but still get to inflict their unfortunate ideas on you. It hurts to say "no" to money, but sometimes that's the only sane option.
160. Bake sales and book sales are fun and make everyone feel involved and appreciated, but they don't bring in much money. Construction projects rely on seriously big bucks from a more limited range of sources.
161. You can't get through any funding for a new library without hearing "The book is dead." Be prepared to point out how packed your library is, but don't expect to convert everyone.
162. Know what you'll do if you end up with the larger library of tomorrow but with yesterday's operating budget.
163. Local nonexperts are frequently eager to estimate construction costs on your behalf. Run away quickly.
164. Some sinks may require garbage disposals, particularly in staff lunchrooms.
165. If you construct an open terrace next to your library, below grade level, you will regret it deeply. Sooner or later the storm drains will fail, and water will fill your library.
166. A happy library is a basement-less library.
167. Install enough electrical outlets. Fire marshals will not appreciate your extension cords.
168. Wall-mounted computer counters with outlets at the back force users to sit with their backs to the room. Lots of users don't like this much.
169. Study rooms and staff workrooms all need individual thermostats.
170. Heating with propane is a lot more expensive than heating with natural gas. If you have a choice of sites, pick one with access to natural gas.
171. Never buy a site or a building without input from an architect (and a consulting librarian, if possible).
172. When possible, use the term *workroom* rather than *office*. It's a lot more accurate and creates far fewer emotions on the part of observers.
173. Floor-mounted toilets are cheaper than wall-mounted toilets, but only if you don't count the cost of maintenance.

174. Always use flush-valve toilets unless your community suffers from low water pressure.
175. Unless your building successfully bans infants, your restrooms will need changing tables. And receptacles for dirty diapers.
176. Even in tiny libraries, staff do not want to share restrooms with library users. Unless you've spent your life working in libraries, you have no right to regard this as an unreasonable attitude.
177. Restrooms must never open directly into reading rooms, program rooms, or staff lunchrooms.
178. The only acceptable restroom floor covering is anti-slip ceramic tile with very dark grout.
179. Be sure all of your toilet stalls are large enough for actual human beings.
180. Written building programs for expanding existing buildings should always be written without regard to those structures. *It's always a matter of what you need, not what you have.*
181. Remodeling and expanding a historic library is difficult. Trying to merge it with a second historic building is seriously scary, but the concept has an evil appeal to the inexperienced.
182. Once they've been expanded, historic buildings frequently have too many floors and too many rooms, with resulting expensive implications for access, supervision, and excessive elevators and staircases.
183. The walls of most historic libraries are uninsulated, and you probably won't be able to do anything about it.
184. The great temptation in dealing with historic buildings is to construct what you can have rather than what you need. Starting with a written building program is particularly vital.
185. A bargain building in a bad location is a bad building. A beautiful building in a bad location is also a bad building.
186. A contemporary addition to a historic building will frequently—with the passage of time—become a painfully dated addition to a historic building, the architectural equivalent of avocado shag carpet.
187. A service desk is a service desk, not a monument.
188. Most service desks need occasional rearrangement, relocation, readjustment, and repurposing. Inflexibility of construction is not a virtue.
189. A matching soffit with recessed downlights over a service desk ensures a strong and happy combination of inflexibility and glare.
190. Atriums are rotten places for service desks.
191. All program rooms need adequate storage closets for all furniture and program supplies.
192. Movable room dividers in program rooms are expensive and hard to maneuver, do a bad job of acoustical separation, change the shapes of rooms in weird ways, and are hard to repair. But outside of that they sound like a pretty good idea.

193. Funny-shaped meeting rooms are less amusing than one might hope. Nature loves rectangles.
194. Very few libraries complain that their meeting rooms are too large.
195. Unless you have a large and pompous library, conference rooms with large and pompous conference tables and with large and pompous chairs tend to look extremely silly.
196. Few public libraries complain that they have too many study rooms, but most of them complain that they have too few.
197. Be careful that parent agencies like universities or city governments don't take over control of your program rooms. And set things up so there won't be any serious security problems when they overrule you and take over anyway.
198. Study rooms need to be terrariums—glass boxes that can be supervised from every possible angle.
199. Good architects can envision solutions to design problems in ways that would never occur to the rest of us. Make your needs clear and then see what happens.
200. When you are planning a library, always ask what additional building codes will come into play when you expand it.
201. All entrances need to be staffed, whether or not they have security gates.
202. Never let your library be a passageway to someone else's turf.
203. The lowest-cost theft prevention system is keeping something that's theft-worthy in an area limited to staff.
204. Avoid creating places where staff and users can be trapped.
205. Workrooms need internal windows with Venetian blinds to adjoining areas.
206. If you plan your new building for thirty years of collection growth but no staff growth, the fact that workers eventually end up on each others' laps shouldn't come as much of a surprise.
207. When people are waiting to see the library director, where will they sit?
208. Access lanes to drive-up book returns and book pickups need to have curves wide enough for real vehicles to handle.
209. Good shapes for staff workrooms are simple rectangles.
210. A staff lunchroom without a powerful exhaust fan is not as gross as a staff restroom without an exhaust fan, but the general principle is the same.
211. Staff toilets located directly next to staff lunch areas are depressingly prevalent and are one of the most easily avoided library design idiocies.
212. Staff mailboxes need to be large enough for 8½ × 14-inch documents. Pigeonholes don't work.
213. A bad site for a nice store is a bad site for a nice public library.
214. Whether you have a campus library, a school library, a business library, or a public library, if you have a great site, everyone always wants to steal it.
215. Never let anyone else relieve you of your vacant land, and never let nearby land slip through your fingers.

Part II
About Library Buildings

3

The Library Construction Process

I. INTRODUCTION

This chapter provides a quick summary of the information in the chapters on programming, design, and construction.

II. MOTIVATIONS

Some library building projects occur because of unanticipated gifts, but most are the result of long-standing space, service, and structural needs.

Ideally, libraries will review the adequacy of their structures every few years and take quick steps to cure problems. However, most libraries struggle for years with inadequate buildings before they are actually able to meet their needs. When the time finally comes to plan expansion, there are usually a large number of existing problems to be dealt with at the same time.

When you are deciding what changes to make in your building, don't make the mistake of assuming that all you have to do is cure one or two obvious problems. Solving problems one at a time is terribly expensive, and you may paint yourself into a corner in the process.

Depending on the type of library in which you work, you may want to start by forming a building committee with members of the governing board and staff members.

III. BUILDING PROGRAMS

The creation of a written "building program" is the first step in a building project. The program specifies how much space of what kinds and in what juxtapositions your library needs. The program should also include a review of the existing facility (including a detailed list of its strengths and weaknesses), a statement of required equipment for each space in your new or expanded library, and information on the special architectural needs of libraries.

Architects tend to view projects in terms of problems and their solutions. From this perspective, programming consists of defining the problem.

One of the primary responsibilities of library building consultants is the preparation of building programs. Unless you have had personal experience writing programs, it is probably a bad idea to do it yourself.

Some architects want to prepare building programs, but this can be a bad idea for two reasons. First, programming requires a strong background in the daily operation of libraries. And second, by using separate consultants and architects, you will have valuable second opinions.

While you are discussing your building program with your consultant, it's important to divorce yourself mentally from the service attitudes and procedures that are dictated by your current building rather than by current and long-term community needs. It's also important to think about functional needs rather than what you might specifically do with your current building. This type of planning literally involves the old cliché, "thinking outside the box." (It sometimes helps to imagine that your current library has been totally destroyed by an impressive storm, and that you need to list everything you need to start over.)

You may want to seek separate citizen, faculty, or student input in addition to the knowledge of local needs that the librarians, managing board, and staff bring to the project. Common approaches include focus groups and questionnaires. Both require professional assistance. (Because it's nearly impossible to develop questionnaires that yield useful and reliable numbers, focus groups are usually a better approach.)

After the building program is complete, use it as a yardstick for evaluating your current building and your various options for expansion or starting over. Remember that until you know what you need, you can't evaluate what you have or evaluate proposed construction options. (It's not a matter of what you have, but what you need.)

It's tremendously important that your program be in print and in detail. As Francis Bacon said, "Truth emerges more readily from error than from confusion." Until the program is actually written, the people involved in your project may mistakenly assume that everyone agrees on everything simply because not every detail has been made clear. A program written in substantial detail helps people to recognize differences of opinion early in the project, at a time when resolving differences involves sorting out details rather than redesigning a structure.

When in doubt, involve more rather than fewer people in programming. Seek inputs widely. And the more people who read drafts of your program, the more likely you are to catch errors and omissions. (Remember that book-shelvers and custodians see the world in terms of the difficulty of doing *their* jobs, and that their problems matter.)

When you are hiring architects, make sure that firms know they will be quizzed on your program at the time they are interviewed. This helps you make sure that they read the entire program and not just the page summarizing square footages.

It's a good idea to devote your first meeting with your architects to a review of the program with the consultant there. If the architects disagree with some aspects of the written building program, the only good time to work this out is in a general meeting with everyone present.

The program will be modified during the design phase of the project, but insist that the architects indicate up front where and how they wish to modify it, and then discuss the change as a group with the building consultant present.

Watch for signs that architects, city fathers, or school administrators are ignoring the program.

For copyright reasons, any modifications to the program should be made only by the consultant.

Always require that all floor plans proposed by your architects be accompanied by tables comparing programmed square footages with plan square footages.

IV. BUILDING CONSULTANTS

To make sure that you have looked consciously at all the problems facing your building—rather than just one or two particularly painful ones—always start your project by hiring a building consultant who has a professional background in the management of libraries.

The job of a building consultant is to help you review your current building and options, and to convert your needs and long-range plans into architectural terms. The result is a written building program. A consultant will also bring the perspective of a working librarian who has special knowledge of how libraries occupy spaces.

In addition to having your consultant prepare a building program, you will want your consultant to attend planning meetings led by your architects and to critique architectural designs from the point of view of library functionality.

A building consultant is not an architect or engineer. Do not expect your consultant to evaluate your HVAC system, design your building, write bid specifications, estimate construction costs, or help administer construction.

Always hire a consultant before you hire architects. And always hire architects before you hire a contractor.

There are many ways to find consultants, including word of mouth, recommendations of other libraries, and lists compiled by state agencies and associations. But just because a consultant's name is on a list, it doesn't mean that they are the kind of people you want.

In order to maintain proper checks and balances, it's important that your consultant NOT be an employee of your architects. The job of the consultant is to view the project as you would if you had more experience with buildings, and to provide you with opinions independent of your architects.

Sometimes part of the job of a consultant is to convince local people that what their library staff and board have been saying all along is actually true. That's just the sad part about experts—none of us is an expert at home.

Hire a consultant with at least a master's degree from a program accredited by the American Library Association and extensive (at least ten years) practical and fairly recent experience working in real libraries. If your consultant is a librarian with a strong background in library architecture, rather than an architect with experience designing libraries, you will have a far better-balanced planning team.

It's always reasonable to ask your consultant for an example of a prior building program. Among other things, check to be sure that it does not consist primarily of boilerplate. It's possible to sell the same consulting report many times over, and you don't want to pay for material that is just repetition.

Make sure that your consultant is committed to following your project through to the end—or at least through the preparation of bid documents. Clarify this, and check on follow-through costs.

Not all architects like working with consultants. As a result, your architects may not suggest including your consultant at meetings, or they may contend that there is "no time" to that your consultant is in attendance at building planning meetings and receives copies of plans in time to review them.

Whether you like the consultant personally is an important consideration. Consultants are there to convert the needs of libraries into architectural terms. To do so successfully, they have to be people that librarians and owners like. If a consultant gives you a major pain during the interview, hire someone else.

Always check references. Ideally, speak with both staff and owners. Prospective consultant candidates should be happy to give you lists of previous clients.

Questions to ask references include the following:

- Were you generally satisfied with the consultant?
- Did you enjoy working with the consultant?
- Did your consultant have a wide range of experience with libraries and library buildings?
- Did your consultant listen to you?
- Did your consultant suggest all kinds of possibilities (even if you rejected many of them)?
- Were your consultant's building program and other documentation complete and detailed?
- Was the program clearly written and easy to follow?
- Was your consultant prepared to attend most (if not all) planning meetings with architects?
- Was your consultant able to review architectural plans and make suggestions for functional improvements?
- If your consultant squabbled with your architects, who in retrospect was correct?
- Was your consultant regarded positively by the grant-giving authorities?

Compared with other construction costs, consultants are very inexpensive. If your consultant averts even one bad decision, you will probably have saved much more than the entire consulting fee.

When hiring professionals—both consultants and architects—never get involved in complex discussions with disappointed applicants about why they were not hired. Say something to the effect that, "We hired the person we felt best met our needs," and do not let yourself be drawn out, just as you would not let yourself be drawn out when hiring personnel for your library.

V. ARCHITECTS AND DESIGN

Avoid the dangerous temptation to go straight to a contractor for any library construction project, whether it's a new building or just a bunch of new windows. Design is almost always more complex than it appears, and if bidding is required under law, bid documents must be prepared professionally. Good architects are always a good investment. For any library project bigger than a woodshed, good architects are an absolutely essential investment. In fact, in many cases you won't be able to get a building permit without plans stamped by licensed architects or engineers.

You can locate possible architectural firms in many ways. Among these are recommendations of other libraries, advertising, looking through building issues of library publications, and talking with your state library or other agencies. (Most firms are always seeking commissions, and once word gets out that you're thinking of hiring architects, architectural firms will find you.)

Depending on the laws in your area, you may have to advertise for architects for your work and/or rank order applicants. Laws may also prohibit low-bidding architectural services. In addition to advertising, you can of course contact firms directly if you like their work.

Request information from at least a half dozen firms.

- Ask them for lists of prior projects, including for *each* project (a) specific work undertaken, (b) references, (c) specific information on what percentage of the project was their firm's responsibility, (d) the current status of the project, and (e) the name of the project architect.
- Many firms will list projects that were studied but never built, projects in which they played extremely minor roles, projects that are under way but not

completed, or projects that were built by a different branch of the firm in a faraway city. Ask for a list of *completed* projects consisting of new buildings or of major expansion and remodeling work, in which the firm was the only architect or the lead architect.
- Ask them to list the key personnel of their firms and what specific people are being proposed as project architects. If not all services are provided in-house, who will provide them?
- If the firm has done a number of libraries, ask specifically which staff member was the project architect for each library. It's frustrating to find out too late that the firm's library expert has moved on.
- Many excellent architectural firms hire outside structural engineers, mechanical engineers, electrical engineers, cost estimators, and so on. The decision of these firms not to provide these services in-house is not a failing, nor does it lead to poorer work.

Request specific information on the library design experience of the individual members of the team that each firm is proposing for your job. This is particularly important in the case of large firms or merged firms, where the number of library projects can be large but the actual library experience of the proposed team can be very limited.

Call prior clients. There are many important questions to ask architects' previous clients.

- Are they satisfied now that the job is completed?
- Do they like the building, independently of whether or not they like the architects?
- Were the architects responsive to their needs?
- Did the architects listen to the owners and staff and other administrators and respond?
- Did they abandon concepts when requested to do so, or did they keep trying to talk you into something you didn't want? (A few architects can be amazingly aggressive and stubborn about pushing their ideas. You will probably not enjoy working with them.)
- Did they work well with the building consultant? If your architect and consultant disagreed, do you have any feeling about who was right?
- Did the architectural firm's staff members who began your project continue through to the end?
- Did the architectural firm practice "bait and switch"? (Did the immensely appealing architect who led the team during the interviews actually do the work, or was the job passed off to a junior member of the firm?)
- Did the building come in on time and under budget?

- Did the architects do a good job administering construction?
- How did the architects respond when things went wrong during construction? What did they do when the problem was clearly their fault?
- How many change orders were due to architect errors and omissions? If an architectural error cost you money to correct, did the architect take fiscal responsibility? Ask your consultant to help you determine what constitutes an "excessive" number of change orders. Also bear in mind that the blame for many change orders can be laid on fickle clients who changed their minds in midstream, or on hidden conditions that no architect or engineer could reasonably have been expected to determine in advance. (Change orders are inevitable and not a sign of poor design work. However, if change orders for an architect's errors alone exceed 5 percent, that may be a sign of problems.)
- Have the architects been back since the ten-month post-construction building checkup to see whether the building continues to function satisfactorily?
- Are there any aspects of the building that cause functional problems? Do you have trouble changing light bulbs? Do you have trouble keeping an eye on back corners of the library? Do you have trouble rearranging furniture and equipment to cope with changing needs? Figuring out how to expand the building? Keeping water out of ductwork? Maintaining delicate building sheathing? Finding places to plug things in?
- Would you hire your architects again?

You can sometimes learn more if you ask your department heads to call their counterparts at other libraries. For example, if your head of maintenance calls the heads of maintenance in other libraries, he may hear very different things than you hear from library directors.

Visit sites of previous work. Talk to staff while you're there—preferably not just the director and owners who were there when the library was built, because they have a lot of ego involved in the project and often cannot (or will not) recognize errors.

Review the team the architects propose for your job. It should specify the "project architect" (who will be in charge of the process) and outside consultants, such as engineering firms. Most engineers will be firms that the architects work with on a regular basis, but the civil engineer should be a reasonably local firm with knowledge of local construction conditions. Watch out for situations where architects propose professional library building consultants other than your own, or where the organizational chart for the project shows your consultant reporting to the architects rather than to the entity in charge.

Interview a limited group of architectural firms—up to three or four. Insist that the person who will be project architect be present at the interview and play an active role. (Some large firms have sales architects and working architects. You want to interview the architects with whom you will work.) Spend one-and-a-half hours interviewing each of a very few firms rather than running many architects through a revolving door. Try to conduct all interviews on a single day, or on an evening and the following day. If you spread out interviews or try to interview more than about four firms, you'll have a hard time getting all your board or building committee members to every interview, and you'll be unfair to the firms applying for your work, since it costs them a surprising amount to make presentations.

Some architects will arrive at interviews with drawings of "your new library." This is an advertising device that you should ignore. Architects can't provide drawings of your library until they have completed extensive study and design work.

Similarly, it's not a great idea to ask architects to bring conceptual drawings of your new library with them to the interviews. Select architects on the basis of past performance, not on the basis of how they will solve your specific problems.

Interviews are not the right time for architects to get to know you and your interests or for them to discuss projects that they are envisioning or planning. You want to know what they've accomplished in the past.

Whether you like the architects personally is a valid consideration. Working with people you dislike is never a good idea. (However, architects you like personally can still design buildings you dislike.)

After the interviews, you will have follow-up questions. Feel free to call architects back for clarification, call their previous clients one more time, or visit additional libraries that the architects have designed.

Be sure you know any state laws affecting how you hire your architects. In general, professionals are not hired by low bid. (Your state may have a QBS—qualifications-based selection—law that provides basic rules for hiring professionals.)

When hiring architects—as in the case of hiring consultants or library employees—never get involved in discussions with disappointed applicants about why they were not hired. Some applicants for architectural services can be extremely aggressive when requesting explanations concerning hiring decisions, and you need to *stand absolutely firm*.

Be sure you have the assistance of an experienced attorney before you sign a contract for architectural services.

Almost everyone uses standard AIA (American Institute of Architects) contract forms, but many issues are negotiable. Among the most important issues to settle in the contract are:

- Basic percentage or flat fee.
- The portion of the total fee that will be billed at each stage of the project.
- Acceptable additional charges. The add-on charges can be extremely expensive, and your lawyer will need to clarify what extra charges will be made (for example) for the preparation of grant-application documents, construction administration, grant administration, attendance at local public meetings, and extra meetings to discuss owner concerns. Clarify "reimbursables," such as travel and postage costs, bid copies of documents, renderings and models, and so on.
- Who is responsible when things go awry? (Some people feel that the AIA contracts are a little vague in this area.)
- Who will be the project architect? Will this person be responsible for project oversight?

There are also things that are good to clarify in the written agreement, including:

- The schematic design must include full furniture layouts.
- The architect will have no residual rights to the structure once the building is complete and the architect has been paid. (If you want to paint the building bright pink, you need to have the right to do so.)

It's possible to contract with a "team" consisting of a local architectural firm and an out-of-town firm specializing in libraries. Sometimes this approach works very well, but there are potential problems. The two firms may fail to work smoothly together, and you may have conflict between the out-of-town designers and the local people who prepare the bid documents and administer the project. It may also be more difficult to pin down responsibility for problems. Before you hire the team, try to find out:

- Whether the team was created to form a better working group or to just make a more effective sales presentation.
- Whether the members of the team have ever worked together before. Did they meet face-to-face for the first time on the morning of the interview?
- How much you will actually see of the out-of-town specialist firm.

- Whether including the out-of-town firm will lead to increased reimbursables. If an out-of-town firm flies half a dozen people in for every meeting, the reimbursable transportation costs can be extremely high.

In your contract, you can specify that the project architect will stay with your project until it is completed. This means that if that architect leaves the firm, the firm will have to hire the architect back to complete your project, or even that the architect may take your project to a new firm. If your decision to hire a firm is based on the presence of a specific architect in that firm, this kind of agreement is particularly important.

The program is your instructions to your architects, and they should treat it as such. *It's extremely important that you keep your consultant involved throughout the design process* to be sure that this happens, and that the plans reflect good library practice. At the same time, it's important to remember that programs are living documents, and that the full planning group (owners, board, staff, other administrators, architects, and consultant) may decide to make useful changes during the design process. Only the consultant who wrote the program should make the actual modifications to the text.

Remember at all times that you are the owner. The building is yours, and the architects are your employees. You are paying all the costs, and you are the one that has to live in the finished library. Unless it's a matter of violating laws or legal regulations, you can always say "no" and stand your ground. (Bearing in mind, of course, that you may possibly be very wrong.)

Treat your architects fairly. Do not let your architects waste their time continuing to develop plans you dislike. Do not expect them to do major extra work not called for in your contract without extra compensation. And do not expect them to create perfect construction documents that require absolutely no change orders.

VI. CONSTRUCTION OPTIONS AND SITE SELECTION

These are often the most difficult decisions in a building project.

Among the issues are choice of site and of construction type (expansion, new construction, or conversion of an existing building).

If at all possible, involve your architects (and consultant, although the architects and their engineers are more critical) in site selection. The sites initially proposed for library use are frequently too small, and existing buildings may be far more expensive to convert than one initially expects. "Brownfield" sites that once were occupied by other buildings may have hidden problems. The usability of sites is also affected by local zoning restrictions, soil bearing capacities, access to utilities, EPA (Environmental Protection Agency) concerns, and other technical issues that your architects will be prepared to evaluate.

If your current building is a historic one, that will limit your options. Check with your state and local preservation agencies and with your local government before going too far with planning.

When it comes to site selection, try to avoid having your library become a pawn in local development or redevelopment. Your library may be good for a neighborhood, but the neighborhood may be bad for your library and for its services to the community.

Renovating existing non-library structures can sometimes (but by no means always) save money and be good for public relations, but be sure that you understand the true costs in terms of both conversion and long-term occupancy. In particular, be sure that the existing building has the following:

- Floors strong enough to carry library weights. Libraries must carry live loads of 150 pounds and up per square foot, and few existing non-library buildings can handle this bearing capacity without reinforcement. In areas where compact shelving is planned, additional weight and floor deflection are both important issues. (If floors are too flexible, compact shelving can roll downhill to the center of a sag.)
- Regardless of initial design, book shelving may need to be relocated during the life of a library building, and *all floors* need to be strong enough to hold books.
- Ability to provide sufficient cable conduit and wiring. Even with wireless transmission, we still need widespread access to 110-volt current and data conduits. Providing wireless access to the staff side of the library's operating systems can make the library more vulnerable to hacking.
- Ability to provide restrooms in the proper locations. (Most small and medium-sized public libraries place restrooms and program rooms off the entry foyer, so that meetings and programs can take place when the rest of the library is closed. Few existing commercial buildings are designed this way.)
- Adequate ceiling height. Anything less than ten feet between the floor and the suspended ceiling grid is a serious problem, for it makes it difficult or impossible to provide the reflected uplighting that works best in libraries. In practice, the need for 10-foot or higher ceilings means there can be no less than about 14 feet between one floor and the surface of the floor above.

- Space for meeting rooms. Meeting rooms typically need higher ceilings than other areas of the library. Because columns to support upper floors severely limit the utility of meeting rooms, most meeting rooms have no floors above them. If meeting rooms are to be used after hours, they need to be directly accessible from the main entry vestibule.
- Absence of extensive bearing walls. Bearing walls support the structure and are consequently hard to alter or remove. If bearing walls force you to create more separate public spaces than you need, you may wind up with a building that is inflexible and expensive to staff.
- Column spacing that works with book stacks. New libraries are designed so that column spacing is in multiples of shelf aisle spacing, so that columns never end up in the middle of aisles. If an existing building has a large number of columns, this may limit its usefulness as a library.
- Ease of meeting accessibility requirements. Many old restrooms and narrow hallways will not meet ADA (Americans with Disabilities Act) requirements, and any variations in floor level can lead to problems.
- Large open spaces for easy supervision. Maintaining the best possible sight lines for your staff will reduce the long-term cost of library operation.
- Structural design that permits humidity control. It is completely reasonable to expect that your HVAC system will maintain relative humidity between 30 and 50 percent at all times. However, many older buildings present particular problems when it comes to maintaining adequate minimum humidity in the winter.
- No major costs for moving people between floors.
- No environmental problems, such as asbestos, lead paint, and underground fuel tanks. All of these can be extraordinarily expensive to correct. Any building constructed before the late 1970s may have asbestos in pipe lagging, floor tile, adhesives, duct lining, and so on.
- An attractive exterior, or one that can be made attractive easily.
- A sufficient number of windows. Readers and staff like natural light. Skylights are a major pain in libraries and are not a substitute for windows.

Probably the easiest buildings to convert to libraries are empty big box stores, which tend to have large open spaces, high ceilings, and single floors.

In general, it is harder to convert existing buildings to libraries than to most other purposes. Consider what universities do. Most new buildings are for science and engineering, for athletic functions, and for libraries. For very good reasons, the humanities, social sciences, and administration—which need primarily office and classroom space—get remodeled buildings.

Unfortunately, some people inevitably see libraries as the solution to derelict building problems. A local government saddled with an abandoned building may see conversion to a library as a way out of the dilemma. Private owners who have been unable to sell empty office buildings, churches, or stores may see the library as their last chance to cash in—sometimes for far more than the building is worth. (In some cases, private owners and their real estate agents have started whispering campaigns, accusing public library boards that have rejected unsuitable buildings of doing so because board members would rather build expensive "monuments to their egos." Your architects and consultant can defend you in these situations.)

Be sure that your new or expanded building can be expanded again in the future. People who want you to use inadequate sites will argue that the electronic revolution means that your library will never need to be expanded again. But they are wrong. Wrong, wrong, wrong.

Be sure your site is large enough. If you will be providing on-site parking—and most libraries do—you will need a site that is a minimum of four times as large as the total floor area of your library. Detention basins (to control water runoff) require even more space. (Obviously this may not apply to central business district libraries in large cities.)

For public libraries, the best sites are usually good commercial sites. If it's not a nice place for a nice store, it's not a nice place for a nice public library. Academic libraries are best with central sites, but because some of them tend to be huge, they have to be constructed on open land on the edge of campus. (In 1970, the University of Chicago built its new library on the site of the football stadium, which seems like a particularly good idea.)

Within buildings, such as schools or office structures, good library sites require floor strength, open floor plans for easy supervision, no unnecessary partitions that cannot be removed, quiet neighbors, and sufficient space for long-term use. Being adjacent to food service areas can make libraries particularly visible.

MOST IMPORTANTLY: To repeat points made earlier, the world is awash with surplus buildings and sites that are white elephants. Many are vacant or undeveloped for very good reasons. Don't let people unload them on your library. Always keep in mind that converting an existing structure to a library can easily cost nearly as much as starting from scratch, and that architects have to charge a higher percentage of construction cost for remodeling work than they do for new construction.

VII. DYSFUNCTIONAL DESIGN CONCEPTS

Although this outline is concerned with the construction process rather than with design issues, there are a number of common design errors that are found constantly in library buildings and are important to mention.

- Skylights. Areas under skylights are too bright by day and too dark by night, and the glare from skylights interferes with reading and computer use. Areas under skylights are noisy. And many skylights leak. (Skylights are touted as energy-saving devices, but to balance the brilliant light from a skylight, you may need to increase artificial lighting in adjacent areas.)
- Windows that face any direction except north and don't have blinds. Many libraries have high windows that produce uncontrollable, blinding light.
- Atriums. Atriums are high-ceilinged spaces connecting two or more floors. They can be grand spaces, and they can help with user orientation within a building. But most librarians dislike them, often intensely. Atriums take up a lot of space, they waste energy, they transmit unwanted noise, they are hard to maintain, they block internal movement on upper floors, and they unnerve people with acrophobia. Some people select library atriums as places to commit suicide.
- Designer staircases. Many libraries have impressively dysfunctional staircases. Watch out in particular for features (such as open or transparent risers or overly long straight runs of steps) that bother people with acrophobia. Other dangerous features include oddly shaped steps, horizontal bars in railings that can be climbed like ladders, handrails that run diagonally to the run of steps, curved or circular staircases, steps that are not enclosed at their ends, and floating staircases where users can bump their heads on the underside of the stairs. Open staircases can also lead to unwanted noise transmission between floors. Making a major architectural statement with a staircase can be a seriously bad idea.
- Courtyards usually cause trouble by interfering with logical internal circulation. Users going from point A to point B often have to circumnavigate courtyards, and courtyards tend to lead to beads-on-a-chain room arrangement. Maintaining courtyard plantings can become a major burden.
- Water features. Water and books are not a good combination. People throw things into water features, and they sometimes fall into them. Some libraries find that the persuasive sound of running water sends staff members constantly to the restroom. And water features have harbored Legionnaires' disease. *Never* agree to an indoor water feature.
- Non-rectangular interior spaces. Virtually everything in libraries is rectangular. Oddly shaped spaces are hard to use effectively and hard to light effectively, and they result in wasted space.

- Downlighting. The right way to light a library is to bounce the light off a white ceiling. Any other form of lighting leads to uneven illumination and glare. Among the many types of bad lighting that cause problems in libraries are recessed downlights and light fixtures mounted on ceilings. Unfortunately, many architects and lighting designers like downlighting and are not bothered at all by the blinding glare that accompanies it.
- Light fixtures that show off dead bugs. No matter how great your maintenance staff members are, dead bugs will always be one hop ahead of them.
- Insufficient electrical outlets. Electrical outlets are needed everywhere, both for opening day and for years to come, when furniture may be rearranged or new equipment purchased. No place in a public service area should be more than six or eight feet from the nearest electrical and data outlets, especially in an age when many users bring laptops with them. Areas where food is served—such as staff break rooms and meeting rooms with kitchenettes—need large numbers of electrical circuits for times when many electrical devices are used simultaneously.
- Bad acoustics. Common sources of serious acoustical problems are atriums, sloped ceilings without acoustic surfaces, and inadequate sound separation between rooms.
- Bad security, including:
  - Multiple public entrances cause problems because each entrance needs to be watched by library staff members. Unstaffed security gates (with or without security cameras) don't work.
  - Dead-end stack aisles, where users can be trapped.
  - Internet computer screens facing away from staff service desks.
  - Single-user restrooms with locking doors. Restrooms with stalls provide adequate privacy without facilitating vandalism.
  - Bad sight lines. Complex spaces that are difficult to supervise can cause many problems.
  - Study rooms with opaque walls.
- Inflexibility. During the 50 to 200-year life of a library building, library services will change many times. Any time a library is designed to work in one way only, trouble results. Common sources of inflexibility are excessive built-in equipment and furniture, too many small spaces, the use of soffits to define the location of desks or other furnishings, and architecturally mounted task lighting.
- Maintenance problems. Perhaps the most common and avoidable maintenance problem in libraries is light bulbs that are difficult to reach. Another is excess glass that needs cleaning by experts. Always show your library plans to your custodians.

VIII. SCHEMATIC DESIGNS

Schematic design (often abbreviated as "SD") is the first architectural step. When this step is completed, you should have:

- Floor plans (including tentative furniture placement) and elevations (drawings of your building seen squarely from each side). It's important that you make clear to your architect that the schematic design floor plans must include all furniture placement. Without this information, a library looks like a bunch of big open rooms.
- A site plan (showing how your building will fit on your site) and a vicinity plan (showing how your site relates to your community).
- Outline specifications.
- A cost estimate.
- A list comparing the square footage of each space in the design with the space allocated for the same purpose in the building program, and a similar table comparing furnishings in the design with those in the program.

Because mechanical systems (electrical, plumbing, HVAC, and so on) can represent from a third to nearly half of the cost of construction, it's a good idea to have basic engineering concepts included in schematic designs.

There are many methods of moving from the needs statements in your program to a schematic design, and different architects have different approaches. But whatever approach is taken, the building design should evolve from a concern with the individual spaces needed and their relationships to each other. No schematic design process should begin with an exterior envelope and then try to stuff all the needed spaces into it.

Much of the creative design work of the project takes place during schematic design. Architects may correspondingly bill a substantial portion of their total fee at the completion of this stage. Although the AIA says that schematic design is 15 percent of the total architectural fees for project, some architects bill a much higher percentage than that. If done well, the schematic design phase consumes a tremendous amount of very expensive architectural time, and to be fair to your architects you need to recognize this.

For the vast majority of libraries, it's important that schematic designs emerge in stages. Libraries do not benefit from architects who work backwards from concept or appearance. If a full-fledged design is delivered at stage one, that's a bad signal. And beware of pretty boxes with muddled or uncertain interior arrangements.

Some libraries, however, are intended more to make dramatic architectural statements than to function in practical ways. If this is your desire, it will alter your approach—and your selection of architects.

The evolution of a schematic design involves at least four essential parties: architects, library board or administration, library staff, and consultant. When design problems occur, one of the best and fastest problem-solving approaches is to have representatives of these four sit down as a group and thrash out specific design issues.

Very few architectural firms will actively encourage you to include your consultant in schematic design meetings, but it is to your strong advantage to do so. Make a point of asking your consultant to attend these meetings.

Owners and architects frequently have disagreements at the schematic design phase. If your architects don't want to change an idea you don't like, insist on specific reasons and reject those reasons if they aren't relevant to your needs or wishes. Librarians know more than architects do about how libraries operate.

If you don't like a proposed idea, stop it as quickly as possible. Unwanted concepts tend to take on a life of their own and need to be brought to a quick halt. You are not doing your architects a favor by failing to say "no" the minute you see something you genuinely don't want, since the longer they work on a design you don't want, the more of their limited time they'll waste. Saying "yes" when you are thinking "no" is unfair to your architects.

Be careful not to get sidetracked in arguments over minor points (such as the shape of a window) when there are major conceptual issues to resolve. At the schematic design phase—particularly at the beginning—concentration on broad issues is important. That's why it's inappropriate to start with half-finished floor plans.

In reviewing schematic designs, watch for the many functional problems that can occur in libraries. Look for problems with security, awkward or confusing physical relationships between areas, bad sight lines, wasted space, non-rectangular spaces, lighting that is not evenly distributed and indirect, difficult maintenance, design spaces that fail to match program spaces in size and location, and so on.

Occasionally, when a library is faced with a number of different options on different sites, it will begin with a "feasibility study" to examine which options are suitable or unsuitable, before beginning work on a schematic design.

By the end of the schematic design phase of your project, you will have enough information for fundraising. For this reason, architectural work should cease when your schematic design is completed while you locate the funds to construct your building.

IX. RENDERINGS AND MODELS

Most library construction projects of any size will benefit from renderings and models.

Renderings are artistic drawings of selected views of the inside and outside of the new library. Unlike the elevation drawings, which are rather mechanical representations, renderings are sketches in perspective. They have all the extra details to which most viewers respond—trees and plantings, passing cars, users, and so on. Some renderings are simple black-and-white sketches or color computer printouts, while others are works of art.

Models are three-dimensional representations of the completed building. Usually models are simplified, and frequently they are stylized. Models can vary from simple constructions, showing little more than basic masses, to complex representations in color, with added trees, pedestrians, vehicles, and so on. Some models are exterior models only, while others have removable roofs and upper floors so that people can see the interior arrangement of each floor of the library.

Sometimes it's to your advantage to keep renderings and models somewhat vague and conceptual. The more detail you give people up front, the more they'll expect to find that specific detail in the finished library. Since models are frequently built early in the project, details can change a great deal between then and the final bid documents.

Since very few people can read blueprints, renderings and models are an important way to show them what the completed building will look like. In particular, voters and donors need to know what their tax dollars and donations will build.

The creation of architectural renderings and particularly models is a skilled specialty, and is not something you can turn over to a friend who draws well or makes hobby models. Modern CADD (computer-aided design and drafting) and BIM (building information modeling) systems can actually rotate views of buildings in space, and these greatly simplify making renderings.

One major issue is accurate representation. Artists who create renderings of proposed buildings tend to gild the lily by omitting ugly mechanical details (such as air-handling equipment or penthouses). They also tend to improve on the surroundings by replacing adjacent used car lots with virgin forests, adding greensward for which there is no actual space, and so on. Sometimes even the client doesn't realize how things will actually look. You will have to decide whether selective artistic vision will hurt or help you in the long run, and make sure you and your architects settle this issue face-to-face before renderings are prepared.

Software exists to provide an animated impression of how it will feel to walk through your proposed building. You may find this a useful promotional device, but remember that it's impossible to re-create the impression of moving through a three-dimensional space on a computer screen.

Renderings and models are expensive. The cost ranges from a few hundred dollars for a simple black and white computer drawing to many thousands for a complex scale model.

Study models, however, fall into a completely different category. These are more rough-and-ready constructions used by architects to study massing or convey ideas to owners. Study models are part of the design process and should not require any additional fees.

X. MONEY

The single most important construction material is money.

Few libraries have enough cash lying around to do the job. It always helps if you have huge unexpected legacies, or atomic power plants in your taxing jurisdiction, but most libraries have to locate extra construction funds.

Before you can raise funds, you will need to know what your project will cost. This is a job for your architects. Be sure the preparation of cost estimates is part of your contract. Frequently, estimates of costs are prepared at the end of each of the three major stages—schematic design, design development, and bid documents.

Be sure at all times that you understand whether your architects' estimates are for "construction costs" or "project costs." When figures are quoted, always ask which they represent. Construction costs are the costs of erecting the building itself. Project costs are substantially higher. They include many additional costs you will have to pay, including paving, landscaping, utility connections, professional fees, furnishings, equipment, and so on. In addition, you may have to cover moving, opening day collections, and other costs. For realistic financing, always use project costs rather than construction costs.

The cost of construction projects usually startles people who are not involved in the planning efforts, and coping with public and political "sticker shock" is frequently a problem. It helps to be able to point out what similar communities or universities have spent on adequately sized new libraries. Frequently, groups in town or on campus that have little knowledge of library space needs or costs will propose clearly inadequate project costs by plucking project figures out of thin air, and once proposed, these figures can take on a life of their own. Other groups will assume that whatever cost a library proposes is clearly excessive and will automatically propose a fraction of that cost. Even if the library is proposing a cheaply built, undersized building, someone is likely to refer to it as a "Taj Mahal." Dealing with sticker shock can be difficult; one way is through very public planning, frequent communication with the media and political leaders while planning is taking place, and printed reports.

Primary sources of funds for public libraries include the sale of bonds, direct allocations from local governments, mortgages, state construction grants, money set aside from operating funds for future construction, and private fundraising. Unfortunately, with the conversion of LSCA to LSTA, federal construction funds for public libraries ceased to be available. (LSCA is the Library Services and Construction Act of 1964. LSTA is the Library Services and Technology Act of 1996.)

- Bonds can be issued by citizen vote or by direct government action.
- Once you know project costs and available government funds, you will know how much you need to raise privately.
- Some basic points about private fundraising:
  - Private fundraising requires an incorporated Friends group or foundation with federal 501(c)(3) tax status. Obtaining this status is not difficult, but the paperwork is initially intimidating. You will need the help of an attorney. (Library boards can also raise funds directly. The problem is that people have read too many stories about fundraising by public boards leading to the transfer of tax money to other projects. Donors may fear that even elected boards with funds that cannot be attached by any higher level of government may spend funds for totally different projects if new board members are elected.)
  - Professional fundraising consultants are available, and some specialize in libraries. Even if you do most of your own work, it's helpful to have

initial advice and planning assistance from an experienced person. Hiring a consultant is much like hiring any other professional; feedback from previous clients is particularly important.
- If you have a major fundraising campaign, you will probably want to hire someone to run it. Fundraising can take a great deal of time. It's unreasonable to assign your fundraising to your current staff unless you hire someone else to do their regular work.
- Fundraisers should always be paid by the hour or by the job, never a percentage of the funds raised.

XI. DESIGN DEVELOPMENT

The best time to spend the money on design development is after you have the necessary funding for your project.

Design development (often called "DD") is the process of expanding the schematic design to include full information on how the building will be constructed. At this point you will get details on casework (built-in furniture), ceiling plans, the locations of all mechanical and electrical elements, detailed furniture location information, and so on.

Some decisions made at this point are critically important to the successful functioning of your library. Among the decisions that should concern you and your consultant most are HVAC, lighting, data transmission, electrical wiring, telephone systems, service desks, shelving, and plumbing.

The importance of these topics makes it vital that *all four players* in the library plan—architects, staff, owners, and consultant—be involved.

XII. BID DOCUMENTS, AKA CONSTRUCTION DOCUMENTS

Bid documents are the package of materials necessary for contractors to make careful estimates of the cost of a project. They have two primary components: drawings and project manuals.

- The drawings (blueprints) show the structural, plumbing, mechanical, and electrical components of the project.
- The project manual is an accompanying narrative text that includes all the specific requirements of the project, including specifications for the types and qualities of all components.

Most bid documents include a few "add alternates" in addition to the "base bid." Add alternates are additional items or features that you would like to have included in the project if the base bids are sufficiently low. By asking for prices on these items as part of the bid process, you will obtain better prices than you would by negotiating prices later with your contractor. (There are also "deduct alternates," but the conventional wisdom is that add alternates lead to lower prices.)

Accurate and complete bid documents are of critical importance. The nature of the low-bid process required for most government work means that contractors will base their prices on the very least that the documents allow them to do. If critical items are omitted from the documents, you won't get them in your library. They will then have to be supplied through change orders, and these will cost much more than they would if they had been properly listed in the bid documents. Bid documents are a job for professionals; do not try this at home.

Many details of room finishes, electrical receptacle locations, door types and hardware, and so on will appear for the first time in bid documents. This makes such documents extremely important to review.

Bid documents are complex and detailed, but do your best to review them to be sure that they include what you want. If you are uncertain about the appearance of any item, such as a light fixture or door handle, ask your architects for a copy of the manufacturer's "cut sheet" for that item.

Having your consultant review your bid documents is an extremely good idea. Almost any error or omission detected—even the most minor—will cost vastly more to correct than you will pay your consultant for a full, final review.

To give your consultant adequate time to review the documents, and to leave time for corrections and questions, send your consultant the 90 percent set in addition to the final version. And never let your architect finish drawings at the last second and then tell you there's no time to review them before bidding.

XIII. BIDDING

This section describes "design-bid-build" projects, the traditional way library buildings are constructed. In a design-bid-build project, general contractors bid on the entire project. (Some of the work is done by the contractors, but much is done by specialized subcontractors, who are hired by the general contractor.)

Other delivery methods, including construction management and design-build projects, are described in a later section.

In a design-bid-build project, your architects and attorney will be involved throughout the bidding process. Each state and locality has specific rules for bidding on public construction jobs, and failing to observe the rules can lead to major problems. Both your architects and your attorney will examine the bid documents, and they will be present when bids are opened to be sure that all legal requirements are met.

The bidding process includes:

- Advertisements announcing that the project is ready to bid. An advertisement will include a date and place when bid documents will first be available, a date for a pre-bid meeting, and a date and time for the receipt of bids.
- Formal opening of bids after the deadline for their receipt has passed. Late bids—even if they are just minutes late—are rejected unopened. Bidders use forms supplied by the architects, certifying that they are bidding on all required components of the project, certifying that they have the necessary bonding, and so on.
- Customarily, the bid goes to the lowest bidder, but there are exceptions to this rule. Consult with your architects and attorney.
- The library always reserves the right to reject all bids and start over. This right is important, particularly if all bids are too high and it becomes necessary to redesign the project.

The pre-bid conference is important. By answering any questions in front of all bidders, the architects try to make sure that no bidders can later claim that they were not party to basic information. Minutes are kept and distributed to all bidders. In many cases, the architects will state at the conference that all oral responses are nonbinding, and that the written response to questions (in the form of an addendum to the specifications that is distributed to all bidders) is the only binding response. Your architects may require attendance by contractors at the pre-bid conference as a condition for bidding.

Most bid documents include addenda issued after the pre-bid conference to clarify questions raised at the conference or other questions raised later. These addenda are a routine part of the bidding process and should not be interpreted as a failure of your architects to do things right the first time.

Because of the importance of formal addenda, it's a good idea to warn your staff not to comment informally to prospective bidders when they visit the library.

Ask your staff to show bidders anything they want to see, but to refer all questions to the architects.

Most libraries will require that bidders be bonded. This protects the library from bad bids. And it keeps contractors with bad reputations from bidding, because the bonding companies won't insure them.

Some projects "pre-qualify" bidders. This involves establishing minimum criteria for bidding and verifying that bidders meet these criteria before being allowed to bid. Prequalification is designed to prevent clearly unqualified bidders from going to all the work of preparing bids, only to be turned down due to lack of experience, inability to get bonding, or similar problems.

XIV. CONSTRUCTION MANAGEMENT

Some large or complicated projects are built by construction management firms rather than by general contractors. Construction management firms are hired much the way architects or consultants are hired. The construction management firm is an employee of the library. While the architects are responsible for construction "administration" (making sure that the library is built as designed), a construction management firm is responsible for the daily operation of construction work, serving much the same role as a general contractor, but not profiting from the ability to cut expenditures.

One important function of construction management firms is "value engineering." Value engineering consists of evaluating construction options to see where savings can be made without impairment of function. Because savings decisions of this kind will best be made fairly early in the design phase of a project, construction management firms can provide greater help if they are hired soon after architects are selected.

Instead of seeking a single bid for most of construction, if you hire a construction management firm, the firm will solicit separate bids for a wide variety of aspects of construction, and there will not be a single bid opening.

XV. DESIGN-BUILD PROJECTS

A very few library projects are design-build projects. In these projects, teams consisting of a contractor and an architect undertake to construct the required building at a specified price. Because controlling construction cost is such a major factor in design-build projects, the contractors tend to be the dominant partners.

XVI. GROUNDBREAKING

Groundbreaking is an important occasion. Take advantage of its positive benefits.

Although the groundbreaking takes place out of doors, it's a great deal easier to entertain people indoors at the end of the ceremony.

If you will be having speeches out of doors, you will need a PA system. Many speakers cannot be heard out of doors, and many people with bad hearing cannot hear any unamplified speakers.

Plan groundbreakings for nice weather, and have contingency plans for rain.

Be sure to invite all the right people. Politicians thrive on library projects because they offer great noncontroversial photo ops. Also, be sure to invite all current and prior board and staff members, all donors, the contractors and other businesses involved with the project, and the consulting professionals on the project (architects, engineers, and consultants). Invite local school groups, clubs, chambers of commerce, faculty, students, and so on.

Invite the news media. Send out invitations in advance, and call, e-mail, or fax them the day before the event to remind them. When they arrive, provide fact sheets listing important names, dates, building features, and so on.

Groundbreakings offer fewer photo ops than ribbon cuttings because there's no new building to see. Provide an attractively photogenic substitute, such as young children participating in the ceremony.

Be sure to prepare the ground in advance. Untouched ground frequently has the consistency of concrete. It's embarrassing to watch a major donor struggle to turn a shovelful of soil. Spade the ground up thoroughly and smooth it out the day before the ceremony.

Give everyone a chance to turn a spadeful of soil. Libraries are egalitarian institutions, and many people want to feel a part of the process.

Don't count on speakers to cover the right subjects without being coached. Among the things to be sure someone covers are:

- Recognition of all politicians (even those who—very frankly—didn't do anything at all).
- Recognition of donors. You may want to point out certain really major gifts, but be careful not to offend those who gave smaller amounts.
- Recognition of all board members, and university officials, including those who served during the planning process but whose terms expired before groundbreaking.
- Recognition of important support groups, such as your library foundation, library Friends, and so on.
- Recognition of the hired folks, including the architects, contractors, consultant, and so on.
- General remarks on the important role of the library in your community and on the features of the new building.

Consider finding an indoor space for post-groundbreaking snacks. This is a good time to display floor plans and renderings away from the weather. (It's also a good time to display in a delicate sort of way brochures asking for funding for specific pieces of equipment or brochures for inscribed bricks for a future plaza.)

XVII. THE CONSTRUCTION PROCESS

In design-bid-build projects, one vital function of the architect is construction administration. In this approach, the architect ensures that the building is constructed according to specifications, that work is carried out expeditiously, that the necessary coordination of various contractors takes place, that problems that arise are dealt with rapidly and effectively, that all shop drawings are approved, and that all payments to contractors are made properly. These are absolutely essential services.

The general contractor will in turn provide a project manager who is responsible for the daily management of construction.

If you hire a professional construction management firm to represent your library during the construction process and actually construct the building, you will need to spell out the relationships between the architects, construction management firm, and contractors. This is important because some roles proposed by construction management firms are traditionally those of architects or general contractors. If you're not careful, you could end up paying twice for some services, or buying services that you may not need.

The project team will consist at a minimum of the architects, the contractor's hired project manager (or the construction management firm, if you employ one), other representatives of the contractor or subcontractors, representatives of the library, and a representative of the owner if the library is part of a larger organization. The library representatives can be the director or a member of the staff to whom the project is assigned. The presence of library staff is essential. It's a good idea to have two library staff members present at meetings, so that the library can maintain a consistent presence when a key staff member is out of town or ill.

Bear in mind that many large construction firms have relatively few employees. They work by bidding, organizing, and supervising projects, not by providing their own employees to do the actual construction work.

The architects (or construction manager or general contractor) will work with the contractors and subcontractors to establish a construction schedule.

During the project, there will be regular weekly or biweekly construction coordination meetings of the project team to be sure that work is progressing on schedule, to coordinate the work of all the contractors and subcontractors, to deal with problems, to answer questions, and to make decisions not requiring action by the full library board or other owner. If the library board or staff have concerns, it's important that they be taken up immediately at these meetings.

The contractors submit pay requests (usually monthly). These are accompanied by "lien waivers" for work done by subcontractors for the prior pay requests. A waiver of lien from a subcontractor assures you that the contractor paid the subcontractor the subcontractor's proper share of the contractor's last pay request, and that the subcontractor now waives the right to file a mechanic's lien for that amount against your library. The architect or construction management firm will oversee the lien waivers to make sure that subcontractors have been paid.

Normally the library holds back a portion of each request (typically 10 percent) to be paid only after all work by that contractor has been completed to the full satisfaction of the owner and architects.

All projects involve "change orders," which occur when unforeseen problems arise, the owners change their minds, or problems with the bid documents are discovered. All owners try to avoid change orders because they are expensive. With change orders, costs are arrived at by negotiation rather than by low bid, and the result is inevitably more expensive. One economical way to help avoid change orders is to do the most thorough review possible of the bid documents before the project is put out for bid.

Because most projects involve change orders—particularly in expansion or conversion projects, where unforeseen problems can be discovered—every project needs contingency funds. Typically, libraries set aside at least 10 percent extra for projects involving remodeling and at least 5 percent for new construction projects.

Be careful to establish and follow the proper chain of command. In the normal chain of command, the subcontractors report to the contractors and the contractors report to the architects and/or construction management firm. If you see a contractor doing something you don't like, or you want to make a change, the proper thing to do is usually to contact your architects. In particular, do not make offhand remarks to contractors or workers that may be construed as requests for additional services.

Occasionally a contractor will make a mistake and suggest issuing a credit to the owner rather than undoing the mistake. Agreeing to something like this is tempting, particularly because doing things properly may delay the project, but by accepting such offers some libraries have permanently limited the effectiveness of their buildings in return for relatively minor compensations. *SO BE EXTREMELY WARY.* This is a good time for a review by both your architects *and* your consultant.

Some remodeling and expansion projects are conducted in two or more phases, with the library continuing to operate in the building the entire time. Construction in phases is a tangled undertaking. Bids are higher because the contractor will not have access to the entire building at all times, and because the contractor will have to work around staff and library users. Users and staff will in turn be subjected to months or years of noises, dust, limited access, bad smells, workers' radios, and other undesirable problems. The contractors may want to stage construction on the library's parking lot, leaving no place for library staff or users to park. Two-phase construction will take a great deal longer than single-phase construction. And with one-year warranties from contractors, the warranties on some parts of the building may expire before the entire building is completed; this is a special problem with HVAC systems. Before choosing two-phase construction, always explore the option of moving out and the comparative costs of two-phase vs. single-phase construction.

At the completion of work, "punch lists" are prepared. The architects and owner (sometimes assisted by the consultant) inspect the project with care, preparing lists of items that must be completed or corrected before the building can be considered complete. When the items on the punch list have been completed to the owner's and architects' satisfaction, the project is considered complete and the retainages are paid to the contractors. It is often a very good idea to get assistance with punching your library, because the architect may be wearying of the entire process and not eager to note all the remaining problems. HVAC systems in particular need expert checking to be sure that everything works.

In complex projects, it's a good idea to keep up with inspections rather than wait until the end of the project to do the punch list. And you may want to provide specific information where construction documents are a little vague. For example, staff may want to write indications of specific electrical outlet locations on the raw concrete floors.

Some contractors will put extreme pressure on owners to pay all but minor amounts of retainages before all punch list items have been totally corrected. IT IS ABSOLUTELY ESSENTIAL THAT YOU RESIST THESE PRESSURES. Once you have paid off all but a very small portion of the money due, contractors will tend to concentrate on large new projects rather than wrap up small details on old ones. The fact that you are holding back far more than the actual cost of making final corrections is the primary leverage you have to be sure that all the last minor items are fixed. The punch list process can sometimes ruin what was a warm and friendly relationship between owner and contractor, but that's the way it goes. Your responsibility is to be sure the library got everything it paid for, and that everything was done right. Always stand your ground. Some punch list processes can go on for years, but that's better than paying too soon and not getting what you paid for.

Before signing off on a project, the owner should receive:

- A full set of operating manuals for the building and its equipment, a detailed walk-through of the building for all relevant library staff, and full training ("commissioning") on the operation of complex systems.
- A set of "as-built" or "record" drawings for the building. These are drawings modified to indicate all situations where actual construction details differ from the original plans. As-built drawings are essential for future repairs and alterations, and they should continue to be modified whenever changes are made. Protect them fiercely. (If you want your architects to provide neatly corrected as-built drawings, write this into your contract and withhold final payment until you receive the drawings.)
- Copies of all shop drawings showing the architects' initials of approval.

As-built drawings should be both on CADD or BIM disks and as a full-sized printout on a permanent medium.

CADD or BIM discs are not an acceptable substitute for actual physical prints. Anyone working on your building at a later time will want to see full-sized drawings, and electronic systems change so frequently that your discs are unlikely to be usable when you finally need them.

Libraries typically find that the construction process consumes a vast amount of staff time. Libraries need to provide extra staff funding if it becomes necessary to hire additional help for the director during construction.

XVIII. MOVING

Moving can be done by hired movers, by staff and volunteers, or by a combination of the two.

Many issues will affect your choice. How far do you have to move? What will the weather be like? Are you moving inside a building, where you may be able to move fully loaded book stacks with stack-moving equipment? Do you have a labor union with complicating contractual agreements?

Small library moves are often done with staff and volunteers. The main challenge is good procedural planning, particularly developing a method for knowing where each container of books goes on the new shelving.

Large libraries are often better off hiring professional movers. Some companies specialize in library moves. You will probably need to bid this service, so a detailed RFP (request for proposal) is necessary.

The most important components of a successful move are a detailed plan and a single person in charge. Be sure your plan includes the current and new locations for each piece of furniture and for all portions of the collection.

Don't underestimate the complexity of relocating computer services. Reestablishing a 100-computer network is a major undertaking.

Moving takes more time than you might expect. Since your library will be closed during most or all of your move, your announced timetable matters. Be sure not to blithely promise overly ambitious reopening dates.

XIX. RIBBON CUTTING

Ribbon cuttings can be wonderful occasions if you plan them properly, but they can be sources of real embarrassment if things go wrong.

Inevitably, you'll need to move in and start using the building before everything is finished. For this reason, don't plan to keep citizens or students out of the new building until the ribbon cutting takes place. When moving day is over, there are almost always items of furniture that have not arrived, punch list items that have not been completed, and workspaces where staff are just starting to unpack.

Libraries, like new stores, are therefore wise to have "soft" openings, providing public access and service for a few weeks before scheduling a major event. When the ribbon-cutting time comes, unveil (for example) the building plaques and the donor plaques rather than the entire building.

It's usually a bad idea to do much out of doors. Weather is undependable and outdoor acoustics are uncertain. If you want to cut the ribbon at the door and then have everyone troop into the new library, be prepared to cut the ribbon first and have speeches indoors afterwards. If you have outdoor presentations, you will need a good PA system and a contingency plan for rain or heavy winds.

Plan ribbon cuttings for nice weather. Midwinter is often a poor time. Out-of-town participants will have a difficult time traveling to the ribbon cutting, and elderly donors may slip on the ice. People will need to enter the library the moment they arrive.

Be sure to invite all the right people. These include politicians, university officials, board members (including those whose terms ended mid-project), staff members, contractors and other businesses involved with the project, and the consulting professionals on the project (architects, engineers, and consultants). And invite all of the citizens of the community.

You may want to have a special event for donors, but don't make it the main ribbon cutting. The entire community needs to feel involved.

Speeches should be brief. Among the important things to cover are:

- Recognition of the key people present. These may include politicians, donors, board members (including those whose terms ended mid-project), library staff members, and hired people who worked on the project.
- The locations of plaques and other forms of recognition.
- Special functional features. Building aesthetics are usually very visible, and you don't need to say much about them. Instead have someone dwell on convenience, services, efficiency, good functional design, and so on—all of which may not be intuitively obvious to non-librarians.

XX. TEN-MONTH POST-OCCUPANCY EVALUATION

Most construction projects carry a one-year warranty.

During the first year of occupancy, keep a careful log of problems that develop and what the contractors did to correct them.

About ten months after the building is completed and accepted, conduct a thorough evaluation. The key people in this evaluation are your architects, your construction management firm (if you have one), your library staff, and even your consultant if you want a completely independent opinion. Of all of these people, your staff members will have the best day-to-day knowledge of where problems exist.

If anything is not working correctly or proves to have been done wrong, it is extraordinarily important that this fact be noted and transmitted to the contractors before the warranty expires.

This is your final chance to have many things done at no charge. (Certain components of the building, such as the roof or some pieces of equipment, may have longer warranties, but don't take any chances.)

As with the punch list, insist that the corrections be made on a timely basis and to your standards. Never let a vendor sweet-talk you into accepting something that is not quite right.

If your project will be conducted in phases, warranties on the first phase may have expired before subsequent phases are completed. Unfortunately, some problems are hard to see when work is continuing. If your project has more than one phase and will last more than a year, you may wish to require your contractor to provide a warranty on the entire project that extends for one year after the total completion of the project. This is particularly important for systems like HVAC that operate in both halves of the building.

XXI. REWARDS FOR THE STRESSED-OUT LIBRARIAN

At the end of your project, your library director will deserve a long vacation. Depending on circumstances, he or she may also deserve a major bonus in pay.

4

Basic Configuration of Library Spaces

I. INTRODUCTION

This chapter provides a quick overview of some general options for the physical layout of library buildings.

Many of the issues discussed here are easy to review when you are going over early versions of schematic designs. If you think your staff, owners, or architects are proposing room shapes and arrangements that may cause functional problems, the time to deal with this is as early as possible in the design process.

If you are going to evaluate a schematic design, it's essential that the design contain furniture placement. Without furniture placement indicated, library spaces are nothing more than large open spaces, and it's impossible to judge their effectiveness.

Occasionally architects will argue that schematic designs should not include furniture placement, which should come later in the process. But they are wrong. Be sure that your contract with your architects makes clear that furniture placement is part of schematic design work.

It's unfair to everyone to keep your mouth shut and let an unfortunate early concept develop and take shape, only to be abandoned when your staff or owners or architects have devoted a lot of time to them.

This floor plan for the Allerton District Library (Monticello, Illinois) illustrates many basic principles of functional library design. The 12,350-square-foot building was designed by Mark Misselhorn (architect) and Julie Coogan (interior designer) of apaceDesign in Peoria, Illinois, and completed in 2016. Fred wrote the building program. The design principles illustrated here apply to libraries in a wide range of sizes.

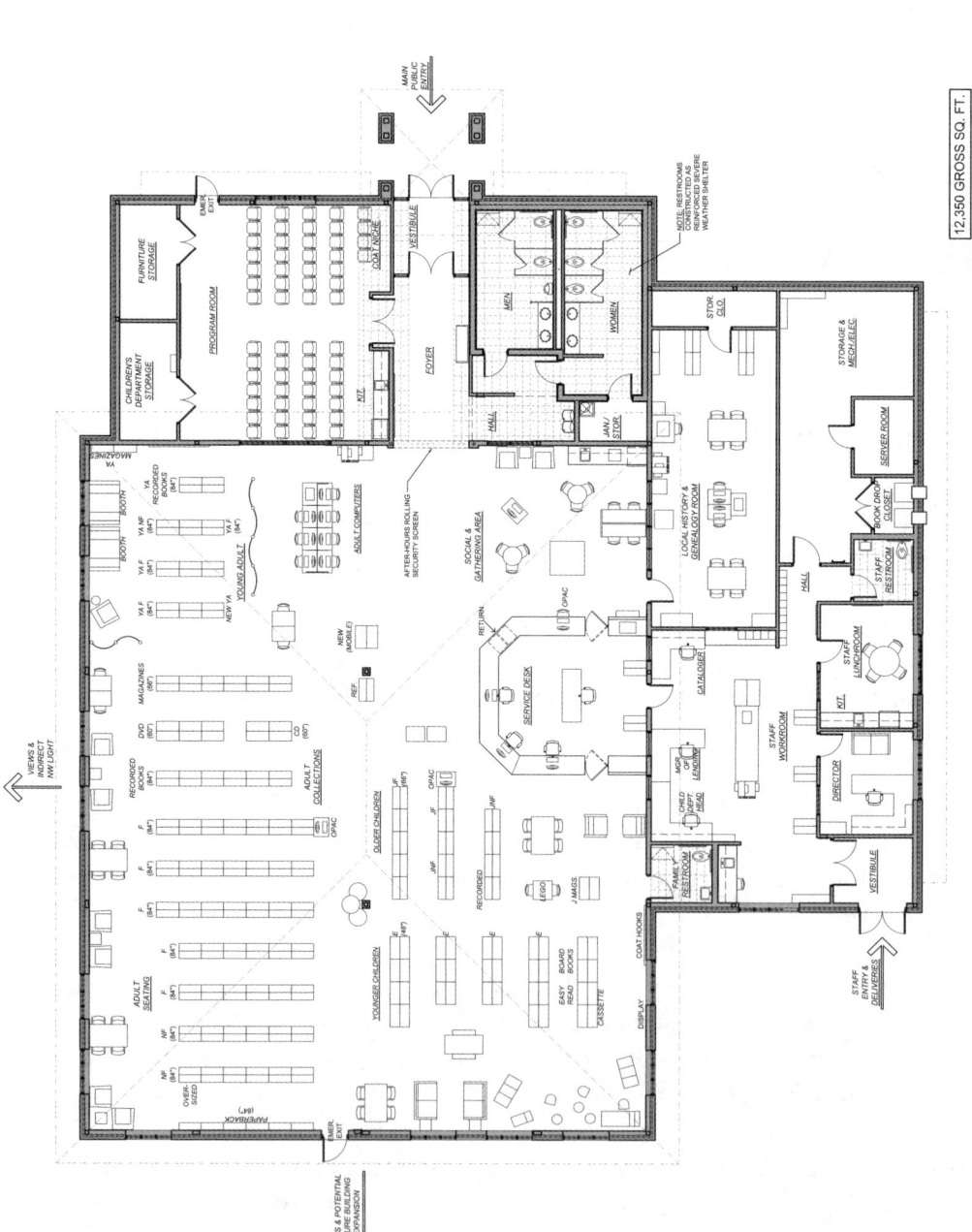

FLOOR PLAN

General Features
- The building consists entirely of rectangular spaces. Triangular and curved spaces are much more expensive to construct and much harder to use effectively.
- The building faces east, sheltering library users and staff from the prevailing winter winds in the Midwest, which come from the north and west.
- The library building is designed for easy expansion to the west by knocking out a single wall.
- The opening between the foyer and the main library room can be closed by a security screen, allowing the program room and restrooms to be used when the rest of the building is closed.
- Because the site is sufficiently large, the building could be constructed on a single level, significantly reducing long-term staffing costs (which are about two-thirds the cost of library operations) and eliminating the very substantial construction cost of staircases, an elevator, and an upper floor strong enough to bear the weight of books.
- The building has no basement, eliminating the high cost of constructing a main floor with a basement below it, eliminating the cost of construction of staircases (and perhaps an elevator), and eliminating the problem of flooded basements.
- The drive-up book drops lead into a room designed to contain fires. (Incendiaries in book returns have caused fires in libraries.)
- The library has a large number of wall and floor outlets (which don't show on the plan, but are vital) and security gates are roughed in for possible later installation.

Program Room
- The program room includes storerooms for furniture and for program supplies. (The functionality of program rooms in many libraries is reduced by the inability to store furniture and program equipment out of the way when it is not in use. Program rooms without adequate storage closets end up with stacks of unused furniture and equipment piled around the edges.)

Main Library Room
- The main library room is a simple rectangle, maximizing flexibility of use.
- The north wall of the library has a large number of windows that provide low-glare north light for reading. The furniture arrangement places readers (who like light) close to windows and books (which don't like light) away from windows.
- The main library room is extremely flexible in design. All of the shelving and seating and computers can be relocated. This is particularly easy because there are only two support columns to get in the way. (It doesn't show in the drawing, but the room also has large numbers of electrical outlets, which are essential for flexibility in modern libraries.)
- The single service desk is immediately visible to users entering the main library room. In turn, library staff at the desk have direct oversight of the main library room, the entry foyer, the local history room, and the entrances to the restrooms and meeting room.
- The connection between the main library room and staff work areas is at the back of the service desk, discouraging library users from wandering in.
- The service desk has two access points, making it difficult for staff members to be cornered behind the desk.
- A public photocopier is located at the entrance to the main library room, making it unnecessary for people who stop by the library just to make photocopies to walk through the rest of the library.
- Public computers are close to the service desk for ease of staff supervision and assistance.

- In accordance with good seating practices, round tables are provided only for socializing, while chairs at rectangular tables are on two sides of the tables only.
- Soft seating includes easy chairs for adults and a mixture of easy chairs and loveseats for children and their parents or caregivers. (Parents and children like reading together on loveseats. Adult readers on the other hand don't like sharing soft seating, and sofas therefore tend to be used either by single readers or used for sleeping and necking.)
- Shelving aisles are a maximum of 21 feet long, making it easy for a user to approach an aisle from the opposite end when another user is blocking the aisle.
- The open design of the room leaves no place where users can be cornered. None of the shelving aisles have dead ends.
- The young adult area is as far as possible from the children's area, a feature young adults strongly prefer. It is also easy for adults to use the YA area, since many adults make heavy use of YA materials.
- The social area is between the service desk and the entrance to the main library room, keeping social conversations away from reading areas.

Restrooms
- The two restrooms are designed to serve as storm shelters, which is particularly important in one-story buildings without sturdy second floors that protect people on first floors below. (The unusual thickness of the restroom walls indicates concrete construction. The ceilings of the restrooms are concrete slabs.) The only rooms that provide good storm shelters are restrooms because they are never used as storerooms. And they can be built without windows, avoiding flying glass shards when storms hit.
- The open space in the wall between the restrooms provides space for brackets supporting wall-mounted toilets. Wall-mounted toilets make restroom cleaning easier because they eliminate the unsanitary joints between toilets and floors.
- The restrooms are laid out so that there are no unwanted sight lines between the access hall and the interiors of the two restrooms.
- Restroom doors swing outward, eliminating the problem users face when trying to open doors as they leave restrooms with freshly-washed hands.
- The mop basin (required by building codes) is located as close as possible to the restrooms.
- The library has a staff restroom. No matter what outsiders think, all but the tiniest libraries need staff restrooms. (Ask any experienced librarian.)
- A "family rest room" is located by the children's area. Restrooms of this type are useful for situations where a person of one gender is assisting a person of a different gender, including parents with children and elderly couples.
- The library's eight sinks are concentrated in a relatively compact area of the building, which simplifies plumbing.

Floor plan by apaceDesign of Peoria, IL
Mark Misselhorn (architect)

II. EXTERNAL CONFIGURATION

A. Structural Shapes

Rectangular structures are less expensive to construct than more complex structures, and they're a lot easier to arrange internally.

Constructing buildings with curved walls is expensive. Curved glass is for people with lots of money. As the chapter on collection storage indicates, trying to fit shelving into curved spaces is a miserable experience. Curved glass walls also tend to lead to weird acoustics.

Similarly, rooms with diagonal walls are hard to use. Libraries with a lot of triangular or trapezoidal spaces have problems with furniture placement.

The other side of the issue is that rectangular buildings can also be more boring to look at, particularly if your designer is in love with buildings with no surface ornamentation. We think that surface ornamentation appeals much more to users than to designers, some of whom appear to writhe in agony at the thought of Georgian, Tudor, Art Deco, Prairie, Arts and Crafts, or any other revivals, sometimes forgetting whose money and library it is.

The main thing is to be aware of your choices. Be sure that your architect reviews your options and relative costs, and be sure that all schematic designs show how your necessary furnishings will fit in.

B. Compass Orientation of Entrances

Except in areas where winter never comes, south entrances always work best.

South entrances help protect your users and staff from wintry blasts when doors are held open.

South entrances also discourage ice buildup right outside the doors because the south sun shines directly on the pavement all winter.

If you can't have a south entrance, strive for east or southeast and do your best to avoid north and west entrances.

> This really matters. Fred worked with one library with a long (and fairly modern) flight of steps facing northwest. The steps are coated with ice all winter (because the sun doesn't fall all that much on staircases facing northwest). As a result, the steps are roped off for about three months a year, and users must enter through a basement door. When the architect was asked why he designed a huge exterior flight of steps facing northwest, he responded, "Don't they look great!"

If you are forced to have a north or west entrance, investigate ice-melting systems with fluid in heated pipes buried below the pavement outside the door. Or do as many libraries with west or north entrances do and budget for substantial amounts of ice-melting chemicals. And have a closet for ice-melting chemicals right by your main entrance.

C. Where to Put the Entrance

It's always better to enter a rectangular building or room on the center of the long side. This allows service desks to face entrances and permits users to divide into separate groups the moment they enter the space. For example, in a small public library, children can immediately turn one way and adults the other, without having to traipse through each other's spaces.

If users have to enter the narrow end of a space, it's much harder for library staff to supervise the space, and users have to walk through more irrelevant spaces to reach the spaces they want. It's a little like entering the airplane through a door right by the cockpit and having to thread your way past endless rows of seats.

D. Number of Entrances

"The right number of entrances to a library is anything up to one" is one of the most central tenets of library design, along with "no skylights" and "don't smirk while you terrify people who have acrophobia."

A few exceptions to the single-entrance rule exist. Huge buildings that consist of hallways leading to lockable departments sometimes need more than one way in. Libraries with historic entrances accompanied by flights of stairs need second entrances that are accessible to users with disabilities.

The primary reason for the single-entrance rule is money. All public entrances need to be staffed at all times by people who are within a few feet of the entrance.

All security gates need to be staffed. (Architects frequently don't realize this fact, which means that librarians and building consultants have to keep an eye on schematic designs.)

III. INTERNAL LAYOUT AND ROOM SHAPES

A. Avoid Labyrinths

Library buildings that have bearing walls and have been repeatedly expanded sometimes end up as labyrinths, but there's no excuse for a labyrinth in a new building.

Staff supervision requires excellent sight lines, and that means the absence of unnecessary walls. Patron orientation requires excellent sight lines, and that means the absence of unnecessary walls. User and staff security require excellent sight lines, and those also require the absence of unnecessary walls.

We've met architects who are mad wall builders. "Beware! Beware!" as Mr. Coleridge might say, were he with us today.

> One interesting version of the labyrinth is provided by a midwestern academic library. The library has two identical two-story spaces, each consisting of a main floor and a central balcony. The trouble is that the two spaces are identical in appearance, and neither one is at the building's entry level. Both are arrived at by elevator or totally enclosed staircases, and users arriving in one of the two spaces may take a considerable amount of time to puzzle out that they are in the wrong space. Fred spent several hours in the building and became lost on a number of occasions. He likes to blame his problems on the building.

> The San Francisco Public Library has two entrances, one from Market Street, and a second from the city hall plaza one flight up. People entering from the plaza walk to the great atrium at the center of the building. Across the way is the children's department. But you can't get there, because there's no way around the atrium. To reach the children's department, users retrace their steps to the plaza entrance, go down one floor, walk the length of the building, pass through security, and then go back up by a different elevator. Fred spent fifteen minutes figuring things out and then spent half an hour watching other visitors struggle with the same confusing layout.

B. Maintain Sight Lines

Many libraries have too many partitions.

Unless you are separating back-of-the-house spaces from public spaces, if you must have walls, glass is a good material. Study room walls need to be glass—not walls with little windows but glass walls. Not glass walls *on one side* but glass walls *on all sides* that face the department or adjacent study rooms.

Staff offices need large windows with Venetian blinds. Staff can always close blinds when privacy is essential, but they can't knock windows through when better sight lines are necessary.

Good sight lines are essential for wayfinding. It's no fun to have to give users complex instructions when they ask how to find things. It's a lot easier to answer the favorite reference question of all time ("Where's the restroom?") when you can point to a distant sign and have the user say happily, "Oh yes, I see the sign!"

> When Fred was a student in library school he ran the main information desk at the historic Chicago Public Library, which is now the "Cultural Center." The building was extraordinarily handsome, but it was so confusing that staff had to give routing instructions on the order of, "Take the elevator up one floor, walk the length of the building, take the next elevator up one floor, walk down the corridor, and turn left." Staff had to refuse to tell users where things actually were, because the users then inevitably got lost.

Good sight lines are also essential for security. Libraries do not benefit from lurking places. Far too many libraries require that librarians take frequent tours around the place, just to be sure that everything is safe. We've had librarians tell us, "We have to be careful who uses that study room" because there's no glass wall facing the reference desk.

If your designers don't like glass walls, they'll have to learn to live with them.

The time to start evaluating sight lines is during the schematic design phase. Sometimes you need to be really aggressive.

C. Avoid Strangely Shaped Spaces

Designers are frequently tempted to create interesting interior spaces by avoiding simple rectangles. Sometimes these work well, but often they don't.

L-shaped rooms are often a bad idea. Some libraries have tried L-shaped meeting rooms, with program locations at the juncture of the two sides of the L. Inevitably, all the members of the audience see the speaker at a 45-degree angle, and no one can see the projection screen well. The audience in one arm of the L cannot see the audience in the other arm. Say "No" loudly.

L-shaped rooms will typically hold fewer pieces of furniture than rectangular rooms with the same square footage.

Triangular rooms also make bad use of available square footages. Shelving and study tables are all rectangular. And nothing fits into sharp corners.

In addition to L-shaped rooms and triangular rooms, we've also seen libraries with banana-shaped rooms, oval rooms, circular rooms, pie-shaped rooms, trapezoidal rooms, and other non-rectangular geometric shapes. In all cases, the rooms worked poorly. In many cases, the owners spoke unkindly of the rooms, despite their strong motivation to speak well of their buildings.

Summing up, funny-shaped rooms cost more to build per square foot. They are hard to light, since rows of light fixtures don't fit well into oddly shaped spaces. Funny shaped rooms often have strange acoustics. Library furnishings are almost all rectangular, and fitting them into non-rectangular spaces is difficult. A funny-shaped room with 3,000 square feet of floor space will probably hold less furniture than a rectangular room with 3,000 square feet of floor space.

Our advice is, don't build funny-shaped rooms if you can avoid them.

D. When Possible, Use "Main Streets"

One convenient way to lay out the interior of a library space is to arrange various elements along a wide central aisle through the space, with individual elements butting up against the aisle. Some architects have referred to this approach to building layout as "Main Streets," and it seems to work very well.

Some libraries have used different carpet colors to indicate main street paths.

E. Avoid "Beads-on-a-String" Designs

Far too many libraries have floor plans that force users to wander through irrelevant spaces.

Sometimes this kind of unfortunate beads-on-a-string room arrangement is the result of putting obstacles such as courtyards or atriums in the way, forcing users and staff to circumnavigate the spaces.

Despite their frequent beauty, courtyards and atriums can be functional pains in the neck.

F. The Wonderful T-Shaped Space

One of the best ways to lay out the interior of a small library building or a department in a large library is to lay it out in a T shape.

The entrance to the room or library is in the center of the wide side of the room. Facing the entrance, about halfway from the entrance to the back wall, is a service desk. Reaching to the right and left of the desk, aisles provide user access to the various areas of the department or library.

Spaces arranged in this fashion maximize interaction between users and staff. Users see the service desk straight ahead when they enter the space, and staff at the desk see arriving users. Staff at the desk can also look down the left and right-hand aisles to see what's going on. And various areas of the library or department can abut the aisles.

G. Let Functional Needs Drive Structural Spaces

Ideally, the exterior shape of the library will be driven by the spaces that have to fit within.

An architect friend of ours said it's a matter of laying out all the spaces you need and then wrapping an attractive exterior around them, rather than creating an attractive exterior and then cramming everything inside any old way.

Courtyards can be beautiful, but they can lead to long, narrow interior spaces that are hard to use and may complicate access to other parts of the building.

IV. TRAFFIC FLOW

When you are evaluating the floor plans of libraries, it helps to consider the flow of users, staff, and books through the building.

Users need simple, efficient routes that don't force them to detour through unwanted spaces in order to reach their destinations. They need simple rather than complex routes, so that wayfinding is as easy as possible.

Most users rely on a reasonable number of directional signs to find their way around buildings. Deciding on the right number of signs with the right wording in the right locations is an art, and there is a considerable literature on the subject. Some of our favorite rules are:

- Always used mixed upper- and lowercase letters in signs.
- Use basic Roman or sans-serif faces.
- Watch out for unfortunate second meanings (show your draft signs to your evil-minded teenage employees, who can thereby earn their pay).

Never give your designers veto power over your signage.

Attempting to have enough signs to tell library users everything they need to know is a little like asking them to listen carefully to the 87 new phone options. Asking a staff member is always easier (and vastly more civilized) than reading dozens of signs in the fond hope that you'll actually find one that answers your question.

Homemade signs are awkward and often unnecessarily ugly. (But at least these are legible.)

- A modest number of well-positioned signs is better than a lot of signs in unhelpful locations.
- When you post a map of your building, be sure that the top of the map is north and that the map is posted on a north wall. There may also be state standards on what safety features need to be included on maps.

While staff routes are often shared with users, all but the smallest libraries have additional routes that are closed to users. Much of this is for security. Libraries don't need users wandering through the service corridors that provide access to staff workrooms, staff lunchrooms, staff restrooms, panel rooms, HVAC spaces, water rooms, custodial workrooms, and so on. Usually these end up being somewhat more complex routes than are routes for users, but it helps to evaluate schematic designs by imagining how staff members will get around and whether the spaces that various subgroups of staff use are conveniently close.

Occasionally, staff areas double as fire escape routes. In this case, doors providing emergency access to staff areas need to be equipped with alarms.

The final major traffic flow in a library building is books. Technical services departments are ideally located near loading docks, although elevators can keep libraries from tying up valuable main floor space with tech services workrooms. The general flow of processed materials from technical services to public shelves is far less massive than lending, and the paths may be longer because of that.

This odd choice of a temporary tripod with a sign pointing the way to the permanent restrooms suggests that the library may have agreed to let the architect dictate all built-in signage forever. (The moral is to never give your architects any rights to your building once the ribbon is cut. If you want to paint it pink, you should never need to ask your architects' permission before picking out the special shade you want.)

Always be sure that extra signs to match those in your new library are available at a reasonable cost. Many libraries are driven to improvisation when it turns out that a group of signs was affordable but a single extra sign is impossibly expensive.

In the alley behind this library, users first encounter a parked bookmobile. Hidden behind the bookmobile is a trash container and then (finally) a book return. For some reason, this stuck some citizens as a dysfunctional arrangement.

Lending operations must deal with major flows of incoming and outgoing interlibrary loans, carts full of returned materials brought from book returns to lending departments, and carts used to return materials to shelves. To be convenient for users, lending desks need to be close to main entrances, but what happens to returned books afterward can vary a lot. Having to trundle quantities of materials by awkward pathways may be an avoidable problem.

One concept with a murky track record is sorting rooms for returned books. For many libraries, these appear to become black holes. Books vanish into sorting rooms, and some of them never emerge. Shelving staff all know that mystery stories are fun to reshelve, but that art books and children's picture books are a pain, and they make their work decisions accordingly.

Once there's a backlog in sorting rooms, books that the database claims are on the shelf are not there, and expensive reference staff are forced to mess around trying to determine if the books are missing, misshelved, or simply buried in the sorting room.

Our experience is that sorting rooms can be serious problems unless a supervisor is around to make sure that book-shelving staff reshelve items in the order in which they were returned. John has had very good luck with this approach.

Fred prefers that libraries avoid sorting rooms altogether. By keeping shelving staff around all day, these libraries can reshelve books almost as soon as they're checked in. Automatic sorting systems *may* also speed reshelving.

If shelving staff can't keep up, public sorting shelves (or "recently returned" carts) allow users almost instant access to recently returned books. (Some users prefer to select their books from public sorting shelves anyway, because they're freshly read and are therefore probably better.)

V. WINDOW PLACEMENT

One constant problem in the layout of library buildings is windows that admit uncontrollable direct sunlight. Any window that doesn't face straight north, no matter how elegant or cute or tiny or symmetrical, needs some kind of adjustable blind. Problems frequently occur with windows that are too high for adjustable blinds or too oddly shaped for blinds.

If your architects propose windows of this type, it is your moral duty as a librarian to ask how direct sunlight will be controlled. If your architects insist it will not be a problem, they may have a good reason to reassure you, but in our experience, it is usually because they like the look of the window artistically and are optimistically hoping for the best. They may also suggest that with "modern glass" it won't be a problem.

When faced with issues of this type, always insist on seeing a similar building or an example of the same brand of "modern glass" at work. If there is no similar building or glass, insist on a different design.

Lots of libraries have been fitted with windows that admit too much direct sunlight and have ended up having to retrofit dark gray film to windows that face east, west, or south. Dark gray film basically eliminates the reason for having a window in the first place.

Here are some basic configurations that cause major problems:

- Skylights. No matter how large or small or cute or supposedly energy-saving, skylights are always a major pain in libraries. If your designers absolutely insist on a skylight (or, if you are really unlucky, lots of skylights), consider an "artificial skylight," one illuminated by electric lighting rather than daylight, or one made of a product like Kalwall, which blocks the majority of light. Every building program needs to say "NO SKYLIGHTS" in large and masterful print, and you need to stop the idea the moment you hear it mentioned.

The following window types cause major problems *if the windows do not face straight north*:

- Monitor roofs—these are roof sections that are elevated above the main flat roof and have windows on all four sides connecting the main roof with the roof of the monitor. No matter how you design a monitor, three sides will face in extremely undesirable directions.
- Chevron-shaped windows connecting two abutting sloped roofs of slightly different heights.
- Windows that are too tall for adjustable blinds.
- Clearstory windows.
- Windows with oddly shaped top panes to which blinds cannot be fitted.
- Windows so high up that blinds can't be reached.

Some libraries have spent huge sums of money retrofitting workable blinds to troublesome windows or adding dark gray film to windows that cannot be dealt with in any other way. How pleasant it is to know that your library is not among them!

Ever since the days of the Bauhaus, walls consisting of monstrous sheets of glass keep turning up. If you have trouble with windows facing in unfortunate directions, imagine entire walls blasting library users and staff with direct sunlight.

When your architects present drawings featuring any of the problem windows listed above, stop things as quickly as possible.

VI. ARTISTIC CEILING SHAPES

Creative ceiling shapes can lead to odd valleys in roofs that may tend to leak, but a more immediate problem is weird indoor acoustics.

A few libraries have had rooms with barrel vault ceilings. A barrel vault is a curved ceiling that runs the length of a room, much like the top of an old railroad tunnel. Barrel vaults can transmit sounds in amazing ways.

> Fred worked with a library that had a reference desk at one end of a plaster-surfaced barrel vault and (about 50 to 75 feet away) a group of armchairs at the other end of the vault. Every word spoken by people sitting in the armchairs could be heard with amazing clarity at the reference desk, and all reference questions could be heard by users sitting in the armchairs.

Circular rooms can have dreadful acoustics. An Illinois public library had a children's program room shaped more or less like a silo, and it was a miserable place for programs. Circular rooms can also function like the Whispering Gallery at St. Paul's Cathedral, where a whisper spoken on one side of the room can be heard clearly on the far side.

Domes also have weird acoustics, transmitting sounds up and down and all around.

Many libraries with cathedral ceilings have serious problems. A "cathedral ceiling" is a ceiling with a center ridgepole and two sloped roof sections, similar to a house with a simple pitched roof. Cathedral ceilings are attractive and homelike, but they tend to have nasty acoustics. Sounds rise, are reflected by one side of the ceiling, are reflected again by the second side, and descend upon innocents below. In buildings with complex patterns of cathedral ceilings, sounds can bounce around in strange ways. Conversations in one part of a library can be heard unexpectedly in areas far away.

All of these problems can be cured (or at least minimized) by using sound-absorbing ceiling materials, but your designers may resist sound-absorbing surfaces because they won't provide the look they want.

> This can come to a real showdown. In desperation, one client of Fred's hired her own acoustical consulting engineers, who reported that without acoustic surfaces, the proposed cathedral ceiling in her library would be an acoustic nightmare. In the process, she forced the architect to grudgingly agree to acoustic surfaces.

VII. CURVED WALLS

Curved walls are the bane of many libraries, but they won't go away.

Curved walls are expensive to build, and library contents don't fit well into curved spaces. With curved spaces it's hard to install lighting, hard to position stacks and furniture, and frequently hard to keep an eye on things because non-rectangular spaces lead to bad sight lines. Curved walls can lead to sounds carrying in undesirable ways.

If your library is constructed with curved walls, they'll be around for the life span of the building, making life miserable for users and staff and maintenance budgets in decades to come. Or you'll spend a lot of money getting rid of them or building a totally new library. Cuteness is not a sufficient excuse for curved walls.

VIII. BASEMENTS

One of the seriously bad ideas in library architecture is basements. Putting things as simply as possible, you don't want a basement in your library.

Unless you are forced to do it, never build a new library with a basement.

Most libraries with basements regret the situation. Basements have humidity problems. Basements leak. Basements flood. Basements are dark. Staff members who are relegated to basement workspaces are not happy staff members. Books that are stored in basements can have short life spans.

As a friend of Fred's who works for a large insurance company says, "Basements are places you put things you really don't want."

In Carnegie-era libraries, first floors were several feet above grade level and basements only a few feet below ground. But in modern libraries with grade-level entries, basement floors may be anything from 14 to 15 or more feet below grade. As a result, modern basements have no natural light (except for the occasional perimeter skylight) and suffer from far greater hydrostatic pressures from groundwater.

Some libraries build basements because they aren't allowed to add extra floors. If you have a limited site and a zoning restriction on building height, you may be forced to have a basement. Outside of this, there seems to be little excuse for basements.

Unlike home construction, basements in libraries are nearly as expensive as upper floors. With basements in houses, the crawl space is just made larger. The foundation walls are simply extended a few feet downward, and a concrete floor is poured. (It also requires footing drains, underfloor drains, a sump, and a sump pump, but they're not a huge deal.)

By contrast, *modern* libraries use slab-on-grade construction. Pouring concrete on compacted fill means that the immense weight of books is born by the soil rather than by a strong floor. But if you add a basement, the slab-on-grade floor must be replaced by a floor strong enough to hold 150 pounds per square foot—a floor just as strong as a second-story floor. The only real difference in cost between a basement and an extra story in a library is the cost of the windows and more attractive sheathing, and from that we deduct the cost of sealing the basement walls. The upshot is that by building a basement instead of an extra floor, you save probably less than 10 percent in construction cost. And you get a dark and potentially dank space, missing the advantages of natural light and the absence of hydrostatic pressure.

Sooner or later, most basements get wet. Wet books don't smell as bad as wet dogs, but they're still no fun. Wet dogs can be dried off, while wet books (unless they have seriously major value) go into the dumpster. When the river is over its banks, it's comforting to know that your library has no basement.

> There's a lot of talk about freeze-drying books as a way of rescuing wet books. For school and public libraries in particular, this appears to be a dubious idea. Freeze-drying is expensive. Books with coated paper can't be rescued, And rescued books never look the same. When you are making plans for disasters, know what the real costs and benefits of rescue are. And wish all of your books were stored above grade.

The other advantage of upper floors over basements concerns flood insurance, which is not offered by commercial insurance companies. For political reasons, the federal flood insurance program is operated at a major loss, but if reasonable premiums are ever charged, you may find it hard to afford them.

The only sane reasons to put a basement in a library are that (a) someone out there won't let you put on another floor, or (b) your existing library has a half-basement and you need to match it in your new addition.

IX. SNAPPY RULES ON THE BASIC CONFIGURATION OF LIBRARY SPACES

1. Funny-shaped buildings may be architecturally interesting, but they're usually expensive and dysfunctional.
2. The right number of entrances to a library is anything up to one. Among other things, multiple entrances cost too much to supervise.
3. Most departmental libraries benefit from a "T"-shaped interior furniture layout. Enter from the center of the broad side of the department, facing the service desk. Walk to the desk and turn left or right for the rest of the department.
4. The same thing works for entire buildings. Enter a library building from the center of one of its long walls.
5. Everyone knows that cathedral ceilings are noisy, but libraries with horrible acoustics sometimes blithely deny that they have a problem.
6. Triangular interior spaces cost a lot more to construct, but they compensate for it by not holding much. The best interior spaces for libraries are rectangles.
7. Unless your library is so far south that you worry about Burmese pythons lurking in the parking lot, you need an entrance that faces south. Under terrible duress, settle for southeast or east.
8. Curved exterior walls lead to all sorts of problems with shelving placement, light fixture location, workroom shapes, weird acoustics, and other good things. On the other hand, they cost a lot more than straight walls.
9. If your name is not "Library of Congress" or "British Museum," you don't need a round reading room or a dome.
10. The reason for reading rooms on top floors is to avoid forests of support columns filling the rooms. Otherwise, main floor reading rooms sound friendlier.
11. All windows that don't face directly north need blinds. "Modern glass" is not a substitute. (You can often expect a fight from your architect, who will be wrong but unusually determined.)

12. You need a good excuse for interior partitions. "Functional necessity" is a good excuse. "Architectural concept" is not a good excuse.
13. Outside of study rooms, program rooms, faculty studies, and restrooms, libraries don't benefit from small interior spaces for public use.
14. Wide, flat, and open makes a happy library.
15. Good sight lines in public areas are essential. Study rooms need glass walls—not windows here and there but glass walls on three sides. Hidden spaces available to library users have an impressive potential for assault (really bad), fooling around (probably fun, but nonetheless not a good idea), and long-term inflexibility. And small rooms without windows can aggravate claustrophobia.
16. Basements in new libraries cost about the same amount as extra floors, but they have many fewer advantages. *As in no advantages whatsoever.*
17. If your library has a basement, sooner or later someone will store books there. And sooner or later, you'll have a lot of soggy books.
18. A "monitor" is a four-sided structure that rises above a roof and has glass on all four sides. Since monitors do not have adjustable blinds, this is three glass sides too many. Stop monitors the first time you hear them mentioned, and say "NO MONITORS" in your building program. (If you have a paralyzing fear of lizards, keep the phrase "monitor lizard" in mind.)
19. An Illinois public library has a young adult study room with one tiny window. The library staff call it the "sex room."
20. North-facing clearstory windows are a great idea. (On the other hand, clearstories facing any direction except north are seriously nasty.)
21. Try to cluster staff workspaces next to relevant public spaces.
22. Main floors are prime commercial space. Don't use them for tech services.
23. If you have to install dark gray film on a window to block the glare, you should probably be asking yourself why you allowed your architect to install the window in the first place.
24. If you have impressively identical public rooms in locations where you can't see both rooms at the same time, your users are likely to become totally confused. This is Not a Good Thing. Consider wildly different paint colors for the two spaces.
25. You always need more storage space than your board of trustees, university administration, school principal, hospital administrator, or architect think you need.
26. A schematic design without furniture placement is worthless.
27. If you arrange things right, the staff at the service desk in a small public library also can see all of the reading tables, can see through the glass walls of the entry foyer (where they can see who's entering the building, who's entering the restrooms, and who's entering the meeting room), can see the screens of the public computers, and can see (through a conveniently

placed glass wall or group of windows) into the meeting room itself. And with a little pacing back and forth, they can see down all the book aisles.
28. If you have study rooms that don't have glass walls and can't be supervised by your staff from their service desks, they'll spend a lot of time running back and forth, peeking into study room windows. This annoys both library users (who by and large don't enjoy being peeked at) and librarians (who by and large don't enjoy peeking).
29. It's a good thing to position shelving so staff members seated at service desks can see down as many aisles as possible. *But never use radiating aisles.*
30. Never arrange rooms like beads on a chain. (One of the reasons to be extremely wary of courtyards and atriums is that they can lead to this arrangement.)
31. There are libraries where it's quicker and easier to go from one room to another outside the building than through the building. This is Not a Good Thing.
32. It's better to lay out all the spaces you need and wrap an attractive exterior around them than to create an attractive exterior and then cram everything you need inside, whether it fits or not.
33. Beware of ornamental columns. They get in the way and block sight lines. Purely functional columns are bad enough, and you don't want any extras.
34. When in doubt, hire an acoustical engineer to review your drawings.
35. Always have your consulting librarian check your schematic design for functionality.
36. Designers frequently assume that they have just invented the concept of reading terraces. Unfortunately, reading terraces have been around for a long time, and they're all unfortunate. The approaches to reading terraces have to be from a point outside the library's security gates. (In defense of their concepts, some designers use the phrase *secure reading terrace*, but it's an oxymoron.)
37. Screen porches in libraries are a romantic idea but also a miserable idea. The need for screen porches ended with the advent of air conditioning.

5

Evaluating Library Buildings by Walking Around

I. REASONS FOR EVALUATING BUILDINGS ON YOUR OWN

a. Librarians, library board members, city officials, university administrators, and others sometimes need to evaluate library buildings.

b. In addition to evaluating their own buildings, people frequently evaluate other libraries when they are considering hiring architects and want to get some idea of the kind of work they can expect from specific firms.

c. Most librarians and library governors who set out to evaluate library buildings do so for practical reasons. They need to determine whether the buildings are successful as functioning libraries.

d. It's possible to tell a great deal about a library building by just looking at it, and you can find out a great deal without asking staff members, board members, or other officials. Many staff members—including directors and governors—are very hesitant to discuss problems. And sometimes they are blinded by the elegance of new buildings. It's useful, therefore, to be able to draw your own conclusions just by walking through library buildings.

e. The items listed below are some that you can evaluate without consultation with library management. Obviously, there are things you can't evaluate—such as staff workspace or storage spaces—without making special arrangements to go behind the scenes. And problems like structural strength, recalcitrant HVAC systems, and so on are not usually susceptible to informal evaluation.

II. THE PROBLEMS WITH ASKING THE STAFF

a. Library staff members often have a very hard time coming to grips with the fact that their buildings have problems. Librarians who participated in the design and construction of buildings are sometimes extremely attached to them, despite dysfunctional problems that are immediately obvious to most other librarians.
b. Library staff members may fail to recognize that functional problems are the direct result of architectural errors.
c. Library staff members may be hesitant to point out design problems. They may be driven by loyalty to their institutions or by administrative requests to not complain.
d. Library staff members are often brilliant at developing workarounds. The building may have major problems, but staff members have figured out how to make things work pretty well in spite of all that.
e. Librarians who specialize in providing outstanding public service may tend not to grumble about things.

III. APPEARANCE

a. Do you find the building attractive? Most people want library buildings that look warm and welcoming. If a building strikes you as ungainly or cold or awkward, this makes a difference.
b. Does the building look nice primarily just because everything is new? It may help you if you try to envision how the library will look when it's somewhat worn.
c. If the building is brand-new, does it look nice because it exhibits the most recent styles? Or does it give the impression that its looks will outlast its newness?
d. Does the building seem suited to its environment, or does it seem discordant? No matter how much aluminum and glass are in fashion, the effect may be out of place on a Georgian campus. Just as a new Georgian library may look out of place in a severely Bauhaus campus.
e. Do the interior and exterior work well together? Is there a sense of comprehensive design?
f. Are decorative elements pasted on, or do they follow naturally from the design of the building? Does it appear that the architect and the interior designer were a team, or that the building was first constructed and then interior elements were pasted on like the crepe paper decor at a sock hop in the high school gym?

g. Do the interior spaces strike you as either too open (like a barn) or too close (like a tunnel)?
h. Do you see signs of water intrusion? Look for stained ceiling tiles, efflorescence, problems around windows, water-damaged drywall, and so on.
i. Whether you personally like the looks of a building is just as important as the opinions of architects or professional critics.
j. If the building won a design award, that doesn't necessarily make it a good library. Most design awards are simply architectural glamour contests and can be heavily influenced by passing design vogues. Award committees may have little or no interest in issues of practical function.

IV. SENSE OF WELCOME

a. Does the building look attractive as you approach it?
b. Is the entryway warmly lit? If you arrive after dark, does the entryway glow invitingly?
c. Can you see staff members when you enter the library, or are they hidden away?
d. When you enter the library, do you immediately feel good about it? Is it pleasant and welcoming?
e. Is there an obvious place to get help? With a real person?
f. Are there enough signs to guide you through the building, but not so many that it reminds you of wading through all the options on telephone answering equipment? (If the signs look homemade, it may be because the architects talked their clients into agreeing that all signs will be designed by the architect, and the result is temporary, homemade signs stuck up in desperation. On other occasions, the original signs were so expensive that the library cannot afford to purchase additional ones of the same type. And some libraries may just not get around to it.)
g. Do you see a lot of places where you would like to sit and read or study? Many readers like armchairs or tables beside windows, but the main thing is whether the library has a place where *you* would like to be.
h. Do the places you want to sit have power for your laptop?
i. Can you get a good Wi-Fi connection everywhere you go?
j. Is the layout of the library relatively easy to figure out, or are you still puzzled after hanging around for a couple of hours? Is it easy to find the area of the collection you want? When you get to 317.8 at the end of a range of shelves, is it obvious where to find 317.9? If the building is complex, are clear maps posted? Are the maps oriented to match the building?

V. STAFF SERVICE POINTS

a. Can you find library staff when you need help?
b. Are service points located with careful consideration to staff supervision of spaces? Do staff members have good sight lines? Is a staff service point located close to every alarmed exit? Although good sight lines are extremely important, they can be overdone. For example, stacks that radiate like the spokes of wheel are a seriously bad idea.
c. Can service points be relocated, or are they monumental constructions? Look for signs of modular desk construction. Matching soffits above service desks are very popular with designers, but they make it extremely expensive to relocate desks.
d. Does the library have more than one entrance in use? Unless one entrance is an inaccessible historic entrance, this may be a design error. In most situations, every entrance has to be staffed, and this can be a very expensive proposition. Security gates are not a workable substitute for a staffed entrance. However, if two entrances lead to a common foyer, which in turn has only one entrance to the library, that is effectively one entrance.

VI. NATURAL LIGHT

a. Can you see the outside world? One of the many reasons not to put libraries in basements is that everyone—patron and staff alike—wants a view. (There are a lot of other reasons, including high cost and moisture.)
b. Are there places where the natural light is unpleasant? All glass surfaces that do not face north need some kind of movable shielding, such as blinds. It's often impossible to install adjustable blinds in high windows, and such windows frequently cause major problems if they don't face north. Sometimes the only solution is to apply extremely dark film to the glass, which makes one wonder why a window was installed in the first place. If direct sunlight hits lending desk staff in the face, there are real problems.
c. Particular problems arise with skylights. Skylights are beloved of many architects, but they always cause serious problems because (among other things) they are too bright by day and too dark by night. If skylights are located over book stacks, people may be blinded by the light and unable to read spine labels. If a skylight is located over a service desk, staff can't move to a different place to avoid the blinding glare. Skylights also cause echoes, and they often leak.
d. "Fritted" glass is very popular now. The general effect is of areas of frosted glass or glass with a pattern of black dots, as used on the upper and lower edges of some automobile windshields. All-over black dots can be effective,

but patterns of frosted glass cause serious problems with glare. If the library has glass with this type of fritting, try to find a window facing direct sunlight to see how things work. If you are blinded by direct daylight anywhere in the library, it's a sign of bad design. Glass with ornamental fritted patterns may also prove to be amazingly expensive to replace if one or more panes are broken. To us, fritted glass is an indication of badly designed windows.
   e. Do the long sides of the building face north and south? At middling latitudes in the northern hemisphere, north light is the best reading light and west light is the worst. Buildings therefore work best if the long direction is east-west and the short direction is north-south, with north windows for reading and with sheltered south entrances. Entrances that face north or west in climates that have snow also suffer from ice.
   f. Are there any signs that the library has had to take extraordinary steps to block light through ill-conceived windows? Look for dark gray films on the glass surfaces of high windows.

VII. ARTIFICIAL LIGHT

   a. Can you see to read everywhere?
   b. Is the light soft, bright, and even? Libraries need pleasant light everywhere. The best library lighting is achieved by bouncing fluorescent strip lighting off white ceilings. (LED lighting will probably take over fairly soon. If the library has LED lighting, can you look straight at the fixtures without being blinded?)
   c. Is light in the stacks bright enough to allow you to read the spines on all of the books—even the bottom rows?
   d. Are there any places where highly concentrated lights shine directly in your eyes? Including when you look straight upward. This is called "direct glare."
   e. Is stack lighting functional? Because book shelving is often high, using a library often means looking at books over your head. If in the process, you have to stare into a bright light fixture or a skylight overhead, you can be so blinded by the light that you can't read the book spines.
   f. Does the lighting allow furnishings to be relocated?
   g. Are there a great many different types of light fixtures? In some libraries, one gets the impression that people went through light fixture catalogs to see how many different fixtures they could use. The result can be far too many different types of light bulbs.
   h. Are any of the lights funny colors? This is easiest to spot where light hits walls or is reflected off ceilings. Funny colors of light typically come from metal halide lighting, but they may come from too many different kinds

of fixtures cluttered together. (In some libraries, fluorescent lamps in a variety of colors have been used in identical fixtures. This is a maintenance problem, not a design problem.)

i. Are there any light bulbs that appear to be hard to reach? Look for high bulbs that are burned out. Ask yourself how you would get at fixtures that are over staircases or in multistory atriums. If fixtures are above book stacks, remember that the lifts that are frequently used to change high light fixtures may have outrigger legs that make them too wide to use in stack aisles. Many buildings have light fixtures that are nearly impossible to service once the construction scaffolding is removed. This is one of the most common and most frustrating design errors in library architecture.
j. Are there shiny surfaces that reflect unpleasant images of light fixtures?
k. If the restrooms have motion sensor lights, do the lights go on before you enter the restroom and never go off while you are in there? Having to grope your way into a dark restroom is a sign of sloppy design.
l. Are any of the light fixtures full of dead bugs? Some light fixtures display every dead bug with cheerful clarity, and no maintenance staff can keep ahead of the problem. Watch particularly for chandeliers with completely translucent bowls; there's no excuse for them.
m. It's easiest to evaluate artificial lighting if you visit a library after dark.

VIII. ACOUSTICS

a. Do any areas of the library echo? Listen for reverberation. When you enter a room, can you hear the openness? (Clapping your hands helps reveal echoes, but you may not be welcome when you do.)
b. Can you overhear distant conversations? Some design features that cause serious problems are hard-surfaced ceilings (particularly sloped ceilings, barrel vaults, and cathedral ceilings), skylights, domes, rooms with curved walls, and hard-surfaced floors. Atriums (open areas connecting floors) often carry unwanted sound in unpleasant ways (in addition to having lights that are hard to change and terrifying people who suffer from acrophobia). On upper floors, atriums often get in the way because people have to detour around them.
c. Do noises from children's areas bother people in adult areas?
d. Are there quiet reading rooms or study rooms for people who want to hold small meetings or get away from the constant noises of telephones, computers, users talking with each other, and conversations at service desks? Do the reading and study rooms have glass walls (not little windows but completely glass walls) to allow staff supervision?

    e. Do walls block noises? For example, see if you can hear conversation from adjacent rooms when you're standing in a restroom or sitting in a study room.
    f. Do staircases transmit sound in unwelcome ways?

IX. ELECTRICAL WIRING

   a. Does the library have enough electrical outlets and data ports? In the era of the laptop, almost every reading table needs places to plug in computers (on the top of the table, not hidden underneath). And armchairs need nearby outlets.
   b. Are extension cords strung about the place for laptop use or other purposes? Are laptop cords stretched across walkways? (Remember that fire marshals regard extension cords as serious evils.)
   c. Are light switches located where users can mess around with them? Typical good locations for light switches are behind service desks or in offices.
   d. Are there outlet boxes in floors as well as around the walls and on the support columns? Is the grid of floor boxes no larger than 10' × 10' or 12'× 12'?
   e. Are floor outlet boxes totally flush with the floor, so furniture can be placed over the outlets until they're needed?
   f. Are there outlets in reserve, in areas that are now used for shelving but may have computers or other equipment in the future?
   g. Are electrical outlets childproof ("tamper-resistant")? This is particularly important in public library adult departments, since it's there that preoccupied parents hand their toddlers their car keys to play with. Look for a blue dot on the receptacle.
   h. Does the library have good Wi-Fi service throughout all public service areas? Your laptop or phone will tell you.

X. HVAC (HEATING, VENTILATING, AND AIR CONDITIONING)

   a. Are places in the library unpleasantly drafty? Do you find yourself changing seats because of drafts?
   b. Are areas of the library too hot or too cold?
   c. Does the library seem stuffy? Is the air stale?
   d. Does overly positive or negative air pressure cause outside doors to stand ajar or be difficult to open? Do you hear whistling air when you start to open a door?
   e. Do study rooms and similar spaces have individual thermostats? One thermostat for two rooms is exactly one thermostat too few.

f. Are space heaters scattered about? Common places are service desks, where space heaters are tucked beneath to keep the legs of staff members warm.
g. If the entire building is too cold in the winter or too hot in the summer, this may represent a management decision to save energy.
h. HVAC systems in new libraries represent about 25 percent of the entire construction cost of the building, and it's a shame that many of the systems perform in unsatisfactory ways.

XI. FURNISHINGS

a. Are the chairs at tables comfortable? Do they slide easily? Many users prefer padded seats and backs.
b. Are tables a comfortable height? Many people prefer about 29 inches.
c. Do the tables avoid aprons? (Aprons are vertical boards attached to the undersides of tabletops and connecting the table legs.) Users in wheelchairs need 27 inches of clear space under tables, and many other people prefer this kind of space. This is impossible with aprons. Ancient library tables may look impressive, but because they usually have aprons, they often have no leg room or they have uncomfortably high tops.
d. Are armchairs the right size for human beings? If you sit in a large armchair, is it so deep that your legs stick straight out in front of you? Is it so low to the floor that you are forced to roll out of it? Can older users get out of armchairs relatively easily?
e. Does upholstery appear to be fragile? Is it stained or worn? Does it give the impression of being hard to clean? (Remember that the age of the building makes a major difference here.) Even poorly selected fabrics can look good when new.
f. Most armchairs in libraries have wooden arms to avoid rapid wear of the upholstery, so rating armchairs down due to wooden arms is not realistic.
g. Are the surfaces on service counters wearing out? (Ordinary high-pressure laminates are too fragile for lending countertops. Unfortunately, that's what you often get when you order from a library supply company catalog.)
h. Are there furnishings that lend themselves to misuse? A common example is the use of sofas in public library adult departments. Strangers won't share sofas, but sofas offer a great place to neck or to sleep.
i. Are the shelving aisles comfortably wide? Aisles as narrow as 36 inches may be legal, but 42 inches or more works better. If a library plans to have 36-inch aisles, inevitably some will be a little over 36 while others are somewhat under 36 (and consequently illegal).
j. Are shelves sufficiently deep? Outside of shelving for pocket-sized paperbacks, most shelving should be at least nine inches ("nominal ten inches")

deep. Many libraries with seven-inch-deep shelving have books that stick out over the edges of the shelves, effectively narrowing aisles. The ends of double-faced shelving units should be at least two feet wide.

k. Are individual shelves sufficiently far apart? Nonfiction books tend to be taller than fiction books. If books are being shelved on their fore edges, the shelves are too close together. Sometimes this overcrowding represents a failure to allow enough floor space for shelving.

l. Were shelving colors selected for functionality rather than to make a decorator statement? Were they chosen to stand the test of time? Are they so dark that they show dust and absorb light? Are they white and hard to keep clean? (Neutral pale gray or cream are ideal colors for steel shelving. They don't show dust or dirt, don't soak up light, and don't interfere with future redecorating.) (Steel shelving is coated with powder paint and is very difficult to repaint, so most libraries get just one chance to pick a color.)

m. Are there any building support columns in the middle of shelving aisles? This is a sign of bad architectural planning (unless, of course, the library has altered aisle width after moving in).

n. Do the tilting shelves for magazines lock up and open, or do you have to attempt to hold the shelf up with one elbow while looking through older issues?

o. Does the library have standard steel cantilever-style shelving? Cantilever shelving has sturdy central posts. Individual shelves hook onto the posts. (One of the tremendous advantages of cantilever shelving is that it can be picked up and relocated fully loaded by using hydraulic stack-moving equipment. Many other types of shelving have to be unloaded and disassembled, an amazingly miserable undertaking.)

p. Is there a lot of overstuffed furniture? The problem with modern upholstered furniture is that it is usually made with polyurethane foam, which is extraordinarily flammable and releases toxic gases when it burns. (Chemicals added to make it less flammable are also toxic.) Overstuffed furniture also provides better lurking crevices for creatures like bedbugs.

XII. STORAGE

a. Are items that should be stored out of sight piled around the edges of rooms? One of the most common places to see this problem is in meeting rooms, which may have furniture and equipment piled around the edges because there aren't adequate furniture and equipment storage closets. The addition of maker space equipment to meeting rooms has made inadequate storage space even worse.

b. In public libraries, do children's services areas appear to be short of storage space? (This is actually a two-edged sword, since some children's librarians are notoriously unable to toss anything out.)

XIII. FRAGILE CONSTRUCTION MATERIALS

a. Are there any signs of fragile materials?
b. Do you see things that appear to be worn or battered because they are hard to repair?
c. Since modern drywall with latex paint is extremely fragile, do walls in public areas have chair rails?
d. Is the building covered with EIFS? (External insulation finishing systems consist of a coat of stucco over Styrofoam. They frequently have trouble with water intrusion. If the wall is stucco, rap on it with your knuckles to see if it sounds lightweight or hollow.)
e. Are door handles, railings, and newel posts finished in colors that are coming off? Tubular metal handles, railings, door knobs, and newel posts need to be stainless steel.

XIV. FLEXIBILITY

a. One of the characteristics of libraries is their tendency to move things around as functional needs change. Some architects enable this, while others make it nearly impossible to adapt to change.
b. Can small service desks like reference desks be moved easily? One thing that makes this nearly impossible is soffits that match the shape of the desk. And some desks are too monumental to move.
c. Do carpet patterns tell you where things must be located?
d. Can you see signs of obsolete and inflexible storage for things the library no longer owns? For example, do lending desks have cutouts in their tops for the card tubs that were used in lending systems a generation ago? Are there special provisions for long-gone card catalogs?
e. Are there outdated decorative elements? The trendier the design, the easier it has to be to change. (Teenagers have the attention span of gnats, and spaces for them need to recognize this fact.)
f. Are spare electrical outlets located everywhere? Many designers balk at providing sufficient numbers of electrical outlets.

XV. FUNCTIONAL ARRANGEMENT OF ROOMS

a. Can you use the library meeting room when the rest of the library is closed? This requires access to both the meeting room and the public restrooms from the main entry foyer.
b. Do you have to walk through the children's department to get to the adult department, or vice versa? Or are there other awkward beads-on-a-chain room arrangements? Adults in children's departments can lead to security problems, and children in adult departments can lead to distracting noise.
c. Are departments divided for no good reason? (This is a better question to ask in entirely new buildings. The expansion of existing buildings can force designers into awkward arrangements of spaces.)
d. Is the flow of materials clear from shelving unit to shelving unit? If a shelving unit ends at 327.1, is the location of 327.2 obvious? (If the Dewey or LC range is broken in illogical ways, people may have a hard time finding books.)
e. Are there perimeter soffits with inset downlights? These are a seriously undesirable design feature leading to dark room perimeters and spotty illumination. To ornament the junction between walls and ceilings, crown moldings work vastly better.

XVI. CEILINGS

a. Are all ceilings white, to enable reflected uplighting? (Some historic libraries have dark ceilings, but there's little excuse for any of that in new buildings.)
b. Are all ceilings acoustic? This is particularly important when ceilings are sloped or curved.
c. Are most ceilings made of acoustic tile? In addition to muffling sound, acoustic tile provides access to the vast quantities of mechanical, electrical, and plumbing equipment located above ceilings. Historic ceilings, of course, are ruined if acoustic tile is added, but in many other situations, acoustic tile is fine.

XVII. ACROPHOBIA

a. Is the library considerate of the vast numbers of people who have at least a mild fear of heights? If you are fearless around heights, be sure to bring someone with you who is not. Are railings by drop-offs made of glass?
b. Can you see downward through staircases as you are walking upward? The vogue for transparent risers has been around for decades and seems to be one of the most permanently disturbing features in library design.
c. Has the library had to install kiddy gates at the heads of staircases?

d. Do you have to skirt the edges of atriums on narrow walkways?
  e. Do staircases consist of vertiginously long runs of steps, or do they double back, reducing images in the minds of those who fear heights of tumbling downstairs head first forever?
  f. Are elevators glass boxes or do they provide a sense of protection?
  g. If staircases are frightening, are elevators nearby, or are they hidden away?
  h. Do the floors bounce underfoot?

XVIII. FLOOR COVERINGS

  a. Are the floors comfortable underfoot, or do you soon find yourself looking for a place to sit and rest your feet?
  b. Is the carpeting of solid colors that show every speck of dust? Most libraries do better with patterned carpeting.
  c. Do the carpets in areas in front of copy machines or service desks show signs of heavy wear? If so, does that appear to be due to the use of broadloom carpet rather than carpet squares?
  d. It's hard to evaluate carpet at a glance because so much depends on maintenance and on frequency of replacement.

XIX. ORNAMENTAL SPACES

  a. Are there any dramatic or decorative areas that appear to be little occupied? (Some huge open spaces like atriums, courtyards, or areas under large skylights aren't much good except as "wow" spaces, and floor openings in the middle of upper floors can lead to awkward room arrangements.)
  b. If the library has a fireplace, is it in a suitable place? Are the controls for staff use only? Does it have a protective glass front?

XX. PROTECTION FROM THE ELEMENTS

  a. In the winter, do blasts of cold air through the front door freeze users and staff? If the library has power assist doors, are both frequently open at the same time?
  b. The best entrances face south or southeast. The worst face north or northwest.
  c. Does the library have trouble with ice forming on shaded sidewalks or (even worse) steps? South entrances prevent many evils.
  d. Does the building have cold drafts? One sign of good architecture is attention to sealants.

XXI. SECURITY

   a. Does the building appear to be easy for staff to supervise? Are there hidden corners? Do study rooms have opaque (bad) or transparent (good) walls? Can you keep an eye on users of the study rooms while you're seated at a service desk? Some libraries have tried to assist supervision by arranging stack aisles like the spokes of a wheel. It turned out to be a singularly bad idea.
   b. Do any of the stack aisles have dead ends? Libraries cannot afford situations where a user or staff member could be trapped in an aisle. Dead-end stack aisles are always a viciously nasty idea.
   c. Can users open the windows? A standard way that thieves bypass security gates is dropping books out of windows and picking them up later.
   d. If the library is over 12,000 square feet, does it have a sprinkler system? The ideal sprinkler system for a library is a pre-action system, but you can't tell by looking at the sprinkler heads.
   e. Are sprinkler heads concealed or are they exposed? Concealed heads are less prone to vandalism. And they're cuter. Look for three-inch white metal discs mounted flush on the ceilings.
   f. Is there only one public entrance? Multiple entrances are the bane of libraries because every one of them must be staffed at all times a building is open. Unstaffed security gates don't work, although designers sometimes don't believe it.
   g. Can people obtain 100 percent privacy by locking themselves into restrooms? Even single-user restrooms can have stalls and provide for better staff oversight. Many libraries now prefer airport-style restrooms, with zigzag entries rather than doors.
   h. Do restrooms have unfortunate sight lines? Watch out both for direct views of fixtures and stalls and for indirect views by way of wall mirrors.
   i. If the restrooms have doors, do you have to grab dirty handles when you leave the restrooms after you have finished washing your hands? A restroom door should swing outward, or there should be a wastebasket by the door where users can drop paper towels after using them to open the door.
   j. Are there railings by drop-offs whose horizontal bars can be climbed like ladders? Children have fallen while climbing handrails. All balusters should be vertical.
   k. Are there places where users can bump their heads, such as the undersides of staircases?
   l. Are there any reading terraces accessible from inside the building? If users can carry books out onto terraces, they can always toss them over the edge and retrieve them later from outside. (No matter what planners contend, there is no such thing as a "secure" reading terrace.)

m. Can library users easily wander into what should be secure staff areas? Lending work areas and technical services areas are particularly vulnerable. (Of course, if you test this by trying doors marked "staff," you may call attention to yourself.)
n. Do all exit doors have illuminated "Exit" signs?
o. Is there a fire extinguisher located near each exit door?
p. Do any exit doors swing inward? (By law, all exit doors must swing outward.)
q. If the library has revolving doors, are they designed so the panels will swing open to create passageways that allow people to exit the building quickly?
r. Do any of the exit doors have double-cylinder locks? (Double-cylinder locks have keyholes on both sides. If an exit door has a keyhole facing inward, this is a serious life-safety problem.)

XXII. EXPANDABILITY

a. Is there space around the library for later expansion?
b. Will expanding the library in the obvious direction involve the removal of small rooms (expensive) or the opening up of large reading rooms (much less expensive)?

XXIII. WATER FEATURES

a. Some designers enjoy installing water features both inside and outside library buildings. A "water feature" is any design element that includes water.
b. If a water feature is inside a building, is it turned off and empty? Some libraries turn off water features almost immediately after construction is completed.
c. Among other things, library users fall into water features. Visitors can plug up water features with coins or debris. Water features can harbor Legionnaires' disease. Water features can leak. And the sound of running water can send staff members repeatedly to the restroom.

XXIV. OMISSIONS

Because of technical complexity, this list of questions does not include many important questions on code compliance, including access for users with disabilities.

6

Dysfunctional Designs

I. INTRODUCTION

This chapter is of necessity a negative one, and you may not want to start reading the book by looking at this chapter. By necessity, it also repeats things found in other chapters.

When we became involved with library buildings, one of the first things we noticed is how many bad ideas are repeated again and again in library building design. Librarians grind their teeth in frustration, but architects (and everyone else involved in the library building process) eternally repeat the same design errors.

In response to seeing endlessly repeated errors, many years ago we began photographing them and talking about them at conferences. Some people thought the tone of our presentations was too apocalyptic, but we think there's something almost biblically evil about the scope of completely avoidable mistakes in library design.

We'd like to say that this section of the book was really fun to write, but the joy of righteous denunciation is tempered by the frustration of seeing bad ideas endlessly repeated.

EIFS (external insulating finishing systems) can be too fragile for many situations. The first photo shows damage from a bicycle (not a really heavy-duty weapon), while the second shows how a vulnerable corner can be disfigured. In both cases the reinforcing fiberglass mesh is visible.

No list of bad design concepts can ever be complete. However, by the end of this chapter you should have enough information to let those involved in your building process know some of the features you don't want in your new building.

One reason that dysfunctional design ideas are endlessly repeated is that they may sound innocuous or even exciting when first proposed. But once the building is finished, everyone knows "a mistake has been made."*

And unfortunately, once the building has been finished, it's often too late to change. A dysfunctional building—designed with careless enthusiasm—may remain in use a century or more, frustrating generations of library users and library staff yet unborn.

> Fred's students claim that they can spot serious design errors in libraries just by looking at the pretty pictures in the new buildings issues of library publications.

One important point to make at the outset is that bad design ideas come from many sources, including architects, designers, librarians, library consultants, and governmental bodies. Blaming all bad designs on any one group is unfair. But you still don't want bad designs.

Bad designs are often pushed with extraordinary vigor. Be prepared for seriously dysfunctional concepts that are beloved favorites of politicians, boards of trustees, faculty senates, architects, and others. As Mr. Yeats might observe, were he with us today, "The best lack all conviction, while the worst are full of passionate intensity."

The great thing is that absolutely none of the bad designs listed in this chapter are necessary. But not all architects agree. A lot of the ideas in this chapter appeared in an article Fred wrote in 2011 for *Library Trends*.** One architect's reaction to the article was to call it a "screed" and to announce that it would be impossible to build a good library without using some of the ideas the article warned against. He may have been right about the "screed" idea, but he was dead wrong about the necessity of using the bad designs.

---

*Lawrence Cheek. 2007 review of the central Seattle Public Library by a local architectural critic who ended by saying, "A mistake has been made."

**"The Dark Side of Library Architecture: The Persistence of Dysfunctional Designs." *Library Trends,* Vol 60, no. 1 (2011): 227–255.

II. COMMON DYSFUNCTIONAL ARCHITECTURAL DESIGN CONCEPTS

A. Skylights

Skylights are generally seductive in description, fetching in photographs, and alluring at first glance, but they almost always cause nothing but trouble.

Skylights are also appealing in concept because they make use of natural light. When conserving energy is a constant concern, the free natural light from skylights seems like a win-win proposition.

Although they are almost always popular with designers and with people who don't actually have to spend much time in libraries, skylights cause endless problems in real life. Here are the most important of them.

- Because of their hard surfaces, skylights reflect noise. Areas under skylights are frequently unpleasantly noisy. This is particularly true because skylights are usually curved or peaked—shapes that increase problems with sound reflection. In many cases, skylights are paired with hard-surfaced floors, which are also noisy, and the resulting spaces can be like boiler rooms. Even worse is the lethal combination of skylight, hard floor, atrium, and lending desk. Sounds are endlessly reflected and magnified, then shared generously with other floors of the library.
- In addition to reflecting noise, skylights transmit noise laterally. If a long, roof-shaped skylight has a reference desk under one end and reading tables under the other, everything said at one location will be heard far too easily at the other.
- Areas under skylights are too bright by day. The level of glare can be reduced by using translucent materials like Kalwall, but the areas under the skylight are still vastly brighter than artificially lighted areas nearby.
- Because of the brightness, books and other materials under skylights may tend to fade badly, and the many users who are blinded by the glare tend to seek other places to read.
- If you are looking up at book spines on a high shelf beneath a skylight, you will be blinded by the light from the skylight and unable to see anything on the spines.
- Work areas under skylights may need special light shielding.

- Areas lighted by direct sun through skylights can be so bright that adjacent areas are hard to see. An artificially lighted area that would be sufficiently bright under normal circumstances is too dim because users' eyes adjust to nearby areas in direct sunlight.
- Skylights cause problems with reflected glare (veiling reflectance). Because skylights are vastly brighter than the ceilings around them, distracting images of skylights are reflected in shiny surfaces such as computer screens.
- Direct glare from skylights can travel across library spaces as the sun crosses overhead, making areas of the library sequentially uninhabitable when they are in the direct light.
- We know one Illinois library that has a cathedral ceiling with a long, clear skylight at the peak. For an hour or so every day, all of the staff computers on a counter below are unusable when the sun falls directly on them.
- Just as areas under skylights are too bright by day, they are too dark by night. If the library has a large skylight, some kind of lighting system needs to be suspended beneath it. To provide effectively even lighting, a lighting system under a skylight may involve a large number of suspended light fixtures that are unsightly during the day. Lighting the area under a skylight is made more difficult by the fact that it is difficult to bounce the light off the ceiling because—even with translucent skylight materials—much of the light that is directed upward will simply keep going, contributing to light pollution and wasting energy. Because of this, areas under skylights are often illuminated by direct downlighting, with all of the dysfunction such lighting entails. Some libraries with skylights have relied on lamps on reading tables, which is a traditional way to light reading rooms with dark ceilings. Table lamps can work, but the area under the skylight will be gloomy at night.
- Some lighting systems have been designed to automatically compensate for the changing light levels under skylights, but librarians report that they don't always work well. This is particularly true on days with scattered clouds when the sun frequently comes and goes.
- Blocking unwanted light from skylights is difficult, since most curtains and blinds are engineered for vertical windows. Libraries are full of examples where staff members have tried to block excessive light from skylights by various awkward devices. For example, Fred worked on a library that had skylights in staff work areas. In each case, the librarians had suspended pieces of colored fabric like awnings under the skylights, trying to block the sun. And catching dust.
- Heavy rain falling on skylights can be amazingly noisy. Even when skylights are made of slightly flexible materials like Kalwall, being under a skylight during a heavy rain can sound like being inside a drum.

- Skylights waste energy. Transparent skylights are far worse in this respect than skylights made of insulated, translucent materials, but the latter are still far less effective than well-insulated roofs. Solar gain from skylights can be pleasant in the winter, but it has to be removed by extra air conditioning in the summer. The areas under skylights can be cold on winter nights—or need extra heat.
- Eventually, almost all skylights leak.
- Tiny skylights (such as "light tubes") cause tiny problems, but they're the same sort of problems. And the light they bring in is more symbolic than actually helpful.

A very common use of skylights is to connect new and old buildings. (We see it proposed so often we think it must be taught in Design 101 classes in architecture schools.) Architects faced with a historic library, for example, are tempted to build a modern library next door and bridge the two with a monster skylight.

Inevitably the result is dramatic. The space under the skylight is huge and bright and open. It showcases both the back of the original building and the front of the new building. When the expanded building opens, everyone is excited.

But then reality intrudes. The space under the skylight is expensive to heat and cool. The intensity of the sun fades everything. The hard surfaces of the skylight provide acoustics reminiscent of old railroad terminals, where reverberations made announcements loud but impossible to understand. Providing even illumination at the right level of brightness is pretty much impossible. The original library and the new are widely separated and poorly integrated. Water soon drips through the skylight. And it's hard to find a good use for the space beneath. While first-time visitors cry, "What glorious light!" the librarians and readers grind their teeth in frustration.

Because of the problems outlined above, many library areas under skylights receive little use. They end up as concourses or serve other non-assigned functions. Unfortunately, few libraries can afford to create large areas of essentially unusable space.

When you are preparing a building program or talking with your designers . . .

- Always begin by saying "no skylights." And do your very best to enforce it.
- If people are determined to have windows in the roof, north-facing clearstories work well. Try to nudge people in that direction.

- If someone proposes a monitor (a raised roof section with windows all around), regard it with severe hesitation because of potential problems with uncontrollable direct sunlight. Check the section on monitors later in this chapter.

If you are going to be stuck with a skylight and can't talk your way around it, here are some things you can do to reduce (but not eliminate) the pain.

- Be sure it is made of some translucent, insulated material like Kalwall.
- Be sure it's very small.
- Be sure it's in a place where a vertical window is impossible, such as the top of a basement wall, where any other form of natural light is difficult to achieve without a window well.
- Be sure nobody has to do anything important under it.

If you inherit a building with a skylight, your options are a lot more limited.

- Occasionally, historic libraries have spectacular stained glass skylights. Good examples are the Tiffany glass skylights in the old Chicago Public Library (now the "Cultural Center"). They have many of the problems associated with skylights, but they're amazing to look at.
- If you have impressive historical skylights, consider roofing them over and lighting them artificially. This allows consistent illumination independent of exterior light conditions and allows you to pick the proper level of brightness.
- Modern versions of this are called "artificial skylights." They consist of translucent ceiling panels lit from behind by electric light. Artificial skylights work far better than real skylights, but it may be difficult to get up inside them to change the lamps.
- If your skylights aren't works of art, you may be able to arrange to have them removed entirely.

Skylights are almost always a mistake. We think that every building program should include the phrase, "There will be no skylights."

B. Atriums

An atrium is a high-ceilinged space connecting two or more floors.

Some atriums are massive, while others can be mere holes in the floor, sometimes with matching tiny skylights above.

Atriums can create suitably grand spaces. They can also help with orientation. Patrons standing in the atrium may better understand where things are located elsewhere in the library.

Atriums also provide great views. If you stand at the edge of an atrium, gazing upward from the bottom floor or down from a high balcony, the view can be spectacular.

If you look in the new libraries issues of library magazines, you will be impressed by the number of photographs that feature atriums. Atriums often make great pictures, pictures that grace library web pages and architects' advertising brochures.

However, most librarians who have to cope with atriums dislike them, often with great intensity, and their complaints fill the library literature. Sadly, librarians' complaints seem to serve little purpose, for atriums crop up with dismal regularity in new libraries.

Here are some of the problems with atriums:

a. Atriums take up a lot of space. Although a hole in a floor is cheaper space than the solid floor that could replace it, it's by no means free.
b. Atriums are inherently noisy. Unless the walls of upper floors are glazed (glassed in), sounds carry amazingly well between floors. If the atrium is over an entryway or a lending desk—two typical locations—there will be even more noise to make its way to the beleaguered reference and reading rooms above.
c. When skylights are installed over atriums, which can be dramatic, the result is even more racket. The skylights add to the basic noisy atrium problem by reflecting rather than absorbing sound.
d. And if the floor of the atrium is ceramic tile or terrazzo (which is often the case) rather than carpet, the acoustical characteristics of the space are even more offensive. Half a dozen simultaneous conversations at the lending desk can fill an entire atrium with reverberations.
e. If they are not glassed in, upper stories overlooking atriums terrify people with acrophobia, particularly if the upper floors have narrow walkways. Few librarians or library users want to navigate narrow balconies beside huge drop-offs.
f. Pedestrian bridges across atriums are even more terrifying for some people. Some libraries have both the bridges and the terrified people.
g. Atriums tempt library users to experiment with gravity. Whether it's something innocuous and creative like paper airplanes, heavy objects like books (which can conveniently be found in many libraries), or distasteful moist

substances, open atriums encourage trouble. And if an atrium is sufficiently tall, it may suggest a practical alternative to leaping from the Golden Gate Bridge.

> We are not making this up. Libraries with high atriums have had suicides.

h. Atriums often get in the way. If an atrium is in the middle of the building, it usually interferes directly with traffic flow. Users may arrive at an upper floor by elevator and stairs, only to find that to reach a service desk they have to circumnavigate an atrium. In this respect, atriums cause some of the same navigational problems as courtyards.
i. Instead of helping with orientation, atriums can actually cause confusion if it's impossible to get from one side of the atrium to the other.

> The central library in San Francisco has a huge atrium. After struggling helplessly to get around it, Fred spent an engaging fifteen minutes watching people try to get from one side to the other, when the only actual way to get across was to return to the entry, go down a floor, walk back most of the length of the library, pass through security, and then come back up by a different route. It was all a little like watching Alice's many attempts to enter the garden.

j. Atriums are notoriously difficult to light, and light fixtures in atriums can be amazingly hard to service. Gazing upward at an impressive light fixture 30 or 40 feet above the floor may be fun, but changing the lamps is usually no fun at all. And because the ceilings are so high, many atriums are equipped with spotlights that put splashes of light on the floor but leave the ceiling dark and cause major pain when people make the mistake of looking upward to see the soaring ceilings.
k. Atriums waste energy. In a time when green features are important, wasting energy heating and cooling a high, unoccupied space seems inappropriate.
l. Atriums can screw up air handling. It's easier to heat and cool a building when floors are separate.
m. In recent years there have been passing enthusiasms for mini-atriums, which are sometimes little more than barrel-sized holes through floors. Although these small atriums don't cause the large problems that large atriums do, they still manage to cause small problems.

The frequency with which architects recommend atriums and their powerful reluctance to give them up makes us suspect that (as in the case of skylights) architectural schools are stressing atriums in Design 101 classes.

- Always start by saying "no atriums" in your program.

If you are going to be stuck with an atrium, and you can't talk your way out of it, here are some ways to make it less noxious.

- Be sure that it is glazed above ground level in order to simplify temperature control, keep people from dropping things over the edge, control racket, and make people with acrophobia less terrified.
- Be sure that the upper levels have opaque walls to above waist level. People with fear of heights are afraid to lean up against floor-to-ceiling glass partitions.
- Be sure all ceiling-mounted light fixtures are on electrically powered drops, so they can be lowered to floor level for servicing.

> It's impressive to see the number of atriums with permanently burned-out lights because the fixtures are too hard to reach.

- Be sure that the atrium is on one edge of the building, such as above an entry foyer. If people don't have to circumnavigate the atrium to get from one side of the library to another on upper floors, this will reduce some of the negative impacts of the atrium.
- Be sure that crucial pathways through the library don't skirt the precipice of the atrium. Your designers may think pathways like this are a neat idea, but many of your staff and users won't.

Although it's possible to design atriums to limit the damage they cause, you'll be a lot better off without having one at all.

What do you do if you inherit an atrium?

- First, follow some of the suggestions above for the evil but inevitable atrium. Be sure the opaque wall sections on upper levels are tall enough to avoid spooking your users and staff, and glaze the rest of the walls. Put the light fixtures over the atrium on drops.

- Consider completing upper floors, bridging over the atrium, and eliminating the multi-floor opening. The cost per square foot gained may be high, but the reduction in racket and bad floor layout and wasted energy may be worth it.

C. Designer Staircases

Photographs of new libraries are filled with pictures of romantic and dramatic staircases. They sweep upwards in atriums, accompany impressive vistas, and form artistic centerpieces of buildings.

However, library history tells us that one area where librarians need to keep an eagle eye and a firm claw on their architects is staircases. Horrible examples abound.

Designer staircases provide special problems because all staircases are prone to problems under the best of circumstances. People trip and fall on staircases with grim regularity, even on staircases that are designed with prime concern for safety. And people bump their heads on the undersides of staircases.

Many designer staircases also terrify people with acrophobia.

> We can't find solid data on what percentage of the population has acrophobia, but we've heard estimates of 5 percent. If that's the case, people with acrophobia may constitute your single largest group of users with disabilities. It helps to consider what would happen to your library if the Americans with Disabilities Act were expanded to cover acrophobia.

Designer staircases can also absorb a lot of space, because they are design features. A huge atrium with a designer staircase can use up a lot of the cubic space in a building while accomplishing little or nothing of value except providing good photos for the designer's portfolio and the library's web page.

Over the years, a number of designer staircase ideas have proven their lack of merit and have been banned by building codes, but others continue to be created. The sad thing about all of this is that designers kept using the dangerous concepts until the concepts were actually banned.

Remember that a staircase is a means to move safely between floors on foot. If it is also a design statement, it needs to be a safe and functional and comfortable and reasonably priced design statement.

Here are some examples of problem staircases.

1. Floating Staircases

These have been popular for years. Instead of being solidly filled in below with useful features like storage closets, floating staircases are engineered to hang in midair, sometimes with no visible means of support except at their tops and bottoms. They may represent real tours de force of structural engineering.

The main problem with a floating staircase is making use of the open space beneath it. If the space beneath the staircase is left wide open, it offers people of every possible height someplace where they can bump their foreheads on the lower edge of the staircase. And there's nothing you can do with the space beneath, once the bottom of the staircase gets to less than about seven feet from the floor.

In some floating staircases, the balusters extend down an inch or two below the lower edge of the stair. In one Illinois library, a staff member received a serious and permanent injury when he jammed his forehead into the projecting bottom of a baluster. In another Illinois public library with a similar staircase, the staff keep display cases under the staircase at all times to protect library users.

Owners of buildings with floating staircases have sometimes had to install curbs or railings on the floor around the base of the staircases to keep people from wandering under the staircases and bumping their heads.

Some architects have installed platforms under floating staircases to keep people from actually stepping under the stairs and bumping their foreheads. Other libraries have storage closets up to the point where the bottom edge of the staircase is high enough to clear most heads.

Anything stored in the open under a floating staircase looks messy. Given the extreme lack of storage space in many libraries, staff members are tempted to eventually give up and put something under the staircase. How much better everything would look if the space were a closet!

Floating staircases are creepy for users with a fear of heights, who may not want to look down on both sides as they climb. Staircases neatly enclosed between walls are far more welcoming.

Floating staircases mean atriums, with the noise and other problems that accompany them.

Floating staircases can't be placed next to elevators, and users who don't want to climb the staircase may have to hunt around before they find the elevator.

2. Staircases with Oddly Shaped Steps

Old Carnegie-era libraries often had basement stairs with pie-shaped steps at the corners, and even experienced staff members took tumbles now and then.

People have known for at least a century that safe steps are rectangular steps, and that all steps in a staircase should be the same size. But odd steps keep turning up in new buildings.

A good example of oddly shaped steps is provided by curved staircases, where the treads are shallower on the inside of the curve than on the outside. Walking up and down on opposite sides of the staircase can provide very different experiences. Curved staircases can be truly elegant to look at, but people want to get a firm grip on the handrail before starting down.

> If libraries were Tara and Vivian Leigh and needed to make dramatic entrances, there might be excuses for curved staircases. But they aren't and she doesn't.

By the same token, treads and risers should have standard dimensions. People are accustomed to a limited range of proportions in steps. Anything different can lead to awkwardness in climbing and descending, and it can encourage falling.

A few libraries actually have old-fashioned circular staircases, the kind with a center column and extremely tight curves. They may look romantic, or appear to be a great way to fit a useful staircase in where you have no space. But just getting up and down staircases like this is a major adventure, even when you're unencumbered with books. Circular staircases for public use are an anathema, and for staff use they're dangerous and impractical. If you must have a circular staircase, be sure you have a lot of liability insurance.

3. Handrails That Are Not Perpendicular to the Run of the Staircase

If a handrail runs diagonally to the steps, people using a staircase have to walk crabwise if they want to hold on to the handrail.

For those people (like us) who are no longer young, being faced with the choice of going without a handrail or walking downstairs diagonally is not pleasant, and it's annoying to once more have to seek the elevator.

4. Staircases (and Balconies) with Handrails That Can Be Climbed Like Ladders

For a number of years, designers have enjoyed creating balcony and staircase railings with horizontal rather than vertical balusters. The effect is a little like a split rail fence.

The problem with these railings is that children can climb the horizontal bars like ladders. And they do. (At one university in Illinois, a small child fell off a balcony during a building's grand opening by climbing a railing.)

> While serving on a design awards committee, Fred had someone argue that climbable railings aren't an issue in buildings not intended for children, but he disagrees. Unless you card everyone at the door, kids will sneak in.

As far as we know, at least some building codes now ban railings like this, but it's always a good idea to make sure. Look at the designs for railings in your proposed building (you may have to check the shop drawings) and veto anything where a child can get an easy foothold anywhere and scramble up and over.

> The architecture building at the University of Illinois has endless balconies. The whole effect is a little like a stage set for *Riot in Cell Block Thirteen*. Because all of the railings on all of the balconies have horizontal balusters, there's literally no safe place for a child above the ground floor.

5. Staircases (and Balconies) with Balusters Too Widely Spaced

In days gone by, staircases and balconies were created with openings between the balusters wide enough for children to fall through.

Modern building codes limit such openings to four inches, but your library may be old and unsafe.

6. Staircases with Open or Transparent Risers

One favorite design element that upsets many people is open or transparent risers.

A stairway is made up of treads and risers. People step on the treads, which are connected by the vertical risers.

In the past, some designers built staircases with open risers. As people climbed the stairs, they could look down between the treads and see whatever was going on many feet below. Not surprisingly, most people disliked this sensation, and people with acrophobia couldn't use the stairs at all.

> After many years, we still can't see any practical or aesthetic benefit to seeing through a staircase by looking down between your feet.

Building codes now limit the size of the opening to prevent small children from falling through, but stairs are still built with partial risers.

Other stairs are built with transparent risers. People can't fall through, but they can still enjoy the vertigo, not missing out on a moment of potential queasiness.

We recommend that you tell your architects from the start that you want closed, totally opaque risers in all your staircases.

7. Staircases with Transparent Treads

Even worse than transparent risers are transparent treads.

Many steel staircases in factories and power plants have semi-transparent treads made of steel bars set on edge. They're safe enough, but for the uninitiated (even those without acrophobia) they're remarkably unnerving.

8. Staircases with Slippery Treads

Some ornamental staircases have hard steps that are slippery when wet. Elegantly polished stone treads may be fun to look at, but they're a lot less fun when we have to get an iron grip on the handrail before we start down.

Staircases work well with carpeted treads, especially if they have plastic nosings to resist wear. Hard-surfaced treads need to have surfaces sufficiently irregular to offer serious traction.

9. Staircases Where the Ends of the Treads Curve Upward into the Walls

This doesn't happen often, but it's another bad idea. Fred tripped on a staircase like this in the main Seattle Public Library, which has lots of signature architecture.

10. Staircases Where the Treads Have Drop-Offs at the Ends

Like staircases with treads that curve up, staircases with treads that just end are also unnerving to users, who can envision stepping off the edge accidentally. (This seems an unlikely design choice, but an important U.S. academic library has staircases designed this way.)

11. Overly Long Staircases

Even straight, crisp staircases can be unnerving if they continue too long in one direction. Especially for people heading down, starting at the top and looking down a flight of stairs that drops twenty-five feet is scary. (If you've ever taken an escalator to a deep tunnel line in the London Underground or Washington DC Metro, you know a little about what this feels like.)

A staircase that has a landing halfway and reverses itself before it goes the rest of the way is far more comfortable than one that runs the entire distance between two floors in one line.

We know of one library with a second-floor children's department reached by a long, straight staircase in an atrium. Library staff members installed a kiddy gate at the top of the stairs.

12. Staircases with Light Fixtures That You Can't Reach

When your library is being designed, always find out how the lights will be changed over your staircases. Ask very specific questions, and don't accept overly vague answers. ("Use a lift" is an overly vague answer.)

One of the problems with changing lights over staircases is finding a place to put the ladder.

The world of public architecture is full of staircases where the lights were installed when scaffolding was in place, and once the scaffolding is removed there's no way to get at the fixtures without erecting a new scaffold.

One easy way to check whether existing libraries have problems in this area is to look for burnt-out lamps in fixtures over staircases. A few of these will almost certainly never be replaced.

> The University of Illinois, where Fred teaches, once erected a new scaffold to change an otherwise unreachable light bulb. When the campus maintenance department figured out what it had all cost, they said "never again," and the bulb has now been burned out for years.

What can you do to keep yourself sane when the time comes to service light fixtures over staircases?

- Have the fixtures on drops, so they can be lowered to the staircase below for servicing.
- Make sure that fixtures not on drops are located above landings that are large enough for tall stepladders, never above steps.
- Have railings at the top that are strong enough to support planks stretched across the opening, so that people can stand on the planks while replacing lamps.

> One library on which Fred consulted has quartz halogen lamps far above the staircase. Lamps of this sort burn out quickly, and even at the grand opening, when the building had been polished lovingly by the staff, several lamps were burned out over the stairs. The director said she feared for the custodian's life every time he changed a lamp.

13. Handrails That Can't Be Grabbed

Until safe handrails were required for compliance with the Americans with Disabilities Act, designer staircases featured an amazing range of impossible handrails.

Most of them were far too large for normal hands to grip. People headed downstairs might be required to hang onto huge timber beams, gripping them caliper style between their thumbs and fingertips.

If you inherit stairs like this, you can probably replace the handrails with something that actually works.

14. Staircases Too Far from Elevators

If a staircase becomes a central design element, there probably will be no good place for an elevator right beside it. Users who take one look at the staircase and say "Not for me" may find themselves searching for an elevator.

Sometimes they really have to search. There's nothing better than a spectacular central staircase with the alternative elevator hidden away down an unmarked hallway.

15. Staircases That Transmit Too Much Noise

Simple staircases with walls on both sides offer the great advantage of limiting noise transmission between floors. If a public library has an adult department on one floor and a children's department on another floor, a staircase that is not located in a huge open space can prevent a lot of unwanted noise transmission.

16. Staircases That (among Other Problems) Waste Space and Energy

In addition to all of the other problems associated with overblown staircases, many of them simply waste expensive space. We've seen drawings for proposed libraries where it looked like a quarter of the building was devoted to atrium plus staircase.

17. Speculation on Why We Have So Many Dysfunctional Staircases

It's hard to know why so many libraries and other public buildings have horrible staircases, but our best guess is that the designers are planning dramatic photographs in company and library brochures.

If you look at almost any architectural issue of *Library Journal* or *American Libraries,* both of which feature photographs selected by architects, you will be impressed by the percentage of pictures that feature huge atriums with monumental staircases and lights that will be nightmares to change.

18. Wording for Building Programs

So very many things go wrong with staircases that it's hard to come up with a concise list to include in building programs. But here's a start:

- Staircases will be designed to allow people to travel safely and securely between floors.
- Staircases will not be installed as central features of huge atriums.
- The undersides of staircases will be enclosed.
- Staircases will proceed in straight lines, not diagonals or curves.
- Staircases will be designed to minimize the effects of acrophobia. They will not have open or transparent risers or treads. Railings will not be completely transparent. Staircases will not make long, straight descents, but will reverse directions at landings halfway down between floors.
- To prevent injuries to children, staircase and balcony railings will not have horizontal bars or balusters that can be climbed like ladders.
- Staircases will be designed to limit noise transmission between floors.

All in all, staircases are a major source of serious accidents. Any cute design that makes them even marginally less safe is a serious mistake.

D. Courtyards

Many libraries have been built with charming courtyards. Some are at one end of the structure, while others are buried in the center of the building.

Courtyards can introduce daylight to otherwise dark interiors. They can also provide a glimpse of nature, not to mention sites for fountains or artwork. In communities with moderate climates, courtyards can provide pleasant places to sit.

Many historic libraries—built in the days when natural light was essential to reading—have courtyards designed to provide additional space for windows. Some of these courtyards are extremely attractive spaces.

In general, however, courtyards tend to cause trouble with circulation (moving from place to place in the building) and with effective room design. Here are a few standard problems caused by courtyards:

- Courtyards in the middle of libraries usually interfere with navigation. When people want to go from point A to point B, they frequently have to circumnavigate the courtyard.
- Courtyards can lead to user confusion. In some buildings, users circumnavigating a courtyard may lose track of how many times they have turned. If they make the wrong guess, they may end up walking three-quarters of the way around a building, looking for the door, when one-quarter of the way around the building would have worked if they had started off in the opposite direction.

- Courtyards in the center of buildings can lead to beads-on-a-string room layouts. Because the building narrows beside the courtyard, the designer may provide traffic flow that leads through one room to another.

> For example, in one Illinois public library with a courtyard, the library conference room could be reached only by cutting through the main meeting room or through a closet reached through a secure local history collection. In another part of the same building, it was faster and easier to go outside and come back in through another door than to walk through the building.

- Although courtyards look like great places for people to read out-of-doors, they appear not to function well for security reasons.
- Courtyard plantings have to be maintained. If the courtyard is small, the amount of light actually reaching the plantings can be inadequate.

An impressive number of courtyards in libraries are simply kept locked. When we tour libraries with courtyards, we always try the doors, and stepping out into the courtyard is almost always impossible.

The easy phrase to put into your building program is "no courtyard."

E. Indoor Water Features

A "water feature" is any architectural ornament that employs water. Water features include fountains, reflecting pools, water walls, and similar ideas.

Water features can be handsome, exciting, refreshing, and musical. They photograph well and are fun to see. Given the choice of sponsoring a fountain or some bookshelves, donors will probably have little trouble deciding.

By and large, however, librarians find water features a remarkable pain.

- Water and library materials are a bad combination. Nothing libraries have or do benefits from water splashing around. If something important in a library is stored one floor beneath a fountain, staff members never sleep well.
- People fall into water features. One major U.S. public library had a reflecting pool in an entry corridor, and people kept taking headers into it. Including the mayor. Many libraries with fountains have to constantly watch small children.

- People throw things into water features. A fountain inside a library is a magnet for coins. Unless the drain is carefully maintained, sooner or later it will plug up, and water will flow over the edges.

In addition to throwing their own possessions into fountains, users may drop in books. Whether they do so accidentally or experimentally, few items that libraries own benefit from being dropped into water.

> John worked in a college library where students continually added fish and frogs to the indoor pools. The pools were eventually drained and covered over.

- Water features can raise humidity to unwelcome levels.
- Water features can harbor Legionnaires' disease. Starting about 2010, a number of hospitals reported encountering this problem in their water features.
- Running water has a powerful psychological impact. One Illinois public library has an attractive fountain near the lending desk. Unfortunately, the musically tinkling sound of running water has a strong psychological effect on staff members, and the library has to keep the fountain turned off to prevent staff from constantly running to the restroom.

The wording for building programs is simple: "No water features."

If you find yourself stuck with an unwanted water feature, the solution is simple, although fraught with potential complaints. Turn it off, drain it, and turn it into a planter.

F. Non-Rectangular Interior Spaces

To create architectural interest, designers frequently create oddly shaped rooms. Some are triangular or trapezoidal. Some have oddly shaped alcoves. Portions of some rooms are designed to project at odd angles from otherwise rectangular buildings. Other rooms have unnecessary curves, ranging from simple sections of circles to strangely undulating, serpentine creations.

Some of these spaces are inherently interesting and appeal to owners, who may find sweeping curves or jutting angles attractive during the design process.

Curves on floor plans look neat from an aerial perspective.

Here are some basic problems with non-rectangular spaces:

- Everything we put in libraries is rectangular. Oddly shaped spaces are at their best inefficient and awkward to use.
- Curved walls may also lead to the necessity of installing curved shelving or work counters, which have the unfortunate ability to combine very high initial cost, long-term inflexibility, and awkward working spaces.
- Book stacks fit extremely poorly into any shape of space except a rectangle.
- Curved or other oddly shaped walls are also a waste of construction funds. Curves are expensive to construct. Replacing glass walls on a curved structure is an extraordinary budgetary adventure.
- Curved walls can lead to unfortunate acoustics, with odd sound transmission. Being inside a small, round room is a lot like being inside an oil drum.
- Curved walls also make later expansion difficult or impossible. Adding on to a building with a straight wall is vastly easier that adding on to a building with a serpentine wall. Since all libraries eventually run out of space, having no logical place to attach extra space leaves a library unprepared for the future.
- Installing lighting in non-rectangular spaces is extremely difficult. By far the best way to light a modern library is by using strip fluorescent or LED uplight fixtures set end-to-end in parallel rows. This is hard or impossible to accomplish in oddly shaped spaces.

Libraries, of course, are not the only institutions to suffer from the impact of non-rectangular spaces. But our shelving makes us more vulnerable than most other buildings.

As with other areas listed in this chapter, we recommend that your building program have an emphatic statement to the effect that *all internal spaces in the library will be rectangular.*

> "The truth of the matter is that it would have been a great deal simpler and more practical to build the cabin as an ordinary three-dimensional oblong room, but then the designers would have got miserable." Douglas Adams, *The Hitchhiker's Guide to the Galaxy,* chapter 11, paragraph 1.

What can you do if your architects or owners want a curved or diagonal wall?

- Begin by asking what part of "no" they didn't understand.
- Ask your engineers or construction management firm to conduct a value engineering study. The extra expense of non-rectangular spaces in terms of cost per usable square foot can be extraordinary.
- Ask for a very specific furniture layout. Do not accept stacks with aisles that are narrow at one end and wide at the other, or stacks where you can't look down the aisles because they shift left or right every few units to eliminate overly wide or narrow aisles.*
- Ask to see the proposed lighting scheme, including calculations of illumination levels. Reject lighting systems that involve oceans of round pendant lights, as well as schemes that result in uneven lighting levels.

What do you do if you inherit curved or diagonal walls?

- Curse and live with the situation. You are not alone. Given the survival time of most library buildings, the walls will continue to be there to torment generations of library users and librarians yet unborn.

G. Bad Lighting

Most bad lighting sneaks up on libraries because it's difficult to spot in construction drawings. Only when the building is finished, the furniture is in place, and the lights are switched on do librarians realize that some truly unfortunate ideas have come to pass.

Bad lighting is also hard to spot in photographs of libraries. Photographs don't show glare and uneven illumination well, and many professionally made photographs of libraries involve lots of supplementary, portable lighting brought in to provide temporary illumination.

1. Downlighting

One major problem that pervades far too many library buildings is the extensive use of direct downlighting.

Recessed downlights (commonly called "can lights") are cylindrical (or sometimes square) openings in the ceiling with lights pointing straight down.

---

*All schematic designs except extremely preliminary rough sketches should include full furniture layout diagrams. If your designers don't provide these, stop everything until they do and until you have approved them.

- Recessed downlights direct almost all of their light straight down. The result is overly brightly lit horizontal surfaces and badly lit vertical surfaces, such as book spines and the pages of books held vertically.
- The light from recessed downlights is spotty, and this becomes increasingly apparent near ceilings. Downlights along walls, for example, provide odd and unattractive patterns of light and dark, a little reminiscent of gum lines. Designers who want to install recessed downlights frequently assume that as long as the resulting cones of light overlap at tabletop, there is no problem with illumination, but that doesn't help libraries.
- Downlights also cast harsh shadows. In some extreme installations, users trying to write find that the shadows of their hands conceal what they are writing.
- Looking up into downlights can be a particularly unpleasant experience. Since people in libraries frequently look up at high shelving, they are often blinded by any downlights, which are highly concentrated. (Because libraries move things around, the harsh downlights that are not over high shelves today may easily be over them tomorrow.)
- For a while, pendant lights with small glass shades were in vogue with designers. Unfortunately, these also direct spots of very bright light downward. If pendant downlights are used, they need to be located where users and staff cannot accidentally look upward into the lights and be blinded by glare. If pendant lights are incandescent, they also contribute to inefficient energy use without providing a great deal of usable light.
- Small perforations (never slots) can be used to let a percentage of the light pass directly through strip uplight fixtures. As long as the center of the fixture is opaque (to conceal the presence of dead bugs) these work well, but perforations are not essential to good lighting.
- Buildings illuminated with downlights can look closed at night. People driving by realize a building is open because the walls and ceilings are lighted, not because the tabletops and floors are lighted.

The most effective way to light libraries always remains strip uplights with standard, four-foot fluorescent tubes, although LED fixtures may replace them.

We recommend that your instructions to your architects include something like the following:

- "All lighting fixtures in public areas and staff workspaces will be pendant fluorescent or LED strip fixtures reflecting most of the light off the ceiling."
- "In particular, there will be absolutely no recessed downlights not specifically called for in this program. In other words, none at all."

2. Architecturally Fixed Task Lighting

Task lighting is lighting designed to provide particularly bright illumination in a specific area. Examples of task lighting are light fixtures attached to book stacks, light fixtures on reading tables, light fixtures on staff workstations, and similar equipment.

As long as task lighting is mounted on furniture, it moves with the furniture when you rearrange your library. (You may still run into serious problems, however, when you find there's no way to plug in the lighting once you've relocated things.)

If task lighted is architecturally mounted, however, it's often impossible to relocate the furniture it illuminates.

Even if task lighting is mounted on furniture, it doesn't necessarily work. Cute round lamps on reading tables, for example, often produce cute round circles of light in the middles of the tables—just where nobody needs them. Table lamps often need to be strip fixtures running the length of the table. It's always reasonable to insist on trying out one of the specified fixtures before you accept the idea.

3. Most Quartz Halogen Lighting

Quartz halogen lighting is described in chapter 25 on "Lighting." Basically, it's incandescent lighting that has extremely white light because it operates at a very high temperature. This is made possible by a quartz glass envelope that resists heat and by the introduction of halogens into the inside of the lamp to enhance filament life.

Compared with other forms of lighting, quartz halogen lamps are extremely bright, extremely hot, and extremely short-lived.

You can recognize quartz halogen lamps because most of them are miniature reflector lamps about two inches in diameter. The backs often glow pinkly because the lamps are designed to let heat escape through the silvered reflectors, and some of the visible end of the spectrum escapes along with the infrared.

When we visit libraries with quartz halogen lamps, lots of them are usually burned out. This is probably a Good Thing.

Unless the light is badly needed, in which case it is an Annoying Thing.

4. Indoor Metal Halide Lighting

Metal halide lighting is described in great detail in chapter 25 on "Lighting."

Metal halide is great for exterior lighting, where we need lots of light, we turn the fixtures on and off only once a day, noisy ballasts don't drive people up the wall, and funny colors are acceptable. And if a lamp blows up once in a while (the engagingly named "catastrophic end of service"), the shreds of hot glass are less likely to land on human flesh.

Unfortunately, metal halide fixtures have also been popular for indoor lighting, especially where designers want to produce a great deal of light from a very small fixture.

In interiors, of course, the bad characteristics of metal halide lighting really make a difference. If people turn lights off, we want to be able to turn them on again without waiting fifteen minutes (the so-called "restrike time" that characterizes metal halide lighting). Noisy ballasts disturb readers. Odd colors are disruptive. And who knows who will get what when things explode.

Metal halide lamps are expensive, and often lamps and ballasts are matched. With four-foot fluorescent tubes, you may have an immense selection of lamps that will fit a specific fixture, but with metal halide you may be stuck with one specific product.

Although metal halide lamps are often more efficient than fluorescent lamps, they're not efficient enough to justify their use inside a library. In addition, replacement metal halide lamps are far more expensive than fluorescent lamps. It's better to specify fluorescent and stand your ground.

When is metal halide the best solution?

- Metal halide lamps shining upward can illuminate large cathedral (sloped) ceilings from a relatively small number of fixtures.

What can you do to stop metal halide lighting?

- As usual, put the prohibition in the building program.
- When the building is being designed, check the schedules of fixture types on the electrical plans. You can also insist on receiving cut sheets for all proposed lighting fixtures and check every sheet for lamp types. (Remember that some fixtures can be ordered with more than one lighting technology so you need to watch carefully.)

What can you do if you've been handed metal halide lighting?

- If you're lucky, you may be able to replace only the guts of your light fixtures, but you will probably have to replace the entire fixtures.
- If the metal halide fixtures were selected because they're compact and round, you may find that this decision was driven by an oddly shaped room where strip fluorescent fixtures won't fit.

5. Dark Ceilings

Libraries with dark ceilings are always difficult to light, because we can't bounce light off dark ceilings.

In addition, dark ceilings make rooms seem low and gloomy.

Coping with dark ceilings is sometimes unavoidable in historic buildings, but there is no excuse for recreating the problem today in modern construction.

Even rooms with light-colored ceilings sometimes have dark soffits (lowered sections of ceilings). If the underside of a soffit is painted any color but white, the area under it is likely to be unpleasantly dark.

> Fred worked with one library that had soffits around the edge of a large room, with the undersides of the soffits painted brick red. All of the shelving around the edge of the room, underneath the soffits, was too dark.

If you have a historic library with a dark historic ceiling, the best approach is probably to do what libraries did a century or more ago in their huge, dramatic reading rooms. Provide chandeliers that supply sufficient ambient light for people to move about safely, and supplement this with task lighting on bookshelves, tables, and service desks.

Remember that historic dark ceilings should be as visible as possible. If you can't make the ceiling lighter, you can use angled lighting that increases the surface modeling. (Fred thinks you could dry brush the edges of dark ceiling details so that they are more visible, but he could be wrong.)

We've seen a number of libraries with dark ceilings that had retrofitted blazingly concentrated downlights, and we think this is a terrible mistake. If you look up at a historic ceiling and are immediately blinded by bright lights, why bother to have a historic dark ceiling at all?

What can you tell your architect?

- With the exception of historic ceilings that must be preserved, all ceilings will be white.
- The undersides of all soffits will be white.
- There will be no perimeter soffits, with or without downlights.

If you inherit dark ceilings:

- Deal with historically dark ceilings as we suggest.
- Replace dark acoustic tile with white acoustic tile. (If you paint acoustic tile, its acoustic properties are ruined.)
- If any hard-surfaced soffits have dark undersides, paint them white.

H. Multiple Public Entrances

Libraries are frequently tempted to create multiple entrances, particularly if access by pedestrians and drivers are on opposite sides of the building or if the building is in the center of a campus.

Unfortunately, all entrances need to be watched, and multiple entrances almost inevitably lead to wasted staff time.

The pressure for multiple entrances appears to come mostly from people in authority. Mayors want access from several directions. University boards of trustees see the library (correctly enough) as the center of the campus, and they want students to be able to enter it from any direction.

If access to the library from two directions is essential, buildings can be efficient if both entrances lead to a single foyer, with a single door between the foyer and the library proper.

> One junior college library in Illinois was envisioned by the architect as the center of campus. It was located in the central core of a large building that sprawled with wings in a number of different directions. Although the librarians liked the central idea, they strongly disputed what went with it, a separate door from each wing of the college into the library. The library had far more entrances than the library staff could possibly watch, and (as the staff had predicted at the time the design was forced upon them) a significant portion of the collection vanished during the first year. The school then did what it could to close all but one entrance, but the design of the building made this extremely difficult.

The situation is different, of course, in large library buildings where access to all collections is through departmental libraries with single doors leading to central hallways.

What can you do if people suggest multiple entrances to your library?

- If you are dealing with your funding authorities, you can explain to them the extra cost of supervising each additional entrance and ask how many additional entrances they are willing to pay for in eternity.

> Fred has this conversation about multiple entrances with mayors every couple of years, often mayors he has never met who are dealing with libraries he has never seen and who can't believe the cost implications he hands them. He never makes these mayors happy.

- If you are dealing with architects who are pushing for multiple entrances, tell your funding authorities exactly what the cost implications of multiple entrances are.
- Remind people that all security gates need to be staffed at all times. Many architects refuse to believe this.

What can you do if you inherit multiple entrances?

- Do what lots of libraries have done, and start converting them to alarmed emergency exits. It will look funny to have entrances out of service, but you may have little choice.

- You will be able to take consolation (perhaps limited) in the fact that many other libraries share your problem, and you can mutter together with other librarians. This is why there are always late-night bars open at library conferences.

I. Architectural Solutions to Furniture Problems

Built-in features are fun to design, and when a library building is new, furniture that is literally part of the building can look neat and tidy and organic.

Unfortunately, however, libraries and their services change frequently, and today's built-in feature may become an awkward white elephant in a few years.

For example, some libraries in years gone by were outfitted with card catalogs or other card files that were structurally part of the building. When card files ceased to be used, libraries were left with special niches or supporting plinths that were difficult to alter.

> Fred knows one library where the designers installed a special niche in a brick wall behind the lending desk to hold the library's registration card files. The first thing that happened was that the library registered vast numbers of new users, and the available drawers no longer could hold all of the registration cards. Soon there were a couple of loose drawers on the floor under the desk. The second thing that happened was that the library stopped using registration cards entirely. Now it had an extremely visible (but unlighted) empty niche behind the desk.

> Long ago, Fred inherited a library where the card catalog fitted between two small wing walls. As the collection grew, the staff piled extra catalog units on top of the original, but eventually things got completely out of hand and the staff had the wing walls ripped out to make space for a larger catalog. (Of course, this led to carpet patches where the wing walls had been, and these never matched the rest of the carpet until the entire carpet was replaced).

A common error has been to create special spaces to house pieces of trendy electronic equipment. Technical equipment changes frequently, however, and long before the building becomes worn with use, spaces created to hold special objects may become obsolete.

Even popular concepts like computer classrooms can become dated. If a library teaches classes for only a few hours a week, it will almost certainly be more practical to use laptops in a multipurpose conference room than to have a room dedicated to classroom functions.

> *Ars longa, technologia brevis est.* (Fake Latin for "Technology is fleeting, but art endures.")

What can you do to prevent these problems?

- When you're preparing your building program, always ask yourself whether technical changes in the use of libraries may make a special-purpose space obsolete. (Don't blame yourself if you don't see changes coming. Most of us were blindsided by the laptop revolution in libraries. But always ask what you think is likely to change in the next twenty-five years.)
- In bold print in your building program, say "There will be no architectural solutions to furniture problems." Insist that you approve all shop drawings, and reject all of those with built-in gadgetry.
- Never use unadjustable shelving or unusually shallow shelving. (Regardless of the type of material to be stored, no shelf less than nine inches [nominal ten inches] deep is ever a good idea.)

J. Non-Acoustic Ceilings

Except in the case of inherited historic ceilings of significant beauty, all library ceilings need to absorb sound.

The usual way to achieve this is by using acoustic tile, which has the advantage of easy removal for access to the increasing variety of mechanical systems we hide above ceilings.

> Although some people don't see stains as an advantage, one of the notable characteristics of acoustic tile is the way it turns brown the instant water falls on it. Few libraries with acoustic tile ceilings are oblivious to leaks from aging roofs, ruptured sprinkler pipes, or condensation.

Many acoustic problems in libraries are due to the omission of sound-absorbing surfaces on portions of ceilings that are not flat. These commonly include:

- Cathedral ceilings. Ceilings shaped like the inside of a roof.
- Shed roof ceilings. Ceilings that slope in one direction only, high on one side and low on the other.
- Barrel-vault ceilings (sometimes called wagon-vault ceilings). Like cathedral ceilings, but curved rather than peaked in cross-section.
- Sloped portions of ceilings that combine flat and sloped elements.

Cathedral and barrel vault ceilings are notorious for their ability to transmit sound. A library with a reference desk and soft seating area 100 feet apart at the ends of a barrel vault without an acoustic surface may find that no conversations are private, and that the conversations of people seated on armchairs far from the staff can be overheard with distressing ease.

Sloped ceiling sections can also do an impressive job of transmitting sound. Sound that rises vertically can be reflected 90 degrees by a sloped ceiling, travel horizontally, and then be reflected downward by another section of sloped ceiling.

In many libraries, ceilings of this type are made of gypsum board (drywall), and they cause serious problems with unwanted sound transmission. But wood is just as bad.

Some libraries have small areas of flat ceiling dutifully equipped with acoustic tile, but accompanying large areas of sloped ceilings made of drywall. Noises carry magnificently.

Luckily, the solutions are easy.

- If the slope of a ceiling is gentle, creating it from suspended ceiling components is straightforward. It's also easy to use acoustic tile on the undersides of soffits.
- For ceilings that cannot be constructed using suspended ceiling systems, spray-on acoustic surfacing is available that works well.
- If your architects insist on a non-acoustic ceiling, get an independent opinion from an acoustical consulting engineer.

How do you prevent acoustic problems?

- Make very clear in your written program that the building will have no new hard-surfaced ceilings of any kind, either flat or sloped. And hold your designers to it.

If you inherit a library where sloped ceilings lead to unwanted noise transmission:

- You can spray on an acoustic surface after the fact. The only problem is that the job is a little messy, and you can't have exposed books, carpet, and furnishings while the work is progressing.

K. Inflexibility

One of the most basic truths about library buildings is that library needs change and buildings must adapt.

Our experience with experts on non-library buildings is that they are continually taken aback by the tendency of librarians to start moving the furniture around almost before the wall paint is even dry.

What can you do to protect yourself and your library?

- Have the program clearly state that all spaces in the library will be planned with long-term flexibility of use in mind.
- List the features that will be avoided:
  - Task lighting that is not attached to furniture.
  - Sections of floor that cannot carry the weight of library books. In years gone by, some academic library reading rooms were constructed with the presumption that the floors would never carry books, but if times change you may need stack sections at each end of a large room.
  - Public areas or staff offices without full access to 110-volt and data service. A library with a poured floor slab needs electrical outlets and data access at frequent intervals in the slab for long-term flexibility of use. Outlet covers must always be totally even with the slab, so that outlets do not limit the placement of shelving and furniture. (Many libraries use wireless data connections for public workstations, but wireless has problems with bandwidth, speed, and reliability. While you're installing wiring in slabs, always err on the side of long-term flexibility and provide data conduit everywhere.)
  - Built-in furniture.
  - Bearing walls. Bearing walls make remodeling and expansion extremely difficult. There is little excuse for them in all but the smallest of modern library buildings.
  - Structural details that make expansion difficult or impossible. Remember that expanding a library usually means enlarging existing spaces, such as adult or children's departments in public libraries, rather than just adding a new addition to one end of the building. If a library can't

open the side of a room to enlarge it, long-term flexibility is seriously impaired. Similarly, if a row of offices is on one side of a floor, they should be opposite the wall that will be knocked out for expansion.
- Structural systems that meet codes when the library is built but will no longer do so if it's expanded. Always specify that the systems used in your building will still meet building codes if the building is doubled or tripled in size.
- Restrooms that are barely large enough to meet codes. If you expand your building, you will very likely be forced to locate additional restrooms in extremely undesirable places.
- Curved or diagonal exterior walls.
- Underground utilities installed in the path of future expansion.
- Multistory buildings with exterior walls that step inward or outward, leaving no place to attach additions.

L. Bad Sight Lines

All libraries—particularly public libraries, school libraries, and college libraries—rely on good sight lines to enable a limited number of staff members to supervise large areas.

If a library has bad sight lines, it seldom can afford the extra staff necessary to keep an eye on hidden corners, and the result is constant problems with the supervision of users.

Some standard ways of preventing bad sight lines include:

- Orienting stack aisles so that staff members stationed at service desks can see down as many aisles as possible.
- In the past, however, some libraries experimented with aisles that radiated like the spokes of a wheel from service desks. These turned out to be unworkable—almost always impressively unworkable.
- Using glass walls to permit staff to supervise people using study rooms, quiet reading rooms, and so on. Study rooms are most effective when they are essentially terrariums. Privacy walls to protect users of adjacent study rooms from seeing each other lead to major oversight problems for librarians. And it makes the study rooms claustrophobic.
- Making sure that public computer workstations that offer Internet access have screens that face service desks.

Chapter 6 ■ Dysfunctional Designs   127

Inflexibility appeals much more to designers than to librarians. Some designers want to build for the ages, while most libraries move things around every few years. For years, this obsolete card catalog blocked an important path between a lending desk and a reference desk because it was perched on a concrete plinth that was too difficult to remove. (The same library had a small display case—which should be a simple piece of furniture—mounted on I-beams sticking out of a wall. Moving it required a cutting torch, and the cut-off beams still stuck out of the wall.)

However, there are also sight lines that are better than anyone really wants.

- Many libraries provide unwelcome views of toilets. Far too many libraries, for example, have single-user restrooms leading directly from reading rooms—or even staff room kitchens—with toilets on full public view whenever the restrooms are not in use. And many libraries provide unwanted views of multi-user restrooms in action whenever the door is opened. Remember that if you can see a wall of mirrors when the restroom door is open, you can probably see most of the restroom reflected in the mirrors.
- Special libraries may need computer workstations with screens that cannot be seen by passersby. Lawyers, for example, may be working on confidential materials. Physicians may need to consult patient records that are made completely private by HIPPA—the federal Health Insurance Privacy and Portability Act.

When you are reviewing building floor plans, always study sight lines carefully. It's amazing how many ill-considered features you'll discover.

M. Excessive Use of Soffits

Soffits are lowered sections of ceilings. They serve to break up what might otherwise be huge expanses of suspended ceiling tiles. Some soffits enclose pieces of equipment, such as air ducts.

But many soffits cause problems.

- Soffits are very frequently used to define the location of desks. *In almost all cases, this is a major error.* It greatly limits the long-term flexibility of space organization, since desks cannot be moved without reconstructing the soffits. Particularly in the case of small service points like reference desks, matching soffits are a real mistake.
- Many soffits are too low. Any portion of the ceiling that is less than ten feet high causes problems with lighting and book shelving. If the ceiling of your room is only ten feet high, you don't want soffits.
- Because soffits are lower than the rest of the ceiling, they are a favorite place for can lights (round recessed downlights). Unfortunately, recessed downlights—as noted elsewhere—provide uneven and unpleasant light. (Recessed strip fluorescent fixtures, however, can work well.)
- Some interior designers paint the undersides of soffits dark colors to provide visual interest. This is a bad idea under any circumstances, but when dark soffits are combined with can lights, the result is almost inevitably a mixture of glare and gloom.
- A common problem in many libraries is dark perimeters in rooms. Perimeter soffits can add significantly to this problem.
- If you decide to rip out a much-disliked soffit, you may have to relocate sprinkler pipes.

We recommend that you include something like the following in your program statement:

- Soffits will be used only to break up overly large expanses of acoustic tile ceilings. In such cases, they will be narrow and will hang down just far enough from the ceiling to be visible.
- Soffits will never be used to define the locations of objects below.
- The undersides of soffits will be white.
- Soffits will never be equipped with can lights (round recessed downlights).

- Perimeter soffits will stop at least ten feet above the floor and will have inset strip fluorescent fixtures to eliminate dark shadows around the edge of the room. (Perimeter soffits are not only a functional problem but also an extremely overworked and trite design idea. Crown moldings are a lot more attractive.)
- Soffits will not be used to conceal ductwork. Space between floors will be sufficient to allow ductwork to be concealed above ceilings at least ten feet high.

N. Balconies

Balconies and mezzanines look romantic and fun. One can stand on a balcony with the wind in one's hair to greet the morning. One can gaze down from a balcony upon a lover. One can admire a soaring atrium from a balcony. Many older libraries had multiple levels of book stacks visible through large openings at the back of high-ceilinged reading rooms, giving users a real sense of how the collections were stored.

But balconies in libraries cause all sorts of problems.

- Whether interior or exterior, balconies offer a great opportunity for people to fall off. Or at least drop things off.
- While some people find the view from balconies euphoric, other people completely panic when they get too close to the railings. Unfortunately, some designers seem to take a special delight in toying with the psyches of users who suffer from acrophobia.
- The use of interior balconies often leads to ceilings that are too low and too high—if not both. If a library consists of a large open space with a balcony around the edge, too often the main ceiling will be high and hard to maintain, or the ceilings under the balcony and on the balcony will be too low for workable lighting. Ceilings under balconies and on balconies always need to be at least ten feet high.
- Balconies, like atriums, are inherently noisy. Sounds carry from the room below up to the balcony and from the balcony to the room below.
- Balconies can screw up HVAC systems. In hot weather, convection movements can lead to cool air flowing like a waterfall off a balcony to the space below, replaced by warm air rising. In its desperate attempt to keep its balcony cool in the summer, for example, a library may freeze the people right below the edge of the balcony.
- In the winter, hot air rises from the center of the area between the balconies and produces stifling heat on the balconies.
- Access to balcony spaces is inherently awkward. For all practical purposes, a balcony that includes public space is similar in layout to a tunnel—a long,

narrow area that must be accessed linearly, since users must follow the balcony rather than cut diagonally across to the other side.
- Because of their linear floor space, balconies can be very hard to supervise.
- Building codes may limit the size of balconies in your library. What's legal today may be illegal after the next code revision.
- Unglazed balconies are unsafe. For example, one Chicago suburban library has a long exterior balcony outside the children's department. Of course, it has to be kept locked at all times. (This was a pet idea of a city official and was included against the better judgment of both the architect and the library staff.)
- Some balconies have railings made up of horizontal balusters. Kids climb up and fall off.

What can you do to prevent this sort of thing?

- Always write "There will be no balconies" in your building program. In large and bold print.
- Battle in particular any design where a narrow balcony provides the basic access to spaces around the perimeter of an atrium.
- If balconies seem inevitable, insist that all interior spaces have at least ten feet of vertical clearance, including both spaces on balconies and the spaces beneath them.
- Insist that interior balconies be separated from the areas below with glazed walls or high, opaque parapets.

And if you're stuck with existing balconies:

- Consider glazing them to help people with fear of heights and improve temperature control and acoustics.
- Raise the height of the parapets and make them opaque.

Unfortunately, there's nothing you can do to eliminate the low ceilings and awkward floor configurations that may accompany balconies.

O. Features That Panic People with Acrophobia

For some reason, designers seem to take a special pleasure in tormenting people who have a fear of heights.

Examples unfortunately abound.

- Staircases with open or transparent risers.
- Staircases with glass sides.
- Staircases that continue endlessly with no turns. A large number of people dislike staring down a run of thirty or more steps, imagining that they could trip and roll endlessly down the stairs like the baby carriage in *Battleship Potemkin*. It's extremely easy to provide a landing halfway down and have the staircase turn 180 degrees at the landing, reducing the number of steps in a single row to no more than one finds in the average home.
- Balconies—particularly balconies that must be used to get from one room to another. Some buildings with balconies around atriums encourage people with even mild fear of heights to walk from room to room rubbing their shoulders against the walls opposite the drop-offs.
- Atriums in general, particularly those without protective glass walls on upper floors.
- Bridges over atriums. People who hate walking along narrow balconies beside drop-offs will have even more fun on bridges directly over the drop-offs. Particularly bridges with glass sides. If you have no fear of heights yourself, you can snicker as you watch the panicked expressions on your library users' faces as they cross the bridges. But snickering is not really good for your personality.
- Staircases floating in open spaces. Staircases between walls are far more comfortable.
- Glass-walled elevators, particularly elevators running up the sides of huge atriums.
- Floor-to-ceiling glass walls on upper floors.

Some designs are so extreme that people who normally have no fear of heights find themselves unexpectedly uncomfortable or even panicked. Few people, for example, are completely comfortable climbing industrial staircases with metal mesh treads, allowing them to look straight down between their feet to areas far below.

No one appears to know what percentage of the population suffers from acrophobia, but fear of heights may be one of the most common of all disabilities. Sources suggest that up to 5 percent of people may have serious problems in this area.

Imagine what could happen to architecture if the ADA were modified to take acrophobia into account. The dull panic that hit librarians when the ADA was first passed in 1990 would return to a substantial percentage of those who manage libraries with more than one floor.

This expansion of the ADA may never happen, of course, but imagine your smug pleasure if it does and—thanks to your leadership—your new library has no uncomfortable drop-offs to review or correct.

> Here's an example of uncomfortable libraries from real life. At a Public Library Association conference, Fred was riding up an elevator in a large public library building in the company of three women. The elevator had glass windows that overlooked the library's large central atrium. The women were already uncomfortable with the unwanted view when the elevator finally stopped at the top floor. All three stepped out, felt the plenum floor bounce slightly underfoot, and said (in unison), "I don't feel good." Opinions can, of course, vary, but it seems reasonable to believe that any library that leads its patrons to say (in unison) "I don't feel good" is not a complete success. (The same library had open risers in its staircases to provide additional not-feeling-good opportunities.)

Coming up with all-inclusive wording for your building program to keep architects from including terrifying heights appears difficult to us, but here's a stab at it.

- "The building will be specifically designed to be comfortable for use by people who suffer from fear of heights. Staircases will have opaque treads and risers, railings will be high and opaque, elevators will be enclosed, staircases will not continue more than 15 steps before reversing direction, exterior windows will stop at least 18 inches to two feet above the floor, and there will be no atriums."

What can you do if you're stuck with a scary building?

- Raise railings to a comforting height.
- If glass walls facing drop-offs continue to the floor, add opaque barricades at least three feet high.
- Fill in all open or transparent staircase risers with opaque materials.

P. Features That Lead to Particular Maintenance Problems

Some popular design features lead to serious upkeep problems. This section lists some of those we see most often.

1. Light Fixtures That Are Difficult to Reach

This is probably the most frequent upkeep complaint that librarians have about new library buildings.

Some library buildings are full of light fixtures that cannot be reached with ordinary ladders. Among the worst are fixtures more than ten feet above the floor and fixtures over staircases.

Unfortunately, unreachable fixtures can be found everywhere, even in tiny libraries.

If asked during the design process, designers usually suggest that mechanical lifts can be used, but this presupposes that (a) suitable lifts can be found, (b) the lifts are available at a reasonable price, (c) the lifts can be fitted through the entry doors of libraries, and (d) the lifts can be moved into position without relocating shelving.

> We read about a British library where all the shelving has to be moved in order to bring in lifts to change the light bulbs.

> "Use a lift" is never sufficient. Always ask "What lift? Where will it be stored? Can it fit through the stack aisles? Even if it can fit through the stack aisles, can it actually be used there?" And insist that designers be extremely specific.

The situation can be made worse by light fixtures that must be partially disassembled to change lamps.

Some people have memories of using a pole with a clamp on the end to change lamps in high can lights. That worked in older fixtures with incandescent lamps (most of the time, except when bulbs snapped off at their bases), but modern can lights may have biax fluorescent lamps that require someone to put his hand entirely into the fixture to change the lamp. A maintenance supervisor Fred knows says that lots of the men who work for him have hands too large to fit into can lights when they're trying to replace biax lamps.

What can you do to prevent problems of this type?

- In your building program, specify that all light fixtures should be reachable from an eight-foot stepladder.
- Specify that fixtures over staircases must be located over landings.
- Specify that any fixture more than 12 feet above the floor must be on an electric drop. (This is not as vital for fixtures mounted on a wall, where you can lean a straight ladder against the wall next to the fixtures, but for fixtures over wide-open spaces, drops are essential.)
- Look carefully at spec sheets for proposed light fixtures (include alternates suggested by your contractors) to be sure that changing lamps while perched on a ladder will not be difficult. (This is a great time to show proposed designs to your custodians.)
- Watch in particular for any proposed use of incandescent lamps, since they burn out while you're at lunch. Modern limits on illumination wattages may end the dismal practice of introducing quartz halogen lamps into libraries, but banning them up front is always a good idea. LED fixtures should work as well and last many, many times longer.

What can you do if you inherit a library with light fixtures that are almost impossible to reach?

- Look for long-life replacement lamps.
- Change all the lamps at the same time. (This is good advice for any building with widespread banks of fluorescent lamps.)
- Replace the fixtures with LED fixtures.
- Retrofit electric drops.
- Install new fixtures in reachable places and let the old ones rest unburnished rather than shine in use.

> LED lighting emerged as a workable option while we were finishing this book. The main problems we've noted are high color temperatures—harsh, bluish light far from the incandescent lighting warmth that many people like—and excessive directness, but they'll probably be cured.

2. White Grout in Ceramic Tile

Professional building-cleaning firms regard white grout in ceramic tile floors as the worst material to keep clean.

All light-colored grout darkens in use because its coarse, porous nature makes it impossible to get all the stains out. Unfortunately, the inevitable result is grout that is much darker near the center of the room than around the edges, advertising to all that things aren't really clean.

Colored grout tends to fade as it ages, so what appears to be a nice, medium color in the sample chart will slowly age to (stained) pastel.

The only way to avoid making this staining obvious is to select a really dark color of grout when you are working with your interior designer.

3. Flush-Tank Toilets

Tank toilets are touchy and difficult to maintain. Library users can also remove the lids and occasionally break them.

By contrast, modern flush-valve mechanisms are amazingly sturdy.

Unless your building has problems with low water pressure, a flush-valve toilet is always possible and always better.

Unlike tank toilets, flush-valve toilets don't need to refill before they can be flushed a second time. They also flush more vigorously and are less likely to jam.

What do you do to make sure you get the right equipment?

- Always specify flush-valve toilets.
- While you're at it, specify *wall-mounted* flush-valve toilets, since they are not only easier to maintain but easier to keep clean.
- If you want to check your floor plans quickly to be sure your architects have included wall-mounted toilets, look for an extra deep wall at the back of the toilets.

What if you inherit flush-tank toilets?

- Retrofitting a flush-valve toilet may be difficult because it takes a larger-capacity water line than the tiny pipe that feeds a tank toilet.
- To combat clogging, you can install tank toilets with power-assisted flush mechanisms. (The downside of these mechanisms is that they are noisy. People are used to them now, but in Fred's library a woman once shrieked in surprise when she flushed one of them while sitting on it.)

4. Built-In Soap Dispensers

Soap dispensers are not lifetime devices. Most of them fail in service, some depressingly soon.

Public restrooms of America are filled with the nonfunctioning remains of soap dispensers. Many of these are pump dispensers mounted in countertops next to sinks, with the arm of the dispenser extending over the sink for tidy delivery of liquid soap. The giveaway that there are problems is the adjacent extra dispenser, either a disposable plastic device stuck to a wall or mirror with double-sided tape, or just a separate home-style bottle sitting on the countertop or sink.

In some restrooms, there are open holes in the countertop where the pump soap dispensers were once located.

How can you prevent this?

- Many libraries fall back on the disposable dispensers that are provided free or at little cost by the companies that sell custodial supplies to institutions.
- Often the best place to mount the dispenser is directly on the mirror over the sink. ADA requirements leave little wall space between the top of the sink and the bottom of the mirror. (You can also mount the dispenser to one side of the mirror, but if you do, a lot of the soap may drip on the floor rather than onto the sink, adding to clean-up fun.)

5. EIFS

EIFS stands for "external insulation finishing system." Basically, it's a skim coat of stucco (or a similar product) over a layer of plastic foam, sometimes with an intervening mesh of fiberglass.

EIFS is popular with some designers because the material is extremely plastic. It lends itself to interestingly complex shapes.

But it also has a miserable track record with libraries. Among the common problems are:

- Water intrusion. Water sometimes gets behind EIFS and can't get out. The result can be mold, rot, or even entire exterior walls peeling off.
- Fragility. EIFS is not particularly resistant to being bumped. It's easily dented in collisions with bicycles and even less durable objects.
- Cost. Despite its fragility and its water problems, EIFS is not cheap. Some people claim that it costs nearly as much as face brick.

If it looks like stucco but may be EIFS, you can almost always tell the difference by tapping it. If it sounds lightweight and slightly hollow, it's EIFS.

EIFS is extremely popular for storefronts and is probably a good choice for this purpose. It's short-lived, but most stores want to redecorate their fronts every 10 or 15 years anyway. As an architect friend says, it's a material for stage settings.

But for buildings intended to last for a century or more, EIFS is an extraordinarily bad choice.

If you are planning a library building:

- Always say "No EIFS" in your building program. Insist that you mean *all* exterior surfaces, even if it's just trim.

If you inherit a building covered with EIFS:

- Have engineers check frequently for water intrusion.
- Be prepared to patch and repaint.
- Be prepared to have to replace the entire exterior surface of the building.

6. Colored Handrails and Door Handles

Metal handrails and door handles are available in a variety of attractive colors, ranging from silver to gold to bronze to other shades.

Unfortunately, anything not stainless steel-colored appears to cause trouble.

Actual brass (or brass-plated) railings are almost always covered with some kind of protective lacquer.

- If your handrails are bare brass, your custodial staff will need to polish them almost daily. (That's what the fancy hotels in Manhattan do.)
- If your handrails are lacquered brass, the lacquer quickly starts to wear off. In spots. The places with lacquer remaining are bright brass, but the places with missing lacquer darken. The result is an unpleasantly piebald effect.

Metal handles on doors often come factory finished in bronze or other colors. Unfortunately, the colors start wearing off in a year or two, leaving bits of the silvery base metal showing through.

As far as we know, the only solution to both of these problems is to replace the railings and handles with stainless steel.

7. Latex Paint on Drywall

Drywall is used almost universally in the United States. It's inexpensive to purchase and install. (If you've got the cash, real plaster is still available, but few new buildings have it.)

Latex paint is strongly hailed for its environmental qualities because it emits no VOCs (volatile organic compounds) while it cures. Latex paint is easier to apply than oil-based paint because it's less runny, and brushes and rollers can be cleaned up with water.

Unfortunately, the combination of latex paint and drywall has the structural integrity of piecrust. A good bump dents drywall, and any slight contact with latex paint can leave a mark. (Schools and dormitories have concrete-block interior walls for good reason.)

What can you do about this when you're planning your library?

- Discuss options for heavy-duty drywall and extra-tough paints with your architect and interior designer.
- Heavy-duty drywall is tougher than standard (class X) drywall, but the products look pretty much alike, and contractors who have temporarily run out of the heavy-duty product may be tempted to use everyday drywall in the hopes that no one will notice. If you have specified heavy-duty drywall, check the wrappings on all of the incoming blocks of drywall to make sure you're getting what you paid for.
- Install chair rails at the correct height to keep the specific chairs in your library from damaging the walls. This is especially useful if you have a lot of chairs of the same height or chairs with sled bases.
- Never use rocking chairs. Rocking chairs are part of a Norman Rockwell America. They evoke visions of grandparents by the fireplace and contented people on front porches. Unfortunately, rocking chairs migrate backwards as people rock, and when the sharp rear end of a rocker makes contact with drywall, it doesn't take long to cut completely through. Rockers can also squish small fingers. However, Fred and John disagree vehemently on rocking chairs. John has had great experiences with them and does not support this section. See chapter 16 on "User Seating."

What if you inherit cheap drywall and latex?

- Install chair rails if your chairs slide easily and damage the paint. Be sure to place the chair rails at the height where your chairs hit the walls.

- Be prepared for frequent repairs. Luckily, drywall is easy to patch with spackle. Sometimes you can feather in new paint over a repaired place, but often the change in color shows, and you'll need to paint up to a corner.
- If you can't throw out your rocking chairs, place them away from walls.

Q. Buildings That Can't Be Expanded

Every time a new library is designed, self-assured people announce that it will never need to be expanded.

Often this contention is used to support inflexible designs or the construction of libraries on undersized sites.

These people could be right, of course, but history is not on their side. Somewhere there are no doubt libraries that are just too large, but in most cases libraries are either brand-new, overcrowded, or both.

In practical terms, libraries should always have expansion plans up their sleeves.

- Sometimes this involves having a master plan, one that shows specifically how the library will be expanded in the future. As the chapter on design indicates, the problem with master plans tends to be vagueness. Too many involve dotted lines outlining a space that cannot actually be incorporated into the library. It's always fair to ask that your master plan include a Phase II schematic design that shows in serious detail what the building will look like when it's expanded, including furniture placement.
- Planning for expansion always includes controlling enough property. University libraries need to fight fiercely when other campus units cast envious eyes on the libraries' expansion land. Public libraries need to own enough land to make sure that expansion is possible.
- Cutting the size of a library to fit a limited site automatically ensures future problems.

Libraries also need to be sure that the architecture of their buildings is compatible with expansion. Among some things to remember:

- Increasing the size of a building can easily place it in another construction code category. For example, wooden components that are legal in the first phase of your building may no longer be legal if the building is expanded. A building may not require a sprinkler system when it is built, but expanding it may require retrofitting sprinklers.

- Flat walls are easier to expand than curved walls.
- Buildings are far easier to expand outward than upward.
- Expanding upward (even if it's possible) usually means hiring more staff to do the same work in order to avoid unstaffed floors.
- Walls intended to be knocked out for expansion should be adjacent to large open areas, not lined with staff offices.
- Be sure that Phase I construction does not include the location of utility lines where Phase II will be located. (This sounds like a silly warning, but we've seen it happen.)

R. Screen Porches

One romantic idea that tends to lead to trouble is screen porches. Many designers suggest them, and clients who have no experience with them are often enchanted by the concept. There's a kind of honest American, eternal-social-verities flavor about a screen porch. The name conjures up images of blissful summer evenings in Iowa, choruses of katydids, courting couples on swings, and people strolling down tree-lined sidewalks, waving to friends taking the air on the porches of houses they pass.

But screen porches in libraries lead to many problems:

- Screen porches are usable only at limited times of the year. Most of the time it's too hot, too cold, too wet, too windy, too dusty, too noisy, too smelly, or too something-or-other.
- Screen porches are particularly unpleasant during heavy rains when wind drives the rain through the screens and onto the people seated there.
- Porches have the potential for adding too much moisture to the air inside the building, as well as for wasting energy. If the porch door stands open for access and for staff supervision, all the wet air comes into the library, along with unwanted heat in the summer and cold in the winter.
- Porches are hard to supervise. If there's only a single door onto the porch, staff have to step into the porch to keep an eye on things.
- Screen materials are fragile and easily damaged. If a user decides to pitch a book out a window to bypass a theft-control system, a screen porch may offer an excellent opportunity.
- Porches are hard to keep clean. Dust and dirt blow in through the screening, turning to mud if it rains.
- Like the original screen porches, screen porches in libraries have been made obsolete by modern air conditioning.

How do you protect yourself from screen porches?

- Say "no porches" in your program.
- When your designers or city fathers propose porches, tell them stories of dysfunctional porches in other libraries. If you don't know of any, ask your consultant, or call us.

What do you do if you inherit a screen porch (or are forced to have one)?

- Do what many other libraries have done and enclose it for year-round use, if necessary opening up the wall between the porch and the inside room, to allow staff oversight. The only trick is making sure that the HVAC system works on the porch.

S. Monitor Windows

A monitor is a raised section of a roof with windows on all four sides (or occasionally fewer).

Unlike a clearstory window, which can be oriented to prevent direct sunlight from streaming in and interfering with vision, monitors usually have windows facing in directions that cause problems—east, south, and particularly west.

If the angles of the roof overhangs in monitors are carefully calculated, it's possible to avoid direct sunlight, but most of the ones we see cause trouble.

The result is staff and users blinded by direct sunlight and computers made impossible to use.

Because of their location, typically high above an open floor, it's almost impossible to add a movable shade to a monitor window.

Ill-considered monitors—and similar windows set into roofs—can be found everywhere.

The problem with monitors, as with so many other architectural problems, is that they are usually not recognized as problems until the building is complete, everyone has moved in, and it's pretty much Too Late.

If people propose a monitor, here are a couple of suggestions:

- Say "no."
- Make sure that the overhangs on the monitor extend far enough to prevent direct sunlight from falling on the windows of the monitor. This means essentially no overhangs on the north, but carefully calculated ones for windows facing in other directions.

If you have a cross-section drawing of your proposed library, you can check your own angles with a ruler.

In case you inherit a troublesome monitor:

- Install exterior louvers to prevent direct sun from falling on the glass.
- Cover the glass with a dark gray film, sufficiently dark to let people stare at direct sun without blinding themselves.
- Cover the glass with something opaque.

T. Use of Esoteric Glass

Glass is vital to good library design.

- Windowless rooms are depressing. Library users like to sit near windows when they read, in order to watch the world go by. When Fred talks with library staff members about their dissatisfactions with their current buildings, lack of natural light is one of the first things he hears. (Skylights cause problems of their own and are not a response to lack of windows.)
- Internal glass is important. Windows between offices can bring borrowed light to what would otherwise be depressingly windowless spaces. Glass walls on study rooms and similar spaces allow staff supervision of what could otherwise be troubled areas.

But it's all too easy to overdo glass exteriors.

- Unshaded exterior glass that does not face straight north leads to serious problems with glare.
- Glass that faces any direction except north can lead to unwanted solar heat gain. The only way to prevent this is to shield the glass from sunlight, since even blinds don't solve the problem. When sun falls on blinds it warms the blinds, and much of the heat is trapped indoors.
- Glass is hard to insulate as effectively as solid walls.

- Glass reflects sound. You can always cover solid walls with sound-absorbing materials, but glass is there for good.
- Exterior glass fails for many reasons. Seals can leak, and multi-pane windows can fill with moisture. Hailstorms or vandalism can break windows. A few buildings have had problems with windows that fall out. Some esoteric glass units with metal foil grids between the panes have simply disintegrated.
- Because of failures, it's essential that you have a practical way to replace exterior glass units that fail.
- The worst problems occur with esoteric glass that is manufactured overseas and cannot be replaced easily. A single unit of special glass may have to be specially manufactured and shipped and can cost a very surprising amount of money.
- Glass has to be cleaned. Frequently.

What can you do to protect yourself?

- For any major installation, insist on being shown other buildings that use exactly the same type of glass in a similar installation. Innovation is by and large for institutions wealthier than most libraries. When it comes to exterior glass, you cannot afford to be the first kid on the block to try out a new system.
- Insist on glass that can be duplicated domestically. Having to go back to Europe for specialty glass may take months and cost an impressive amount of money.
- Watch out for proposals that buildings be glass boxes. Consider the implications for energy use and maintenance and glare.
- Beware of assertions that "modern glass" can cure all of the problems associated with excess use of glass. Always insist on seeing a comparable installation using the same type of glass.
- Be particularly wary of proposed glass walls that are not straight. In addition to causing many problems associated with non-rectangular spaces, curved walls may require a variety of custom glass units.
- Require that your architects provide a projection of maintenance costs associated with the proposed glass exterior. What will it cost to clean it? What will replacement wall units cost?
- If your glass will need lots of fritting (frosting) to reduce glare, you have too much glass.

What can you do if you're stuck with a problem-laden building with too much exterior glass, or too much unusual glass, or glass that's busy fogging up?

- Check the warranties on your glass units. They may be longer than the typical one-year warranties on new buildings.

- When esoteric units fail for reasons of bad design, don't simply duplicate them. Find a less complex solution.
- Don't let your architects off the hook. Even if it's been a decade, if the building is failing, demand that your architects solve the problem. (You may be stuck with paying for the replacement glass, but we think you should expect your architects to come up with a workable solution at their expense.)
- It may be possible to reduce the total glass area by redesigning the building, but a building designed to be a glass box may look odd when glass units are replaced by opaque panels. (This was commonly done with school buildings, where to save energy, large, traditional windows were replaced with opaque inserts with small windows. The result was gloomy interiors and spectacularly ugly exteriors.)

U. Dysfunctional Service Desks

A surprising number of libraries have service desks that cause problems.

Service desks are covered in another chapter, but some of the most common dysfunctional features are listed here.

- Fragile surfaces on lending desks. Both wood and standard high-pressure laminate are insufficiently sturdy for the tops of lending desks. Real wood is fragile and will need regular refinishing to avoid looking battered. Printed wood grain or other colors on high-pressure laminate will begin to wear off in a year or two from the friction of books being pushed back and forth.
- Some libraries protect wooden desktops with transparent plastic or glass. Unfortunately, plastic sheets quickly become scratched from the friction of sliding books, while glass-topped desks have serious problems with breakage and reflected glare.
- Badly positioned book return slots. Many lending desks have book return slots located where people stand to have books checked out. Setting up a library that places users on constant collision courses is a really bad idea. Some desks have book return slots at the far end of the desk from where users enter the library. Slots need to be the first thing that users encounter when they reach the desk, not the last thing.
- Low book return slots. Book return slots need to be in counters about forty inches high in order to leave space for receiving bins. Unfortunately, a number of libraries have book return slots in low desk sections, and the result is endless problems with returned books.
- Difficult exit from behind the desk. Staff members need to be able to step out from behind desks, and this means exits at both ends. No one wants desks where staff can be trapped behind them.

- Lending desks too far from security gates. Anything more than about fifteen feet is too far. Security gates need to be in the direct line of sight of library staff. Staff members need to be able to hear alarm signals and (if necessary) get to the gate quickly. (Obviously, if your library has separately staffed guard stations by its security gates, the location of the lending desk is not a security issue. But few libraries can afford that.)
- Desktops that are either white or very dark. Dark desktops (like dark tops on reading tables) cause eyestrain due to contrasts between paper and the desktop. White desktops reflect too much light and create unpleasant glare.
- Lending desks that make it completely unclear which areas are for staff only. If your users wander behind the desk, you will have major security problems with held books, cash drawers, and so on.
- Lending desks with raised barricades between the library staff and users. This sounds like a great way to keep desks looking tidy, but barricades make it hard for staff and users to see each other. If there is no break in the barricade, staff members will have to hand books out at arm's length rather than simply pushing them across the countertop, and one can imagine the eventual problems with repetitive stress. Providing completely flat desktops with small translucent shields to hide the backs of the computers used for lending appears to be a very successful approach.
- Desks that cannot be expanded if you run out of space. Always ask what you will do if the proposed desk proves to be too small. Depending on your procedures, you can need a lot of space behind desks.
- Desks that cannot be shrunk if they turn out to be too big.
- Funny-shaped lending desks. Many historic libraries, for example, had semicircular desks. Desks shaped like half-doughnuts take up a lot of floor space but have virtually no space inside for staff to work. Too many modern libraries have the same problem. To leave adequate space for both users and staff, lending desks work best if they are relatively straight.
- Reference desks that can't be relocated because of matching soffits or other permanent architectural details. While lending desks are fairly permanent due to their location facing entrances, reference desks may need to be relocated as space uses change or more staff space is needed behind desks.
- Lending desks that leave staff no opportunity to do alternate work between customers. Efficient staffing of lending desks requires that staff check books in or do other work during inevitable slow moments. (This is one of several reasons why lending desks set up like supermarket checkout counters are a failure.)

How do you avoid problems?

- Never simply turn the design of service desks over to your architects or to anyone else who doesn't work in libraries. Few non-librarians really

understand work flow in libraries. Examine proposed designs in light of your professional experience or ask your consulting librarians.
- When desks are being planned, it's an important time for staff to list features needed (and to be sure later that the features are actually included).
- Make sure that surfaces and structural materials are sufficiently tough. Desks made of chipboard will probably chip. Lending desktops are best made of plastic products like Corian.
- Never allow anyone to install soffits over your service desks.
- Prefer modular desks that can be expanded or shrunk as the library's needs change.
- If your building consultants have extensive real-library experience (and we think all library consultants should), have them help with the desk design.
- Visit other libraries and size up how their desks work.
- Make clear to the architects that while the front surface of the desk may be theirs to design, the top and guts of the desk are yours.

> A service desk is first and foremost a service desk, not a monument.

V. Reading Terraces

One idea that is constantly brought up by designers is reading terraces—elegant outdoor spaces where library users can sit and read when the weather is nice.

Although reading terraces might be pleasant and even popular places, the problem is that designers always want them to be directly accessible from inside buildings. Once this happens, if access to the terrace is from within an area protected by security gates, users can carry books out to the terraces, hop over any fences or walls, and simply walk off with the books. If the barricades are higher, users can toss the books over the barricades, leave the library (passing through the security gates empty-handed), and retrieve the books from the bushes outside. It's similar to the problems caused by windows that users can open.

On several occasions we've pointed this out to architects, only to have the plans altered to say, "*Secure* reading terrace." And when we ask how this security is to be achieved, we're basically told that it's none of our business.

The only ways we can think of to construct secure reading terraces are:

1. Enclose the entire terrace—walls and roof—in metal mesh with openings small enough so that books cannot be pushed through the mesh. We're convinced that the general effect of reading in an area entirely enclosed by metal mesh will be a little like occupying the buzzard enclosure at a zoo, but some people like evocative designs.
2. Put security gates at the door out to the terrace, with a staff member there to supervise the gates. What the staff member will do between users is an interesting question, but security gates have to be staffed.
3. The only good answer is to provide a reading terrace but to have it accessible only from outside the library or from an area inside the library but outside the security gates. Users who want to read on the terrace will need to check their materials out, leave the library, and walk around the building to the terrace. Or pass through the security gates and only then enter the reading terrace.

All of this discussion should be unnecessary, but reading terraces occur to designers with dismal (and depressing) regularity. And once they think of them, designers fight fiercely for them, denying all of the security concerns that librarians raise. In several library projects Fred has seen, designers simply refused to remove the reading terraces. (We're not sure how to fight this, but we think telling designers that reading terraces are embarrassing clichés might shame them into dropping the idea when issues of failed security don't concern them in the least.)

W. Problem Features Yet to Be Invented

Lots of bad ideas have a natural history. For some there's a pattern of invention, experience using them, and banning by life-safety codes. (Others are not banned, of course, and we fall back on the shared experiences of librarians.)

However, designers are impressively inventive, and we confidently expect something new (and bad) to turn up.

Here are some examples of amazingly rotten ideas, all of which have in common their creation by internationally famous architects.

- A public library was constructed with room partitions that all stopped short of the building's ceiling. This included restroom walls.
- A public library has book stacks based on the principle of the Guggenheim Museum, with baffling lateral access to the middle of the spiral to reach specific parts of the collection.

- Art museums intended to provide an unobtrusive background for the display of great art instead reinvent themselves as great art, attempting to draw visitors' attention away from the art to the building itself.
- One architect wanted to divide the book collection among dozens of tiny rooms, each with fewer than ten shelving units.

Although you can list the most common dysfunctional design concepts in your building program, there are always bad ideas that no one expects. The best advice we can give is to be ever alert. Stop bad politically motivated ideas as quickly as possible. Show any innovative concept to people who know library buildings before you accept it.

> In 1957 Jean Kerr wrote the bestselling book *Please Don't Eat the Daisies*. The title came from an episode where she was expecting lunch guests and announced a long series of "don'ts" to her children. When the visitors arrived, Jean found the children had eaten the daisies on the centerpiece. "I had told them not to eat the daisies on the dining room table."* Similarly, it's hard to tell your designers everything you don't want because there are always new (but bad) ideas.
>
> *Jean Kerr. *Please Don't Eat the Daisies*. Doubleday, 1957. Page 27.

III. IN DEFENSE OF DESIGNERS

It's always important to remember that dysfunctional designs come from many places. Blaming them all on architects is easy but seriously unfair.

- Bad locations for new buildings are usually proposed by owners—universities, cities, and others. Chapter 10 on "Site Selection" lists many locations that cause problems.
- Undersized sites also have a strong political element. People recognize a good place for a library and are undeterred by the fact that the available land is too small, or that a library placed there can never be expanded.
- Design decisions can be made without any input from anyone who knows anything about library buildings. Having the city council or the university's board of trustees pick the design helps increase the possibility that the building will have functional problems. (Your library staff and the consulting librarians who prepared your building program may be the only people on the project with extensive firsthand knowledge of how libraries occupy spaces. Always have them review your plans.)

- Decisions to remodel existing but unsuitable non-library buildings are sometimes made without wide input. Remodeling is almost always far more expensive than most people outside the building professions expect, and many non-library structures lack the basics that libraries require: strong floors, wide-open spaces, adequate ceiling height, windows on all sides, and the ability to provide electrical outlets everywhere. This situation is especially a problem for public libraries, because many communities have a stock of buildings that are standing empty for very good reasons, and whose owners are desperate to sell.

So while librarians tend to rail against what they see as foolishly—if not willfully—dysfunctional design choices, we need to sympathize with designers.

- First, some really bad ideas are thrust upon designers.
- Second, given the cost of labor in contemporary construction, ornamentation of any kind is almost prohibitively expensive. The kind of architectural detail that was possible a century ago is no longer affordable. An architect seeking some way to make a new building not look like a bunker or a pole barn has few options.

The fact that some of the options just don't work, therefore, is not always an indictment of designers but rather a result of attempting to work within the limiting circumstances of modern construction.

But you still need to cut this kind of thing off at the pass.

- If outside forces propose dysfunctional ideas, expect your architects and consultants to explain why these ideas won't work. (You shouldn't get caught between a rock and a hard place. When local folks propose bad ideas, have your hired guns tell them why they're wrong.)
- Include a solid list of forbidden design options in your building program and (if necessary) point it out firmly to your architects during the selection interview or at the first planning meeting. Then make a very angry noise the first time you see any of the items in the list.
- When you are calling architect references, ask the firms' previous clients whether they had to battle vigorously against unwanted design concepts.
- As part of the review process in selecting an architect, have your head of maintenance call the heads of maintenance at other libraries.
- Pick your battles. Some bad ideas are pernicious, but others are just wastes of money. If the city manager or the university's board of trustees wants to build a new library but plans to meddle in the design, decide what dysfunctional features you can live with and which ones are totally unacceptable. A dangerous exterior balcony can always be kept locked, but 200 light fixtures you can't reach will drive you seriously crazy.

IV. THE GOOD NEWS

The good news is that none of the unpleasant, troublesome, or dysfunctional design concepts discussed in this chapter are essential in any way whatsoever. You can have an architecturally exciting and elegant building without any of them. And a great many libraries do.

So be of good cheer. But stand your ground. And get help when things start running amok.

V. SNAPPY RULES ON DYSFUNCTIONAL DESIGN

1. We've tried to make this chapter cheery, but it turned into a litany of complaints. We apologize and hope that you can maintain a lighthearted attitude as you read it, especially if your library has been spared the problems listed here.
2. If users have to shield their eyes from glare anywhere in a library, something is wrong.
3. Try to prevent your staircases from becoming major design elements.
4. If you stand at the top of a staircase, looking down, and start fantasizing about tumbling down head over heels, this is Not a Good Thing.
5. Water features may be exciting and desirable, but only in someone else's library. If you're stuck with one, convert it to a planter.
6. "How will we change the light bulbs?" is a legitimate question. "Use a lift" is not a sufficient answer.
7. If a railing can be climbed like a ladder, someone will climb it. And fall off.
8. Good libraries shouldn't terrify people who have a mild fear of heights.
9. When designers suggest a feature that gives you qualms, always ask where you can see one already installed in another building. Being the first kid on the block architecturally can lead to joy, but it can also lead to eternal misery.
10. No matter what people say about electronic books, libraries always run out of space sooner or later. Before you construct a new building, know how it will be expanded.
11. If your library's spectacular atrium tempts people to leap into the void, sooner or later someone will. "Splat" is not a reassuring sound to hear on a busy afternoon.
12. "Secure reading terrace" is an oxymoron.
13. Perimeter soffits are an overworked and distressingly dysfunctional design cliché, whether or not they have recessed downlights. Never allow anyone to

put perimeter soffits in your library. If you need perimeter ornamentation, crown moldings are vastly better.

14. Perforated vinyl white roller blinds are an amazing cure for blinding sunlight. And you can still see images of the outside world.
15. Unless it faces directly north, any exterior pane of glass needs a blind. If it's just a tiny pane of glass, it needs just a tiny blind.
16. Before you agree to an unusual kind of glass, ask to see an installation and talk with the owner.
17. Cylindrical spaces are noisy.
18. If your architects want to install a skylight in your new library, ask to see the skylights over their drafting tables.
19. No matter how your designers complain about lists of "don't do its" like this one, none of the problem areas listed in this chapter is essential to a well-designed library.
20. Skylights are too bright by day and too dark by night, and they are noisy. But they make up for all that by leaking.
21. Atriums are fun, but only at first glance.
22. If your library has a dramatic floating staircase, you'll need a clearly marked elevator close by.
23. Railings that can be climbed like ladders should be banned by building codes. Even if your codes don't forbid them, you still don't want them.
24. Staircases with open risers appear to be designed on the highly dubious assumption that people climbing stairs enjoy looking down between their feet to the floor below.
25. Screen porches sound romantic, but they aren't. Always say "No."
26. Book stacks don't fit into non-rectangular spaces.
27. Recessed downlights are easy to forbid up front, but they come sneaking and slithering into your plans when your back is turned.
28. The right number of entrances into a library is anything up to one.
29. Don't put in a little window where you need an interior glass wall.
30. Colored metal door grabs look good for a few months. Grabs with the color wearing off are not cute.
31. No matter what people say, almost all libraries sooner or later run out of space.
32. Good sight lines are vital, whether they're cute or not.
33. Glass surfaces are a lot noisier than drywall surfaces, and you can't install sound-absorbing panels over them.
34. Nasty glare is not a characteristic of good lighting.
35. Rooms with dark ceilings are hard to light. Historic dark ceilings probably need to be preserved, but we don't need to create new ones.

7

Converting Non-Library Spaces to Public Libraries

I. INTRODUCTION

This chapter deals with the conversion of non-library buildings to public libraries. It also applies conversions to other kinds of libraries, but proposed conversions to public libraries appear to be by far the most common.

When a community needs a new public library building, people frequently suggest the conversion of existing (usually vacant) structures to a new library. Occasionally these are structures that can be converted to good public libraries, but much more frequently they would make terrible libraries. The situations are often complicated by extreme political pressures, and libraries need to be prepared to explain to their communities why or why not conversions are good ideas.

As with all such situations, if your library has to deliver unwelcome news, always let your hired experts do it, especially if they can go home to other towns at the end of the meeting.

In all conversion situations, one of the major problems involves the building shaping the library rather than the library shaping the building. If too many of the basic functional needs of libraries are compromised by limitations imposed by existing spaces, the result is at best dysfunction and at worst an amazing waste of money.

When possible conversions loom on the horizon, libraries need to be prepared. Among the most important things libraries can do is have building programs ready and waiting. By the time a conversion is proposed (or occasionally simply announced), it may be too late to begin planning. It's also important for libraries to have an architect selected ahead of time, particularly if you are subject to laws (such as QBS—qualifications-based selection—laws) that prescribe a time-consuming process.

Converting non-library spaces to libraries has a lot in common with remodeling and expanding existing libraries, but it's a far more perilous undertaking. Many of the proposed spaces may lack many of the basic needs of libraries, such as ceilings high enough for reflected uplighting, sufficient power supplies, workable configurations of spaces, desirable natural light, good sight lines, sufficient floor strength, flexibility of design, and the many other special needs that set libraries apart from most other buildings. Unfortunately, citizens, planners, and owners of unoccupied buildings are frequently smugly confident while lacking even the foggiest ideas of how libraries operate.

As we keep saying to the point of being seriously boring, when you realize that you need larger space and need to do something about it, always start by preemptively preparing a building program. Once you have a program in print, it can be used as a yardstick for evaluating possible conversions. If you don't have a program in print, inventive people will start pointing out what interesting features could be provided in certain existing structures. By and large, these will be interesting features you don't need.

Unless you have a lot of experience with library building construction, always hire a building consultant to write your program—an experienced professional librarian with a degree accredited by the American Library Association and not an architect. See chapter 8 on "Programming."

You will also want to take a look at chapter 13 on "Remodeling and Expanding Library Buildings."

II. PLANNING CONVERSIONS OF NON-LIBRARY SPACES

If you are considering converting a non-library space or building to a library, it's essential that you start with a completed building program. If you have a program, you can use it as a yardstick to determine whether the proposed conversion provides the spaces and technical features you actually need.

Conversion ideas can be sprung on libraries abruptly, and for this reason having a written program almost instantly available is important. Although programs can be written quickly, it's a lot better to be ready when the time comes.

Because there are many issues in library planning in addition to space needs, building programs need to be detailed, with information on required floor loading, accessibility, lighting, acoustics, furnishings, shelving, floor coverings, electrical supplies, sight lines, exit control, security, flexibility, and other areas.

Chapter 8 on "Programming" has a lot of general information on writing programs. If there appear to be no construction plans in the offing, it may be difficult to convince people of the importance of spending money on a library building consultant, and librarians may be forced to struggle through on their own, even if it's a bad idea.

Once conversion is suggested, however, libraries have a good reason to insist on spending the money to have help with program preparation. Experienced programmers should be able to work quickly when time is tight if library boards are able to meet frequently. It's important that programmers be experienced librarians rather than architects or other people with no personal experience fitting library operations into spaces.

Programs should always be written without regard to available spaces, so that the programs can be used as measuring sticks to test the feasibility of using a specific proposed space. There will inevitably be compromises, but starting with the ideal program helps everyone become aware of what these compromises are.

III. RATIONALES FOR CONVERSIONS

There are good and bad reasons for converting existing spaces to libraries rather than starting over.

A. Good Reasons for Conversions

There are a number of reasons why conversions can be a good idea.

- Location. Sometimes the best locations already have buildings, and some of these buildings may be politically impossible to remove.
- Existing parking. If a building has an existing parking lot in good repair, the library is spared the cost of constructing a new lot.

- Existing utility hookups. The cost of bringing water, natural gas, electric power, data, sanitary sewers, and storm sewers to a new site can be very high. If everything is already in place, conversions will be less expensive. (Of course, if you have to relocate all the utilities as part of the conversion, conversions can be painfully expensive.)
- Modern buildings available for conversion. A building constructed after about 1980 is likely to be accessible to users with disabilities and not suffer from asbestos, lead paint, or other problems that will be extremely expensive to overcome. (Even better is a building built after 1990.)
- Buildings that are in good shape and fairly easy to convert. The best examples are probably modern big box stores, particularly if their MEP systems are in good condition and generally suited to library use. ("MEP" stands for mechanical, electrical, and plumbing. "Mechanical" in turn is HVAC—heating, ventilating, and air conditioning.)
- Political necessity. In some cases, a city may announce that money will be available if and only if the library converts a specific building to a new library. If this version of Hobson's Choice is presented to a library, it's possible that things may work out well. Alternatively, the library may be faced with balancing undesirable options: stick with an obsolete current library building or convert a much-less-than-ideal building to a library.
- If a building is available at no cost, that makes conversion more attractive, but there are a lot of "free" buildings that should not be converted to libraries on a dare.

B. And (of Course) Bad Reasons for Conversions

- Although some buildings can easily be converted, many conversion jobs make no economic sense.
- One frequent rationale proposed for conversion jobs is saving money. Few people, however, have any concept of how much it costs to convert an old building to a library, but they eagerly (and sometimes aggressively) promote a bad idea. Things can get particularly nasty when the owner of a building (or real estate salespeople) see big profits to be made in palming off a white elephant on the public library and hence on the taxpayers. The nation abounds in buildings that are standing vacant for very good reasons. Library owners need to keep reminding people that almost all conversions will involve constructing new restrooms, replacing existing lighting, adding electrical outlets, upgrading or replacing HVAC systems, providing new plumbing in staff work areas and lunchrooms, removing unwanted partitions, adding windows, improving insulation, and so on. The structure proposed for conversion must have both expansion space and off-street parking space.

- Many towns have landmark structures that are standing vacant. Citizens are always scouting about for possible conversions. Some of these buildings are vacant for very good reasons, and converting them to libraries makes no rational sense.
- Some proposed conversions may come with unacceptable limitations. The donors of the building must have *no rights of any kind* whatsoever over the subsequent use of the property. The library needs full title to the building, including the site, allowing it to make any changes it wants and to sell off the building and site and move on at any time it wants. *Any proposed limitations must be total deal killers.*

IV. COMMON PROBLEMS IN CONVERSIONS

A. Poor Natural Light and Insufficient Windows

Modern public libraries need windows for light and for openness. Libraries typically place reading tables and chairs next to windows, where users can see the outside world while they work.

Unfortunately, many existing commercial buildings proposed for conversion to public libraries have almost no windows. This may meet retail sales needs, but libraries need windows on all sides. If the commercial building in question is part of a row of structures, adding more windows may be impossible. And skylights—one of the True Evils in Library Design—are not an answer.

B. Unwanted Partitions and Floors

Libraries tend to consist of large, open spaces, both for readers and for collection storage. Libraries of less than 30,000 or 40,000 square feet tend to work far better if they are on one floor, to simplify floor loading problems and to avoid the permanent costs of elevators and of staff to supervise additional levels.

Any structure that introduces unwanted but immovable partitions or unnecessary levels is one to avoid.

C. Bad Locations

Bad locations for public libraries abound.

Chapter 10 on "Site Selection" provides a great deal of information on what constitutes good and bad sites.

The quick, easy measure is to ask whether library users would want to go there in general, and whether the location is compatible with their daily travel patterns.

A bad location for a nice store is a bad location for a nice library.

D. Obsolete or Nonexistent Air Conditioning

A library without air conditioning is a miserable library.

Unfortunately, adding HVAC systems to ancient buildings can be extraordinarily expensive, especially when there are no air ducts and there is insufficient space to install them.

Window air conditioners are friendly warning signs of structures you want nothing to do with.

Even if a building has an HVAC system, it may be out of date or simply worn out. HVAC equipment is expensive, and its expected life is about twenty years.

E. Insufficient Floor Strength

Many proposed conversions simply ignore the problem of weak floors. With the exception of warehouses and factories, few existing buildings have the strength in upper floors to carry the weight of books.

Existing slab-on-grade construction will probably be strong enough for books, although a structural engineer will need to verify this.

But upper floors are in almost all cases insufficiently strong. Among those floors that are usually not strong enough are church floors, regardless of how massive the pews appear.

One solution to weak floors is to use lower shelving units and wider stack aisles, but this will require more floor space, and the floor space projections in your building program will have to be increased.

Some floors can perhaps be reinforced, but the supporting columns and column footings will need to be capable of handling the extra weight. In many cases, providing the extra strength may be more expensive than starting over.

F. Lack of Utilities

Older buildings may lack essential utilities. As part of evaluating the potential of an existing structure, check for the provision of natural gas, electric power, water, telephone, data, sanitary sewer, and storm sewer.

A building heated by propane rather than natural gas will be extraordinarily expensive to operate, and the inability to supply natural gas should be an automatic deal killer in a town that has natural gas available elsewhere.

On the other hand, many existing buildings will have all necessary utilities already connected, eliminating what can be the very high cost of extending utilities to a new building.

You'll need engineers to check the quality of utility provision and the condition of the connections. For example, if the building's water supply is provided by a lead pipe, you'll have to rip it out and replace it.

G. Lack of Expansion Space

An existing structure that completely occupies its site may be a very poor choice for conversion to a library, unless the building is substantially larger than the space specified in the library's building program.

When some large buildings are converted to libraries, not all the available space may be needed immediately. The available space stands empty or is used for storage until it is needed at a later time.

Unfortunately, there have been cases where the extra space was converted to a non-library purpose rather than kept in reserve, eliminating any possibility of long-term expansion.

H. Accessibility Problems

Many older buildings are inaccessible to users with disabilities, and the extra cost of providing the necessary restrooms, elevators, and entrances may be greater than the value of the converted building.

In general, attempting to convert a building constructed before the Americans with Disabilities Act and never modified to provide accessibility may make very little sense.

I. Parking Problems

When you are considering a building for conversion to a library, parking is a major consideration. Looking at a specific building, always ask:

- Where will users and staff park? People who are pushing for a specific conversion project may claim that parking is not an issue, but they are wrong. On a lovely spring day, a few users may decide to walk to the library. Kids may stop at the library on their way home from school. But most users drive most of the time. The failure to provide good parking may lead to the failure of the entire library.
- Will the library control parking, or will it be at the mercy of other owners or agencies? It's hard to know where, but at any specific time somewhere, someone has a brilliant community development plan that involves eliminating library parking.
- Will the front door of the library face the parking lot, or will the parking lot be behind the library? If the lot is behind the library, users will insist on two entrances, one facing the street and one behind the library facing the parking lot. And this violates one of the primary rules of library design. Unless the two entrances lead to a shared hallway, with a single door from the hallway to the library, staff are in a bad position to both greet users arriving at the library and to supervise entrances.

Convenient parking looms large in citizen evaluations of community services, and any situation that leads to inconvenient parking will alienate users.

Don't underestimate public library parking needs. As a first quick estimate, a public library parking lot needs to have the same square footage as the library. This means that a two-story library with a 25,000-square-foot footprint will need about a 50,000-square foot parking lot. If the library will house major public meeting spaces, or if there is no overflow parking on an adjacent street, its parking lot may need to be even larger.

Zoning may also affect parking requirements.

J. Bearing Walls

Bearing walls are walls that hold up a building, as opposed to curtain walls, which simply fill the spaces between support columns.

Older buildings with bearing walls rather than curtain walls may prove to be extremely difficult to convert because interior bearing walls cannot be removed to create larger spaces. If the proposed building has bearing walls, you need to be sure that the spaces you need already exist. Having to work with a number of small spaces when a library needs a single larger space is a mess.

If you are attempting to expand an old building, you may need to be careful about not digging too close to the existing footings. You'll need the input of an architect and a structural engineer.

K. Basements

Old basements are a lot less useful than many people imagine. Century-old retail structures may even have dirt-floored basements. Humidity in old basements may be so high that almost nothing can be stored there. The presence of a basement may indicate that the main floor is not strong enough to support the weight of books.

Occasionally, main floors with wooden joists can be strengthened by putting props under the joists, but it's a pretty makeshift approach if you're converting a building to a library.

Slab-on-grade construction is a lot more useful in libraries.

L. Cheap Construction

Some commercial buildings are built to minimum standards. The price may be attractive because the building is pretty much junk. Buildings sheathed in sheet steel, for example, may have a relatively short life before rust begins to eat away at the sheathing. Similarly, EIFS is a sheathing material with an uncertain reputation. There may be little or no insulation. HVAC systems may be primitive. Wiring may be minimal. Floor slabs may even be of substandard quality.

We've looked at a number of strip malls proposed for library use, and most of them had extraordinarily flimsy construction, with exterior walls made of 2 × 4s and no fire walls between units. Renting space for a library branch in a building like this may be okay, but you don't want to own it.

If it looks cheap to you, it probably is. But even if it looks great, you need the opinion of a structural engineer.

M. Code Compliance Problems

Building codes change constantly, and the older a building is the more likely it is to be seriously out of compliance.

As long as changes to a building are minimal, remodeling may take place without bringing a building up to code, but with significant changes it may suddenly become necessary to make radical upgrades. You may have to add a sprinkler system, provide all-new electrical service, introduce automatic fire doors, provide an elevator, add fireproof staircases, construct new and larger restrooms, and who knows what else.

If you want to provide an addition to a building, you may need to add fire doors between the old and new areas, leading to problems with awkwardly divided spaces.

This is a particularly good reason to have architects, engineers, and programmers size up a building *before* you decide it can be converted to a library.

N. Asbestos, Lead Paint, and Other Pollutants

Any structure built before the late 1970s may be awash in asbestos and lead paint. And the soil may have serious contaminants. Before you agree to any reuse of an older building, you need to have qualified experts check for these and estimate the cost of remediation. It's easy to simply say, "No buildings with asbestos."

> The easiest chapters to write are those with unequivocal messages, such as "There are no snakes in Ireland."

O. Converting Historic Structures

It's hard to convert non-library structures to libraries, but it's even harder if the structures have historic significance. Unless a building has spaces, windows, ceilings, floors, and accessibility that already match those in your program, you may find yourself in a situation where reworking the structure to serve as a library is nearly impossible and frighteningly expensive.

If you do commit to converting a historic structure, you may have to deal with a wide variety of additional pressures. Historic preservation committees and agencies will demand that you seek their approval. Self-appointed local groups may want to step in.

Many communities have vacant historic buildings in search of a purpose. Given the very specific structural and staffing needs of libraries, there may be another purpose for those buildings that works better.

Why might a library decide to convert a historic non-library structure to a library? First, there may be no other good place to build. Second, *large* amounts of money may be available *if and only if* the library agrees to repurpose a historic building. ("Large" is a key word here. If you don't tremble with ill-concealed anticipation when you hear the amount, it's probably not enough.)

And third, of course, historic buildings are often worth saving and may possibly become functional libraries as well.

P. Buildings "Designed for Adding an Extra Floor"

Owners of one-story commercial buildings frequently assure prospective buyers that their buildings were designed to allow an extra floor to be added. Your reaction should always be:

- Friendly disbelief. Many people constructing buildings originally considered providing the stronger footings and columns necessary to support a second floor, but they abandoned the idea when they learned how much extra it would cost. Thirty years later, they remember talking about a second floor but forget that the idea of a stronger structure was abandoned. If you're serious about the building and the second floor matters, you'll need a structural engineer to check things out. Remember that even surviving drawings may not be accurate.
- Suspicion that—even if the columns and footings for a second floor were installed—they may not have been designed to carry the weight of a library. A second floor perfectly fine for office use can be completely unacceptable for library use.
- Questioning whether an extra floor would be better than a larger main floor. A 30,000-square-foot main floor is vastly better than two 15,000-square-foot separate floors, for with a single floor you will avoid the high (and continuing) cost of an elevator, the cost of staircases, the fact that it's much more expensive to build an upper floor strong enough to hold books than it is to house books on a floor slab, and (probably worst of all) the high cost of supervising an extra floor.

All in all, the only good reason to build upward rather than outward is that (a) you are desperate for more space, (b) there's absolutely no way to expand the footprint of your building, or (c) no one will let you move.

Q. Insufficient Electrical Wiring and Outlets

Retrofitting electrical outlets to buildings can be difficult, and buildings converted to libraries may end up with far too few outlets. Modern libraries need electrical outlets everywhere, not just in places where power will be needed on opening day. The cost of providing sufficient power may substantially increase the cost of converting a non-library building to a library.

Adding outlets to slab-on-grade buildings requires saw-cutting floors, inserting outlet boxes and conduit, and filling in around the new conduit. Because of the cost, libraries may end up with power poles instead. Power poles connect to the ceiling grid and are screwed to the floor. Although they work, they are ugly, inflexible, and fragile.

R. Unworkable Lighting

Library lighting needs tend to be very specific, and most conversions require the complete replacement of lighting systems.

A possible exception is some big box stores with modern lighting that may be bright and even enough to meet library needs.

Since people have to look nearly straight upward in libraries to view top shelves, harsh downlighting is unworkable. One way to test the light in a building is to look straight upward at the ceiling. If it blinds you, you'll need different lighting.

S. Low Ceilings

The absolute minimum ceiling height for libraries is 10 feet, and 11 or 12 feet is better.

Light fixtures for reflected uplighting need to hang at least 2 feet below the ceiling. Allowing 8 feet for clearance, this means 10 feet.

Sprinkler heads usually need to be up to 3 feet above the tops of the book shelving. With 7-foot-high shelving, this also means 10 feet.

Low ceilings don't work.

T. The High Cost of Conversions

Probably the single greatest problem with conversions is unexpectedly high costs. Remodeling and modernizing an old building can easily cost as much as starting over, and if the result is less efficient to operate than a new building, the high costs can continue for the life of the structure.

It's extremely easy to underestimate the cost of remodeling and modernizing an existing building. If a building needs an all-new HVAC system, all-new wiring, all-new plumbing, a sprinkler system, abatement of asbestos and lead paint, addition of an elevator, removal of interior partitions, addition of windows, addition of code-compliant exit staircases, and other miscellaneous code compliance work, it can easily cost as much as or more than new construction—and cost far more to operate than a new building of similar size.

Architectural fees are also likely to be higher for conversions than for new construction.

If you have a choice between converting an existing two-story building and constructing a new one-story building of the same total square footage, the one-story building will be far less expensive to operate.

Local citizens are unlikely to believe the high cost of conversions. Libraries will need to rely on their programmers, architects, and engineers to provide a realistic idea of what kind of money will need to be spent.

However, some architects can be equally ignorant. Fred knows one remodeling and expansion project where the architect's estimate was one-third of the lowest bid.

V. TYPES OF BUILDINGS THAT MIGHT BE CONVERTED TO LIBRARIES

This section reviews some of the building types that are frequently suggested for conversion to libraries.

A. Schools

Abandoned school buildings are frequently proposed as locations for public libraries.

Empty school buildings abound. Unfortunately, most have been abandoned for very good reasons: they were abandoned because they have outlived their natural life or were badly designed to begin with. Local residents have probably been speculating for years on how these buildings can be recycled, but that doesn't mean they'll make workable libraries.

Most old schools will fail to meet a wide variety of building codes. Schools dating back to the 1970s or before may be awash in asbestos and lead paint. Most will have accessibility problems, perhaps requiring the addition of elevators. Most will be badly insulated. Despite the stability of schools, floors will probably not be strong enough to carry the weight of books.

In order to provide enough space, some school conversions have included the addition of balconies. Balconies cause far more problems than they solve, and you will not enjoy them.

Schools are often not in good public library locations. Schools are typically built in residential areas away from local businesses, but the best location for a public library is a good location for retail business.

Parking lots around old high schools may be reasonably adequate for library use, but grade schools and middle/junior high schools may have only enough parking spaces for the faculty.

If a town that needs a new public library has an old school building, people will inevitably propose that the school will be a great place for a new library. Unfortunately, with rare exceptions, they are spectacularly wrong.

About the only space in an old school building that can be converted to a workable library is the gymnasium. Classrooms are no good for most library purposes. Some gyms have been converted to attractive and functional libraries, but that presumes that the gym is large enough to meet the need for all those library functions that need to be in a single, open space. In a small public library, for example, the service desk, adult area, and children's area all need to be in a single room. If a balcony has to be added to a gymnasium to provide essential floor space, the library will be at a disadvantage forever. If the elevator is in a different part of the building, there will be a second (and probably unsupervised) library entrance leading directly to the balcony, violating the basic single-entrance rule.

An even larger question is, once the gym is converted to a library, what happens to the rest of the school building? The last thing a library needs is to be part of an otherwise abandoned building.

B. Banks

Some communities have successfully converted bank buildings to public libraries.

Some banks appear to be more strongly constructed than many other commercial buildings, and they may be capable of carrying the weight of books without extra reinforcement. But always assume they aren't strong enough and have an engineer check.

Modern banks will be at grade level. Older banks may have steps up to the front door, and you do not want them.

Most bank conversions are faced with what to do with old vaults. Vaults are strongly built and will probably be too expensive to remove. In the conversions we have seen, most vaults have been used for storage or office space. Obsolete vault doors may make interesting reminders of the building's history, but you'll at least have to disable the locking mechanisms and install some kind of bolted-on flanges on the floor that prevent the doors from swinging.

Most banks will have more small interior spaces than libraries need, and part of the evaluation of a possible bank conversion will involve checking to see how easily partitions can be removed.

Many banks have drive-through service windows. In small banks, these are frequently on back walls so that staff at a service counter can simply turn around to assist customers at the window. It might be possible to convert bank service windows to book pickup windows, but drive-up service windows in libraries are not always successful because library users sometimes treat them not only as places to pick up held books but also as short-order windows, where library users can request items that are not on hold but have to be searched and retrieved from throughout the library. Exterior pickup boxes may work better in this case, and you will probably be better off taking the windows out of service.

One of the appeals of converting banks is that they may have been maintained in better repair than many other structures.

C. Department Stores

Some communities have converted abandoned department stores to public libraries. With the coming of big box stores and shopping centers, department stores tend to become available for other uses.

Because department stores may have been focal points of traditional city centers, there may be warm memories among older citizens and strong political interest in conversions. If a community cannot find alternate uses for a major department store that is now standing vacant, sooner or later someone will think "library!"

Department store conversions may be aided by existing elevators, eliminating the high cost of retrofitting new elevators.

Department stores typically do not have floors strong enough to carry library loads. If a department store has a basement, perhaps only the basement is strong enough for book stacks. In order to reduce loads, it may be necessary to use shorter shelving units and space them more widely apart, significantly increasing the amount of space necessary to store a given number of books. Lack of floor strength may be one of the greatest challenges in converting department stores to libraries.

Older department stores may have the windows libraries need, but if windows were removed at some time in the past to provide wall space for merchandise display, the library may be faced with a choice between spending a great deal of money installing replacement windows or having to live in what feels like a basement.

In addition, most department stores have too many floors. Instead of a wide, single-level space, a store may have several floors. If the resulting library has more floors than the library needs, supervision may be extremely expensive.

D. Strip Malls

Strip malls have been proposed as public library locations.

There are some possible advantages. Strip malls may be in highly visible locations, and placing public libraries next door to retail stores is good for both.

But there are a number of potential problems.

Strip malls come and go. A dying strip mall is no place for a public library, and one sees dying strip malls everywhere.

Just as good commercial neighbors can be of great benefit to libraries (and libraries can greatly benefit the nearby businesses in strip malls), businesses can change quickly. Because libraries in strip malls are right next to the other businesses, if the clothing stores, paint stores, toy stores, and bookstores are quickly replaced by liquor stores, tobacco shops, video gambling parlors, and bars, the desirability of the libraries' locations can quickly change.

As speculative commercial structures, strip malls may be very cheaply constructed and quickly thrown up. If someone is proposing a planned strip mall as a location, you'll need your architects and engineers to check out the quality of proposed construction, just as you will want them to evaluate completed buildings.

Some strip malls do not have fire walls between stores. As a result, a fire that starts in one store can quickly spread to adjacent stores through the attics of the stores.

Because buildings in strip malls share common walls, there is no possibility of adding additional windows on the sides of the stores.

Expansion is probably impossible without acquiring an adjacent unit, and fire codes may make it impossible to join two units together.

As with old stores on courthouse squares, retail spaces in strip malls may be too deep and narrow for good library service.

In general, the only good public library use of strip malls may be as rented spaces for library branches or as temporary locations while main libraries are being rebuilt.

E. Big Box Stores

Of all the projects for converting non-library buildings to libraries, conversions of big box stores are among the most successful. In addition to being practical, at least one has won an ALA interior design award.

Modern big box stores have a number of advantages:

- Grade-level entries.
- Single floors, eliminating the need for elevators and staircases and reducing the number of staff required for supervision.
- Concrete slab-on-grade floors, making it easy to carry the weight of books. (But always have an engineer check to be sure the slab will handle the load.)
- High ceilings, making lighting far easier.
- Post and beam construction, meaning that there are few if any interior partitions that cannot easily be removed.

- Large parking lots, typically as close as possible to the public entrance. Modern designers know that parking lots need to be in front of buildings, not behind them, and you are most likely to find this arrangement in big box stores.
- Utilities connected. Most big box stores will have electric power, natural gas, water, sanitary sewer, storm sewer, and data connections already in place.
- Modern wiring.

There are also some potential problems:

- Virtually no windows. How easily windows can be retrofitted will depend on the type of construction. And the evil allure of skylights may always lurk around the corner.
- Potentially undesirable locations. Libraries need big box stores where chains went bankrupt, not where a store moved out because the location was far from ideal.
- Cheap construction. If a mall was designed with a twenty-year service life in mind, it won't be a happy choice for a library.

Big box stores were designed to meet the retail needs of modern populations, and these have a lot in common with the library needs of modern populations. Which makes the entire conversion project a lot easier.

Since big box stores are economically constructed, however, you will need engineers and architects to evaluate the condition of a building you are considering. It may just be worn out.

F. Historic Stores on Courthouse Squares

Although this section says "courthouse squares," it applies to all historic retail spaces that are deep and narrow and trapped between adjacent buildings.

Former stores on courthouse squares have sometimes been converted to public libraries. While locations adjacent to retail businesses are very functional, there are large numbers of challenges in conversions of this type.

- Former stores tend to be narrow and deep spaces. This is a bad configuration for public libraries. Users have to thread their way through successive areas of the library. If the adult department is in the front of the store, children must walk through the adult area to reach the children's area, with consequent implications for disturbing adult readers. If the children's area is in the front of the store, all adults must walk through the children's area—a possible security risk. Fitting in meeting rooms can be difficult, because a store may be so narrow that it is wide enough only for the meeting room and a hallway to bypass it. Service desks will probably be located halfway to the back of the store, between the children's and adult areas, making it difficult for staff to see the front entrance and greet arriving users. Public libraries work better if users enter the center of the wide side of the building.

- Former stores typically have small shop windows in front and perhaps alley windows at the rear, but no side windows due to adjacent buildings. If the former store is narrow and deep, this means a general absence of natural light. Skylights—one of the Great Evils in library architecture—are not a solution.
- The appeal of courthouse squares comes in part from unbroken lines of facades facing the squares on all sides. Maintaining these lines of storefronts is not compatible with library functional design.
- If an old store has partitions, they may be in unsuitable locations and difficult to remove for structural reasons. Although the library may need partitions for a meeting room, restrooms, and staff workroom, existing partitions are unlikely to be in the right place.
- Historic stores will probably have wood joist floors that are not strong enough to support the weight of books. However, if one-story stores have unused basements, existing wood joists can possibly be propped from below to strengthen them. (Metal bar joists, by contrast, are far more difficult to strengthen.)
- Old historic stores may be approaching the limit of their reasonable life. They may have antiquated MEP systems. Few buildings will have restrooms suitable for library use. Wiring may be ancient. Just replacing all of these components may cost half as much as starting over with a new building.
- An old store building may have a couple of parking spaces on the street in front and more off an alley at the rear of the structure. Users may want to park in the alley and enter the library through the back door, a major violation of the single-public entrance rule.
- If the library needs additional parking, it will have to go behind the library, making the double-entrance problem a lot worse.
- If the building has a second floor, this will introduce a wide variety of problems. Ideally, it can be just used for storage. Using a second floor for public services means an elevator and staircases (including new exit staircases) that meet fire codes, second-floor staff (an extraordinary and permanent expense if the staff would not be needed in a single-story library of the same total size), supporting an insufficiently strong floor when there is no space for props below, dealing with what may be very low second-story ceilings, and so on.
- Some old retail spaces are a step or two above sidewalk level, introducing access problems. Sidewalks have been regraded to provide entry ramps, but it's not a great solution. Among other things, it can lead to incredibly high curbs by the ramp.

- Often the main reason people want to convert an old retail space to a library is that business around the courthouse square is dying, and local residents hope that the presence of a library can revive it. Basically, this means using the library as a cat's-paw. The same features that make businesses want to relocate will also make the library wish it had never gone there.

Even if a courthouse square building of this type is available to the library at no charge, it will be very far from "free." Unfortunately, political pressure to accept gifts of old buildings can be strong, with persistent advocacy from people who have no real idea how libraries work.

If the presence of the library on the courthouse square is essential, the best solution is probably to obtain a row of commercial buildings (including a corner structure), demolish them all, and build a new library facing the courthouse. Even then there are likely to be parking problems. If a parking lot is constructed behind the library, there will be pressure from users to enter the library both through a door facing the courthouse and through a back door facing the parking lot. *This violates the one-entrance rule, and you won't like it.*

All in all, attempting to convert ancient retail spaces to public libraries is likely to be extremely expensive, and the resulting structures are highly unlikely to be satisfactory.

G. Churches

Some churches have been converted to libraries.

Generally, this involves converting the sanctuary of the church to the main area of the library. Churches usually have a number of smaller rooms, including Sunday school rooms and small meeting rooms. If the church has a fellowship hall, it may be large enough to use as a multifunction room, but the remaining rooms may be large enough only for offices and storage. Support spaces in churches may also be located in extremely awkward places, such as separate wings.

One advantage of converting sanctuaries to libraries is that the ceilings are frequently high enough for good lighting.

Another advantage can be good natural light. Many churches have big windows, and stained glass windows can easily be retained if they have sufficiently abstract designs.

The easiest sanctuaries to convert are modern ones built at grade level on concrete floors. Fred worked on one small-town library where the board came in at night and removed a front platform and baptismal tank, added better lighting, patched the front carpet, and then moved it, all for very little cost.

Some churches have sloped sanctuary floors, and these are impossible for conversion to libraries.

If the church is not a modern structure with concrete floors, always assume that sanctuary floors are not strong enough. (Some people insist that a floor that can carry the weight of heavy pews will surely be strong enough to carry the weight of books, but they are wrong. Or, more accurately, WRONG.)

If the sanctuary has religious symbols they should probably be removed. This is easy with most decorations, but it's a shame if there are strongly religious stained-glass windows.

As with all conversions, modern structures with concrete floor slabs, grade-level entrances, and curtain walls are the easiest to work with.

H. Houses

A number of small-town public libraries have been located in converted residences, including homes donated for the purpose, existing historic homes, and other houses.

Although some of these are charming, there are inevitable challenges.

- Making the floors of houses accessible to users with disabilities can be extremely expensive. If the main floor is more than a foot or two above grade, the result may be a virtually endless entry ramp. Even then, libraries may be limited to main floors for everything except storage. The other solution is an elevator, which is a very expensive device.
- Older houses may be badly insulated, with single-pane windows and uninsulated walls. Unless it's done with care, replacing the windows of a historic house with unmatching modern windows may damage the historic appearance of the building.
- Floors may not be strong enough to hold books. It may be possible to strengthen wooden floor beams with props if there's an unused basement below where the props can be placed, but that doesn't work with upper floors.
- Most houses consist of many small rooms, which may lead to supervision problems and to collections awkwardly divided between rooms. Because the

partitions between rooms may be bearing walls, opening up larger spaces may be extremely difficult. And it may also spoil the historic architecture of the home.

Houses of the mansion variety may have considerable charm, but they may also be serious white elephants.

I. Automobile Salesrooms

Some communities have converted former auto sales facilities into public libraries.

Auto salesrooms have the advantage of strong floors (but double-check, because books are heavier than cars). They frequently have open floor plans and single levels.

But you will still have to deal with all of the other conversion issues—lighting, wiring, HVAC, restrooms, and the rest. And it's hard to find a use for an old grease rack in a modern library.

J. Abandoned Government Buildings

Some communities have converted former government structures to public libraries.

Sometimes this can be very successful. A town in Illinois, for example, converted a former air force base bowling alley to a public library, but the bowling alley was no ordinary bowling alley. It was a huge and sturdy structure with high ceilings and no bearing columns to get in the way.

Lots of former government buildings are cut up into many offices, and these are bad choices for conversion to libraries. An old city hall, for example, may have a council chamber surrounded by a rabbit warren of offices. A fire station may have a large and high-ceilinged first-floor room, with a second floor filled with small rooms and with no elevator access.

Former city garages may offer lots of wide-open spaces and good parking, but public works garages may not be in suitable locations for public libraries.

Our experience is that old city buildings were often abandoned for good reason. New buildings were constructed because the old ones were seriously inadequate. The old buildings may be awash in asbestos and lead paint. Parking may be inadequate for public library service.

Even worse, cities may run old buildings into the ground once new buildings are underway. If maintenance stops for the last year, there may not be much left, certainly not enough to make the conversion to a public library economically sensible.

VI. SUMMARY

Converting non-library buildings to public libraries is done all the time.

Sometimes everything works out beautifully, but on other occasions the library ends up spending far more on a reworked but dysfunctional building than it would spend on a brand-new building, and in addition is saddled with higher operating costs for the life of the building.

How do you keep out of trouble?

First, always have a building program in hand, one that lists in detail what spaces you need when the project is done. As soon as people start talking about conversion and there's no program, "What we could do with this space" takes over from "What spaces do we need."

Next, have a good idea of what kinds of buildings lend themselves to conversion. Many of the basic issues are covered in this chapter. Remember that the ADA came along in 1990 and that buildings built before the late 1970s may be full of asbestos and lead paint. Buildings constructed before 1990 are a gamble, and you are unlikely to be offered buildings newer than that.

Remember that HVAC machinery has an expected life of about twenty years. And it's expensive to replace.

Be sure that there is space for the expansion of services and sufficient off-street parking. Many proposed conversions lack both.

Be sure you will have total ownership of the property. One thing that has led to major problems with conversions is limited title to the property. If, for example, you are offered a building with the understanding that if it ever ceases to be a library, the building will revert to its previous owners, walk away as quickly as possible.

When people pressure you to accept or purchase an existing building, always get help before saying "yes." Because the pressure you face will frequently be political, outside help is particularly important. The help you will need includes:

- A written building program listing all the spaces you need when you are finished. The program should not be written with any conversion job in mind. Once it is finished, the program can be compared with the proposed building to be sure that the spaces you need can be provided there. Sometimes a building will be so unsuitable for reuse that your consultant's opinion may be enough to stop things. Remember that programs should always be written by experienced librarians.
- An architect to help you evaluate the building to be sure that it is in good condition and can be converted to a functional, modern library at a reasonable cost. Among other things, your architect will review code implications to be sure that modernizing the building will not embroil the library in a maze of code compliance issues. Your architect can also check for EPA concerns, such as asbestos, possible buried fuel tanks, and so on. In many cases, a quick examination by your architect will lead to the rejection of the proposed conversion project.
- Your architects may bring in engineers to evaluate the structure of the building, the condition of MEP services, any hidden threats (such as asbestos), the ease of opening up internal spaces, any difficulties involving accessibility, and so on.
- If the project passes initial checking, your programmers, architects, and engineers will need to review the ability of the building to meet all specified functional needs.
- At this point, your architects will also need to develop a cost estimate. This is a dangerous area, particularly when it comes to remodeling. There may be pressure on your architect to lowball costs. In all cases of this type, your architects and other experts will need to report on projected remodeling costs, functional compromises that would result from remodeling, and the likely cost of building a similar structure from scratch.

Rejecting a proposed conversion job may be unpopular with your community. This is one area where your hired outside experts will prove their worth. They can deliver the bad news and then go home to distant communities where their annoyed neighbors will not snarl at them at the supermarket.

If all of this chapter sounds negative, it's because there are so many pitfalls in conversion projects.

Luckily, we have some examples of really excellent libraries constructed by converting other buildings, so it's a matter of caution rather than outright rejection. In general, fairly new buildings with wide-open spaces, high ceilings, good windows, sidewalk-level entrances, concrete slab floors, high-quality construction, up to date MEP systems, and sufficient parking seem to offer the best possibilities.

VII. SNAPPY RULES FOR CONVERTING NON-LIBRARY SPACES TO PUBLIC LIBRARIES

1. Owners who can't unload vacant buildings often have special epiphanies about what wonderful libraries they'll make.
2. Big, open, one-story spaces with high ceilings tend to make workable libraries. Complex, multistory spaces tend to make seriously bad libraries.
3. *Never* buy an existing building or agree to a conversion job without the help of both a consulting librarian (a programmer) and architects who have had serious experience with functional library design.
4. Any existing floor that is not slab-on-grade construction is unlikely to hold the weight of books.
5. The cost of converting an existing building can be higher than most people want to believe. The right price to pay for a building to be converted to a library is often free—and even that may be a bad deal.
6. Unfortunately, there's often no such thing as a "free" building, and lots of "free" buildings can end up costing more than starting over from scratch.
7. When a building is standing vacant, there is likely to be a very good reason. Or many very good reasons.
8. Be very afraid of proposed conversions that would involve your library sharing space with another agency. Anyone with a key to your library must report to the library director.
9. The cost of an unnecessary second floor can be extraordinary—and an extraordinary waste.
10. As shopping patterns have changed, American cities are full of abandoned downtown department stores. Converting them to libraries is not a job for institutions with limited construction funds or limited operating budgets.
11. Converting retail buildings to libraries will usually require adding a lot of windows. Find out the cost implications before agreeing to anything.
12. Political pressures to convert unsuitable structures to public libraries can be intense and sometimes amazingly nasty. Get professional help before you sign, and let your professional helpers take the blame.
13. With the exception of rented space for branches, public libraries need to own their buildings, including full titles to the sites. Always avoid situations where the library does not have permanent and clear title to the property.

A number of libraries are in situations where the property will revert to someone else if the library ever moves out. This leads to wretched messes, and you don't want to have anything to do with it.

14. Never trust anyone's offhand estimate of conversion costs. People can be wrong by a factor or five or ten and feel no guilt afterward.
15. Always be wary of proposed conversions, and sometimes be very afraid.
16. Converting a building that has no expansion space and no off-street parking space involves making two impressively major errors at the same time.
17. Age matters. Buildings constructed before 1980 are likely to be EPA nightmares. Buildings constructed before 1990 may not meet accessibility codes, and lots of those constructed after 1990 may not either.
18. Just because buildings look huge and massive, that doesn't mean their floors will support the weight of books. (In the engineering trade, the huge and massive part concerns "dead load," and floor strength concerns "live load." Some historic buildings are barely able to hold themselves up, let alone hold any extra weight of contents.)

Part III
Basic Steps

8

Programming

I. INTRODUCTION

A "building program" is a written description of the spaces required in a new or expanded building. For each space, the program provides information on the functions of the space, the required contents of the space, the corresponding square footage required, the physical nature of the space, and its relationship to the locations of other spaces in the proposed building.

Programs can vary from very brief outlines to detailed and comprehensive statements of what is needed and why.

Programming achieves a number of important things:

1. The act of getting all the details into print helps make sure that all participants agree on what the library needs. Sometimes they don't know they disagree until the library's needs are spelled out clearly.
2. Programming is usually an excellent way to sort out disagreements among members of the planning group. Often taking time to talk things through thoroughly solves a lot of problems.
3. Building programs provide a way of establishing a library's needs before another agency decides to take unilateral action.
4. Having a building program on file in college, school, hospital, or city administrative offices can also remind everyone that the library has space needs and that it has done its homework.

5. Having a building program can help with selecting an architect. If you interview an architect who (a) has never read the program or (b) clearly disagrees with it, this *is* useful information.
6. Building programs provide yardsticks for evaluating whether buildings can be realistically remodeled and expanded, as well as for evaluating whether proposed architectural designs correspond with the library's needs.
7. Programs serve important functions during architectural design work. Without a program, the decisions about how the library will operate may be driven by what looks good rather than by functional needs.
8. Having your library building consultant present at architectural meetings provides an essential evaluation of the design from the point of view of a librarian with personal knowledge of how libraries function in space.
9. Written building programs provide strong support for grant applications and may be required by the agencies giving the grants.

Programming is an absolutely essential first step before any consideration of actual building design takes place. If a building project is undertaken without this comprehensive review of long-term needs:

1. Essential spaces and features needed by the library may be omitted.
2. Features the library doesn't need or want may be included.
3. Spaces may be located awkwardly in relationship to each other.
4. Functions that should occupy a single large space may be divided among multiple small spaces.
5. Functions that need to be separated may be placed awkwardly together in a single large space.
6. Spaces may have dysfunctional features that a program could have warned against.
7. In the process of solving some problems, the architect may make it impossible to solve others.
8. Instead of asking what spaces you need, your owners and architects may begin by asking what kind of building will look best.

It's unfortunately easy to come up with real-life examples of these problems:

1. Omitted spaces: Libraries designed without programs commonly have inadequate storage space and staff workspace.
2. Unwanted "wow!" features: Dramatic spaces that interfere with the library's functions may be included.
3. Omitted details. Libraries have specific needs that may not be included unless they appear in print in a building program.

4. Awkwardly arranged spaces: Courtyards may lead to beads-on-a-chain room arrangements, with people forced to thread their way through awkwardly arranged spaces.
5. Functions divided unwisely: Fred saw a proposed academic library floor plan where the architect wanted to divide the book collection among dozens of small rooms.
6. Dysfunctional features: Architects frequently decide that outdoor reading terraces would be a wonderful feature, although the result is a total lack of all security for the book collection and any equipment not nailed down.
7. Solving some problems while creating others: As an example, a town with a historic Carnegie public library building was concerned about lack of accessibility for users with disabilities. The mayor asked a local architect to develop a design that would provide elevator access between levels and provide two accessible restrooms. Unfortunately, accessibility was the only requirement given the architect. The architect's resulting design would have made the library accessible, but it would have permanently ended any chance of expanding the building. Luckily, the board of trustees knew that accessibility was only one of a number of problems facing the library building, and they turned down the proposed design.

The basic points are:

- One of the main benefits of programming is actually getting things into print in detail. When written words replace conversation, differences in opinion stand out. As Francis Bacon observed, "Truth emerges more readily from error than from confusion."
- Never start a building project by drawing pictures. Always begin with a written building program—a detailed description of the spaces you need in the completed building.
- Always have a librarian who has a lot of experience with buildings act as your library building consultant and write your building program. This means someone with a library degree and at least five or ten years of experience running actual libraries and experience with actual building planning.
- Always have your consultant participate in design decisions. With a few wonderful exceptions, architects don't really understand everything that goes on in libraries. Having your consultant around at planning meetings saves a lot of planning time and backtracking. And it often eliminates errors that can never be corrected once construction has taken place.

> We've settled on the term *library building consultants* for people who write building programs. We probably could have said *programmers* instead, but we think libraries are best off using specialists for this work. Besides, we're both library building consultants.

II. PURPOSE OF BUILDING PROGRAMS

A. Cookbooks for Library Design

The primary purpose of a building program is to convert the service needs of the library to a detailed and thorough list of architectural spaces.

A building program provides a detailed list of all the spaces required in a structure, including their sizes, physical characteristics, adjacencies to other spaces, and contents.

The written program provides the owners with a chance to see whether everyone agrees on what is wanted. Without the formality of a written program, the various parties involved can never be sure that they are all talking about the same thing. Once things appear in written form, unrealized differences in understandings become more obvious.

The written program also provides the architect with a "cookbook" for the new or expanded library. Using the program, the owners and architect can test whether all of the spaces required are included in the proposed design.

When libraries are limited by existing structures, programs are particularly important. The temptation is always to start by tweaking the existing building or by adding a few features that emerge from short discussions, and in the process other essential needs and features may be ignored. In particularly unfortunate situations, the new features may actually prevent the addition of other important features.

A program allows the library to step back and ask what the library actually needs. This in turn allows a creative architect to find solutions to problems by undertaking rearrangements that no one foresaw.

The failure to foresee possibilities can occur particularly if library staff members have spent years coping with an inadequate building and thinking about how it might be tweaked to make it function more effectively. The kinds of changes that emerge from this approach are often too narrowly focused and miss out on the opportunities for major reassignment of spaces that starting with a written building program makes possible.

Due to the presence of existing buildings, successful programs must be carefully written to specify needed spaces rather than to make plans and suggestions for the use of existing spaces.

It's essential to avoid confusing the terms building *programs* and building *plans*. The purpose of a program is to define the problem, not to develop a solution to the problem. A program is a written document, not a drawing. A "plan" in turn is a drawing illustrating architectural spaces. These are common definitions used in the architectural community. If you keep referring to your building program as a "plan," sooner or later one of the experts you hire will get confused about what you're talking about.

In architectural terminology, the consultant defines the problem, and the architect develops a building design that solves the problem.

Once you have a written program, you should expect your architects to design spaces that respond to the program. If they disagree with the program, it is their professional responsibility to tell you so before design work begins.

Occasionally architects will present designs that clearly fail to meet programmatic needs but will not point this out to the owners. This is why it's useful to have your consultant present, and it may be a good reason for reconsidering your relationship with your architect.

Programs also help owners separate functional architectural design from razzle-dazzle. It's easy for owners to be enchanted by a dramatic staircase or swoopingly curved wall when a quick check of a written program might remind them that those features have nothing to do with library needs.

B. Presentations to Your Community

A building program provides an early way to show members of your community what you have in mind.

Unfortunately, comprehensive programs can be pretty dry reading. To combat this, programs should always include *executive summaries*. Because summaries are really for library users and for administrators of larger service units, they can stress details that will be of particular interest to library users and academic or city planners.

Even if many readers will not read past the executive summary, distributing the entire program is important because it provides evidence of the careful and comprehensive planning that supports the summary. Readers who want more detail about an area in the executive summary can page back to the full explanation.

C. Proactive Statements of Needs

Programs often benefit from being created proactively, particularly for libraries that are part of larger organizations, such as school libraries, special libraries, academic departmental libraries, and so on.

Decisions to alter or relocate libraries that are small elements located in large buildings can come with virtually no warning, and librarians need to be prepared. By the time the head of a library learns that change is planned, there may already be an architect drawing plans. In situations like this, having a building program on file long in advance may help.

The situation is made worse by space poaching. In large buildings with small libraries, someone always needs space and is casting covetous eyes on desirable locations.

To deal with situations like this, it's useful to have building programs on file with administrative offices, or to be able to whip one up at a moment's notice when possible changes are announced.

> As an example, a medical library with which Fred worked found out on a Friday morning that a meeting had been scheduled for the following Monday afternoon to review relocating a number of hospital units, including the library. The director of the library and Fred spent the weekend on the project, and by Monday morning they had a program in the hands of the hospital administration. While the other departments turned up only to complain and to demand more space, the librarian was able to smile and say, "Here's what we need."

D. Required Documentation for Grant Applications

Depending on circumstances, written building programs may be required as part of construction grant applications or for other purposes.

For this reason, a program may contain information not strictly needed by the architect, such as brief descriptions of the business, university, or town to be served; executive summaries to enable quick reviews; or comments on how the program matches the requirements of external agencies. A program for an academic library may need to demonstrate that it meets the requirements of an accrediting agency or a professional group from which the school is seeking accreditation. A program for a public library may need to demonstrate that the library meets state standards for public libraries.

Because all programs are written on word-processing equipment, quick program revisions to match the special requirements of various grant proposals are easy to accomplish.

E. Sorting out Differences of Opinion

It's highly unlikely that all the players in a library project will agree. Frequently, extensive discussion among all of the planners can help sort things out. On occasion, it reminds us of discussion with citizens who want books removed from libraries—often being listened to carefully disarms tense situations.

F. Providing an Opportunity for User Input before Design

Programming is a good time for user input because it separates discussion of the library's service and space needs from possible arguments over locations and sites and building design. In some cases, members of governing boards and communities have strong and widely divergent views about where libraries should be built and what buildings should look like, or whether old buildings should be expanded or replaced, and starting with a program focuses attention on functional needs rather than artistic decisions.

Getting people involved in planning how the library will work and what kind of space is needed can help the same people realize later that certain options they originally liked are simply not workable.

Many library users want to be heard, and asking them early in the process can bring about a great deal of "buy in" on projects.

III. INPUT ON PROGRAMS

A. Observations by Consultants

Many consultants will want to begin by simply exploring existing library buildings, either alone or in the company of library administrators and staff. Programs should describe existing buildings, and whether the libraries expect to remodel and expand them or start over. A lot of this description can be prepared by consultants without major input from library staff.

See chapter 5 on "Evaluating Library Buildings by Walking Around."

B. Interviews with Staff and Management

The most direct way to figure out what spaces are needed in a new or expanded library is to simply ask the staff and administration.

It's the responsibility of the consultant in this situation to know enough about libraries to be able to ask endless "do you want this" sorts of questions.

Sometimes, library staff members have trouble divorcing themselves from the existing library building. After many years of asking themselves, "How can we tweak this building to make it more functional?" they may have problems thinking of new buildings in the abstract. One approach Fred has used is the tornado approach: he asks library staff to imagine that a tornado has demolished the library and to tell him what kinds of spaces they need in a new building. (Consultants who take this approach need always to warn owners in advance, so that the owners don't assume that the consultant is trying to tilt things toward an entirely new building rather than possible remodeling.)

> This need for a tornado analogy is not imaginary. In one library Fred worked with, a department head's response to "What do you need?" always resulted in "I want to move that wall." When Fred said it would be a new library and the wall wouldn't be there to move, the department head was unable to respond, and the assistant department head and Fred ended up working together to enumerate the necessary features of the new department.

Another problem with discussions of needed spaces occurs when library staff who have developed ingenious workarounds for badly designed buildings want to repeat those workarounds in new buildings.

> In one library Fred worked with, the space for cataloging was completely insecure, and the cataloger kept a cart of uncataloged DVDs in the computer server room near her cataloging workstation. This was an ingenious solution, and she insisted that the server room in the new library be located next to technical services so she could continue storing DVDs there. When Fred suggested that a locking storage cabinet or closet could be provided in the technical services room, the staff member instead insisted on using the new server room.

Some library staff have a tendency to omit from the program statement things they already have. When consultants ask, for example, "Does your department need a storage closet?" staff members may respond, "We already have one." This puts a lot of pressure on the consultant to make absolutely certain that staff members are not omitting things they need, since anything not listed in the program won't be included in the design for a new building. Once again, the "tornado" approach may help.

One problem with evaluating options occurs when the library's staff, governors, and users disagree on what the library needs. To take a public library example, storing children's picture books in flip bins with the front covers of the books exposed leads to vastly higher use, but library staff may dislike the idea because this browsing-friendly arrangement can make it harder for staff to keep books in order or locate individual items.

Avoiding assigning specific uses to specific existing spaces in programs is important because an ingenious architect may end up reassigning all existing spaces.

Our experience has been that the best way to discuss needed features is to ask librarians and owners about long lists of possible features the library might want.

One pitfall with distributing lists of possible features is the desire of owners and staff to get together without the consultant present and decide on answers for all of the questions. The problem with this approach is that the questions cannot explain all of the implications of decisions. If board members of a public library, for example, get together to decide all by themselves, they may select features without realizing how things might work. And once they've decided, they may balk at changing.

A solution to this problem is to not give people time to meet in advance of discussions of library needs. Fred often sends libraries the lists of options just a few days in advance, specifically asking library directors to distribute the questions to board and staff members just long enough in advance for the board and staff to quickly skim the lists before they meet with Fred.

Lists of options can come from many sources. Fred usually develops them himself, but a good source is the sixth edition of Sannwald's *Checklist of Library Building Design Considerations* (American Library Association, 2016).

The following sample list of possible discussion questions is for a children's department in a small public library, but the same approach works for all sorts of library spaces. The main challenge is to list every possible feature that might affect the size and layout of the department—not because the library may want the feature, but to give the library the opportunity to consciously reject it. Thinking of possible features only after construction has been completed is not much help.

One important point in figure 8.1 is that there are often a vast number of possible space-consuming features to consider. No list of planning options is ever complete, but you should expect your consultant to describe a large number of possible options.

The main point of including this extremely detailed list is to emphasize how extensive the possibilities are for even one department of a middle-sized public library. Failure to review (and accept or reject) as many possibilities as possible can result in omitting features from architectural designs. It's frustrating to complete a building and only then realize that useful things have been omitted.

C. Focus Groups

Focus groups are small discussion groups drawn from the public the library serves that are assembled to look at specific planning issues. Typically, focus groups have a comfortable number of people—enough people for a lively conversation and not so many that most people sit silent. If you have more than twenty individuals in a focus group, it will be difficult to acquire useful information.

Many focus groups consist of people with similar interests, such as parents of preschool children for a public library, nursing training staff for a hospital library, or student study groups for a college library.

By assembling a group of people with similar interests, the people leading the focus group can get them to discuss how they prefer to see services offered and how they may differ among themselves. If each group consists of a full range of library users, it's much harder to discuss specific details.

FIGURE 8.1

Possible questions for planning a children's services department in a medium-sized public library

- How do the children of your town use the library?
- What kinds of needs result from public school classes?
- Do the schools have libraries?
- If so, are the school libraries available to children after school hours and during weekends and vacations?
- What age or grade range of children will use the department?
- Do kids hang out in the library after school?
- If kids don't hang out in the library, does the community have a need for this kind of after-school environment for kids?
- Do you want a separate children's service desk?
    - Will the children's desk provide lending services, or will lending take place centrally?
    - Will there be one or more self-check stations?
    - Do you want a modular desk for long-term flexibility?
    - Will the desk have seats for users?
    - What about seats for staff? How many will you need at peak times, such as enrollment for summer reading, when you may have several volunteers in addition to regular staff? Or will volunteers sit at reader tables?
    - Will you need space for a ready reference collection?
    - Will you need space for books held for teachers?
    - Will you want double monitors for staff computers, so that users can see the information that staff are looking up?
    - Will you need all areas of the desk limited to 29" high to enable staff seated there to see the entire department?
    - If you want all areas of the desk 29" high, do you want to keep all shelving and files around the desk also 29" high, so that staff can rotate their chairs and see the entire department?
- How will you provide computer service for children?
    - In the children's services area, or in an area for all library users?
    - Will you have separate computers for younger and older children, or shared computers?
    - How do you want to provide for printing? For reserving computers?
    - Do you want multifunction or single-function workstations?
    - What about office suite software, computer games, Internet access?
    - Do you want separate OPACs? (Some libraries have separate OPACs because users searching the Internet leave no workstations free for short-term use)
    - Do you want computers with bench seats for two people, such as kids playing video games together or parents and children working together?
    - Do you want provisions for staff oversight of computers? Line-of-sight views of Internet-enabled computer screens?
    - Self-check lending equipment?
- Card catalog?
- Do you want to have group seating and materials for younger children in one area of the department and seating and materials for older children in another area? Or do you want all materials in one area and all seating in another area?

- What kinds of materials do you want to provide? And how do you want to house them?
  - Junior fiction books (chapter books)? On 60" shelving? Or something else?
  - Junior nonfiction books? On 60" shelving? Or something else?
  - E-books (picture books)? On 48" shelving? In flip bins? Or something else? (48" shelving is tall enough for 3 shelves of E books, but the 42" shelving often recommended by vendors holds only 2 shelves)
  - Board books? On shelves or in bins?
  - Leveled readers? On shelves or in flip bins?
  - Current magazines? On tilt shelves? In plastic bins on shelves? In wall-mounted plastic pockets?
  - Magazine back issues? Stacked flat on 60" shelving? Bound?
  - Videocassettes? On shelves? Or something else? (If you still have any videocassettes)
  - DVDs? On shelves? Or something else?
  - Audio books on CDs? In flip bins? Or something else?
  - Video games?
  - Audiocassettes?
  - Books on tape or CD? On shelves? Or something else?
  - Cassette/book sets, CD/book sets, and similar products?
  - Games, puzzles and toys? On shelving units? In bins? In a staff workroom?
  - Circulating kits? In plastic boxes on public shelves? In a staff workroom? In a storeroom?
  - Displays of new materials? Divided by age group or format of materials?
  - Do you want slat-wall end panels?
  - Do you want canopies on shelving to provide shelf-top areas for displays? On all shelves, or just 48"-high shelves?
  - Do you need to isolate any portions of the collection for security? (Video games are a common example)
  - Will you provide publicly accessible shelving for held books? Where?
- What size of collections in each of the above areas do you want to provide space for?
- What kind of user seating do you want to provide for children and their parents or caregivers?
  - Do you want electrical outlets on all tables and by all soft seating?
  - Toddler-size tables and chairs?
  - Primary-size tables and chairs?
  - Adult-size tables and chairs?
  - Carrels?
  - Diner-booth style seating?
  - Game tables?
  - Children's-size soft seating, such as miniature armchairs and sofas?
  - Window seats?
  - Sprawling and play space for very young children? With ornamental rugs?
  - Adult-size armchairs, love seats, or rocking chairs, for adults alone or for adults to share with children?
  - Special reading structures?
  - Study rooms?
  - Other types of seating?
  - Is there any kind of seating you want to ban? Three-legged chairs? (Which tip over) Reading pits? (Which cause serious problems of the falling-into variety)

- Play areas:
    - Playhouses?
    - Miniature kitchen sets? Or similar items?
    - Lego tables? Lego Duplo tables for younger children?
    - Brio train tables?
    - Beads-on-wires tables?
    - Other play equipment?
- Exhibit spaces?
    - Exhibit cases? Rotating exhibits or permanent displays?
    - Small exhibit cases for children's collections? Inset in walls?
    - Wall space for artworks? (Review hanging options)
    - Bulletin boards? Number? Sizes? Locations? (Spaces planned for bulletin boards can end up being prevented by thermostats or fire alarms if not nailed down in advance)
    - Pinnable walls?
    - Exhibit lighting?
- Space for pets?
- Project tables for daily crafts?
- Departmental lighting needs? Brightness? Glare prevention?
- Departmental electrical outlet needs? Childproof (tamper-resistant) outlets? Outlets in the center of the floor?
- Coat storage? Hooks or rods?
- Stroller parking?
- Features the library specifically does not want?
- Craft and story room?
    - How many children?
    - Parents as well?
    - Separate story and craft spaces, with seating space in both, so that children can move from stories to crafts?
    - Floor coverings? Washable floor plus area rug for stories? Permanent carpet and tile areas?
    - Coat storage?
    - Parental oversight? High windows? In-room parent participation?
    - AV equipment?
    - Locking storage cabinets and drawers? (No chipboard components)
    - Sinks? At two heights?
    - Refrigerator for snacks?
    - Projection equipment? Ceiling-mounted projector? Screen? (Motor-driven with key control?)
    - Lighting? Different lighting for program presenter?
    - Electrical wiring? (Especially outlets in the center of the floor, which may be impossible to add later)
    - Storage closets for furniture and equipment?
    - Restroom?

- Family restroom? (for use in particular by adults helping children of the opposite genders)
- Children's restrooms?
  - Do you want to make it impossible for children to lock themselves into restrooms and create trouble?
  - Child-size fixtures in addition to standard adult-sized fixtures in the restrooms?
- Provision for nursing mothers?
- Staff workroom?
  - Do you need a sink? (Sinks are the only items that require built-in counters)
  - Refrigerator? (For staff lunches? For snacks for kids?)
  - Windows with Venetian blinds for department? For department head's workroom?
  - Space for a clothes washer and dryer for cleaning hand-puppets, dress-up clothes, and anything else that may harbor bedbugs or other infestations? (Important to decide while writing program because of the necessary provision of power, water, dryer vents, and drains)
  - Workstations for individual staff members? Required components of each workstation?
  - Shared computer equipment, such as printers?
  - Worktables?
  - Extra chairs for visitors or for staff meetings?
  - Work counters? (Tables are more flexible in use than built-in counters)
  - Provision for staff to eat lunch in the workroom?
  - Space for special equipment, such as die cutters and dies? Paper shredder? Paper cutter?
  - Shelf list? (If such still exist)
  - Storage shelving?
  - Storage cabinets?
  - Filing cabinets? Vertical or lateral? Number of drawers?
  - Storage for office supplies, such as printer paper, printer cartridges, and so on?
  - Storage for unusually large items used for programs?
  - Storage for posters and poster supplies?
  - Bulletin board(s)?
  - Wall space?
  - Lost and found? (What items will you automatically throw away, such as knit caps?)
- Staff restroom? (Access through staff corridor, not directly from staff workroom?)
- Department head's workroom?
  - Desk?
  - Credenza?
  - Worktable?
  - Sink?
  - Personal computer printer?
  - Bulletin board(s)?
  - Chairs for visitors?
  - Filing cabinets? Vertical or lateral?
  - Small refrigerator?
  - Wall shelving?
  - Wall space? (For art? For family photos? For diplomas?)
  - Department head's restroom?

- Departmental storeroom(s)?
  - Will the storeroom have shelving? (Will the library have obsolete shelving it can retire to storerooms?)
  - Will the storeroom be adjacent to staff workroom? To craft and story room? To public areas of department?
- Will you want to store program supplies in a closet off the meeting room instead of in the department? Or in both?

In addition to reviewing library services, focus groups can also help develop community support. People who have participated in focus groups will have a vastly greater knowledge of the library's needs and plans, and their response is likely to be positive.

Focus groups usually take place by public announcement, but invitations are also essential. Without inviting participants and confirming attendance, libraries sometimes find that almost no one turns up. While having too many people attend a focus group session can make things somewhat unwieldy, even worse is having almost no one turn up.

John has improved attendance at invited focus groups by paying participants a modest fee, making it more difficult for them to just not bother to show up.

It's sometimes difficult to make sure that focus groups include a real cross-section of the service community. Once Fred was asked to lead a focus group of junior high and senior high students for a public library, only to find that the library had invited only honor students, all of whom saw the library as a place to study alone rather than to hang out with friends, read Manga, or play video games. To counter this problem, John used a college business department with access to census data. Using this data focus groups were developed that enabled the library to receive information from a broad segment of the community; it's also a good thing to be sure that friends and supporters of the library are present in focus groups. If all the people who attend a focus group session are anti-construction, it won't be a productive meeting.

Focus groups need to be driven by questions to which the library needs answers. Sometimes the group can be given a list, or the library may simply prefer to have a list of questions on hand.

One reason that focus groups work much better than surveys is that the person leading the group can take time to explain concepts. For example, one of the most popular innovations in library design in recent decades is study rooms, but they require some explanation before people in the focus group can be asked whether they might use them.

It's important that the leader of the focus group not serve as a scribe to record the session. People leading focus groups don't have the time to pursue ideas and to keep notes at the same time. (Consultants talking with library staff can pause while they write down staff responses, but with focus groups consultants need to keep going and not break the flow of conversation.) Consultants who are planning focus groups will arrange to have someone take notes or make an audio recording of the meeting.

Focus groups are intended to gather input, not to make decisions. This is usually understood, but occasionally someone will say something to the effect of, "Well, what are you going to do about this?" Or, "Well, are you going to have a coffee shop or not?" Occasionally, one or two aggressive people attempt to take over a focus group, making one point repeatedly and arguing that everyone else is wrong or that the library is clearly up to something. At times like this, the group leader needs to find a way to say something equivalent to "You've made your point, and we need to hear from other people."

It's sometimes hard for leaders of focus groups to avoid arguing with seriously bad suggestions from the group. Even if as librarians we know that a specific idea has been a disaster in other libraries, the purpose of focus groups is to find out what people think. If someone in a focus group is enthusiastic about an unusually bad idea, we can smile, write it down, say thank you, and then not act on it.

> For example, when Fred led a focus group for a public library, one of the people present talked about the importance of a coffee bar as a fundraiser, but also talked about the importance of keeping prices lower than in coffee shops. Fred was tempted to point out that, even charging full prices, coffee bars in public libraries are almost always money losers, but he managed to force himself to keep his mouth shut and say "Thank you."

It can be distressing for libraries when new ideas that particularly excite librarians and owners fall like lead balloons in focus groups. Sometimes the participants in the groups just don't get it or happen to be the wrong group of people. But it's also possible that the new ideas really don't appeal much to the community.

You may want to consider listing focus group members in your written building program, particularly if there are a reasonable number of names. However, it's not always an easy decision. Listing a total of eight people suggests that your focus groups were really a failure, while listing 300 may take up an unreasonable amount of space.

Some libraries have summarized focus group input and posted it on their websites, along with thanks to all the people who participated.

If focus groups work well, they may lead to changes in building programs, but even if that doesn't happen, people always like being asked, and in that way focus groups can help bring good will to the library and remind everyone of the necessity of the proposed project. It also gives libraries the opportunity to point out that members of the public were indeed consulted.

D. Surveys

When the time to plan arrives, libraries frequently discuss using surveys to help determine what the students, faculty, citizens, lawyers, or medical staff want. Surveys sound like great devices, but they have a large number of potential pitfalls—some of them sufficiently serious to make the resulting data completely worthless.

Surveys are complex undertakings. Designing reliable questions for use on surveys is difficult because it takes work to be sure that questions are clear and unbiased. Drawing a random sample is difficult, and if it's not done right, the results of the survey are inaccurate. Unless you have a large sample, confidence intervals may be so wide that your results don't help much. (National opinion surveys typically survey over 1,000 people and have confidence intervals of about plus or minus 3 percent.)

When we first drafted this book, we included a long section on survey design and administration and analysis. (Fred worked for the National Opinion Research Center many years ago and took courses in survey design and analysis. So he had fun writing a how-to-do-it section on surveys.)

But the more we reviewed the situation, the less we wanted to recommend surveys. Surveys can work with a handful of narrow questions (such as where users park), but are too rigid for more broad-spectrum questions and don't lend themselves to asking complex questions.

So we eliminated the section on surveys.

Some libraries do informal surveys. A stack of questionnaires on the lending desk in a public library, for example, may lead to a report on how local citizens feel about a new library building. If you report on questionnaires of this kind, you need to say something like, "Of the people who stopped by the library to fill out questionnaires, 73 percent felt that the current library building is too small." This makes clear that you surveyed foot traffic in the library and not the entire community.

Librarians need to be careful not to exaggerate the accuracy of survey data. If 342 people filled out questionnaires and 248 said the library is too small, it's tempting to do the math and say that 72.5146 percent said the library is too small. But with a sample of 342, the margin of error is about plus or minus 3 percent, so it's important to round things off to the nearest whole percent, or 73 percent. To be even more accurate in light of confidence intervals, say "about three quarters."

There's always a danger of what are called "push surveys," surveys designed to lead respondents to reply in specific ways. The world of politics is awash in push surveys. The main thing to do is to not let people know what answers you want. We've seen surveys like, "Help our library qualify for a grant by telling us how you like our service," and no one should do something like that.

If your library wants statistically valid surveys of the entire community—particularly the citizens served by a public library—it needs to hire a professional survey firm.

However, we think there are better ways than surveys to find out what people want—including, in particular, talking with library users in focus groups and talking with library staff—and we recommend that you don't try to use survey data.

IV. TYPICAL CONTENTS OF PROGRAMS

This section uses the children's department of an imaginary library to demonstrate how information can be clearly presented.

A. Table of Contents

Figure 8.2 is a table of contents for a possible building program, showing the types of topics that need to be covered. This particular program is for a medium-sized public library, but programs for academic, school, and special libraries have somewhat similar contents.

The program in this example was written by Fred, who tends to include information on what people participated in programming, the library's technical needs in various areas, and the history of the library as a service institution.

("Springfield" is supposedly the most popular town name in America, so it seemed the least prejudiced name we could use.)

FIGURE 8.2

Building Program for the Springfield Public Library

Table of Contents

I. Executive summary
   A. Introduction
   B. Strengths and weaknesses of the current building
   C. Planning numbers of specifications
   D. Spaces in the expanded building
   E. Estimate of total required space

II. Introduction
   A. Purpose of this program
   B. About the community of Springfield
   C. About the Springfield Public Library
   D. List of planning participants
   E. Optimal design and construction timetable

III. Strengths and weaknesses of the current building
   A. Strengths
   B. Weaknesses

IV. Planning numbers, specifications, and applicable standards
   A. Collections
   B. Furnishings
   C. Construction details

V. Library spaces
   A. Vestibule
   B. Main service desk
      1. Public spaces
      2. Staff spaces
   Summary of service desk spaces

   C. Adult Services
      1. Service desk
      2. Collections

3. User seating
4. Study rooms
5. Quiet reading room
6. Computer workstations
7. Coffee bar
8. Display facilities
9. Staff workspaces
10. Departmental storage spaces

Summary of Adult Services spaces

D. Young Adult Services
1. Service desk
2. Collections
3. Seating
4. Computer workstations
5. Staff workspaces
6. Departmental storage spaces

Summary of Young Adult Services spaces

E. Children's Services
1. Service desk
2. Services for younger children
    a. Collections
    b. Seating
    c. Special equipment

Summary of spaces for younger children

3. Services for older children
    a. Collections
    b. Seating
    c. Computer workstations

Summary of spaces for older children

4. Services for children of all ages
5. Display facilities
6. Craft and story room
7. Staff workspaces
8. Departmental storage spaces

Summary of Children's Services spaces

F. Local History and Genealogy
1. Collections
2. Seating
3. Computer and microform workstations

G. Meeting room
1. Seating
2. Space for presenters

           3. Coat storage
           4. Kitchenette
           5. Storage closets
   Summary of meeting room spaces

   H. Public restrooms
   I. Staff workroom
   J. Director's workroom
   K. Staff lunchroom
   L. Staff restroom
   M. Records storage closet
   N. Server room
   O. General storage
   P. Custodial spaces
           1. Mop closet and cleaning storage
           2. Garden supply closet
           3. Ladder storage
           4. Storage for gasoline-powered equipment
   Q. Book return and pickup facilities
   R. Exterior details

VI. **Total estimated space**

B. Description of the Agency the Library Will Serve

A brief description of the library is usually a good thing. It helps architects looking for commissions to understand something about the university, city, or other agency planning a new library building. And it helps grant committees gain a quick understanding of the nature of the project.

Usually a description of the agency to be served will include basic numbers:

- The number of students, researchers, citizens, or employees.
- The number of users of specific age or occupational groups.
- The size of the collection to be housed. Or the sizes of the collections to be housed, if different materials require separate housing.
- Whether most of the students study in the library or in their dorm rooms, and how many are likely to crowd into the library during exam weeks.
- Expected future changes. Anticipated changes in student body size, public library service populations, the boundaries of service districts, and many other areas can help clarify the long-term needs of libraries.

This is also a good place to include some very basic information on the library's existing building.

C. Long-Range Plans as They Relate to Space Needs

A few elements in long-range plans apply directly to space needs, and these plans always need to be taken into account during programming. One of the responsibilities of the building consultant is to sort out those elements that need to be reflected in space projections.

For example, if a long-range plan calls for more public computer workstations, extra space needs to be provided. But if the long-range plan calls for access to an increased number of databases, this has little or no space implication, unless it will lead to a reduction in the sizes of reference collections or to a greater number of computer workstations.

Although they are important to planning, existing long-range plans are extremely insufficient to serve as programs because they do not examine every aspect of library operations and do not convert plans to space needs. For this reason, long-range plans are an important input to programming work but provide far too little information.

D. Review of Applicable Service Standards and Restrictions

Depending on circumstances, there may be applicable standards that will affect the library. Some states may specify minimum user seating and minimum collection sizes for public libraries. Accreditation standards may apply to academic libraries. Some professional associations may specify book collection sizes for academic programs seeking accreditation.

This is a useful place to list the library's actual planning numbers, clarifying many of the numbers in the program.

For example, see table 8.1 for seating for a totally imaginary small college library, demonstrating that the seating meets an applicable standard (also imaginary).

See table 8.2, which shows collection sizes for the imaginary children's department. The "minimum standards" are also imaginary.

TABLE 8.1

Total Seating

Type of seating	Number of units	Total chairs
4-person tables	40	160
2-person tables	20	40
Armchairs	25	25
4-person study rooms	10	40
Total	**95**	**265**

TABLE 8.2

Children's Collections

Type of material	Total collection size
Board books	250
Picture books (E-books)	4,000
Junior fiction	3,000
Junior nonfiction	3,500
Recorded books	500
Total books	**11,250**
DVDs	1,000
Music CDs	500
Total recordings	**1,500**
Periodical subscriptions for younger children	10
Periodical subscriptions for older children	20
Total subscriptions	**30**
Kits (boxed sets of circulating materials)	**20**

Note that the table focuses on materials that require physical space for storage. For this reason, it does not include electronic books. If the collection looks paltry to you in your program, you may want your consultant to reassure readers in a footnote that the library will also own or provide access to e-books or that it offers extensive interlibrary loan service.

Public library children's departments tend to have materials in a wide variety of formats, and the table for a real library would probably list many more types of objects.

E. Functional Evaluations of Current Facilities

Whether the program calls for the reworking of an existing library or the construction of a new library, a functional evaluation of the existing library is always a useful feature of a written building program.

When architects set out to remodel and expand an existing library, detailed information on the functional failings of the current library will help them design a structure that improves on the current building. Although architects usually do a good job noting problems with existing structures, they are not librarians, and they may overlook serious functional problems that can be identified by a consulting librarian working with the staff and owners.

If the library plans to abandon its current building, a written evaluation of the functional problems with the current space helps the owners explain to the community why abandoning the existing library is a necessary decision. Sometimes the number of functional problems posed by a building can be overwhelming when everyone involved takes the time to enumerate them.

A written evaluation of an existing building can also help owners and architects decide whether expansion is even feasible at all.

F. Structural Evaluations of Current Facilities

In addition to a functional analysis, the owners may also want a structural analysis of an existing building. In general, this calls for a very different set of skills and a different report. Determinations of such things as structural soundness, condition of heating and ventilating systems, conditions of roofs, presence of asbestos and lead paint, adequacy and condition of power supplies, problems with water infiltration, and so on go far beyond the scope of building programming and call for hiring separate technical experts in these various fields.

Before a final decision can be made regarding the remodeling and expansion of an existing library, or the conversion of a non-library building to a library, owners will need to know all of this information.

However, we believe that engineering studies should be part of the design process, not the programming process. The purpose of the program is to provide a careful description of all the functional spaces necessary to meet the library's long-range needs. Deciding whether to abandon an existing building or remodel and expand it is a job for the entire planning team—owners, staff, architects, engineers, and building consultant.

When the program is complete, it can be used as a yardstick to evaluate the suitability of a proposed site or building. But architects and engineers will need to review each specific site or building to be sure that it also meets the library's structural needs.

G. Enumeration of Required Spaces and Contents

For each space in the library, the program should provide a written description, including the purpose of the space, the activities that take place in the space, the contents of the space, and notes on adjacencies—the location of the space with regard to other spaces in the library.

We strongly recommend that programs provide for each space in the library a table listing the elements in that area that lead to the recommended size of the space. If programs don't do this, people can say, "Let's cut it by 10 percent," without having any idea of what that will actually mean. If the program has a list of features for each area, libraries can use the list as a shopping list if they have to reduce the size of the program.

Space calculations for a space in the library might look something like table 8.3. Once again, the example is for a children's department in a small public library. (The abbreviation "sf" always stands for "square feet.")

TABLE 8.3

Program Section on Services for Older Children

Functions

1. Seating for older children
2. Seating for parents, caregivers, and teachers
3. Collections for older children

Placement

1. On the opposite side of the service desk from services to younger children

Features and equipment

1. *Two adult-sized reading tables, each with four side chairs.* Tables will be three by five feet, with two chairs on each long side. Tables will not have aprons. Table legs will be attached with metal-to-metal fasteners. Tables will have high-pressure laminate tops and bottoms, with solid lumber core construction. Side chairs will have metal-to-metal connections between their aprons and legs.
2. *Two armchairs*
3. *Game table with printed chessboard pattern, with two side chairs*
4. *Two computers on individual tables.* Computer screens will be oriented to face library staff at the departmental service desk.
5. *Storage for 3,000 junior fiction books* on the equivalent of eight double-faced 60" shelving units (assuming 40 books per shelf and five shelves vertically)
6. *Storage for 2,000 junior nonfiction books* on the equivalent of five double-faced shelving units (assuming 50 books per shelf and four shelves vertically)

Estimated space required

2 reading tables @ 100 sf	200
2 armchairs @ 40 sf	80
Game table @ 60 sf	60
2 computers 30 sf	60
13 shelving units @ 23.5 sf	306
Subtotal	706
Circulation space	69
TOTAL	**775 square feet**

Comments on table 8.3

1. All public areas need circulation space in addition to the space required for the specific items of furniture to allow more elbowroom for users to move around. For public areas, 10 percent is often adequate, but if the library has non-rectangular spaces or wants a feeling of openness, substantially more circulation space may be necessary. ("One of the reasons we like to use the term "lending desk" rather than "circulation desk" is that architects use the term "circulation" the way we have here, and saying "lending" helps avoid confusion.)
2. We prefer to round off spaces for individual areas of libraries, in part to make clear that all of these numbers are estimates. In this case, we assume that all space estimates in the program were rounded off to the nearest 25 square feet.

The list of spaces for the entire building could look like this:

Foyer	unassigned space
Lending	875
Adult department	5,900
Young Adult department	600
Children's department	3,150
Program room	950
Public restrooms	unassigned space
Director's workroom	150
Staff workroom	725
Staff lunchroom	300
Server closet	100
Storage	900
Custodial spaces	unassigned space
Total assignable space	13,650
Unassignable space (25% additional)	3,450
TOTAL GROSS SPACE	**17,100** square feet

See section V, "Methods of Space Estimating," below for definitions of "assignable" and "unassignable" space.

H. Things That Don't Belong in Programs

The danger in writing programs is that authors may become bored with describing what's needed and start designing the building.

The purpose of the program is to define needs in extremely thorough detail but not to start drawing pictures. This occasionally happens when architects try to write building programs, because they tend to think in terms of design rather than more abstract descriptions. Building programs benefit from functional diagrams showing the relationships between spaces, but they should never have floor plans.

As an example of things that don't belong in programs, we've seen programs that provide a lot of information about landscaping decisions that are really a matter of architectural design rather than functional space needs.

One exception to this general rule of separating functions and aesthetics is the owner's desire to have the library fit in with the existing architecture of a campus, civic center, or historic neighborhood. In this case, the program might say (for example) that "the new library will match the Georgian Revival architecture of the rest of the campus." Among other things, this statement may warn off architects who would rather die than match campus architecture. (Or, more likely, they will take the job and then strive in every possible way to ditch the requirement. See the section on selecting architects in the next chapter.)

> If the new library doesn't match the rest of the campus, it may look great when it's new and trendy, but thirty years later it may stand out like white brick with turquoise doors or like avocado shag carpet.]

V. METHODS OF SPACE ESTIMATING

An essential component of all building programs is an estimate of the space required for each section of the library.

Although space estimation is sometimes viewed as the great challenge of programming, it can be a fairly mechanical undertaking. The real challenge is determining what features and items are needed in the library to meet the library's long-range plans and needs, and the final estimate of the space that all of these features and items will take requires far less thought.

A. Sources of Planning Numbers

In preparing space estimates, consultants typically rely on standard figures for the space required for a wide variety of furniture and other items found in libraries.

Lists of the spaces required for various items are found in a variety of publications, including *Building Blocks for Functional Library Space*. Some of these lists are very useful, but many contain puzzling items as well.

Some space estimates in square feet that we have used frequently include the following.

3-foot double-faced shelving unit with 36" aisle	22	sf
3-foot double-faced shelving unit with 42" aisle	23.5	sf
3-foot double-faced shelving unit with 48" aisle	25	sf
Large A-frame for new books	100	sf
Map case		range
3 × 5 foot 4-person reading table	100	sf
3 × 6 foot 4-person reading table	115	sf
4 × 6 foot 4-person reading table	130	sf
6-person index table	160	sf
3 × 3 foot 2-person reading table	60	sf
1-person carrel	40	sf
Table and 4 chairs for toddlers	40	sf
Table and 4 chairs for preschoolers	60	sf
Upholstered armchair	40	sf
Love seat	60	sf
Sofa	80	sf
Computer workstation	30–35	sf
Stand-up computer workstation	20–25	sf

The problem with numbers like those above is that everyone copies from everyone. A (somewhat) fascinating research project would involve tracing back the histories and evolutions of these numbers, looking in particular for misprints that are repeated, much as typographical errors in the bibliographies of scholarly works are copied verbatim by sloppy authors who pad out their bibliographies with books they have never examined—or when the books listed do not actually exist.

B. Planning Space for Collections

Precision in calculating space needs is far more important when libraries have many identical items. For example, if a library will have 2,000 double-faced shelving units, the accuracy of calculating the space needs for each shelving unit will be far more important than the accuracy of the space estimate for a single display stand.

One important step in space calculations is converting from long-term collection numbers to storage needs. It's basically a matter of simple arithmetic.

- Remember that a 36-inch-long shelf is full when about 30 inches are occupied.
- Determine the number of books of each type that will fit in 30 inches. The results can sometimes be surprising. For example, collections in research libraries often contain thinner books than those in public libraries. The important thing to remember is that the average number of books per shelf varies from library to library and from collection to collection.

> We read about one research library that got itself into planning troubles by basing all calculations on the works of a famous local author, not considering whether those books were typical in size for the collection as a whole.

- Determine the number of shelves vertically that each type of material requires. For shelving for children, this requires deciding how high shelving units will be and what impact this has on the number of shelves possible. A 60-inch-high unit, for example, may hold five shelves of juvenile fiction but only four shelves of juvenile nonfiction, since nonfiction books tend to be taller. In public libraries using 84-inch-high shelving, a single shelving unit may be able to hold seven shelves of adult fiction but only six shelves of adult nonfiction.
- Calculate shelving needs separately for all areas of the collection that will be stored separately.
- Some libraries have based shelf need projections not on collection sizes but rather on how many books are actually in the library at a given time. The trouble with this approach is that one has to base calculations on times when the maximum number of books are on the shelves. (August and December for public libraries, and summertime for academic libraries.) In addition, if different areas of the collection are out at different times, the staff will have to do a lot of back-spacing to make things fit.
- Adjusting shelving on the basis of circulation strikes us as a potentially dangerous idea.
- Decide how the library will cope with oversized books. Separating oversized books can greatly diminish use, particularly in public libraries, but integrating them with other books can lead to fewer shelves vertically or occasional fore-edge shelving. The usual practice is to allow more vertical space in the 600s and even more in the 700s, although it's always a pain interfiling the *Pocket Guide to Michelangelo* with an eighty-pound *Life Work of Michelangelo*, even if they both fit. Some libraries stack oversized books flat on the bottom shelves of shelving units. Others simply avoid really big books.

- If the library will have separate subject areas, but older books are retired to the main book stacks, this makes it possible to have fixed sizes for subject areas.
- The space required for individual shelving units depends on the aisle width in stacks and the frequency of cross-aisles.
- Building programs need to pay close attention to whether sources of planning numbers specify square footages for single-faced or double-faced shelving units. We like double-faced, but the main thing is to be consistent and to make things extremely clear. After a bad experience with an architect who converted the specified number of double-faced units to the same number of single-faced units, Fred began using phrases like "double-faced 84" shelving units" every time he mentioned shelving.
- Written building programs need to specify aisle width and the frequency of cross-aisles. (When you are reviewing your schematic drawings, double-check that your architects provide these.)
- Programs always need to specify that there will be no dead-end book aisles.

C. Additional Space

One of the serious challenges of space estimating is what takes place after the determination of the space required for contents.

One way to estimate extra space is by using standard planning formulas.

- Circulation space. Most standard figures for estimating the space required for furnishings don't provide the extra space needed to allow people to move comfortably between the furnishing. If a college library reading room has 30 four-person tables, each occupying the recommended number of square feet, the room will be an undifferentiated mass of tables with no walkways between them. Depending on the feeling the owners want, the extra space may range from an extra 10 percent for a comfortable feeling to even 20 or 30 percent for a sense of real spaciousness. A good name for this type of extra space is circulation space, the architectural term for the space provided to allow people to move around.
- Assignable space. "Assignable space" is the total space required for all of the library functions, including reader seating, collection storage, service desks, staff workspaces, storage, and so on.
- Unassignable space. In addition to these functions, however, there are many other things that require space, including hallways, staircases, restrooms, elevators, MEP (mechanical—as in HVAC—electrical, and plumbing) spaces, and so on. After adding up all the assignable space, consultants need to add a factor for unassignable space, typically somewhere in the range of 25 to 30 percent of assignable space, but it can be much more if the library wants a lot of ceremonial open space.

If the issue of open space is not settled, or if the building has a lot of historic spaces that are hard to use, your written program may want to stress the fact that unassignable space is a very rough estimate.

We very strongly recommend not merging circulation space and unassignable space into a single planning number, since the circulation space may then be used for other purposes than where it is needed to provide extra elbowroom for basic library functions.

Space estimates must be based on an enumeration of contents. If estimates are merely offhand guesses, there is no reason to believe that the space listed for each section of the library is sufficiently accurate for the architect to follow.

D. Putting Numbers Together

The space estimate for a small adult reading room in a public library might look something like this:

8 armchairs @ 40 sf	320
2 reading tables @ 100 sf	200
Fireplace	50
Small counter for coffee service	25
Subtotal	595
Circulation space (about 10% extra)	55
Total	**650** square feet

And a shelving area might look something like this:

64 double-faced shelving units @ 23.5 sf	1,504
3 OPACs on stack ends @ 20 sf	60
Subtotal	1,564
Circulation space (about 10% extra)	161
Total	**1,725** square feet

Note: Although it's possible to use an exact 10 percent, rounding things off to the nearest 25 square feet is close enough and makes presentation simpler. Since estimating methods lead to estimates, not ironclad figures, it's probably more honest anyway.

The actual space that many items require depends on how many users will cluster around them. In many cases, for instance, heavily used materials need to be spread out onto extra units. For example, a new book display on 90-inch shelving with seven packed shelves vertically concentrates so many high-interest items into so little space that users will start elbowing each other out of the way to get at the books.

> This is not imaginary. Fred once watched in fascination for 15 minutes in a busy suburban library near Chicago while otherwise civil adult library users snarled at each other in front of an overly compact new book display.

Some program writers specify overly precise sizes. For example, a reading area may be listed as 427.75 square feet. Although this may be the exact outcome of using available estimating information, it is a figure with some seriously insignificant digits. Space estimates with numbers this specific are a bit of a fraud, because none of the planning numbers are that accurate to begin with.

> One good way of describing inappropriate precision is "Measuring a hot dog with a micrometer."

> Commercial businesses have used the overly specific number technique for years in sending bills. Even though $3,000.00 is sufficiently accurate, the company knows that a bill for $2,987.58 is (a) more attractive because it's just under $3,000.00, which seems like more of a bargain, and (b) more credible because the unusual number implies extraordinarily careful calculation. Some people feel that this technique is particularly evident in their telephone, hospital, and funeral home bills.

No matter what source of square footages is used, consultants always run into situations where no data is available in published sources, and they have to make estimates. The main thing to remember is that most of the space required by a piece of furniture is due not to the furniture itself but to the space around it, both for people to sit or stand and for people to circumnavigate the piece of furniture and the people sitting or standing there. In the case of items that are associated with crowds—such as new book racks or video selection areas—this extra space can be considerable.

Consultants who have to deal with a piece of furniture or equipment for which no space estimates are available have to develop their own. One way is to draw a floor plan of the space occupied by the item and then determine how much space will be needed around it to allow people to come and go without bumping into the item or each other.

Consultants may also be tempted to include unneeded items in building programs just because they can find suitable square footages for them listed in a guide. Obviously, this is a bad idea.

While working on space estimates, consultants sometimes find recommended square footages that make very little sense, and consultants have to develop their own numbers.

Space projections in programs can be reasonably accurate, but the final test is always the design of the building. Sometimes problems are due to inaccurate programming, but they can also be due to adventurous designs that make it difficult to arrange furniture without wasting space. For example, an office that is not a simple rectangle will probably include square footage than cannot be used effectively, and the room will need to be larger as a result. Almost any space with curved or diagonal walls will be less efficient.

VI. WHO SHOULD WRITE YOUR BUILDING PROGRAM?

A. Programs by Building Consultants

Programming is a common service provided by independent library building consultants. Usually these are professional librarians with a great deal of experience in working with library buildings.

Having a librarian rather than your architects prepare your building program has some significant advantages:

- A librarian will have a different perception of space needs than your architect. No matter how excellent your architects are, they may tend to see buildings in terms of architectural spaces rather than of library services.
- If you hire a consultant who does not work for your architect, you have a much better chance of hearing an essential second opinion on a problematic design concept. (And if things get dull, you can encourage your architect and consultant to argue with each other.)
- Although architects can create exciting and interesting library spaces, they sometimes fail to understand how libraries occupy spaces on a daily basis.

- Working with a consultant will give you someone to critique proposed floor plans and building designs. This is a critical function of consultants, because very few practicing librarians or governing bodies have extensive experience with library designs.
- Be alert to architects who try to prevent your consultant from attending planning meetings or critiquing drawings. If your architects balk or always say, "There's no time," be prepared to inform them otherwise.

Building consultants occasionally get behind schedule and have trouble catching up. This happens for a couple of basic reasons:

- Some consultants are library administrators who do consulting on the side. Their experience as library administrators makes their input valuable, but they occasionally get swamped on their day jobs.
- Many consultants work as individuals rather than as part of firms, and even if they are part of firms, it's possible that no one else in the firm has the same expertise in the functional design of library spaces. So if the consultant is ill, there may be no one who can take his or her place.

B. Programs by Architects

There are at least two problems associated with having your architect prepare your building program.

The first is that by having your project architect program your building, you lose the vital second opinion that comes from separate people or firms doing the programming and design.

The second is that architects and librarians see library buildings in different ways. Apart from any unproductive contentions about who is right and who is wrong, having two different perspectives on your building is almost certainly a better idea than having only one.

Unless your architects . . .

- Have masters' degrees in librarianship accredited by the American Library Association, and
- Have worked for many years *as librarians,* and
- Have designed a number of successful library buildings

. . . you may find that their knowledge of libraries and how library contents occupy space and what goes on every day in libraries may be extremely inadequate.

We feel strongly that most architects are not qualified to write building programs. If your program is written by an architect rather than by a librarian, your program and your design may share similar misapprehensions about how libraries work.

C. Programs by Owners

If you are experienced in program writing, you may want to prepare your own building program, but it's a good idea to have a consultant check your work.

For example, when Fred wrote a building program for his own library, he had written about fifty earlier programs for other libraries. Nonetheless, Fred insisted that his library hire a second consultant to review Fred's own work. In the process, the second consultant discovered a couple of places where Fred had been myopic—or just not thinking clearly.

If you don't have experience writing several building programs for other libraries, it's almost certainly a serious mistake to write a program for your own library unassisted.

Because programming is the first step in library design and construction, taking the time to do it right is very important. Errors and omissions are amazingly cheap to correct during the program stage but increasingly expensive and difficult to correct as architectural design work progresses. By the time the building is built, it's basically too late.

> On a couple of occasions, Fred has been asked to do post-occupancy evaluations of recently completed buildings. Unfortunately, he usually encounters architectural concepts that should have been headed off at the pass long before and are now too late to correct.

VII. HOW TO HIRE BUILDING CONSULTANTS

One of the best ways to find out about consultants is through professional word of mouth. Talk with directors and governing board members of other libraries.

State library agencies may have lists of people who have served as consultants on library design projects, but they are unlikely to provide any evaluations of the quality of consultants.

When you speak with other libraries, there are a number of obvious questions you can ask them about their consultants.

- Did your consultant have essential basic credentials, including
  - A master's degree in librarianship from a program accredited by the American Library Association.
  - A minimum of five to ten years of library experience as an administrator.
- Were you generally satisfied with the consultant?
- Did you enjoy working with the consultant?
- Did your consultant have a wide range of experience with libraries and library buildings? Did your consultant have a number of years' experience as a library manager? Was this your consultant's first building program?
- Could your consultant answer your questions about how libraries work inside buildings?
- If you called your consultant with quick questions, could your consultant answer them?
- Did your consultant listen to you?
- Was your consultant adept at sorting out differences of opinions among library staff and between library staff and governing bodies? (Sometimes this is nearly impossible when members of governing bodies are strongly against spending any money whatsoever and have no real interest in library services, but in most cases it goes surprisingly well.)
- Did your consultant suggest all kinds of possibilities? (We think that one of the jobs of a consultant is to give you a chance to consider a wide variety of options. If you reject many of them, at least you won't find yourself asking later why you'd never considered them.)
- If a staff member insisted on an ill-considered idea, was your consultant able to deal effectively without making the person angry and at the same time not simply giving up and putting the idea in the program?
- Was the building program complete, clear, well-organized, and literate? (Given that we're librarians, literate seems particularly important.)
- Did your consultant answer quick questions at no charge? (Could you call your consultant at 10:00 p.m., get a quick answer to your question, and not hear a billing clock ticking in the background?)
- Was your consultant prepared to attend most (if not all) planning meetings with your staff and architects? (Some libraries try to save a small amount of money by not having their consultant attend design meetings. This is typically a very serious mistake.)
- Was your consultant familiar with architectural drawings? Was your consultant able to review drawings and make suggestions for functional improvements?

- Did your consultant have an extensive knowledge about what kinds of architectural features are successful and what kinds tend to cause trouble?
- If your consultant squabbled with your architects, who in retrospect was correct?
- Could your consultant help you present your project to your community? (Remember that it's the job of your consultant and architects to take the blame when people are angry, leaving the library staff and government to take any credit.)
- Was your consultant regarded positively by the grant-giving authorities?
- Was your consultant willing to help with punch listing?
- Could your consultant help with practical advice on groundbreaking and ribbon-cutting events?

Your state may have legal requirements that limit the ways in which consultants can be hired by public agencies. Check with your state library or university administration or an experienced library attorney.

VIII. PROGRAM-WRITING METHODS

A. Successive Program Drafts

No building program is complete and correct the first time it is written. It's hard to be complete in initial conversations. And participants sometimes don't realize they disagree when they're talking in groups.

Getting drafts into print is therefore essential. When programs are in print, missing elements are far more likely to stand out, and the people providing input are much more likely to realize that they disagree.

For this reason, good programs cannot be completed in a single, intensive working session. For a small library with a limited budget, having a consultant who is close enough to make three or four visits is very much to its advantage.

Because programs may go through many drafts, it's vital that you can identify specific drafts. For that reason, all program drafts must have page numbers and running heads that include the date of the draft.

> Before word-processing software was commonplace, the constant revision required of good programs presented unpleasant technical problems for the consultant. Fred's first program was written on a typewriter. As revisions continued, he retyped altered paragraphs, cut and pasted, and photocopied the result. Some pages in the program had five or six layers of paper. He still has the original, which provides quaint memories rather than a useful example.

B. Cutting Building Programs

The majority of building programs need to be cut in size.

Although the contents may be appropriate and logical, by the time libraries have listed everything they need and want, things are usually larger than people can afford.

The right way to cut a program is in a meeting with the owners, staff, and consultant. If the program is well constructed, every section shows how estimated space requirements were developed, as in the example above, and it's possible to work through the program crossing things off as you go.

Some things can be cut almost by rote, with space for collections, user seating, and other parts of the building cut by a fixed percentage.

A few things, however, can't be cut by simple formulas. Workrooms for individual staff members, for example, will usually need to be cut in number rather than reduced in size.

Our experience has been that unless people fight to retain certain features undiminished in size, even large programs can be cut in a few hours. Usually the owners, staff, and consultant decide what needs to be cut, and then the consultant revises the written program accordingly.

One thing that makes the space-cutting process less painful is the percentage add-ons. If each area of the library is increased by 10 percent to provide circulation space, and then the entire program is increased by 25 percent to allow for unassignable space, cutting 100 square feet of space from user seating may result in cutting about 138 square feet from the total program. For example:

User seating reduction	100
Additional circulation space deleted (at 10 percent)	10
Assignable space deleted	110
Additional unassignable space deleted (at 25 percent)	28
Total space deleted	**138** square feet

C. Final Review with Architects and Library Building Consultants

One of the first working meetings with your architects should include a review of the building program. A program review provides your architects with an opportunity to raise questions about your program. Your architects may find some aspects of the program unclear, and they may have alternate suggestions.

This meeting is an important step. Your consultant may have made errors, and your architect may have interesting alternatives to suggest.

The most vital aspect of this meeting is that your consultant be present to respond to suggestions or questions from your architects, and to question them in turn.

It's also a good thing to make clear to your architects from the beginning that you expect proposed changes in the program to be discussed directly in this meeting. Very occasionally, architects will employ a form of passive resistance, ostensibly accepting the written program but then presenting drawings that ignore or violate sections of the program. Fred has had a couple of experiences where public library boards were nearly driven to distraction by long series of proposed designs that ignored the boards' programmed spaces.

Occasionally, architects will balk publicly at written programs, contending that the consultant is "designing the building." This can be a genuine problem, but in our opinion it is completely reasonable for a program to include a list of objectionable design features that have failed widely in other libraries. A program that specifies a "two-story Prairie School revival building" may be intruding in design, but one that says "no recessed downlights, no atriums, and no indoor water features" is dealing with function, not design.

IX. TWO-PHASE BUILDING PROGRAMS

Frequently, libraries cut the sizes of their building programs not because the programs include unneeded features but because the results will simply be too expensive to construct at one time.

Rather than simply cut a building program in situations like this, we strongly recommend that you ask your consultant to prepare a two-phase program, listing first all the spaces for the Phase I version of the building and then all the spaces of the Phase II version.

A good two-phase program will include:

- Notes throughout the Phase I version on what changes will be made for Phase II.
- Recognition that many smaller spaces cannot be stretched between Phase I and II. While large reading rooms are easy to expand, meeting rooms, public restrooms, staff workrooms, and similar areas are hard to expand.

Some solutions to the inability to stretch small spaces in second phases include:

- If you have two meeting rooms, omit one from Phase I.
- If you have only a single meeting room, you'll almost certainly need to construct it full size in Phase I or put up with the smaller size in Phase II.
- If your state plumbing code dictates the number of toilets in your restrooms, have your architect calculate how many will be necessary in Phase II. To avoid having extra toilets placed in unfortunate locations in Phase II, build your Phase I restrooms large enough to handle Phase II needs. (Having to add extra toilets can be a serious problem. Extra restrooms in libraries that should have all restrooms in one location can lead to library users trudging from restroom to restroom, hunting for toilets not in use, or small extra restrooms in unfortunate locations.)
- General storage spaces can easily be added to piecemeal, with a second storeroom constructed in Phase II rather than expanding an existing storeroom.
- For staff workrooms for groups of staff, it may be possible to build a single workroom in Phase I, shared by staff from two areas of the library, and then construct a second workroom in Phase II, allowing separate spaces for the staff of each area.

Fred has written a number of two-phase programs. He finds them complicated to write (with tricky calculations of spaces) but very useful for libraries. Library needs outweigh consultant comfort.

X. WHAT TO DO WHEN YOUR ARCHITECTS IGNORE YOUR PROGRAMS

Most consultants have had experiences with architects who simply ignore the aspects of programs they don't like.

When architects disagree with programs, the proper thing to do is sit down in a room with the owners, library staff, architects, and consultant and review differences of opinion.

Some common methods for preventing designers from ignoring programs include:

- Hold a formal program review during the first meeting with your architects, with your consultant present. If it becomes apparent at the meeting that the architects have not read your program with care, this is the best time for a serious discussion of what you expect from your architects. (Actually, you should try to find out during interviews with architects if they have read your program. If they clearly have not done so, don't hire them.)
- Require that every schematic design be accompanied by a table comparing the designed square footage in each area of the building floor plan with the square footage in the building program. This is extraordinarily easy for an architect to do, and resistance or outright refusal can easily be an indicator of serious trouble.

> In one of Fred's projects, the architect flat-out refused to provide such a table. He was later replaced on the job for being unwilling to do what the owners wanted in a number of other areas.

- Include your consultant in all architectural planning meetings. It's amazing how fast planning progresses when owners, library staff, architects, and consultant sit around the same table. Among other things, having your consultant present can stop ill-considered design ideas before they become so established that it's difficult or impossible to change them.
- Insist that your architects provide enough time for your consultant to review construction drawings.

XI. QUICK SPACE ESTIMATES USING FORMULAS

There are formulas for providing space estimates based on projections of collection size, user seating, number of staff workstations, and meeting room and conference room capacities, with the totals increased by fudge factors for unlisted items and for unassignable space.

A space estimation formula can give you a vague idea of how much space your building may occupy, particularly if it is a small, single-story building.

Unfortunately, quick estimates based on formulas are not good for much more than vague ideas. The techniques involved are quick in and quick out, and they include too many leaps of faith.

The serious problem with using formulas to estimate space needs is that owners may be tempted to skip full programming and go directly to an architect with their quick space estimate.

But because the space estimate contains almost no detail:

- It may be very far off the mark in estimating necessary space.
- It leaves virtually all of the programming decisions up to the architect.

If the architect in turn makes these programming decisions without the long conversations and review associated with serious programming, the owners may find that the building is missing many features they actually want.

In the process of preparing building programs, we've inherited a number of prior "space estimates," and all of them had to be simply discarded.

One of the main purposes of estimates based on formulas appears to be to get the consultant's foot in the door. The space estimate isn't good for much, but it's an inexpensive introduction to the full programming services to follow.

If you need a quick estimate, hire someone to write your program and ask that person to include a quick estimate. The extra cost should be minimal (if not free), but the numbers will be of limited accuracy because hundreds of questions will not have been reviewed.

XII. CONCLUSIONS

Programming is a vital step in the design and construction of library buildings. Never be tempted to save a few dollars and a few weeks by launching directly into architectural design.

Well-built library buildings are characterized by permanence, and many serve for over a century. Ill-considered books or software can be discarded, but an ill-considered building can live to torment multiple generations yet unborn.

It's essential that the planning team include people (a) who are librarians with a strong knowledge of the functional aspects of library buildings and (b) who do not report to your architects. In addition to programming, one of the major functions of library consultants is to provide comments on the functionality of proposed designs.

XIII. SNAPPY RULES ON PROGRAMMING

1. Having the same firm write your building program and design your library is always a seriously bad idea.
2. Some consultants make their money by selling the same reports over and over. When you read sample programs and studies and preliminary space estimates, look for reports that could apply to almost any library, or for reports that tell all about the consultant's methods and almost nothing about the specific library in question.
3. When you are hiring a consultant, always ask for a sample building program.
4. If your consultant gets on your nerves, you will not enjoy programming.
5. Some consultants have one solution to all problems. When you talk with previous clients, ask if consultants refused to listen to their special interests and needs.
6. Avoid quickie space estimates based on formulas or templates.
7. You will have a far better-balanced project if your consultant is a librarian with a knowledge of buildings rather than an architect with a knowledge of libraries.
8. Never have an architect write your program. With a tiny number of wonderful exceptions, architects don't know enough about libraries, even if they've designed a few. And few architects can totally divorce themselves from design issues.
9. If your architect and programmer/consultant are the same person, you lose the tremendous advantage of having them argue with each other.
10. Even though the word *survey* sounds scientific, most homemade surveys are not. Add rule #12 to rule #10

11. If your consultant is a librarian with a deep knowledge of library buildings, always use that person to provide ongoing functional reviews of your developing building plans.
12. Focus groups are a good way to talk with library users, but you can't just count on people just turning up. Make sure they attend, and make sure that some of them are real friends of the library.
13. The best sources of programming ideas are staff and administration, rather than users. But even if you don't learn much from user input, it's still important.
14. The two least expensive elements in building a new library are programming and selecting an architect, but both take time. If you're not sure when you'll have to hit the ground running, prepare a building program, go through the legal steps in selecting an architect, and then wait to see what happens next. (Programs cost money, but selecting an architect shouldn't cost you anything except your time.)
15. Programs with big blocks of text are miserable to read. Programs structured like outlines work best and are easiest to follow. You don't want important points buried in the middle of long paragraphs.
16. If you are writing a program, always use running heads that include the date of the version of the program and the page numbers. Programs are constantly revised, and there's nothing less fun than finding out that different people are using different versions of a program.
17. In addition to writing your building program, a good consultant can help you hire your architect, take part in architectural planning meetings, provide the perspective of a professional librarian when reviewing proposed architectural designs, and help with grant applications.
18. If a program needs to be cut in size, the right group consists of the owners, staff, and consultant.
19. If you know you'll be expanding your new library, write a two-phase building program and have your architects prepare schematic designs for both phases. If you don't do this, you may find that you've painted yourself into a corner, and that your Phase I design makes it impossible to construct Phase II.
20. If people above you in the hierarchy insist that each section of your written building program be limited to a specific length, ignore them. It's a seriously bad idea.
21. Writing and revising building programs can take a lot of paper, since everyone needs to get a copy of each version in type large enough to read. This is a bad time to save a tree. (Try telling yourself it's an evil tree.)
22. Getting things into print helps clarify situations where people don't agree—or don't even know that they disagree.

9

Design

I. INTRODUCTION

Most library building projects involve four steps: programming, design, construction, and occupancy.

Almost all design work is done by architects or by people employed by architects.

Always avoid the dangerous temptation to go straight to a contractor for any library construction project, whether it's a new building or just a couple of windows. Design is almost always far more complex than it appears. If a building is larger than a specified minimum size, or if the project consists of more than cosmetic improvements, laws and regulations will require that construction documents be prepared professionally. Preparing bid documents even for something as straightforward as a storage closet is a complex undertaking.

In addition to needing the good advice and experience that an architect will bring to the job, state law may require that bid documents for a government construction be sealed by a licensed architect or engineer.*

---

*A "sealed" document carries a replica of the official seal of the supervising licensed professional.

State law may also specify how public bodies may hire architects. Your state library may have information on the subject, as may the American Institute of Architects (AIA) group for your state or your building consultant.

Good architects are always a good investment. For any project bigger than a woodshed, good architects are an absolutely essential investment.

Design is a complex undertaking because it involves the interaction of a wide range of people and agencies. For example, a project may easily involve most (or even all) of the following:

- Governing bodies, ranging from university boards of trustees to faculty library committees, school boards, public library boards, city councils, school superintendents, and corporate officers responsible for structures
- Library users
- Librarians
- National, state, and local codes and their enforcement agencies
- Other regulatory agencies
- Programmers (library building consultants)
- Architects
- Construction management firms
- Contractors
- Engineers (structural, civil, mechanical, electrical, etc.)
- Campus architects, city engineering firms, and other local experts
- Self-appointed community pressure groups
- Friends of the Library groups
- Library foundations
- Donors
- State agencies, such as historical preservation agencies
- LEED and other freelance programs

But you can't give all of these folks a direct role in your project.

II. THE ROLE OF THE ARCHITECT IN THE BUILDING PROCESS

Although this chapter covers design work, architects also provide many vital functions during the construction process and during occupancy. For the role of architects in programming, construction, and occupancy, see the appropriate chapters.

Among other services, your architects will:

- Help you determine whether your site is suitable for the building you have in mind. This is a surprisingly complex undertaking, as chapter 10 on "Site Selection" indicates.
- Evaluate your existing structure, if you are considering expansion rather than starting over. (Your programmer should have already done this from a library function point of view, but your architect will bring additional viewpoints, particularly the technical feasibility of expanding your building and bringing it up to current codes.)
- Develop a design for your building.
- Help with presenting your design to voters, the local press, and so on.
- Convert the design to construction documents—drawings and written specifications that will assure that bids from different contractors are for exactly the same structure.

During construction your architect will usually do the following, as described in chapter 12 on "Construction." (If you hire a construction management firm, however, much of this work may be done by the construction manager.)

- Supervise bidding, making sure that all bids are responsive and responsible. Bidding for public construction usually is subject to laws providing for competitive bidding. Private construction does not require this, but competitive bidding will almost certainly bring private owners a lower price and prevent situations where the brother-in-law of the college president is allowed to install woefully substandard carpeting.
- Provide construction administration. In particular, this involves making sure that the building described in the construction documents is the building you get. (Note that "construction administration" is not "construction supervision," which is the job of the general contractor or construction manager.)
- Sort out problems during construction. If the owners and contractors disagree, the architects are the people who need to explore the situations and propose solutions.
- Deal with change orders. Sooner or later in every project, the contractor is asked to build something that was not in the original specifications. Your architect will write the change order and help you negotiate a price with your contractor.
- Approve "draws" from your contractors. These are bills for work completed. Your architect will verify that the work was actually done.
- Manage waivers of lien from subcontractors to be sure that the general contractor is paying them for their share of the work covered in the draws.
- Carry out punch listing at the end of the project.

Architectural fees include engineering services. Some architectural firms have a variety of engineers on their staffs, while others subcontract almost all of these services. Firms with many engineers claim that this improves their services, but firms with no engineers on their staffs do very good work as well. Our personal feeling is that both ways work.

Be very careful that your agreement with your architects includes necessary engineering work.

Most engineering specialties required for building construction fall into the general area of "civil engineering." The name is an ancient one and comes from the distinction between military and civil engineering. In the modern architectural design and construction industry, however, "civil engineering" most commonly refers to site design and engineering, including such areas as site utilities, earthwork, paving, storm water drainage, and so on.

Among the sub-areas of building engineering are:

- Geotechnical engineering, concerned with soils, drainage, and foundations. (Frequently identified as "civil engineering" in architectural documents.)
- Structural engineering.
- Engineering of MEP systems—mechanical (HVAC—heating, ventilating, and air conditioning), electrical, and plumbing.
- Acoustical engineering, which is almost always underutilized in library design projects. (Acoustical engineering is a specialized area of expertise. Except for auditoriums, acoustical engineers are often not involved in library projects, although they may be needed in situations with sloped ceilings that don't absorb sound.)

When you build a library, your involvement with your architects will be intense. You need to find a firm with architects who are competent, who are creative while being responsive to your desires, and who understand library design. You will also want to work with architects you like personally, or it will be a very long and unpleasant process.

A. Program Review or Verification

A written building program is a detailed description of all the spaces in your proposed library, including their functions, sizes, furnishings, and adjacencies. Before architects start design work, it's essential that everyone involved in your library project—governing boards and library administrative staff—understand the program and agree on its contents.

The creation of written building programs is covered in detail in chapter 8 on "Programming."

Usually the first meetings with your newly hired architects will involve review of your building program. This is a critical meeting, because your program defines in serious detail what you want in your new library building.

In many cases, architects do not agree with everything in building programs, and this first meeting is the proper time to sort this out. You need to let your architects know that you expect them to either speak up at this time or follow your program as it is written.

To make this meeting work, it is essential that your consultants (or whoever wrote your building program) be present to explain the reasons for the information in the program. And to sometimes stand their ground.

One thing that can go seriously awry in architecture is if the architects disagree with the program but prefer to quietly ignore the program rather than face issues directly. We've worked with libraries that had to fire architects who persistently ignored programs without admitting they were doing so.

A few architects clearly resent building programs. Frequently these architects are people who want not only to design a library but also to determine what it will do. Unless your architects have an impressive track record building highly functional libraries, their desire to redefine your library's purpose and intent should be a chilling experience—a dangerous sign of hubris that needs to be stopped before things get seriously out of hand.

One way to work with your architects in making sure that the proposed building is compatible with your building program is to ask your architects to indicate on their drawings, or in tabular form, which items in the program have been added, deleted, or relocated. In some drawings, you'll notice icons for items of furnishings floating in midair around the edges of the drawings, outside the enclosed floor area of the building, indicating that the items are in the program but don't fit into the drawings.

Keeping your library building consultants around during the design process is an extremely good idea, because they may be the only people who have the knowledge and experience to question your architects' concepts.

> Little white lies may make the world go more smoothly in many areas of life, but the only way architecture succeeds is if all issues are faced directly as soon as they emerge.

Occasionally, a firm of architects will provide both programming and design. *We think this is an extremely bad idea.* If your programmer is a librarian who has wide experience with library architecture rather than an architect, the program is more likely to be driven by functional needs. In addition, if your programmer and architects work independently rather than as members of the same firm, you will have a valuable second opinion on design concepts.

Having said all this, good architectural firms tend to welcome well-thought-out building programs because programs help them understand clients (and sometimes save them a lot of work).

B. Evaluation of Existing Structures

If you are considering remodeling and expanding your current library building, or converting a non-library structure to a library, one of the first and most important functions of your architect is evaluating your structure. Your programmers may have included evaluations in their reports, but these are likely to be from the point of view of effective library service. Your architects will add to this an evaluation of the library as a physical structure, including the opinions of professional engineers as needed.

If your architects disagree with the evaluations provided by your programmers, you need to sort this out with both parties as quickly as possible.

Among the many questions that need to be answered before buildings can be considered for expansion are:

- The physical stability of the structure. Engineers will examine footings, the condition of walls, windows, roof, and so on. For example, if brick walls need to be completely reworked, the cost of moving into an existing building can be greatly increased.
- Floor strength. Library buildings require greater floor strength than almost any other type of structure. In particular, if a non-library building is being considered for conversion to a library, an evaluation of floor strength is vital. Outside of slab-on-grade structures, few non-library buildings are strong

enough. In addition, *some* libraries have floors that are strong enough to hold books in some places but not in others, and you need to find this out immediately.
- Problems with water infiltration. One of the most serious problems with buildings is water. Your architects will inspect your roof, walls, windows, and foundations. They will check the condition of flashings, caulking, mortar, and other elements that resist water problems. If you have maintained your building properly, you will be aware of many of these, but lots of library buildings have structural problems that have been politely ignored. It's important that you tell your architects about any problems your library has had with water infiltration and what was done about them.
- EPA problems that will require expensive remediation, such as asbestos and lead paint. EPA issues will apply not only to existing structures but also to undeveloped sites, particularly sites that have had previous uses. (Typically, your architects will arrange for inspections for asbestos and lead paint by licensed third-party firms.)
- The condition of MEP systems. Remember that the cost of mechanical, electrical, and plumbing systems can be about 40 percent of the cost of building a library, and HVAC alone about 25 percent. In many older buildings, all MEP systems are obsolete and will need to be replaced.
- Conformance with local zoning. Zoning is not usually a major problem for libraries that are government-owned, but you still need to face problems before you begin spending serious money. For example, if you intend to open a small coffee shop in your new library, zoning may have to be altered to make this retail function legal. If your building is in a residential neighborhood, height and setback regulations may apply. In many cases, zoning may specify required off-street parking. And so on.
- Conformance with current building codes. Because codes are numerous, overlapping, and frequently updated, your building may no longer be entirely legal. This is the time to find this out and to look at the legal implications of expansion.
- Whether your building currently meets codes but will not do so if it is expanded. For example, if expansion will increase your building from 10,000 to 15,000 square feet, you will probably need to retrofit a sprinkler system to the entire building.
- Although zoning can sometimes be negotiated, most governments will be unyielding when it comes to code compliance for a public building as heavily used as a library.

Your architects' findings at this stage of your project can have a major impact on your planning. If, for example, you will be required to bring your building up to code requirements when you expand it, it may prove to be massively expensive to do so. Or bringing the building up to code may compromise the design features that made people want to expand the building rather than just start over.

See chapter 13 on "Remodeling and Expanding Library Buildings."

C. Feasibility Studies

Owners sometimes ask architects to conduct separate studies evaluating whether specific buildings can be converted or specific sites utilized.

Even if certain ideas are obviously preposterous, you may still need to check them out in order to convince your community that you have checked all possible options. People often turn up and accuse libraries of not considering specific options, and it helps a great deal to be able to say, "Our architects checked this possibility, and we had to reject it for the following reasons."

Feasibility studies are a valuable architectural service. If you are doing much more than a series of quick trial sketches, you should expect to pay extra, particularly if there have to be a large number of studies or if they have to be very detailed.

Feasibility studies cannot be undertaken before programs are prepared. The whole point of a study is to explore whether a specific building or site can be used for your library, and this cannot be done until your architects have detailed information on what kind of library you need.

D. Schematic Design

The standard AIA (American Institute of Architects) contracts divide architectural services for building projects into five steps:

1. Schematic design
2. Design development
3. Construction documents
4. Bidding
5. Construction administration

Bidding and construction administration are covered in chapter 12 on "Construction."

Schematic design involves the basic decisions about how the building will solve the problems described in detail in the building program. By the end of the schematic design phase, the owner will have received:

- Floor plans (with furniture layouts, which are absolutely essential).
- Elevations (drawings of the building's exterior seen squarely from each side).
- Cross-sections if needed to clarify the proposed structure of the building.
- Outline specifications (a description of the major systems, materials, and quality standards anticipated for the project. Systems include such items as structure type, MEP, and enclosure—walls, windows, roofs, etc.)
- A preliminary cost estimate. It's important that costs be project costs, not just the much lower construction costs. Project costs will include such items as furnishings, site work, fees, contingencies, and escalation (estimated inflation in costs by the time the project is bid).

Some architects contend that furniture layouts are part of design development rather than schematic design, and your agreement with your architects must make clear that furniture layout is part of schematic design. Without furniture layouts, a schematic design for the public areas of a library can be basically a big empty rectangle. You will have no idea of how book stacks, seating, workstations, and service desks fit into the space, or even *if* they fit the space.

Some architects propose oddly shaped spaces that actually have the right square footage but won't hold the furnishings listed in your program. By insisting that the schematic design include all furnishings, you will protect yourself from embarrassing news later.

The understanding that furniture layout is included in schematic design should be made clear in your written contract. When you are dealing with architects, watch carefully that required furnishings are not altered in the schematic design. Rectangular tables must not be converted to square or (even worse) round tables. Double-faced shelving units must not be converted to single-faced units. Square footages must not be altered without discussion involving owners, architects, and consultants.

> Fred has experienced such problems as oddly shaped spaces and missing furniture layouts repeatedly during the schematic design phases of various building projects.

Architects will want to know at the schematic design stage whether you plan to seek a LEED rating for your library, since that has implications for building design and costs. (LEED stands for Leadership in Energy and Environmental Design.)

By the time schematic designs are complete, owners have enough information to raise money. They can show donors or voters what the building will look like and be able to tell them what it is likely to cost.

For this reason, most owners temporarily stop architectural services at the end of the schematic design phase.

Although schematic design is supposedly only about 15 percent of total architectural services, it involves many of the most important decisions on a project, and it can often cost more, particularly because *schematic designs for libraries must include furniture layout*. Projects involving complex remodeling of existing structures can also cost more. Because of both of these factors, it's can be reasonable for schematic design charges to be about 20 percent.

In preparing schematic designs, architects should meet extensively with owners and staff to study ways in which the functional requirements in the building program can be converted into actual designs. Even for a very small library, this can involve several long meetings.

Having your building consultant (programmer) attend design meetings will do a great deal to speed the process, avoiding wasted meetings where the architect brings designs to a library board, the board approves one, the programmer later points out serious functional problems, the architect then redraws the design, and on and on. Some of the most successful design meetings we have seen involve four critical groups sitting around the same table at the same time: owners, library staff, architects, and building consultant.

One popular method of developing design ideas is a process called a "charette." In a charette, architects will lead group discussions, posting all sorts of ideas in the form of quick sketches all over the walls of a room.*

Charettes provide a great way of getting a lot of ideas into print quickly.

Charettes also have a downside. Some suggestions made in haste during the enthusiasm of a charette may be regretted later in the cold light of the morning after. If the architects treat the outcome of a charette as the final word, ill-considered ideas may be difficult to eliminate.

---

*"Charette" is a French word for "cart." Its application to architecture comes from the concept of tossing all sorts of ideas into a cart.

Another method used by some architects is to create a series of cutout squares, perhaps mounted on foam core board, each representing the size of an element described in the building program. By pushing the blocks around, library staff and owners can theoretically try out various arrangements of components. (We don't think it works very well, because few spaces in finished buildings are squares. But it's probably fun.)

Some architects lead off the design process by asking owners to list words that describe the library the owners want. The result may be a dozen or two dozen words, ranging (as possible examples) from "traditional" to "friendly," "important," "spacious," "inspiring," "permanent," and "educational." And so on. We've seen this done frequently. It may help designers get a feel for what you want, but it may also be just a way to get conversation started.

Unfortunately, sometimes the importance of the words themselves as objects takes over in the minds of the owners. When libraries make their descriptive words permanent parts of their new buildings, things have gotten seriously out of hand.

All schematic designs should always progress through a series of steps, from simple layout concepts to more carefully developed floor plans. Architects should begin with a large number of rough concept sketches, showing how various approaches might work. Many ideas can be discarded at this point, but you'll want to keep all of the sketches so you have a response to people who propose design ideas that you've rejected for good reason.

Beware, beware of architects who want to present finished floor plans as the first drawings you see. Starting with finished drawings tends to stifle discussion and move things along too quickly. If architects are working on a flat fee basis, starting out with a finished drawing may save the architects' time and improve their income per hour, but it's a major disservice to the client. When the first thing a client sees is a finished drawing, the tendency is to get hung up on discussions of small details rather than of basic conceptual issues.

Architects who skip preliminary sketches and begin with semifinished drawings are not earning their money and are stifling the proper consideration of options. It's intimidating to find yourself looking at a finished drawing and realize that you need to reject the entire thing. The mere fact that the drawing is elegant is no reason to accept it. If you feel it doesn't meet your needs, you need to say so immediately, even if it means tossing out a finished-looking piece of work.

In all dealings with architects, it's vital to stop ideas you dislike as soon as possible. The longer your architects work with an idea, the more time and imagination and money they will have invested in the concept, and the harder it will be for them to abandon it. If things you don't like go on too long, the architects' time has been wasted, and that's not fair to them.

Occasionally, you may deal with architects who essentially refuse to abandon design concepts you dislike. You need to put a stop to this quickly and firmly. We've seen stubbornness over design ideas lead to the dismissal of architects, and you should be prepared to do so if your architects consistently ignore your instructions. Luckily, things seldom get to this point.

You have a right to expect technical explanations from your architects. If you ask for a specific feature and your designers say you can't have it, or if your designers propose something you don't like, it's completely reasonable to expect a full explanation.

> One librarian Fred knew had a great way with designers. Although she understood a great deal about construction, when she saw concepts with which she disagreed, she'd say something like, "I'm sorry, but I'm new at all this, and I really don't understand why it has to be this way. You'll have to take time to explain to me why we can't do things another way."

One thing that helps a great deal during the schematic design process is to ask your architects to provide a small chart comparing the space required for each major area of the library in the building program with the space provided in the design. Fred once worked with an architect who categorically refused to provide this information. The library board eventually severed the relationship.

At all meetings with your architects, someone must prepare minutes of the meeting. Typically, architects will prepare minutes and circulate them for signatures by the owners or other parties involved. We think it's a good practice for owners to do the same thing, making sure that things important to them are not omitted from the minutes, and also collecting signatures.

"Outline specifications" are summaries of the types of construction proposed. They may be as short as two or three pages for a relatively small project. They are important because the cost of buildings depends heavily on materials. If you've been thinking of a limestone exterior and the architect is thinking of precast concrete or even EIFS (external insulation finishing systems—basically a skim coat of mortar over Styrofoam), you need to know this right away.

Cost estimating is vital at every stage of a design project and should become more accurate at the end of each stage—schematic design, design development, and construction documents. When you are researching possible architectural firms to hire, their track records in cost estimating are of serious importance.

Some designers will attempt to present schematic designs without furniture placement. Because libraries consist of a lot of big, open spaces with furniture, schematic designs without furnishings are worthless.

In the trade, schematic design is often referred to as "SD," as in "We're in SD right now."

E. Estimating

Accurate cost estimating can make the difference between joyous and miserable construction.

By the time bidding takes place, you will have found your site, presented your plans to your public, lined up your funding, completed your construction documents, and be ready to go. If your low bid is triple your estimate, there is no way that omitting some add alternates will fix things. You will then be faced with returning to your funding source, completely redesigning your library, or some other desperate measure. If donors find out that their gifts will purchase only a third of what they were promised, they may decide to skip the whole thing. If you have government grants, you may find yourself trapped in situations where you are required to start construction by a specific date or lose the grants.

Total screwups in estimating don't often happen, but even minor screwups can lead to major problems. (Buildings that cost three times the estimated amount sound impossible, but it happened to a library Fred knows.)

Because of the critical importance of estimating, many architects use separate estimating firms or rely on construction management firms for help. Estimating firms have a reputation for being hard-nosed rather than optimistically hopeful that things won't be too expensive, and that's a good reason to use them.

As we've mentioned in other places in this book, it's vital that everyone agrees on what "budget" means. Actual construction is only one part of the cost of building a new library. Be sure everyone agrees that all budget numbers discussed will be for a "project budget" or "comprehensive budget," including not only construction but all the other inevitable costs, including site work, permits, furnishings, professional fees, contingencies, utility connections, moving, and so on. If the project won't start in the near future, budgets need to provide for escalation—expected inflation in costs. Construction costs alone may be interesting to know in an abstract sort of way, but they aren't helpful in planning.

As an unusually competent architect friend of Fred's says, "Estimate early and estimate often."

F. Assistance with Fundraising

Many architects are skilled in helping clients make presentations to donors or to voters.

Architects are very aware that buildings can't be constructed without funds, and that their incomes and reputations depend on the completion of projects. Having a resume consisting only of schematic designs for structures that were never built does not indicate a successful architectural firm.

1. Renderings

Many architects will prepare renderings, which are pretty pictures of completed buildings. These are vital for elections and donors because relatively few people can look at architectural drawings and visualize the resulting structure. Even owners who work extensively with architects may be surprised by the way things actually look.

Preparing renderings used to be a job for highly skilled artists who could see in their minds' eyes how completed buildings would look, but the coming of computer-aided drawing and design changed all of that, and modern design systems can easily show you how buildings will look from a wide variety of angles of view and perspectives.

One of the downsides of computer-generated renderings is that they can look very mechanical and even stilted. But they have the advantage of costing very little extra. Computerized drawing programs can provide people, automobiles, landscaping, flagpoles, blue skies with white clouds, and other persuasive details.

Many architectural firms will use computers to generate drawings with the proper perspective and then redo them in a more artistic medium, typically with hand-drawn lines and soft watercolors rather than hard computer colors. This can be expensive, but the artistic images can exert a powerful appeal that computer-generated images cannot.

One of the major criticisms of renderings is their tendency to lie attractively. The used car lot next to the library site is magically transformed into virgin woodland. The ungainly HVAC penthouse on the roof of the library conveniently vanishes. If the front of the library will actually be butted against the curb, the rendering may include an elegant but imaginary expanse of green lawn between the library and the street.*

The problem with misrepresentation in renderings is that people may call you on them. You hope this happens only after the building is completed, but it's embarrassing to be caught lying when a tax referendum is just around the corner.

A similar problem occurs because most completed library buildings do not match the renderings exactly. Since renderings will usually be prepared at the end of the schematic design phase, the actual buildings are likely to be somewhat different. However, this seems to be a much less severe problem than deliberate misrepresentation.

Because renderings are never exactly like the finished buildings, some people argue they should be vague. But users need to see what they'll get.

The power of renderings is impressive. People who look at floor plans and elevation drawings may say, "Very nice," in a controlled sort of way. But when shown the same thing in perspective as a rendering, they cry, "That's what we want!"

2. Models

Some library construction projects, particularly those that require fundraising or referendums or competitions, also include models.

Architectural models can be lovely objects and persuasive when it comes to convincing people that their money will be well spent on the new library. Some models even have lift-off roofs to allow people to see the interiors of buildings.

In design competitions, models are of critical importance, and they may be required as elements of submissions.

Models are sometimes displayed in libraries at times leading up to referendums. Others migrate about like garden gnomes, sitting in windows of local businesses, attending PTA meetings, and so on.

---

*These are common misrepresentations in renderings, all drawn from Fred's consulting experience. In the case of the green lawn, the architect angrily insisted it would be there when the building was finished. But it wasn't.

Architectural models are impressively expensive. A simple model of a small library may cost as little as $5,000, but a large model of a major structure may cost $50,000 or more. Many models are displayed in custom-made enclosures of heavy transparent plastic.

Simple models can be built in architectural offices, but large models are often built by firms that specialize in architectural models.

Even transporting large architectural models is difficult. We hear of them being transported in vans or occupying a couple of first-class seats in airplanes.

Once the building is constructed, the owners have to decide what to do with the models. Many of them kick around library administrative workrooms, protected by their original transparent plastic boxes. Others—particularly those from design competitions—end up on permanent display. Because models are extremely expensive, no one wants to chuck them out. (And most are too stylized to serve as scenery on model railroad layouts.)

Make sure your contracts with your architects specify who owns the models when the project is completed.

3. Participation in Public Meetings

Architects are often gifted at making public presentations. This is particularly true of those architects who specialize in representing architectural firms at job interviews. Having your architect attend public meetings can add a strong dimension to your presentation, as can having your consultant present. In fact, having your consultant first describe your needs at a meeting, and then having your architects show the proposed building and explain how it will enable the library to meet its needs, can make an effective presentation.

Always find out in advance what your architects and consultants will charge you for attending meetings of this type.

4. Responding to Questions from the Media

Architects often deal effectively with reporters because the information they have does not have to be filtered through the owners of the building.

And, as mentioned repeatedly in this book, architects can explain why the beloved ideas of some local people won't work, secure in the knowledge that the architects do not live in town and won't have to confront angry faces at the next Rotary meeting.

Dealing with the media requires spokespeople who are knowledgeable and not given to off-the-cuff responses. Your library will want to designate a small number of people who respond to media questions and tell other participants that all questions will be handled by this group.

G. Design Development

The second phase of architectural work as specified in AIA contract documents is design development.

From the point of view of the community, this is a far less exciting time than schematic design, because most decisions about room arrangement and exterior appearance have already been made.

In design development, a wide range of technical decisions are made. What kind of physical structure will the library have? How will the HVAC system work? How will the building be lighted? What provisions will be made for electrical power? How will foundation problems be dealt with? And on and on.

If schematic design is typically only about 15 percent of total architectural services, design development is 20 percent. Sleazy architectural firms will sometimes skip design development and move from schematic design straight to construction drawings. Don't put up with this (and don't put up with a firm that wants to do it).

Even if the questions raised for design development may not excite the outside world, from the owners' point of view they are of major importance, and you should expect to be deeply involved in the planning that moves your project through design development. It is here that functional or dysfunctional lighting can be selected. Electrical outlets can be plentiful, or they can be so few that users will be tripping over laptop cords everywhere. The floors can be solid, or they can bounce underfoot because of HVAC plenums beneath. West-facing windows may have perforated vinyl blinds, or they may have partial fritting (patterns of printed dots) that results in spotty but blinding glare.

If your building program is a complete one, it should have some information on what technical solutions are of particular importance to libraries, but vast areas of decision making will be left to the architects and their engineers to develop and make recommendations.

Librarians should approve design development documents, just as they approve schematic designs. You can also involve your programmers.

Just as schematic design is often referred to as "SD," design development is called "DD."

H. Construction Documents

Construction documents are used by contractors both for preparing bids for constructing your building and for actually constructing the building. The documents typically include both a set of drawings and a book of specifications.

Construction drawings are grouped by the area of construction they represent. Some groups of sheets may be prepared by engineers or other specialists, rather than by your architects. Individual drawings are often identified first by the series (such as A for architectural, M for mechanical, etc.) and second by the number in the series.

Typically, a set of drawings might include:

- A cover sheet, identifying the library and listing all the drawings that comprise the complete set.
- Site plans, showing how the library building will occupy its site.
- Structural drawings.
- Architectural drawings, including elevations, floor plans, footing plans, reflected ceiling plans, roof plans, framing plans, construction details, cross-sections, and so on.
- Plumbing drawings, showing the details of installation of fixtures, diagrams of piping, and so on.
- Sprinkler system drawings. (Fire-suppression systems are typically specified separately and installed by specialist contractors.)
- HVAC drawings, showing the location and sizes of HVAC ductwork, heating and cooling equipment, and so on.
- Electrical drawings, including lighting, switching, power distribution, communications, fire alarms, and so on.
- Furniture layouts should be included for informative purposes to remind everyone where things will go, even though furnishings will be bid separately. (These are left out of some sets of construction drawings, making the drawings far harder to interpret.)

For remodeling work, there will also be:

- Drawings of the existing building. This is an area where rushed work by architects can lead to problems if they use surviving original plans that may

not represent what was actually built or what has been changed since the building was new.
- Demolition drawings, showing which existing parts of the building need to be removed during the construction process.

Remodeling is amazingly complex, and it's reasonable for your architects to charge a higher percentage of construction costs for remodeling than for new construction.

Although construction drawings do not typically include furniture placement drawings, it's a very good thing to specify that a sheet showing furniture placement be part of the construction drawing set. Because libraries frequently consist of large open spaces, knowing how the furniture will fit is vital. (Such drawings will be marked as for information only, since your construction firm will generally not supply your furniture.)

The preparation of construction documents is an immense job because nothing can be left vague or uncertain. If your library is requesting competitive bids, each prospective bidder must sift through the drawings and specifications, asking how the building can be built for the least possible cost while still meeting specifications. If there is a nice feature you want, but it's not in the drawings or specifications, you won't get it.

Because of the amount of labor involved, construction drawings are assumed to be about 40 percent of the entire cost of architectural services.

Modern construction drawings are prepared by computer, with much of the work done by young architects and engineers who grew up using computer design systems.

Almost all construction drawings are created by computer. CADD systems (computer-aided drawing and design) have been around since the 1970s, and these have frequently been updated to BIM systems (building information management). BIM systems have the added advantages of keeping better track of competing locations for ductwork, wiring, and plumbing. They also make it easy to generate lists of materials in buildings, which in turn help with accurate cost estimating.

Much of a bid set or construction set is not drawings. Specifications, contained in a "project manual," are verbal instructions on material selection, installation processes, and quality assurance standards. Assembling the specifications should involve as much participation by the library as the construction drawings.

All planned items of manufactured equipment, such as light fixtures, plumbing fixtures, and so on will be illustrated with catalog pages called "cut sheets." Insist on seeing all of these before they are included in your bid documents.

Often the specifications will include two or three acceptable brand names and model numbers for each item required. This promotes competition, which helps to control prices. The acceptable models, however, should not lead to sacrifice of performance or durability. If different items are proposed, be sure you receive and approve cut sheets.

State or local laws may require that the owners accept alternative equivalent products in addition to those specified. Be sure to require that any substitution of equipment proposed by the bidder or contractor includes the provision of new cut sheets for your approval. The burden of proof in establishing equivalence is on the contractor. Serious problems can result when a contractor talks the owners or architects into using an inferior product, claiming it is an "equivalent."

Be sure that your library building consultants (programmers) see all the construction documents and let you know if they see any potential problems. Let your architects know that you want your consultants to see the drawings, and insist that your architects leave enough time for this to take place. Occasionally, your architects may contend that there is "no time" for your consultants to review drawings, and you will need to refer your architects to your prior agreements.

The next steps in your project and your use of the building for decades to come depends on the quality of your construction documents. Thorough review is essential.

As chapter 12 indicates, the construction drawings are the basis for "shop drawings" for construction details or for individual pieces of equipment supplied by outside firms. These may include structural steel, hand railings, cabinetry, and many other areas. Architects approve large numbers of shop drawings during the course of a project and initial them to indicate their approval.

If you don't keep an eye on first the construction drawings and then the shop drawings, as they are submitted, you may have unwelcome surprises when these components are actually installed. Your arrangement with your architects should include your notification of all approved and initialed shop drawings, plus photocopies of selected initialed shop drawings for the library's records. (Among other things, the copies of *initialed* drawings assure you that your architects haven't fallen behind and letting approval of shop drawings slide.)

III. HIRING AN ARCHITECT

Finding and hiring the best architects for your project is one of the most critical tasks facing library owners. If you hire the right architects, the whole process can be relatively straightforward and extremely rewarding. By the end of many projects, librarians are convinced that their architects can walk on water (or at least barely get their ankles wet).

But with the wrong architects—firms that know little about libraries (and don't admit it), ignore your requirements, fight you at every turn, or let cute design enthusiasms overcome functionality—the experience can be miserable.

A substantial number of architects specialize in library buildings, and this can be very much to your advantage. Although architects who know little or nothing about libraries can design functional libraries, they have a great deal to learn on the job, and you may wish they hadn't done so at your expense on your project.

If your architects don't bring significant knowledge of libraries to the job, you will need other people who have this knowledge. The most common people are your library building consultants, who you will probably need to attend many design meetings. Some libraries also hire "owner's representatives" with extensive experience in library design to provide this double-checking.

One major problem is that some architects are unwilling to admit that any special knowledge is required to design a library. This is why it's so very important to do extensive research on the prior work of firms before selecting one.

> The approach of some architects to library design reminds us of someone's comments on women's shoes in Britain: "They look like they were designed by someone who had often heard women's shoes described but had never actually seen one."

One of the main reasons to hire architects with little or no library experience is because you want to hire local architects. In situations like this, local architects without library experience frequently form "teams" with out-of-town architects who are library specialists. The local architects serve as the local point of contact and are always nearby during construction when things go wrong, but the out-of-town library architects are present during the design process to be sure that good library practices are followed. Working with teams is not always a great experience; see the later section in this chapter on "Special Problems with Teams."

Special and school libraries, of course, frequently have to deal with architects who have no particular knowledge of libraries, because the library is just one small element of a much larger project. In this case, having a very detailed building program ready before design work begins is particularly vital—as is finding a way to make sure that the architects pay attention to your program. Having your consultant around may also help, particularly if you have your consultant play the "bad librarian" role and fight the architects and administrators when dysfunctional library design ideas are proposed.

Some states have very specific laws concerning how public bodies hire architects. Your state library may have this information, or if you have in-state consultants, those people may know. When in doubt, you need to check with your attorney.

> Good librarians can be annoying to those architects who start off with little intention of listening to them. One architect who specializes in schools told Fred that school librarians were the hardest crowd to deal with during school design. Fred cheered, but to himself, in a polite sort of way.

A. Locating Architectural Firms

Typically, architectural firms keep a constant ear to the ground. If you are considering a new or expanded library building, many firms will find out about it through the grapevine.

Many state library agencies keep lists of library architects, and these can be a useful starting point. Such lists, however, often contain all firms known to have designed libraries in the state. Because the lists are not evaluative, they may not be of much help until you get to know the individual libraries personally.

Many librarians rely on word of mouth from other libraries. A morning on the telephone, calling libraries that have recently completed buildings, may give you a quick idea of who the major players are, including which architects librarians tend to like and which ones they dislike. Be careful at this point, however, since many librarians are in love with their new buildings—even buildings that are surprisingly badly designed—while other librarians can be crabby about reasonably workable projects.

Independent library building consultants are also good sources of information, since they spend much of their time with library buildings and keep up with library architects.

One of the potential dangers for library building consultants is their developing overly close ties with architects, since they may see them on many successive jobs. Consultants work for owners and should always take the owners' sides and be deeply committed to the owners' needs, even when the architects involved are old friends. It's good to ask other libraries about this when you're hiring a consultant.

Many architects have booths in the exhibit halls at state library conferences, and you can make contact with excellent firms this way. Since architects usually practice regionally, you are more likely to encounter them at state than at national conferences, unless this year's national conference happens to be in your part of the country.

Unlike, for example, some insurance or copy machine salespeople, architects are generally too civilized to seize you by the arm and draw you into the dark recesses of their exhibit hall booths at library conferences. But they will be interested, friendly, receptive, and given to keeping in touch extensively after they meet you.

Libraries can publish advertisements indicating their interest in hiring architects. Depending on the laws in your state, government-owned libraries may be required to do so.

For all architects, one of the biggest challenges in the profession is actually getting the job—beating out other firms for commissions. Once hired, relatively few are fired, even on those occasions when they thoroughly deserve it. Because of the critical importance of getting commissions in the first place, some architects spend a lot of money on marketing.

B. Investigating the Prior Work of Architectural Firms

Before you send out requests for proposals to architectural firms, or after you've received proposals from firms you don't know, you want to conduct personal research on the work of the architects you are considering.

Librarians have a tremendous advantage here because they tend to have long-term, friendly social contacts in the profession. If you are evaluating an architectural firm that specializes in libraries, there's a good chance that someone you've known for years has worked with the firm.

This is why it's important to have the right people call references. Library directors speaking with library directors are more likely to get a straight response, because none of us likes lying to friends and colleagues.

However, it's sometimes very hard for directors who had libraries built under their aegis to admit that things went badly. In this case, a tour that includes informal conversations with rank-and-file staff may lead you to hear about features that everyone hates. We've both had experiences touring new libraries where the directors were busy telling us how well everything worked while staff members were muttering about major dysfunctions. (At one major library conference, staff members giving tours of a new library building had to admit to using flashlights to read call numbers in the stacks.)

Your library building consultants can organize tours of appropriate library buildings.

For a different and useful view of libraries, it can be a very good idea to have your maintenance staff call the maintenance people at libraries designed by the architects you are considering hiring. Your maintenance people are the ones likely to hear about light bulbs that can't be changed, floor coverings that are impossible to clean, and other expensive maintenance miseries.

Your consultant may also help you evaluate firms, but consultants have to work with architects, and you should expect quiet private comments rather than loud public comments.

> Consultants are nervous about this sort of thing. Once Fred worked for a library board that pressured him for comments on a specific architectural firm. After they promised him they would never tell anyone what he said, he said some bluntly negative things, and the board didn't interview the firm. When the head of the architectural firm asked why the firm wasn't being interviewed, the board said, "Fred told us not to."

You can learn a lot about architects by visiting their libraries, and that's an important part of fact-finding. A good firm, however, can deliver a variety of building styles, so it's dangerous to base your entire opinion of a firm on one building you think looks a little weird. If you don't like the aesthetics of a building, consider that the architects may have done their best to give the clients what they wanted.

While you're visiting a library, ask staff members about how the project went. Did the architects listen to them when they made suggestions? Did the architects have pet ideas and refuse to abandon them? Did the architects know anything about libraries, and, if not, were they aware of the fact?

It always helps to look for some of the architectural features that make good libraries:

- Good sight lines for library staff, including lots of interior glass partitions
- Long-term flexibility of use
- Single public entrances
- Easy navigation
- Impressive numbers of electrical outlets, including the tops of all reading tables and in the middle of open floors
- Soft, bright lighting
- Pleasant places to sit
- Comfortable acoustics
- North light
- Blinds on all exterior glass that faces any direction except north (including tiny blinds on tiny areas of glass)
- Light fixtures that are easy to reach
- Adequate staff workspaces
- Adequate storage space

You can also carry a checklist of architectural ideas that almost always cause problems in libraries. It's probably safe to assume that when you find these in a library, most of them were suggested by architects rather than librarians. Common errors in library architecture are mentioned throughout this book, but here for quick reference are a few of the worst (and—unfortunately—most beloved by designers):

- Atriums
- Skylights
- Balconies
- Courtyards
- Reading terraces
- Indoor water features
- Non-rectangular rooms
- Monumental staircases that cause functional problems with such features as oddly shaped steps, open risers, places beneath to bump one's head, overly large openings that transmit sound between floors, and so on

- Features that terrify people with acrophobia
- Railings that can be climbed like ladders
- Architecturally mounted task lighting
- Intense downlights, including recessed downlights of all sorts
- Soffits that determine the location of service desks
- Perimeter soffits
- Dark ceilings (except for historic ceilings)
- Non-acoustic ceilings (except, again, for historic ceilings)
- Insufficient electrical outlets
- Windows of any size, shape, or height that can admit direct sunlight but don't have blinds

All of these are covered in detail in the chapters on

- Dysfunctional design ideas
- Evaluating libraries by walking through them.

C. Requests for Qualifications

When you are considering hiring an architect, a standard way to gather information is to formally request information from architectural firms. Most libraries will send out something variously identified as an RFP (request for proposals), RFI (request for information), or RFQ (request for qualifications).

When you send out an RFQ you embark on what sometimes approaches a game. You are trying to find out a number of things, while architects will try to convince you that whatever they have done in the past is exactly what you want.

Here's what you ideally want to know about each firm:

- **How much actual library work the firm has done**
  Finding this out can be surprisingly difficult, because firms tend to list every library they've ever touched, ranging from major new buildings designed and completed to preliminary studies for remodeling men's restrooms, when nothing was ever done. One way you can deal with this is to ask the firm to list only new library construction jobs or major library remodeling and expansion jobs. If you ask that all the projects be already completed, you will avoid a great many preliminary studies. But firms with little experience may dodge this question. Some firms will want to talk about buildings currently being designed or under construction. These may be interesting, but you can't drive over and take a look at them. And some turn out to be a lot less

fantastic when completed than when described. We suggest that when you schedule interviews, you ask to hear about finished projects only and avoid hearing about projects that are just in the planning stages. When two firms merge, even if their offices remain scattered across the nation, they often combine their lists of previous projects. For any firm with more than one office or with a recent merger, your job becomes one of finding out which people in the firm built its library reputation and whether those specific people will handle your project—or are even still with the firm. Some firms will include in their responses to your RFQ libraries that were worked on by the engineering firms they propose to work with. This information can be somewhat useful, but it can also be regarded as serious resume padding.

- **What people the firm is proposing to do your work**
  In your RFQ, you want to request specific biographical information on the people who will lead your project. In particular, you want to know about the "project architect." Who will be responsible for the actual work? Who will be present at all planning meetings? If the firm has an overworked star library designer, you sometimes need to watch out for "bait and switch" situations. The star attends the initial interview with the owners, but the rest of the crowd does the actual work. Often these stars have tremendous personal charisma, and you need to be wary of situations where you won't see much of them once the contracts with your architects are signed. You also want a list of the architects' subcontractors or sub-consultants. Common ones include engineers and estimators. Geotechnical engineers are frequently hired locally, because they know local soil conditions and have necessary equipment, but in many cases other engineers will be from out of town. (In architects' submissions, you will frequently see geotechnical engineers identified as "civil engineers," although civil engineering is actually a much broader field.) Increasingly, architects hire independent cost estimators, since the volatility of the construction business makes it hard to project costs accurately, and since owners seldom forget the experience of receiving a low bid three times larger than the estimate.

- **Whether the firm's clients are satisfied**
  Some architects will send photocopies of letters from clients. However, clients who like their architects socially can be "satisfied" with dysfunctional buildings, so you need to tread carefully.

- **How much work of this type the firm has done**
  As noted above, some firms list projects that no one currently associated with the firm ever worked on. When you have doubts, ask which member of the current staff was the project architect.

- **Whether the buildings the firm designs actually work**
  Instead of asking previous clients, "How do you like your architects?" ask "How do you like your building?" It also helps to ask specific questions. Do the staff members like their workspaces? Do users find the building confusing? Is it hard keeping an eye on things? Are there maintenance problems (such as difficulties maintaining light fixtures)? Is the building inflexible? Does it have problems with acoustics and with overly direct sunlight? Are people with acrophobia uncomfortable when using the building? Is energy usage exceptionally high? What was the most frustrating thing about your experience constructing this building? Because owners are typically in love with their new buildings, it helps to visit and judge for yourself. If the building is brand-new, try to see past the gleam of fresh carpet and clean paint and look for places where trouble can occur. Directors of new libraries can actually be extraordinarily defensive. On several occasions, we've asked whether a specific feature causes trouble, and the director's response has been a completely irrelevant, "You should have seen our old building!" or "But it's so much better than what we had before!" Don't buy into this kind of talk. Successful building design is not a relative thing. A bad design is not better because your building used to be a lot worse.

- **Whether previous clients found the architects in the firm responsive to client requests. This is an extremely important point but sometimes a surprisingly difficult one to get at.**
  As a profession, architects have developed a reputation for being poor listeners. It's impressive how many times owners get into a situation where their architect appears with a design idea, the owners say "no," the architect returns with new drawings featuring the same idea, the owners say "no" again, and the architect ignores them and brings back the same idea a third time.

The architect for one library Fred worked with was in love with atriums. The first suggested design had an atrium. The board of trustees responded, "No atrium, please." The second design still had an atrium, but in a different location. Only mildly testy at this time, the board repeated, "No atrium." The cycle continued through *eight successive designs with eight different atriums*, until the board president, a woman given to modest speech, pounded her fist on the table in fury and shouted, "NO DAMN ATRIUM!" The architect's feelings were hurt. The ninth design had no atrium, but one could clearly see where an atrium could be inserted when the members of the board changed their minds. The board eventually found a different designer.

The moral is, when project architects ignore clients, it's time to talk with the firm bluntly about (a) whether the architect will follow the client's wishes, (b) whether the firm will assign a new architect, after that person meets with the client, or (c) whether the client will hire a new firm.

When you are interviewing firms, most will tell you what good listeners they are. Many may be. A few may not be. And some stress "good listening" because, as a group, architects can be notoriously bad listeners.

- **Whether artistic design tends to trump function**
Everyone wants library buildings that are great looking, but libraries have to function as well. To us, the real challenge of library design is having libraries that look great but also work well. A knock-your-socks-off library that doesn't do its job is a failure rather than a success. Library design awards are given for appearance rather than function, and this is a good reason to pay only limited attention to them. It's also a good reason to ignore publications that consist just of pretty pictures of new library buildings.

- **Whether the firms tend to have an excessive number of change orders due to sloppy preparation of construction drawings**
Change orders are due to many things, and many of them are no fault of the architect. Innocent change orders are particularly prevalent in remodeling, where unexpected problems are frequently found when walls are opened. Other innocent change orders are frequently due to clients changing their minds. Sometimes this happens only after a feature is constructed and the owners shout, "What is this? We hate it." (One could also argue, of course, that if owners are that surprised, *their* architects failed in their communication roles.) Other change orders result from extra money. If bids come in unusually low, a library may decide to add extra features, and these may appear as change orders. But other change orders are the result of total designer screwups. If the construction drawings are simply wrong, or if features everyone agreed on turn out to be missing, it's the architect's fault. Omissions may not be a big deal if the missing items can be added later at no extra cost. But changes that are necessary and expensive and leave the library with nothing extra should be regarded by architects as their personal responsibility. Omissions that can be rectified later by simply adding things rather than also ripping things out are sometimes called "betterments." The general idea is that under betterment situations owners are not paying for things twice. They just didn't get them the first time around. The implication is that owners should have to pay for things that were never in the original construction contracts. The problem occurs when adding things retrospectively costs a lot more than if they had been included up front in the original contract. At what point should architects be held responsible for the extra cost of what amounts to a change order rather than part of a competitive low bid? At any rate, what you want to find out is: If your architects get you

into alteration trouble because of careless work, will the firm take fiscal responsibility for the extra costs? Unfortunately, very few do.

In interviews with prospective firms, try a question on the order of, "If you specify the wrong size of window, and it doesn't fit the space where it goes, will your firm be responsible for the cost?"

> In one project John was involved with, the architects forgot to provide ventilation in a restroom. The result was grim. The architectural firm contended it was not at fault, but after strong words of the what-in-the-Sam-Hill-were-you-doing-designing-a-restroom-without-ventilation variety, they paid for retrofitting the proper ventilation.

Local contractors know which architectural firms tend to make a lot of errors in their drawings, and they may bid extra low to get a job, knowing that they're sure to make a good profit on change orders. If you have a connection among local contractors, you can ask them about the reputations of various architectural firms for accurate drawings.

- **Who the firm is proposing as the team to do your work**
  All but the tiniest of firms have several architects. If the firm's reputation as a library designer is based on the work of one or two architects, you may want to be sure that those particular people are on your job.

- **Who will do construction oversight?**
  In some firms, the project architect also takes the responsibility for ensuring that the building is being constructed in accordance with the drawings, but other firms have employees who provide this service. We think having the actual designers keep an eye on things works better because they know the actual design far better and they're more personally involved in the success of the project.

To get at this information, what can you ask for in your RFQ?

1. A list of completed projects, particularly libraries

This can be hard to get at, since project lists from architectural firms tend to be full of projects that involved remodeling a restroom, doing a preliminary study for construction that never took place, and so on.

One way to nail things down is to ask for (a) a list of library construction projects that are completed or under construction, (b) the scope of each project, (c) whether any other architectural firms were involved in each project, and (d) if other firms *were* involved, which firm was the lead architect.

Some firms submit impressively long project lists but have relatively few completed buildings. There's nothing necessarily wrong with this, but you want to know specifically about completed buildings.

2. Accreditation

If your state accredits architects for state work, you can ask firms for copies of their accreditation forms. Even if your library is not a state job, the state may have worked up some good ways of asking questions.

Architects who are members of the American Institute of Architects will consistently place "AIA" after their names. In most cases, you will want your project to be led by someone who is a member of the AIA.

You will occasionally see "FAIA" after the name of an architect. This stands for "Fellow of the American Institute of Architects." It's a major honor for architects to be named fellows, but it reflects more service to the AIA as an organization than architectural achievement, and you may wish not to be swayed by it.

Architects are licensed to practice in specific states. If the proposed project architect is not licensed to practice in your state, you will want to know what's going on.

If you plan to construct a LEED-certified building, you can specify LEED-accredited architects. Most architects with LEED accreditation put the initials "LEED" after their names, after "AIA."

3. A list of the people who will make up the team proposed for your project

For all the members of the team, you want to know their credentials, training, and personal experience.

You can also ask for a list of projects this specific team has completed. Known compatibility is important. (Fred has attended architect interviews with teams who scarcely had been introduced to each other before the interview.)

You should expect the relevant credentials for each individual team member.

4. As part of this list, specific information on who will be project architect

Watch out when responses to this question get vague, or firms say something like "In our firm, everyone works on everything." Someone has to take the lead, and if this is the first time for that person, you want to know it.

5. List of outside consulting professionals in the team

Few architectural firms have a wide range of engineering skills within the firm, and this is not a reason to discount the capabilities of the firm.

Among the firms you may find mentioned are structural engineers, mechanical engineers, geotechnical engineers, electrical engineers, lighting consultants, construction cost estimators, and so on. It's common that geotechnical engineers will be from your immediate area, because knowledge of soil, drainage, and local construction conditions is very much a local specialty, but the other firms will probably be from the architects' area and work with the architects on a regular basis.

Some architectural firms with little or no library experience will list the library experience of their engineering firms. This is relevant, but not very relevant, and you want to watch out for it.

Watch out in particular if an architectural firm lists your library building consultant as reporting to the firm. If this is how they're thinking, the result can be serious trouble, since they may hope to squelch people who disagree with them.

6. Directions on where to send copies of proposals

If your library building consultant will be participating in architect interviews—which is always a good idea—you will want to ask firms to send copies of their proposals to your consultant so that you don't have to repackage them and ship them yourself.

Also include the following specific information in your RFQ:

7. The specific day and time that proposals are due

Always make this time a time when your library will be open and staff members will be present to note when proposals turned up. "Midnight" is never a satisfactory time because you have no one present to receive and time stamp submissions. (This may seem a petty requirement, but in case of controversy, it's important to know who was on time and who was not. When it comes to formal bids of any kind, this information can have major importance.)

8. The number of firms you plan to interview

The right number of interviews is about four. In extreme circumstances (such as irresistible political pressure to interview a firm you wouldn't hire on a dare) you might have five interviews, but we don't recommend it.

If you plan to interview a large number of firms, it will make your job far less attractive to architects. When firms feel that there is little chance of being hired, they will be less likely to spend the money to submit credentials and attend your interviews.

If you try to interview too many firms, you will not give each firm enough time to make a good presentation. You may forget who said what. And you may be tempted to interview them over a period of days or weeks—always a bad approach, because the people doing the interviewing will not always be the same group, and the people doing the interviewing may forgot their impressions of some firms.

9. The day on which interviews will take place

The time to tell firms about interview schedules is far in advance, so that they can pencil the interviews into their calendars, and so the interview team will also commit to those times.

If you tell them at the last minute, you'll have a far poorer chance of interviewing every firm on the same day.

Don't schedule interviews for days when travel conditions are likely to be poor. Keep away from winter months if your part of the country has snow and ice in the winter.

By announcing interview times far in advance, you also prevent attempts by a handful of firms to angle to be the last firm interviewed. (Some firms feel that the last firm interviewed is the one most likely to be selected.)

We think it's also a good idea to let architects know that you are planning serious interviews, not twenty-minute wonders. If you say in your RFQ, for example, that ninety-minute interviews will be conducted at 9:00 a.m., 11:00 a.m., 1:30 p.m., and 3:30 p.m., architects will know they have a reasonable amount of time to describe themselves and their services, and that the half-hour break between interviews means they won't be treading on the heels of other firms.

10. Sources of additional information

Architects need to know where to go for additional information not included in your RFQ. Usually this is a hired professional—a library director, university architect, or similar. You want this to be a single person for consistency of responses. (You also want to warn your staff to refer all architect questions to this single person. Staff members making offhand and partially informed comments to architects who "stop by" can lead to problems.) So provide the mailing address, phone number, e-mail address, and so on of the person who will be available to answer questions.

Expect that architects who are seriously interested in your project will want to *visit* your library for a tour and conversation. This is a very reasonable request, and you should make time available.

You should also offer to provide interested architects with copies of your building program, including contact information for your building consultant. (Since architects routinely contact consultants, you will want to let your consultant know if you would prefer to handle all contacts with architects personally. Most consultants will be happy to simply tell architects that questions are being handled by the library, but you have to warn your consultant in advance.)

D. Proposals from Architectural Firms

Most architectural firms will send you elaborate pamphlets in response to your requests for proposals. Most of these are plastic spiral-bound and in full color.

Proposals will include photos and resumes of key staff members, with specifics about their professional experience. Proposals will also include pictures and floor plans of completed projects, information on the firms' track records in the areas of accurate estimating and change orders, statements of design philosophies (which are pretty much slogan writing), and other materials.

Many firms will provide an organizational chart of the planning team. This will help clarify the relationships. It can also warn you of potential problems if people you regard as reporting to you directly (such as your building consultant) appear in the chart as reporting to the architects.

We strongly recommend that you request physical copies of proposals rather than electronic copies, and that if you need up to a dozen or so copies, you expect architects to provide them. To avoid handling problems, include in your requirements that each firm send a *hard* copy of its proposal directly to your consultant.

E. Special Problems with Teams

Some architects submit proposals involving multi-firm teams. "Teaming" is standard jargon in the field, although not necessarily grammatically elegant.

A common multi-firm team arrangement involves local architects with little library experience and an out-of-town firm with more experience.

Multi-firm teams can be great, especially if the out-of-town firm is experienced and plays a major role in the work.

However, we often suspect that the team is formed for reasons of competition with other firms, not because the local architects have any doubts about their ability to design a library all by themselves. The local firm needs the out-of-town firm's credentials to get the job, but it may plan to use the out-of-town firm as little as possible thereafter.

What can you ask when faced with a team proposal?

- Have the two firms ever worked together before? If this is a first time, it may be a marriage of cynical convenience in order to line up a job in a competitive environment rather than a healthy working relationship.
- Which specific people are the members of the team?
- How much will you see the out-of-town firm during the project? We've seen situations where the out-of-town firm attended a single meeting and never turned up again. You should expect the out-of-town firm to be present in particular for all schematic design meetings.
- What is the implication of the team for your costs? Will the two firms be willing to split a reasonable fee, or will they want extra money? Will the out-of-town firm expect expensive travel costs to be paid as a reimbursable item? We prefer the situation where the out-of-town firm is listed as a consultant to the local architect, since that clarifies the relationship.

> Unfortunately, in some cases the out-of-town expert is mostly window dressing. The one time that Fred teamed with an architect, it turned out that the architect needed Fred's credentials to get the job, but thereafter he expected Fred to shut up while the architect informed the client about all things library. When Fred sent a report to the architect, the architect simply deep-sixed it and told the client the opposite. In desperation, Fred sent a report directly to the library. The architect then screamed at Fred over the phone, claiming that Fred had no right to speak with the client. And the team ended.

Sometimes mild confusion occurs because the word *team* is used in slightly different ways by architects. Some architectural firms will refer to the group that will be assigned to your project as a "team," while other firms talk about working with a second firm as "teaming." (From a purely grammatical point of view, we think "teaming" is an embarrassment, but this is probably a bad time to bring this up.)

F. Evaluating Proposals

Once the proposals have been received, typically representatives of the owner will evaluate them in order to select firms to be interviewed. Among the things you can look for are:

- Does the firm have a company style, or does it do a variety of different designs? There's absolutely nothing wrong with a company style if you like it, but if, for example, you think serpentine glass walls are too expensive (and they *are* expensive), you will in all likelihood be unhappy with a firm whose previous buildings all have serpentine glass walls.
- What kind of library experience does the firm have? Remember that you want to find out what library projects have been *completed,* or are at least under construction. And you want to know about new buildings or major expansion jobs, not minor remodeling. If your RFP is worded correctly, the proposal should contain this data.
- What library experience do the people in the team proposed for your project have? You particularly want to know about the project architect, the person who will be in charge of design on a daily basis. Sometimes it's hard to tell this from proposals, and that's a good time to ask the firm for *written* clarification. (It's perfectly fine to respond to architects' submissions with specific questions, particularly in areas such as prior experience with libraries, where firms can be amazingly evasive.)

Sorting out experience is much harder with very large firms, which may have library experience scattered among many offices and many architects. What you want to know is what *your* office and *your* architects have done.

This is also a time to start sorting out the working architects from the sales architects.

- Is the group proposing to replace your library building consultant with one of their own? This is a bad sign.
- Much of evaluation consists of contacting people listed under previous projects to see whether they are happy with the experience.

Because librarians are basically sweet people, it's sometimes hard to get unvarnished opinions. They may also be unwilling to say anything negative about their new library buildings.

A firm may feature two or three libraries, providing the names and phone numbers of directors. Call them, but also call libraries that are not featured, because they may be less successful projects.

Remember that more librarians like their architects than like their buildings. So it's always a good idea to ask about the building itself.

- Your gut reaction matters. If you find staff members of an architectural firm to be dishonest, bullying, evasive, or poisonously full of themselves, don't bother with an interview, because you would never want to work with them.
- If you haven't done so already, try to visit buildings designed by the firm in order to judge for yourself. This is especially important because many owners and directors may fail to level with you.

Take a copy of chapter 5 on "Evaluating Library Spaces by Walking Around" with you.

- Architectural firms with no library experience will sometimes argue that their lack of experience is a Good Thing. They may be right, but we don't think so.
- Ignore AIA awards and most other design awards. Although recognition from the American Institute of Architects and other groups is always impressive, these awards may not be for things you find important. If you want a library that is cozy, pleasant, functional, easy to maintain, architecturally in keeping with your community, and popular with your users, you will probably find that awards are not given for any of these attributes.

G. Interviews

The first and most important rule for interviewing architects is to strictly limit the number of interviews and provide enough time for each firm to make a reasonable presentation.

We recommend holding a maximum of four interviews. By the time you interview a firm, you should feel that the firm is a strong potential candidate. This is why it's essential to do your homework *before* scheduling interviews and select only firms you suspect would do good work for your library and would be a good fit.

One of the worst ways to interview architects is to run a large group of firms through at high speed, meeting a new firm every few minutes. This wastes the firms' time and money, and it gives you no time to evaluate them.

It costs architectural firms a substantial amount of money to attend interviews. The best firms are therefore much more likely to be interested in your project if they learn you plan to interview only three or four firms. This greatly increases their chance of being selected and makes the investment in the interview less of an expensive long shot.

Although you may assume that the large number of interviews is just the architects' problem, it can hurt you as well, because some of the best firms may simply lose interest if they learn that you plan to interview more than four or five.

For this reason, we think it's important to tell firms in your RFQ both when you plan to conduct interviews and how many firms you plan to meet.

Remember also that (as with marriages) there will be more than one firm out there with whom you could probably cohabit happily. By the time you interview, you should be feeling around for the best fit, not wasting everyone's time talking to firms you know you would never hire.

Any interview less than ninety minutes long is unfair to everyone concerned.

We recommend that you:

- Strictly limit the number of firms interviewed to about four. However, one thing that can occasionally lead to additional interviews is the presence of local firms that politics say must be interviewed but that the owners of the library don't want to hire. It may be better to interview an extra firm than to antagonize the local community. If a firm drops out at the last minute, invite another firm. You want to interview an absolute minimum of three firms.
- Interview all of your architectural firms in a single day. Among other things, this ensures that all members of the interview group will meet all of the architects. It also helps keep all of the firms fresh in everyone's mind.
- Be sure that the same group of evaluators is present for all interviews. People who miss some of the interviews are of no help when the time comes to select a firm.
- Schedule interviews at two-hour intervals. Two hours leaves time for a 45-minute presentation by the firm, 45 minutes for questions and answers, and 30 minutes for the first firm to pack up and depart, the next one to set up,

and the interviewers to refill their coffee cups and/or rush to the restroom. (Under duress, one hour and 45 minutes also works, but you may feel rushed.)
- Be prepared for high-tech presentations. Virtually all firms of any size will have PowerPoint presentations. They may bring projection screens with them, but many expect you to have one. You will also need proper electrical supplies and a way to partially darken a room. (Libraries that have meeting rooms with two light levels—blazingly bright and medieval dark—will have trouble meeting architects who want to simultaneously show pictures and converse with you.)
- Some architects take all their own photographs of the buildings they design, while others hire professional photographers to focus on one or two areas of the building that were designed to be particularly photogenic. It helps to know what's going on, especially because professional architectural photographers tend to bring in portable lights that completely change the look of the spaces photographed. You can always ask at interviews whether the pictures were taken with available light or whether the photographers brought in their own lighting equipment.
- Many architects will also bring boards with mounted photos, samples of carpet and tile, and so on, all of which have to be set up on portable easels. (You should not be asked to provide easels, but you'll need to provide adequate floor space.)
- Prepare sets of questions in advance. To be sure you cover the same material with each firm, prepare advance questions. (Many of these will usually be answered by the architects in their presentation, so you will need to pick and choose when the time comes for Q&A.) A list of possible interview questions appears below.
- Select the order of interviews yourself. Some architectural firms are convinced that the last firm interviewed is the one most likely to be hired. Most firms that ask for later interviews have valid reasons for doing so, but occasionally a firm will angle to be last for a perceived advantage. (It's always considerate not to schedule the farthest-away firm for the first interview of the day.)
- Have your building consultant present at the interviews. Consultants can bat cleanup, asking questions that have been omitted in the conversation. They're also good at asking questions no one wants to ask, such as "Is your firm currently subject to any litigation?" or "What went so terribly wrong in the job in Port Amazing?"
- Be sure that the people asking questions know how libraries work. The great danger in having architects selected by (for example) university boards of trustees is that boards of trustees usually know absolutely nothing about libraries. The result may be the employment of an architect primarily on the basis of glamour.

What are you trying to find out at interviews?

- The interview gives you a chance to meet the members of the architectural firm. Everything else being equal, it's always better to work with people you like. If you can detect signs of serious egomania, that's useful information.
- The interview is designed to show you what the team can do for you by what it has done for other libraries in the past. It can also show that the team understands the special challenges facing your library. The team may even bring along a couple of idea sketches to show that they've been thinking about you.

> The term *team* can carry a number of meanings. When they introduce the employees of their firm that they propose to work on your project, architects usually refer to them as a "team." If the architects bring in people who are not employees, such as architects from another firm or various consultants, they also refer to the group as a "team." Usually things are pretty clear, but always ask if you are unsure.

- Pay far more attention to the firm's completed work than to descriptions of work in progress. Or ask firms not to talk about work in progress at all. We've listened to hundreds of architect interviews, and it's interesting to see how some excited descriptions of great works in the planning stages vanish from presentations once the buildings have been completed and things didn't work out quite as well as the designers had hoped.
- The interview is not a time for the architect's team to present a design for your library. The team may show a few concepts, indicating that they are already thinking about your problems, but the presentation should stress their awareness of your problems and their past successes with other difficult situations, not the solution to your library's problems. Stress on your library's specific needs may also indicate a lack of previous experience.
- Any architectural team that arrives at an interview with an elaborately finished rendering of "your library" either is trotting out a cynical sales pitch or is the kind of team that leaps to conclusions. There's no way most firms can learn enough about your library before the interview to allow them to come up with a serious conclusion about designs. You are interviewing for demonstrated aptitude in past efforts, and the work to design your library is still to come.
- The interview is also not a time for the architects to learn more about your library and its needs. It's always fun and good for the ego to talk about your library, but the purpose of the interview is for you to learn about the

architects. Having architects learning about your needs comes during previous visits to your library and after you've selected a firm.

- By watching the interactions within the architect's team, you can often learn how they work together—and sometimes that they've never worked together before. (A good question to ask during the interview is the prior experience of the proposed team as a working group.)
- Watch for demonstrated flexibility. You want a firm that can design the kind of building you want, not one standard structure.
- Watch for indications that the firm may fight your aesthetic ideas. If you want a Prairie Style building or a Georgian Revival building, you want to find out whether the firm will fight you.
- Watch for signs that the members of the firm listen to you. You can find out some of this during the Q&A period. Try to base your opinions on how they respond to the questions rather than exclusively on what they say.
- Watch for signs that the members of the firm have reviewed your building program, and be very concerned if they have not. It doesn't hurt to ask the team specific questions about the program. (If your program has some controversial features, it's interesting to see how the team deals with them.)
- Watch for signs that the members of the firm dislike working with experts on library design. For example, if they clearly bridle at the consultants who wrote your building program, that can be a bad sign. And it's a *very bad* sign if they want to bring in their own consultant. (If you have your special needs in print, you don't want an architectural firm that has no interest in responding to them.)
- Discount standard architectural talk. The world is full of architects who have a "passion" for libraries. In addition, many firms will stress in their presentations what good listeners they are. This is nice to hear, but we think firms say it because too many architects have well-earned reputations for not listening to their clients.
- You may not want to ask the following important question because it seems impolite. But ask anyway. Or stick your consultant with it. Are you currently subject to any lawsuits or litigation? You want to know whether a firm is being sued, and whether it's for a good reason. If the last library the firm built has filed suit because the building has a wet basement, leaky roof, malfunctioning detention pond, terrible acoustics, bad lighting, and expansion space that's unusable (this describes a library Fred knows that sued its architects), you want to know about it.

In actuality, most firms are probably sued because workers are hurt on the job and the workers' lawyers sue everyone involved in the project. Once things get sorted out, the suit against the architect is usually withdrawn. So always follow through on this question and find out the nature of the legal problem.

H. Possible Questions for Architect Interviews

Here are some questions you can use when interviewing architects. Many are intended to help you pin things down if you feel that people are avoiding responding to questions.

If you divided your architect interviews into formal presentations and then Q&A, many of these questions will probably be answered during the interviews. But you want to ask questions that are not covered during presentations.

A couple of libraries have interviewed architects simply by asking questions, with no opportunities for the architects to make preliminary presentations. Architects have told us they found this a very unsettling and somewhat random experience. We suspect it's not a good idea.

The italic items are the actual questions and the rest are just comments.

1. *Who will be your project architect? How long has this person been with the firm? For what other projects has this person been project architect? Who will be present on a regular basis at all planning meetings? Are there any occasions when the project architect will not be present?*

If the project architect is not present at the interview, or plays no real role in the interview, find out why. If you prefer that another member of firm than the one proposed as project architect serve in that capacity, you can make that a condition of employment. If someone in the team suggests there will be no project architect—saying something like "We all work on projects together"—that's just being evasive.

In your contract with the firm, you will want to specify that the project architect lead all of the planning meetings.

2. *Is your firm prepared to guarantee contractually that this person will continue as project architect throughout the job?*

Architects leave firms for many reasons. If you are selecting the firm because of a specific person, you want to have contingency plans. Midway through your project, you don't want to hear an offhand, "By the way, XXX has just left the firm, and we'll be assigning YYY to finish your project."

3. Who will your consulting engineers and other specialists be? If these are not employees of your firm, what prior experience have you had with these firms?

Commonly, firms hire their geotechnical engineers—whom they sometimes identify as "civil engineers"—locally, so they may not have worked with them before.

4. Who will be your interior designer? Is that person present at the interview today? What experience has this person had with library design?

Interior designers are far more than interior decorators. For instance, they may be responsible for all of the furniture layouts in your library, for specifying furnishings, and so on. Meeting the designers is important.

5. Do you do your estimating in-house, or do you hire the work done? How accurate have your estimates at the end of the schematic design process been in recent projects? How about your estimates at the end of the construction document phase?

Estimating is vital. Many architects rely on specialized firms to do the work, but architects with geographically concentrated practices—particularly in areas of similar small towns—often can do a good job estimating.

Architects should be prepared to provide examples of projects including initial estimate, final estimate, and actual cost.

6. What are you prepared to do for us if the low bid for our project is higher than your estimate? Will we be billed for the extra costs?

7. Are you prepared to design a building that makes an architectural statement in accordance with our preferences? In keeping with the character of our campus or town?

You can always try out some kind of design you suspect they will not like, just to see how they react. If they say, "It's a terribly passé design, but we can do it if you want," that's a good sign. (White brick with bright turquoise doors is a 1950s enthusiasm that should make good architects wince.)

If you say, "We want an addition that matches our existing building," and they say, "We'll design the kind of addition your original architect would design if he were working today," this is a seriously weaselish response and not a good sign, because it places no limits whatsoever on the architects.

8. Are you comfortable with designing a building that does not feel contemporary? That appears strongly influenced by earlier designers?

Some architects are extremely uncomfortable with the appearance of lack of originality. This is a good time to watch their reactions.

9. We will continue to use our building consultant as our agent throughout the design process. We intend to have him or her present at most if not all planning meetings. Will you accept this working relationship?

Watch out for firms that hope the consultant will butt out during the design process, even though they are unlikely to ever say so outright, particularly during an interview with the consultant sitting right there.

10. Do you have any questions or problems with the written building program?

Try to figure out whether the firm has actually read the program. For instance, you can ask what they think of a proposed feature without describing it. You can also ask your consultants to raise questions about elements they think the architects may not like, in order to see how they respond.

11. What experience has your firm had designing libraries? Libraries of our specific type? How many have been completed? Were any of these projects carried out by a different office of your firm? Were any done by a firm you acquired after the projects were designed and built?

Firms with little experience can be straightforward or evasive. Personally, we're very fond of straightforward. Although a track record of good library buildings is always the best thing, firms with little experience can do a great job if they know their limits and your consultants are actively involved during the project.

12. How much experience has your proposed project architect had with library design projects? For which of those projects was he or she the project architect?

13. Of your library building projects, how many have been completed? Of these, how many in the last ten years?

14. What libraries have you completed in about our size range?

A good way to describe size is in gross square feet.

15. What design errors have you seen in recent library construction projects? What design mistakes do you foresee tempting us in this project?

This is a somewhat mean question, because you are asking the firm to criticize current designs. Architects hoping to be hired will be very wary of stepping on the toes of those people conducting the interview. You should expect the response not to simply repeat problems with your structure that are listed in your building program.

16. Can you help us with presenting our design to the community? What experience have you had in this area?

17. What is the capacity of your firm? What other projects are currently underway? How major a role will our project play? What other projects will your proposed project architect be working on at the same time?

Architects can end up either hunting for extra work or being overextended.

A standard response can be "Our services are in high demand, but we can fit you in." But it's still a good question to ask.

18. Of your last five library projects, how many came in on time and under budget? If they were not on time or under budget, what happened?

If the firm has had fewer than five library projects, broaden the question to a larger category, such as campus buildings, city government buildings, and so on.

"On time and under budget" is a magic phrase in building construction. In the case of library construction, over budget leads to particular problems. (Our impression is that some of the poorest records in this area are held by the firms with the largest international reputations, but we could be wrong.)

19. Is your firm currently party to any lawsuits or litigation? Please explain.

No one likes asking this, but it's a good question. If you don't want to ask it, get your consultants to do it.

20. Are you prepared to make frequent trips here if this proves essential for design work or for construction administration? If something goes really wrong on the job, how fast can you be here?

21. What experience have you had with construction grants?

22. The library will reserve the right to alter the building in any way it sees fit after construction is over. Can you live with this?

Some architectural firms have managed to get libraries to agree that all changes of any kind—even colors on workroom walls or signs saying "restroom"—will be controlled indefinitely by the firms. This is a seriously crummy situation.

23. If you are proposing a team project with another architectural firm, have your firms ever worked together in the past? If so, what buildings have you completed? How often will we see the second firm? Will there be extra charges for that firm's attendance at meetings?

24. Are the architects in your team all members of the AIA? Are they all licensed to practice architecture in our state?

This should be clear from credentials, but if the credentials are vague, you need to know.

25. What's currently happening in the construction industry that may impact this project?

All kinds of things affect construction costs and schedules, ranging from changes in the labor market to shortages of materials like drywall. This should be an easy question for busy architects.

26. Why are you the best firm for the job?

Ask your consultants, attorneys, or state library whether there are any questions that are illegal. In Illinois, for example, you cannot ask firms what they will charge for the work until after you have rank-ordered the applicants and are ready to enter trial negotiations with the top-ranked firm.

I. Final Selection

The final selection is completely in the hands of the governing body.

- Frequently, you will have a pretty good idea of who you like best by the time the interviews are over. If you did your homework before scheduling interviews, all the firms have good reputations, but you still will be strongly influenced by the proposed project architect and design team, by the degree to which responses are straightforward rather than evasive, and by your perceptions of where overweening egos may make it difficult for you to work smoothly with a particular firm.

- Some owners find themselves ready to make a decision as soon as the interviews are over, while others find that they have additional questions they want to ask previous clients.
- Either way, it's a good idea to make a decision reasonably soon, while memories of the interviews are still strong. And within a few days of the interviews, the firms you met will start to call to see if you've made a decision. Making a reasonably speedy decision should not lead to timetable problems because the fact that you've designated a preferred firm does not obligate you to start work at any particular time.
- In fact, if laws in your state make hiring architects a slow process, it makes very good sense to hire them early, so that you can start design on almost a moment's notice, or carry out a quick study of some kind.
- Despite occasional hints from architectural firms that they have a special political relationship that should be recognized, you are limited only by existing laws, regulations. and contracts. (Our reaction to claims of political connections is to take deep offense, but every situation is different).
- It's useful to have first and second-choice firms, in case something happens that makes it impossible to hire your number-one firm. If, for example, the project architect you want is no longer available at your preferred firm, or if you cannot arrive at a satisfactory contractual agreement with the firm, it's better to have a second firm in mind than to start over.
- There is no legal obligation to hire anyone at all. If you are unhappy with all of the firms you interview, you have the right to start the entire process over. (However, if you have brought in what appear to be the best firms, you may not be any happier with a new group. And because it costs firms a great deal of money to attend interviews, libraries that get a reputation for jerking firms around may find a significant loss of interest among good firms the second time around.)
- Once you have made a decision, let everyone know which firm was your first choice. For architects, the major hurdle is being hired in the first place, and all of the firms you interviewed will be eager to know your choices.
- Architectural firms that are not hired will frequently ask you why. They will ask, for example, how they might improve their presentations or proposals. We recommend very strongly that you do not ever get involved in discussions of this type. Hiring an architectural firm is like hiring a library employee, and the correct response to, "Why wasn't I hired?" is always a friendly but noncommittal, "Because we felt that the firm we hired was the one that best met our needs for this project."

Even if you were singularly unimpressed with a firm, it's a good idea to be friendly and nonjudgmental, since you never know when you'll need help with something else. You can always tell firms that you appreciate their taking time to attend the interviews and that you enjoyed meeting the team, but getting involved in specifics of evaluation is a major mistake.

J. Contracting with Architects

Although in some states it may be legal to select architects by low bid, this always strikes us as an extraordinarily bad idea for several reasons:

- The scope of the architectural process is elastic. If your architects want to renegotiate their contract every time you request a small additional study, this may be counterproductive.
- Architectural services are far less specific than construction. When you are constructing a library building, your architects will spend months preparing detailed bid documents, leaving as little as possible open to interpretation. By contrast, your contract with your architect will of necessity involve some generalities.
- The personalities of your architects and their approach to design are important because you are exploring ideas together. By contrast, contractors execute projects already described in detail. If you hire your architects by low bid, you may have to take whatever annoying person they send you.

In the United States, most contractual relationships with architects are by means of standard contract forms prepared by the American Institute of Architects. These standard forms are part of a family of agreements that will cover the future steps in the project, such as the owner's agreement with the contractor or construction manager, and with other entities such as furniture vendors.

The family of documents also includes the "general conditions" that apply to all parties to all the agreements. This is a set of basic definitions and responsibilities. Unfortunately, it is often overlooked in the contract review.

The problem, of course, is that these are AIA forms, not ALA forms, and they tend to be worded in favor of architects. As a result, some universities and units of government have their own forms. If this is the case, be sure to find out whether the unit of government also has its own versions of the various "downstream agreements" that are part of the AIA family.

If you will be using AIA forms, you will need the assistance of an attorney who has a thorough knowledge of the forms.

The AIA forms divide the process into the five steps mentioned elsewhere in this book. The contract should specify the percentage of the contract amount attributable to each step. For example, it may be:

Schematic design	15%
Design development	10 to 20%
Construction documents	35 to 40%
Bidding	5%
Construction administration	25 to 30%

We have run into several situations where architects insisted that schematic design did not include placement of all furnishings. For libraries in particular, schematic designs without furniture placement are worthless, and you will need to make extremely clear in your contract with your architects that your definition of schematic design includes furnishings. (Some architects may feel this calls for a higher percentage of total fees.)

In addition to these costs, your architects can reasonably expect to have a separate contract for feasibility studies if a number of alternate sites need to be formally evaluated and tested for their ability to hold the sort of library you want.

Here are some things you want to be sure are covered in your contract with your architects:

- Your intent to stop work after the completion of the schematic design and not continue until construction funds have been raised. Schematic designs are all you need to raise money, and if you fail to raise the money you need, you don't want to pay for unneeded design work.
- The schematic design will include scale drawings of the floor plan, elevations, and perhaps cross-sections, plus a preliminary cost estimate and outline specifications.
- The floor plan of the schematic design will include furniture placement. (Architects will sometimes argue that furniture placement is not part of schematic design, but—to repeat ourselves endlessly—library floor plans without furniture placement are truly worthless.)
- What happens if the architect makes an error that will cost you money? This means a mistake that has to be rectified by tearing something out and replacing it. Simple omissions are not mistakes of this type, because you can still add the item to the project. But if the construction drawings put the footings in the wrong place, and they have to be ripped out and poured again, will the architect take responsibility?

- Who will be the project architect? Because many architectural firms have charismatic sales architects and more humdrum working architects, you want to make this very clear. (This doesn't mean that the humdrum architects will be disappointing, but you want to be sure about the firm's commitments. Bait and switch is a very serious possibility, particularly with very large firms.)
- If you select a firm because you like the proposed project architect, what happens if that architect leaves the firm and goes to a different firm? Among other things, you may want to have the right to transfer the project to the project architect's new firm.
- How will fees be determined?
    - Many contracts with architects start with an understanding of general fee levels based on a percentage of construction cost. Typically, small remodeling jobs have the highest percentage fees and large jobs with repetitious elements (such as dorm rooms) can have substantially lower fees.
    - One of our favorite methods is to agree on a time-and-materials-not-to-exceed charge, where you and the architects agree on a maximum cost and a schedule of fees for individuals of the firm. The firm then bills you for its time and costs not to exceed the agreed-upon fee.
    - Another method is a flat fee method. This is particularly common for preliminary studies (such as feasibility studies) or even for schematic designs.
- What expenses are reimbursable? These are amounts that will be billed in addition to those covered in the basic percentage or dollar contract. Typically, renderings and models and printed sets of bid documents are billed separately to the owner, but find out if you will be billed for mileage, lodging, meals, and other costs. Travel and lodging costs can be a major item if the architects have a long way to travel. (If you select a team that includes both a local firm and an out-of-town firm, you may be asked to pick up a lot of extra airfare and lodging costs for the second member of the team.)
- What activities will involve extra fees, and how will these be determined? This is a tricky area. Will your architect charge you extra for evaluating alternate sites, helping with referendums, attending public hearings, preparing master plans for long-term expansion, and other essential services that are not exactly part of designing and constructing the building?
- What is the schedule of payments? As with contractors, you want to be sure that the bills are not running ahead of the work. For example, if your contract says that schematic design will be 15 percent of architectural fees, you want to be sure that at the end of schematic design you will have not paid more than 15 percent of total fees.

- What will you do if the architect does not deliver everything promised? This can happen when firms never get around to providing record drawings ("as-built" drawings). As with contractors, you may want to hold back a percentage of fees until all the work for which you've contracted is delivered. Record drawings are a particular problem because the work is over, exciting new projects are beckoning your architects, and this kind of tidying up is a bore.

A problem can also occur when architects feel that schematic design work is getting nowhere and (despite the lack of progress) they feel they've done all the work their fees justify.

> Fred knows one firm that handed the library a collection of rough sketches and contended that this constituted a "schematic design." The library hired a new architect.

- What will happen if the low bid is substantially greater than your architects' estimate? Contracts with architects may specify (for example) that if the low bid is more than a certain percentage over the architects' estimate, they will redesign and rebid the library at their expense.
- How will the contract be dissolved? As with your library building consultants, you want to be able to pay your bills for work to date and walk if you become dissatisfied.
- Who owns the plans, and what does "ownership" mean? Can the architect use the plans to build an identical building for another library? Can the library sell the plans to another library?
- What happens if the library decides to paint the building pink three months after it's finished? Some contracts give architects residual rights to buildings, and this is a disastrous idea. It's your university or town or high school and your library and your money, and the architects work for you. If they don't like your *new* signage or color scheme or whatever, they're just out of luck.

To repeat: developing a contract with architects is not an amateur undertaking. You will need an attorney who is familiar with AIA contracts. This may be a university attorney or city attorney, but it may also be an independent attorney with significant experience in the area.

K. Understanding Architects

There's no way to walk on thinner ice than to conduct amateur psychoanalysis of a profession, but here goes.

When library construction projects are complete, librarians are sometimes unhappy with the experience and the results.

They complain about many of the things mentioned throughout this book: architects who won't listen, buildings that are nightmares to maintain, buildings that terrify users with acrophobia, buildings that are hard to supervise, buildings that end up on the covers of architecture magazines but fail as libraries, buildings with gimmicky details that get in the way of performance, buildings with oddly shaped rooms or confusing floor plans, complex buildings that require too many staff members to supervise, and so on.

We think part of the problem is that while architecture is a graphic art, some architects want it to be a fine art. Libraries hire architects for the same reason they hire graphic artists—they have an idea of what they want, but they don't have the skills to create it. Just as they expect graphic artists to bring them a variety of concept drawings for them to choose among, they expect architects to bring them a variety of possible solutions to the problems outlined in their building programs, so that the owners can select what they want.

Vast numbers of architects perform brilliantly in finding ways to design the buildings that libraries would design for themselves if only they knew how.

A very few architects, however, want to create Great Art, and they regard the functional needs of their clients as nuisances to be ignored when Art is underway. This attitude appears to be far more characteristic of "signature architects" or "starchitects" than of the great mass of the profession, but it can also be found almost anywhere, particularly among young architects who are short on practical experience and long on exciting visions of design.

Some architects are also deeply offended by the idea of imitating the work of previous architects. The arguments that architects raise against matching existing architecture are legion. Some of these are perfectly reasonable—clients may not be able to afford the styles of 1910—but we suspect that underlying this argument is the powerful desire not to be seen imitating the styles of other times. As a result, for example, university campuses that maintained a fairly uniform Collegiate Georgian or Tudor Revival look through the Second World War now feature odd conglomerations of buildings representing a variety of fleeting post-World War II design enthusiasms.

An architect with a vision or "concept" you dislike can be hard to derail. It helps to say "no" the first time you see something you dislike, but you may have the feeling that you are reacting too negatively too soon, or failing to grasp the innovative brilliance of the idea. By the time you are convinced that you are right and that the concept is a disaster, things have moved on and are hard to divert.

Remember that you are doing no one a favor by letting unwanted design concepts continue. Your architects will end up wasting their time pursuing a concept you have no intention of using, and you will waste expensive meeting time and perhaps delay your project.

As we often suggest, some architects are modern Svengalis, entrancing owners—particularly public library and university boards of trustees—with exciting architectural details that will lead to serious functional problems or terrible cost overruns.

Other architects strive to speak only with people who don't understand libraries. They bypass librarians, public library boards, campus architects, faculty library committees, library building consultants, and similar people to speak directly with city fathers, university boards of trustees, and school boards.

These are major reasons why libraries can benefit from having relationships with people who know construction and/or library building needs extremely well but who do not work for architects. These people may include independent building consultants, construction management firms, and similar specialists.

IV. DESIGN COMPETITIONS

For major projects, owners may occasionally hold design competitions.

The greatest problem with design competitions is that they lead to the choice of a design on the basis of external appearance rather than function. They are pretty much glamour competitions and nothing more.

Design competitions can be exciting, but they can lead to problems if aesthetically popular submissions are also clearly dysfunctional.

If your circumstances call for a design competition, one thing you can do is provide a very detailed building program and require that proposed designs meet the program. It will help if your program specifically bans some of the features that are popular with designers but cause real problems in libraries, such as skylights, atriums, direct lighting, terrifying staircases, and so on.

A *major* problem with design competitions is that they may not bring out the best firms, who may be too busy with work to take time out for what looks like something little better than a lottery. It's a shame when entrants in the competition are all folks with time on their hands.

Moreover, the world may regard design competitions for less than highly prestigious jobs as simply examples of the owners' overwhelming hubris.

Our strong recommendation is that when the phrase *design competition* occurs, everyone involved in the project shouts "No!" in unison.

V. PLANNING GROUPS

Most building planning takes place in a series of meetings between architects and owners.

The library owners need to be represented by:

- Representatives of owners, including public library boards, school administrators or school boards, campus architects, and campus administrators. Usually this amounts to one or two people—not enough people from any one board to make the planning meetings subject to your state's open meetings act.
- Library staff. In order to have essential continuity, you need two administrators, so you can count on at least one being present at every meeting.
- Hired experts on the functional design of library buildings. Someone in the library's group needs to be an expert on how libraries occupy spaces. This can be your library building consultant, construction management firm, or owner's representative. The main thing is that someone in the room in addition to the architects needs to have serious expertise. (Library staff members can sometimes fill this role, but there needs to be someone in addition to the architects who knows what's going on.)

The main problem is that a wide variety of groups have an interest in the design of your new library:

- Governing boards, such as city councils and university boards of trustees
- Library staff, particularly directors and managers
- University architects, city project managers, and so on

- Library building consultants
- "Owners' representatives," library building specialists who are hired when libraries don't have enough staff to represent them in planning
- Donors
- Library support groups, such as library foundations and Friends of the Library
- Regulatory agencies
- Self-appointed pressure groups
- Library users

Most of these will have no representation on the planning group, but they may expect to be informed on progress and decisions. Sorting all of this out can be interesting.

Planning groups can easily become too large. For everyday meetings, probably a maximum of six to eight people in addition to the architects is recommended. With occasional meetings to report to all the major players.

Architects will take minutes of each meeting and circulate copies for everyone to sign.

Libraries should do the same. Take your own minutes of the meeting and have everyone present—including your architects—sign copies. If anything goes wrong, having the library's own records helps.

VI. WHAT CAN GO WRONG WHEN YOU WORK WITH ARCHITECTS?

Although architects are absolutely essential to any library design and construction job, things don't always go well between librarians and architects. Both groups can be at fault.

A. Loss of Control to Architects

Sometimes architects try to bypass librarians and city or university engineers and deal with people as remote from the project as possible. Make clear from the beginning to whom the architects report, and stop any attempt to go around you.

One serious source of trouble is the delegation of major design decisions to people who know next to nothing about library functions—for example, most mayors or university boards of trustees—bypassing library directors, library boards, campus architects, and other experts. The fact that a library architect you are thinking of hiring wants to immediately talk to the mayor rather than to your library board should send serious warnings of the "hire someone else" variety.

Stop concepts you don't like instantly.

It helps to take your own minutes at meetings with your architects. Send copies of your minutes to your architects and make sure that they sign to indicate their agreement, just as you sign their minutes.

B. Architects Who Ignore Building Programs

After spending months discussing every aspect of your library's planned services and having this converted to an extremely detailed document, you have every right to expect your architects to read and follow your written building program.

If your architects disagree with the program, you should expect them to do so in a meeting with you and your library building consultant, so that the architect and consultant both get to explain the reasoning for their different views.

Frequently, a program review is included in the first meeting with architects. Some architects take this very seriously, but others totally blow it off. Be sure to ask your architects formally if there is anything in the program with which they disagree, and get their response into your meeting minutes. If you have a good program, it will include a list of those design features librarians hate but some architects love, and you don't want a firm that says, "Sure. We agree," and then proceeds to include some of the features you specifically don't want.

In all of this it's important to remember that the best projects are collaborative. If the owners, library staff, architect, and building consultant are all present at planning meetings, the chances of having everything go right are greatly improved.

C. Architectural Firms That Substitute Personnel

All but the smallest architectural firms have a number of architects. If there is one specific architect you want to work with—particularly if you are considering hiring a larger firm—you will want to make sure that the architect you want is the architect you actually get.

Unfortunately, some firms have sales architects and working architects, and a few firms can be amazingly evasive when it comes to telling you who will be assigned to your project. In the worst cases, the situation is very much one of bait and switch. Evasiveness about personnel is a very bad sign.

In some cases, the architect you want turns up at meetings now and then, but the actual planning work is in the hands of someone else. Your contract with your architects should forbid this.

As indicated above, contracts with architectural firms may include the provision that if the project architect leaves for a different firm, the client has the right to sever relationships with the original firm and follow the project architect to the new firm, or simply to start over with a new firm.

D. Architects Who Refuse to Listen to Owners

One of the reasons why so many architects stress what good listeners they are is that a few architects have well-earned reputations for ignoring their clients.

If you feel that your architects are refusing to listen, here are some things you can do:

- Keep your own minutes of design meetings and have all the parties sign testifying accuracy. Architects do this all the time, but you should do it too in order to be sure that your wishes are clear in the minutes. Even if you don't have bad feelings about how things are going, bring someone to meetings to take notes on your behalf.
- Don't put up with situations where you turn down a design concept but the architect ignores you. If a concept that you totally rejected comes back again, it's time to sit down immediately with your architects and discuss the nature of your future relationship.
- If your architect keeps coming up with ideas you don't like, keep asking why things have to be this way.
- Ask point-blank why the concept you suggested is not the one the architects are presenting. Occasionally, a library's architects will dislike the entire concept that the library has in mind, but instead of being up-front about things they will bring out one alternative after another, hoping that one will appeal to the owners and make it unnecessary for the architects to openly reject the owners' ideas. This happened to one library board Fred worked with, and the delays and frustrations wasted a year while the architects passively resisted the library board, coming up with one unwanted alternative concept after another.
- Find a new architectural firm. This is the most extreme response, but occasionally it's the best one.

> Some architects brush off what librarians want by saying, "You just don't understand architecture." Your response is to force them to explain why their ideas are essential, ideally with your library building consultant present. In addition, a few architects under these circumstances would benefit from what a woman librarian friend of Fred's calls "A pop in the snoot."

E. Owners Who Refuse to Pay Attention to the Process

Sometimes things go wrong because clients don't pay sufficient attention to the process.

For instance, we've had a number of experiences with librarians who let the short-term pressures of daily life dominate their lives during building planning. Faced with decisions that may affect the library and its work for 50 or 100 years, librarians announce that they have no time to review plans because they're "busy with summer reading."

For good planning to take place, libraries need to enable their administrative staffs to devote themselves nearly full-time to architectural projects, and librarians in turn cannot hide behind familiar activities. This means that the governing boards of libraries must make specific plans for the extra expenditures that will result from tying up their most expensive employees.

Having library building consultants or owners' representatives fill in for administrators helps, but the focus of an administrator has to be the new building.

One useful thing some administrators do is to maintain a diary of the entire process, both design and construction, listing major events and dates. If disagreements later arise, it helps to know what happened and when it happened.

F. Owners with No Practical Experience with Buildings

Most day-to-day library building planning includes frequent meetings between architects and owners. For practicality, the owner's group has to be of reasonable size, anything from a half-dozen to a maximum of perhaps eight people.

Among those representing the owners at these meetings has to be someone who knows about the practical side of buildings, particularly library buildings, someone who can understand proposed designs and who can point out potential problems.

Some libraries have a professional staff member with wide experience in the functional design of library buildings.

- Public libraries can sometimes find building committee members who are retired contractors or school superintendents, or they can arrange to have their building consultants, construction managers, or owners' representatives attend all meetings.
- Universities can rely on campus architects, construction management firms, or building consultants.
- Other libraries rely on their library building consultants.

The reason these people are important is that planning committees must include members who understand everything architects say, and who occasionally point out the problems with suggested ideas.

One great way to keep library owners from being Led Down the Garden Path is for them to have their own experts on hand.

> At one public library Fred worked on, the owners' members of the committee included a former contractor who was a member of the board of trustees, a library director who was forceful and knowledgeable, and Fred. At least once or twice in every meeting, the three said "No!" in unison to proposed ideas. The good thing is that they were always right. The building was successful, but the architects skipped the ribbon cutting.

G. Owners Who Are Painfully Indecisive

Occasionally, owners are nearly unable to make up their minds or keep changing their minds, and the architectural design process slows to a halt.

To be fair to your architects, be available for meetings at reasonable times and make sure that all decision makers turn up. If you don't like a proposed idea, say so immediately, before your architects have spent many hours pursuing a concept that is doomed from the start. If a new member of the planning group wants to throw everything out and start over, you may have to tell that person that *it's too late*.

If your architects are working for a fixed fee, creating endless delays by being unable to attend planning meetings or make up your mind is seriously unfair.

H. Owners Who Want to Do Illegal Things

Good architects have an intensive mastery of the vast array of legal standards that surround buildings and construction. Building codes, prevailing wage laws, accessibility codes, zoning regulations, and other regulations place severe limits on the freedom of action of library owners.

Occasionally, owners push pet ideas that are strictly illegal, placing their architects in awkward situations. For example, Fred has encountered library boards that want to evade prevailing wage acts, ignore or argue about building codes, not install required sprinkler systems, or cut corners on accessibility.

Occasionally, owners and directors want to steer work to family and friends. We've seen it happen particularly with interior work and furnishings, but there are probably all sorts of other bad examples out there.

If you and your architects are facing off, good sources of insight may be your construction management firm and your attorneys.

I. Architects Who Do Sloppy Work

Many architects do painfully accurate work, creating construction documents that represent carefully accurate engineering and impressive consistency in detail and that lead to projects with a minimum of change orders.

A handful of architectural firms, however, create careless construction documents. Things that you want may be missing, sections of the drawings may be out of agreement with each other, or measurements may be off.

In some towns, some architects have reputations for sloppy drawings, and local contractors submit lower bids because they assume they can make things up with change orders.

When you are selecting your architects, try to find out through the grapevine which ones tend to be careless. Your construction management firm or building consultant may have experience. But do not expect them to comment on the record.

J. Owners Who Refuse to Be Realistic about Costs

Architects tell us about problems with owners whose desires are larger than their finances and who balk whenever architects start providing cost estimates.

Libraries are inherently more expensive than many other types of buildings. They need high-quality air-handling systems, lots of light fixtures, a huge number of electrical outlets, unusually solid floors, ceilings a minimum of ten feet high, and many other features that set them apart from inexpensive structures like many retail stores. Library owners need to come to grips with this.

K. Owners Who Think They Know It All (but Don't)

We'd like to think that all librarians and library governors are modest and well-informed, but the field has a few amazingly unjustified egos.

We've seen it primarily in public library boards. Individual board members can be amazingly insistent on dysfunctional ideas.

Sometimes it's logical. For example, basements in library buildings are a really bad idea, but they make good practical sense in private homes constructed in areas with low water tables. Board members who have a good understanding of the construction of houses can insist on similar concepts in libraries. And it can be hard to dissuade them. Even though they're wrong.

L. Architects Who Cut Corners to Save Their Own Time or to Increase Profits

Occasionally we encounter architects who see ways to make extra money on fixed-price projects by simply skipping essential steps or moving ahead when owners aren't ready.

Initially, all projects involve a lot of noodling around, trying out sketches of various possible designs and reviewing functions and likely costs. If your architects start with a completed schematic floor plan, they are cutting off valuable (and time-consuming) discussion. Instead of asking whether the entire concept needs rethinking, owners can end up debating the shape of a window.

Some architects try to keep building consultants from attending planning meetings or commenting on designs. This may streamline the process, but it eliminates one of the owners' major sources of professional opinions on how libraries occupy spaces, and on what kinds of features work and don't work.

Some architects find projects more time-consuming than they want and try to get owners to accept bundles of loose sketches as "schematic designs."

Some architects don't want to stop with schematic designs but get on with design development or construction documents before schematic designs are final. Remember that a schematic design (including the cost estimate that accompanies it) is all you need to raise funds for your project. If you are unable to find the money, any money you spent on design development or construction documents is wasted.

Some architects move directly from schematic design to construction documents, skipping the vital area of design development. At best, this is sloppy. At worst, there are all sorts of important decisions that are never discussed.

Some architects blow off punch listing, turning in a page or two of uselessly vague remarks like "Repair damage to wall finishes" when every specific dent needs to be mentioned (and ideally photographed), so that contractors can't claim at a later time that all the dents are the fault of the owners.

M. Architects Who Are Bullies and Raging Egomaniacs

While most architects are great, it's also a field that attracts more than its share of egomaniacs, people who are spectacularly full of themselves, often with no justification and frequently with little or no knowledge of libraries and how they work.

Over the years we've met architects who feel that they are slumming by dealing with librarians. Architects who feel justified in ignoring everything librarians say. Architects who come up with impressively dysfunctional designs and then angrily refuse to budge. Architects who want to deal only with people who know nothing about library buildings, bypassing librarians in the process. Architects who insist that their contracts allow them to ignore librarians and do whatever they darn well please. Architects who truly feel "Function be damned."

Some architects can be amazingly arrogant when dealing with librarians, who they clearly regard as their serious intellectual inferiors. One architect we know (not even hired yet) called the director of a library "little missy" and threatened her with dismissal if she didn't shut up and do as he said. (The fact that she was well educated and had extensive experience in both business and library management didn't slow him down.)

Some architects announce that they are a part of the community power structure, and that nothing will get done if they don't personally approve.

Some architects feel that they are slumming by doing anything less than the Library of Congress, and that the least the local folks can do is shut up While the Great Men Are at Work.

It may sound like we're exaggerating, but problems with rampant and unjustified egos abound in the profession.

Our personal feeling is that people who hire architects should be extraordinarily sensitive to this kind of thinking. Never hire architects who are too full of themselves, and immediately sever relationships with architects who forget whose library it is and whose campus or town it is and whose money it is.

Architects are like graphic artists. Their job is to design the building you would design for yourself if you had the training, not to bring the blazing light of their amazing brilliance to shine upon your pitiful and ignorant existence.

One useful function of library building consultants with strong credentials is to have them attend all or many of your planning meetings with your architects. Egomaniac architects will probably want to trample all over your consultants as well, but it's easier for consultants with a hundred library projects under their belts to look architects in the eye and say "Hogwash!" And if everything blows up, it's a lot better for librarians if their consultants get fired than if the librarians get fired. If necessary, sacrifice the outsiders.

VII. SNAPPY RULES ON DESIGN

1. For any library construction project larger than a bicycle shed, you need an architect.
2. Treat your architects fairly. Don't expect them to take on major unexpected tasks for no additional money.
3. Some architects have a brilliant ability to mentally envision complex structures in three dimensions. Watching them work is fun.
4. You can have a comfortable and functional library. You can have a library designed by a world-famous architect. But you can't have both.
5. Communication is the soul of architectural planning. Always speak up.
6. If you hire a team consisting of two architectural firms, be very sure you know who will actually be doing what and when—and what the extra costs will be.

7. If your architects have little or no library experience, decide how you will fill the gap. The consultants who prepared your building program are the most likely people.
8. Of all architectural words of tongue or pen, "We will reinvent the library" are among the most terrifying.
9. Good librarians can be seriously annoying to architects who start off with little intention of listening to them.
10. You have a right to understand what's going on. Although mansplaining is passé, even a remark like "Don't worry your little head about it" is totally unacceptable.
11. Saying "I'm sorry, I don't understand these things, so you'll have to explain to me why we need to have this in words I understand" is a great technique.
12. Always be sure you know who your project architect will be. Evasive answers during interviews or contract negotiations are a sign of serious problems.
13. Always beware if the first drawing you see is a completed drawing rather than a few conceptual sketches. Rushing things this way may save your architect time, but it does you no favors.
14. If your architects refuse to answer your questions about their designs, you have a serious problem.
15. Be particularly wary and aggressive when your library is a small element in a large building. Do proactive programming. Insist on being heard.
16. Be sure that decisions made in meetings are reflected in plans. Take your own minutes in meetings and have everyone sign off on them.
17. If you see a building that has some seriously awful concepts, the fault may lie entirely with the client rather than with the architects. Find out before you jump to conclusions.
18. You will often see architectural awards hanging in the offices of architects. None of the awards were given for outstandingly functional buildings.
19. Charettes are fun, but they can lead to serious rushing to judgment.
20. Sometimes the word *concept* should bring terror to your heart.
21. When you are interviewing architects, always be alert to bait-and-switch tactics. Insist that the proposed "project architect" be the main presenter at the interview.
22. Clarify contractually what will happen if your project architect leaves the firm.
23. Clarify contractually what will happen if your lowest bid is significantly higher than your architects' estimate.
24. Clarify contractually that *your architects have no rights to the building once it's completed*. This is a building, not fine art. You must have the right to alter anything you want at any time you want, whether your architects like it or not.

25. Clarify contractually that all color schemes, signage choices, and similar aesthetic decisions are your library's business. Your designers provide suggestions, not orders.
26. If an architect brings a picture of "your new building" to an initial employment interview, ignore it.
27. Many states have specific laws concerning how government agencies employ architects. Check with your lawyer or library building consultant.
28. Complete honesty in renderings is of mixed value. Sometimes it's better to leave off the HVAC penthouse.
29. One way to design a library building is to lay out all the needed spaces and then wrap an attractive exterior around them. Another way is to design an attractive exterior and then cram all the library spaces into it. The latter approach was invented by Procrustes, and you will not enjoy the results.
30. When your designers talk about "modern glass," ask to see an existing installation. Too many new libraries have had to replace their windows or cover them with dark gray film.
31. Soaring spaces with monumental staircases provide a few moments of "wow," followed by endless years of problems with heating, lighting, maintenance, acoustics, getting from point A to point B, unusable but expensive space, and (for many users) paralyzing fear of heights. Say "no" early and often.
32. Things will work vastly better if you hire programmers and architects separately rather than as part of a single team, where you will not have the benefit of independent opinions.
33. Make sure that your library staff have enough free time to work on the project. Even if your director's responsibilities can be handed off to other staff members, those staff members may need to pass things off in turn. At the bottom end of the handing-off chain you'll need more staff hours somewhere.
34. Don't pressure your architects to do something illegal. (Unfortunately, it happens.)
35. Schematic designs without furniture placement are worthless, particularly in libraries, which are basically large open spaces. Make sure that your contract with your architects specifies that your schematic design will include furnishings.
36. If your program calls for rectangular 4-person tables but your architects' schematic design converts them to round 4-person tables or square 4-person tables, you have a very serious problem, probably involving trying to cram too much furniture into too little space. Shout "Stop that!" immediately.
37. When you are interviewing architects, find out where your project fits into their work. If you are their only project, things are not well with the firm. But if they have too many projects, yours may receive short shrift.

38. If your architects have to labor mightily to talk you into their design concept, it may be because it's a crummy concept. Ask people who have worked in library buildings, such as the library building consultant who wrote your building program.
39. If your architects infuriate you on a regular basis, tell your colleagues. That's one of the great strengths of the social networks of professional librarians.
40. Design competitions for less than truly major libraries may simply drive off good architects. (For smaller libraries, design competitions come across as manifestations of excessive owner pomposity and ego.)
41. When you have planning meetings with your architects, always have your own expert on library buildings in the room.
42. Working with your architects to list words that will define your project is fun, but don't engrave them on the front of your building.
43. Just because you can manage to build some kind of library with your limited funds doesn't mean it's a good idea.

10

Site Selection

I. INTRODUCTION

The two largest challenges that face most library construction projects are site and money.

Library sites can be hard to find both because libraries occupy large quantities of space in crowded towns, schools, campuses, or businesses and because successful libraries require desirable locations for which other agencies are in competition.

Generally speaking, all libraries need sites that are central, easily reached, safe, convenient to similar services, sufficiently large, relatively quiet, provided with adequate parking (if relevant), and not adjacent to problem areas.

Because other agencies are in competition with libraries for good sites, people with other plans for the most desirable sites will argue that libraries (a) have plenty of space already or (b) don't really need attractive sites. Unless libraries and librarians are able to hold their ground in the face of political and social pressure, libraries often end up in poor locations.

Examples of bad sites are found everywhere.

- Public libraries are sometimes built on sites that have no room for expansion—let alone parking. They may be built in locations far from other heavily visited buildings. They may be built on soil unsuited for structures, particularly massive structures like libraries. They may have neighbors that lead to endless troubles. They may be in locations that users are afraid to visit after dark.

- School libraries sometimes have common walls with gymnasiums or band practice rooms. They may be located in places buried deep within buildings, guaranteeing that they can never be open when the rest of the school is closed. Or they may be designed to serve as passageways to other areas of the school, completely ignoring the necessity of security for collections and equipment.
- College and university libraries are sometimes built far from the center of campus or in locations with no room for expansion. They may be divided into scattered elements, not because service plans call for libraries on separate subject areas, but because there's not enough space for a single central library. High-density storage units are too often in remote locations rather than right next door, resulting in substantial delays in the delivery of requested items.
- Special libraries are sometimes built so far from the center of corporate life that nobody finds them. Because they are located in buildings not engineered to hold the weight of books, special libraries can be buried in odd corners of basements or find themselves severely limited as to where shelving can be installed.

Unfortunately, most library locations involve compromises. The important thing is to be aware of what compromises are involved and when it is essential that you stand your ground.

> One good way to protect your library from inappropriate sites is to have a carefully prepared building program ready and circulated (or better yet, accepted) *before* site issues arise.

II. EVALUATING POTENTIAL SITES

This section is concerned primarily with selecting physical sites for the construction of buildings. It therefore applies primarily to public and academic libraries.

Careful evaluation of a site is vital because construction decisions can last for a century. Or several centuries.

Unfortunately, while you are investigating sites, people will be pushing you to approve sites that may represent extremely poor choices. This is particularly true for public libraries, where political pressures to purchase sites that are too small, in inappropriate locations, or involve the remodeling of unsuitable existing buildings can be immense.

A. Always Employ Professionals

Although it's tempting to simply pick a site, there are so many technical considerations involved that libraries *always* need professional assistance. Among other things, your architects, engineers, and building consultant (all three, not just one or two) will help you determine:

- **How much space you actually need (consultants and architects)**
  Remember that if you cannot afford to build enough space now, you need to set aside for future growth both the extra space you need to build a sufficiently large building today *plus* the additional space you need for long-term expansion, including not only structure, but also parking, setbacks, landscaping, water runoff control, and so on. A carefully prepared building program will help you defend your space needs. One of the reasons for programming early is to be prepared when people abruptly start talking about sites. If you can spell out and defend your space needs when the topic first comes up, you can prevent other people simply taking over your planning for you. Nevertheless, some people will blithely assume that all of your planning work is of no merit, even though they (a) have done no actual space planning themselves and (b) know little or nothing about libraries. In our experience, the political pressures to occupy undersized sites can be immense.

> A two-phase building program is an important tool to make sure you have enough space not only for construction but also for long-term expansion. See chapter 8 on "Programming."

- **Whether you can physically construct a building on the proposed site (engineers and architects)**
  The world abounds in sites that are unsuited for massive structures. The most convenient location in town is not a good choice if the library slowly sinks into the ground. (In actuality, relatively few libraries sink, but the extra cost of building on bad soil can be immense.)

> One of the persistent rumors in the wide world of urban legends concerns hundreds of different libraries where the architects and engineers supposedly forgot to calculate the weight of the books when the buildings were designed, and the libraries are now sinking into the ground. This appears to be total hogwash, but it's fun to say, "And now as our library sinks slowly into the earth, we say goodbye to plans for long-term service."

The input of local civil engineers (specifically geotechnical engineers) is particularly essential here because they know the idiosyncrasies of local sites.

- **Whether the shape of the site lends itself to the construction of a library (architects and consultant).**
  Long, narrow sites, for example, may technically have sufficient square footage but will not lend themselves to the construction of functional libraries with easy access from parking lots. If local zoning requires setbacks, long narrow sites may have little land on which buildings can actually be constructed.

- **Whether zoning and code regulations and other laws will allow you to build there (architects).**
  Zoning and building codes will specify setbacks, total square footage (frequently as a percentage of site size), maximum building height, minimum off-street parking, water detention, construction types, and many other aspects of your library building. Often libraries are able to obtain necessary rezoning, particularly because they are not regarded as detrimental to neighbors, but you will be in bad shape if you purchase land on the assumption that you can have it rezoned, only to find that other interests stand in your way.

- **Whether existing buildings you plan to remove or alter are protected by federal, state, or local historical preservation regulations (architects).**
  Constructing a library in a historic district is almost always a challenge. You may find, for example, that groups insist that a specific structure on your site remain there forever, even if the new library will have to coil in a serpentine fashion around it.

- **Whether your location in a historic district will permit you to construct the library you need (architects).**
  The limitations imposed by historic districts can be significant. Typically, you will need to deal with local agencies that have significant authority to allow or deny a wide variety of aesthetic and land occupancy considerations.

- **Whether there are any concealed historic remains on the site that can prevent its development (architects and local or campus historians).**
  Previous burials or other hidden archaeological remains may limit or prevent use of the site for construction of a library. For example, if your site has Native American graves, you are highly unlikely to be able to use it.

- **Whether you can afford the extra technical costs of building on the proposed site (architects and engineers).**
  Coping with difficult soil situations or distant utility connections, for example, can have a major effect on construction costs. And so can having to relocate existing utilities in your site.

- **Whether adjacent land uses will operate to the detriment of the library (consultants and architects).**

- **What the likely cost of removing any existing buildings is likely to be (architects and engineers).**
  Removing buildings can be far more expensive than many people expect.

The following sections of this chapter examine the practical implications of a number of these issues.

> Always consider using your hired professionals to deliver the bad news about proposed sites. They can make everyone mad and then leave town.

B. Soil Conditions

When you are considering a site for your library, you will need to know whether the soil is suitable for construction. Some sites that initially appear lovely are vacant because they are unbuildable.

If you manage a public library, always begin by checking with your city engineering staff. Because they are involved with issuing building permits, they often know where problematic soil conditions exist.

Before you purchase property for your library, you will want your architects and engineers to test the ability of the soil to bear loads. This is done by boring holes in a number of locations around the site, removing core samples, and having them checked in a laboratory.

A number of additional problems emerge if the site is a "brownfield" site that has been used for previous buildings. In such a case, you will want to check to be sure that the site has clean fill rather than buried chunks of demolished buildings. Examples of bad sites are legion:

- Fred's hometown library purchased an urban renewal site that the library board was promised was a clean site. But when the time came to install foundations for the new library, it turned out that the site was full of buried debris from a previous structure—a tangled mass of concrete chunks and rebar. The urban renewal agency eventually had to clear the site at its own cost, but the library board had to first bring suit.
- An older library that Fred worked with had been built on the site of a previous library that burned down. Apparently, rubble from the previous buildings was not completely removed from the site, and the result has been uneven settling of the new building.

Soil conditions will also affect your ability to use geothermal heating systems. If you are considering a geothermal heating and cooling system, it's extremely important that you have an engineering firm evaluate your site for that purpose before you purchase it. Your architect can arrange this.

C. Utilities

One of the major costs of constructing a building is bringing utilities to the site.

Libraries commonly need access to:

- Water
- Gas
- Electricity
- Storm sewers
- Sanitary sewers
- Telephone
- Data

If a site is half a mile from all of these utilities, the cost of connecting them to the library may be very high.

While bringing distant utilities to a site can be expensive, so is relocating utilities to make way for a new structure.

- Relocating utilities is often necessary when libraries are expanded or are constructed on brownfield sites. As with bringing utilities to a new site, the cost of relocating utilities can be extraordinary.

- Utilities are typically located under streets or alleys. If your library plans to expand across a street or alley, your architects and engineers will determine which utilities must be relocated and how much this is likely to cost. The locations of modern utilities can be located electronically, but some stuff is seriously hidden.

> Some cities have only limited knowledge of what's underground. In the past, they prided themselves on not wasting money maintaining maps of underground utilities. Even if determining the location of utilities after the fact costs ten times as much as making maps in the first place, one still had the advantage long ago of bragging about not wasting taxpayers' money.

Occasionally, libraries are constructed or expanded without relocating utilities that cross the building footprint. For example, sewer lines or even small brooks are sometimes located beneath floor slabs.

> Fred worked with one library that had two basements divided by an underground stream running through a large pipe. Ironically, it was the newer basement that filled with water a couple of years after it was built.

The cost of locating and relocating utilities is a particular problem because many people who give you forceful good advice on your project may have no idea how much money is involved in utility connections—or even that utilities are needed. This is why you need opinions from your architects, engineers, and city or campus engineering staff as soon as any site is seriously considered.

Even your planners may fail to mention the cost of connecting utilities while they are involved in the early phases of design, because utility connections are considered part of project costs but not construction costs. This is another reason why it's so important to be sure your architects are quoting you full project costs rather than just construction costs from the very first.

Occasionally, architects will indicate future expansion areas on site plans, then proceed to locate utilities directly under them. Always compare your architects' dotted-line "master plan" for future expansion locations with your engineers' utilities plans.

> Errors in this area can be amazing. For example, in one library Fred worked on, the designers planned to locate all of the utilities and the AC compressors on (and under) an area that was designated for future building expansion. From this experience, Fred concluded that the architects' indication of a building expansion area was a matter of lip service rather than genuine interest.

D. Surface Water Runoff Detention and Retention

Local regulations may require that your site include an area where rainwater can accumulate temporarily until it can drain away. If you need to provide a detention basin, this can add substantially to the size of the site necessary to construct your library.

- Detention basins: Detention basins are low areas designed to control the accelerated water runoff that occurs when natural growth is replaced by buildings and pavement. The basin fills with water during rainstorms, and the water slowly drains away or evaporates later.
- Alternatives to detention basins: Depending on local ordinances, you may be able to avoid providing a detention basin if you are building on a brownfield site and you will not increase the total space occupied by buildings and paving. In essence, the non-absorbent percentage of the site is grandfathered in.

There are also engineering alternatives to detention basins. For example, some parking lots have permeable paving that slows water runoff and performs the same function as detention basins. Green roofs may also meet local requirements for controlling runoff. Your local building authorities are the people who know the available options.

> Detention basins in subdivisions have led to a major ecological shift in the United States. Faced with the attractive new habitat offered by thousands of new detention basins, many Canada geese have become year-round residents rather than migratory waterfowl. People who once rushed from their houses to marvel at V formations of geese passing overhead now rush from their houses to curse geese passing in their yards.

- Estimating detention basin areas: Calculating the area required for surface water detention requires the assistance of architects and engineers because the size of the basin required depends so heavily on the size and the construction of structures and paving.
- Retention basins: Some basins are designed to always hold water. They're cute, but be prepared for the inevitable side products of goose populations.

E. Subsurface Water

Subsurface moisture conditions are also important, even if you don't plan to create any basement space. Moisture can affect footings and lead to water infiltration.

> Fred worked with one Carnegie library that had been constructed next door to a concealed underground stream. Seventy years after the library was built, groundwater had undermined the building's footings. The result was stairstep cracks in the brick walls, massively cracked and heaving terrazzo floors (the library covered the worst cracks with heavy rubber mats), and roof beams that were pulling apart. When dropped on the floor, round pencils inevitably rolled off into dark corners.

Water infiltration in basement walls can lead to hidden mold formation, particularly if the library furrs out the walls and installs a vapor barrier.

We argue against basement space elsewhere in this book. If you have an old library, you may be stuck with basements, but there's a very great deal to be said for not doing any more of that sort of thing, particularly because adding an extra floor costs very little more than adding a basement.

> You can laugh at subsurface seepage a great deal more easily if your library does not have a subsurface.

F. Floodplains

Although it's possible to build on floodplains with the right sort of design, you don't want to do it. Ever. Or, more specifically, EVER.

Given world climate changes, it seems possible that floodplains will expand in the future, and even building *close* to a floodplain may be a dangerous idea.

A more extensive discussion of libraries built on floodplains appears in chapter 30 on "Security."

G. Site Configuration

Most libraries fit best on fairly square sites. Mere acreage is not enough. The longer and thinner the site, the less chance there is of fitting a successful library onto it.

Non-rectangular sites are also difficult places to locate libraries. Some architects have thought it was fun to build buildings with curved or diagonal walls in order to echo sites with curves or diagonals, and the result is almost inevitably a Very Bad Idea.

When a site is proposed for your library, one of your architects' responsibilities is checking to see whether it's possible to actually fit the building you need on the site. This is another important reason to hire your architect before you make a final site selection.

On the other hand, you may need your consultant to fend off your architects' enthusiasm for non-rectangular buildings.

H. Site Topography

Although the world frequently looks like a fairly flat place, it seldom is. Even a city block that looks almost totally flat may slope a dozen or more feet from one side to the other. As a result, libraries must be fitted to the contours of sites, and many plans are developed in response to existing conditions.

Sloped sites offer both problems and opportunities. For example:

- Will the site lead to a multilevel building when your programmatic needs called for a single-level building? Multilevel buildings need elevators, staircases, and second stories that are strong enough to bear the weight of books. And all are expensive. In addition, overseeing a multilevel public library building may require extra staff and therefore raise occupancy costs forever.
- What are the implications for accessibility for users with disabilities? A long uphill ramp from the parking lot or the street to the library entrance may be technically legal, but it will also be uncivilized.

- If the site slopes down from the street front, will it lend itself to a construction of a parking area under the building? On a site like this, the parking area beneath the building may be open to daylight on at least one side and therefore be less spooky to library users.
- Are there opportunities for green construction using bermed walls, green roofs at grade level, and so on?
- A number of libraries have been built on slopes with the entrances and reading rooms on the top floor and book stacks beneath. This permits the high ceilings and open structures that make reading rooms attractive. (By contrast, many great research libraries constructed on flat ground have reading rooms far above entry level, to eliminate the problem of masses of columns supporting heavy floors above the reading rooms.)

Again, before you commit to a site, you will need (a) a building program to define the necessary functional spaces, and (b) preliminary studies by your architects and engineers to test how the library you need might be fitted to the site. Once your architects have completed their studies, you can ask your consultant to double-check the functionality of the possible structures that can be fitted to the site.

I. Brownfield Sites

A site that has existing buildings (or has been occupied by previous buildings) is often referred to as a "brownfield site." By contrast, sites that have been used only for agriculture or wild vegetation are called "greenfield sites."

There are several major dangers in dealing with brownfield sites.

- Existing structures: The first problem with brownfield sites is existing structures. Even if the structures have no historic merit, they may be very expensive to remove, particularly if they have asbestos or lead paint. Taking down a medium-sized old school building, for example, can easily cost half a million dollars, all of which must be deducted from the value of the empty site when the purchase price is considered. Remember that any building constructed before the late 1970s may have asbestos or lead paint. That's why old school buildings often stand empty for years. The cost of taking them down can be greater than the value of the resulting empty site.
- Buried remains of previous buildings: Brownfield sites that appear innocuous are sometimes full of hidden remains of previous structures. In the past, buildings may have been knocked down, the resulting rubble pushed into basements, and everything covered neatly by a clean layer of dirt. Unfortunately, all of this will have to be dug out and removed and replaced with

compacted fill before you can construct a building there. One constant fear when excavations for new buildings begin is that workers will discover buried fuel tanks, forgotten until work begins. Removing fuel tanks is not very expensive if they're empty, but if they have ancient fuel in them, the whole issue falls under the jurisdiction of the EPA—the U.S. Environmental Protection Agency.
- Serious pollution: Many brownfield sites are badly polluted. Although it's perfectly possible to construct a library on what was once an EPA Superfund site, the cost of cleanup can be spectacular. And as with the demolition of asbestos-laden buildings, the costs of cleaning up a polluted site can be vastly more than the value of the resulting empty land.

> Never make assumptions on the costs of site cleanup, and always get prices in writing.

Polluted sites are jobs for serious experts. Never commit in any way to a polluted site until you know what the problems are and who will be cleaning things up *before* you own the site. Hire experts and rely on them.

The main thing is to be sure your site is genuinely clean before you acquire it, and that you don't get stuck with any of the cleanup costs.

- Who's responsible? As part of the evaluation of your proposed site, your architects and engineers should do a historical check to evaluate the likelihood of underground problems. Libraries are well equipped to participate in such studies if they have long runs of old city directories, old Sanborn atlases and similar fire-insurance publications, or other historic materials. For example, if a review of old city directories indicates that there was once a gas station or a manufacturing plant on your proposed site, the chance of a forgotten underground storage tank or of general site pollution increases immensely. Fire insurance atlases give diagrams of buildings' footprints and provide information on type of construction, helping you to know where to explore for problems. If a large building once stood on the site, you need soil borings to check that it was totally removed rather than simply pushed down into the basement and covered with earth. Despite people's best efforts, however, some unknown hazards sneak through. For example, buried tanks for heating oil for homes or small businesses may never have been documented and may still be lurking. This is one of many reasons why all projects need

construction contingency funds. Whenever libraries are dealing with old buildings or previously occupied sites, there's always a chance of an unexpected mess turning up and requiring extra expenditure.
- REALLY bad ideas: When faced with polluted buildings or sites, a few owners are tempted to conduct midnight removals. "The old high school is full of lead and asbestos," someone argues, "so we'll bring in a backhoe on Saturday night, knock the structure down, load it into trucks, and dump it in the crick." (In other words, an unauthorized landfill.) This kind of activity will almost certainly lead to an intimate acquaintance with the EPA. You will not enjoy an intimate acquaintance with the EPA.

J. Good and Bad Neighbors

Just as homeowners worry about inappropriate neighbors, libraries have to ask what adjacent property uses are likely to cause service problems.

> One of the villains of Walter Scott's *Ivanhoe* is Sir Philip Malvoisin—which can be translated as "bad neighbor." This section is dedicated to his memory.

Public libraries are particularly vulnerable to bad neighbors because they are legally open to everyone, but all libraries can suffer from inappropriate next-door activities.

Some bad neighbors that affect all kinds of libraries include:

- Noisy neighbors: Although libraries are not as quiet today as they were in years back, people still need to find quiet corners and study rooms.

> Fred worked with a school library where every iteration of the architect's drawings included a new (but always noisy) neighbor next door to the library, with the two spaces sharing a common wall. First it was the band practice room (remember that the sound of people learning the saxophone sounds a lot like seriously unhappy cats) and then it was the gymnasium. In desperation, the library finally arranged to have the wall between the library and the gym consist of a row of athletic department offices and library storerooms.

> Another school library Fred worked with occupied part of a large room that had originally been a garage. To keep the cost of HVAC modifications down, the school had years earlier built a partial partition between the library and the rest of the garage. Because the partition ended about six feet below the ceiling, all sounds were shared.
>
> Many neighbors would have been good neighbors. Office personnel would have been fine. So would sewing classes, or plane geometry, or studio art.
>
> Unfortunately, the school used the space for the weight training room for high school athletes. As a result, users of the library were treated to the constant grunting of students attempting to hoist heavy weights, punctuated occasionally by the ringing crashes of barbells being dropped by young athletes who had bitten off more than they could hoist. Each time a barbell dropped, all the occupants of the library leapt as if electrocuted.

> Fred worked with another library next to a busy railroad track with about three unit coal trains passing every hour—each one a string of honking diesels followed by about 125 heavy cars. In addition to the constant noise, the vibrations from passing trains caused objects to fall off shelves, and sections of the building eventually started pulling apart.

- Polluting neighbors: Pollutants can range from dangerous chemicals (for example, benzene) to bad smells (such as pig farms). Unfortunately, pollution can spread widely, and moving the library may not help a great deal.
- Homeless shelters
- (For public libraries) Junior high schools
- And many others . . .

K. Size

When the time comes to build your academic or public library, many people will have difficulty believing how much acreage you need.

The important point is that the library building itself often occupies a relatively small portion of the site.

Here are some of the factors that contribute to necessary site size.

1. Building Footprint

The "footprint" of a building is the physical space it occupies.

Your building program will give you a rough idea of the likely footprint of your library. Because libraries are inherently flat structures, for anything up to about 30,000 to 50,000 square feet, begin by assuming that the building will be all on one floor, and that the footprint will therefore be as large as your programmed building size.

When they get a great deal larger than 50,000 square feet, one-story libraries start resembling Walmart. Horizontal distances become too great, and libraries start expanding upwards.

Public libraries need to limit the total number of public floors in order to limit the cost of staff oversight. For a medium-sized public library, two floors are ideally enough for public areas, although offices, workrooms, storage, HVAC, and other functions can be on a third floor.

For a public library of anything from 40,000 to 80,000 or even 100,000 square feet, you might start by guessing a 40,000-square-foot footprint. For an academic library, more vertical stacking may be feasible, since supervision is a less significant issue.

Estimating footprint size is complicated by the fact that certain areas of a building—typically public library meeting rooms—may need to be in single-story sections of the building. Meeting rooms need to be at grade level to allow after-hours access and easy emergency exits. Placing other functions above meeting rooms is difficult or impossible because making the upper floors strong enough will probably lead to unwanted columns in the meeting rooms, and meeting room ceilings often need to be higher than other ceilings in the building.

The real test of required footprint, of course, is the actual building design.

2. Parking and Driveways

Virtually all academic and public library buildings require space for parking and driveways.

- On-site parking: The amount of parking required for academic libraries will depend on campus planning. Many academic libraries use shared parking rather than library parking. Public library parking is strongly affected by local zoning requirements. If your public library is in an area that requires off-street parking, you may have to provide two to four parking spaces for every 1,000 square feet of library space. (Even if you are in a central business district location where zoning does not require off-street parking, you still need to know where your users will park.) Assuming that each parking space requires 300 square feet, a library in a town that requires four spaces per 1,000 square feet will have a parking lot larger than the library. If you are planning for expansion, don't forget that if you expand your library building by 75 percent, you will probably also need space to expand your parking area by 75 percent. Under conditions of extreme crowding, some libraries save space by providing parking beneath their structures. Be sure to review all of the implications with your architect, consultant, and local planning officials before assuming that you can save space this way. Know the extra cost. And keep in mind that the idea of parking underground spooks many users because they are concerned about who may be lurking in the dim recesses of the garage.
- Drive-through services: Drive-through book returns and similar services require far more turning space than is often provided, and the world is full of libraries with drive-up services that simply don't work. Unfortunately, designers often underestimate required turning radiuses for cars that need to pull up closely to book returns. (If you stand and watch people using drive-through returns, it's impressive to see how many have to get out of their cars because they can't get close enough to the returns to reach the chutes through open car windows.)

> Fred dealt with one library where the twisted drive-through lanes required contortions that no driver could manage. When Fred complained to the people who designed the drive-through, they said that the lanes were fine but that the drivers were "timid."

- Deliveries, trash removal, and so on: All libraries need additional driveway space for deliveries, staff arrivals, dumpsters, and so on.

3. Setbacks

Except for central business districts, most zoning codes require that buildings be set back from the street to provide open space and a uniform line of facades along streets.

If zoning in your area requires that your library be set back thirty feet from the sidewalk, you will require a substantial amount of extra land.

Checking to be sure that your site can contain the library you need while maintaining legal setbacks is a job for your architects. Don't guess without them.

4. Plantings and Landscaping

Public and academic libraries need to set aside space for grass, trees, flower beds, foundation plantings, terraces, fountains, statuary, and other civilized details. These also require space.

Depending on zoning codes, you may be required to include plantings around your public library building.

Some public library branches in cities are installed in storefronts that are located directly on sidewalks, but many of these are rented spaces rather than custom-built libraries.

5. Surface Water Detention

If your library will need to provide space for a detention basin on its site, your site may need to be substantially larger.

The provision of green roofs or permeable pavers in parking lots may change requirements if your site would otherwise be too tight.

Your architects will need to review these issues with city authorities.

6. Expansion Space

As we mention frequently, one of the major mistakes libraries make is assuming that they will never need to expand.

Spending a vast amount of money on a new library with no possibility for future expansion is a great demonstration of the power of short-term thinking.

It's hard to know how much space to allocate for long-term expansion, but with a brand-new building, planning for a 100 percent increase in size is not unreasonable.

When you are planning a new library, well-meaning (and frequently very aggressive) people will insist that your library's next construction job will be its last. These people are inevitably wrong, but they are hard to deal with. Many of them deeply believe that they are right, and this gives them righteous conviction. Others have axes to grind.

There are a number of solid reasons why you should always plan space for outward rather than upward expansion.

a. Expanding Outward

Remember that when it comes to expanding library buildings, outward expansion is almost inevitably better than upward expansion. People who argue that *if* you run out of space you can easily expand upward know pretty much nothing about library buildings.

The approaches here are obvious:

- NEVER build a library with an architectural design that prevents outward expansion. Of all errors that prevent expansion, this is by far the most easily avoided, for it simply involves holding designers to the requirement that buildings be designed for expansion.
- ALWAYS obtain and protect sites large enough to accommodate expansion, make clear from the beginning that the empty site is reserved for expansion, and fight any group that proposes alternative uses for the space. This can be a special problem on crowded campuses, where academic units are always casting greedy eyes on open spaces.
- Be extremely wary of expansion underground.
- If you can see that your library will need to be expanded in the foreseeable future, a two-phase building program will help you make sure that expansion will be as easy as possible.

Expanding a two-story public library outward can work particularly well if (a) the adult and children's departments are on separate floors, and (b) offices and other small rooms do not abut the wall to be removed. (All of this, or course, requires proper planning of the original building.)

b. Problems with Expanding Upward

You will encounter many problems if you try to expand upwards.

- Upward expansion requires massive surgery. Roofs have to be removed and replaced with floors that can hold the weight of books. One-story libraries will require the addition of elevators and staircases in proper locations.
- Frequently, existing footings and columns are not strong enough to support additional levels, despite beliefs to the contrary. When people tell you, "Our building was engineered to carry an additional floor," *never* believe them. Among the reasons for disbelief are:
  - When the building was initially planned, the owners may have discussed providing footings and columns capable of holding additional levels. These were deleted to save construction costs, but the memory of the change is overwhelmed by the memory of the original concept.
  - If the building was initially planned for anything other than library functions, the footings may still not be strong enough. Footings strong enough for a two-story office structure are usually too weak to support a two-story library.
  - Columns in the building may not be strong enough to support an additional floor. This is particularly true with one-story buildings, where the existing columns have to support only a roof.
  - In a one-story library, supporting the weight of books on a concrete slab on grade is easy. When we have to build upward, it's suddenly a different structural world because we have to support the weight of books in midair.
  - In some libraries, sections of the floor that were not initially intended to hold book stacks are too flimsy to do so. This violates one of the most basic principles of library design, but it happens all the time and can have a major impact on the ability to rearrange functions.
  - When additional stories are mentioned, always have a structural engineer verify that this can be done. Never believe anyone else.
- For public libraries, upward expansion may increase the number of floors to be supervised. Operating a public library with an unsupervised floor is a recipe for major problems. To make extra public floors work, you need a service desk on each floor. Unless these are desks that currently exist and are staffed whenever the library is open, you will have to hire additional staff members just to watch the new floor.
- If you need to expand upward, it may be much cheaper to demolish all or part of the building and build a new two-story or three-story section from scratch.

c. Few Critics Are Disinterested

Much of the talk against the need for expansion comes from people with axes to grind.

Public libraries can be victimized by people who have white elephant buildings to unload. If the proposed building and site are too small, the owners will argue that expansion will never be needed. Often the owners will pitch their arguments directly to local governments or to chambers of commerce, contending that the only reason the library doesn't want the owner's building is the desire of the board of trustees to build an expensive monument to its own ego.

For example, Fred worked with a public library in a town that had an abandoned church that would have made an incredibly poor library. Not only was the church building unworkable, but the site was too small, even if the building were demolished. The congregation hoping to unload their former church at a high price formed an unholy alliance with a local real estate firm, which started a whispering campaign against the library board. Fred ended up having to document all of the reasons why both the building and the site were unworkable and why the cost would be greater than starting over with an empty site, and then holding public meetings to explain everything. (After the public meetings, the only holdouts were the real estate agents, who saw some really major sales commissions going down the tubes. When the building was eventually sold to another congregation, it brought only a small fraction of the price the real estate firm hoped to extract from the library.)

In general, when public libraries are seeking new sites, boards of trustees need to be prepared in advance with responses to the "Why haven't you considered X building or X site?" sort of questions. Armed with a written building program and a list of likely suggestions, architects can help boards by preparing beforehand lists of the "Yes, we considered X, and here's why it won't work" variety.

Always be prepared to tell everyone in advance the absolute and non-negotiable basics of functional library design:

- Floors that can uniformly hold 150 pounds per square foot (and much more for compact shelving and microfiche storage)
- Wide-open floors for easy supervision and stack placement
- Rectangular spaces

- Ceilings at least ten feet high (higher for meeting rooms)
- Vast numbers of electrical outlets
- Single entrances

> One classic example of turf problems occurred at the University of Illinois in Urbana. In the 1960s, the university wanted to construct an undergraduate library adjacent to the main graduate library. Unfortunately, the only available site was located between the graduate library and a historic agricultural experiment plot. The agriculture department had enough political clout to force the new library underground, where it would not cast a new shadow on the corn.

d. Necessity of Strong Floors

Expanding school and special libraries requires access to adjacent space strong enough to carry appropriate loads.

While academic and public libraries need open land reserved for expansion, small libraries that consist of rooms in large buildings need to expand horizontally into adjacent areas.

For many special libraries, however, relocating the library to a larger space may be simpler and cheaper than trying to expand an existing library. As usual, the major problems may lie in:

- Finding space strong enough to support the weight of books.
- Finding a space that facilitates use of the library by members of the organization.

School libraries can sometimes be expanded by absorbing adjacent classrooms. Here the problem may be as much one of completely opening walls as of the ability of floors to carry loads. Given limited staffing and the variegated social enthusiasms of students, school libraries cannot afford to be complex places with areas that are difficult to supervise. Basically, a good school library space is one big room.

1. Always Buy (and Keep) Adjacent Land

One of the most common mistakes that public library boards of trustees make is to not acquire adjacent land when it comes on the market. Many boards have turned down the opportunity to buy land next door to the library for a song, only to find that when they desperately needed it ten years later it was not available at any price—or at least not at a rational price.

Buying land when the owner wants to sell also keeps libraries away from the ugly face of eminent domain. Although a public body can often take needed land against the will of the owner, the resulting bad feelings and bad publicity can linger for years.

If you have land for future expansion next to your library, be careful that it isn't converted to a temporary asset that becomes a permanent asset. For example, if a local garden group constructs a mini-park on the site, the area may take on a life of its own and be harder to convert to library building functions when the time comes.

Existing buildings can be used temporarily for storage or leased out until the time comes to demolish them, but there are always pitfalls. Although a building was purchased for expansion, it may come to be regarded as an asset of value. And leasing out space turns the library into a landlord—a function some libraries enjoy more than others.

With the passage of years, existing buildings of no distinction scheduled for eventual demolition may also slowly gain status as "historic" structures.

Leasing space to a local business can lead to problems if the local business becomes popular with the community and local citizens want the business to stay where it is forever.

> If a library has no immediate need of an adjacent structure, it can always lease it temporarily, but there's a lot more to be said for quick demolition and conversion to parking while the demolishing is good.

2. Rules of Thumb for Estimating Site Acreage

People will frequently push you to specify a site size before you know anything about the nature of available sites or about your library design.

The only good way to come up with an opinion on site size is to involve your architects, engineers, and consultants. If you're under severe pressure to respond prematurely, here are a few suggestions:

- Tell people that you cannot make a commitment or even a comment without professional input. If you have a written building program and an architectural site study, you will be far more able to tell whether a site is large enough to actually work.
- As with all situations when you deal with the news media and politicians, never make any offhand comments, and never agree with other people's proposals until you have solid information. Never respond "Yes" to any "Would you say X?" question. And there's no shame in repeating, "We won't know until our architects and consultants have studied the situation."
- Guess big to start. It's a lot easier to eventually agree you can get by with less space than to have to say, "Oops. We *meant* to say that the space you suggested actually isn't big enough."

But if you guess too big, that can lead to bad publicity as well.

- If anyone pushes you, it's not unreasonable to suggest that the site should be six times the total programmed floor space of the library, always repeating that this assumes (1) a detention basin and (2) a flat, reasonably square site that allows construction anywhere on the site. This means that a library of about 45,000 square feet may need a site of up to six acres.

L. Historic Buildings and Neighborhoods

Any site with existing buildings needs to be investigated for possible historic protection. Although it's perfectly possible to demolish structures regarded as historic, trying to do so can sometimes lead to bad feelings and/or legal entanglements.

The most difficult problems occur when existing libraries need to expand onto adjacent property with historic structures, because the library may feel that it cannot simply elect to build elsewhere. For a more extensive discussion of expanding historic libraries, see chapter 13 on "Remodeling and Expanding Library Buildings."

If there's a historic building next to your library, many people will contend that you can solve all of your space problems by linking the two, both saving money and protecting a community treasure.

As a basic rule, remember that (no matter what local enthusiasts claim) it can be extremely difficult and expensive to join a library to a historic building—especially one that was never designed to be a library—and that the resulting structure is far more likely to be very seriously dysfunctional. You will almost certainly have major problems with different floor levels, overly divided interior spaces, and difficult oversight.

Nothing here is meant to suggest that a handsome historic structure cannot be converted to a handsome and functional library building, but it will almost certainly be a complex and expensive job. Once again, it helps to have a building program in print and approved and ready to be used as a yardstick for evaluating options *before* discussions of possible conversions begin.

1. Players

One thing that complicates dealing with historic structures is the number of different groups that can be involved.

- Depending on circumstances, existing buildings can be protected by federal, state, or local laws.
- Many states have historical preservation agencies and many municipalities have preservation ordinances.
- Buildings and neighborhoods may be listed on the National Register of Historic Places.
- Whether or not they are on the National Register, historic neighborhoods can have extremely specific legal limits on construction and remodeling.
- Even in the absence of legal limits and controls, ad hoc local preservation groups can be avidly involved.

While federal and state rules and regulations are usually straightforward, local preservation ordinances can be unpredictable. Sometimes local preservation groups can be far more emotional and difficult to deal with than state or federal agencies because they are less process-bound and see themselves as protecting their local communities.

If your library is considering a new site with surviving structures, it will be wise to check with local and state preservation groups to see whether you are likely to encounter adverse reactions. Until you have completed a building program and at least architectural feasibility studies, *NEVER* let yourself be cornered into agreeing to retain existing non-library structures as part of a new or expanded library. Connecting two buildings is extremely difficult and likely to lead to complex structures that are on too many levels and have too many irrelevant and disconnected spaces. It may also involve difficult problems with codes, because construction types in existing buildings may not meet code requirements for larger buildings—or may not even meet requirements at all. The gross square footage of an expanded or combined building will probably be much larger than the gross square footage of a comparable new building that meets the same program needs.

Existing laws may allow the adverse (against the wishes of the owners) addition of old structures to registers of historic buildings, particularly if the structures are publicly owned. This means that a public body can purchase a privately-owned structure not listed as historic, only to find it suddenly added to the National Register of Historic Places.

2. Sources of Assistance

When your proposed site has historic buildings, a number of people and agencies can help.

- State historic preservation agencies. Well-developed state historic preservation agencies can be of great assistance. They are prepared to balance competing interests, they have a broad perspective that comes from dealing with large numbers of historic structures, and they may have experts on library design who understand how libraries occupy spaces. If you have a historic library building, get to know the library expert in your state preservation agency.
- Local planning agencies. Local government agencies are good sources of information on actual local codes and local preservation ordinances.
- Experts on historic architecture. If you need a strong person in your corner, or just an impartial observer, one place you can turn to is architects with expertise in this field.

If you see problems with historic structures arising in your project, you can limit your search for architects to firms that have resident experts.

- Local activist groups. In our experience, if older buildings need to be demolished, the greatest difficulties can be found in dealing with local activist groups. They are more likely to be passionate and unreasoning and to lack the balance that comes from the wider experience and professional training of state agency staffs.

> On the other hand, if you are seeking to expand your historic library and are convinced you can do it with proper support, local preservation groups can be powerful friends. But there's always the danger of loose cannon behavior.

- Issues of standing. Not all agencies and groups have legal standing. Even if a building is listed on the National Register of Historic Places, it's possible that no state or federal agency will have standing if you will not be using state or federal money on your project. Many local activist groups have no standing at all.
- Politicians. Every once in a while, a library finds itself in a situation where it becomes the prisoner of a decaying or ancient-but-unworthy structure on an essential site. In situations like this, sometimes the only feasible course of action is to bypass the preservation process and seek political relief. John has done this in the past.

M. Archaeology

In addition to visible structures, ostensibly empty sites may have buried remains that limit or eliminate their use as library sites.

1. General Archaeological Issues

If your site has any historical significance, you can rest assured that you will need an archaeological study.

Depending on circumstances, you may be required to have an archaeological compliance survey conducted of your property. The field of cultural resources archaeology has expanded rapidly in the last forty years, with contract archaeologists conducting, for example, rapid surveys of proposed highway rights of way for evidence of possible archaeological significance.

One of the major careers available to professionally trained archaeologists is checking sites for possible archaeological significance.

Your architect can assist you in finding necessary experts and complying with relevant laws.

2. NAGPRA

The discovery of Native American graves on your building site will probably end any possibility of constructing a library on the site.

The Native American Graves Preservation and Repatriation Act (NAGPRA) of 1990 was designed to eliminate the practice of treating Native American burials as little more than engaging sites for archaeological investigations.

Reactions to NAGPRA have varied widely. Some people regard the act as a tremendous handicap to the study of American history, while others see it as a long overdue way to keep people from simply poking around in ancestral graves, much as more recent inhabitants would resent the scientific excavation of their church cemeteries.

From the library construction point of view, it's best to assume that if there are Native American burials on your property, you won't be able to build there.

For this reason, it's important to:

- Do some preliminary historical checking. Ask local government officials, local civil engineers, and local historical societies about stories of local Native American burials. Stories may be little more than unfounded rumors, but they may give you the impetus to do further checking.
- Include a statement in your bill of sale that the site is warranted not to include Native American graves.

N. Orientation to the Compass

Frequently, sites dictate how library buildings can be oriented. The comments here apply to temperate areas of the northern hemisphere, such as the contiguous forty-eight states.

Generally speaking, the best sites permit:

- **Library buildings with south or southeast entrances.**
  In many parts of the United States, prevailing winter winds from the north and northwest make sheltered entrances on the south or southeast sides of buildings far more practical and comfortable. If the wind howls into your library every time the door is opened, even a foyer or vestibule may not be enough to prevent bitter blasts from hitting the staff facing the entrance. And if the sun doesn't hit your entrance in the winter, you may end up fighting The Ice That Never Melts. Icy steps and ramps are particularly vicious.
- **Library buildings with north light for reading.**
  In the northern hemisphere, the only natural light that is dependably pleasant for reading is north light. If the back side of your library faces north, this provides an opportunity for rows of windows and bright but low-glare light. Depending on latitude, even north windows may be a source of direct sunlight, particularly around the summer solstice. As part of preliminary design sketches, your architects should indicate when north sunlight might be a problem.

- **Library buildings with the least possible west light**
  In most of the United States, western sunlight is nasty for much of the year, particularly the summer. Most libraries are closed for business until long after summer sunrises, limiting the problems of eastern light, but they are open when the sun sets, and the brutal light blasting in from the west is enough to sear retinas. If you have western windows in your library, they will all need effective shades, including in particular cute windows set far above the floor. This is frequently forgotten by architects, who blissfully install small clearstories in sloped ceilings, ornamental curves above rectangular windows, and monitor windows facing in all directions. The fewer western windows you have, the easier it is to avoid the very worst that natural daylight has to offer.

- **Library buildings with their long axes running from east to west**
  In order to maximize northern and southern exposure, and to minimize western exposure, most libraries do best if the longer dimension of the building runs east-west rather than north-south. (However, most small library buildings are somewhat square.)

- **General problems with excess glass**
  If you are worried about excess glass in your building, beware of the assertion that "with modern glass" glare is no longer a problem. We've heard this for decades, but when the buildings are complete, unshielded glass hit by direct sunlight is *always* a problem, regardless of how modern it is. When your architects tout "modern glass," always insist on seeing an existing installation using the same glass.

O. Easements

Easements are legal rights to use someone else's property. Typical uses might include driving through the property to access another piece of property, running a sewer through the property, or running power lines over the property.

Other easements limit the ability of a property owner to affect neighboring property, such as agreements not to block the view.

Libraries need to be aware of any easements on their proposed sites.

P. Land Ownership

Occasionally, libraries construct buildings on land they do not own.

This is always an extraordinarily bad decision. If libraries do not own their sites, any money spent on their buildings is essentially thrown away, for the libraries cannot sell their buildings if it becomes essential to move.

Fred has worked with a couple of small public libraries caught in this situation. Any investment they make in their buildings will be lost if they leave their buildings. This is very much like the dilemma of farmhouses for tenant farmers; the tenants don't want to spend money on buildings they don't own, and the owners don't want to spend unnecessary money fixing up tenant farmhouses.

The rule is a simple one: Never build a library on a site to which you do not have full and clear title. Or, more clearly, NEVER BUILD A LIBRARY ON A SITE TO WHICH YOU DO NOT HAVE FULL AND CLEAR TITLE.

III. SPECIAL SITE NEEDS OF VARIOUS TYPES OF LIBRARIES

In addition to the issues listed in section II, a number of site selection concerns apply specifically to certain kinds of libraries.

Most of the issues listed here apply primarily to public libraries, since these are the primary libraries to have completely independent sites. The locations of academic libraries, school libraries, and special libraries are limited by the institutions they serve, which both define a limited range of sites and protect libraries as part of larger buildings or campuses.

A. Public Libraries

Public libraries in particular need to consider security issues when selecting sites, but all libraries can be affected by the problems that result from insecure locations.

Public libraries are particularly vulnerable to neighborhood problems because they are open to anyone who wants to enter the library. By contrast, academic institutions, schools, and the proprietors of special libraries can usually turn away people who are not authorized to enter their buildings.

The problem with many of the issues raised in this section is that they sound illiberal. But they all are based on extremely widespread problems.

Here are a handful of site situations that affect primarily public libraries.

1. Retail Sites

About seventy-five years ago, Joseph Wheeler argued that the best place for a public library was a good place for a dime store. His basic point was that libraries benefit from being located where people go shopping. While a school may benefit from a slightly out-of-the-way location, public libraries benefit from being highly visible and accessible.

In turn, commercial sites benefit from nearby libraries. For example:

- Fred consulted for a library that moved into a couple of empty stores in a nearby strip mall during construction. When the library moved in, merchants in the strip mall varied from indifferent to concerned about competition for parking. But when the library moved out a year later, the local merchants were dismayed to see it leave. Sales had boomed while the library was there.
- Naestved, Denmark, has a library that shares a large, two-story building with a supermarket. The first floor is retail and the second the library. Both are entered through the same door, with library users taking the stairs or elevator to the upper level. Both the store and the library are packed with users.
- When Fred surveyed the patrons of his own downtown library, they commonly noted that they would do less business downtown if the library were not located there.
- The sad thing about all of this is that too few people recognize this extremely useful juxtaposition.
- Merchants are frequently surprised to find that business increases when libraries move in nearby.
- Mayors and city planners want to save good retail sites for the exclusive use of businesses, not realizing that public libraries boost business and would improve the mix of land uses.
- Governing bodies may also want to reserve the best sites for property tax-paying entities.

2. Government Sites

Frequently, developers of new sites for local government suggest including libraries. Often the plan is to provide a "campus" arrangement for the city hall, police department, fire department, and public library.

Libraries can benefit from being adjacent to other governmental buildings.

- Public libraries may find it easier to find large new sites in a government campus. With luck, the site will be free to the library.
- A group of new government buildings will be attractive, reducing the risk that the library may end up with run-down neighbors.
- Of all the buildings in a government campus, the public library may be the most popular with local taxpayers. This may provide local government with a greater incentive to fund the new library building as part of the project.

- Certain difficult neighbors, such as homeless shelters and bars, may be avoided because they are unwelcome to the people who write the zoning codes, who may be eager to protect the government center in general.
- Because a number of governmental buildings are located together, the cost of the library's access to utilities may be paid by the municipality.
- A location next to the police department may increase users' and librarians' sense of security.
- When libraries are adjacent to local government buildings, opportunities for shared meeting spaces are possible. For example, a city government and public library may share a large meeting room.

There are also a few potential problems.

- Shared governmental sites offer few opportunities for citizens to make multiple-visit trips that include the library. Stopping by the hardware store, the cleaners, and the library on a single trip makes sense, but there are few shared visits to libraries and other local government buildings.

> It's hard to imagine people saying, "Since we're stopping by to see Uncle Joe at the jail, let's get some books from the library. It's right next door."

- Because total space may be limited, developers of shared government sites may announce that the library's required space is unreasonably large, or that no expansion space can be provided. Libraries need to have carefully developed building programs in order to be prepared to defend their space needs, and they need to stand their ground.
- To obtain a uniform appearance among buildings, local governments may insist that their architect serve as the library architect, regardless of prior experience. In such situations, public libraries can agree to match the general exterior appearance of the other government buildings in the site, but it's absolutely essential that libraries have their own architects and their own consultants.
- A shared meeting room can be a major problem if an agency other than the library takes over the management of the room or if the room is buried in the library.
- Shared parking can be a problem at times of heavy use of adjacent government buildings.
- While the logic of grouping municipal government buildings is attractive, the logic breaks down because there are always a few types of buildings that are excluded, such as those dealing with utilities or sewage.

On balance, local government sites can be very successful locations for public libraries. The important factors are visibility, access, independence of architectural design, adequate acreage for expansion, and independence of meeting room management.

3. "River City" Sites

Some people have idyllic images of sort of Norman Rockwell libraries, not unlike the River City public library in *The Music Man*.

When public libraries are seeking sites, or considering abandoning undersize sites, someone will inevitably attack all change, painting a rosy picture of a sort of Never-Never-Land Public Library—a classic building with pediment and columns, facing the courthouse, close enough to homes so all children in town can walk to the library and obtain improving books.

Some sites of this type are still around and work. Historic libraries can feel wonderful.

However, many such surviving libraries stand on sites that are far too small and offer far too little parking.

If you sense that the "beloved traditional tiny central library" argument will arise, you can be prepared in two ways:

- Have data prepared on how many people actually walk to the library. One way to develop data is to conduct a parking survey, asking (in the course of the survey) whether users walked or drove to the library the day of the survey. If you know that only a small percentage of your users walk, even given the library's perfect traditional location, you will be in a much better position to argue. Doing the survey twice, once in summer and once in winter, may provide persuasive data if people never walk except in nice weather.
- Have a building program prepared to defend your space needs and describe your building's current shortcomings. One problem with all library locations is that *someone* always lives nearby and doesn't want the library to move. If that person speaks passionately enough in a public hearing, however, other people in the room will realize that *they* don't live close to the library, and that may help take care of things.

4. Sites near "Homeless" Shelters

Never build a new library near a homeless shelter.

This is absolutely critical. Not only should public libraries never be built within less than a few blocks of homeless shelters, but library officials need to maintain constant vigilance to prevent homeless shelters from being established nearby after the library opens.

Many times, shelters are in church basements. The seemingly innocent church across the street may suddenly become a source of major problems when it adds the function of homeless shelter to its mission. This is one of several reasons why churches can be far less desirable neighbors than one might imagine.

Before building a new public library, try to arrange for zoning around the library that does not permit shelters. Impress on your local zoning administrators how the presence of a nearby shelter can seriously limit the effect of the money the municipality devotes to library service.

Library staff and board members who have not had experiences with homeless shelters as neighbors may not realize how many problems shelters bring with them. Typically, shelters close for the day just about the time that libraries open in the morning. The residents of the shelter, who are seeking comfortable seating and temperatures, migrate en masse to the library, where they spend the day sleeping on (and mistreating) the library's soft seating. Some libraries are forced to eliminate their soft seating as a result.

Some homeless people come to the library to use its resources, and libraries need to help them as much as they would help more fortunate users. But many homeless people are simply looking for a comfortable place to sleep. Any library should be able to cope with a couple of people sleeping, but when the building is completely taken over it can cease to function as a library.

The situation is made worse by the fact that many "homeless" people are actually non-institutionalized mentally ill and substance abusers. Librarians are not trained to provide services to these groups, library buildings are not designed to serve them, and libraries are not funded to serve them. Society has treated these people shabbily by simply dumping them on the street, but providing housing in public libraries is not the right answer.

Having to deal with vast numbers of homeless people tends to lead libraries to adopt policies that are unfortunately harsh. For example, some libraries do not allow sleeping, and any retired persons who nod off over the *Wall Street Journal* are immediately awakened and told that they must stay awake or leave.

Because the impact of homeless shelters can be extreme, even when you're not contemplating construction, you need to keep alert to the quiet introduction of homeless shelters near your library. Be sure your city zoning staff members know the library's legitimate concerns in this area, for the implications of a shelter near the library may simply not occur to them when the issue is raised.

> One structural option for dealing with homeless people who spend their days in libraries but don't want library services is to create an alternate day shelter. John collaborated in a project like this when he was director of the public library in Decatur, Illinois, and it worked well.

We've devoted a lot of space to this issue because it is such an important one. The basic points are:

- The creation of a homeless shelter near a library can have a really major negative impact on library functions.
- Actually, building a brand new public library next to an existing homeless shelter is measurably foolish.
- The issue is not "homelessness" but rather people who need assistance with mental illnesses or substance abuse but have simply been dumped on the street. This is a failure of social policy, and libraries should not be cornered into taking the blame.

5. Secure Locations

Never build on sites that people are afraid to visit.

No matter how attractive your new building, people won't go there if they regard its location as unsafe.

- A library in a park, for example, seems charming by daylight, but few people want to enter parks after dark. This means that any library in a park must be located on a sidewalk at the edge of the park with the entrance on the sidewalk.

- Depending on the neighborhood, if the library is surrounded by bushes or trees, users may worry that people are lurking in the underbrush, waiting to leap upon passersby.
- Underground parking also spooks many users.
- Some planners envision libraries as pawns in the redevelopment or improvement of unpleasant neighborhoods. Although the presence of the library in a rough area may eventually bring other desirable functions to replace the drug dealers and prostitutes, in the short run most people won't want to visit the library (or let their children walk there unescorted). And few public libraries offer the kind of hardship pay that will make up for staff having to park behind chain-link fences topped with concertina wire or having to be accompanied by armed guards wherever they enter or leave their libraries.
- If you are planning a library building in an area that people find insecure, be sure to factor in the added long-term operational cost of extra security measures and get a commitment from local government to foot the extra cost on a permanent basis.

6. Locations near Schools and Churches

- Beware of building next door to high schools and (particularly) middle schools. Although all public libraries are eager to serve students, libraries need to be far enough from school buildings to give kids a chance to unwind and calm down before they reach the library. If a school and a library are half a dozen blocks apart, students can easily walk to the library, but it's not the first thing they encounter when they leave school. Middle school and junior high school students are generally the most difficult to cope with. Grade school students are generally sweet, and high school students have grown up a little, but middle school students can represent major behavioral problems. Local citizens are unlikely to understand the problems that libraries encounter when they build next door to middle schools, and they may see a proposed library location next door to a middle school as one that will benefit the entire community. Similarly, school officials will envision the placement of a public library next door to the school as a win-win situation, particularly if they hope to be able to reduce expenditures on school library services once the public library is located down the block.

> One public library we know was built next door to a middle school. While the newly opened library was struggling to cope with after-school uproar, the principal of the middle school was proposing a tunnel of terror connecting the middle school with the library.

- Some libraries also encounter problems when they are located close to churches. Many public libraries are wary of locations near churches. Churches can take over all available parking for blocks around during services. This is seldom a problem on Sunday mornings, but cars parked for weddings and funerals can make it almost impossible to use nearby libraries. As mentioned above, if the church decides to provide a homeless shelter, the impact on the library can be extreme. As with locations near middle schools, citizens are unlikely to understand why libraries are wary of building too close to churches. Funeral homes can have the same effect as churches. When funerals take place, every parking space for blocks around may be taken. All of this is made more complex by the fact that many churches and funeral homes have inadequate parking to begin with. Obviously, when weddings and funerals are not taking place, library users can take advantage of unused church parking if the two institutions come to a cooperative agreement. But the tradeoffs can be severe for the library.

7. Adjacent Transportation

Always consider the implications of adjacent transportation.

Both highways and railroads offer problems (and occasional benefits) for public libraries.

- **General implications**

    A busy highway near a library can bring visibility and (depending on signaling) easy access, but it can also bring noise and concerns about safety. If a toddler wanders out of a library, a nearby highway can pose a real threat. Railroads provide noise, and those without grade separation lead to blocked crossings. Towns located on suburban railroad lines complain endlessly about the noise of locomotive horns, even though they are usually essential from a life-safety viewpoint. Towns on freight lines complain about the rumble and noise of passing trains and about long interruptions of automobile traffic as freight trains pass slowly through town. The transport of massive amounts of crude oil by train means that derailments can be major disasters.

> The distant whistles of passing trains are a lot more romantic if they're genuinely distant.

- **Changes in traffic patterns**
  Railroad traffic patterns change. The fact that a railroad line is lightly used today does not prevent it from becoming a major thoroughfare tomorrow. Road traffic patterns can also change abruptly, particularly if highways are relocated or streets widened.

For example, one library with which Fred worked purchased a much larger site than it actually needed. The board of trustees envisioned selling part of the site for housing, but within a few months the state department of transportation announced that it was taking about a third of the site for road realignment, leaving the library with just the right amount of total space.

Although most transportation routes are well established, it's impossible to predict all changes, and compensations for heavier traffic or widened rights of way may be inadequate. For example, if a highway project takes most of a library's parking lot, the library may be compensated only for the value of the lot. If the library cannot acquire compensating space at a similar price, it may find that it owns a building that is almost unusable.

- **Anticipating changes**
  The best way we know to predict what will happen next is to keep as many communication lines open as possible. Make sure that everyone knows how your library is vulnerable. Talk with local, county, and state traffic planners. Have friends in engineering firms. And talk with local railfans, who often have a pretty good idea of what railroads are likely to do (and who aren't subject to corporate confidentiality requirements).

B. Academic Libraries

Because campuses are controlled environments, academic libraries face fewer special location issues.

However, because academic libraries require a lot of turf, finding an adequate space can be difficult, and this may push the library to an undesirable part of campus. Libraries need to be central, not off in a far corner behind the stadium.

Academic libraries may have particular problems protecting their expansion space.

Once in a while, an academic library lucks into a central space. In 1970, for example, the University of Chicago opened its new library on the site of what had been Stagg Field, the university's one-time athletic field. All of this was helped, of course, by the university's earlier decision to get out of interschool athletics.

In recent years, many academic libraries have constructed high-density storage units. Some of these are located on inexpensive land, far from their main campus libraries, introducing delays on the order of twenty-four or more hours for retrieving materials. Others, however, have been constructed directly next to their main libraries, sometimes allowing retrieval even more rapid than from the main stacks.

C. School Libraries

In addition to the problem of nailing down sufficient space, school libraries are constantly threatened with being located next to truly undesirable functions.

One problem school librarians encounter is that their libraries are just one element in a complex mix of school functions. In many cases, spaces for many different functions are planned simultaneously. School librarians angling for good sites are up against science, athletics, music, drama, computer instruction, and lunch, in addition to all the departments that just need better classrooms. In this kind of space-needs free-for-all, getting the attention of the superintendent of schools can be a struggle.

In addition, while academic and public libraries are usually designed by architects with special experience in library design, the architects designing school libraries are selected for their general knowledge of school design challenges and regulations. Compared to the difficulty of laying out gymnasiums and band rooms and wet labs, libraries may appear to deserve just a quick glance.

One common problem is planners' visions of shared spaces. For example, they may decide that the library can be part of an all-hours learning commons, a cafeteria, or a social center, with all the potential security issues. (To be fair to designers, some school libraries have been intended all along to be part of larger centers.)

Or the library may be viewed as the center of the school, with doors entering the library from multiple directions. This violates the basic principle of library design that libraries need single entrances, but the planners may simply try to overrule the librarians.

> Avoiding multiple entrances seems logical, but politicians and architects have ignored this basic security need over and over again.

Another common location problem that school libraries face is noisy neighbors. If walls aren't designed to block sounds, a beginning saxophone class next door can contribute to the general library atmosphere in unsavory ways. The worst neighbors tend to be:

- Music rooms. A common wall with a music room can lead to perpetual unwelcome noise in the library.
- Athletic spaces. The noisiest spaces in schools are probably gymnasiums, but other athletic spaces can cause similar problems.

If you are stuck with noisy adjacencies in a proposed new building, here are some things you might try to add to reduce possible problems:

- Introduce an intermediate row of storerooms between the athletic or music or cafeteria space and the library. You might also suggest athletic or music department offices or cafeteria storerooms.
- Make sure that the entrance to the noisy neighbor space is not immediately adjacent to the entrance to the library.
- Be sure that the dividing wall is designed to diminish sound transmission. As noted elsewhere in this book, some common methods include staggered stud walls, double walls, and making sure that the wall between the library and the noisy facility continues past the ceiling to the bottom of the roof above.

D. Special Libraries

Because most special libraries occupy relatively small spaces, finding a site is often a matter of finding a space that is large enough and that can bear the weight of the collection.

Many special libraries are located in basements, where the weight of the books doesn't threaten the poured concrete slab-on-grade floor.

As with public libraries, a good special library location is often a busy location that staff members of the organization frequently pass. A hospital library, for example, may be far more successful just down the hall from the cafeteria than in a somewhat larger space in an outbuilding.

Because professional organizations are frequently pressed for office space, special libraries are occasionally asked to fit into smaller spaces. The success of this change typically depends on whether the library can give up hard copy of long runs of such materials as medical journals or court reporter series without diminishing service to its clientele.

Both to protect turf and to be prepared for sudden developments, special libraries may want to have completed building programs ready for rapid deployment at all times. Unlike school libraries, public libraries, and academic libraries, where the mills of governmental gods grind slowly, special libraries may find themselves in situations where the response to proposed change must come virtually overnight.

Once the director of a hospital library and Fred put together a quick building program over a single weekend. Although the hospital abandoned its plans to relocate the library, the fact that the library appeared with a written study while the other departments appeared only with angry arguments left the library looking particularly good to the administration.

IV. SUMMARY

When the time comes to select a site for your library, it's important to include your architect, engineers, and consultant in addition to your governing board and local campus, school, or municipal officials. Each party sees things somewhat differently. Even if you choose to ignore the advice of one or more people you hire, it's always worthwhile getting their input and having specific information on why they object.

It's extremely important to have a building program ready before you begin site discussions. You and your architects will need to know in specific detail what kind of space your library needs. Without a program, you will have a hard time convincing the rest of the world that you really need that much space.

It's also vital to have architects. You may be sorely tempted to agree to a site without the help of architects (and the engineers they retain), but you are likely to make serious errors. For example, architects can create quick sketches to test how your library might fit on proposed sites, and engineers can check whether the site can support a library.

When people argue with you, always use your hired professionals to deliver the bad news. And always deliver your own good news.

When deciding between a number of possible sites becomes difficult, your architectural firm may have a scoring system for giving points to various aspects of each site.

However, there are certain aspects of sites that are essentially non-negotiable. Regardless of other considerations, your site has to be large enough, capable of supporting the weight of books, convenient to users, and safe.

V. SNAPPY RULES ON LIBRARY SITE SELECTION

1. Preemptive programming is almost always essential. When people start talking seriously about specific sites, you will need a building program to explain your space needs, but it may be too late to start writing one. Hiring a consultant to write a program is cheap, and delaying can lead to troubles.
2. A bad site for a nice store is a bad site for a nice public library.
3. Most empty buildings suggested for conversion to libraries are empty for very good reasons.
4. Whether you have a campus library, a school library, a business library, or a public library, everyone always wants to steal your site. Be wary and unforgiving of interlopers. One advantage you may have is psychological surprise, since many people don't expect to encounter librarians who go for the jugular.
5. Most sites suggested for libraries are too small. But the people who suggest them will refuse to believe you. Have a building program handy to show them why they're wrong, and an architect to explain how much acreage it will take to house the library described in the program.
6. The electronic revolution does NOT mean that your library will never run out of space.
7. Keep away from river banks, seacoasts, and floodplains. Even without global warming, "hundred-year floods" seem to come along about once every two or three years.
8. Even if it's more conveniently located, you will regret building on a low area of your site. You will not enjoy the scenic effect of seeing water run downhill straight into your library.
9. If your site is so limited that your library will need to plunge underground, you will have windowless and wet basement spaces that staff and books and users will all hate. (Remember that basements in libraries cost nearly as much as extra floors above ground.) Robert Frost, were he with us

today, would no doubt remark that something there is that does not love a basement.
10. Wet books are even less fun than wet dogs.
11. High-density storage next to your library is infinitely better than high-density storage two counties off.
12. Charming, historic sites for public libraries are no good unless their charming, historic parking lots are large enough to hold everyone who wants to use the libraries.
13. Converting an existing non-library structure to an academic or public library often costs just about as much as starting over. If the result is a cumbersome or awkward library, no one wins except the person who sold you the structure. Among possible choices for conversion, empty big box stores are probably best.
14. Sites required for new academic and public libraries can be very large and will frequently involve the demolition of other buildings. Expect squabbles.
15. Neighbors matter.
16. Homeless shelters cause terrible problems for nearby public libraries. (Homeless people are frequently avid library users and fun to talk with. The problem is that many non-institutionalized mentally ill and substance abusers are mislabeled "homeless" by people who don't want to come to grips with serious social issues.)
17. One of the truly fine places for a special library is next door to the cafeteria.
18. Never let anyone else relieve you of your vacant land, and never let nearby land slip through your fingers. Never sell off part of your land to help fund construction; in the long run, the money is trivial and the space is irreplaceable.
19. People with axes to grind will challenge your program. The credentials of your programmer may therefore be politically important.
20. Many proposed sites look sweetly benign but are truly evil below the surface.
21. Never build a library on land you don't own. Land that reverts to someone if the library leaves is nearly as bad. Never get involved with either situation.
22. State law may make hiring an architect for public work a slow process. You can run through the selection process at almost no cost, then lie in wait to pounce when people pressure you for quick designs.
23. Whenever architects quote building costs, always make sure you know whether they're talking about construction costs or project costs, and always insist on project costs.
24. Never agree to a site for a public or academic library without the advice of your consultants and architects.

25. If a library has no immediate need of an adjacent structure it owns, it can always lease it temporarily, but there's a lot more to be said for quick demolition and conversion to parking while the demolishing is good.
26. If your library is close to a homeless shelter, it will become a homeless shelter.
27. The right price to pay for a building to convert to a library is often free, and sometimes that's too much.

11

Zoning, Covenants, and Codes

I. INTRODUCTION

Even if you own your site and it's paid for, there are a lot of rules that limit what you can build there.

- **Zoning**
  Zoning controls the types of uses allowed in specific areas of land. Zoning is provided by local laws and planning maps. Most cities have zoning, but smaller communities may not.

- **Covenants**
  Covenants are similar to zoning, but consist of private legal agreements attached to deeds for property. Typically, covenants can be more restrictive than any existing local zoning, but not less restrictive.

- **Building codes**
  Codes may be national, statewide, or local. They are primarily concerned with issues of life safety, and many of them were originated by insurance underwriting associations. Depending on your state, there may be state electrical codes, fire codes, and so on. Local communities typically adopt codes written by national associations, such as the IBC (International Building Code) and the SBC (Standard Building Code).

In addition to life-safety codes, in recent years a number of energy-usage codes have emerged. Some of these are well thought-out, while others make life extremely difficult for libraries. Pay particular attention to codes affecting library lighting. If your architects are enthusiastic supporters of energy-usage codes, try to find a cynic to provide a contrasting view.

This chapter makes a few basic points about zoning and codes, but these are all technical areas. You will need to rely on your architects and engineers to sort things out, but you'll still want to know why your library is required to do specific things. Keep an eye on what's going on and challenge structural details you think will make your library dysfunctional. If you are arguing with your architect, it's a good time to seek input from your building consultant.

Remember that while saying a building "meets all applicable codes" sounds great, it actually means that "nothing in this building is so bad as to be actually illegal."

In many situations, as buildings increase in size, codes become more stringent. For example, libraries need sprinkler systems when they exceed 12,000 square feet. In situations like this, some libraries have carefully constructed buildings that slip under codes, such as an 11,900-square-foot building to avoid required sprinklers. Inevitably, of course, the day comes when the building needs to be expanded, and now the library has to retrofit sprinklers to the entire structure—which is probably more difficult and expensive than installing sprinklers in the first place.

Sprinklers can at least be retrofitted, but other codes limit the amount of wood that can be used in framing, and this had led to libraries that can't be expanded without firewalls between various sections.

The moral of the story is to not cut corners. A high percentage of libraries are remodeled and expanded someday, especially when major funds for brand-new libraries may initially be limited, and you don't want to make this expansion extremely difficult or impossible.

II. ZONING

Zoning controls the types of use that may be made of land. Zoning can prescribe legal uses of land, the maximum heights of buildings, setbacks (the distances between buildings and the street), maximum square footage of buildings, signage, required off-street parking, control of water runoff, and many other things.

Paying attention to zoning is vital. For example, an area that is zoned to permit the construction of a public library building may not allow the operation of a commercial coffee shop within the library.

When zoning was first introduced, landowners objected because they felt limits on their use of their land violated the takings clause of the Constitution. But zoning was supported by the U.S. Supreme Court in 1926 in *Euclid Ohio vs. Ambler Realty*, and it has been legal ever since.

Zoning will be of concern primarily to public libraries. Academic libraries are single elements in campuses, while school and special libraries are rooms in larger buildings.

Zoning is usually not a major problem for public libraries unless the libraries have strained relationships with the communities in which they are located. On the other hand, libraries that request exemptions to building codes may be sorely disappointed. Zoning merely controls what can go where, but codes protect life safety, where local governments will take a far dimmer view of cutting corners. But so should libraries.

One library Fred worked with had a disagreement with its architects, who wanted a complex entryway with a winding exterior ramp, something the board of trustees did not want. The architects' publicly expressed concern was that avoiding the ramp would force the library to extend an entry structure closer to the street than zoning setbacks permitted. At that point in the meeting, the board president excused himself. In three minutes he was back, having called the mayor at home and having been assured the violation of setbacks in this case was just fine.

Another library Fred worked with was pleased at the willingness of the city to negotiate on zoning and subsequently taken aback by the city's unwillingness to budge on code issues.

Buildings that do not conform with zoning requirements are frequently "grandfathered" in when zoning changes. A neighborhood bar, for example, may continue to exist because it has been there forever, even though current zoning codes do not permit new bars in that area.

Zoning may have a strong impact on the size of lot you need for your specific building. Including off-street parking, traffic access, water detention, setbacks, height limits, and other requirements, you may need a site with a buildable area five or six times the square footage of your building.

The secret to dealing with all of these problems is your architects, who upon starting work will make friends with everyone in the city, learning about all zoning and code requirements and making sure you can do what you want where you want.

The basic rule is: never buy property until you know what you need (a written building program by your consultants) and have the appropriate experts (aka your architects) make sure you can actually do it there.

III. COVENANTS

Covenants are one of several categories of legal agreements that may affect your ability to use a piece of property as you plan.

Covenants are common in American towns and cities. For example, many subdivisions have subdivision covenants placing various limits on what owners can do with their land. Often these are administered by homeowners' associations. Covenants that pertain to pieces of property regardless of who may own them at a later time are said to "run with the land."

In general, covenants can be more restrictive than applicable zoning but not less restrictive. Covenants can require greater setbacks, require that homes be of large minimum sizes, limit numbers and types of pets, limit vehicles, and so on.

The existence of covenants is another reason to have someone check your proposed site legally to be sure that you can actually do what you want with it. For example, if a covenant on the deed permits only residential use of the site, you probably won't be able to build a library there.

Some pieces of property will have covenants that cannot be enforced because they are illegal. For example, decades ago, some residential neighborhoods had codes excluding racial or religious groups. But the best thing to do is to know what you might be getting into.

IV. CODES

A. Building and Life-Safety Codes

Codes can be national, statewide, or local. It's a real tangle, one that your architects and engineers will need to sort out for you.

Codes constantly change and they never become simpler. Every time there's a major catastrophe like a nightclub fire, city officials wonder what rewrites of codes will take place, but a lot of catastrophes are due to willful disregard of codes (such as chaining exit doors shut to keep people from sneaking in without paying), making the issue one of enforcement rather than modified codes.

Municipal codes are basically published books written by private agencies, and municipalities adopt specific dated versions of the codes (much as some libraries adopt specific editions of Dewey). Some municipalities add additional local requirements to building codes.

Many American municipalities adopt the IBC (International Building Code). If your community has no comparable code, you may want to suggest to your architects that they follow the IBC. (The IBC is the former BOCA—Building Officials and Code Administrators—code.)

It's important for your planners to know which versions of which codes your municipality has adopted, and what modifications to those codes they have made.

A general knowledge of code requirements is to your advantage, but you will need to rely on your architects and engineers to be sure that your building is in compliance with applicable codes. Your job is to be sure your engineers and architects are up to date on codes.

If your proposed library has a feature you don't like that's based on building codes, talk seriously with your architects and engineers. There may be a different option.

B. Energy Codes

In recent years, energy conservation codes have been adopted by U.S. cities. The most common appears to be the IECC, the International Energy Conservation Code.

Very much unlike building codes, which are designed to ensure life safety, energy codes tend to specify required ways of conserving energy. Sometimes these lead to functional problems. From the library planning point of view, we've had problems with codes that limit lighting wattages per square foot and that specify various kinds of automatic switching.

Some wattage limits are so low that even fluorescent lighting is too dim for reading, and the only option left for libraries may be LED lighting. Until very recently, LED lighting featured extremely unpleasant bluish white light, but white light is now available—even if startlingly white instead of the warm white to which most people are accustomed.

Switching is another problem. While everyone expects some kind of energy-saving switching in research library book stacks, it's unnerving to find it in public library reading rooms, with lights going off and on apparently randomly in various areas of a single room as they are activated and deactivated by motion sensors.

> One can only imagine the outraged uproar if sections of retail stores were subject to the same code for motion sensors. We think librarians are inclined to be too polite when they are pushed around.

As an alternative to motion sensors, the energy codes to which you are subject may allow timers rather than motion sensors. Timers are acceptable as long as they are easily overridden without any reprogramming. It must be possible to leave lights off during a holiday, turn lights on for cleaning or special evening events after regular library hours, and make other easy adaptations.

> In one public library Fred knows, the staff and board became so annoyed at the sensors turning lights off and on in the main reading room that they first sent a book shelver running around the main reading room every few minutes to reactivate all the sensors. When they got tired of that, a board member came in one weekend and replaced all the sensors with light switches.

C. Accessibility Codes

The Americans with Disabilities Act of 1990 forced many American libraries to come to grips with the fact that users with disabilities could not enter or use their buildings.

In addition to the ADA, many states have accessibility codes, some of which may set higher requirements than the ADA.

The ADA covers a wide range of problems, but for libraries the main issue has been access to buildings, including parking, restrooms, aisle width and other clearances, elevators, and other basic issues. Library building constructed since the passage of the act are usually in compliance, but many older buildings still are not, even though over a quarter of a century has passed since the signing of the act.

For most libraries, the most significant requirements of the ADA include the ability of people who use wheelchairs to get in and out of library buildings, use collections within the buildings, and use restrooms.

The fact that your library delivers books to the curb is regarded as a friendly gesture, but not one that eliminates the need to conform to the ADA.

For some small libraries of the Carnegie era, bringing the library into full conformance with the ADA and other codes may cost just about as much as building a new library. For towns where historic libraries are among the most revered structures in the community, this presents tough choices, particularly since Carnegie-era buildings—even after they have been made accessible—may also be unusually expensive to heat and cool, difficult to supervise, and inflexible in use. See chapter 13 on "Remodeling and Expanding Library Buildings."

Our experience has been that people who use wheelchairs are sometimes amazingly good-natured about things—far more good-natured than we would be under similar circumstances. Friends of Fred's with disabilities told him, for example, that some things like drinking fountain heights are not a major issue. However, if people with disabilities cannot park close to your front door, cannot get into your library, cannot get to the book shelving, and cannot use your restrooms, library users in wheelchairs have every right to demand that things change.

People with disabilities can also be stubborn and angry if libraries simply blow off accessibility issues. Libraries that made no effort to improve accessibility or refused to even make long-range plans have lost lawsuits and have been given limited times to comply. (If your mayor makes snotty remarks about accessibility in public meetings, expect trouble.)

Inevitably, conditions that make it difficult for users in wheelchairs to use your library will also affect users with other limitations. While steps, for example, are impossible for users in wheelchairs, they are also extremely difficult for users with walkers, parents with children in strollers or baby carriages, or for users who simply feel uncertain on staircases.

Note that the ADA requires access to all shelving aisles but does not require that most shelving be low enough for access from wheelchairs.

Reading up on basic ADA issues is a good idea, but you'll need the advice of a professional to take action. This is another occasion where you need architects and engineers.

V. LEED

The LEED system recognizes buildings for commitment to green ideas, including energy saving, recycling, local sourcing of construction materials, and so on. LEED stands for Leadership in Energy and Environmental Design. The undertaking is administered by the United States Green Buildings Council.

In the last few years, the LEED system has become well established, and architects who have gone through LEED training sometimes list "LEED" after their names, just as they list "AIA" for "American Institute of Architects."

The administrative cost of obtaining a LEED plaque can be extremely high, in addition to the cost of making the design changes. It can cost tens of thousands of dollars—or even hundreds of thousands—just for the required LEED paperwork.

There are various levels of conformance with LEED suggestions, ranging from "conformance" to silver, gold, and platinum plaques. Our personal preference is to go with the lowest level you can get by with. You can still review all of the recommendations and pick the ones that make the greatest sense to you.

From our experience as consultants, we find that LEED can be an expensive game, with points awarded not only for solid achievements but also for all sorts of miscellaneous gimmicks (including putting up permanent advertisements for the LEED rating system or installing staff showers that no one ever uses). In this way LEED is very different from building codes, which provide absolute safety requirements. It seems to us that if LEED concepts don't save energy or preserve the environment, things have gone too far.

Our personal preference is for being aware of LEED while designing your building and treating the whole thing as good advice. However, your area may have passed laws requiring that public buildings conform to LEED, or there may be substantial political pressure.

When LEED gives points for avoiding polyurethane foam (which is amazingly flammable but a standard in the furnishings industry) and for avoiding vinyl tile (manufacturing polyvinyl chloride is a major source of toxic pollution), we'll be more impressed with the LEED system.

Unfortunately, there are endless chemicals used in the building industry that have never been evaluated for toxicity or flammability. Others are known to be dangerous but are fiercely defended by industries that make heavy use of them. Until more data is available and enforcement is better, all undertakings like LEED may be handicapped.

VI. SNAPPY RULES ON ZONING, COVENANTS, AND CODES

1. Beware of constructing buildings that are just small enough to slither under code requirements. Sooner or later you'll want to expand, and the cost for upgrading the existing building can be painfully high.
2. Trying to weasel out of building codes is not a good idea (as our choice of verb suggests).
3. City fathers may be willing to negotiate on zoning, but they'll be far less good-natured about building codes.
4. We suspect that some authors of energy-saving codes have never seen libraries.
5. Some energy-saving codes think it's a great idea to have light too dim to read by, or to plunge library users abruptly into stygian darkness. There's often a rational way out of these situations, but you may have to put pressure on your architects and engineers if they turn out to be energy-code enthusiasts.
6. When you're faced with some sort of technical gadget for your building, the UL seal mounted on it is a comforting detail.
7. Never design a building that would fail to meet codes if you increased the size by 100 square feet. At the time you build it this may sound like a great way to save money, but sooner or later you'll need to make the building larger, and you may find it horribly expensive (or even impossible) to expand.
8. Building safety codes are almost always there for very good reasons. Don't quibble.

9. Meeting accessibility codes is pretty easy with new construction, but it can be a bear when you're expanding and remodeling old buildings. This is another place where you'll need professional help.
10. Some states may compromise on some codes when it comes to historic structures. You'll have to decide whether this is good or bad.
11. Some serious code violations—such as double-cylinder locks on the front doors of libraries—are quick and cheap to fix. If it's hard to find a good excuse for delaying, why not do it right away?
12. Some of the worst losses of life have occurred in buildings where the owners purposely violated important safety codes. This is a case for criminal prosecution, not altering codes.
13. If your public library has a history of getting along well with local government, you'll have a much better chance of getting minor exemptions to zoning requirements when you need them.
14. Before you buy a piece of property, make sure that the applicable zoning, code requirements, and covenants allow you to construct the building you need. It's not much fun to find out that you can't build the library you need on the site you've selected. Get input from your architects and building consultants before you commit yourself to a site.
15. If you are criticized for failure to meet codes, a soft answer turneth away wrath far better than an angry defense.
16. People in wheelchairs can be amazingly tolerant of the failures of libraries to fully comply with accessibility codes if you approach the entire situation with the intent of doing your very best. When things are against you, start with the ability to get into and out of your library, and with restrooms that work, and then talk with people about what else they need most.
17. Local organizations specializing in access for people with disabilities can be amazingly helpful. If you have an old building with ADA problems, seek out their advice.
18. The ADA is a civil code, which means someone has to sue you. If your library is inaccessible and you blithely write the whole situation off, you'll lose the suit. (Government agencies can sue on behalf on unnamed complainants.)
19. In our opinion, LEED deals with extremely important issues but becomes too much of a game and too much influenced by manufacturers.

12

Construction

I. INTRODUCTION

For librarians, construction is a far different experience than programming or design. The thousands of decisions that fill programming and design are replaced by oversight and watching for errors and omissions.

At the outset of the process, you will work with your architect to determine how construction will take place. The traditional approach is "design-bid-build," where the information on the project is made available to general contractors who submit "bids," prices they will charge to complete the project as it is described.

For larger or more complex projects, many libraries use construction management firms, which supervise the work and bid it out in many small increments.

All projects have frequent meetings between the architects and contractors and either owner's representatives or consulting librarians, and library staff need to attend all of these meetings. Accompanying the library staff may be designated members of governing boards or building specialists from parent organizations.

Because many things are left only vaguely specified in construction drawings, there are large numbers of "shop drawings" that provide details of specific items, and librarians need to know what's going on with these as well.

Things inevitably go wrong. There will always be change orders, situations where there are errors in drawings or where there turn out to be hidden problems with existing buildings. Contractors may ignore the construction drawings or simply make mistakes, and architects may have to make them rip things out and do them over. Or contractors may make mistakes and offer owners cash in lieu of ripping things out and doing them over. Contractors or subcontractors may go bankrupt partway through the job, and bonding companies may have to step in to protect the library from loss. Some feature of the library may come as a horrible surprise to the owners, who did not recognize it in the construction documents and decide to spend the money to change it immediately.

Library staff also need to participate in "punch listing," the listing of items that need to be corrected before the final payments are released to the contractors.

Construction is a long-term process. A quick remodeling job may take only a few months, but the construction of a straightforward frame-on-slab building can take nine months or more, while a complex, two-phase expansion and remodeling job may take two or three years.

Accompanying construction are ceremonies such as groundbreaking and ribbon cutting. These are usually organized by library staff, foundation officers, public relations (PR) offices, and other groups that do not report to the architects or contractors.

As mentioned in the chapter on design, it's always a good idea to keep a diary of the project, with dated entries on meetings, decisions, problems, weather delays, and so on. If problems lead to finger pointing, having a record of meetings held and decisions made during the building process can be invaluable.

II. STANDARD STEPS IN THE CONSTRUCTION PROCESS

A. Construction Documents and Specifications

Construction drawings and specifications are prepared by your architects and engineers. They are described in detail in chapter 9 on "Design."

Drawings are the basis for both bidding and construction. They provide in tremendous technical detail all of the information required for your new library building or for the rooms it will occupy. ("All" is not really correct, since many additional "shop drawings" will be prepared during construction.)

Sloppy construction drawings can be a nightmare for owners, for they lead to omissions, to features you didn't want, to the absence of features you want, and—expensively—to large numbers of change orders.

For a large structure, construction drawings can be a huge roll of prints, but even the smallest library will have 20 or 30 sheets of drawings.

All construction drawings are accompanied by specification books that list applicable standards for all components of the building. National standards exist for virtually every item or construction material in your building, and by citing appropriate standards, your architects protect you from the substitution of cheaper and lower-quality products. (Actually, contractors sometimes try to pull fast ones hoping no one will notice the substitution, but the specifications protect you.)

Even for a small building, the spec book can be an inch-thick stack of double-sided 8½ × 11-inch paper.

Most specification books are primarily boilerplate, standard information that applies equally to a wide variety of buildings, but they also contain important information specific to your project.

B. Bidding

If you are following the traditional design-bid-build approach, your architect will normally manage the bidding process for you.

If you are using a construction management firm, the CM (construction manager) will handle the bidding.

With design-build projects the bidding will be between individual contractors and the design-build team. See later sections in this chapter for discussion of construction management and design-build.

1. Advertising for Bids

When you are ready to bid a standard design-bid-build project, your architects will arrange for advertising aimed at general contractors. Laws may specify where advertisements must appear.

In days gone by, contractors interested in bidding on your project would pick up sets of drawings and specification books from the architects' office, but now these items are more likely to be sent electronically for contractors to print out in their offices. (For libraries, this saves a great deal of money, since there would be many sets of the documents, and the libraries were responsible for paying to have them reproduced.)

2. Items Excluded from General Bids

One thing that you and your architect will determine in advance is which items in your library will not be provided by your general contractor. Typically, construction bids exclude fixtures, furnishings, and equipment (FF&E).

These items are excluded because you may want tight control over some things that do not have to be carefully integrated into the construction process. For instance, some electronic systems may prove to be difficult to specify for low bids if no two have exactly the same features. In addition, for some systems, the vendor's reputation for maintenance can be vital.

3. Add Alternates

Most bid documents include "add alternates." These are extra items you'd like to have if you can afford them.

A contractor competing for your job will supply a price for the basic project and then a price for each of your add alternates.

Add alternates have to be items that can be added to the structure without much redesign work. For example, you may ask for the extra cost of vinyl wallpaper as opposed to painted drywall, or a standing seam metal roof as opposed to asphalt singles.

It's tempting to get carried away by asking for prices on too many add alternates, or for prices on items that are tricky to price. You don't want to drive off good contractors by giving the impression you could be a pain to work with as an owner.

Contracts with architects can require free redesign by the architects if the base construction bid comes in over the estimate. We think this is an excellent idea. One way that architects protect themselves in these circumstances is by converting part of the project to add alternates, so that the base bid has a better chance of being lower than the estimate.

If bidding is highly competitive and bids submitted by various contractors are very close, it is possible that the winning low bidder may be determined by which add alternates are selected. You may want to check on the legal implications here.

4. Deduct Alternates

It's also possible to have "deduct alternates," where contractors tell you how much less they'll charge if you deduct specific items from the contract.

The general wisdom says that you'll get a lower-cost project by using add alternates, but not everyone agrees with this.

5. Prequalification of Bidders

In many circumstances, particularly bidding situations where there are known contractors with bad reputations or inadequate experience, owners and architects may choose to "prequalify" bidders. Only bidders who have proved they can meet the owner's basic criteria are allowed to submit bids.

Your architect should handle prequalification for you. Typically, it might involve checking to be sure that the contractor has undertaken projects of your scope (you don't want a tract home builder constructing a 100,000-square-foot library), has an unblemished fiscal reputation, is not involved in litigation, has the necessary licenses, and so on. When advertising for bids, your architect will specify that bidders must meet certain qualifications. Obviously, these need to be objective (for example, previous experience with buildings in excess of 25,000 square feet) rather than subjective (no bad vibes among folks in town).

Instead of prequalification of bidders, some architects may include a list of minimum qualifications with the bid documents. As part of the approval process for low bidders, these qualifications are verified by the architects.

Prequalification of bidders is essential.

6. Bonding

Bonds are insurance policies purchased by the contractor to protect owners if things go wrong financially. Since contracting can be a fiscally risky undertaking, things go wrong on a fairly frequent basis.

Since bonding companies are unwilling to insure contractors with weak reputations, requiring bonds helps protect owners from the problems inherent in rejecting companies on the basis of their bad reputations.

When owners advertise for bids, therefore, bonding is frequently a requirement.

Requiring bonds will increase bids because it increases costs for contractors. But it's a good practice and worth the cost. We think it's important for all library projects.

a. Bid Bonding

Many owners—particularly the federal government—require "bid bonds" from contractors submitting bids. Bid bonds protect owners by guaranteeing that the lowest bidder will do the work rather than simply dropping out. Bid bonds guarantee that the owners will be able to obtain the work for the price of the lowest bid. If the lowest bidder is unable to do the work, the bonding company picks up the difference in cost between the lowest bid and the next lowest bid.

Bid bonding, as with other forms of bonding, also protects owners because construction firms with iffy reputations will not be able to obtain bonding from the companies that specialize in these products.

If contractors object to the requirement for bid bonding, performance bonding, or payment bonding, it's a good time for your architect to suggest they may be happier working on other projects. Bonding companies have little interest in dealing with contractors with poor reputations, and by requiring bonding you help protect your library.

b. Performance Bonding

Many bid documents require that contractors obtain performance bonds.

Performance bonds guarantee that the contractor will complete the agreed-upon project. If the contractor or a subcontractor goes bankrupt, the bonding company will pay the extra costs involved in finding replacement firms, to be sure that there is no extra cost to the building owner.

Although performance bonds can increase construction costs a little, they can save owners incredible legal messes if contractors go bankrupt partway through construction.

> Bankruptcies happen a lot more often than one might imagine. For example, in both of the two construction jobs Fred was associated with in his own library, contractors went bankrupt and bonding companies had to step in. The general contractor went bankrupt in the middle of the first job and the HVAC contractor halfway through the second job.

Requiring bonding will increase your construction cost, but if you have a problem contractor it can save you major agonies and protect you from substantial extra costs.

c. Payment Bonding

Payment bonding covers situations where contractors do not pay their subcontractors, who then file mechanics' liens against the owner of the building.

Some protection for owners is provided by the requirement for lien waivers (see below), but there can be situations where a general contractor has collected money from the owner and abruptly goes bankrupt without paying his subcontractors.

d. Bonding Is an Important Sifting Device

Having bonding companies determine whether a contractor is reputable is a good thing, but things can go wrong. Unfortunately, some low-cost bonding companies are sharks. Some states have rules for bonding on public projects. Ask your architect or your local government.

7. Pre-Bid Meetings

At a time before the bids are due, the architects will schedule a pre-bid meeting where they answer questions raised by bidders. In order to prevent disappointed bidders from contending that other bidders were given information privately, questions clarifying the construction documents are answered only at this meeting, when all bidders can be present.

Typically, the architects will answer all questions in writing and insist that oral answers given at the meeting are not binding. This prevents contractors who mishear or misunderstand the architects' answers to their questions from contending at a later time that the written answers differ from those given at the meeting.

Particularly in the case of expansion and remodeling jobs, contractors will want to stop by the library to see the building. Often contractors will raise questions during tours, but librarians need to limit their responses to showing contractors where things are.

The importance of avoiding even a hint of favoritism is why library staff members should show bidders anything they want to see but should refrain from answering any questions except directional ones.

Typically, the director or a designated staff member will show contractors around, and all other staff members will be directed to refer all questions to the single person giving tours. Often libraries will designate times available to contractors for tours to prevent people from stopping by at odd moments and demanding immediate attention. The times available need to be reasonably extensive. For example, four hours a day for five weekdays should be sufficient.

If you are keeping a diary of the project, you will want to note which firms toured the building and how long they spent looking at it.

8. Receipt Deadlines

As with all serious projects involving bids or quoted prices, a specific and absolute deadline is essential.

For this reason, deadlines for bids always are set at times when library staff members (or city, university, school, or corporate staff members) will be present to note precisely which bids arrived on time and which arrived late.

This seems like overkill to many owners, but it's an important way to avoid lawsuits from disappointed bidders who contend that the winning bid actually arrived five minutes late and should have been disqualified. Since contractors tend to submit bids at the last moment, this is an important issue.

To protect your library, bid deadlines have to be enforced with brutal exactitude. The basic rule is that if a bid is due at 3:00 p.m., check the accuracy of your clocks and reject all those that arrive at 3:01 p.m. or thereafter.

9. Bid Openings

Maintaining secrecy over all bids received is absolutely essential, and for this reason they are never opened or examined until after the deadline for receiving bids. The purpose of bidding is to get the best possible price, and this requires both a competitive bidding environment and ignorance on the part of all bidders concerning what the competition is up to.

Bids can be opened almost immediately after the deadline for submission. Because the contractors submitting bids want to know as soon as possible who is likely to be doing the work, an immediate bid opening can be a very good idea.

Publish bid opening times at the time that bid deadlines are announced.

Bid openings for government work are public events. Expect the contractors to have representatives present.

At bid openings, one person—probably one of your architects—opens each of the bids, checks that all required items are included, and reads the amounts. This is done without comment on which bids appear to be lowest. Everyone in the room can hear what's read, and holding off gives the owner and architect a chance to be absolutely sure that the bids are completely in compliance with requirements and to determine which add alternates will be accepted.

10. Bidding Errors

Typically, all bids are reasonably close together, but occasionally one is significantly lower.

Often this is the result of a mistake by the contractors, who failed to include some important feature in his cost estimate.

Since contractors' bids are legal documents, you can force the lowest bidders to build your library and lose their shirts in the process, but it will be a rotten working relationship. Underbidding may lead to sloppy work, not to mention a barrage of change order requests for trivial items that would be ignored under better circumstances.

For this reason, if the lowest bid is a great deal lower than a cluster of fairly similar bids from other contractors, the owner may choose to allow the low bidder to withdraw its bid. (This does not mean, of course, that the low bidder gets to submit another and higher bid. The bidder is simply off the hook and out of the running.)

If the project involves bid bonding, if the low bidder bows out, the bonding company picks up the difference in cost between that bidder and the next lowest bidder.

11. Avoiding Bidding

If your library is privately owned rather than a government entity, you will probably not be required by law to hire a contractor by low bid. But you will want bidding in order to push contractors to give you the best possible prices.

Asking contractors to provide bids also prevents the project from being given to the nephew of the mayor or of the college president as a fond gift.

12. Local Contractors

Many owners—especially small-town public library boards—are concerned that local contractors get local work. As a consultant, Fred is asked this question on almost every job. In most low-bid situations for public work, however, the only legal way a local general contractor can get the job is to bid lower than the out-of-town competition.

When it comes to subcontractors, general contractors will usually ask for prices from firms they know and trust. This may also make it hard for local firms to get bids if they are not known to the general contractors.

When a construction management firm is involved, many portions of the project are bid separately, and there may be a better chance for a small local firm to get part of the project. See the "Construction Management Firms" section at the end of this chapter.

C. Awarding Contracts

The general presumption is that the bid goes to the lowest qualified bidder.

A common phrase is "the lowest responsive, responsible bidder." "Responsive" means that the bidder agrees to meet all the requirements and specifications, and "responsible" means that bidder is competent and above-board.

However, things are sometimes more complex.

Depending on applicable laws, owners may be able to select bidders who are not low bidders. This can happen when the cost of an item is below a certain cutoff amount, or when contractors cannot obtain a specific product. "Sole source" bids, for example, may be allowed when a library already has a specific type of equipment (for example, shelving) and new equipment has to be the same brand.

Bids for government work may also be affected by "prevailing wage" laws, which specify that all work will be done by workers paid not less than a specific wage.

Fringe benefits may also be specified. Prevailing wage laws go back to the federal Davis-Bacon Act of 1931, although some states had similar laws as early as the late nineteenth century. Many states have separate prevailing wage statutes. In many jurisdictions, prevailing wages are basically union scale. Laws may also exclude a requirement for union labor, but in practice, specifying prevailing wages probably means union labor.

Some owners are dismayed by the idea of prevailing wages, but there are serious advantages to using union labor in projects as complex as libraries. Unions tend to have required extensive training for their members, and this in turn helps ensure rapid and more error-free work on complex jobs.

Running a job with a mixture of union and nonunion labor can be a procedural tangle.

Awarding construction contracts is a job for lawyers, architects, and construction managers. Libraries must not try it alone.

D. Construction Administration

One of the major responsibilities of your architectural firm will be construction administration.

Construction administration is not the same thing as construction management. Your architect is not responsible for providing daily supervision of the project, which is the job of the general contractor or the construction management firm.

However, the architect is customarily responsible for:

- Helping the owners determine which is the low bid. As noted above, in very tight bidding situations with add alternates or deduct alternates, the order of bids can be changed by the alternates selected.
- Being present at all construction coordination meetings to maintain communications with the contractors and subcontractors.
- Receiving and approving "shop drawings." Shop drawings are detailed drawings showing exactly how a piece of work will be accomplished. Most construction drawings are not sufficiently detailed, and shop drawings provide the extra information. Architects are expected to review and approve all shop drawings, and owners should require a complete set of drawings for the library's files, in each case showing that the architect approved the drawing. (Some people feel that this is serious overkill, but it will help you to know what's going on and that your architects are on top of things.) Shop drawings are also helpful for future maintenance and alterations.

- Monitoring the work to make sure that the contractors are following plans and bid specifications exactly.
- Dealing with situations where the work to be done turns out not to match the construction documents. This can happen fairly often. For example, an architect friend of Fred's made a roofing contractor replace a new roof twice in a row because the contractor did the job "his way" rather than the way it was described in the drawings and specifications.
- Receiving and approving periodic bills, (draws) from contractors. For all bills, the architects first determine that the contractors have actually completed the work before authorizing payment. Typically, a percentage of each draw is "retained" or "held back" by the owner. Retainages are paid upon the successful completion of the entire job. (See "Punchlists.")
- Receiving and monitoring lien waivers, legal documents that certify that the contractors have been paying their subcontractors.
- Maintaining contact with local authorities, to be sure that all inspections and permits are properly undertaken.
- At the end of the project, preparing a "punch list" of items to be completed before the contractors' holdbacks are paid.

As the owner or administrator of the building, you will want to be sure that all of this is taking place properly. Plan to have two library staff members assigned to attend all meetings between your architects and contractors, so that at least one of the staff can always be present. Check the building frequently during construction, and if something appears to be wrong, talk with your architects or construction management firm immediately. At the end of the project, prepare your own punch list.

A substantial portion of the total architectural fee for a project is for construction administration, and the list above tells you why.

E. Design-Bid-Build Projects

The traditional way to construct government buildings is by the design-bid-build process.

In this approach, the architects provide copies of the construction documents to contractors, the contractors bid on the project, and the lowest responsive and responsible bidder constructs the building.

The general conduct of the work takes place as described below.

1. Construction Coordination Meetings

All construction projects have frequent construction coordination meetings, which are usually held by the contractor or construction manager. For larger projects, these meetings will be weekly, and for small projects probably biweekly.

The main purpose of these meetings is to make sure that everyone is aware of the state of the project and the times at which each of the subcontractors needs to be ready to do its work to keep the project moving along on schedule. Because a lot of contracting work is of the we-can't-do-X-until-Y-is-done variety, the inability of a critical subcontractor to appear on time can mess up the project schedule.

The construction coordination meeting will be led by the general contractor or construction management firm and attended by representatives of the subcontractors and the architectural firm. Some architectural firms have separate staff members who provide design services and construction administration services, while in other firms the project architect will be present in person at the construction coordination meetings. If architectural firms have separate construction administration staff, these people will probably have backgrounds in construction.

In our opinion, having the project architect serve as construction administrator leads to a more coordinated approach where fewer things slip through the cracks.

The library owner should always have one or more people present at each of these meetings. Even if the library staff don't say much, it's important that everyone see them there and be aware of their continued interest and involvement. Because no single library staff member can plan to be present at every meeting, it's a good idea to designate two library staff members and make sure that no occasion occurs when both are away from town at the same time.

As with all other major steps in the project, this is a good time to maintain a diary.

If the library has hired an owner's representative, that person will be present at all meetings as well. A few libraries ask their consulting librarians to be present at construction coordination meetings.

At each coordination meeting, the general contractor or the construction management firm will review the status of the work and discuss when things will be ready for each of the subcontractors. Because much of construction work is sequenced, making sure that various trades are ready at the right time is vital. For example, the electricians may not be able to install electrical conduit until the steel studs are in place, the drywallers won't be able to work until all of the wiring conduit is in place, and the painters can't work until the drywall is installed.

At most construction coordination meetings, the various subcontractors will review the status of their work.

Often general contractors or construction management firms will prepare charts showing when they expect each of these interdependent steps to take place.

You need to control the people who turn up for construction coordination meetings. They should not be media events, and you don't want so many members of your governing board turning up that applicable open meetings acts apply. You also don't want members of the general public, some of whom may turn up because they want to argue with your experts.

2. Draws, Lien Waivers, and Holdbacks

On most construction projects, the general contractor and subcontractors will submit monthly draws, which are bills for work completed to date.

One major responsibility of the architect is to make sure that the work for which bills are submitted has actually been completed, and that all of the participating subcontractors have been paid by the general contractor.

Problems can occur in several areas. For example, if a construction firm is running short of cash, it may start billing for work that is almost—but not quite—finished. Architects quickly learn which firms are jumping the gun, just as they (very) occasionally learn which firms have to be prodded to submit bills.

Any contractor who does requested work and does not receive payment may file a "mechanic's lien" on the completed building. The problem sometimes occurs when a general contractor collects money for work by subcontractors but does not pay them. As part of the construction administration process, therefore, architects require that the general contractor provide "waivers of lien" from each of the subcontractors, certifying that they have been paid and that they therefore waive the legal right to submit mechanics' liens on the building. During the course of the project, lien waivers can amount to a substantial amount of paper. (As mentioned above, payment bonds also protect owners in these situations.)

One way in which librarians involved in construction projects can be of assistance is to watch for trucks with the names of possible subcontractors and be sure that the architects know about these firms, keeping notes in project diaries.

As soon as the library pays for any part of the work, it now owns that section of the building. To protect the library from liability and losses, the library purchases "builder's risk insurance." Because losses are more likely during construction than after the building is occupied (think cutting torches), builder's risk insurance is more expensive than everyday insurance on library buildings.

By contractual arrangement, owners hold back a specific portion—typically 10 percent—of each draw, for payment at the time the building is completed and accepted and all punch list items have been corrected. By the end of the project, this can be a very substantial amount of money, and it some cases (again by arrangement) this may be reduced to something like 5 percent when the project is nearly done.

Some contractors constantly angle for payment of holdbacks before work is completed, and owners need to stand extraordinarily firm against them.

3. Verification That Construction Matches Drawings and Specifications

One of the major jobs of the architect is making sure that the construction is in accordance with the drawings and specifications.

A large library building is an amazingly complex undertaking, and there will be thousands of details for architects to check against the drawings. One of the signs of a good architect is constant verification that construction is in accordance with drawings.

Some of this work consists of making sure that the dimensions of the building match the drawings, that concrete passes tests proving that the cured product meets specific standards, that flashings and roofing have been installed correctly, and that all MEP (mechanical, electrical, and plumbing) systems are correct. Architects will sometimes bring in engineers to verify that very complex systems (particularly HVAC—heating, ventilating, and air conditioning) are properly installed.

Owners assist with this by visiting the building frequently and raising questions with the architects or construction manager if things appear to be incorrect, but they should not deal directly with workers or subcontractors.

4. Resolving Claims of "Equivalencies"

Depending on laws, government construction projects may be required to list a range of products that will be acceptable for a specific situation. For example, a bid set may list three acceptable electrical fixtures, specifying brand names and model numbers.

Problems can occur when the construction documents are required not only to list several alternate fixtures but also to state "or equivalent." This opens the door to contractors' claiming that some other product is the equivalent of the ones specified by brand and model. Unfortunately, the suggested equivalents frequently fail to be equivalents. Contractors may find similar products that are being discontinued and available for far lower prices. Or they may hope to slip in less expensive products of genuinely lower quality.

Almost every week, your architects may be asked to rule on substitutions of this type. Our experience is that architects need to regard such suggestions with an extremely wary eye, usually saying "no." Unfortunately, contractors can wear architects down, and you may end up with items you really don't want.

Library staff can also insist on being included in all discussions of "equivalent" items. Insist on seeing cut sheets of the substitutes. Make sure that there is no difference in required maintenance. You may have to insist on seeing a sample of the item or comparing the specified and "equivalent" item side by side.

A "cut sheet" is a catalog sheet with illustrations of items and all technical specifications.

> Fred's bad experiences in the area of equivalencies have centered on light fixtures, where easily maintained fixtures were replaced by fixtures almost impossible to service, and where the fixtures supplied were out of production and could not be matched.

5. Shop Drawings

In many cases, not all construction details appear on architects' construction drawings. Additional drawings with extensive additional construction details are prepared by contractors and submitted to architects for approval.

As a librarian, you want to keep track of these "shop drawings." While many are merely technical, others involve decisions on details that may matter significantly to the library owners and staff.

Protect your library by insisting on receiving copies of all approved shop drawings—all with the architects' indication of review and approval—for inclusion in the library's permanent files on the project. (Some architects have a reputation for falling behind on approval of shop drawings—or simply initialing drawings without careful review—and having a set of approved drawings helps protect the library.)

Shop drawings also provide essential information when the time comes to modify buildings.

> Many architects may suggest that libraries planning to keep copies of all shop drawings is overkill. We think that it can never hurt, and it's good to be seen keeping an eye on everything, but you can still be selective.

6. Change Orders

Change orders are agreements between owners and contractors to add or alter items in the contract for an additional charge.

Change orders inevitably cost more than if the item had been part of the original contract. Prices for the original contract are arrived at by low bid, where the contractor is in competition with other contractors in order to get the job. But the price of change orders is set by negotiation, leading to prices much less advantageous to the owners.

Change orders become necessary for a variety of reasons:

- Architects make mistakes. Drawings are inconsistent, necessary items are omitted, or incorrect features are specified. For example, the ceiling of a room may be too low for the compact shelving scheduled to be installed there, resulting in the need to raise the suspended ceiling grid and alter the location of sprinkler piping.
- Unexpected conditions are encountered. This happens frequently in remodeling jobs. For example, a wall believed to have no wiring turns out when it is opened to have electrical lines that need to be relocated before a door can be installed. Since contractors were told they would not have to relocate wiring in order to install the door, the extra cost of moving the wires leads to a change order.

- Owners change their minds. Owners read about new features they would like to have in their libraries, they change their minds once they see what something actually looks like, or they find they have extra money and decide to improve some feature of the building. Occasionally, owners misread the construction drawings, are surprised and disappointed when they see what's actually constructed, and then pay extra to have it changed.

Architects whose projects are characteristically accompanied by vast numbers of change orders do not develop good reputations. Since it's impossible to draw up anything as complex as building plans without making mistakes, a few architectural errors are par for the course. But endless change orders mean sloppy designing. (Supposedly, contractors who know an architectural firm's reputation for excessive change orders will submit lower bids on the presumption that they'll make up their losses in change orders.)

Expecting any set of architectural drawings to be completely correct is unreasonable, for even a small building may involve tens of thousands of details, and the cost of getting everything absolutely consistent is too high. For new construction, change orders due to architectural errors shouldn't be much more than 3 to 5 percent of construction costs.

Unexpected conditions are always encountered, but better examination of existing buildings can prevent some of them.

Fickle owners are responsible for the results of changing their minds. Architects, however, can take time to be sure that owners realize what they're actually getting.

Change orders are one of the many reasons that all construction budgets include contingency funds. Typically, these are 5 percent for new construction. For remodeling and expansion, contingency funds may be 10 percent, since the chance of discovering unexpected conditions is much higher.

Contractors who seriously underbid projects are notorious for constantly demanding change orders. It's interesting to hear architects tell contractors things to the effect of, "We're going to have to do this a little differently, but it's no more work, and I don't want to see any change orders."

It's extremely important that all change orders be documented. Your relationships with your architects need to specify who is authorized to agree to change orders, and that change orders must always be in writing, not simply conversations between the architects and contractors. All change orders must include specific prices. (This is another good place to keep a diary of action taken on the project.)

7. Resolving Contractor Errors

Occasionally, contractors will make major errors and suggest a cash settlement in lieu of correcting the errors. If architects are primarily in a hurry to get things done, unholy alliances of architects and contractors can form in opposition to the library.

This happened with Fred's first building consulting job, decades ago. Fred specified a network of electrical and data conduit in the concrete floor slab to permit the flexible location of computers and other equipment. When this kind of work is done, the conduit for the wiring is first supported in place and the concrete slab is then poured. Unfortunately, the contractor got concrete into the open ends of the conduits, making it impossible to use many of them for wiring. Faced with the major cost of ripping out the floor slab and conduit and starting over, the contractor offered the library a small cash settlement instead, and the architects encouraged the library board to take the settlement. Which it did. Because the building had a cathedral ceiling, power poles were not an alternative for power and data. So the library ended up with a tremendous loss of long-term flexibility, all for a small payment from the contractor.

What disturbed Fred most was that he was never asked or told about this until long after it was too late, and that the architects were complicit in the situation, encouraging the board not to fall behind on their schedule (using up the architects' time and delaying their final payment in the process).

To balance this, something went wrong in another library project where the library board president was head of quality control for a large factory. Even through the architects—the same architects, as a matter of fact—encouraged him to take a (minor) settlement for a serious omission, he refused to budge until the work was redone according to specifications.

Owners and architects can deal with contractor errors, but so can building inspectors, who have the authority to insist that construction stop until problems are addressed.

8. Code Inspections and Occupancy Permits

At key points during construction, the work will be inspected by code enforcement officials, who are typically employees of local government.

For example, when wiring is complete but drywall has not been installed, electrical inspectors will go through the building making sure that the wiring has been done in accordance with local codes.

Building inspectors have the authority to stop construction until a problem has been addressed.

Note that these inspections do not determine whether outlets have been omitted, but only that those installed have been done properly from a life-safety viewpoint. Code inspection, therefore, does not substitute for the architects' determination that everything called for in the construction documents is present and properly done.

When the building is complete, the local government will issue an "occupancy permit," allowing the library to use the building. At the time the permit is issued, minor things may remain to be done, but key safety items (for example, hand railings and outlet cover plates) will all be in place.

9. Construction Site Maintenance

Your contractor or construction manager will need to clarify who is responsible for removing construction trash and debris. Construction sites can become dangerously cluttered almost overnight, and you don't want accidents for workers or owners. If you see trash everywhere on the construction site, this is a good subject to bring up at a construction coordination meeting.

Your contractor or construction manager will also need to establish job site security, particularly overnight. Construction sites have expensive tools and supplies lying around.

Most construction sites have temporary fencing of some kind with controlled gates for the entry of workers. (If you have a mixture of union and nonunion workers, you may have to have two gates.) Fencing can also control blowing trash.

Remember that as you pay off the building during construction, the responsibility for insurance rests with the library rather than with the builder. See the section on "Builders' Risk Insurance" in chapter 30, "Security."

III. CONSTRUCTION MANAGEMENT FIRMS

Traditionally, libraries were built on the design-bid-build system. The architects designed the building and prepared construction documents, general contractors were invited to bid, and the lowest responsive, responsible bidder was awarded the job. Construction was managed by the general contractors, who hired subcontractors to do the work their employees did not do.

A second approach has become more prevalent in the last twenty years. In this approach, the library hires a construction management firm that does work similar to that of a general contractor, but acting as an employee of the owner. The construction manager (CM) runs the entire project, coordinating the activities of all of the specialized contractors. Each specialized part of the project is bid separately, with coordination between contractors managed by the construction management firm rather than the general contractor. Instead of subcontractors reporting to general contractors, who bill the library for both their work and the work of all the subcontractors, with a CM the library or the CM contracts directly with a wide range of firms for various segments of the work.

One source of comfort when dealing with a construction management firm is that the firm has no financial incentive to cheapen the project.

There are two general approaches to contracting with a construction management firm, straight construction management and construction management "at risk."

With the exception of small or simple jobs, we think construction managers are a great idea.

A. Traditional Construction Management

In traditional construction management, the construction manager acts as an agent of the owner. The construction manager bids out each segment of the project on behalf of the owner, and the owner contracts directly with each contractor. The CM supervises every aspect of the work, overseeing the work of all of the subcontractors to be sure that all work is workmanlike and in accordance with the construction drawings. The CM sorts out any difficulties, such as problems that arise with a mixture of union and nonunion subcontractors.

B. Construction Management at Risk

In some construction management projects, the CM undertakes to construct the building for a sum not to exceed an agreed amount. In this case, the CM contracts directly with all the individual contractors. The CM is said to be "at risk" because if the building cannot be constructed for the agreed-upon amount, the CM takes a loss on the project.

The usual arrangement is that the CM's profit is limited by agreement. If the CM is able to construct the building for substantially less than the agreed amount, its profit from doing so is limited.

There are some problems with construction management at risk.

- The CM is now in the same position as the contractor in a traditional design-bid-build project, because low bids are to its personal financial advantage.
- Since the agreed amount for the entire project is arrived at by agreement, in essence the project is not undertaken by low bid. This may or may not be legal for government work where you live.

C. Value Engineering

Construction management firms often do "value engineering" for their clients. Value engineering involves analyzing the architects' plans to ask whether a very similar effect with equally high-quality functionality could be achieved at a lower price by changing details.

For example, a CM may point out that the curved I-beams your architect is specifying could be replaced by straight I-beams at a very substantial reduction in cost. You may want the curved I-beams, in which case you do nothing, but it could also be that they are not all that important to you.

To be effective, value engineering needs to take place early in the design process, where a simple change may bring about substantially lower costs. If value engineering waits until the end of the design process, it can result in simply substituting cheaper components rather than finding major savings by altering construction concepts or methods.

For this reason, if you decide to hire a CM firm, you are better doing so early in the design process.

D. Hiring Construction Managers

State law may control methods for hiring construction management firms. For example, you may be required to advertise for firms and rank order applicants.

Hiring a construction manager is similar to hiring an architect:

- Place advertisements in suitable publications.
- Provide an RFQ with questions about the firm's past achievements. You will want to know about the variety of projects it has completed, in order to be sure it has done projects in your general size range. You will want to know if it has been sued, and, if so, the outcomes. You will want to know

the histories of any labor disputes. You will want to know its history of bringing in projects on time. And you will want a list of completed projects with contact information.
- As with architectural firms, the specific people assigned to the project can matter. It's appropriate to ask about the person who will run the project for the CM firm and check that person's references.
- The RFQ will specify response time. As usual, deadlines for submissions should be midday times on weekdays, so that the library will be able to say whether individual responses were on time or late.
- Review qualifications.
- Talk with references.
- Interview a maximum of four or five firms. Expect to meet the people who will manage your project, not their public relations staff or sales representatives.
- Select a firm.
- The process should NOT be by low bid. As with an architect, costs are important, but expertise and past successes count for far more. (Your state laws for government work may specify the equivalent of the QBS process used for selecting architects.)

What can you look for in a potential CM?

- General range of experience
  - Does the firm have a wide range of experience with projects?
  - Has it done a number of projects in your size range? (You need the firm to be comfortable with projects like yours, but you don't want it to regard your project as a trivial one.)
  - What unique processes does it incorporate into its projects? How many libraries has it built?
- Past jobs
- References from previous clients. Among the questions you can ask are:
  - Did the CM estimate costs accurately? (CMs should be the real experts on construction costs.)
  - Did things move smoothly on the job?
  - How effectively did the CM handle change orders?
  - Were there any union problems on the job site?
  - Was the job site kept clean, or was it a physical mess?
  - Did you ask the firm to provide value engineering services? Were they able to find ways to cut costs without just cutting quality?
  - Did the firm maintain tight quality control? Did they keep a close eye on the work of all of the contractors and subcontractors? Were they painstakingly aware of details? Did they catch architectural errors?

- Did the CM attempt to self-perform? Did the CM want to use the CM's own employees for parts of the work? (This is a major conflict of interest, since it avoids bidding.)
- Does the firm use modern software, such as BIM?
- Possible interview questions
    - What unique processes do you incorporate into the process? If we called your references, what would they say about your firm?
    - How many libraries have you built?
    - How is your company going to make the administration's life easy during this process?
    - How do you handle change orders?
    - How do you prevent schedule slippage?
    - How do you communicate during the process?
    - How will you protect our best interests?
    - How do you handle adversarial or controversial situations?
    - What challenges do you see with our project?
    - What ideas do you have to deliver this project for less cost than it currently is?
    - What is your approach to managing tight sites?
    - How do you work with governmental authorities?
    - What is your approach to pre-construction?
    - How do you ensure timely close-out of projects?
    - How do you keep a job running smoothly when difficult circumstances arise?
    - What process do you employ to screen and pre-qualify bidders?
    - How do you ensure quality in the field?
    - How do you handle clients who are very busy both professionally and personally?
    - Give us an example of a difficult situation with a client, architect, or project, and how you handled it?
    - How do you view your role as our CM after the warranties expire?
    - How do you handle union versus non-union situations?

IV. DESIGN-BUILD PROJECTS

Most libraries are built on the design-bid-build system or by construction management firms, but a few are design-build projects.

In a design-build project, a team consisting of a contracting firm and an architectural firm agree in advance to construct a building for a specific price.

The advantage of the design-build process is that design-bid-build projects can come in far above the architects' estimates. This may be a particular problem with signature architecture, but it can also happen in fairly modest projects, where bids can come in at two or three times the architects' estimate.

Relatively few libraries are built by the design-build process. The only one with which we are personally familiar is the Harold Washington Library—the Chicago Public Library's central building and the largest single public library structure in the United States. The city held a design-build competition in 1988, with the building completed in 1991. Five teams competed for the job. The four losing teams each received $100,000 for their costs, but that probably paid for little more than the elaborate submission models.

By and large, architects appear unenthusiastic about design-build projects, for it places them essentially in the role of being the employees of contractors.

From the point of view of librarians, design-build projects can be primarily glamour contests, placing vastly more emphasis on appearance than function. If the winning design turns out to need various kinds of functional tweaking, do these alterations all become high-priced change orders?

V. MOVE-OUT VS. PHASED CONSTRUCTION

When libraries are expanded and remodeled, one of the major planning decisions is whether to move out during the course of construction or to do the work in phases, with the library moving contents around to keep out of the way of the contractors. Typically, this involves two-phase construction, where the library constructs a new addition, camps out in the new addition while the existing building is remodeled, and then moves back into the original building.

While many phased projects involve two phases, some have many phases, with the library endlessly moving stuff back and forth to keep out of the contractors' way.

Most projects in really large buildings end up being done this way, for there is no practical way to move out during construction.

In general, you should expect much more attractive bids if you move out of the building during construction. From contractors' points of view, the job is much simpler. They have access to the entire building. They don't have to provide safe access for library users and staff. They can use your parking lot for their construction office and for stacking construction materials and dumpsters. They don't have to deal with complaints from users and staff. The various trades (such as electricians, plumbers, HVAC workers, drywallers, painters, and so on) have to come only once rather than return for each successive phase.

From your point of view, the project will go substantially faster if you move out. Your staff and patrons will be spared dust, bad smells, noise (ranging from the crashes of falling objects and the whine of saws to the unfortunate choices of music on workers' radios), disruption of services, awkward access through temporary entrances, and limited parking.

Most importantly, if you move out during construction, the bids for your project will almost certainly be substantially lower.

If you do not move out, you will need to determine who controls what happens on the site. Where will library users, library staff, and construction workers park? Which doors will be open for staff and public use and when?

Moving out also helps avoid a major problem with your HVAC system. If a library is expanded in two phases, the HVAC system for the first phase needs to be switched on at the completion of that phase so the library can operate in the new space. If remodeling of the original building requires a year, by the time the library moves back in, the standard one-year warranties will have expired on the equipment in the new addition. Subsequently, if the equipment in the new addition and the equipment in the original building fail to function properly as a single system, you're pretty much out of luck.

A solution to the HVAC problem is specifying in your construction contracts that warranties on all HVAC equipment commence at the completion of the final phase of the project, but you may have trouble obtaining this.

Moving out requires leasing temporary quarters for your library. Empty big box stores make good temporary locations if their MEP systems function.

Some libraries find that the available temporary spaces are too small. In this case, it's possible to put the least-used portion of the collection in storage. Most computerized lending systems can provide lists of the least-used items in the collection, which can be pulled from shelves and boxed for storage.

VI. THE LIBRARIAN'S ROLE IN CONSTRUCTION

Librarians can play a more active role in construction than many books suggest, and the result can be a better building.

It's worthwhile walking through the construction zone almost every day. Ask for a white hard hat (denoting an important personage) and try to keep an eye on things. If nothing else, just be visible. If you see problems, bring them up in construction meetings rather than attempting to deal directly with workers. (If you see a major problem, call the architects immediately.) Posterity loves an alert and intrepid owner.

You can learn a lot by unobtrusively observing workers. Are things being done in a sloppy manner? Is there trash lying around everywhere? What do you hear people saying? (If you're around all the time, people may almost forget you're there.)

Maintain a friendly relationship with workers. Learn their names and greet them. But don't tell them what to do or slow them down with irrelevant conversation. If you bring snacks, let the general contractor or construction administrator decide how to distribute them.

If you have seen work you don't like in other libraries, make clear from the beginning what you expect from your contractor and subcontractors, and what things you will bring up in the punch list process.

For example, floor boxes for electrical outlets set in concrete floors are frequently twisted out of square. If you want them in dead-straight lines, make this clear from day one. Your electrical contractor will be annoyed, but he'll have trouble arguing that sloppy is fine.

The placement of items in walls—electrical outlets, fire alarms, thermostats, HVAC grills, and so on—is often somewhat vague in construction drawings. If you have plans for shelving or a bulletin board on a wall, you may know exactly where you want the outlets and other devices to be located. As soon as the steel studs go up, use a marking pen to note the exact location of each item on the raw concrete floor. (Most items will be at standard heights, but there is room for a lot of sideways slop if you aren't extremely specific.)

You may also find that walls are located slightly off where they belong. If a filing cabinet will be located in a narrow alcove, check to be sure that the alcove will be wide enough. If shelving needs to fit between a door and a wall, check to be sure that the door isn't half an inch too close to the wall. The precise location of steel stud is easy to tweak when it first goes up, and that's the time to check.

VII. PUBLIC CEREMONIES

A. Introduction

One of the really fun things in library construction is ceremonies—brief shining moments of hope and victory and widespread congratulations in between barrages of plaster dust, the crashing of falling objects, strongly scented glues and finishes, workers' radios, and who knows what else.

Ceremonial construction events serve many purposes:

- They provide newsworthy events.
- They keep your community focused on your progress. Because the construction of major library can take two or three years, you may need to have something of note happen not only at the start and at the finish, but also while you are underway.
- They satisfy community curiosity about what's going on behind the construction fences. Looking through peepholes in fences is less satisfying than one might expect.
- They provide opportunities to thank all of those whose support made the project possible, including granting agencies, individual and corporate donors, administrations (university, city, school, hospital, etc.), and politicians.
- They provide opportunities for prospective donors (who never thought the project would get off the ground but have had their minds change by seeing things actually under construction) to reconsider making serious donations.
- They allow the public to recognize all the local people who have done the work: library and university and school board members, fundraising groups, and so on.
- They provide opportunities to note the achievements of the hired guns, including library staff members, employees of parent organizations, architects, contractors, consulting librarians, and construction workers.

Ceremonies involving buildings require extra planning in advance. Be sure to consider:

- What will you do if it rains?
- Can speakers be heard?

- Will speeches bore listeners to death? Ceremonies are better shorter than longer. (Try to avoid speakers who have reputations for never shutting up. It's always possible to just point out notoriously loquacious people, speak briefly about them, ask them to wave to the crowd, and then move on.)
- Will you have copious treats?
- Is your event schedule compatible with somewhat uncertain construction timetables? When contractors are at work, you can't tell them to stop for 10 days or to do 10 weeks' work in 2 weeks because of a scheduled event.
- If there is earth to turn, will you have loosened it first?
- Will you recognize everyone who expects to be recognized?
- Have you invited all the politicians, even those who gave you no help at all? After all, they may help you another day.
- Have you prepared fact sheets for the media? (However, despite your best efforts to give everyone all the names and numbers and dates, someone will still get it all wrong.)
- Have you involved cute children?
- Do you have a competent person in charge to plan your events? Disorganized events can be embarrassments.
- Have you checked out all of your technical equipment in advance? It's embarrassing if the big day arrives only to have the PA system shrieking and howling or the flagpole have a permanently jammed pulley, and have 300 people watching while the folks in charge struggle to get things working.

B. Groundbreakings

Groundbreakings are times of hope and glory. After many years of space planning and design and fundraising and bidding, things are actually underway.

The major problem with groundbreakings is that they are out of doors. But there are lots of other things to keep in mind.

- Schedule groundbreakings for nice weather. Basically, April through October in temperate parts of the country. Since you want to get as much work as possible done before winter, spring groundbreakings are a practical idea from the construction viewpoint as well as the pleasant weather viewpoint.
- Groundbreakings are not the actual start of construction. You can work around being either early or late.
- Invite all the politicians, whether or not they helped. Library groundbreakings are great political photo ops, and you never know when they'll pay you back. (Library buildings are the kind of positive projects that lots of politicians love to be seen hanging around with.)

- Invite all the support groups—foundations, donors, Friends, staff, boards, councils, faculty senates, library employees, and all of the rest.
- Invite all the hired types—architects, engineers, consulting librarians, contractors, surveyors, and other specialists.
- Make sure the media are there. Announce in advance. A good way to remind them is to call the day before, just to be sure that you have "prepared everything they need."
- Have a fact sheet ready for the media. Reporters need names, numbers, schedules, and other information.
- Have your own photographer. In the digital world, there's no such thing as taking too many pictures.
- Have public handouts listing all the participants and supporters. List all of your donors, right down to those who gave five dollars. Print lots of copies. (Keeping precise track of donations is a job for a precise person. Omitting a donor from a list can lead to years of unhappy memories.)
- Have a pavilion or other shelter available. If rain comes unexpectedly, it's too late to plan quickly for alternative action.
- Have places for elderly donors to sit. Preferably under the pavilion.
- Have a PA system. Some crucial speaker will have a voice that can barely be heard in a small clothes closet, and very few people can talk loudly enough to be heard out of doors.
- Have renderings of the building-to-be on display somewhere. Your architects will supply them. Have extra copies for the press. Have releases assuring the press that they have the right to reproduce the drawings.
- If you're still raising money for furnishings or opening-day collections or mortgage retirement, let people know. People who won't give to vaguely promised projects may be positively motivated by signs of actual work.
- When in doubt, be brief. You can be just as joyous in fifteen minutes as in an hour. You may need to remind speakers in advance of your intent to keep things moving.
- Provide food. There are probably some kinds of happy events that are not improved by food, but we are not aware of them.
- Consider some kind of souvenirs of the occasion.
- Loosen the earth in advance. An elderly donor struggling helplessly to turn a spadeful of earth is not an auspicious sign.
- Ask your contractor about fancy shovels. Most have a supply, often chrome-plated. If they don't, spray some brand-new garden spades with gold paint.
- Let everyone have a chance with a shovel. Take lots of pictures.
- Involve cute children, who are far more photogenic than politicians, members of governing boards, or hired professionals. (One library Fred worked with featured a small boy who gave the building fund six months of his allowance and was a hit.)

C. Laying Cornerstones

A cornerstone is an ornamental stone block set fairly close to the ground where two exterior walls of the building meet. The block may be inscribed with the date and with whatever else the owners want to see there.

Many cornerstones have hollow cores with boxes of documents and other memorabilia, for recovery at some unspecified future time—perhaps when further construction makes the relocation of the cornerstone necessary—or just to provide a good excuse for looking inside. In this respect, cornerstones serve something of the function of time capsules, but without the recommended opening date. (When ancient cornerstones are opened, people often find that water has intruded, which is one of the advantages of indoor time capsules.)

The name comes from the idea that the cornerstone is a basic supporting element in the structure, sort of like the keystone of an arch (even though the arch would collapse with the removal of any individual stone). As a result of the implication of essential underlying support, "cornerstone" is a popular element in the names of many organizations.

In the United States, cornerstones were often laid by members of the Masonic Order in their role as ceremonial masons. The stone might be placed on an element in the foundation or a masonry wall, or it might be slipped into a prepared opening in a wall. Old cornerstones sometimes list the name of the Masonic Lodge that placed the stone.

Most modern cornerstones appear to simply display the date of the building.

While older buildings frequently have cornerstones, we're not sure how many library construction projects include cornerstones these days, or how many of the libraries that still install cornerstones actually hold special events when the cornerstones are put in place. Our suspicion is that some of the other events in this section have supplanted them.

D. Signing Beams

Some projects include a ceremony where library governors, staff, construction workers, and others all sign a steel beam. This can be the final beam, which is signed before it is lifted into place. Or it can be a beam that has already been installed but is within reach of people standing on the floor. In some cases, people sign columns rather than beams.

The presumption is that the signed beam will be hidden by later finishes. You may be tempted to make a permanent display of your signed beam, but many are fairly ugly.

Beams intended for signing need to be painted white in advance.

Since the beam may be covered up later, extensive photography is important.

E. Topping Out

"Topping out" is a traditional ceremony that focuses on construction workers. It customarily involves mounting a fir tree on the very top beam of the building when the beam is installed. If the building has no top beam, the ceremony may revolve around a ridgepole, the last roofing piece, the last brick, or some other element. Obviously, topping out takes place long before the ribbon is cut, for much of the curtain wall construction, window installation, MEP equipment, and interior work may remain to be done.

Sometimes the beam is painted white and signed by all the workers, staff, owners, and others before it is hoisted into place.

In addition to a fir tree, the top beam may also be decorated by an American flag. In some parts of the country, the tree is omitted if any construction workers died from accidents during the project.

Frequently the contractor or owner will treat the construction workers to a meal as part of the ceremony.

Topping out is a traditional ceremony focusing on the construction workers, but on many projects it becomes a media event as well, with owners seizing the opportunity to report to the community on the status of the project.

As with all ceremonies, public relations opportunities abound. If you decide to make a big deal of the ceremony, be sure that every suitable person is invited—public library or school board members, university officials, political supporters, donors, foundation members, all sorts of members of the press, library employees, and so on.

But the meal may be limited to the workers. Sometimes (for example) it is served on a newly poured floor in an upper area of the building not yet open to the general public. Medieval topping-out ceremonies supposedly included alcohol, but you may want to think about liability issues before trying that route.

The main point is that the focus of topping out is on construction workers. Who deserve the attention.

F. Phase I Completion Events

Some phased projects involve constructing an addition to the library, camping out in the addition while the original library is remodeled, and then moving back into the original library.

When the new addition to the library opens, it's possible to hold an event recognizing the newly completed work. This obviously depends on the size of the new addition. For example, if a library is tripled in size, the new addition is a very significant achievement.

One possible ceremony is having tours on the first days that the new addition to the library is open.

Sometimes when libraries camp out in new additions, however, the result is a crowded and very much half-finished space, and visitors may need help envisioning what's still to come. Or you may want to wait for the final ribbon cutting.

G. Tours of the Work in Progress

Some libraries provide tours of construction sites before the work is finished. These may be for staff, members or governing boards, media, and other people who want to see how the work is progressing. Often staff members are particularly curious about new spaces.

Tours are difficult for safety reasons. Until staircases and hand railings have been installed, access to upper floors of the building will be by ladder, and neither the library nor the construction firm will be happy about the risk of injuries. Tours are difficult to conduct until construction workers have left the site for the day, which means late afternoons or weekends.

While some contractors maintain very clean sites, there are always construction materials lying about for people to trip over.

In general, tours of buildings under construction are probably a really bad idea for large groups. Visitors touring the site may need to be herded along to keep them away from inevitable drop-offs without railings.

Most visitors will have trouble envisioning how things will look when the work is completed. A stretch of bare concrete floor with steel studs and wiring conduit, and suspended ceiling grids without acoustic tile and with air ducts and sprinkler pipes lurking above tells more about the inner workings of the structure than about how it will look when it's finished. For this reason, tours when the building is nearly finished may be more useful.

If visitors have to wear hard hats and goggles while touring the building, they may find the whole experience more empowering. You can always do it when things are about 95 percent complete and still have the same fun.

H. Construction Plaques

There are a lot of decisions in this area:

- Every new library needs one or more plaques by the front door to recognize all the right people. Determining who the right people are is more complicated.
- For public libraries, plaques usually list the name of the library, the date of completion of construction, board members, library director, architect, contractor, and programmer. If you had a construction grant, you may be required to list it on the plaque.
- Private academic libraries will need the university board of trustees and president, but public universities may also need the names of state officials, recognition of construction grants, and so on. Be sure to check on the required wording.
- If the library had a single, major donor, that person's name will usually appear on the plaque.
- If you have a lot to say, it's fine to have more than one plaque.
- Some architects find consulting librarians annoyingly independent and will not want to share plaque space with them. Tough.
- Getting names right is complicated, but one wrong name on a bronze plaque is an expensive mistake. Insist on receiving draft versions of everything and have lots of people read them. Including teenagers with raunchy senses of humor, who may see troublesome second meanings where more sober adults do not.
- Time capsules are trite, and most have painfully boring contents. Fight both tendencies. Ask yourself what kind of stuff would be fun to discover inside a just-opened 50-year-old time capsule. Old toys are more fun than old lists of old people. Any digital media will probably be too old to read.

This sounds silly, but there are some amazing howlers out there. One city had to remake a major stone monument in front of its new city hall because it referred to the women on the city council as "aldermen."

Here's a plaque for a completely imaginary public library:

THE WILLIAMSTOWN PUBLIC LIBRARY 2015

[The date is usually the date of the ribbon cutting]

BOARD *of* TRUSTEES

[Names of board members go here. The problem is whether you list current trustees only, or whether you list all trustees that were involved since the beginning of the project. If a couple of board officers who inspired and led the project end their terms three months before the ribbon cutting, you don't want to omit their names. But if you include their names, you then need a consistent way of dealing with the names of other former board members.]

DIRECTOR

[If you changed directors in mid-stream, will you list both of them? Who goes first? If an associate director played a major role, do you list that name too?]

JOHNSON AND WILLIAMS | *Architects*
WILLIAMS AND JOHNSON | *Contractor*
WILLIAM JOHNSON | *Consulting Librarian*

[Up until now, things are pretty standard. Depending on the situation, you may want to list donors, local government officials, a second architectural firm, grant agencies that require they be listed, university boards of trustees, government officials, and so on. Sometimes two plaques are needed to cram everyone in.]

[One of Fred's libraries took years to plan and build. A plaque listed all board members who had been associated with the project since the beginning of planning. The names filled a plaque all by themselves, but the people deserved to be mentioned.]

I. Donor Recognition Plaques

All sorts of donor recognition plaques are available commercially. Many are designed for adding extra names over the years, but some libraries create final plaques at the time the building is completed.

Lots of libraries recognize major donations by mounting individual letters on walls. Unfortunately, major problems occur when they have to repaint the walls or relocate the letters. Be sure your donor-recognition letters are engineered for easy removal and reinstallation.

Your fundraisers will need to figure out what level of donation results in that level of recognition. Be consistent. See chapters 14 ("Building Costs") and 15 ("Funding").

J. Donor Receptions

Many libraries have special receptions for the donors who contributed to the project. Sometimes these are evening events with special food, wine, and so on.

Receptions provide time for more personal attention to donors. If a ribbon cutting is a mob scene, you may not have the chance you want to take time to talk with each major supporter of the project.

However, don't let a donor reception become the major celebration or a substitute for a ribbon cutting. The vast number of members of the community need to be welcomed as well.

K. Ribbon Cuttings

Ribbon cuttings are fun. Have a great time, but prepare for common problems.

- Some libraries have grand openings with people seeing the library for the first time, but they're tricky to bring off. Like retail stores, you may want to have a "soft opening" and unveil something like recognition plaques at the grand opening.
- Be prepared for things not being entirely done. Furnishings frequently arrive late. Some furniture manufacturers swear that everything's nearly ready to ship while they haven't even begun production. Somewhere there'll be a missing ceiling tile with wires hanging down.
- Punch lists are almost never resolved in time for ribbon cuttings. But there's so much to see in a new building that we hope that lots of people won't notice failings.

- Publicize the ribbon cutting full blast.
- Just in case something goes wrong with construction, it's probably a bad idea to pick the date months in advance.
- Invite all the people you invited to the groundbreaking: politicians, donors, boards, foundations, faculty senates, friends groups, students, employees, hired experts, and the rest. We need to be consistent here. Omitting people is a far greater sin than inviting too many, so invitations are vital. Back them up with mass e-mails.
- Make sure the media are there, although ribbon cuttings are reliable sources of media activity because they are good photo ops.
- Print booklets listing everyone, particularly all donors, volunteers, and supporters. No donation is too small for recognition.
- Keep speechmaking short. People want to see the building. But take time to thank everyone. It takes only seconds to say, "Our great architects are here," and ask them to wave.
- Be sure that a speaker points out the functional features of the building. Everyone can see the handsome architectural features, but they may not be aware of how well things work.
- Schedule ribbon cuttings for nice weather, both to allow people to congregate out of doors and to allow people from out of town to attend the occasion.
- Hold ribbon cuttings on convenient days—basically Saturday and Sunday at 2:00 p.m. A Thursday evening ribbon cutting is antisocial.
- You may want a special event for donors, but the main event should be for everyone.
- Hold most of the event inside the building rather than keeping everyone hanging around outside in the rain. Unless it's a seriously lovely day, traipse in first and cut the ribbon second.
- If necessary, the ends of the ribbon can be handheld rather than anchored to the building.
- With proper staging, 20 people can cut one ribbon at the same moment. It's fun to watch 20 bits of ribbon fall to the ground at the same time. (Make sure your 20 pairs of shears are all sharp.)
- Even if everything takes place indoors, you'll still need a PA system.
- Take endless photographs.
- Try to have the donor recognition plaques installed in time for the ribbon cutting. For some donors from out of town, this may be their main visit to the library, and it's a great time to have the maximum number of people see the plaques.
- When you put up donor-recognition letters and other items, consider how you will repaint the walls on which they are mounted. Individual letters look great on walls until repainting day arrives, when you'll want them to be easy to remove and replace.

- Have staff present to give tours or to introduce people to what goes on in their departments. Write lists of key points for the staff to make, rather than just leaving everything to chance.
- If you need money for extra stuff, have information available. (One library Fred worked with had booklets with maps of the building showing each piece of needed furniture, with prices marked on each object. It worked.)
- Feed people. Even if it's just candy corn and circus peanuts (although you can almost certainly do better).
- If you can afford it, spend money on an opening day collection to make the shelves sparkle. (Some ill-advised public libraries, however, have pitched out all their older books to make their shelves seriously sparkle, making citizens wonder why they bothered to build a new library in the first place.
- People may want to see the back rooms, but probably more out of general curiosity than an overwhelming interest in library staff functions. Most people want to see things they will use personally, and this does not include tech services, staff lunchrooms, panel rooms, water rooms, loading docks, or storage.
- During a grand opening, people will try every available door. If you don't want visitors wandering in, keep doors locked.
- When you cut the ribbon, the library is brand-new. Outside of things that didn't turn up on time or punch list problems, the building will never look better.

VIII. PUNCH LISTS

At the end of projects, before the contractors receive the money that's been held back from all of their payments during the projects, the owners give the contractors final lists of things that need to be corrected before the holdback funds are released.

Lists of this type are called "punch lists," and the process of preparing them is called "punching," as in "We punched the first floor wiring last week."

Final punch lists are notoriously unwelcome to contractors. They're finished with the buildings, ready to pack up and be paid, and suddenly the owners give them what they regard as picky lists of unreasonable complaints. Frequently punch lists involve bringing back all the trades involved in the project, so the cost and nuisance for the contractor may be considerable. If your social relationship with your general contractor has been warm and wonderful, the punch list may cool things off.

Like contractors, architects are also ready to wrap things up and get on to the next project, and their punch lists may occasionally be perfunctory. Because of this, punch listing is one area where you may want to bring back your programmer (building consultant) or hire an independent outside expert. If you have an owner's representative, that person may provide constant quality oversight.

Depending on your architects, your punch list may be much more detailed than theirs. This does not mean you have done a bad thing.

It's important to do punch listing before you've moved anything into your library. Many of the problems in final punch lists are concerned with minor dings and scrapes, and if you've been doing anything inside the building except walking gently through, your contractors may contend that everything was great when they left, and that any damage was your doing. Because latex paint on drywall is impressively fragile, it's easy to cause unintentional damage, and your contractors may be right.

Punch listing requires a systematic approach. Make lists of things to inspect, then check them one by one in definable areas of the building. If you have big areas to check—such as ceilings or walls—you can "paint" the surface with your eyes, sweeping them systematically back and forth to cover an area. Some things to look for are:

- Dents, scrapes, and lumps in paint. (If you want to be really demanding on dents, go in at night with a flashlight and hold it flat against the wall, making irregularities in the finish stand out like the Mountains of the Moon.)
- Rough surfaces. Check in particular painted windowsills, where construction dust can settle in wet paint.
- Damaged ceiling tiles. Tiles in suspended ceilings are fragile, and workers sometimes leave them in chipped or stained condition.
- Sloppy trim. If moldings are crooked or meet badly at corners, if there are wide gaps between trim and the adjacent surfaces, or if there are gaps where pieces of trim are supposed to meet snugly, all of these should be corrected.
- Bad carpet seams or wrinkles.
- Electrical switches and receptacles that don't work properly. Watch for substitutions of cheaper products (for example, regular receptacles substituted for childproof tamper-proof receptacles). It's easy to buy an outlet tester and send a low-paid employee to test every outlet in the building.
- Crooked electrical fixtures, outlets, and switches. (Flush floor boxes are particularly prone to be laid out irregularly, and you will need to tell your electrical contractors up front that you won't accept them. Forcing contractors to rip out floors to correct crooked boxes may be regarded as unreasonable.)

- Restroom floor drains that don't drain properly. Try pouring water on the floor near the drain and see what happens.
- Restroom fixtures that don't function properly. Automatic faucets should operate when hands get generally near them. Automatic toilets should flush consistently and enthusiastically. Automatic towel dispensers and hand dryers should not require you to repeatedly wave your hands about trying to get them to work. If these gadgets don't work perfectly at punch listing time, they almost certainly will not improve with age and experience. Don't be lenient with them.
- Faulty fixtures and equipment provided as part of the contract. Test everything, particularly automatic switches, which can easily fail to work correctly.
- Motion detector lighting (if you are unfortunate enough to have it) that activates only after people have entered the area in question and that turns off too eagerly. Door motion should activate restroom motion detectors.
- Items out of plumb, crooked walls, skewed windows, and so on are best if you note them immediately rather than waiting for the final punch list, but if that's the first time you spot something, bring it up.
- Crooked windows.
- HVAC systems are so complex that you will want to hire an expert to check them out. Fred once paid an expert about $10,000 at the end of a construction project and found out in turn that about $60,000 in work had been left undone or incorrectly done. In situations like this, make sure that your expert is totally separate from the firms doing the work.

Ideally, you will maintain good communications with your contractors throughout the project, letting them know in construction coordination meetings what type of work you expect and noting problems when you first encounter them.

Occasionally, local architects and contractors appear to tacitly agree that problems very visible to the library staff simply don't exist. If this happens to your library, you will probably have to be a complete pill to protect yourself.

> One library Fred knows found that the architects, engineers, contractors, and city inspectors were all local and all buddies and all blithely insisted that major problems simply didn't exist. The library had to hire an out-of-state engineering firm with a nationwide reputation and with enough professional clout to get past the good-old-boy blockade.

One of the most serious errors a library can make is not sticking by its guns at punch list time. Although your building will come with a one-year warranty, getting things corrected is a lot easier when you're sitting on someone's money.

Punch lists need to be in print and fully detailed. If you tend to pick nits, you have just the right sort of mind for punch listing. Software is available for documenting punch lists, including photographs of all problems.

Frequently your contractors will contest some of the items in your punch list. If so, offer to walk through the library with them and review each item.

> Fred had this happen once. When he offered to meet with the contractor and remove any unreasonable item from the punch list, the contractor replied that the point wasn't unreasonable items but simply too many items. Things were somewhat tense after that.

Running through all the items in a punch list can take months or sometimes even years. Throughout the process, you may be under continuous pressure to release nearly all of the holdback money. Your contractors will contend, for example, that you are sitting on $100,000 of their money while the total remaining work is perhaps $5,000, and that this would be a good time to pay all but the $5,000. However, if you do this, you are unlikely to ever see your contractors again. The thing that keeps contractors coming back is the leverage of the $100,000. The proper response is always to assure your contractors that you are very eager to release the entire $100,000, and you hope that the $5,000 worth of work can be completed quickly.

In addition to final punch lists, all jobs require ongoing punch lists. Construction managers, architects, and owners frequently spot things that are not correct and stop payment on those items until they are done properly. As the owner, you can keep an eye on the building as it goes up and bring up things that appear to be wrong.

If you maintain a diary of the project with specific, dated entries, this also provides a source of items for your punch list.

IX. POST-OCCUPANCY INSPECTION

In the construction industry, the standard warranty period is one year. After that, you are generally on your own, although manufacturers' warranties for individual components of your building—such as the roof and windows—may be longer.

Warranties are useful but far less powerful than holdbacks, because you are no longer sitting on the contractors' funds. And you may have no recourse if the contractor has gone out of business.

To take advantage of your warranty, you need to keep careful track of problems during the first year of occupancy. Frequently, owners and architects get together about ten months after buildings are completed to work up lists of items that should be corrected under the terms of the warranty.

It helps if you remind your staff to let you know during the first year about anything that appears to be wrong.

X. SNAPPY RULES ON CONSTRUCTION

1. A badly constructed building is a pain forever. Or until it falls down, whichever comes first.
2. Everything else being equal, union labor is more technically competent than nonunion labor. If prevailing wage laws mean you have to pay the same price for both, union labor is a good idea.
3. Punch listing tries the previously warm social relationships between owners and contractors.
4. The failure of architects to provide correct details on plans is not the contractors' fault.
5. Contractors and construction managers tell workers what to do. Owners do not.
6. In some parts of the United States, no workers turn up on the first day of deer season or trout season.
7. Holding a contractor to a mistakenly low bid may lead to nothing but trouble.
8. A happy construction situation is when everyone gets along together and no one is losing money on the job.
9. If you want to provide cookies for the workers, talk with the contractors. A large crew taking time off work to line up for cookies in mid-morning can cost a contractor hundreds of dollars in lost production.

10. Contracting is a perilous undertaking because the job goes to the lowest bidder, who then has to try to still make money.
11. Someone from the library staff needs to be present at all construction coordination meetings.
12. If you know you will be a real stickler on a certain area, tell people up front. (Fred insisted that all electrical boxes in the floor be square and in rows. He was never popular with the electricians, but the result was a lot less sloppy looking than most jobs of that kind.)
13. If the contractor messes up, be extraordinarily careful about accepting cash in lieu of corrected work. You have a right to a building that works the way it is supposed to, and it's easy to bargain away proper performance for far too little money. If your architects encourage you to accept a cash settlement, always talk to your owner's rep and programmer.
14. It's a good thing if the project architect is the person the architectural firm sends to attend the construction coordination meetings.
15. If you have named categories for various sizes of donations to your project, be careful how you name them. "Supermen" and "Sharecroppers" are probably not good choices.
16. Short public ceremonies with extensive eating make everyone happy.
17. If your designers want to mount individual donor-recognition letters on walls, ask them how the letters can be removed for repainting the walls ten years from now. (Latex paint on drywall has the durability of piecrust, and you will have to repaint.)
18. If you decide to have a cash bar at public events, you'll need dram shop insurance, which the press may find entertaining to report.
19. It's almost impossible to have everything completed in time for your ribbon cutting. Luckily, you will be far more aware of what's missing or wrong than will the people seeing the building for the first time, and incomplete details may not register.
20. It's hard to find the right place between having too few public ceremonies and having so many ceremonies that the press and bloggers start having fun at your expense.
21. At public events, what people want to hear is probably more important than what you want to tell them.
22. Settle in advance what kinds of advertising from designers, contractors, and other participants can be posted on the construction site.

13

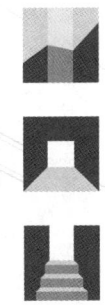

Remodeling and Expanding Library Buildings

I. INTRODUCTION

This chapter deals with the special problems encountered in remodeling and expanding existing library buildings.

One of the most satisfying undertakings in library design can be the expansion and remodeling of historic libraries. When owners walk into projects with a firm idea of functional needs and the special challenges of dealing with existing buildings, the results can be outstanding.

However, although the logic of preservation and conservation leads to strong public interest in the reuse of existing structures, the costs can be extremely high, and the results can be disappointing from a functional viewpoint. If, in addition, the historical qualities of the original structure are compromised or ruined, not much is gained by reuse.

If you are considering expanding an existing library, one absolute prerequisite is a completed building program, one based on long-term functional needs rather than on your existing building. If you have a program, you can constantly use it as a yardstick to determine whether proposed modifications and additions provide the spaces you actually need. Without a program, you are likely to provide features because you can, rather than because you need them.

While remodeling and expanding existing libraries can be a positive experience, converting existing non-library structures to libraries is often a perilous undertaking. See chapter 7 on "Converting Non-Library Spaces to Public Libraries."

II. COMPARATIVE COSTS

It's extremely easy to underestimate the cost of remodeling and modernizing an existing library building. If a building needs a new HVAC system, new wiring, new roof, new lighting, new plumbing, a sprinkler system, abatement of asbestos and lead paint, provision of accessibility, and substantial other work to bring it into compliance with building codes, the necessary work can easily cost as much as new construction—and sometimes substantially more.

In addition, the increased space taken up by air ducts, larger restrooms, legal clearances between furnishings, removal of historic but inaccessible book stacks, retrofitting of electrical outlets and data conduit, addition of an elevator, and provision of additional staircases required to meet safety codes means that the existing building will almost certainly hold substantially less after remodeling. This means that remodeling historic libraries without simultaneously expanding them is unlikely to be successful unless the libraries have a great deal of currently unused space.

One of the problems that accompanies possible remodeling and expansion is public pressure. Even if your building is clearly unworkable, few people will believe that reworking it involves throwing good money after bad.

When you are considering remodeling and expansion, therefore, you will need:

- A written building program listing the spaces you need when you are finished—not those you think you can create by the conversion of existing spaces. Existing spaces will have to be considered later, but they should not affect your initial description of what constitutes a suitable building for your library.
  All of us who live in existing buildings are constantly thinking of ways they might be tweaked to improve things, and it's hard to suppress these ideas and think instead of everything we actually need. To protect yourself in situations like this, always make sure that your program is designed to be equally suitable for both remodeling and new construction.

- The opinions of architects and engineers on the physical condition of your current building and its suitability for expansion. This kind of analysis can be complex. The unfortunate thing is that even if your building is only 10 or 20 years old, it may still be unsuited for expansion.
- A schematic design prepared by your architects, showing how your building can be expanded and remodeled to meet the needs specified in your building program.
- A review by your consultant of your architect's design for expansion and remodeling, to be sure that there are no resulting functional problems.
- A solid cost estimate for the project.
- For comparison, your architects' estimate of the cost of starting over with a completely new building.

> Estimates for the cost of remodeling and expansion can be extraordinarily inaccurate. One Illinois Carnegie library found that its lowest bid was three times the architects' estimate.

If discussions about the need to start over on a new site get ugly, it's important to let your hired professionals—your architect and your programmer—take the flak. Remember the basic rule: the library should always deliver any good news, and hired professionals should deliver the bad news. The professionals will probably be more believable, but the important thing is that they can leave town at the end of the meeting.

III. PROBLEMS WITH THE REUSE AND EXPANSION OF OLD LIBRARY BUILDINGS

A. Changed Building Codes

Unless your library is very new, it can easily be out of conformance with existing building codes. As long as you don't change it much, it may be considered to be "grandfathered" as an existing building. But if you carry out significant expansion or remodeling, you may be required to bring it up to code.

Determining what you can and can't do is a technical undertaking that will require conversations between your architects (and engineers) and local code enforcement officials.

Inevitably there are gray areas. Officials may be willing to bend on zoning, but asking that building code matters be waived is not welcome. (Sometimes historic buildings may be allowed to vary from codes, while more recent buildings of less architectural significance may not.)

B. New Code Categories Resulting from Expansion

Many building code requirements vary with the size of the structure.

You may find, for example, that your building is perfectly legal as a 10,000-square-foot structure but no longer legal as part of a 30,000-square-foot structure.

This can frequently happen if the construction materials in your building are inappropriate for a larger structure. For example, existing wooden structural components may not meet local fire codes for significantly larger buildings.

If this is the case, it's possible that you may not be allowed to expand your building. Or you may be required to construct what amounts to two separate buildings with a narrow opening between them, equipped with doors that close automatically in case of fire. A narrow opening between two sections of the building may work well if each section is the right size to correspond with one of the major spaces listed in your building program. But if the resulting spaces don't match your program, you may find it difficult or impossible to develop the functional spaces you need. And if a department is divided between two essentially separate spaces, this may introduce expensive problems with staff oversight.

Another frequent requirement when buildings expand is the addition of a sprinkler system. The IBC (International Building Code), for example, specifies that any library over 12,000 square feet must have a sprinkler system. Libraries have been built just under 12,000 square feet in order to avoid this requirement, but when the time comes to expand, they are faced with the additional complexity of retrofitting sprinkler systems to buildings that may never have been intended to have them.

Be sure your architects determine what this situation is before you make any public announcements about your plans.

C. Asbestos and Other Pollutants

Almost any building constructed before the late 1970s is likely to contain asbestos and lead-based paint.

Outside of its health risks, asbestos is a great material. It makes good pipe insulation, strengthens materials like vinyl floor tile and plaster, absorbs sound, and does many other desirable things.

But you still don't want it, and in many cases you will have to have it removed (remediated) during construction. (Even if you plan to tear your old library down and build a new one on the site, you will still have to remediate the asbestos.)

Actually, asbestos that is not in danger of being dispersed in the air can sometimes be left in place. A good example is vinyl asbestos floor tile (VAT) that is intact and not crumbling and will be covered by new material.

You are most likely to find asbestos in pipe lagging (insulation), vinyl asbestos floor tile (always suspect the worst of 9 × 9-inch tile), tile mastic (the glue that attaches tile to the floor), fireproof enclosures (look for concrete asbestos board called Transite), acoustic ceiling tile, and some drywall and joint compounds. Asbestos was banned for construction in various stages during the 1970s.

Lead paint was banned in interiors in 1978. As with asbestos, lead paint was great except for its poisonous qualities. If it's stable and not attached to crumbling surfaces and not powdering off, it may not be a major problem. But it can be nasty if you need to modify things. For example, sanding wood that has been painted with lead paint leads to airborne lead dust.

The most common poisonous metallic compounds used in paint are lead pigments (red lead, white lead, chrome yellow, chrome orange, chrome green), cadmium pigments (shades of red, orange, and yellow), vermilion, Paris green, and so on. Lead pigments are by far the most common.

As part of remodeling a building constructed before the late 1970s, you will need to have it assessed for lead and asbestos. Architects can recommend firms to do this work or arrange to have it done.

D. Bearing Walls

"Bearing walls" are walls that hold up a building.

If your library has load-bearing walls, it will be far more difficult to open up larger spaces. While it's almost always possible to create openings where solid walls exist, this can be expensive and may even require strengthening foundations where the remaining portions of walls are carrying more concentrated weight than the footings below them were intended to support.

One of the standard solutions when expanding historic libraries is to convert existing windows to doors, because the lintels over the windows are already in place. Cutting out a section of wall to essentially lower the windowsill to the floor may have little or no impact on the structure of a building and may therefore be a relatively inexpensive alteration.

The expansion of old buildings with small rooms and bearing walls can lead to larger structures that are labyrinths, with too many rooms and too many invisible corners to supervise.

Many historic small libraries of the Carnegie era have front reading rooms and back offices or stacks. If the offices all have bearing walls, it may be difficult to open up the back of the existing library. And the artistic character of the formal reading rooms may be hurt if they are enlarged. If a new wing is added at the rear of a library of this type, the old offices may create a wasp waist between the original reading rooms and new public spaces at the back of the building. The danger in such a situation is that the original reading rooms may become forgotten adjuncts, spaces down the hall and around the corner. And they may be hard to supervise.

E. HVAC

Many historic buildings do not have the ductwork necessary for modern heating, ventilating, and air conditioning systems. This is particularly true of Carnegie-era buildings, which were built with radiators but without cooling systems.

If a historic library has two floors—a main floor and a basement—it may be fairly easy to add ductwork to heat and cool the main floor because many old buildings have substantial attic spaces that provide sufficient room for ducts.

If a library has two floors plus a basement, there will be no attic space available for ductwork to provide air to the main floor. Hanging ductwork from a historic ceiling is an abomination, so the only option may be installing ducts in the basement.

Whether or not they must house ductwork for the floor above, basements in old libraries are often a serious problem for modern HVAC systems. If a basement has an eight-foot ceiling, for example, the addition of ceiling-mounted ductwork will make basement spaces too low for occupance. However, sometimes it's possible to install perimeter ducts that leave the center of the basement usable.

Many historic library buildings are energy hogs. Solid masonry walls have no insulation value, nor do single-pane windows. Rooms with high ceilings are more expensive to heat than those with low ceilings. The lack of entry foyers can expose users and staff to blasting winter winds. If old skylights still exist, they can radiate heat in the winter and bring in unwanted glare, especially in the summer.

Unfortunately, ill-considered responses to this problem can ruin attractive buildings. Some historic windows have been replaced with modern windows with different muntin patterns, essentially ruining the historic appearance of the building. Some libraries have added cheap aluminum storm windows, which are ugly but at least do not result in the destruction of the original windows. Handsome ceilings with elegant cornices have been hidden by suspended acoustic tile ceilings. Awkward foyers have been added to the front of historic buildings to block winter winds.

Although it's more expensive, existing small-pane windows with single glazing can be replaced by double-pane windows that look essentially identical.

Many historic libraries have large attic spaces, making it easy to insulate ceilings.

If high ceilings lead to the concentration of heat, paddle fans can often be installed that suit the era of the buildings

Historic skylights can be covered over and lit electrically, or they can be provided with translucent protective covers.

F. Electrical Wiring

Old libraries can have extraordinarily tangled wiring that has been frequently cobbled together over many years and is sometimes in spectacular noncompliance with even rudimentary building codes.

It's still possible to find old libraries with working knob and tube wiring, often with its original insulation happily cracking off.

Knob and tube wiring uses ceramic tubes to separate wires from wood when they pass through structural members, and ceramic knobs to support wires away from wood and other surfaces. The system was generally used from about 1880 through the 1930s. Because wires were held away from surfaces, they radiated heat well. But by separating positive and negative wires, the system led to greater magnetic fields around wires. And knob and tube systems do not have ground wires. Insurance companies may not want to insure your library if it has knob and tube wiring, and some building codes may ban it. You don't want it in your library.

Because historic buildings often have solid masonry walls, it's tempting to add new wiring by attaching metal conduit to the surface of the walls. Unfortunately, the result can be extraordinarily ugly. If you care enough to preserve and expand your historic library, you should care enough to hide the new wiring.

The attractive way to add wiring is to channel through the plaster (and sometimes part of the masonry beneath) to provide space to bury electrical conduit in the walls.

If you are remodeling and expanding a historic library, it may already have a variety of unsightly exposed electrical conduit, added piecemeal over the years as occasional new outlets or light fixtures were needed. A major remodeling job is a great time to get rid of the mess.

When remodeling historic libraries, designers need to bury new electrical conduits as much as possible, although it's tempting to save money by surface mounting ugly wire mold on the walls. In the first picture, the three electrical items were installed by chiseling through the plaster (and the brick beneath), installing the conduit, and then covering the conduit with new plaster. In the second picture, the conduit emerges to pass over the historic dark marble baseboard because the designers were concerned about possibly ruining the baseboard if they tried to remove and reinstall it.

Reflected uplighting can be installed in historic library rooms without creating aesthetically jarring effects. Designers are sometimes tempted to install clusters of chandeliers, but the effect can be overdone. (And lots of chandeliers do a great job of displaying dead bugs.)

G. Windows

One of the most important sources of character in historic buildings is their windows. The dimensions of the frames and muntins, and the number and proportions of the windowpanes, play a critical role in the appearance and aesthetics of historic libraries.

One of the worst things that has been done to historic buildings is replacing historic windows with modern windows that do not match the originals. Removing small pane windows, for example, and replacing them with large sheets of glass can alter the appearance of a building destructively.

If modern aluminum sash windows are used to replace original steel sash windows, the result is likely to be unfortunate. For reasons of strength, aluminum windows will probably have bulkier muntins than steel windows, and even if the pattern of windowpanes is similar, the new windows will look distinctly different.

Obviously, the best thing is to leave historic windows in place, but they often have serious problems. Old wooden windows may be rotting out. They may have been destructively modified in the past. They may be totally uninsulated or equipped with ugly storm windows. The best solution may be to use photographs of the original building to create custom-made, insulated windows that match the originals as closely as possible.

If your library is subject to the oversight of a historic preservation agency, it will probably pay special attention to what you plan to do with your existing windows.

H. Cheap or Fragile Construction Materials

It's fun to believe that historic buildings were always well built, but that can be far from the truth.

For example, many Carnegie libraries have cornices that resemble stone balustrades but are actually made of painted sheet steel. If this material is rusting out, or if more is needed, details of this kind can usually be matched in fiberglass or similar materials.

One of the most attractive features of classical library buildings is architectural terracotta, ornamental details made of glazed ceramic material. Eventually, some terracotta develops major crazing and cracks and has to be replaced. Other terracotta simply needs matching on additions. While replacement terracotta is available, the cost can be significant, and some architects have been very successful at matching historic terracotta details by making molds from the originals and using them to produce replicas from materials like fiberglass.

I. Poor Functional Locations

Some otherwise great library buildings find that with the passage of time, the buildings are no longer in functional locations.

This seems particularly true for public libraries, which can interact strongly with their neighborhoods. If all of the retail stores around the library have closed and relocated to preferred areas, the library loses much of the synergy that occurs between libraries and commercial neighbors. If the houses that surrounded the library are replaced by industries, or if a homeless shelter has been established close to the library, it may be time to move away rather than undertake major remodeling.

If the library has a functional location, it may need extra land not only to expand its building but also to add off-street parking.

See chapter 10 on "Site Selection" for more information on location.

J. Matching Historic Exteriors

- *Brickwork*. Matching exterior brickwork is a special problem, since many types of brick used a century ago are not easily available. For example, the slender Roman bricks with thin horizontal mortar joints that are sometimes found in late nineteenth and early twentieth-century buildings are particularly hard to match. Taking the time to thoroughly investigate brick sources is important, and the rush to select brick quickly may lead to gross mismatching that grates on the eyes forever. One standard approach to satisfactory expansions of historic buildings is to never place new and old bricks directly adjacent to each other. If two areas of brick are separated by a new architectural element perhaps 10 to 20 feet wide, it's much harder to tell that the two types of brick don't quite match.
- *Stonework*. Limestone can sometimes be matched, and it may even be available from the same quarry that provided the original stone. A greater problem than matching stone can be matching the carving on the stone. The work can still be done, but the cost can be higher than libraries can afford.
- *Windows*. Another problem with historic buildings is that windowsills are often too high to allow users to see the outside world. A century ago, the main function of windows in libraries was to provide natural light, and book shelving was frequently located along perimeter walls beneath windows. However, library users today often want to read in locations that let them see the outside world pass by. Larger windows also make it easier for passersby to see what's going on inside the library. In our opinion, constructing additions with windows that match those in the original buildings but have lower sills does not destroy the historic look of the buildings, particularly if the tops of the new and old windows all align, the framing elements match, the muntin patterns are as identical as possible, and the widths of the new and old windows match.
- *Architectural styles*. Opinions differ strongly on whether historic buildings should have matching additions or have distinctly different modern additions. The argument against matching additions is that the building exemplifies the intent of the original architects, and any addition should be obviously an addition, a structure that no one will assume was part of the original architects' vision for the building. We find this contention a silly one, something that bothers primarily design professionals who are either historical purists or offended by the prospect of imitating an older building style. Usually everyone else, particularly the users of the building and the residents of the area it serves, is happy with a matching or very similar

Expanding historic buildings is frequently made difficult by problems with matching old and new brickwork. On the left in the first photograph are the Roman bricks in this Carnegie-era building, while the new (and very different) Norman bricks are on the right. One standard way of limiting the obviousness of the mismatch is to place some kind of structural element between the two areas of brick, as illustrated in the second photograph. (Bottom photo by apaceDesign, Peoria, Illinois.)

addition. One of the problems with unmatched modern additions to historic buildings is that they age badly. When the new addition is constructed, the building consists of a historic library and a cute modern wing, and the two function comfortably together. But after thirty years, when styles for contemporary architecture have changed, the building consists of a historic library and a painfully dated addition. (Not unlike an antebellum mansion with avocado shag carpet.) Admittedly, some historic buildings have oddly matched sections built at different times in different styles. Hampton Court palace provides an example. But why take a chance? Your architect may also contend that matching an original look is impossible because it will be too expensive. This can be the case, but one suspects that the real motive is often a desire to make an original design statement rather than be derivative. Original looks can be matched in somewhat simplified form, skipping for example the most expensive stonework details. We are convinced that being talked into an unmatched addition to a historic building is almost always a terrible mistake. The words "talked into" are the right ones. In every case we've seen, the owners are talked into an ill-considered and unmatched addition by the architects.

K. Adjacent Land

In many cases, the ability to expand a library building is hampered or prevented by the lack of adjacent land.

- Some libraries have been built on sites too small to support expansion. This is one of the worst mistakes that can be made in library planning. At the time the new library is built it seems huge—a building that will last forever. But in 10 or 20 years, the library is packed solid. Library collections—particularly university library collections—grow remorselessly. When campuses add new programs, substantial new collections may suddenly be required. Public libraries introduce new services, services that were never anticipated when the library was designed, and the services need new space. When a public library finally constructs a new building after many years of desperately forced weeding, collections may grow surprisingly quickly.

    Needing to expand a library when the available space is too small leads to hard decisions. Libraries cobble on crowded additions. They try to build upwards, which is almost always impossible or badly advised. They put high-density storage units miles away rather than next door, where books can be accessed quickly. Or they delay and delay before finally cutting their losses and starting over on new sites.
- Other libraries have had expansion space, but they sold it or gave it away. On a scale of bad planning from plus 10 (great planning) to 0 (seriously awful

planning), this rates about a minus 10. On crowded campuses, somebody always wants the empty space next to the library. Protecting it for long-term library expansion can be a major political problem, with avid departments coveting the prime central land surrounding the library. Unfortunately, once land is lost to the library, it is almost certainly gone forever. Part of the problem on campuses is that library planning is a very long-range undertaking. Holding empty land for half a century or more may be difficult. Public libraries sometimes purchase large sites and immediately sell off some of the space to raise construction money. Inevitably, when the library needs to expand, the space it sold off is no longer available, or available only at an unaffordable price.

- Changes in zoning may make a library's current site too small. A good example is the requirement that libraries detain water runoff. At the time the building was constructed, on-site water retention may not have been required, but when the time to expand arrives, the library may find out that new zoning requirements have made most of its available land required for ponds. (There may be solutions to the problem. Existing structures may be grandfathered in, with only land being converted from turf to building requiring retention ponds. In that case, if the library demolishes an existing nearby building to construct a library addition, the net decrease in turf may be small. In some communities, green roofs count as turf rather than as structures.)

The moral of all this is a simple one:

- Never let land around your library go, particularly for a short-term (and often minor) cash infusion.
- Never let available land next to your library slip through your fingers. You may not need it for 10 or 20 or even 50 or more years, but when the day comes you'll be ready.
- Never sell off land to pay for construction, for your successors will shed bitter tears.
- Someone will always contend that with the coming of electronic books, libraries will never need to expand again. Often these people have axes to grind (they hate taxes or covet your land), but libraries need to combat them vigorously. There are no doubt libraries out there that are awash in unneeded space, but they are probably few.
- Pay particular attention to proposed developments near your library building. Chapter 10 on "Site Selection" contains information on the types of neighbors that are likely to undermine the functions of your library.
- On campuses, fight all attempts to convert empty land around your library to non-library purposes.

L. Accessibility

Any library built before the passage of the Americans with Disabilities Act or similar state statutes may have serious problems with accessibility.

Libraries are full of steps, ranging from essential staircases for movement between floors to irrelevant steps introduced because the designer thought they were cute. All of these have to be overcome.

Many libraries also have inadequate clearances to allow wheelchair traffic. These can range from narrow doorways to narrow stacks, cramped restrooms, and other common problems.

1. Historic Entrances

A large number of historic libraries have entrances that do not meet modern requirements for accessibility for people with disabilities.

There are no quick and easy solutions.

Many people will suggest adding an entrance ramp, but unless the difference in height is only a foot or so, the ramp will be endless. Remember that moving two feet vertically requires a ramp a minimum of twenty-four feet long. An exterior ramp will be miserable or impossible to negotiate in the winter, and it will make a significant contribution to the architectural destruction of the building.

Even worse is an unenclosed exterior ramp leading to a basement entrance, because sooner or later the drain at the foot of the ramp will clog or back up, and rainwater will flood the basement.

The only practical solution for access to the vast majority of historic libraries is to provide a second entrance at grade level, with an elevator inside that can transport people to the various original levels of the library. Usually entrances of this type are on one side of the building, often about where the original building and new addition meet.

Larger libraries usually have multiple elevators, one to move people from street level to the main floor, where they can pass through a security checkpoint, and then additional elevators to move people between floors.

It's important that entrances to new parts of buildings be at grade level, with movement between floors all internal. As a bad example of poor design, when one Illinois public library was expanded, the architect added a huge new exterior staircase, supplemented by a ramp down to the basement level. The results were miserable. The staircase faced northwest and was covered with ice all winter, forcing the library to rope it off for weeks at a time. The exterior ramp down into the basement channeled rainwater into the building, leading to frequent floods. The fact that the library had two new exterior entrances forced it to provide two lending desks. With a single entrance, a library can arrange to have all users pass a single desk before being transported between floors, but this library found it impossible, and the result was having to staff two desks at times of the week when one would have been sufficient. (The addition of self-check equipment can make the situation even worse.)

Once a new entrance has been provided, it's tempting to take the historic entrance out of service. Watching two doors is expensive, and the original entrance may be poorly sheltered from winter weather.

Unfortunately, a major architectural message of historic buildings is frequently "this way in." If historic doors are taken out of service, the building may lose essential navigational clarity.

If you are forced to take a front door out of service, about the only acceptable thing to do is to convert it to an emergency exit but otherwise mothball it, leaving it strictly alone, so it can be used as an entrance once again if times change.

Probably the worst thing architects and owners have done with historic entrances is to simply brick them up. Bricked-up historic entrances are simply ugly. At this point, one is tempted to ask why anyone bothered to keep the old building at all.

M. Basements in Expanded Historic Buildings

Most basements in historic library buildings have low ceilings, severely limiting the use of basement spaces.

When these buildings are expanded, the solution to the problem is usually to drop the level of the basement floors in the new additions to provide adequate ceiling height. The change in level may be only a couple of feet, so elevator service may not be essential. If the building will have an elevator anyway, it may be possible to have it stop at both basement levels.

If staffing is limited, use basements for services that don't require constant supervision. Common uses include meeting rooms, restrooms (although there can be supervision problems there as well), storage, equipment rooms, workrooms, and so on.

IV. PHASING EXPANSION PROJECTS

When libraries need to expand, one major decision is whether to stay in the building during expansion work or to move out temporarily.

If the library continues to provide service in its building during expansion and remodeling, the result is a "phased" construction project.

A simple phased project may begin with the construction of a new wing. When construction is complete, the library may camp out in the new wing while the existing library is remodeled. Then the library moves back into the remodeled space.

Some projects involve more than two phases, and planning them becomes reminiscent of planning complex military campaigns.

With really large buildings, phasing may be the only practical option, but it always deserves careful evaluation and review.

A. Advantages of Phased Construction

The main advantage of phased projects is that libraries don't have to move out during construction.

And that's about it.

B. Problems with Phasing

Phasing a project introduces a number of problems:

- *Extended construction time.* Phasing a major construction job can more or less double the time required for the project.
- *Lack of space for staging construction.* Construction companies need space for their construction trailers, for parking for workers, and for piling construction materials. A common way to provide this space is to cannibalize the library's parking lot, leaving staff and patrons no place to park during construction. If your library has trees you want to preserve, you will need to take special and very firm steps to keep contractors from piling construction materials around the trees—and very likely killing them.
- *Discomfort for patrons and staff.* If you are trying to operate a library while construction is going on behind a plywood partition, you can expect to

be subjected to a constant barrage of the sounds of masonry drills, falling objects, loud conversations, and workers' radios, which they will turn up loud enough to be heard over the drills and falling objects. There will also be bad smells. Because of construction, you may also have problems getting patrons and staff in and out of the building. Entrances will vary as the project continues. Temporary staff parking and even patron parking may need to be blocks away, particularly if the contractor needs your parking lot for a construction trailer, working parking construction materials, and dumpsters. Construction dust will inevitably make its way into the inhabited part of the library, making some staff members and users ill.

- *Phasing and good design.* The better integrated the new and old sections of the building are, the greater your problems are likely to be. If the new addition is almost totally separate from the original building, phasing may be easier, but the resulting building is likely to be somewhat dysfunctional, with essentially two libraries where one would be better.

> An example of miserable failure in integrating an addition is provided by a large American academic library. The library was expanded in the late 1960s by a major Brutalist addition to the original historic library. The new addition is connected to the original library only by a basement tunnel and a link into the back of a departmental library. The fact that the new addition is impressively dysfunctional didn't help.

- *Higher bids.* Phased projects cost more. Contractors don't like to have owners and users underfoot, and they will spend more money bringing all the trades back at least a second time. If they have to work slowly due to phased construction, they will worry more about inflation and increase their bids accordingly. Because of this, bids for single-phase work will almost certainly be lower. For smaller libraries, it will probably be cheaper to move out during construction, even with the extra costs of renting temporary space and hiring commercial movers. Your architects or construction management firm may be able to help with comparative cost estimates for one-phase and two-phase work.
- *Problems with warranties on equipment.* Extended construction can lead to major problems with HVAC equipment. Because the equipment in the new addition may have to function together with new equipment added to the original building, you won't know if they work properly together until the project is completely done. The problem is that you will need to turn the equipment on in the new addition while you are camping out there. If a year passes during the second phase (remodeling the original building), by

the time the project is completely finished, the one-year warranties on the Phase I equipment will have expired. If the total system doesn't work right when the project is done, you will have trouble because half of the equipment will already be out of warranty. This sounds like a minor point, but it's not. Modern HVAC systems are extraordinarily complex and expensive. In a library construction job, the cost of HVAC may be 25 percent of total construction cost. Commissioning the system (making sure that everything works correctly and that the library staff members know how to operate the system) is a major undertaking. You will not be happy if, when HVAC components in the Phase I part of the job don't work right when the total project is over, the contractor informs you that the Phase I part is now out of warranty, and that it was working just fine when he turned it over to you fifteen months earlier. One solution to this is to have your agreement with your contractor provide that the warranty on the HVAC system will commence at the completion of the final phase of construction, but because equipment warranties may all run just one year, you may have trouble obtaining this requirement.
- *Additional moves.* If you move out during construction, you'll move just twice, but if you phase construction you are likely to have to move a number of times.

C. So Why Phase Your Project?

- No space available for temporary housing for the library. If you are faced with the absence of a space large enough to house your library temporarily, it may be a lot better to put part of your collection in dead storage for a year than to try to live in a building under construction. Any automated lending system should be able to give you a list of the least-used items in the collection.
- Pay as you go. Some owners want to extend the project time to match cash flow. If this is important to you, phased construction may help. But it's important to be aware of the extra costs that accompany phased construction. When all is said and done, pay-as-you-go construction may actually be a bad fiscal choice.
- You have a really large building. Small public libraries, school libraries, and special libraries are all better off clearing out, but a large academic or public library may have no choice except phasing the project and living with the mess.
- Timing can help a phased project. Some libraries have started construction at the end of the spring semester, worked through the next academic year, and wrapped things up at the end of the following summer, being closed for one academic year and two summers.

V. SNAPPY RULES ON REMODELING AND EXPANDING LIBRARIES

1. Remodeling always costs more than 99 percent of the world expects.
2. Written building programs for expanding existing buildings should always be written without regard to existing structures. One good approach to dealing with staff and users and owners is the "tornado" approach, asking what they would need if the building were destroyed by a tornado and they had to begin completely over.
3. Matching historic construction materials can be nearly impossible, but experienced architects can do a lot to conceal the differences between new and old, often by separating them physically.
4. Remodeling and expanding a historic library is difficult. Trying to merge it with a second historic building is seriously scary, but the concept has an evil appeal to the inexperienced.
5. Once they've been expanded, historic buildings frequently have too many floors and too many rooms, with resulting implications for access, supervision, and excessive elevators and staircases.
6. Retrofitting wiring, plumbing, and (particularly) air ducts may require serious surgery. Dropping historic ceilings to conceal air ducts is not an acceptable aesthetic compromise.
7. Trying to get along with inadequate electrical outlets is not an acceptable functional compromise.
8. Expanding a historic library will frequently mean maintaining a historic but inaccessible entrance, in addition to at least one modern entrance. If you can't afford to watch the historic entrance, you can mothball it by converting it (reversibly) to an emergency exit.
9. The walls of most historic libraries are uninsulated, and you probably won't be able to do anything about it.
10. Older libraries typically have bearing walls, which make remodeling and expansion far more difficult.
11. Moving people between floors requires real elevators. Ramps don't work, and lifts of one sort or another are only marginally civilized.
12. Be considerate of aesthetics when reassigning spaces. Converting historic reading rooms to book stacks (which happens) is nasty.
13. Most surviving plans for older libraries are at best inexact. Record drawings from the original construction may not exist, and there may be no record of subsequent alterations. In a firm sort of way, discourage your architects from relying exclusively on old drawings.
14. Remodeling is far more complicated than new construction, and your architects will need increased payment to compensate them.

15. Excavating next to the footings of old library buildings can be tricky. Experienced architects will plan transitions in ways that eliminate expensive reinforcement of original footings. For example, the floors of new additions can be cantilevered to keep them from adding stress to original buildings.
16. The great temptation in dealing with historic buildings is to construct what you can have rather than what you need.
17. When someone says excitedly, "We could put an X here" or "We could use this room for a Y," always ask yourself whether you actually need an X or a Y. Often you don't.
18. A prom date with an ugly guy lasts only a few hours, but an ugly building can last long past the fiftieth wedding anniversary.
19. If your historic building needs new lighting, new wiring, a new HVAC system, and new plumbing, just fixing those can be 40 percent of the cost of a brand-new building.
20. Some historic preservation enthusiasts have big plans for other people's money. Ask yourself whether you can afford to be one of those other people.
21. A bargain building in a bad location is a bad building. A beautiful building in a bad location is pretty bad as well.
22. Changing window muntin patterns in historic buildings is often an abomination.
23. A contemporary addition to a historic building will sometimes—with the passage of time—become a painfully dated addition to a historic building, the architectural equivalent of shag carpet.
24. The decision to expand an old building can lead to tossing out needs listed in the building program, often without full discussion by everyone involved in the project.
25. Despite all the problems, a remodeled and expanded library can be a resounding success and a focus of community pride. Just be careful.

Part IV
Money

14

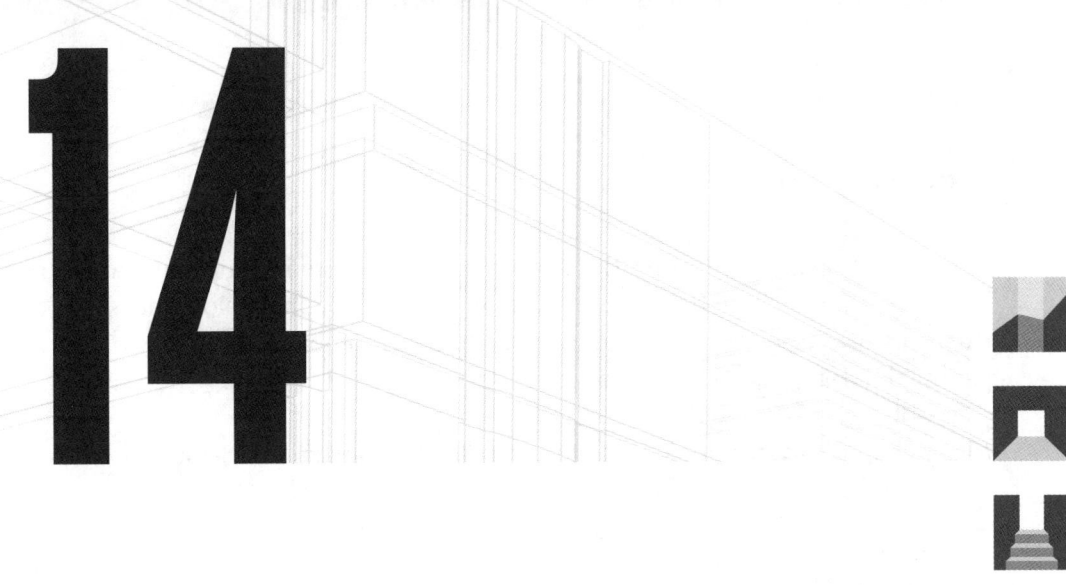

Building Costs

I. INTRODUCTION

Buildings are expensive.

This chapter reviews the various expenses involved in the design and construction of library buildings. It also discusses the tradeoffs between initial expenditure and long-term operating costs.

For information on coming up with the money, see chapter 15 on "Funding."

In general, public libraries may be most on their own when it comes to money. Most special and school libraries are components of larger buildings. Academic libraries usually have the benefit of campus fundraising offices, although universities may have their own priorities, and they may have decided which wealthy donors will be approached for which projects, leaving needy libraries waiting in the wings.

In general, there's a tendency to underestimate construction and operating costs. Architects may quote "construction costs" to library boards, not explaining from the start that total project costs may be 40 percent higher. Library owners may not anticipate increases in operating costs that will accompany new or expanded buildings, or they may not evaluate designs with regard to their implications for long-term operating costs. Well-meaning local citizens may claim that total project costs will be vastly lower than reality.

II. CAPITAL COSTS

Capital costs are all of the one-time expenditures required to construct a library building. They include the costs of land, construction, professional fees, FF&E (furnishings, fixtures, and equipment), site development (utility connections, paving, landscaping, etc.), and other costs.

Many chapters in this book relate to capital costs. In particular, you might want to read the chapters on:

- Programming
- Site selection
- Design
- Construction
- Remodeling and expansion
- Conversion of non-library buildings to public libraries
- Funding

A. Projecting Building Costs Prior to Design

Anticipating costs is less simple than some people suggest, particularly when projects involve remodeling.

Some people want to establish project costs in advance, often before planning has taken place. Sometimes they simply pick cost figures out of midair. When these figures prove to be unrealistically low, unfortunate confrontations occur. This is a bad process. Even when huge bequests are involved, expenditures are usually not absolutely fixed.

Our experience is that library building costs often involve a degree of negotiation. A library develops a building program, hires an architect, creates a schematic design, and then evaluates likely costs. At that point, everyone reviews the project and sorts out costs and benefits. Commonly, the program is cut somewhat to reduce costs, and the owners come to grips with the fact that things are still going to be more expensive than they had hoped.

B. Estimating

One of our architect friends always says, "estimate early and estimate often." Before you begin the fundraising process, you need to have a fairly good idea of what funds you will need to complete the project. Unfortunately, all long-term estimates need to be taken with a grain of salt because estimates are only estimates. In making estimates, your hired experts are projecting into the future. Assumptions are being made on the future costs of materials, land, labor, borrowing, and whether construction will be in a boom or bust cycle.

Never do your own estimating. Unless you are a professional in the area of building design and construction, leave the entire enterprise to hired experts. You should particularly avoid informal but aggressive requests for estimates from local governments and other agencies, since the figures you come up with today may return to haunt you later.

The failure to estimate accurately leads to endless troubles. This seems to be a particular problem with big-name architects, who tend to have no realistic grip on costs and to enmesh their clients in horrendous cost overruns. As a result, really major projects are sometimes built using the design-build system, where teams consisting of a contractor and an architect commit to building a specific project for an agreed-upon price.

Because cost estimating is so vital, some architectural firms employ outside cost estimators. In addition to specializing in this process, cost-estimating firms are more likely to be uninvolved emotionally and will not optimistically guess-a-bit-too-low-and-hope-for-the-best.

When plans are preliminary and vague, cost estimates are of necessity rather general. But as projects move from schematic design through design development to bid documents, the increasingly specific detail enables more accurate estimates.

Some professional publications provide extremely general information on likely costs. For example, you can look up the likely cost per square foot of a library in a specific part of the country built to various levels of quality. It's easy to be overly optimistic when using publications of this sort, so take the cost figures with a grain of salt. Libraries can assume, for example, that their high-end plans are actually low-end plans and lowball costs accordingly.

While using published cost figures may work for informal discussions, an architect or construction manager with experience building libraries in your area will provide far more accurate cost projections.

Cost estimates involve a number of items:

- Construction cost estimates. Construction costs are the costs of building the actual structure. Since project costs will always be significantly higher, insist that your planners and designers always speak in terms of estimated total project costs.

- Project cost estimates. As opposed to construction costs, project costs include parking lots, driveways, sidewalks, utility connections, landscaping, professional fees, FF&E (fixtures, furnishings, and equipment), water detention, and so on. These can add 40 or 50 percent to the total cost of a project.
- Site acquisition costs. Usually the site is acquired before projects begin, but some libraries obtain options on their proposed sites and purchase the sites if and only if their tax referendums pass and they obtain sufficient funding for the entire project.
- Allowances for contingencies. All cost estimates include allowances for unexpected construction costs. Commonly this is 5 percent for new construction and 10 percent for remodeling and expansion, but other percentages are possible. Unexpected costs can come from many places, including changes in materials costs, unknown underground conditions, changes in labor contracts, and so on.
- Allowances for escalation. If a project will not be bid out for a year or more after the estimate is prepared, the estimate must include cost increases due to inflation. Materials and labor will almost certainly increase in costs. If building codes also change, escalation can be even greater.
- Add and deduct alternates. In order to prepare for bids being higher or lower than expected, projects usually separate out some elements for separate bids. If the base bids are attractive, the owners may decide to add one or more of the extra items to the project. If the bids are too high, the owners may select deduct alternates or decide against any or all of the add alternates. Alternates are attractive to owners because the prices are arrived at by bidding rather than negotiation, which always costs more. Examples of add alternates might include sidewalks with pavers rather than concrete, better roofing such as standing-seam metal, or completing interior spaces originally planned to be left unfinished.
- FF&E (furnishings, fixtures, and equipment). These items are usually not part of construction contracts, but libraries need to be able to purchase them. Among other things, FF&E includes all of the shelving in the library, which can be a major item for research libraries.
- Collections. Public libraries in particular are inclined to purchase new books to fill out their shelves on opening day.

C. Components of Building Costs

1. Site Acquisition

Site acquisition costs are primarily an issue for public and academic libraries. Most school and special libraries are located within buildings that are a responsibility of larger units.

In cases of congested areas, such as cities and urban university campuses, the cost of real estate can be a major component of total library building project costs.

In all cases, never (as in *NEVER*) purchase a site without a written building program and the assistance of an architect. Among other things, you need to be sure that:

- The site is actually large enough for the building, parking, driveways and sidewalks, landscaping, water detention, and long-term expansion. Many nonprofessionals seriously underestimate necessary site sizes—and some of them do so very aggressively.
- The site is buildable. There can be all sorts of hidden problems, including soil (such as peat) that won't hold the weight of a library, pollution (which is why old filling station sites stand vacant forever), floodplains or high water tables, underground obstacles (such as sewers), distance from utilities, street access, and so on.
- There are no zoning or code problems. Once you hire architects, one of the first things they do is get to know the folks at the city who implement zoning and code requirements. Some code and zoning enforcement is pretty standard, but other requirements like historic preservation can vary widely from community to community or from neighborhood to neighborhood. It's also important to have an idea about what sorts of changes in zoning or codes are likely to come along.
- The site permits a building entrance facing south—or at worst east. North- and west-facing entrances lead to problems with ice on sidewalks and with winter winds buffeting users and staff whenever outside doorways are opened.

Architectural firms evaluate sites on an everyday basis. Let them help you with it. Also ask your building consultants. (As the saying goes, "Do not do this at home.")

And *never* buy an old building to convert to a library without vast amounts of technical advice from your architects, engineers, and building consultants.

In many cases, libraries in need of sites run into owners of white elephant buildings who decide that their long-vacant structures would be perfect for libraries. This is an interesting but perilous situation. Make use of your out-of-town experts, who will be far more immune to local political pressures.

See chapter 10 on "Site Selection" and chapter 7 on "Converting Non-Library Spaces to Public Libraries."

2. Construction

Construction is expensive. Unless site costs are immense, construction will be the single most significant cost in creating your new library building.

If you will be using a construction management firm, be sure you hire them shortly after you hire your architects so you can take advantage of their abilities to estimate costs and to conduct value engineering studies—suggesting how changes in design can diminish construction costs without diminishing functionality.

3. Utilities

Libraries require access to a wide range of utilities, including natural gas, electric power, water, data, sanitary sewers, and storm sewers.

If utilities are not available at the library site, the extra cost of bringing them to the site (or just rerouting them around your building) can become a major component of total project costs.

If key utilities cannot be brought to the library site at all, that can have a major impact on long-term operating costs. Relying on propane rather than natural gas to heat a building, for example, can vastly increase heating costs. The absence of storm sewers can lead to problems with flooding and may make it particularly important that the library occupy high ground.

4. Site Development

Site development includes all those things that have to be done to the land surrounding the library. The list can be considerable and can be strongly affected by zoning and codes.

- Parking lots. If you have a 40,000-square-foot public library, a good guess is that you'll need a 40,000-square-foot parking lot. And if there's no available overflow parking or you have unusually large meeting rooms, you may need even more. By the time your designers have worked out how to build parking lots that will drain properly (and therefore not be covered with ice in winter) and not crack the first time someone drives a truck onto them, this can be a major investment.
- Driveways. Driveways can be complex, particularly when libraries include places where users with disabilities can arrive easily, loading docks, drive-through book returns (which may require one-way driveways), and discreetly hidden sites for dumpsters.

- Sidewalks. One of the major criticisms of some new libraries is that—in an effort to save money on paving—pedestrians and vehicles share the same pavement.

> This is only a slightly relevant point, but beware the tendency of some designers to create artistically meandering sidewalks that simply encourage users to ignore the sidewalks and cut directly across the grass. Supposedly, some campuses delay installing sidewalks until they can pave the worn places where students have followed the path of least resistance while trudging from building to building.

- Utility connections. Bringing utilities from the street to the building is typically a site cost, not a construction cost. The absence of convenient utility connections can have a major impact not only on costs but also on building design.
- Utility relocation. Some sites have buried utilities that will need to be relocated before construction starts. Sewers can provide special problems.
- Ornamental stuff, such as fountains, statuary, and so on. (Librarians by and large dislike fountains because they have images of users falling in. This seems paranoid, except that users *do* fall in.)

> Library legend has it that the mayor of a major city fell into the public library's "water feature" on opening day.

- Detention and retention basins. Many zoning ordinances require detention basins to control the speed of water runoff. Retention basins are permanent ponds that serve similar functions.
- Landscaping. (As a professional group, landscapers tend to resent the fact that—when money is tight at the end of a project—landscaping is often the first to go. Owners also recognize that you can easily add landscaping later, but that expanding the building later is a major expense.)

5. Fixtures, Furnishings, and Equipment (FF&E)

In addition to the cost of site, utility connections, and construction, most libraries need to purchase furnishings and equipment. These costs are not included in architects' estimates of construction costs, and in many cases, they are not part of general bids on the project.

If you follow the advice in this book and avoid built-in furniture wherever possible, this will lower the base bid on your project (because built-ins will be excluded) and raise your furniture costs.

Some of the common items in this category include:

- Shelving and other collection storage equipment
- Service desks (we prefer movable modular furniture to built-ins)
- Reading tables and chairs
- Office furniture
- Meeting room furnishings
- Computer systems
- Automated book-handling equipment and associated anti-theft systems
- Video surveillance and other security equipment

Your architects will need to provide a reasonable estimate of your costs for FF&E.

6. Opening Day Collections for Public Libraries

Many public libraries purchase "opening day collections" to help fill the empty shelves with sparkly new books.

Library book jobbers are accustomed to meeting needs for such collections. They can supply books preprocessed and provide the necessary database information. In the stresses of remodeling and moving, few tech services departments can handle the stress of large numbers of new books, so the services of jobbers are vital. If you'll be placing a large order, negotiate a good discount.

One serious pitfall involves discarding worn-looking books to make the shelves really glisten on opening day. Some of your users won't appreciate the fact that the depth they found in your collections in the past is no longer there.

7. Professional Fees

Your total project cost will include a number of professional fees.

- Consultants. Programming fees charged by library building consultants tend to be modest, and they come very early in the project. You will also want your consultants to review your schematic designs and construction drawings from the point of view of experienced librarians, but that as well comes long before groundbreaking.
- Architecture and interior design. The range of services provided by architects is impressively large (see the chapters on design and construction), and

fees can be about 10 percent of construction costs—or more if your project consists primarily of very tricky remodeling.
- Construction management. Increasingly, libraries use construction management firms to substitute for general contractors in project delivery for major projects. The general belief is that the cost of the two approaches is roughly similar, but ask around your area.
- Surveys. You may need to have your site surveyed to verify its exact boundaries.
- Some engineering fees are excluded from architectural fees. You may be billed separately, for example, for soil testing. (However, most architectural fees include structural, electrical, HVAC, plumbing, and other engineering.) Make sure which fees are excluded from your contract with your architects before you sign.
- Permitting. Building permits involve a great deal of work by municipal employees and can be expensive. Permit fees can also be a major source of cash for cities. As benign public institutions, libraries should always attempt to have these fees waived.
- Fundraising. If you hire a professional fundraiser or provide staff for a library foundation office, costs will be involved. If your library is tax-supported, you may be limited by law in how you use public money for these costs; check with your attorney.

III. ANTICIPATING OPERATING COSTS

Even with well-designed spaces and the best possible equipment, operating the new library can be a lot more expensive than operating the old one.

Two-thirds of the cost of operating a library can be salaries. Any structural decision that leads to fewer staff can pay for itself quickly. This means that complex designs that may save a little money up front can be fiscal long-term disasters because they require extra staff just to keep an eye on things, even when no service to users is required. Basic strategies for controlling staff costs without compromising on quality of service include:

- Avoiding unnecessary partitions. It's a lot easier to watch big, open spaces than nooks and crannies.
- Keeping walls of study rooms and quiet reading rooms transparent for easy staff oversight. (A small window is not "transparent.")
- Maintaining single entrances, because all security gates must be staffed.
- Using generally horizontal rather than vertical building designs, because moving people between floors is expensive and all floors have to be staffed.
- Avoiding complex mechanical gimmicks that promise high long-term maintenance costs.

- Remembering that vast expanses of exterior glass are expensive to clean and can increase energy costs (among other serious problems).

A larger building means larger areas to clean. It usually means more restroom fixtures. It means more light fixtures (and sometimes, in badly designed buildings, a huge variety of different tubes, LEDs, and light bulbs). It may mean new and dramatically high spaces, with all the extra maintenance they require. It will almost certainly mean more glass to clean.

Modern HVAC systems are often far more efficient than the older systems they replace, and libraries may find that the cost per square foot of space is significantly less, even if the size of the new building means an increase in total energy costs.

While most buildings come with one-year warranties from contractors, and some components like roofs and windows have longer warranties, repairs and upkeep begin almost immediately. Even if the first year is nearly free, with everything both brand-new and covered by warranties, soon things change. Latex paint on drywall is fragile and may need to be repaired almost as soon as the building is opened. Light bulbs fail, although fluorescent lamps can last for a couple of years. LED fixtures probably last a lot longer, but you need to know your options when LEDs start failing. Attic stock of frequently damaged items like acoustic ceiling tile can run out, and matching replacements may not be available. Carpet has to be cleaned once or twice a year and it will eventually wear out, although carpet tile from attic stock can replace quickly worn areas like floors in front of service desks and copy machines. Some modern devices have a short working life; for example, while old-fashioned electric switches may go on working for many decades, sensors used for automatic switching may fail in a few years. Many systems and equipment have annual upkeep costs and maintenance costs. Elevators, HVAC systems, book-handling systems, and others may have substantial annual maintenance charges.

In the long run, major construction items wear out. HVAC equipment is expensive and is considered old after twenty years. Roofs can serve well for decades, but eventually they need to be replaced. Double-pane windows can leak and fog up and have to be replaced.

Many architectural firms can create documents projecting upkeep and maintenance costs, including the long-term replacement of key architectural components. Having this kind of information at hand is useful and can help avoid situations where predictable repairs have not been planned for. (This is an extra service at extra cost and is not part of standard contracts with architects.)

Because some libraries find it easier to find construction funds than operating funds, they adopt a strategy of buying all sorts of automated equipment up front, hoping that it will save on staff costs in years to come. A typical example is highly automated lending systems. The problem with this approach, of course, is the maintenance overhead on expensive equipment and its eventual replacement.

If you don't know what it will cost to maintain complex equipment, a first guess is 10 percent of the purchase price per year.

The issue of operating costs arises in particular for public libraries in states that require separate referendums for construction funds and for operating funds. If the voters are willing to spend money for construction but not for operations, libraries can find themselves in fiscal hot water: the new building is finished but the old operating budget is all that they have. For this reason, good planning calls for buildings that require staff to do the necessary work but not to supervise overly complex structures.

IV. SNAPPY RULES ON BUILDING COSTS

1. The single most important construction material is money.
2. Unless you do this kind of thing all the time, you'll suffer from instant sticker shock.
3. If you hire a world-famous architect, you'll probably get a lot less library than you pay for and have a lot higher operating costs than you hope for.
4. Always think in terms of project cost, never in terms of construction cost. And make sure that all your hired help does the same. (Unfortunately, some architects never mention project costs until it's too late to reduce total expenditures by eliminating flashy concepts.)
5. Remodeling is almost always more expensive than either your critics or supporters expect.
6. Before you undertake remodeling, always ask your architects to estimate what it would cost to simply start over. Sometimes there isn't a vast difference, and sometimes starting over is cheaper, with lower operating costs to boot.
7. Some people suggest you begin with your project cost and design a building that can be built for that cost. This is almost always backwards thinking. It works only if you begin with a realistic project cost rather than with a hopeful lowball guess. (Lots of proposed project costs are hopeful lowball guesses.)
8. We much prefer starting with needs, estimating costs, asking whether you can afford them, and only if and when you decide it's too expensive, compromising on needs.

9. Today's terabyte is yesterday's megabyte. Don't let building size alone scare you.
10. Preparing building programs and hiring architects can take a surprising amount of time and cost surprisingly little up front. It's a lot easier to have a program completed and an architect waiting in the wings than to suddenly have to rush madly about.
11. NEVER BUILD A LIBRARY ON LAND TO WHICH YOU DO NOT HOLD COMPLETELY CLEAR TITLE. (Government construction grants may require this, demonstrating that these governments really know what they're doing.)
12. You can't get through any funding for a new library building without hearing "the book is dead." Be prepared to point out how packed your library is and that tablets are not the ultimate solution to educating the youth of America. But don't expect to convert everyone.
13. Any project larger than a woodshed will be called a Taj Mahal and a monument to the inflated egos of members of managing boards. It's good to have people ready to point out the actual modesty of your plans.
14. Know what you'll do if you end up with the larger library of tomorrow but yesterday's operating budget.
15. Local nonexperts are frequently eager to estimate construction and remodeling costs on your behalf. Run away quickly.

15

Funding

I. INTRODUCTION

Money is the single most important construction material.

Sometimes things are wonderful:

- Wealthy donors who love libraries drop in on college presidents bearing large checks.
- Two or three new factories are constructed in a public library's taxing jurisdiction, and the resulting increase in property tax cash flow is inspiring.
- Totally unexpected bequests brighten otherwise gloomy November afternoons.
- You have a referendum to issue bonds for a new library building and 80 percent of your voters support it.

But because money is almost always an emotional issue, emotions can run high while buildings are being planned, financed, constructed, and operated. We don't have any data, but we've run into a number of situations that involved annoyed people.

Some everyday problems involve:

- Local governments try to redirect library construction funds to other projects. Here's where library foundations can earn their keep, since they are totally independent of local governments and can simply say "No."

- Major donors attempt to impose dysfunctional design ideas on projects. A few libraries have had to simply turn down gifts.
- Belligerent antitax groups make life miserable for everyone involved. The abuse of freedom-of-information acts can be spectacular.
- Local library boards lose their nerve and are unwilling to even ask their neighbors to support projects.
- Whether or not a university library has independent access to funds, the university may insist on determining the library's construction priority.
- Local agencies or university units with no funding (and no chance whatever of funding) attempt to merge themselves physically with libraries. Unfortunately, the last things libraries need is non-library agencies hanging out in their buildings.
- Some libraries can get funding for construction but not for operations. This is why wide-open spaces and wonderful sight lines are so important: they reduce the number of staff necessary in a building. If your library gets a larger building but the same operating budget, you have to be able to cope somehow.

Luckily, almost all of these complications are surmountable. At least, by reading this chapter you'll be forewarned (and sometimes forearmed).

II. SOURCES OF MONEY

A. Money on Hand

Some projects can be funded with cash on hand. Some smaller projects such as special libraries, school libraries that are not part of large projects, departmental libraries in universities, and public library branches may be modest enough to be paid simply out of pocket.

When projects are small enough to be paid for with cash on hand, preemptive (or perhaps "proactive") programming becomes particularly important. If the library's needs are well known and in print and are sitting around administrative offices, this may help prevent offhand conversion planning from taking place without input from the library staff. Many special libraries are corporate and are part of corporate budgets. These special libraries may find themselves under pressure from other agencies within the business that also need better or more advantageously located spaces. If the libraries' needs are on file, it may give the libraries advantages over other corporate agencies that complain but aren't as well organized.

B. Savings Set Aside from Operating Funds

Depending on how funds are handled, some libraries are able to set aside surplus (or carefully hoarded) funds to meet long-term remodeling needs. For instance, libraries may set aside funds for occasional "refreshing" to update specific areas or to repurpose spaces that are no longer relevant to the libraries' needs.

Public libraries tend to be the most frugal of all local government bodies and the most likely to have money in the bank. Often they have enough to at least pay for remodeling or to hire programmers and architects to carry out initial plans.

Unfortunately, the result of money in the bank can be other governmental bodies casting greedy eyes on library savings, with a consequent reduction in the availability of construction funds. For example, antitax types have sometimes demanded that library funds set aside for construction be redirected to reducing annual operating costs, thereby reducing tax levies.

C. Referendums and Bond Issues

Many public libraries and school libraries are built with money from bond referendums, although some states allow bond issues without referendums under specific circumstances.

A bond is a private loan to a government body, authorizing taxes to be levied over a number of years to retire the loan. Usually the bond issue specifies the number of payments and the amount of each payment. If the assessed value of taxable land in the jurisdiction increases more than anticipated, this may lead to the bonds being retired before the expected number of years has passed, which makes everyone happy.

The library's parent organization will need professional assistance with developing legal language for the issue that appears on the ballots, for merchandising the bonds (selling the bonds to investors), and so on. All of these things require professional legal and technical assistance. Laws regarding issuing bonds are complex and vary from state to state, so the individual prior experience of non-experts cannot be relied on.

Timing of referendums is important. Fundraising consultants may be able to help. And because the successful passage of bond referendums is essential to their income, banks that market bonds to investors frequently provide expert advice to libraries on holding successful bond referendums. (Banks that specialize in this work are typically not paid until they merchandise the bonds.)

Government bonds can be attractive to investors because income from the bonds can be exempt from federal taxes and sometimes exempt from state taxes. In addition, most governments are good for the money because they are backed by taxable real estate. (But a few governments are bad risks, as some fiscal meltdowns in recent years demonstrated. Leave any concerns in this area to the agency marketing your bonds.)

Because income from bonds can be tax-exempt, libraries that issue bonds can offer lower rates of interest and still be attractive to investors.

All libraries need legal advice on the roles they can play in bond referendums. As a typical example, public funds cannot be used to influence the outcome of an election. Your lawyers will insist that paid staff members cannot be advocates for the bond issue, and that library money cannot be used for the production of promotional materials advocating "yes" votes. Public money can *typically* be used to provide neutral information about the proposed election, but people and materials advocating positive votes must be strictly independent of public funding and paid for by library foundations, friends groups, or other nongovernment support groups. Here again, consistency is vital.

Depend on your lawyers and bankers all along the way. They can tell you how to get issues on the ballot, how to word issues, what to do next if your issue passes, how to legally select a firm to market your bonds, and what other special steps you need to take to be sure that everything is done in painfully accurate compliance with the law.

In some states, the total indebtedness of political jurisdictions is limited by law to a relatively small fraction of total assessed property value, and this can lead to the creation of multiple overlapping jurisdictions in order to (for example) be able to build new schools and libraries and fire stations at the same time. Know what your local situation is before you progress too far with planning.

D. Bequests

Some libraries are constructed with large bequests. Other, smaller bequests are enough to fund a part of a library, with donor recognition based on named features of the building, such as meeting rooms.

Some bequests carry requirements with them, including specific uses of the money. For example, a donor who knows how governmental units tend to operate may specify that the money be spent for new construction rather than for remodeling or repairs.

Remodeling and repairs can constitute a major portion of the cost of library expansion projects, and to some donors, this part of the work may seem similar to pouring money down a rat hole. It's not a rat hole at all, but it's much more fun to envision the Johnson Wing of the new library than the Johnson HVAC replacement project. And because the library may have to find the money to fix the HVAC system regardless, the limitation of the donation to new construction may increase the net construction money available to the library.

A bequest large enough for an entire building may specify the design of the library, the name of the library, or pretty much anything else that the donor wants. Some requirements may not be legally enforceable, but that's why we have library lawyers.

Many bequests are totally unexpected, but others are the result of long-term cultivation of donors by library fundraisers. Because bequests can have an immense impact on library buildings, libraries should at least make their needs known. The offices of attorneys who specialize in estate work may welcome information on library needs. (Some professional fundraisers talk about long-planned bequests as "maturing," but that seems somewhat tacky.)

Large bequests can lead to sudden projects in campuses and communities that never anticipated constructing handsome new library buildings.

Some bequests may have time limits attached, of the "If you don't break ground or complete the building by whenever, the money will be taken away from you and given to a home for cats" nature. If these time limits are realistic, there is time for essential steps in programming, design, and construction. If enough money is involved, work can go surprisingly quickly, but it means that university or public library boards of trustees or other authorities can't dawdle.

A bequest can also lead to an attempt by a local government to take tax money away from a library to compensate for the bequest, thereby undermining the intent of the donor. A well-written bequest will anticipate this kind of buccaneer approach to local government. So will having the bequest come to a private 501(c)(3) foundation rather than directly to the library.

Often bequests will not be large enough to construct a new building, but they can have a powerful effect in motivating bond referendums or reallocation of university assets, particularly if they are for one purpose only and have a time limit for taking action before the offer is withdrawn.

> We've seen one-time state incentive grants for public library construction that motivated otherwise extremely antitax communities to vote for new projects.

Stories abound of bequests given for specific purposes but simply redirected by the agency that received them. We suspect that libraries would never do that sort of thing, but there are a lot of non-libraries out there that might succumb to temptation. It's hard to imagine, however, that misdirecting a bequest helps with future bequests.

E. Mortgages

Laws on the use of mortgages for construction of government-owned libraries will vary from state to state. Sometimes mortgages cannot be used at all, but in other cases at least a specific portion of the project can legally be supported by a mortgage.

The problem with mortgages is that they need to be paid off from operating funds or from ongoing fundraising. If your library has seriously ample—if not almost excessive—annual cash flow, a mortgage may be usable.

In our experience, mortgages have been used not for major funding but rather for last-minute extra cash when projects run somewhat over budget.

As with all mortgages, be sure your arrangement with the lending agency allows you to retire your mortgage at any time with absolutely no penalty for paying in advance of scheduled payments. You may also want to build into the mortgage language that prevents the lending agency from selling your mortgage to another lending agency.

You will probably have no trouble finding a bank happy to provide a mortgage, particularly if your library is supported by authorized taxes on real estate.

F. Fundraising

With the exception of some special libraries, most library construction projects involve fundraising, even when libraries are also supported by bonds, grants, massive donations, or other sources of funding.

If you have a public library, citizens may sometimes respond far more positively to requests for donations than to bond referendums, especially in times or places where antitax sentiments are strong.

1. Fundraising Consultants

In some libraries, fundraising campaigns are managed by library employees or by university employees. But expecting directors of small public libraries to find the extra time to take on fundraising in addition to their usual management responsibilities can be extraordinarily unreasonable.

Some libraries hire fundraising consultants. Depending on needs, consultants can perform such services as:

- Estimating the amount of money that can be raised. The accuracy of such projections can vary. For example, Fred's library raised several times the amount its consultant estimated.
- Managing campaigns, including solicitations for donations, donor recognition, donor social events, and other functions. A campaign manager may play a major role in the wide variety of special events described in chapter 12 on "Construction."
- Preparing grant applications.

People hired to raise money need to be extraordinarily well organized and socially gracious. The thanking of donors must be meticulous. Checks must not go astray. The voice on the phone must be warm and welcoming. The fundraiser's office must be clean and attractive but not imply any significant outlay of funds for overhead.

If you are considering hiring a fundraising consultant, one good place to begin is talking with other libraries. Because library fundraising is a highly specialized area, you may also want to consider people who have worked on similar government or cultural projects.

It also needs to be clear from the start that fundraising consultants are paid agreed-upon fees and NEVER a percentage of the funds raised. Paying a fundraiser a percentage is regarded as extremely unethical, and you don't want to have anything to do with anyone who suggests it.

2. Capital Campaigns

When planning projects, some libraries hold capital campaigns, in which they attempt to raise the needed funds in a period of a few years or less. These apply particularly to public libraries, which will probably not have the ongoing fund-raising efforts that characterize colleges and universities.

Many campaigns begin with planning studies, which typically identify amounts that can probably be raised, what aspects of the project will be most appealing to donors, and which community leaders might participate. Work on planning studies also helps make communities more aware of library needs.

Because most campaigns involve identifying which potential donors have how much money and how they can be convinced to donate to the projects, publicly funded libraries that are subject to open meetings acts or to freedom of information act requests are in a very awkward position, because these conversations can't be carried out in public. This is another reason to set up a 501(c)(3) foundation where fundraising can legally be discussed in privacy.

A fundraising campaign is often carried out by a team. See the section below on how fundraising groups are typically organized. Remember that people who are selected for their ability to give money and ask others to give money must not be expected to do any clerical work.

3. Lead Gifts

Typically, campaigns begin with the quiet solicitation of "lead gifts," significant donations that help launch campaigns and provide the majority of funds. Big gifts are essential. One runs into various numbers, but a common claim is that 10 percent of the donors may give 90 percent of the funds. Another common presumption in fundraising campaigns is that out of even hundreds of donors, the top donor may provide 10 percent of the total funds and the next two donors an additional 15 percent. Perhaps 45 additional donors provide the following 65 percent, and all of the other donors combined provide no more than 10 percent. So despite the good feelings that widespread support engenders, a relative handful of major gifts provides the majority of funds.

Book sales and bake sales are socially rewarding occasions and make everyone feel like part of the project, but the money that they raise is relatively insignificant.

All solicitation of major donors is in person, and the selection of who will make the request for funds is particularly important. The traditional approach is to ask who—out of all possible people—could be the donor who will have the greatest trouble turning down the request.

Large donors are usually a great thing, but problems can arise:

- Some donors want to take over the design of the project, including determining the functions of the library. This puts the university or public library in a bind, and some have had to turn down money because of the unacceptable strings attached.
- Some donors insist on a particular architectural firm. This can be just fine, but if the architects are (a) very ego-driven and (b) feel that the owners have little say in what they do, since they're really working for the donor, the owners can lose control of the functional aspects of the project.
- Architects with dysfunctional designs in mind have sometimes claimed that this is what the donors want. It's frustrating for universities or cities to find out after the fact that the donors never said any such thing. Beware if architects attempt to separate you socially from the donors.

All campaigns need careful follow-up work to be sure all the funds are collected, that all donors are thanked, and that public recognition—such as naming opportunities—goes off without errors.

As noted in the next section, most serious public library fundraising campaigns require a 501(c)(3) foundation. Colleges and universities should already have fundraising units with this or similar status. Public libraries that don't have foundations should probably set them up in advance.

4. Making the Ask

In all fundraising—particularly raising funds for significant gifts—which person makes the appeal matters a great deal. One of the things members of foundations do (in private, since they are not government bodies) is ask themselves who are the right people to ask for money and who are the right people to do the asking. Obviously, the caller should be the one person in the world to whom the would-be donor will have the greatest difficulty saying "no." Callers do better if they themselves are donors, because people being asked for money are likely to ask, "How much are *you* giving?"

As a result of their qualifications as people who can make large donations and have friends who can make large donations, members of foundation boards are likely to have very limited responsibilities—basically writing a check and making a few calls. All the organizing and record-keeping work is done by foundation staff.

Because they are often selected because they have substantial personal wealth, most foundation board members can be very different from Friends of the Library members. Friends of the Library are typically working groups, not people with big bank accounts. Occasionally this is a socially touchy area. One solution is to have, for example, the president of the Friends of the Library be an ex officio member of the foundation board.

5. Record-Keeping

All fundraising foundations need staff members to do the work of arranging mailings and correspondence, setting up social events, keeping painfully careful track of donors and donations, and being the smiling face of the foundation whenever people call. Expecting people who were appointed to the foundation board because of their ability to donate and ask for donations to also keep track of organizational details is inappropriate.

Some library foundations keep the shopping list for naming opportunities private, but others simply post it in the library and report good results.

Keeping track of all donations is of vital importance. Even extremely minor errors can cause serious problems, and a few donors with seriously hurt feelings can jeopardize a fundraising campaign.

6. Donor Recognition

Finding good ways to recognize donors is important. Most donors are extraordinarily public-spirited, but few of us are made happy by total anonymity.

Many libraries seize upon "naming opportunities" as a way of recognizing major gifts. This requires careful advance planning by the agency raising funds, which needs to determine in advance what individual items will cost. Planning ahead will lead to costs that are internally consistent, so that a small conference room and the main university reading room don't carry the same price tags.

The result of this kind of planning can be a shopping list of features, each with a price attached. People asking prospective donors for money will start high and then work their way down the list to items the donors can pay for.

Planning in advance this way helps prevent situations where naming opportunities take place in an unplanned, free-for-all atmosphere, frequently resulting in either annoying inconsistencies or in donations so low that the library runs out of naming opportunities long before making an actual dent in its costs.

One thing planners will have to ask themselves is the relationship between the size of the donation and the actual cost of the space. If (for example) a building is projected to have a project cost of $300 per square foot, should the naming of a 1,000-square-foot meeting room require a donation of $300,000?

One question all owners need to ask themselves in advance is what it will cost to actually change the name of the library. To have "Hazelton Library" replace "Jamestown University Library" should require a substantial donation, far more than the "Hazelton Wing of the Jamestown University Library."

In addition to library names and building names, libraries typically offer naming opportunities for departments (children's, Slavic languages), meeting rooms (auditoriums, classrooms), reading rooms (massive reading rooms, quiet reading rooms), special features (study rooms, library cafés), and so on.

Of course, lots of essential library spaces don't lend themselves to donor names. Few people want to be remembered as the sponsors of hallways or restrooms.

Sometimes donors make substantial gifts and don't really care about naming, and others may not want their names mentioned at all. The important thing is honoring the wishes of the donor.

7. Recognizing Smaller Donations

In addition to named buildings and spaces, libraries need ways to recognize what may be hundreds of individual donations. A wide variety of plaques are available commercially, some with individual tags that can be inscribed as gifts continue to come in.

Some libraries have raised funds through the sale of inscribed paving bricks that are used to create patios or other features. There are a couple of important points:

- Be sure you know what it will cost to have an inscribed paver made and installed before you settle on prices. Fred worked with one library that priced pavers so inexpensively that it made no money whatsoever on the project—although the pleasure of seeing one's name on the patio has goodwill value.
- Be sure you have an index to paver locations. If you have a patio with 200 pavers, donors will come to a service desk inside the library and complain that their pavers are not there, when in reality it's just hard to find them.

Every once in a while, a library will receive an unexpected late gift when the building is already planned and under construction, and the foundation board needs to have contingency plans.

Be careful about putting donor plaques on items that can be damaged. In the case of reading tables, for example, a library can mount a plaque on the wall saying "Ten of the tables in this room were made possible by donations from the following . . ." By not identifying who gave what tables, the library spares itself dealing with an unhappy donor whose personal table has been vandalized in some way. As long as a few of the tables were paid for from general library funds, libraries can maintain the happy fiction that the damaged tables were paid for by the library, not by donors.

Chapter 12 on "Construction" includes a list of possible social events for donors. There are a lot of great possibilities. (Two to avoid are events with cash bars—which means dram shop insurance—and final ribbon cuttings held for donors only.)

The important thing is to find ways to recognize all donors, regardless of donation size.

G. 501(c)(3) Foundations

All kinds of private groups can raise money for library construction. However, there may be strict legal limits on how much they can raise and hold, depending on their federal tax status.

The most common legal status for fundraising groups—such as library foundations—is 501(c)(3) tax-exempt status. This status allows groups to raise substantial sums of money and to hold it until the time comes to spend it. 501(c)(3) foundations are under the supervision and control of the Internal Revenue Service.

501(c)(3) status is available to not-for-profit organizations with a variety of purposes, such as charitable, educational, religious, scientific, and so on. Libraries fit neatly into the educational category.

To obtain 501(c)(3) status, you will need the assistance of an attorney to help set up a foundation that meets IRS requirements for tax-exempt, not-for-profit status and to file the necessary application. Once formed, the foundation must follow record-keeping and reporting requirements.

The federally certified tax-exempt status of 501(c)(3) organizations is essential to fundraising. Some organizations and businesses will probably refuse to donate funds if you do not have a 501(c)(3) foundation.

Foundations and other groups of this type are independent by law and are not controlled by library boards, city councils, university administrations, and so on. There's always a danger, of course, that the board of the foundation may disagree on how money is to be spent, but there appears to be a greater benefit in the fact that local politicians or university administrations cannot loot the assets of the foundation. If a mayor, for example, congratulates the foundation on its fundraising and proposes that local government can now cut its support of a project accordingly, the foundation board can simply say "No" in a way that a local public library board could probably not do because foundations can be totally separate from local government. (We don't have data on the frequency of politicians' attempts to loot foundations, but we've both seen it happen.)

Foundations also have the benefit of being able to hold private meetings, without which their speculations on who can give what would be impossible.

Colleges and universities have their own foundations that can take over fundraising responsibilities, but individual academic libraries can have their own foundations.

Laws controlling 501(c)(3) foundations require that foundations provide for the disposition of funds if the foundations choose to disband. This comes up because some libraries find little use for their foundations once funds have been raised, buildings have been constructed, ribbons have been cut, and donor receptions have been held. (Our personal feeling is that it can be surprisingly few years before serious fundraising needs to take place again, and having the foundation in place can be a good idea.)

H. Grants

Depending on political and business climates, grants can be a major source of construction funds.

Many construction grants for libraries are government grants, but privately funded foundations also have grant funds available. In particular, consider approaching companies that do business in your community.

Many government grants are competitive, which means that your library will need to make a more impressive application than other libraries in your state.

As with all grants, pay attention to required items. Typical grant applications may require:

- Written building programs.
- Schematic designs. (Remember that it's *essential* that schematic designs include furniture layouts. A library floor plan without placement of furniture is basically an empty square.)
- Cost estimates (which should accompany schematic designs). Good cost estimates are vital for grant applications. (Know your architect's reputation for accurate estimating, and check with your construction management firm if you are using one.)

> Fred knows a public library where the architect's estimate was about one-third of the actual low bid. The library had a state construction grant, and by the time the project was bid, the state had irrevocably committed the funds. Things were eventually sorted out when the library was able to locate the extra money, but it was an amazing political mess. In addition, the higher cost of the project threw the project into a different grant category requiring extra documentation and planning documents from the library. To make things worse, after all the tangles had been surmounted, the resulting building was a functional disaster.

- Project narratives, explaining the need for the project.
- For government grants, sign-offs from specific government agencies. For example, a state grant may require a sign-off from the state's historic preservation agency.
- Demonstrations that proposed projects meet minimum state standards for libraries. Depending on the state, standards that affect schematic designs may include collection sizes, seating, accessibility, and so on.
- Except for some challenge grants, where the announcement of the grant is intended to spur donations and referendums, certification that local matching funds have already been raised. (Some applications even require photocopies of bank records to prove that local funds are in place.) In many cases, nothing messes up agencies administering government grants more than libraries that receive grants and then admit they don't have their share of the money.
- Certification that the library has clear title to its site.

> Public libraries occasionally are constructed on sites to which they have rights only as long as they occupy their buildings. This can lead to extraordinarily bad situations where the library doesn't want to spend money on its building because the building really belongs to another agency. It's a lot like the problems with tenant houses on farms.

- Letters of support may be useful. (A letter from a powerful local politician may be just what you need, or it may just annoy a committee of librarians. Ask around.)
- If the grant application permits them, photographs of your existing library may be a powerful addition, particularly if you can provide images depicting an honest and hard-working library coping bravely while encumbered with a neatly maintained but painfully obsolete structure.

All of these things take time. A good building program can be developed in a couple of months, but for a public library, working that fast may require a long board meeting every week. Three or four months is a much more practical aim. If your state has a QBS law for public buildings, hiring an architect may also take a couple of months. It's hard to develop a schematic design in less than three or four months after the completion of a building program. And sign-offs from overworked government agencies can take longer than one wishes.

Because all of this work can take half a year or more, it can be hard to complete everything in the time between the announcement of a grant program and the due date for applications. This is another reason for doing the low-cost part of the work—preparing a building program and selecting an architect—well in advance.

Corporate grants for library construction will typically require far less documentation than government grants, but they will almost certainly require strong local financial support and a 501(c)(3) foundation to guarantee to donor corporations that their grants are tax deductible. You will probably want to start with industries associated with your community, but persistence sometimes pays off in unexpected ways. A board member of a public library with which Fred worked sent serious inquiries to a couple hundred corporations and eventually turned up a major grant. (He was retired and found the whole process an entertaining challenge.)

For libraries expanding their historic Carnegie buildings, it can be disheartening to recognize that the Carnegie Corporation's major grant programs for totally free buildings ended about 1915.

As with all grants, clarity and completeness of applications are vital. If the grant application form lists 15 numbered items, a good application lists all 15, labeled and numbered and in the same order, so overworked employees or grant committee members can do a quick conformance check to be sure that all required items are present.

Deadlines for government grants are usually ironclad. It's fun to drive your application to your state library on the due date and run into folks from a dozen other libraries who are there for the same reason, but a sudden flat tire may make you wish you had gone the day before.

The terms of some grants may include specific wording for recognition of the grant. For instance, a plaque somewhere in the building may need to say something like, "This construction project was made possible in part by a grant of [program name] funds made possible by the following [government agency, corporation, political person]." If there's a politician you don't like in the group, keep it to yourself, remembering that recognition is a miniscule price to pay for substantial financial assistance.

I. Special Appropriations

America being America, sometimes the best way to get money for construction involves pure politics. As with private fundraising, knowing whom to ask and when and how to ask is important.

Often, special appropriations occur as riders on bills.

From politicians' point of view, libraries have the advantage of being a lot less expensive than interstate exits and providing far better photo ops.

If emergency money is running around after a catastrophe, get yours for your library.

III. SNAPPY RULES ON FUNDING

1. The single most important construction material is money.
2. Unless you do this kind of thing all the time, you'll suffer from instant sticker shock.
3. There are no new Andrew Carnegies providing libraries for all. For most libraries, this means finding your own money, although wonderful individual donors come along.
4. When it comes to bond referendums, making sure that your friends vote works a lot better than trying to convert your enemies.
5. Firms that market bonds sometimes have staff members who study voter behavior and can advise you on the timing of referendums.
6. You have only one chance with naming opportunities. Plan first and negotiate second. All too often, libraries initially give things away too cheaply and find themselves trapped.

7. Thank everyone. For some donors, $100 was a greater stretch than $100,000 for other donors.
8. For most citizens, a new public library is a lot more important than a new city hall or a new public works garage. This annoys city government folks, but they'll have to get over it.
9. Donors would rather pay for a new college library (think shining city on the hill) than a new dormitory (think restrooms on Friday nights). This is probably why dormitories are often named after early college presidents.
10. Before you start mounting donor-recognition letters directly on drywall, ask yourself how you'll repaint the wall. (Some systems for mounting letters allow the letters to be removed when it's time to repaint.)
11. Campuses may have priority listings for capital projects. In the wrong fiscal climate, libraries can hover indefinitely at number two or three.
12. Grant applications tend to expect local matching funds.
13. When you have money, move right along. Construction costs tend to increase faster than the value of money in the bank.
14. Applications for government construction grants may lead to the required involvement of additional government agencies. This may not be fun.
15. Some donors come equipped not only with money (good) but with weird structural ideas they want to inflict on you (bad). Some want to pay only part of the cost of the building but still get to inflict their unfortunate ideas on you. It hurts to say "no" to money, but sometimes that's the only sane option.
16. For public libraries, know the spirit of your community. Some angrily anti-tax people can be amazingly generous when asked for voluntary donations.
17. People reading grant applications may have backbreaking jobs. Make their lives easier by writing clearly, by helping them match their questions to your answers, and by including all the required support documents in the right order.
18. Bake sales and book sales are fun and make everyone feel involved and appreciated, but they don't bring in much money. Construction projects rely on seriously big bucks from a more limited range of sources.
19. Legitimate fundraising consultants always work for agreed fees or hourly salaries and never (as in NEVER) for a percentage of funds raised.

IV. BIBLIOGRAPHY

While the literature on the practical design and construction of functional library buildings can be sparse, the literature on money and fundraising is extensive. Among the works you may find helpful are:

Dowlin, Ken. Getting Money: *How to Succeed in Fundraising for Public and Non-Profit Libraries.* Westport, CT: Libraries Unlimited, 2008.

Hall, Richard B. *Winning Library Referenda Campaigns: A How-to-Do-It Manual.* New York: Neal-Schuman, 1995.

Rawlins, Stephanie, and Pamela H. MacKellar. *Grants for Libraries: A How-to-Do-It Manual with CD.* New York: Neal-Schuman, 2004.

Swan, James. *Fundraising for Libraries: 25 Proven Ways to Get More Money for Your Libraries.* New York: Neal-Schuman, 2002.

Part V
Library Spaces

16

User Seating

I. INTRODUCTION

Most libraries provide seating for their users.

Over the years, we've run into a handful of people who feel that library users should come to the library, get their books, and go home. But this is hard to justify, given that the people who are paying for the libraries want to sit there and read there and socialize there.

Some users are driven away by lack of adequate seating. In one public library Fred was working with, he saw groups of teenagers stop by after school, see that there was no seating anywhere, and leave. (This library had one reading table and a conference table that doubled as a board table and a computer table, so it filled quickly.)

Many libraries have obsolete seating. It's pretty easy to chuck it out if it's old and battered and ugly. But it's a lot harder if it's historic (even if it's awkward and ugly and inaccessible) or if it's fairly new (but dysfunctional). Getting rid of bad seating is important, but it can be politically difficult.

Over the years, libraries have made bad decisions on seating.

- Some have purchased armchairs so large that people who sit up against the backs of the chairs end up with their legs sticking straight out like those of four-year-olds in adult chairs.
- Some have purchased armchairs so low that almost no one who gets in can get back out again.
- One public library in Illinois had its armchairs upholstered in imitation suede, which absorbed body oils like a magnet and had to be replaced within months.
- Some public libraries install sofas, only to find that the two major uses of sofas in public libraries are sleeping and necking, neither of which corresponds closely with most Long-Range Plans.
- Some libraries have purchased discount store seating and had it fall apart in a few months.
- Some libraries purchase seating upholstered in garish colors du jour, only to find that the colors scream passé long before the upholstery wears out.
- Some libraries have purchased side chairs for reading tables, only to find that the chairs tore the carpet to shreds. Sled bases or casters help.
- Some libraries have let their architects design chairs without trying out a preliminary version for comfort.

The list of snappy rules at the end of this chapter is a fairly long one because the world of library administration abounds in shared stories about unfortunate user seating.

At one public library with which Fred worked, the president of the board spoke out firmly against user seating, although users attending the meeting wanted more. She contended that people should pick up their books at the library and then read them at home. She also spoke out against popular materials. When a young mother attending the meeting complained about the absence of picture books for young children, the board president pointed out that the library had just purchased the *McGraw-Hill Encyclopedia of Science and Technology*. The mother didn't ask the obvious question—who's paying the taxes around here?—but she was clearly thinking it.

Luckily, there's lots of really great seating out there.

Some libraries pick out and order their own seating, while others rely on their architects and interior designers for help.

Library conferences usually have booths by furniture firms. Even if you have no immediate need, it's good to be familiar with what's out there. Try things out. Collect catalogs. If you're immersed in planning, ask companies for binders (collections of brochures in monster three-ring binders).

In addition to traditional wooden tables and chairs, there's a wide variety of less formal furniture available from firms that specialize in equipping offices and schools.

Although there's a lot to say about furniture, as far as we're concerned, the most important things are:

- Buy strong. Home strong is not library strong.
- Chipboard (aka particleboard) is not library strong. Chipboard is a mixture of sawdust and glue. Always avoid it. (One magic phrase for solid tabletop construction is lumber core.)
- Always sit in chairs at least fifteen minutes before selecting them.
- If your architects want to design your chairs, never just say "yes." Have one made up to their design and try it out extensively. The chances of its being seriously comfortable are pretty low.
- Buy soft seating that is not too low, not too deep from front to back, not too soft, and not too hard to climb out of. And wide enough.
- Buy tables that are accessible to users with disabilities. Among other things, this means no aprons. (Aprons are vertical boards attached to the undersides of tabletops and connecting the table legs. They strengthen cheap tops and provide a flimsy connection to table legs.)
- Don't buy round tables except for coffee shops.
- Buy tables with 110-volt electrical outlets—and ideally also cell-phone charger jacks—on top. (Who knows, even toddlers may need electrical outlets on their tabletops any day now.)
- Make sure that multi-person tables provide enough space for individual users. A rectangular space 18 by 30 inches per person is minimal with four-person tables.
- Buy from manufacturers rather than from office supply firms.
- Buy tables that are rectangular and have chairs on only two sides. Never agree to rectangular tables with chairs on all four sides, round tables, or strangely shaped tables.

It helps to know some basic vocabulary in chair design:

- *Apron*. The vertical boards that connect the style and front legs and support the seat
- *Corner bracket*. Diagonal brace that connects the aprons to the styles. This joint is the most vulnerable to damage and is often a metal-to-metal joint in chairs designed for library users
- *Rail*. Horizontal board that connects the two styles
- *Splat*. Vertical flat board in between the styles that provides a smooth surface for people to lean against
- *Stretchers*. Boards that connect the styles and the legs, or the two front legs, below the level of the seat
- *Style*. The upright post at the rear of the chair.
- *Top rail*. Horizontal board at the top of the back of the chair, connecting the top ends of the two styles

II. HOW MUCH USER SEATING?

One major decision when buildings are planned involves the quantities and types of seating. Since seating takes a lot of space (one 3 × 5-foot reading table with four chairs occupies about the same space as 1,000 books), building programs are strongly dependent on numbers of tables and chairs. (A 3 × 5-foot reading table is the smallest possible four-chair table for people older than about seven years.)

What are some sources of information and ideas?

- Published standards
- Current overcrowding
- Seating in similar institutions
- Expected growth in college enrollment
- New seating ideas that strike librarians as exciting, such as collaborative study spaces
- Projected changes in public library service populations

Specify furniture very precisely in your building program. For example, "ten reading tables" could lead to almost anything. A better specification might be:

- Ten three by five-foot reading tables, each with two chairs on each of the two long sides and no chairs at the ends.

- Electrical outlets in the center of each table, with enough sockets for four people to plug in their laptop computers at the same time.
- Tabletops with lumber cores, and with high-pressure laminates on both sides. Chipboard will not be used for any table components.
- Rectangular table lamps running the length of each table, designed to cast bright and even light on the entire tabletop.
- Tables will not have aprons. Tabletops will be about 29 inches above the floor, and clearances beneath the tops will be enough to meet requirements for access by people with disabilities.
- Table legs will be held in place by metal-to-metal connections, with metal plates bolted to tabletops and steel posts inside the legs. Screws running diagonally through angled corner plates into wooden legs will not be used.
- Table legs will not have crossbeams at the ends of the tables. It should be easy for users to pull extra chairs up to the ends of the tables.
- The glides on the ends of the table legs will screw in and out to adjust for irregularities in the floor.

We've had a number of experiences with designers who try to cram too much seating into too little space. Some have converted larger tables to smaller tables while keeping the same number of chairs. Some have converted rectangular tables to round tables, which can be crammed more closely together (but are no good for serious work). Some have placed tables too closely together, which challenges librarians to double-check clearances.

> One architect Fred worked with changed the schematic design by taking out a six-foot section of shelving in a stack unit and drawing in a reading table. Unfortunately, it wouldn't have worked. With 42-inch aisles and two-foot-deep shelving units, the total space opened up between the two rows of shelves would be 9 feet. However, a small reading table takes up 3 feet for the tabletop, about 6 feet for seated readers, and another 7 or 8 feet for people to get past the seated readers and get at the books on the shelves. All of this leads to a table needing 16 or 17 feet of space. Trying to cram it into a nine-foot opening requires seriously sloppy arithmetic.

III. HOW LIBRARY FURNITURE IS ORDERED

A. Inventories of Existing Furniture

Unless you intend to chuck everything out and buy all new, you will end up inventorying your available furniture and deciding what will be reused and what will be discarded.

Often this inventory is done by the architect's interior designers. A careful study will identify all existing furniture and indicate where each piece will go in the new or expanded library building—or whether it will be tossed out.

If your library has pieces of furniture you want to retain at all costs, or items you hate and never want to see again, this is a good time to discuss things with your interior designer.

If cash is tight, it's better to make do for a year or two with old furniture, since it's easier to find the cash later for new furniture than to try to stretch the building a little.

B. Selecting New Furniture

Furniture is bid separately rather than provided by the general contractor, so it will not be part of your construction bid.

Rely on your interior designer whenever possible. If not, there are sales reps who can deal with factories on your behalf. Nonetheless, verify everything. In particular, you want to make sure that all selected furniture is comfortable, which means obtaining samples from manufacturers.

A lot of good library furniture is built to order, so you can't delay ordering until your building is nearly finished. In fact, furniture is notorious for not turning up on time for ribbon cuttings.

> An architect told Fred about a library project where none of the furniture was delivered in time for the grand opening. The architect called the company every few days and was always assured that the furniture was almost ready to ship. But at the time of the grant opening, the factory had not even begun to start building it.

Because good-quality library furniture is built to order, most libraries obtain it directly from the manufacturer or from a manufacturer's representative. (Little stuff, like computer tables, can be an exception.)

Don't miss opportunities to see furniture on display and try it out. Manufacturers often have booths at major library conferences. Some furniture suppliers have showrooms at the Merchandise Mart in Chicago. Or consider attending Neo Con, held at the Mart every year. Talk with your interior designers.

If you'll be ordering a lot of furniture, ask the makers to send you samples of the items you like. (Our experience has been that manufacturers are happy to send samples. The trouble doesn't lie in getting the samples but in getting the manufacturers to remove their samples after the library has made a decision.)

Cheap furniture won't survive library use. A library table should be strong enough to drag down Main Street or across the main quad on one leg without the leg joint loosening.

> Many years ago, a staff member in Fred's library bought a handful of ultra-cheap footstools at a discount furniture store. In a few weeks nearly all had completely disintegrated, as in nothing left but worn-out shreds of fabrics and bits and pieces of wood.

IV. TABLES

A. Configurations

Tables are available in a wide variety of configurations:

- *Single-user tables.* Single-user tables need to be a minimum of three feet wide, but they work better when they're four feet wide, particularly in academic libraries, because the combination of a laptop, open book, and notepad takes up more than three feet.
- *Carrels.* Carrels are single-user tables with vertical panels like short walls on three sides to provide a degree of privacy. Carrels in academic libraries need to be four feet wide, just as with single-user tables. Our experience has been that carrels with raised barricades work well in academic libraries but not in public libraries.

- *Square tables for two users.* Square tables need to be 3 × 3 feet or larger, with chairs on only two sides. One thing that goes wrong with furniture layouts is architects trying to save space by putting four chairs at a two-person table, one on each of the four sides, resulting in each user's working space being a small triangle. Watch for this in schematic designs and stamp it out quickly.
- *Rectangular tables for four users.* These call for two chairs on each of the long sides, not one chair on each of the four sides. The absolute minimum size for a four-person table for adults is 3 × 5 feet, but lots of four-person tables are larger, particularly in academic and research libraries. Many people question the need for four-person tables, but we think four-person tables are important. Most adults prefer to sit one per table, but single users at four-person tables have more room to spread out than they would at one- or two-person tables, making four-person tables more attractive. When every four-person table in the room has a single occupant, a second person will usually sit down at a diagonal corner from the first occupant. Teenagers, on the other hand, make great use of four-person tables. They enjoy sitting four to a table, and they often drag over extra chairs from adjacent tables to create five- or six-person tables. (This is one reason why crossbeams connecting table legs at the ends of tables are a seriously bad idea.)
- *Rectangular tables with dividers.* Academic libraries sometimes purchase large reading tables with low dividers (perhaps three inches high) to define user spaces. Four by six feet is probably a minimum tabletop size.
- *Round tables for two or more users.* Round tables are intended for socializing, for drinking coffee, or perhaps for reading novels or magazines, but not for work. Among other things, round tables have no working surfaces. Users need to be able to spread things out in front of themselves, and with round tables, things that are spread out to the left or right simply fall on the floor. Architects frequently draw in round tables where libraries have specified rectangular tables, either because they look cute or because they allow more tables to be crammed into a limited space. Be prepared to reject (firmly) all round tables that are not in coffee shops or social areas.
- *Index tables.* In the heyday of the *Reader's Guide to Periodical Literature* and other long sets of books that people consulted as a group, libraries purchased huge tables with double-faced two-shelf dividers down the center. Only a few sets of materials—such as *Consumer Reports* and financial services—survive in hard copy and need tables of this type (some of these are high-theft items and are kept only at reference desks). We suspect it's been many years since many libraries have purchased index tables, and most existing index tables have had to be repurposed. We've seen some excess index tables converted to computer tables. And no doubt other useful uses have been found, such as Lego tables in children's departments.

- *Custom computer tables.* Computer tables come in a variety of non-rectangular shapes. A common shape is hexagons, with user chairs on six sides and all of the computer wires funneled through the center of the table to simplify wiring. However, it can be hard to arrange hexagonal tables effectively. Computer tables also come in unusual shapes with lobes for individual computers. For users who need space for books and papers beside their computers, these appear not to provide what people need, but we've never really studied them.
- *Machine tables for computers.* Unlike wooden single-person tables, machine tables can be specifically designed for computers, with wire management troughs to keep wires from dangling. Many libraries purchase machine tables from firms specializing in furniture for offices and schools rather than from wood furniture firms.
- *Game tables.* Game tables often have chessboard or backgammon patterns printed on their high-pressure laminate surfaces. They look neat, but cardboard game boards may make your seating more flexible.
- *Tables for very young children.* These can include toddler-height tables for preschoolers and primary-height tables for lower grades.

When designers suggest tables other than rectangular tables with chairs on two sides, always check to see the actual working space available to individual users. A good way to do this is to make a sketch of the top of the table and then indicate the surface space available to each person at the table by drawing dotted lines on the tabletop. If the lines end up diagonal and the work areas triangular, pick a different table design.

B. Requirements

What do library reading tables require?

- *No aprons.* Aprons are vertical boards located under the tops of tables. Inexpensive tables have metal plates (or strips of wood) installed diagonally between aprons at the corners of the tables. Diagonal bolts connect the plates to the table legs. Unfortunately, tables built this way aren't strong enough for library use. While cheap tables with aprons are usually flimsy, massive tables with aprons can be extremely difficult to use, for the thickness of the aprons either leaves no room for users to get their legs under the tables or raises the tabletops to uncomfortable heights.
- *Adequate leg clearance.* Tables for use by adults should have at least 27 inches of leg clearance, as required for use by people with disabilities.
- *Tops about 29 inches high.*

- *Adequately large tops.* Four-person tables in public and school libraries need to be a minimum of 3 × 5 feet, and tables in academic and research libraries can be 4 × 6 or 4 × 7 feet.
- *Durable tops.* Although some beautiful library tables are available with wooden tops, they're expensive and may prove to be high-maintenance. Lots of libraries appear to prefer tops made of high-pressure laminates, which are not strong enough for lending desktops but seem to work well on reading tables.
- *Edge banding is sometimes used to keep laminate tops from chipping.* On wooden tables with lumber cores, this can be a strip of wood, but on some tables the edge bands can be plastic resins cast in place. Wooden edge banding tends to need occasional refinishing.
- *Matching laminates on the undersides of tabletops, to prevent the tops from warping with changes in humidity.*
- *Tabletops that are neither black nor white, both of which cause eyestrain.* Colors like birch or pale gray appear to work best.
- *No chipboard tops.* Chipboard is a mixture of sawdust and glue. The phrase *built for the ages* does not apply to it.
- *Electrical outlets.* All reading room tables for adult and young adult use (except game tables) require electrical outlets, ideally in the center of the top. Some tables have outlets hidden beneath the tops; in a computer age this seems to be a triumph of aesthetics over function. Tabletop reading lamps can have electrical outlets built into their bases.
- *Outlets for charging cell phones may not be essential, but they're a polite idea.*
- *No beams connecting the legs.* Students using library tables may want to pull extra chairs up to the ends of the tables. If the legs are connected by beams, this doesn't work. (In well-engineered tables, beams between the legs are cute rather than functional.)
- *Legs at the corners of the tops rather than inset.* Inset legs get in users' way and provide no compensating benefits.
- *Legs on four corners rather than pedestal legs.* Tables with corner legs are a lot more stable than tables with pedestal legs (center legs), and pedestal legs get in the way of human legs. Our strong feeling is that pedestal legs are a bad idea. Tables with single pedestal legs also offer opportunities for upset.
- *Adjustable glides at the bottom of legs.* If glides screw in and out, they can be adjusted to compensate for unevenness in floors. (More floors are uneven than one would expect.)
- *Very large wooden tables, such as index tables, may have additional steel stiffeners mounted on the undersides of the tables,* running down the centers of the tables.

Shiny tabletops lead to distracting reflections of ceiling fixtures. Glass is particularly undesirable, but so are white surfaces of any kind, which can be unpleasantly bright. Tabletops and service desk tops need to be of gentle colors, neither black nor white.

- *Large reading rooms in academic and research libraries sometimes have long tables lined with chairs on both sides.* (Or shorter tables butted together end to end.) Outside of requiring a little more walking around, they seem to look and work just as well as two- or four-person tables, and they save some floor space. They tend to look particularly elegant with rows of reading lamps on their tops.
- *Some research libraries have long, single-sided tables, arranged in parallel rows so that all readers face the same way* rather than staring at each other across the tabletops. We've seen these in European libraries.

Many historic reading tables are unsuited for modern library use because they have uncomfortably high working surfaces and aprons too deep for accessibility. If they are also dramatic in appearance and admired by local folks, you may have a problem. Some libraries have converted tables of this type to display areas for new books and other materials. Others have simply sold them at auction or put them in storage until they're forgotten.

C. Options

A handful of options are available:

- Table lamps. Some libraries add table lamps mostly for romantic atmosphere, but in other libraries (particularly those with historic dark ceilings) table lamps may be essential. The main tricks with table lamps are:
- Bolt them down.
  - Make sure that they cast light on the entire tabletop. This is most easily done with straight fixtures that run the length of the tabletop. If you would rather have round fixtures, get hold of a couple and see if they cast light in useful places. A couple of round circles of light in the center of the tabletop won't help readers.
  - See if you can find lamps with electrical outlets in their bases, which may limit the amount of clutter on your tabletops.
  - Check with your engineers concerning electrical codes. Can you have a table with a pigtail lead connected to a floor socket below? Or do you have to have a permanently mounted metal conduit?

> We're not kidding about table lamps installed for atmosphere. We know one academic library where the prominent table lamps provide so little light that they might as well not be there, even during the Dark of Night.

- Privacy panels. Many carrels for single readers have raised panels on three sides. Selecting panels high enough to provide a feeling of privacy without appealing to a reader's sense of claustrophobia may take a little research.
- Wire management troughs. Some more modern tables are available with wire management arrangements to conceal the worst of the dangling wires.
- Provisions for laptop security. See what systems are available to protect library users' laptops during restroom breaks. We've seen locking cabinets at the back of user workspaces where laptops can be shoved back and locked in without being turned off, but things change constantly.

D. Adaptations Based on Age of Users

There are some adaptations based on the ages of users:

- Some furniture companies offer slightly shorter versions of adult tables with slightly shorter chairs for use by older children. Our experience has been that

As this historic fixture shows, lamp fixtures on reading tables can be elegant and welcoming. However, some work well while others provide no useful light. If you are planning tables with lamps, always obtain a sample lamp in advance and try it out in an otherwise dark room. (If your table lamps have electrical outlets for laptops, users will be even more happy.)

these are not different enough from adult tables to justify their existence. Unless the children's and adult tables are visibly very different, they tend to get intermixed, with some tables too low for adult chairs and others too high for children's chairs.
- A variety of special seating for preschool children and for children in lower grades is available, often with fanciful designs cut into the chair backs by laser cutters. The catalogs and websites of furniture manufacturers are full of examples. Libraries typically purchase children's tables and chairs at two heights, primary tables suitable for perhaps ages five through seven, and toddler-height tables for younger children.
- Some libraries have purchased stools for children. If you do, avoid three-legged stools, which tend to tip over.
- For over a century, children's libraries have purchased slope-top reading tables with lips to keep books from sliding off. The general idea is that large picture books can be laid flat on the tabletops while kids read them. We both tried them out when we were small children and found them unpleasant places to sit, so you don't want to hear our opinions, which remain extraordinarily negative. Despite our opinions, slope-top tables still turn up in new public libraries with regularity, but when we visit libraries we see them used for displays rather than reading. If you think we're

wrong, please let us know. In the meantime, we suggest you avoid them. Slope-top tables seem to come equipped with backless benches more often than with chairs.
- Seating for infants. Many parents arrive in children's departments with children ranging in age from a few months to perhaps sixth grade. The youngest children may be too small for even toddler tables, but a wide range of printed carpets are available that can be inserted flush in broadloom carpet or carpet squares.

V. CHAIRS

A. Soft Seating

Almost all libraries try to provide comfortable seating, particularly for people who want to read without taking notes.

As many libraries become destinations as well as book warehouses, comfortable seating is even more important.

1. Armchairs

For adults, the most workable soft seating is armchairs.

Armchairs come in a wide variety of styles. Because library furniture is usually made to order, almost any upholstery is possible. Furniture manufacturers will offer their own range of fabrics, but they will also use fabrics purchased by their customers. ("COM" stands for "customer's own materials" in the trade.)

Many armchairs are too deep from front to back. It's no fun to slide back into the rear of a chair, bracing your back against the back of the chair, only to find that your feet stick out straight, like a three-year-old on the family sofa.

In addition to being too deep, many armchairs are too low for library use. Your octogenarian users will need to arise from armchairs without assistance. Having to roll out of a low armchair onto the floor, then struggle to get to your feet, is not a heartwarming experience.

If armchairs have heavily padded arms, it's hard for users to put their weight on the arms to emerge from the chairs. And upholstery on the arms of chairs can wear out quickly and get dirty even more quickly.

One source of good armchairs for libraries is companies that make waiting room furniture for medical offices. Often, they offer both regular widths and slightly wider widths for more comfortable reading. Unlike some overstuffed armchairs, waiting room-style chairs are high enough to allow people to get back up again, and they have wooden arms because clinics don't like shabby arms any more than libraries do, and because inflexible wooden arms are easier to use to lever oneself out of a chair.

An increasing need in America is the need for truly wide chairs. A manufacturer of high-quality wooden furniture told Fred that bariatric chairs were a great new area for sales. If you've visited a doctor's examining room recently, you may be impressed at the width of the chair provided for patients. Libraries may need to provide ultra-wide chairs as well.

Some libraries have had trouble with users dragging armchairs around so that they serve as footstools. You can fight this by making armchairs heavy and hard to move or by not putting two armchairs close together. You can also buy footstools, although they may tend to get in the way.

Buy institutional furniture. There is no theoretical upper limit to the number of teenagers who can occupy a chair.

2. Love Seats

Love seats seem ideally suited for parents and children to sit together in children's departments. And they're too short for adults to nap on.

When equipped with wooden arms, love seats don't take a huge amount of space.

3. Sofas

Sofas look attractive and homey, but as a general rule they cause problems in public libraries. Often serious problems.

In children's departments, they're almost always too long. A parent with one or two children can fit comfortably into a love seat.

In areas for adults, sofas are a problem because users who don't know each other well don't want to share. One person sits alone at one end of the sofa, while the rest of the sofa is empty and wastes floor space.

4. Rocking Chairs

Fred and John are usually civil in their social relationships, but they disagree strongly on the subject of rocking chairs.

Fred thinks that rocking chairs in libraries are seriously evil. Libraries tend to put rocking chairs in children's departments, where the fingers of toddlers are constantly at risk.

> Fred knew a children's librarian who was forced to tell stories to children while seated in a rocking chair given by a donor so important that the chair could not be replaced with something sane. She said she spent the entire time frozen in place, terrified to move because children were gathered tightly about her with their fingers right by the rockers.

The other problem Fred found with rocking chairs was their tendency to creep backwards in use. One library user in Fred's library slowly backed the chair into a wall, whereupon the back tip of one of the rockers ended up cutting a six-inch vertical slot right through the drywall.

In contrast to Fred, in all of his library administrative jobs, John found rocking chairs benign and harmless. The things that dismayed Fred never happened, users enjoyed rocking alone or with their children, and all was well.

Either way, local groups love presenting gift rocking chairs with brass gift plates to libraries. If you are like John, you will be gratified, and if you are like Fred, you'll probably be stuck with more of that sort of thing than you want, because staff members accept the gifts without clearing things with administrators.

5. Problems with Soft Seating

Soft seating is important, but libraries have occasional problems with it. Lots of the problems are avoidable with adequate planning.

- Flammability. As mentioned in several places in this book, most upholstered furniture made in the United States has polyurethane foam padding. Unfortunately, polyurethane form is impressively flammable, and it exudes unpleasant chemicals like cyanide when it burns. To meet flammability standards like CAL 133, flame-retardants are sometimes added, but they can also exude nasty chemicals. The moral seems to be that one might want to avoid seriously overstuffed furniture.
- Worn-out arms. Upholstered arms in soft seating tend to wear out quickly, and libraries do a lot better when their armchairs have wooden arms, or at least wooden inserts at the points of greatest wear.
- Excessive depth. Some soft seating is so deep from front to back that people can't sit with their backs against the backs of the seats without their legs sticking straight out in front of them, much in the manner of toddlers on living room chairs. (This is one reason you want to try out chairs before purchasing them.)
- Excessive general bulk. Some armchairs are impressively huge, with massive stuffed arms, eighteen-inch thick backs, and an amazing ratio of total bulk to actual sitting space. They make a statement, but we're not sure what kind. If you decide you want huge armchairs in your library, increase the minimum estimated space per chair in your building program.
- Overly soft arms. It's much easier to arise from an armchair if it has firm wooden arms.
- Overly low seats. This is yet another reason you want to try out chairs before purchasing them.
- Infestations and urine. Libraries have had to destroy soft seating that became infested with bedbugs, or that was urinated upon or into. (Although one hates to sell college and law libraries short, it appears to be a public library problem.)

> One librarian Fred knows vowed to never buy another computer chair for public use that wasn't totally washable—basically a molded plastic seat with metal legs. (She never explained why people with bedbugs appeared to be particularly drawn to computer chairs, but that's where the bedbugs turned up in her library.) Other libraries try to fight part of the cleanliness problem by using plastic upholstery that is less easily ruined.

B. Chairs for Seating at Tables

"Side chairs" (chairs intended for seating at tables) are available in a variety of options:

- Often you have a choice of chairs with arms or without arms. If you're interested in chairs with arms, have several people of different heights and diameters check them out.
- If the arms won't slide under the tabletops, you'll have a lot of empty chairs sticking out into aisles. Since cleaners often put chairs upside down on tabletops when they are cleaning floors, if you select chairs with arms, you may want to be sure the arms allow the chairs to be placed legs-up on tabletops without falling off or blocking aisles.
- Importance of strong joints. It must be possible to tip back and forth on chairs all day long without causing any damage. No cheap chairs (and few expensive chairs for home use) can withstand this.
- Two-position chairs. Chairs are available with bases that allow users to sit straight upright or tilt backward a specific amount. Apparently younger users like them, but older adults like Fred panic when the chairs start to tilt back (even though he has tried a lot of them and has never flipped over backwards).
- Four separate legs vs. sled bases. Some side chairs have two wooden pieces that connect the bottoms of the legs on each side of the chair. They provide extra strength and may limit carpet damage.
- Casters. Some libraries equip the chairs at their reading tables with casters to make it easier for users to slide chairs in and out from under tables and to limit damage to carpets, particularly tearing carpets up at the seams. Chairs with casters are common in places like the dining rooms of retirement centers.
- Padding choices. Typical options include padded or solid seats and padded or solid backs. Padding is more comfortable if your library is not panicked about dirt and/or bugs.
- Smooth or spindle backs. Some good-looking chairs are available with spindle backs, like Windsor chairs. Try them out for comfort.

An architect specified these bucket seat chairs for a library conference room without ever trying one out. Although the chairs were from a major manufacturer, they were a disaster. The library staff concluded that the intent was to select chairs so painfully uncomfortable that meetings would last as short a time as possible. Sooner or later, everyone found alternative seating, and the chairs migrated throughout the building, ending up being inflicted on library users.

As with all chairs, trial sitting is vital. No matter how lovely or historic or modern a chair looks, if it hurts to sit on it, it's a failure as a chair. If the chair has a spindle back, are the spindles comfortable to lean against, or do you find yourself wondering about the availability of pads that can be tied on?

If you're equipping a library with identical chairs, furniture vendors will lend you examples. Remember that no matter how cute it is, if it isn't comfortable, it's not "cute" in the deeper and more philosophical sense of the word. Go for comfortable.

C. Padded Benches

Libraries occasionally have small padded benches for users.

Some are just places to sit and rest a moment, away from regular tables and chairs. It there's a long hike between seating areas, users may appreciate intermediate seats.

One use of benches is to provide places for parents and children to sit together at computer workstations. (Or for two kids playing computer games together.)

Another place for benches is lobbies, for people waiting to be picked up.

D. Booths

Some public libraries have installed diner-style booths, particularly for teenagers.

Diner booths have some advantages. They encourage a feeling of group support and privacy (even though if the booths are viewed end on, library staff can see every toe wiggle). Four-person diner booths can take up somewhat less floor space than four-person reading tables.

Some libraries have used a combination of freestanding tables and freestanding bench seats with high backs. All of this can be arranged to create diner booths, with the knowledge that if fashions change, it's easy to rearrange the furniture.

E. Window Seats

Many public libraries have window seats. Window seats are welcoming and easy to build. Basically, they're just upholstered benches located beside windows, or in the embrasures where windows are located.

Problems with window seats occur when storage is provided inside the benches, with seats that lift up for access. Unfortunately, users (particularly kids) can lift up the seats and then drop them, where they slam on other people's fingers or startle nearby readers with crashing noises.

Our preference is not to bother with trying to provide storage in window seats. If you can't resist, provide access through sliding panels on the fronts rather than from above.

F. Novelty Seating for Children

Some companies offer a wide variety of colorful seating units for children, snug places to sit and read where parents don't really fit. One company with a large catalog is Gressco.

Other libraries purchase backyard buildings in molded plastic, sometimes changing them seasonally.

This attractive bay window includes a window seat for children, an armchair for an adult, and an unusually delicate light fixture that provides strong uplighting.

Many libraries purchase stools for children and young adults. Be wary. Three-legged stools are far too tipsy for library use. High stools for use at counters seem hard to justify: lots of people don't like them, and they seem not to confer any benefit.

All sorts of unusual new chair designs turn up every year. Many furniture companies display them in their booths at library conferences because they attract attention. This is a good place to sit on one. Page through, in a leisurely fashion, the catalogs available in the booth while you see if your body is happy with the sitting experience.

VI. PLACEMENT OF USER SEATING IN LIBRARY BUILDINGS

A. Adequate Clearances

While some libraries have furniture comfortably spaced, too many libraries have inadequate clearances between furnishings.

- Sometimes inadequate clearances are a result of designers paring down the spaces listed in building programs. A first way to check for troubles of this type is to ask your architects to provide for each department or major area in the library a list comparing the programmed and designed spaces for each area of the building. If your architects don't want to do this, expect to find trouble. (We think it's a good reason to find new architects, but we've become sensitized over the years.) Frankly, a lot of building programs don't allow a lot of extra space, so cuts can quickly become problems.
- No one who uses a wheelchair should find any aisles too narrow.
- Some architects faced with space limitations start changing the dimensions of furnishings, particularly reading tables, or adding extra chairs to tables that are already sufficiently small. Make very clear in your building program what minimum sizes of tables you want in terms of the dimensions of the tops, and make sure that things don't change on you. Watch out for rectangular tables suddenly becoming round or chairs suddenly appearing at the ends of rectangular tables.
- The size of the tabletop has far less to do with necessary floor space than the area available for seated readers and the aisle space between occupied tables. Watch in particular for adequate aisle space.
- Sometimes administrative powers—such as school principals or superintendents—suggest library spaces that are simply too small to hold the necessary furniture. Your architects should step forward and announce that things won't work. But if they won't do it, you'll have to. Or get your building

consultant to do it, since having your consultant fired is a lot better than having yourself fired.

B. Seating Next to Shelving

Never place seating so that chairs—particularly chairs at reading tables—back up against shelving.

No seated user should ever block access to adjacent shelving or seating. Comfortable clearances are about four feet. If a user seated at a table occupies 3 feet of space, the total space from the edge of the table to the nearest fixed object needs to be about 7 feet. If we allow 3 feet for each user and a four-foot aisle, the space between the tops of adjacent tables with user seating should ideally be about 10 feet.

Having chairs backing up toward book shelves is often an extraordinarily bad idea because designers do not allow enough space for both readers at tables and people looking for books on shelves. One still finds it in century-old Carnegie-era buildings, where it's a source of serious dysfunction. But modern academic libraries have experimented with the use of shelving to separate reading tables, simultaneously creating chairs that block access to shelves and endless small sections of shelving where the call number order is a total mystery.

If seated readers block access to shelving, users looking for books have to ask the readers to move. It's hard to find anything really nice to say about the idea of having seated readers block access to shelving, so building programs need to ban the concept in firm terms.

C. Seating by Windows

Generally speaking, people like daylight and books don't. If your library has a limited number of windows, you can deal with both books and readers by making sure that there are armchairs or reading tables by all of your windows.

We can't say this too often, because the problem turns up eternally. All exterior windows that face any direction except due north still need adjustable blinds, so the mere fact that there are no nearby books doesn't end the need for controlling direct sunlight. Of all areas where architects and librarians end up in conflicts, the failure by architects to control direct sunshine is one of the most common.

D. Movable Seating

The vogue for information commons and easily rearranged seating places even more stress on essential flexibility.

If students or other users are going to (a) rearrange the furniture and (b) nevertheless use their laptops, you'll need:

- Even, all-purpose lighting. The closer your space comes to an evenly lighted ceiling, the fewer problems you will have with glare and shadows. Occasional rectangular light fixtures won't do the job unless the ceiling is far higher than in most library reading areas. In our experience, what works best is strip uplight (or at least two-thirds uplight) fixtures with ceilings an absolute minimum of 10 feet high. Eleven or 12 feet works better.
- Electrical outlets all over the place. Talk with your designers and electrical engineers about what's available and meets codes. We assume that a floor grid of totally flush outlets that is a minimum of 10 × 10 feet is important in all public service and staff work areas, but in areas with movable seating this may be insufficient.
- Furniture on casters.
- Sometimes it's hard to tell what's a fad and what's a trend, but information commons have been around for a while, and they may be a genuine trend.

E. Seating without Users' Backs to the Room

In general, people don't like sitting with their backs to the room, especially when clearances are tight and other people are standing or walking right behind them. Even in an environment as pleasant and warmly sociable as a library, people don't like the feeling of unseen strangers brushing up against their backs.

This is one of the downsides of placing computer workstations on countertops along walls, especially if there's not much clearance between the countertops and other furnishings.

> Fred knows one library where users would never sit at the countertops, and the library had to use them for storage.

The main advantage of computers on wall-mounted countertops, of course, is they make it easy for staff to keep an eye on users' web use practices. But that seems a high price to pay if your users are all uncomfortable.

Instead of providing what amounts to a single, long table against a wall, consider setting a number of single-user-sized tables perpendicular to the wall. Now users at the tables have a shoulder to the room behind them rather than sitting with their backs to the action.

In general, tables are almost always better than countertops because it's easy to move tables, while relocating counters can take major surgery. It's almost always better to solve functional problems with furniture than with built-in stuff.

VII. SNAPPY RULES ON USER SEATING

1. Few things are better than sitting in a comfortable chair by a window in a library, reading a new book, and drinking coffee and watching the world go by. All of this is possible in any library, with the possible exception of rare book rooms and archives, which take a dim view of both coffee and sunlight.
2. The only good way to serve all of your users all of the time is to make all tables for all adults accessible to people with disabilities.
3. With the possible exception of small children, all users need easy access to electrical outlets.
4. Beware of built-in stuff. Don't rely on architecture to solve furniture problems.
5. Library users don't like sitting facing walls with unseen people walking closely behind them. Things are a lot more comfortable if you rotate desk surfaces 90 degrees, with users' shoulders facing passersby.
6. Many impressive historic library tables are unsuited for current library use. Sell them for a good price.
7. Even the sturdiest of library users need to use restrooms occasionally. Make provisions for the security of their laptops while they are away.
8. If a group of carrels looks like a swastika when seen from above, the fact that it twirls the wrong way will not palliate the offense.
9. Since the coming of universal laptops, study carrels need to be four feet wide.
10. You don't want sofas in your public library. Children and their parents can do well with small love seats with wooden arms, or with padded window seats. Adults who don't know each other won't share sofas, so the only uses for sofas in areas for adults are for sleeping and necking.

11. Older users have trouble getting out of low-slung soft seating.
12. Round tables are for conversation and for relaxed reading, not for work. Beware (as in be very afraid and extremely uncooperative) when your designers start converting the rectangular tables in your building program to round tables.
13. Standard library tables are rectangular, with two chairs on each of the long sides. If your designers try to convert them to tables with chairs on all four sides, stop them. If they try to convert them to round tables, take more serious action.
14. All tables need electrical outlets boldly installed in the centers, not hidden away discreetly out of sight on the ends.
15. If your college dormitories are noisy and crowded, you'll need more study space in your library. Know what you'll do if 75 percent of your student body tries to crowd into the library during exam week. (If your public library is near a college, you may have experienced study-space overflow at exam times.)
16. Most upholstered furniture is padded with polyurethane foam, which is seriously evil stuff when it comes to fires. Flame-retardant chemicals are available but are nasty. So far, the score on polyurethane foam appears to be furniture industry 100, federal safety standards 0.
17. The current vogue is study areas with movable furniture. This means electrical outlets everywhere. When your designers ask, "Where will you put computers?" the answer is always "Anywhere we want."
18. To check user space allocations on reading tables, draw dotted lines on sketches of the tabletops to show who gets what space. Any tables that end up with diagonals need to be rejected as possible purchases.
19. Users need to walk between reading tables when all the chairs are occupied. Some designers don't leave enough space. Check on everything, and show the drawings to your building consultants.
20. Lamps on reading tables are a great idea. Even if the light isn't essential, it feels warm and comfortable. Rectangular lamps that run the length of tables are more functional. Round lamps are more attractive, but too many don't shed much of any light on readers' books. Experiment with sample fixtures before ordering a roomful.
21. Square reading tables are for a maximum of two users. Laptops with open screens provide helpful barricades between two users facing each other.
22. Library users tilt their chairs when reading. Yelling at kids won't help, so buy chairs that can take it.
23. Never place reading tables so that users can block access to shelving. The ends of tables that don't have chairs should face the shelving.
24. Never buy a chair until you've spent at least fifteen minutes sitting on it.

25. If your designers want to create custom-made chairs for your library, be extremely wary. Insist on trying out samples that you can actually sit on, and compare them with standard industry products for comfort. Or just say "No" to your designers and buy standard seating.
26. If you visit a library and see that all the users seated at the reading tables are resting on their elbows rather than leaning back in their chairs, there's a good chance the library has lousy chairs.
27. Junior-sized tables for public libraries are available about one inch shorter than adult-sized tables. Avoid them, for the difference is inconsequential, and the usual outcome is the junior and adult-sized tables and chairs simply getting intermixed.
28. Armchairs in libraries need wooden arms. Upholstered arms turn filthy overnight and threadbare after a few months.
29. With the exception of folks playing video games, computer users need elbowroom for books and papers.
30. Since users like light and books don't, put reading tables and armchairs by windows.
31. Posed promotional photos from the architecture and furniture industries sometimes show library users reading happily in direct sunlight. Yeah, right.
32. If each area of your library is assigned its own individual furniture color scheme, you'll soon have piebald mixtures as you need to regroup furnishings.
33. Tables for use with several computers, such as hexagonal tables, offer the advantage of feeding a lot of wiring through a single opening in the floor. But the workspaces for individual users can be pretty cramped.
34. You can almost always have your upholstered furniture made up with your own fabrics. ("COM," as in "customer's own material," is a good phrase to know.)
35. Most good-quality wooden library furniture is made to order, so don't expect to select from available stock. Production will take several months.
36. When you're selecting upholstery fabrics, look at swatches from at least a dozen feet away. Some fabrics with attractive up-close detail look muddy from a distance.
37. You can always buy some of your furniture later, but you can't build your library undersized and make it a little bigger later. And some generous people may offer to pay for extra furniture when they see the building actually going up.
38. The most fragile joints on a chair are the ones between the vertical posts at the rear (styles) and the horizontal supports of the seats (aprons). Good library furniture makers reinforce these joints on wooden chairs with metal-to-metal connectors.

39. Furniture manufacturers are notorious for being late. Lots of library grand openings take place with substitute furniture.
40. Never buy a chair with fewer than four legs. No matter how cute they look in the catalog, or how cute they sound in the vendor's booth at a library conference, or how cute they sound in your designers' descriptions, all three-legged chairs tip over. When your users are abruptly dumped on the floor, you are unlikely to be happy.
41. Some of the most uncomfortable library seating we've ever encountered was custom-designed by architects. Always have a single chair built to your architects' design and then try it out extensively. Or just save time and money and say "No."
42. Buy strong. There is no theoretical upper limit to the number of teenagers that can occupy an armchair.
43. Always avoid architecturally mounted task lighting. If users move their chairs, you want the light to be just as good wherever they move them.
44. Ungainly historic reading tables can make attractive display units, but nine-tenths of your tables need to be actually usable.
45. Americans are getting more ample, and available seating reflects this. For example, wider versions of medical waiting room chairs are user-friendly and designed for easy exiting.

17

Collection Storage

I. INTRODUCTION

Selecting the best shelving is an important decision because of the significant cost and the impressive longevity of the product. Steel shelving made in the nineteenth century is still in use in American libraries.

Because high-quality shelving will last the life of a building, decisions are forever. Trendy colors, for example, vastly outlast their popularity.

Even though shelving will occupy only part of a library, all library floors need to be strong enough to handle at least the weight of standard shelving loaded with books—150 pounds per square foot. The tricky planning part comes when we use storage systems that require more strength—including compact shelving and microfiche cabinets. The easy thing is to put these on a slab-on-grade floor, but sometimes they need to be on upper floors. Your engineers and shelving manufacturers will need to work together to be sure there are no problems.

Back in the days when books were scarce and precious, shelving could line the walls of libraries. But even the tiniest modern libraries have parallel rows of shelves with aisles for access.

Shelving mounted flat on walls is attractive, but the ends of reading tables need to face the shelving. If the sides of tables with chairs face shelving, users tend

When people enter a library, they want to see books and staff. This bookstore has book shelving almost immediately inside the entry doors. A staff desk is close by but not visible in this photograph.

to push their chairs back and block access to the shelving. Old Carnegie-era libraries tend to have serious problems with this, but some modern designers still try to lay out furnishings that way.

High-quality cantilever steel shelving is the standard of the library industry. Old wood shelving can be handsome, but for most librarians it tends to be a serious pain.

In addition to covering the basics of shelving, this chapter also mentions some of the standard ways non-book materials are stored.

Selecting stack aisle width is one of the most important decisions in library design. To avoid having building columns end up in the middle of stack aisles, leading to all sorts of awkward shelf placement and wasted space, the on-centers structural column spacing of library buildings needs to be a multiple of the on-centers column spacing of book shelving units.

Plastic sheeting in this book stack unit protects shelving from water leaking through the terrace above by channeling the water into a variety of large containers, which need to be emptied during rainstorms. Unfortunately, the expensive circus tents retrofitted to the terrace didn't help with leakage. Over the years, as the rebar in the terrace began to rust, the water leaking into the shelving below turned the color of tea. (For those who are wondering, the leaking terrace and circus tents and plastic sheeting and receiving containers and tea-colored water are all still there, but the shelving has been removed.)

II. STEEL CANTILEVER SHELVING

The standard of the library industry is steel cantilever shelving with decorative end panels. Except for situations where seriously ornamental shelving is required, we believe that anything else is a serious mistake.

Cantilever shelving has center columns with shelves that hook onto the columns. The name comes from the fact that individual shelves are cantilevered out from the central column. Typically, a shelving unit consists of a rectangular inner frame, feet that extend from the frame to support the unit and keep it from tipping, and individual shelves hooked onto the vertical members of the frame.

The two main varieties of cantilever shelving are starter-adder shelving and welded frame shelving.

With starter-adder shelving, the columns and spreaders are separate pieces. In a range of shelving, the first unit (the "starter") consists of two columns separated by two spreaders. Additional units ("adders") are each created with a single column and two spreaders.

With welded frame shelving, each unit consists of a rectangular welded frame. Multiple units are simply bolted together.

A. Advantages of Steel Cantilever Shelving

Steel cantilever shelving is fairly easy to assemble, much like working with an Erector or Meccano set.

Cantilever shelving has leveling screws, often at the ends of the transverse feet. Leveling screws are important because poured concrete floors are seldom as flat as we would like them to be. If you relocate cantilever shelving, you will probably need to readjust the leveling screws. In fact, because floors are uneven, you may find that if the screws are adjusted for a different part of the floor, when you relocate shelving, things will be worse than having no leveling screws at all until you readjust the screws.

One of the advantages of cantilever shelving is that moving firms with hydraulic stack lifters can relocate whole ranges of fully loaded shelving. If you are recarpeting your library, not having to unload, disassemble, reassemble, and reload shelves can save you vast amounts of money in staff time.

When the time comes to recarpet, many libraries that chose not to purchase cantilever shelving end up cutting the old carpet around the edges of each shelving unit, leaving the old carpet under each unit, and simply replacing the carpet in the aisles. Among many other things, this makes attempting to relocate any shelving unit by even a fraction of an inch an unfortunate undertaking.

Cantilever steel shelving has the advantage of being capable of being repeatedly disassembled and reassembled. Welded frame shelving in particular is compatible with this treatment. With starter-adder shelving, however, the spreaders (crossbars that connect the vertical posts) may loosen eventually after many disassemblies and reassemblies.

B. Specifying Steel Cantilever Shelving

About a half dozen U.S. firms manufacture cantilever steel shelving. The products can be remarkably similar, to the point where shelves by one company may be compatible with posts made by another. (One way to tell brands apart is by the vertical ends of individual shelves, which tend to have individual patterns.)

The thickness of sheet steel is measured by "gauge." Somewhat counterintuitively, the smaller the number the thicker the metal. However, we think the best way to compare shelving is in terms of mils, thousandths of an inch. Always inquire about the thickness of components in mils. The feet of shelving units will be the thickest, followed by columns, and then by actual shelves.

Many architects specify shelving the way they specify lighting fixtures, listing a preferred item and a couple of acceptable alternatives.

1. Paint

Standard finishes on high-quality steel shelving are electrostatically applied powder paint that is fused in place. For this reason, you can't repaint steel shelving unless you have someone that can apply powder paint in what amounts to a factory setting. Spray-on finishes, such as those in auto body shops, won't do. The abrasion on steel shelving is too great, and automotive-style paint will soon begin to rub off.

Because powder paint is extremely tough and permanent, and because repainting is difficult, libraries often sell off shelving in unwanted colors rather than trying to repaint it.

The point of all of this is that you don't want shelving in funny colors. ("Funny colors" includes trendy colors.) It's easy and cheap to repaint walls or change carpet, but changing shelving colors is another story.

The best shelving colors are those that are light enough not to show dust, light enough to not soak up all the available light, dark enough not to show every fingerprint, and neutral enough not to fight any future color decisions. We prefer pale gray.

2. Standard Dimensions: Heights

Cantilever steel shelving is available in a variety of heights. If you order a lot, you can have pretty much anything you want, but there are advantages to selecting standard heights, because you can order a few more sections without paying a fortune for a special order.

For adults, the standard shelving heights are 7 feet (84 inches) and 7 foot 6 inches (90 inches). Many people find 90-inch shelving uncomfortably high, and 84-inch shelving is probably the more popular.

If you're stuck with 90-inch shelving units you don't really want, you can of course just attach the top shelves a little lower than the column heights allow. The spreaders between the posts will always stick up too far, but if you don't have unusually low ceilings, about all the difference it makes is a somewhat awkward appearance.

Since cantilever shelving operates in a fashion similar to Erector sets, you can often replace individual components you don't like with new pieces from the same manufacturer. For example, with welded frame shelving, you can buy a new welded frame but use all the other components over again, including the individual shelves, feet, and front kick strip. (But verify this with the manufacturer.)

Lower shelving is used for children's materials, and you may be required to use lower shelving for accessibility reasons for reference books and current magazines. Check with your architect or state library or attorney.

For children's picture books, many catalogs recommend 42-inch-high shelving, but it's too low for three shelves vertically. If you use 48-inch shelving, three shelves of picture books will fit.

Many libraries use 60-inch-high shelving for children's books for upper grades, basically chapter books and junior nonfiction.

With 84-inch shelving, there's room for seven shelves vertically of adult fiction and six shelves of adult nonfiction.

You can actually use seven shelves vertically for adult nonfiction, but you'll end up with a lot more oversized books. If oversized books are shelved in a different part of the building, most users will never find them. It's also possible to store oversized books flat on the bottom shelf, but this means dedicating a lot of shelves to the purpose, and this will in turn affect your space projections for shelving. And users may still not find the oversize books when they're just a few shelves down. Areas of the collection that run extensively to oversize books—such as art books—usually end up with only five shelves vertically.

With all of these recommendations on the number of shelves vertically, always experiment with your own collection before ordering shelving.

Staff members of new library buildings frequently leave the top and bottom shelves empty, so that 6 or 7 shelves vertically begins its life as effectively 4 or 5 shelves vertically, with the remaining 2 shelves available for long-term collection growth. Short users appreciate not having to deal with high shelves, while older users with limited vision or creaky knees appreciate not having to inspect bottom shelves.

Some librarians worry that the public will criticize new libraries for wasting space with empty shelves, but most people understand the concept of room for growth.

3. Standard Dimensions: Depths

The individual shelves that hook onto the support frame come in a variety of depths.

When selecting shelving, it's important to realize that shelving comes in actual and "nominal" depths. For example, if you want shelving 11 inches deep, you may need to order nominal 12-inch deep shelving. Once again, check carefully with your vendor.

The nominal 12-inch deep description is based on the premise that there is a gap at the back of the shelf, corresponding to the thickness of the support column. The manufacturer takes credit for the open air at the back of the individual shelves. For example, with a nominal 10-inch-deep shelf, the 2-inch space between shelves where they are separated by support columns gets credited to the actual shelves, with each actual 9-inch shelf getting credited for an extra inch.

Most cantilever shelving uses 11-inch (nominal 12-inch) deep shelving for bottom shelves. This covers the cross feet that support the frames and the filler piece that connects the ends of the feet and fills the gap between the bottom shelf and the floor. Depending on needs, upper shelves in the unit may be either 9 inches (nominal 10 inches) deep or 11 inches (nominal 12 inches) deep.

Shelving can be purchased with shorter base feet and shallower shelves. We've seen libraries with cantilever steel shelving as shallow as 5 inches (nominal 6 inches) or 7 inches (nominal 8 inches). Unfortunately, this often results in books sticking out over the fronts of the shelves.

On those rare occasions where books are all of the same depth (such as pocket-sized paperbacks), libraries have put blocks at the rear of shelves to keep all of the books aligned neatly at the front of the shelves. (One library Fred knows uses lengths of 2 × 4 lumber for pocket-sized paperbacks, which turned out to be just the right dimension.)

Shelving depths are usually described in terms of the upper shelves and the base shelves. For example, nominal 10-inch shelves with a nominal 12-inch base shelf are usually described as 10 over 12. If the shelves are all nominal 12-inch, it's described as 12 over 12.

Shelving shallower than nominal 10 inches is a bad idea, and base shelves should be nominal 12 inches deep. By using shallower base shelves, double-faced shelving units can be less than the standard two feet deep, but the space is skimpy, the units are less stable, and the saving in floor space is very modest. The libraries we've visited that have such shallow shelving don't like it.

4. Standard Dimensions: Widths

Virtually all cantilever steel shelving is sold in units three feet wide, and there are large libraries with many thousands of essentially identical units.

Occasionally, libraries will order narrower units to fit very specific situations. Because these are specialized and seldom sold, they tend to be more expensive than standard three-foot-wide units.

5. Bookends

Most cantilever shelving is available with some devices to keep books from tipping over on the shelves.

Companies may offer standard steel bookends, typically painted to match the shelving and perhaps with anti-skid bases, such as cork.

Some shelving is available with slots that run the length of the shelving, with bookends that slide in the slots. Some very small books may want to fall into the slots, but in general they appear to work fairly well.

Other shelving comes with sliding wire book supports that run in the folded-over bottom edges of the shelves above. By squeezing the front and back wires together, library staff can slide the supports snugly up to the last book on the shelf. If you want to have a support like this on the top shelf, you'll need a canopy over the top shelf. Check with the vendor to make sure this works.

Libraries often are concerned about the possibility of slender bookends damaging books that are forced carelessly into the bookends. Some people call this "knifing." Purchasing bookends that have wide front edges helps.

Our personal preference from years of personal experience putting books away is that the sliding wire supports are the easiest to use and the least likely to fall on the floor.

6. Accessories for Steel Cantilever Shelving

All sorts of accessories are available for cantilever steel shelving.

- Lips to prevent books from falling off the back of individual shelves into the gap between front and rear shelves, vanishing into the murky depths at the bottom of shelving units. Some of these are simply pieces of metal bent upwards at the back of the shelves, while others are separate pieces that are held in place between the shelves and the support columns.
- Tilting shelves for periodicals. Shelving of this kind is designed to display the current issue vertically. By flipping up the display shelves, users can access stacks of earlier issues on flat shelves beneath the tilt shelves. Tilt shelves allow current issues to be in display binders, which is important if the library does not lend them. If you buy tilt shelving, be sure that the tilting shelves lock open. Shelves that just depend on balance tend to drop down on the hands (or heads) of people looking for back issues. There's nothing more annoying than having to hold a tilt shelf up with your shoulder while you use two hands to sort through the magazines underneath. Unfortunately, in our experience, tilt shelves are the only components of cantilever steel shelving that tend to go bad.
- Flip bins that hook onto cantilever shelving support columns. The most attractive ones pull out like drawers, to allow users to flip through materials like CDs that are too thin to shelve like books. Be careful to be sure how many items the bins you select will actually hold and still allow easy flipping.
- End panels or end caps. The ends of cantilever steel shelving units tend to look pretty industrial, and many libraries add end panels. For large stack areas, manufacturers will offer steel end panels painted to match the shelving. They may also provide simple panels covered in high-pressure laminates. For browsing or for open stacks, many libraries create custom-designed wooden end panels. Some have panels of laser-cut steel.
- Decorative wooden end panels are frequently designed by architects to accompany the general interior look of the library. You can also specify them yourself. You will need to consider:
    - *Veneer.* What kind of wood do you want? Do you want slip matching or book matching? (Book matching can look neat, but if the front and back of the veneer takes stain differently, you can end up with zebra-striped end panels.) You will need to specify veneer thickness.
    - *Edges.* Veneer is too fragile to run right up to the edge of end panels, and you will need some kind of solid wood banding to prevent damage to the sides and top. Anything thinner than half an inch is probably too thin. Some manufacturers have equipment that will do automatic edge band application, and you may want to ask around to see how thick the banding can be before manufacturers have to do it all by hand.

- *Kick blocks.* The bases of end panels are subject to more abuse, and edge banding will probably not be sufficient to prevent damage. One possibility is solid wood end blocks three or four inches high and the same thickness as the panel.
- *Finishes.* Many clear finishes are too fragile. Other finishes are so inflexible that they can separate from the wood beneath if the finishes are bumped, leaving little white spots. (A lot of companies use pre-catalyzed lacquer. You can specify a coin test for the finished product, consisting of dragging a coin over the finish to make sure it doesn't separate from the wood below.)
- *Inside material for the end panels.* Usually this will be some kind of manufactured board. The section of board for each end panel is veneered, fitted with edge bands and kick blocks, stained, and finished. The quality of manufactured board can vary from impressively strong and permanent to total crap. Get help from someone who knows current products.

Remember that aisle width is measured at the narrowest point in the aisle, which is probably the distance between the two end panels, unless you have an oblong book sticking out.

- *End panels sometimes have slat-wall inserts to allow books to be displayed on the ends of shelving units.* If you are ordering slat-wall end panels, be sure that the slats are lined with metal channels to prevent chipping the wooden edges of the slat openings. Plastic brackets are available from library supply firms for use with slat-wall end panels. Be sure the front of the bracket (away from the end panel) is lower than the back, so the books slip down to the front and tilt backwards. (Some brackets are designed in such a way that books slip to the back of the brackets and tilt forward, making it hard to see the covers.)
- *Canopies.* Canopies are steel or wooden tops that go over the top bookshelves. With low shelving, such as that in children's departments, they provide places to display books or other objects. With high shelving, canopies shield books from dust, but they prevent the occasional extra-tall book from sticking up slightly above the top of the shelving unit, and they can block light and make the aisles feel darker. For areas like children's departments in public libraries, canopies are often custom-made to match end panels.
- *Divider shelves.* Individual shelves are available with high backs and with slots in the backs and shelves. Flat metal sheets fit into the slots and provide dividers to keep materials from tipping over.
- *Bottom shelves that angle upward, making the spines of the lowest books easier to read.*

Although this is a door rather than an end panel, it illustrates the problems that can occur while staining book-matched veneers. Avoid unwanted stripes by specifying slip-matching or by specifying that adjacent veneers will show no signs of different staining.

C. Compact Shelving

Compact shelving consists of ranges of shelving running on rails. It's tremendously popular with large academic collections, with archival collections open only to library staff, and for other situations where a relatively small number of people are using a large amount of shelving.

With compact shelving, perhaps one aisle provides access to ten or twenty ranges of shelving, with the ranges moving back and forth to open up aisles where they are needed. Compact shelving permits far more efficient use of space.

Occasionally, libraries use compact shelving in ill-considered places. If you are planning a small or medium-sized public library, a small college library, or an undergrad library, you may find that compact shelving is a seriously bad idea. Users become annoyed if their access to a specific area of the collection is made impossible because other users are browsing in different aisles. And you may not want teenagers in your public library horsing around with compact shelving.

The two common varieties of compact shelving are "mechanical assist" and "power-driven." Mechanical assist shelving has hand cranks. Inside the end panel is gearing to make the shelving easier to move. (And requiring correspondingly more cranking to get somewhere.) Typically, the mechanism involves the equivalent of sprocket wheels and bicycle chains. It's usually possible to move an impressive number of ranges at the same time.

Librarians tell us that it's important to get mechanical assist shelving that can be repaired by popping off the front of the end panel rather than having to unload books from behind the back side of the end panel.

Power-driven shelving uses electric motors to move the shelving back and forth. One advantage of power-driven shelving is that it comes with safety switches to prevent people trapped in aisles from being compressed in unpleasant ways. (Mechanical assist shelving can simply keep squeezing as long as someone is turning the crank, another reason you don't want seventh graders using compact shelving.)

Power-driven shelving can take a long time to get operating correctly. If you are considering a brand of power-driven shelving, talk with directors of libraries that have the same brand.

Archivists have told us they much prefer mechanical assist shelving, but in many archives, shelving is accessible only to library staff.

Be sure to plan for the extra height of movable shelving. Rails are no more than an inch high, but the carriages that run on the rails are several inches high, and the steel cantilever shelving ranges are mounted on the carriages. Check with the designer of your sprinkler system to be sure that there's adequate clearance between the tops of the compact shelves and the sprinkler heads. Eighteen inches appears to be an absolute minimum clearance, but larger clearances result in less expensive sprinkler heads.

And be sure to plan for the extra weight. Converting from fixed shelving ranges to compact shelving can significantly increase the weight of fully loaded shelving per square feet, and if you don't plan in advance, floors may not be strong enough.

The weight of compact shelving can also cause floors to bend. The official name for this in building design is *deflection*. If your floors bend, your compact shelving will want to roll downhill to the lowest point, probably halfway between support columns.

For all of these technical reasons, you need to talk with technical reps of compact shelving manufacturers and with your structural engineers if you are considering a compact shelving installation.

Because compact shelving involves constantly relocating aisles, lighting for compact shelving consists of strip lighting fixtures installed end-to-end, perpendicularly to the shelving aisles. No matter which aisle is opened, lights will be located above the open aisle.

III. ALTERNATIVES TO STEEL CANTILEVER SHELVING

A. Shelving with End-Supported Shelves

One great feature of cantilever-style shelving is that the weight of the books holds everything tightly together. The books on individual shelves maintain the tightness of the joint between the flat surfaces and ends of the shelves, and in turn the weight of the books on the assembled shelf units keeps the connection between the shelves and the support columns tight. If components of the shelving shift, nothing falls down.

By contrast, in cheap shelving units, the individual shelves are often supported by the end panels. The shelf ends rest on pegs or clips extending from the end panels, or the shelves are slipped into slots in the end panels. In either case, if the end panel shifts a half inch or so, the end of a shelf may no longer be supported, and the shelf can simply fall.

> Fred once broke a rib when a handful of heavily loaded shelves in a cheap shelving unit fell on him, so he knows whereof he complains.

Some shelving with end-supported shelves uses metal tracks mounted vertically on the end panels, with metal clips that snap into holes in the tracks. On the better shelving of this type, the tracks are inset into the end panels, but on really cheap shelving, the tracks may be simply screwed to the surfaces of the end panels. As a result, books can catch on the tracks as the books are slid in and out of the shelving, tearing the bindings or dust jackets.

Steel shelving units with slide-in shelves are sometimes made of metal scarcely thicker than tin-can metal.

> Fred once inherited a children's department with shelving of this quality, and it would collapse without even being touched. Nothing is more fun than being in the library after hours and hearing unexpected crashing in the next aisle.

Although some physically attractive shelving is made with end-supported shelves, particularly shelving with heavy wooden end panels and painted steel shelves, we think it's a poor choice, even though it looks more attractive than cantilever shelving. (We see it most often in school libraries and in very small public libraries, where we suspect librarians may not have much input on decisions.)

B. Wood Shelving

Although steel end panels are available for cantilever shelving, most libraries have ornamental wooden end panels for use in public areas. This gives the libraries the strength and effectiveness of cantilever shelving with the attractiveness of wood.

Shelving made completely of wood seems to be a different matter. The libraries of the nineteenth century had access to first-growth timber, but modern wood is a less sturdy product.

> Fred once worked with a library that had wooden shelves that tended to sag. Every few months, the library would unload sagging shelves, flip individual shelves over so that they humped rather than sagged, and then reload them.

Good wooden shelving is also expensive, far more expensive than cantilever shelving.

Cheap wooden shelving may consist of chipboard covered with vinyl paper with wood-grain patterns. The problem is that chipboard varies from fairly durable to material that breaks as easily as soda crackers.

Our personal feelings are that wooden shelving is a bad idea.

C. Non-Library Shelving

Because good shelving is expensive, some libraries have experimented with other kinds, such as retail shelving, that are not designed for book storage. Most of these experiments are pretty awful.

Fred worked with one library that had shelving designed for use in hardware stores. The units were only about five feet high, they had no ends to keep books from falling over, and the shelves stepped inward as they moved up. As a result, the library could hold only about two-thirds of the books that could have been held by standard 84-inch shelving, and because the individual units had no ends, books were shelved in endlessly long rows, with bookends only at the end of each row of shelving units. Since a row of units was about thirty feet long, that meant a great deal of running back and forth by library users hunting for books.

The easy rule is, never purchase shelving not specifically designed for books.

IV. SHELVING PLACEMENT

A. All Library Floors Need to Be Strong Enough for Books

Floor strength is vital and non-negotiable. Regardless of initial intent, libraries need to be able to store books anywhere they want, and buildings must be compatible with retrospective rearrangement.

Floor loading capacity is a major problem with repurposing non-library spaces. With the exception of slab-on-grade floors, few non-library spaces can hold the weight of books. See chapter 7 on "Converting Non-Library Spaces to Public Libraries."

> In the case of one Illinois public library, the architect ignored the program's requirement that all floors be strong enough to carry the weight of books. When the time came to add additional shelving, the library had a structural engineer check the floors, and only those areas designated for books on opening day were strong enough. As a result, the library had to reengineer about half of its floor area, a tremendous waste of money.

B. Be Careful with Perimeter Shelving

Historic libraries often have walls lined with books. For reading rooms in great university libraries or the front rooms of Carnegie-era libraries, the effect is scholarly and elegant.

But perimeter shelving causes problems.

First, if a room has perimeter shelving, all adjacent reading tables need to be arranged with the ends that have no chairs facing the shelving. If the table sides with chairs face the shelving, readers will push their chairs back and block access to the shelving. This appears to be a particular problem in historic public library buildings. Historic university library reading rooms appear to more often have rows of tables running perpendicular to the perimeter shelving.

A second problem with perimeter shelving is that it has historically been installed on walls beneath highly set windows. In the days when windows in libraries were intended primarily to bring in daylight, this was a great idea, but in many modern libraries users want to see the outside world while they work.

Another problem with perimeter shelving is that architects are tempted to set up perimeter soffits, often with recessed downlights and sometimes with the undersides of the soffits painted dark colors. The result is spotty light on the books located on the perimeter shelving. (When your architects mention perimeter soffits, assure them that you want crown molding instead. It's far more elegant, and it doesn't screw up your lighting.)

All in all, perimeter shelving belongs in historic reading rooms, but it's not a great idea in modern libraries.

C. Ranges of Shelves Belong in Parallel Rows

A handful of libraries have arranged shelving in radiating rows, something like the spokes of a wheel. This appears to have been done mainly because architects selected non-rectangular interior spaces as a design concept.

The results of this approach range from disastrous to merely an extremely serious annoyance.

If ranges of shelving are not parallel, space is inevitably wasted, with aisles wider than necessary as they radiate outward. Sometimes the situation is so extreme that partial ranges are tucked into the widest spaces between shelves.

A major university library in Illinois has circular stack towers. In an attempt to make better use of the spaces, the spoke-like stack ranges consist of alternating full ranges, 1/3 ranges, 2/3 ranges, 1/3 ranges, and then full ranges again. Even then, a lot of space is wasted at the outer ends of the ranges, and the aisles in the inner ends are too narrow to comply with ADA requirements.

Other libraries attempting to fit stacks into circular spaces have provided breaks resulting in aisles that jog every few shelving units. This limits visibility and complicates the provision of continuous call numbers.

The basic rule is that purposely creating non-rectangular spaces for shelving is a really dumbass idea. If people on your project bring up the idea, deal with them rapidly and severely.

D. Absolutely No Dead-End Stack Aisles

One serious mistake libraries make when space is tight is to create dead-end stack aisles. Dead-end aisles seem to occur when libraries are out of space and decide to fill the gaps between the ends of shelving ranges and walls by adding one more shelving unit to each range.

The problem with dead-end aisles is that users can be trapped at the ends of aisles. Unless the aisles are at least four feet wide, users who are blocked in aisles by other users have to ask the other users to vacate the aisles so they can get out. Even with really wide aisles, squeezing past another user is embarrassing.

To envision the problems caused by dead-end aisles, imagine a fifteen-year-old girl at the dead end of an aisle with her only way out blocked by an older man who appears to be only pretending to look at books. Instead of slipping away into an adjacent aisle, she's left with the option of waiting him out, forcing her way past him, or screaming. All of which are uncomfortable choices in a creepy situation.

If you make every other aisle a dead-end aisle, the girl can at least slip into an adjacent aisle. But that's a far less happy choice than having two available aisles, and it gives the creepy guy an opportunity to simply step into the next aisle. The right thing to do is to have no dead-end aisles whatsoever.

E. Aisles Oriented for Best Practical Staff Oversight

Staff oversight of shelving areas can be improved by orienting shelving so that the staff at service desks have the best possible view down shelving aisles.

The usual way is to place shelving so that the end panels face service desks. It's a lot easier for staff members at service desks to walk back and forth a few feet, looking down all of the shelving aisles, than to walk the entire length of a block of shelving to see into each aisle.

Some libraries have set up blocks of shelving on the diagonal to improve staff oversight. This seems to work well, although it requires a little more floor space. Aisles must be parallel.

An extraordinarily dreadful idea that occasionally reemerges is radiating shelving aisles laid out like the spokes of a wheel, with a service desk located where the aisles converge. See the section above on the importance of parallel shelving units.

F. Electrical Outlets Everywhere

Except for major book stacks, which are intended to remain unchanged for generations, shelving areas need recessed electrical outlets, ideally in flush-topped floor boxes. Libraries are always moving stuff around, and what is a shelving area today may suddenly become a reading or computer area tomorrow. Retrofitting the necessary electrical outlets is never as satisfactory, since the usual way is to core drill through the floor slab, and the result is an outlet raised at least a quarter of an inch above the floor slab. If the floor is slab-on-grade construction, things are even worse, since trenching through concrete slabs to retrofit electrical conduit is a major fiscal undertaking.

Some libraries install light fixtures mounted directly on shelving units. If power isn't available through the floors, the only other source is unsightly electrical conduit running up to the ceiling.

G. Unbroken Call Number Ranges

When a user comes to the end of a shelving range, and the last call number is somewhere in the middle of the Dewey or LC call number range, it should be obvious where the call number sequence continues.

The need for simplicity is one of a large number of major arguments against locating shelving in a number of small spaces.

> We saw a proposed architectural plan for a small college library that divided the collection among many dozens of separate small rooms, not out of necessity but because the architect liked having many dozens of separate small rooms. And all the rooms were to have opaque walls. This is a spectacularly stupid idea.

Continuity of call numbers is one of the problems that emerges when shelving ranges are set at right angles to each other. How things continue from one range to the next can be mysterious. When ranges of shelving are set up in parallel rows, it's tempting to have the rows end not by a wall, but instead to have an additional single-sided range flat against the wall, but libraries that arrange things this way have to be sure that the contents of the extra range are clear to users.

Obviously, call number ranges cannot be continuous in libraries with stack decks. Ideally, numbers would start at the top deck and work down to the bottom, but with huge collections this is often impossible due to the cost of rearranging large collections. While major segments have continuous call numbers, these segments are not always in order.

Occasionally, expanded libraries will have historic library rooms with odd bits and pieces of shelving. One solution is to use these rooms for whatever sections of the collection will fit, possibly new books, current magazines, or some other inherently small collection. The other approach, of course, is to use relatively small historic rooms exclusively for seating rather than shelving.

H. Lighting Stack Aisles

Permanently mounted lighting works only if shelving is also permanently mounted. Permanent shelving is typical of research libraries, academic libraries, and large public libraries.

Light fixtures can be installed over the aisles in stack units. Typically, these fixtures are installed end-to-end. To prevent the books at the top of shelving units being far more brightly illuminated than those at the bottom, library fixtures are available that distribute the light more evenly. Be sure to review with the manufacturer how much variation in aisle width the fixtures can handle or borrow a light fixture and experiment.

Lights parallel to aisles can also be mounted on shelving ranges. Typically, lights are mounted on alternate ranges of shelving, with arms that stick out from both sides of a range to support rows of lights over both aisles.

One of the best ways to light stack aisles in small or medium-sized libraries is with fluorescent or LED light fixtures installed end-to-end and perpendicularly to the aisles. If the fixtures provide 100 percent uplight, like the ones in this library, users never have to look directly into a bright light source when they are looking at high shelves. The end panels in this library have slat wall inserts for displaying a handful of books cover out.

The designers of this library failed to provide ceiling light fixtures close enough to the side wall to light the last row of books, forcing the library to retrofit a strip fluorescent fixture. (The best way to light shelving of this type is to use strip fixtures running from wall to wall, perpendicularly to the aisles. If the aisles are made wider or narrower, the lighting is still over all the aisles.)

Other lighting schemes presume that aisles may be relocated occasionally. One way to do this is to set up rows of fixtures perpendicular to the book aisles, so that there are always light fixtures over every aisle and aisles can be shifted to make them farther apart or closer together.

Many light fixtures in the book stacks of large libraries have some sort of mechanisms for turning off the lights when no one is in the aisle. You can use:

- Simple manual light switches. These presuppose proper human behavior, something in which automatic switch fanciers may not believe.
- Push buttons that turn lights on, with timers to turn them off again. These are annoying when they go off too soon, forcing users to return to the beginnings of aisles. And if users finish very quickly, they may want to find a way to turn the lights off when they leave.
- Motion sensors. These can be amazingly annoying to users who tend to stand still while looking at books.

By attaching stack lighting on arms extending from shelving, this library made it possible to relocate shelving and maintain the same lighting. Notice the curved brackets attached to the columns. Every other row of shelving needs brackets. (Of course, when the shelving is relocated, there will have to be some place in the floor to plug it in. And changing the width of stack aisles may not work.)

- Pressure sensors in the floors of stack aisles. This approach offers the advantages of having lights always go out as soon as users leave the aisles, combined with *never* having lights go off when users are in the aisles. It seems to be the best of the currently available options.

Cross aisles will need to have lights on all the time, in order to (among other things) not plunge stacks into annoying darkness.

We think that automatic switching of lighting on the shelving of smaller libraries can be a very poor idea, especially if the automatic switching turns everything off rather than reducing the lighting level to perhaps half of regular levels.

The selection of light levels is always a battle between those who want to use libraries for reading and those who are concerned primarily with energy savings.

Designers sometimes forget that light needs to fall on the spines of books (where the titles and call numbers are located) rather than on the tops (where the cut edges of pages seldom require bright light).

Light falling on the spines of books (as measured pointing outwards, horizontally to the floor) shouldn't ever be less than about 20 foot-candles on the bottom rows. Vertical light, for users checking the contents of books, should be at least 50 foot-candles.

I. Stack Aisle Widths

As indicated in the introduction to this chapter, selecting stack aisle width is one of the single most important decisions in planning library buildings.

Because selected aisle width can have a strong impact on column spacing, libraries need to designate aisle width during the programming phases of their projects. Basically, the center-to-center distance between building support columns needs to be a multiple of the center-to-center distance between book shelving columns. If this is not done, building support columns end up in the middle of aisles.

Accessibility requirements include minimum legal aisle widths. The ADA requires minimum widths of 36 inches and recommends 42 inches. Individual states, however, may require wider aisles.

These shelving units in a European library have unusually wide aisles, empty bottom shelves, and reasonably low top shelves, making user access impressively easy. (As a result, of course, the shelving holds a lot fewer books per square foot.)

Aisles are measured at their narrowest points. Sometimes this is between the end panels at the end of ranges, and sometimes it's where books stick out into the aisle. At any rate, even if your steel shelving is all perfectly legal, your effective aisle width may not be acceptable.

It's also difficult to lay out aisles so exactly that they are genuinely parallel. If you're aiming at 36-inch aisles, one may end up 36½ inches wide while the next one is 35½ inches wide. Being legal on the average is not enough, since every individual aisle will need to be legal.

The moral is to never crowd minimum standards. If your minimum legal width is 36 inches and space is tight, you'll probably need 38 or 39 inches to stay out of trouble. But that's still pretty narrow.

J. Cross Aisles

Since most aisles are too narrow for users to pass each other, all shelving arrangements need cross aisles. The main decision is how many connected shelves a library should have before a cross aisle becomes necessary. If a first user needs access to a book and the aisle is blocked by a second user, the first user needs to circumnavigate the second user and come in from the opposite end of the aisle. Obviously, aisle segments need to be short enough so that third users aren't involved.

Our experience in public libraries has been that a cross aisle after every seven attached shelving units is about right. Small college libraries will probably do all right with about the same spacing.

The number of cross aisles required in large academic libraries may be fewer. Because circumstances can vary widely, the best approach may be to hang out in your current book stacks for a while to get an idea of how frequently users find their way blocked by other users.

Cross aisles need to be at least four feet wide, and you may want wider aisles to make access comfortable for users in wheelchairs.

K. Seismic Issues

Most double-faced shelving simply sits on the floor, but in areas with seismic activity some kind of stabilization is required. From the point of view of mechanical advantage, hanging onto the tops of the posts makes vastly better sense than bolting the feet of shelving units to the floor.

Protecting book stacks from tipping over during earthquakes is vital but beyond the scope of this book. Talk with your architects, engineers, and shelving suppliers.

L. Multi-Deck Shelving Supported by Shelving Columns

Many (if not most) early stack units used the vertical columns in the shelving units to hold up more than one level of shelving ranges. Walkways in the upper levels were supported by the columns.

Some early stack units had translucent glass floors to allow light from below to seep up through the glass and illuminate the spines of books in the bottom rows of shelving units. Interestingly, relatively few of these glass floor sections broke, and nineteenth-century stacks with glass floors are still in use.

Many libraries with multi-deck shelving units have retrofitted boards between the walkways and the adjacent bottom shelves. According to popular explanations, this was to (a) prevent books from falling from one level to the level below, (b) combat feelings of acrophobia on the part of users who didn't really want to look down to lower levels right next to where they were standing, and (c) keep guys from trying to look upward through the gaps between walkways and shelves to see up girls' dresses.

Some of the old multi-deck shelving systems we have seen are impressively inaccessible to users with disabilities. They are probably also fire risks, since with open spaces between floors and shelving units, fire could race upwards, and there's no vertical space for sprinkler systems.

The old multi-deck shelving units had narrow aisles, very low ceilings, narrow staircases, and occasional extra-tight places. When these units are removed and the space reused, the result is vastly less shelving per square foot.

Some manufacturers of cantilever steel shelving may still offer multi-deck equipment. In our experience, this kind of equipment tends to be inaccessible to people with disabilities and awkward and a fire hazard. *If you have it, you don't want it. If you don't have it, you* really *don't want it.*

M. Marking the Contents of Shelving Ranges

End panels on shelving ranges need small signs to indicate the contents of the ranges. Traditionally these were holders for 3 × 5-inch cards, although larger holders allow end signs that are easier to read.

Until the coming of attractive computer printer output, libraries had endless problems keeping range content labels up to date and attractive. Libraries were full of labels crudely altered with markers. Some companies merchandized ingenious shelf-marking signs with movable plastic letters, much like Lego bricks.

Today, range markers are easy to maintain. Plastic label holders are available with transparent plastic fronts and slots for computer printout, and keeping things up to date is easy. The main challenge is keeping up with changes.

Labels change because sections of collections do not remain the same forever. New subject areas arise or old subject areas shrink, and both lead to shifting call number ranges.

Over the years, libraries have experimented with a variety of typefaces for range contents indicators, and librarians have learned things in the process. The fonts used in range indicators need to be extremely legible rather than artistic, and the contrast between lettering and background needs to be substantial—basically black lettering on white backgrounds. We know of one library that had signs with artistic script lettering done in dark gray on a light gray background, and users had to peer closely at the signs attempting to make them out. Permanent range indicators (such as the floor mats at the end of the aisles in the Seattle Public Library) seem like a recipe for eventual irrelevance (or forced sign-based weeding).

Overly specific call numbers may also lead to signs that are continually out of date. It doesn't cause problems if libraries shorten the call numbers on signs slightly. Users can easily check a shelf on each side of the end panel to see where the exact call number break actually occurs.

N. Shelving on Casters

Some libraries—particularly children's libraries—use shelving on casters to allow the rearrangement of spaces for programs.

Although this works, it strikes us a desperate measure in the face of the lack of necessary program space.

Among other things, shelving on casters is inherently unstable. It's okay for children's books, which tend to be on low shelving, but imagine the instability of seven-foot-high shelving units on wheels!

V. OTHER TYPES OF STORAGE

A. Flip Bins

Flip bins are useful for extremely slender publications with spines that are difficult to read if the items are shelved like regular books. Some prime candidates are CDs, 33 rpm records, children's picture books, and graded readers in public libraries.

Librarians tell us that the impact of using flip bins on the borrowing of picture books is powerful, but some library staff oppose the idea because the books are more difficult to keep in order and locate. Our feeling is that user enthusiasm (measured in vastly increased lending) trumps staff inconvenience, but not everyone agrees.

Unlike cantilever steel shelving, flip bins do not always have standard dimensions. Your interior designer should be able to help you calculate the capacities and required square footages for a product you select.

Remember that a flip bin can hold only part of its capacity if users are going to flip through the contents of the bin.

B. Spinners

Some libraries store books on spinner racks, which are basically central posts with attached pockets or with additional spinners at the end of extension rods. Although somewhat larger pockets are available, small pockets usually mean rack-sized paperbacks.

Spinner racks may offer a cheerful and less daunting alternative to masses of seven-foot shelving. Spinner racks with transparent plastic pockets also allow users to see the front covers of a lot of paperbacks. Considering that paperback publishers can spend as much on the cover as on the contents, this allows library users to appreciate the art.

The small pockets in spinners may keep paperbacks from falling out as easily as paperbacks on regular shelving.

In general, spinner racks are high-maintenance objects from the point of view of those who put books away. Because the pockets are small, putting a book back in the right place can involve moving a lot of books around forward or backward to create space in the right place.

Because spinner racks have so many pockets, it can be hard for users to figure out the filing order.

Spinner racks can be easy to tip over. (One major library supply firm sold good-looking spinner racks with four plastic spinners on the end of arms that stuck out from the central column. When the spinner racks tipped over, the plastic spinners often broke, frequently enough that the supply firms' catalogs listed replacement plastic spinners. Library basements used to have abandoned spinner racks standards with all of the plastic spinners broken and discarded.)

Enthusiasm for spinner racks seems to come and go. They're probably most commonly used as racks for paperback fiction, where keeping things in proper order may be of less importance to library staff.

Our experience with spinner racks as library directors has not been positive.

C. Atlas Cases

Atlas cases are furniture units designed to store atlases and provide surfaces where atlases can be opened and read. They're important because many atlases will not fit on standard shelving.

Atlas cases are usually intended for users to stand up while consulting atlases. The top of the case will be sloped slightly, with a lip at the bottom to prevent atlases from sliding off while being consulted. Shelves beneath the top have space for storing additional atlases. Some shelves pull out on rollers to make it easier to retrieve atlases.

Some libraries have tried to cope with atlases by creating wide surfaces consisting of aligned shelves on both sides of ranges of double-faced shelving units. This creates a flat space about 24 inches deep and 34 inches wide. Although this technically works, it leaves it up to users to locate the atlases, pull them off the shelving units, and haul them to a nearby flat surface to view them.

Because maps don't lend themselves well to digital substitutes (except for wayfinding), atlas cases will probably remain standard items.

Atlas cases need enough free floor space for users to stand and to pull out shelves.

D. Map Cases

Map cases consist of stacks of large, flat drawers, typically in units consisting of five drawers. Drawers usually have sheets of fabric attached to the back of the drawers and designed to clamp to the inside of the drawer fronts to hold loose maps in place and prevent them from curling up and being caught in the drawers.

Important features of map cases include double-extension suspension systems in drawers so that drawers are relatively easy to pull out. Good-quality map cases will have mechanisms like those in filing cabinets to prevent more than one drawer from being opened at a time and overbalancing the unit. (Being squashed by a map case that tilts and falls is probably an unpleasant fate.)

In some map libraries, cases are stacked so high that users must stand on stools to access maps in the top drawers.

Most map cases available today are made of enameled steel. As with other steel products, libraries are probably better off purchasing all cases in a standard light gray color because they'll go with everything and can be moved from area to area of the library without creating odd patches of unmatched colors.

As with atlas cases, map cases take up a fair amount of room because the drawers have to be pulled fully out for users to retrieve individual maps.

E. Dictionary Stands

Dictionary stands were developed because unabridged dictionaries are too large for ordinary shelving and require flat surfaces for consulting. Most stands are made of wood and are designed for users to consult while standing. Dictionary stands have sloped tops with small ledges at the front to keep dictionaries from sliding off.

The tops of dictionary stands are intended for single dictionaries, but shelves below the top hold additional dictionaries. As long as copies of *Webster's New International Dictionary*, Second Edition, survive, libraries will probably want stands to hold them.

F. Microfilm and Microfiche Cabinets

The future of microforms may be something less than forever, but libraries still have large collections.

Microfilm is still used extensively for newspapers and census records. Fiche is used for journals and other publications.

Microfilm cabinets will store either 16mm or 35mm microfilm. A standard cabinet from a firm like Russ Bassett will hold over 500 rolls of 35mm film, and you can buy an extra cabinet that balances on top of the main cabinet to hold another 200 or so rolls.

Because fiche can be packed so closely together, a fiche cabinet can hold 125,000 individual fiche and may weigh 300 pounds per square foot when fully loaded. If you will be installing a number of fiche cabinets, ask your engineers and the cabinet manufacturer to be sure that your floors will be strong enough to support the cabinets.

Basic requirements for film and fiche cabinets include:

- Ball-bearing double-extension hardware on all drawers.
- Locking mechanisms designed to prevent more than one drawer from being opened at the same time. (Nothing's so much fun as opening too many microfilm cabinet drawers at the same time and having the entire thing fall over on top of you.)
- Powder paint finish in some innocuous color like light gray. (Strangely enough, the same color we recommend for cantilever steel shelving.)
- Label holders on all drawers.

Film and fiche cabinets are available in a variety of sizes, ranging from desktop units to floor-standing units with additional units on top with drawers that pull out like shelves. If your cabinets will be used for local newspapers, you may never actually throw any film away, so plan for expansion.

G. Pamphlet Files

In the days before the Internet, many libraries had large collections of pamphlets—sometimes important pamphlets, but many times pamphlets that were saved just because they came along.

Ordinary vertical file cabinets were a standard way of storing pamphlets.

Except for specialized collections, most pamphlet collections in academic and public libraries probably vanished by about 1990 or 2000. The libraries we know kept only a few things not available on the Internet, such as full-sized road maps.

If you are buying filing cabinets, the traditional requirements remain. Legal-sized cabinets hold larger objects than letter-sized cabinets. Full-suspension cabinets are essential. Five-drawer cabinets hold 25 percent more than four-drawer cabinets without being too tall for most people to use. Ideally, drawer mechanisms will prevent more than one drawer being open at the same time. As with shelving, neutral colors (such as pale gray) work best. If you have different colors of cabinets in different places in your library for purposes of aesthetics, sooner or later you'll have to move them around and end up with groups of cabinets in oddly variegated colors.

H. Tubs for Board Books

Among the books that defy easy storage, probably nothing is much worse than board books for preschoolers. Board books come in a wild variety of shapes and sizes. Some have attached gadgets, such as wheels attached to books about vehicles.

Most public libraries give up and simply store board books in plastic tubs. The effect is usually somewhat chaotic, but collections are often not huge.

I. Display Shelves

1. Low-Density Shelving for Intensive Browsing

While steel cantilever shelving is the standard of the industry, there are circumstances where it's too compact.

A good example is new book shelving in public libraries. Some libraries have used 84-inch steel shelving for new books, and the results have been ugly encounters between users trying to see new books at the same time.

One standard substitute has been wooden A-frame shelving with three or four shelves vertically on each side. The shelves are all at a comfortable height for browsing, and because the shelves all tilt inward, it's easy to arrange books spine out or cover out as crowding permits. Multiple copies of popular titles, for example, are easy to display cover out.

2. Novelty Displays for Children's Books

Children's books lend themselves to novelty display units. Check manufacturers' catalogs and websites.

Our main concern is that it's easy to get carried away, substituting a variety of shelving for standard steel shelving.

VI. HIGH-DENSITY STORAGE

High-density storage is based on warehousing principles, with bins of books lifted by machinery and tucked into high-storage shelving units. Some are lifted by forklift trucks and others by cranes running on tracks.

The great advantage of many high-density storage systems is their use of standard warehousing machinery rather than machinery developed for a vastly smaller library market.

High-density storage is a separate and highly specialized area, one that we regard as beyond the scope of this book. A specialized literature exists, but if your library is planning high-density storage, you will need to visit other libraries to see it in use.

Our main comment is that high-density storage adjacent to main library buildings is infinitely superior to high-density storage in another county. Being able to request a book and have it in your hands in ten or fifteen minutes is a vastly better way to serve library users than making them wait two or three days.

VII. ESTIMATING REQUIRED SPACE FOR COLLECTION STORAGE

Estimating the required space for collection storage is very much a matter of estimating. Needed space depends on aisle width, number of cross aisles, number of shelves vertically, average size of books, and other issues.

For basic information on space estimating for shelving, see chapter 8 on "Programming."

VIII. SNAPPY RULES ON COLLECTION STORAGE

1. Every area of a library needs to be strong enough to bear the weight of books. Flimsy floors are not a good way to save money. Question your architects specifically on this subject, for some have failed to make floors uniformly strong while not informing their clients of the decision.

2. One of the first and most vital decisions in library planning is stack aisle width, because it determines structural column spacing.
3. Don't ever buy cheap shelving. Steel cantilever shelving is the standard of the library world, and if you buy anything flimsier you will end up throwing it out. Or (more likely) wishing you could.
4. High-quality steel shelving can last a century, but it's extremely difficult to repaint. This tells us why bright orange and vivid purple are such seriously bad color choices.
5. No matter how short your library is of space, never (as in NEVER, under penalty of being cornered by a faceless fiend) have book aisles with dead ends.
6. All shelving aisles need indicators listing what's stored in the aisle. This changes frequently, so permanent markings are a dumb idea. Modern location signs have plastic fronts and accept computer printout, which makes things easy to alter.
7. To the intense chagrin of some designers, end panel indicators you can actually read are far more important than indicators that provide aesthetic gratification.
8. Shelving does best in long, continuous ranges. Dividing it up into lots of separate bits and pieces in separate spaces is A Very Seriously Bad Idea.
9. Shelving needs to be in parallel rows. Some libraries have arranged shelving like the spokes of a wheel, and this proved to be an Extraordinarily Wretched Idea.
10. If you arrange shelving around the walls of a room, know how you will prevent people sitting at tables from blocking access to the shelves.
11. It's hard to shelve books in spinners, because there are so many small pockets. Spinners also tend to tip over in the presence of enthusiastic teenagers, who may be uninterested in putting all the spilled books back in order.
12. Cheap wooden shelving tends to sag, resulting in annual flipping. Libraries unload individual shelves, turn them bottom side up, and then reload them. If the end panels on cheap wooden shelving flex, the individual shelves also tend to fall. You will not like cheap wooden shelving.
13. If you're desperate for shelving and can't afford it, look around for libraries that are remodeling and have old shelving to dispose of. If you get it really cheaply, you can replace it without guilt when you have money (and pass it on to another desperate library).
14. We think the right price to pay for shelving that is not steel cantilever shelving is free, but the world is not always a perfect place.
15. Compact shelving places unusual loads on buildings. Your structural engineers will need to consult with the shelving manufacturers.
16. In bygone days, the support columns in cantilever shelving were used to hold additional decks of shelving. If you are pressured to consider something

like this, check on code implications, especially for fire suppression and for accessibility for users with disabilities.
17. Some libraries purchase shelving that is difficult to move and then recarpet by cutting around the shelves and replacing just what's exposed. If you do this, you'll never be able to relocate shelving, because every time you do it you'll expose some unmatched carpet.
18. Know how cantilever steel shelving is specified before ordering any.
19. When as a library user you're trotting along a range of shelves and they end at 327.8, it should be extremely clear where to find 327.9.
20. All book stacks require cross aisles to allow users to bypass each other. We think a cross aisle after about every seven shelving units works out best for heavily-used collections, but your experience may vary.
21. There's always some new oddball collection format you'll want to store in your library. Hope for stuff that fits on standard bookshelves.
22. Cantilever steel shelving is an add-on system, and you can count on having to add on some day. Generally, it's not really practical to purchase lots of attic stock. When the time comes to match shelving, you will appreciate having shelving that's made in the United States and can be matched.
23. Canopies are closed tops for shelving units. They're great on low shelving units, where they can be used for displays, but on high shelving the main thing they do is make things darker.
24. Shelves supported by clips on the end panels, supported by pins sticking out of end panels, or slipped into slots in the end panels, have a tendency to fall, dumping books on the place (or persons) beneath. Don't depend on end panels to support your shelves.
25. If the end panels on cheap shelving flex, the individual shelves tend to fall. You will not like cheap shelving.

18

Public Service Desks

I. INTRODUCTION

Functional service desks are a vital aspect of library design. Many staff members assigned to public duties spend the majority of their time at service desks, and badly designed desks can be a source of serious problems.

One of the most serious problems with service desks is the temptation to let monumentality replace functionality. Too many service desks make architectural statements at the expense of practicality.

Service desks need to be flexible, because library functions constantly change. It's tempting to assume that we've been changing for decades, but now all of that's over, and we know where we're headed. Unfortunately, we don't know where we're headed, and if we can't modify our service desks we're likely to be out of date in a matter of months.

Planning new service desks needs to involve the library staff members who spend their lives working behind them.

It also needs to involve library administrators, who know where libraries are headed.

Particularly in the case of service desks, planning needs to involve the library consultants who develop building programs, because they have long experience working in libraries. (We constantly warn against hiring consultants with little or no experience working in libraries. This is another reason to hire consultants who are librarians with long personal experience in the field.)

Architects are important contributors, but because almost no architects have any personal experience working in libraries, their input may be less valuable.

One problem with service desk design is the ability of library employees to develop workarounds when faced with badly designed service desks. When the time comes to design new desks, staff may want to repeat workarounds rather than start from scratch.

II. TYPICAL FUNCTIONS OF PUBLIC SERVICE DESKS

Libraries use public service desks for many fundamental functions. Among these are

- Lending, including checking books in and out, issuing borrowers' cards, collecting charges for late books, and other familiar functions*
- Reference (answering factual questions)
- Reader guidance (advice on selecting fiction)
- Assistance with collection access
- Computer assistance
- Concierge services[†]
- Supervision of spaces
- Entrance and exit control (including checking user identification in limited-access libraries)

> Private university libraries often have staffed desks to control access to buildings.

---

*Throughout this book, we have used the term *lending* rather than *circulation* for situations where users borrow library materials. In architecture, circulation means the movement of people through spaces. When librarians use the term circulation to mean lending books, confusion eventually occurs.

[†] Some libraries have desks where staff members greet arriving library users, provide directions to various parts of the building, and provide other front-line assistance. Although some libraries call these *information* desks, we think that the terms *concierge* or *orientation* are less likely to be confused with *reference*.

- Access to sequestered collections (including deliveries from remote storage)
- Provision of held books, including interlibrary loan items
- Telephone switchboards
- Registration for library events
- Staff workspaces

In small libraries, all of these services may be provided from a single desk for efficient use of staff, while large libraries may have a number of service desks. In almost all cases, however, some of the functions listed above will be combined in single desks.

The functions of service desks are frequently in flux. Traditional reference is replaced by computer assistance, sometimes combining desks in the process. Lending desks shrink as self-check workstations multiply. Concierge desks are created, shifting duties from lending, or concierge desks are abandoned and their functions returned to lending. Reference and reader guidance functions are separated or combined. Staff members in some libraries are cross-trained, resulting in fewer and less specialized desks, while staff members in other libraries develop greater specializations, resulting in more desks.

All of these changes make the monumental, inflexible desks that many designers love an increasingly bad idea. Although designers find them uninteresting, modular desks that can be expanded, shrunk, rearranged, and relocated are probably least likely to become obsolete long before they wear out.

Although service desks are fairly simple in basic concept, they tend to share fairly standard problems. Many of these problems are due to designers seeking architectural monuments, placing desks in inappropriate locations, or just failing to understand what goes on in libraries.

The basic rules when undertaking the design of service desks are:

- The key people in desk design are library staff members and library building consultants (but only if the consultants are librarians and not architects).
- A service desk is a service desk, not an architectural monument.
- While the architects or interior designers may recommend the exterior appearance of a service desk, the physical configuration and interior contents of a desk are strictly up to the librarians involved.
- Desks require detailed program statements. Be sure the statements are written before anyone starts design work.
- The most functional desks are simple rectangles.
- Be sure that desks comply with accessibility codes.

- All desks need access to electrical power and data. If your building has power and data everywhere, relocating desks will not involve major surgery.
- All desks need two ways out. It's essential that staff members cannot be trapped behind service desks.
- The functions of service desks constantly change, and flexibility is important. Modular desks installed on top of carpet are far easier to rearrange and move. Architectural details (such as matching soffits or special lighting) that limit relocation are a mistake.
- When in doubt about the proportions of a proposed service desk, build a simple mock-up from corrugated cardboard and try it out.
- Stress to your designers (and cabinetmakers, if you hire them directly) that service desks are more like modular furniture than kitchen counters.

Taking time to make exhaustive lists of the equipment and features required for service desks is a central part of library space planning.

III. PLACEMENT OF PUBLIC SERVICE DESKS

In general, public service desks function best when they face users entering the library or a department of the library. Staff members at such desks are best positioned to greet users and answer questions.

- The ideal physical arrangement for an area with a service desk is to place the entrance to the area in the broad side of a wall, with the desk set back from the entrance, facing the entrance.

Many libraries have T-shaped circulation pathways in such spaces. A pathway from the entrance leads to the desk, and a cross pathway running the length of the space to the right and left of the service desk provides access to all the areas in the room. If access to all elements in the space is provided by the two pathways, the result is basically a "main street" concept.

One downside of this layout is that it may be more difficult to provide an essential staff workspace immediately behind the desk. This can be of significance with lending desks, which frequently need space for a number of features and staff.

Entering large public service areas from their narrow ends compromises effective functions.

- Unfortunately, some libraries have desks that require users to make 180-degree turns after they enter a library room in order to see the staff, who are basically hiding behind people entering the room.

No one likes this sort of thing.

> Walking into a library, only to find that the staff are hiding behind you, may not be seriously creepy or annoying, but it's still far from ideal.

- In any library open to the general public, each architecturally separate area (such as a floor or a very large reading room) will benefit strongly from the presence of a service desk that can also provide supervision.

Part of the design effort for a building is to make sure that each service desk is not only conveniently located for its assigned function, but also contributes to the oversight of the entire library. For example, a three-story public library might have a lending desk on the entry floor, a children's desk on the second floor, and an adult desk on the top floor.

Glass walls greatly improve the ability of service desks to supervise areas. All study rooms need glass walls, but meeting rooms can also have windows facing service desks.

"Glass walls" means glass walls, not opaque walls with small windows. We've had a number of architects battle against glass walls in study rooms, but as librarians we know that glass walls are just fine. (Codes require a transverse muntin with glass walls. This is easy to provide, but we've had architects contend that glass walls are banned by codes, when in reality all that the codes require is a crossbeam. Architects shouldn't try to deceive their clients.)

- Because desks are extremely expensive to staff, planning for the most effective and efficient placement of service desks is extremely important.
- If there are two desks on a floor, the one serving the greater number of users will ideally be closest to the point where people arrive on that floor.
- All public nonemergency exits need to be staffed, whether or not they have book theft-detection systems. Much of the challenge of service desk placement

in libraries lies in making sure that desks provide exit control in addition to meeting other needs.
- If you have more than one service desk on a floor, it's great for safety if the staff members of the two desks can see each other.

IV. ESSENTIAL FEATURES OF PUBLIC SERVICE DESKS

Although service desks have a variety of functions, they all have similar needs.

- All service desks perform two essential functions—provision of service to the public and provision of staff oversight of public areas of the library. All desk planning needs to keep these dual functions in mind.
- In many libraries, service desks also serve as staff workstations, where staff can work on projects between users. This can be as simple as having staff at a lending desk check materials back in between users. But in a small library, staff may even do cataloging or processing at a lending desk. The more that service desks multiply and become specialized, single-purpose devices, the more that libraries may find them unaffordable because the desks do not permit the essential multitasking that takes place in almost all libraries.
- All service desks need two ways out, in addition to any door to a back room. You don't want any of your staff member trapped behind a desk, and if they have to step out from behind a desk, you want them to have a direct route. If the staff members at a lending desk are responsible for the library's security gates, they need to be able to get to the gates quickly.
- It should be clear to library users which areas of service desks are for staff only, and there should be no need for users to be behind desks. Unfortunately, vast numbers of poorly designed desks make it impossible to separate staff areas from user areas. Traditionally, many libraries have had problems with users who wander behind service desks, and it should be immediately apparent to users approaching desks which areas are for staff only. In some older libraries, materials intended for public access were directly behind desks. For example, book stacks were reached by walking through openings in lending desks. (In defense of designers of a century ago, some of these stacks were originally intended to be closed stacks but were converted to open stacks for reasons of staff economy.) For whatever reason, if users routinely walk through lending desks to get to book stacks, special attention needs to be paid to security. Books sequestered behind desks may need special storage. (Some libraries have locked them in drawers or stored them in nearby staff workrooms.) Cash drawers can also present problems. Although historic accidents cannot always be corrected without major surgery, there is no excuse for this kind of ambiguity or intersecting pathways in a modern library.

- Service desks should never be designed in ways that encourage library users to take shortcuts behind or through desks. Often a quick check of proposed floor plans will show where this will be a problem.

> One library Fred worked on had a desk designed in such a way that users could save 40 or 50 feet of walking by cutting through the staff area of the desk. In addition, the alluring walkway through the desk had a pedestal electrical outlet in the middle of the shortcut. Not only did users routinely cut through the desk, but they routinely took headers when they tripped over the pedestal. In desperation, the library placed a table over the outlet, forcing both staff and users to detour.

- Small swinging doors can help define staff areas, but they can lead to problems. If your library has swinging doors in desks, be sure that you provide latches to hold the doors open. Once your regular users understand the situation with the new desk, they're much less likely to wander in, and you can skip the nuisance of the doors. Swinging doors need to be designed to swing in both directions, so that staff members can always push their way through. Swinging doors in desks always need to consist of single panels hinged on one side rather than double panels with hinges on both sides. Trying to push a book cart through double doors is pretty much impossible without bashing the doors, since the operation requires three hands. The architect in one library Fred worked with installed double doors of this type at the new lending desk, and the library ripped them out in the first month of operations. Since you may eventually decide to eliminate your swinging doors, be sure they are designed so there are no unsightly unfinished areas revealed when the doors are removed.
- Be sure that your service desks can accommodate a wide variety of electronic equipment. Because we have no idea what's coming in the next twenty years, the best we can do is provide wide-open spaces and outstanding wire management. Be sure desktops are sufficiently deep (between the user and the staff member) to house any necessary equipment. At the least, all desks will require space for telephones, keyboards, and computer monitors, and you may need a variety of other equipment. Desks need interior raceways for both 110-volt wiring and data wiring. Remember that the two types of wiring cannot share the same trough. Both for security and for reliability and speed of transmission, you cannot assume wireless transmission for such confidential internal functions as lending, user databases, and catalog maintenance. All desktops will need grommets—openings where wires can pass through the top of the desk to wire management troughs beneath. Be

sure your desktop material allows you to add more of these in years to come. For libraries that do not use thin client units, there needs to be space under desktops for computers. Metal racks for holding computers can be bolted to the undersides of the desks, protecting the computers from being kicked or bumped. It's amazing how designers of desks can be aware of the incredible changes in libraries in the past twenty years but assume that there will be no more changes in the coming twenty.

> An insect frozen in amber can be an object of art, but an obsolete service desk built for the ages is not.

- Almost all service desks need built-in storage. The specific provisions for storage should be worked out by library staffs, assisted by their consultants (if the consultants are librarians). All drawers should have double-extension ball-bearing hardware. Double-extension hardware keeps drawers from wobbling from side to side, and it allows them to be pulled all the way out. (Beware of cheap double-extension hardware without ball bearings, because dragging the drawers open and shut will be a pain.) The interiors of drawers and cabinets should be light-colored, so that staff can find things.

> Ornamental black interiors can turn ordinary storage drawers into mysterious, stygian pits full of obscure objects.

- Lending desks in public libraries often have cash drawers. Some ingenuity may be required to make sure that users cannot reach over desks and into cash drawers. Possibilities include latches that are located under cash drawers and cash drawers in separate pieces of furniture behind lending desks. A cash drawer could probably be equipped with a bell that rings whenever it is opened, but it might not be the most popular feature in the library. All cash drawers need ball-bearing, double-extension hardware. Storage cabinets often work best with pull-out shelves in the style of kitchen cabinets. Be sure they also have ball-bearing, double-extension hardware.
- Staff members need knee room. This is essential in desks at seated height, but some staff members may want to sit on high stools at standing-height desks, and they need somewhere to put their knees.

- The fronts of service desks need toe kicks to make it more comfortable both for users to stand close to the desks and to avoid scuffing the fronts of the desks. Toe kicks are recesses in desk fronts to allow people to stand closer to the desks by sliding their toes under the front edge of the desk. Sometimes toe kicks are omitted to give desks a more finished look, but the bottom edges of the desks are soon battered and embellished with black marks from rubber shoes. And the absence of toe kicks will make users surprisingly uncomfortable.
- The tops of service desks need to be a lightish color, never either black or white.
- There are significant advantages to modular service desks, which allow libraries to rearrange and relocate desks as changing needs dictate. The downside of modular design is that desks may be less aesthetically interesting. As a result of this, despite some very significant advantages to modular desks, designers are not fond of them, and very few libraries have them. This is one of many areas where you may have to (always exhibiting the patient good nature for which librarians are inevitably known) stomp firmly on your architects.
- Service desks need to be made of suitably durable materials. See the discussions later in this chapter.
- Many service desks have raised front sections, barricades designed to conceal equipment and materials on top of the desk from library users. Although desks of this type have some advantages, they also cause significant problems.
- Some service desks require a lot of equipment at each staff workstation. For example, each staff workstation at a lending desk may require desktop space for a computer monitor, mouse and mouse pad, caddy with miscellaneous office supplies, credit card reader, receipt printer, and so on, plus space for books being checked in and out. If books are checked in at the workstation, it may require floor space for a bin full of books to be checked in, a shelving cart of books checked in, and so on. And inside the desk may be desensitizing equipment for a theft control system, a computer box on a hanger, and perhaps a bin of security boxes for audiovisual items. This is a great time to enumerate in your building program everything needed at each workstation and then create a full-sized model of the desk to be sure everything will fit.
- Service desks may also require shared equipment. A number of staff lending workstations in a public library, for example, may share a single cash register or a single printer.
- Some service desks, particularly reference desks, have chairs where users can sit while talking with library staff. Some library staff members are enthusiastic about seats for users, while others (perhaps remembering some unusually adhesive conversationalists) would rather skip chairs for users. On the other hand, at reference desks where library staff are seated, user chairs allow library staff to look users in the eye rather than look awkwardly up at them.

Planning for user seats requires only a little extra floor space, so it's probably worth doing. If user seats turn out to be a mistake, you can simply remove them. Lending desks are another matter. We've seen a couple of libraries where chairs were provided at lending desks for users to sit while being served. The effect was very civilized, but the chairs appeared to be little used. The implication was that people borrowing books want to complete the transaction and get on with things.

V. TESTING PROPOSED PUBLIC SERVICE DESKS

A. Evaluating Schematic Designs

When your architect brings schematic designs for you to evaluate, here are some things you can look for in service desks. Even a simple floor plan gives you many opportunities to verify functions.

- Evaluate sight lines. What areas of the library are invisible to staff members at service desks? How could you rearrange shelving, convert opaque walls to transparent walls, or make other changes to improve sight lines? Are service desks immediately visible to users entering major areas of the building? Some designers are tempted to arrange shelving like the spokes of a wheel, radiating outwards from a central service desk, so that a staff member seated at the desk has simultaneous views of all aisles. Although it sounds tempting, this concept has led to extraordinarily bad space utilization, extreme difficulty in figuring out call number sequences, poor lighting, and many other serious problems. Say "no" the first time you hear this idea suggested.

> Good shelving is strictly parallel shelving.

- Make sure that the plans take maximum advantage of your limited number of staffed service points. If you have three service desks and two are immediately adjacent to each other, you may be wasting oversight opportunities.
- Make sure that columns do not block access to any service desk. A library Fred visited has a column so close to the lending desk that it essentially divides the desk into two separate desks.
- Make sure service desks that will be staffed at all times are close to all security gates. The people planning or governing your library may not want to face the fact that *security gates are worthless if not closely supervised*. But that's

the way it is. In many libraries, this supervision is provided by the main lending desk. If other desks—such as concierge desks—are proposed for this purpose, ask yourself whether you can count on always having enough money to staff them. Even if you do not plan to have security gates when your library opens, times may change, and you may need them later. See chapter 30 on "Security" for information on space and staffing requirements of security gates.

B. Using Trial Models of Desks

Because service desks are expensive and have many ergonomic implications, always make a dummy desk out of old corrugated cardboard if you have even the slightest doubt about the functionality of a proposed design.

If a column will be located near the desk, dummy it up as well, to see how it affects the ability of people to move around it.

With a dummy desk, you can verify:

- **The adequacy of the space for staff members**
  Remember to allow for simultaneous activities, such as one staff member pushing a book truck behind a desk while a second staff member is helping users. If a staff member pulls a return bin over to a workstation in order to check books in and place them on a shelving cart, will everything fit? (Some desks don't even have walking space, let alone space for bins and carts.)

- **Adequacy of desktop space**
  Will there be physical space for all of the objects on the desktop?

- **The adequacy of user space**
  When users stand at the desk, is there space for other users to pass behind them? (Don't forget that if you decide to add magnetic security gates, they will stick out about six feet into the space inside the exit doors.)

- **Collision courses for users**
  For example, will users returning books to book return slots get in the way of users waiting to check books out? This is a depressingly common problem in lending desk design.

- **Ergonomic arrangement of desk features**
  Will the desk allow staff to access checkout workstations, cash drawers, telephones, and other features comfortably? Will the desk make it easier or harder for staff to keep an eye on nearby areas of the library?

- **Suitability of height**
  For example, most standing-height desks are about forty inches high, but your staff may have different wishes. (But beware of politically powerful staff members who are unusually short or tall.)

- **Whether the desk should be in a different place**
  Although this kind of design testing sounds like overkill, it can be an essential step in the process of designing service desks. Some proposed service desk designs simply won't work, and it's hard to convince everyone of this fact without actually trying things out.

Once a service desk is constructed, it may be a generation or more before your library can justify the cost of major alteration or even replacement. As with all planning, the time to check everything out is before the big expenditures begin.

VI. TYPES OF PUBLIC SERVICE DESKS

A. Lending Desks

Lending desks are found in almost all libraries, with the exception of some special libraries or research libraries that do not lend any materials. In a small library, lending is often only one of the many functions provided by an all-purpose public service desk.

Because lending desks can be focal points of mass movements of materials, they require far more planning than other kinds of desks for functional layouts and for position in relation to such building functions as public entrances, delivery entrances, sorting operations, and so on.

1. Lending Desk Functions

The major functions of lending desks include:

- **Checking library materials out**
  This is the most basic function of lending desks. Virtually every library lends materials and requires some sort of service point where lending can take place.

- **Self-check workstations**
  In public libraries in particular, self-check workstations are increasingly common. As long as a library continues to offer staffed checkout stations for users who need extra assistance or prefer the social interaction with library

staff, self-check seems to be a very workable option. Because lending desk staff members provide exit control in many libraries, a conversion to 100 percent self-check has major implications for controlling exits. If there are no lending desk staff present, who will monitor the security gates? Remember that staff members need to be within fifteen feet or so of security gates, a fact ignored by many designers. Self-check workstations require sufficient elbowroom for users to line up, as well as access to both 110-volt and data service.

- **Checking library materials back in**
  In some libraries, materials are checked in at lending desks, while in other libraries they are checked in by staff members in lending workrooms or by automated equipment. Where your library will check books in has major implications for the design of lending work areas. Wherever items are checked in, you will need floor space for bins of materials waiting to be checked in and for carts where materials are placed once checked in. In the case of automated equipment—such as RFID (radio-frequency identification) systems with conveyors—you will need space for return slots and transport mechanisms. Automated check-in systems can move slowly, and if library users are expected to return their items personally, backups can develop when people are returning large numbers of items, such as children's picture books. Be sure that your building layout and handling system are compatible with the addition of extra return slots, or that you have an alternative non-mechanized return system available. The advantage of checking materials back into the library in a separate room is primarily one of reducing the size of the lending desk and reducing the associated clutter of book bins full of books to be checked in, book carts for materials just checked in, paperwork on delinquent loans, and so on. If your library telephones users who have materials waiting for them to pick up, doing so in a workroom may assist in maintaining user privacy. The major disadvantage of processing returned items in a back room is the loss of staffing efficiency. One of the basic characteristics of lending is the somewhat unpredictable workload. Although libraries know when to expect the load to be generally heavy or light, things are never really consistent. At one moment, there will be twenty people waiting to check items out, and all the lending clerks racing to keep up. But ten minutes later there may be no users at all. If multiple functions are carried out at the lending desk, employees always have something to do between users. But if staff members have absolutely nothing to do except check materials out, they'll just sit around between users, waiting for the next one to turn up. And cost your library money. Some libraries have provided two separate lending desks, one for checkout and a second for check-in. Our impression is that these concepts made inefficient use of staff and were sometimes abandoned.

- **Greeting library users**
  A primary function of many lending desks is greeting people who arrive at the library. This is also why hiring friendly lending staff members is so important. One of the extremely negative aspects of completely self-service lending is the loss of this important social contact.

  Sooner or later, almost every library hires a lending staff member who shouldn't be inflicted on library users. Library users can remember bad experiences with this sort of turkey for decades. Transferring ill-tempered staff members to technical services to get them away from library users is tempting but is nevertheless a Seriously Bad Idea compared to Not Hiring Them in the First Place.

- **Issuing borrowers' cards**
  Public libraries typically issue borrowers' cards at their lending desks, while other libraries will probably rely on academic or corporate IDs. Libraries may also issue special cards for computer use or other activities. Some academic libraries issue campus IDs at the library, both centralizing services and bringing all new students into the library at least once.

- **Supervising the entrance to the library or department**
  Most lending desks are responsible for overseeing a portion of the library, including in particular the entrance to the building.

> As noted many times in this book (because architects keep ignoring the problem, and we hope that repetition will help), security gates need to be staffed. A theft-detection gate 30 or 40 feet away from the lending desk is worthless. A theft-detection gate out of sight of the desk is just plain silly. At the same time, make sure that the electronics of the theft-detection system and lending system do not interfere with each other, which happened in one of John's libraries.

- **Dealing with holds, interlibrary loans, and items retrieved from storage**
  In most libraries, lending desk staff members handle books held for borrowers. Dealing with incoming held books happens automatically, since lending staff members are alerted to holds when they check books in. Because books received on interlibrary loan are handled in similar ways, the lending staff may intermingle these with held books. And from the point of view of users, there should be little visible distinction between the two. Although many

libraries use automatic e-mail notification for people who have books waiting, many still telephone users. Even if notification is automatic, there will always be a few users who do not use e-mail. Holds and interlibrary loans need to be housed somewhere. The two practices now are either shelving behind the desk, for staff retrieval of items, or self-service public shelving, with books wrapped in paper for privacy and the borrowers' names or ID numbers written on the paper with a marking pen. Wherever holds and interlibrary loan items will be stored, libraries need to plan space for suitable shelving. To keep lending areas neat, some libraries have placed shelving for holds and interlibrary loans in back rooms, but the result is a great deal of time wasted by staff running back and forth to fetch them. The quantities can be impressive. Fred's library sequestered holds, interlibrary loans, CDs, and DVDs on shelving immediately behind a lending desk (not in a back room), and taken together these items represented well over half of total lending. One way to limit the appearance of disarray behind lending desks is to orient storage shelving so the ends rather than the sides of the shelving units face library users.

- **Serving as a library telephone switchboard**
  In many small and medium-sized libraries, general telephone calls are answered at lending desks, and for this reason libraries need to make provisions for a telephone at every workstation. Some libraries deal with incoming calls by installing automatic telephone-answering equipment. Since encountering gear of this type is probably the single most infuriating aspect of dealing with American businesses, we think this is amazingly short-sighted. For public service institutions that rely on the good will of the people who control the money to cavalierly aggravate them just in order to avoid modest expenditures seems amazingly foolish. Whatever libraries decide to do, no library should paint itself into the kind of corner where a reversion to real human beings answering phones is made impossible by building design decisions or by equipment decisions.

- **Providing a place to sequester high-theft items**
  Certain items in libraries are predictably stolen. In public libraries, problems predictably occur with nonprint materials, particularly video games, and with books on topics like the occult, sex, auto repair, and do-it-yourself anarchy. Other materials are constantly mutilated. In public libraries, the worst problems usually occur with old high school yearbooks because library users cut out pictures of friends or of graduates who went on to fame and fortune.

Ill-advised mass assignments by secondary school teachers can lead to the theft of books when 150 teenagers are forced to share the same dozen books. While most teachers understand that the laws of physics make this kind of sharing impossible, a few of them never learn. Luckily, electronic access to many materials has limited this problem.

For standard materials like single-disk CDs and videos, security boxes are available to limit theft. Security boxes contain the markers used to activate theft-detection systems and are designed to be extremely difficult to remove without a special tool kept at the lending desk. Libraries that plan to use these systems have to allow for space to store the security boxes when they are removed, until they are needed for items being returned. They also need to provide workspaces where security boxes can be replaced during the check-in process.

As a side note, it's critically important to try out security boxes before actually purchasing an entire system. Some turn out to be painfully difficult to operate, with staff members wasting time or running the risk of repetitive motion syndrome. Testing library security boxes is fun to do in exhibit halls at library conferences.

Security boxes work better when they're transparent, since staff don't have to stress their wrists opening every box to be sure the right recording is there.

Instead of using security boxes, libraries can simply store DVDs in plain lending boxes on shelves behind lending desks. Users bring empty DVD boxes to the desk, and staff members simply swap these for plain boxes with the actual DVDs, saving a great deal of handling.

One of the major challenges in planning lending desks is planning what kinds of materials will need to be stored behind the desk and how much space will be required. In general, assuming more rather than less is probably safest.

- **Reserve reading functions in academic libraries**
  In years gone by, separate reserve reading rooms with separate staffs were common in academic libraries. Although modern electronic reserves are making this function largely obsolete, copyright restrictions may result in hard-copy reserves never entirely disappearing. If reserve functions in your library have been combined with lending functions, or are likely to be combined in the future, your lending desk will need to be planned with additional storage shelving in mind.

2. Lending Desk Nomenclature

Although most people use the term *circulation desk* rather than *lending desk*, we strongly recommend that you call yours a "lending desk" during building planning and construction.

In the architecture trade, the word *circulation* applies to the movement of people within spaces. When architects speak of "circulation space" in a large reading room, for example, they mean the space required to create aisles between the reading tables wide enough for people to walk comfortably.

Making this change in nomenclature sounds like overkill, but we have experienced a number of situations where communication went haywire during library planning because of confusion over the term circulation.

3. Lending Desk Placement

Unless a library has a separately staffed security gate, it will almost certainly depend on lending desk staff to supervise users coming and going from the library.

To function effectively, security gates need to be close to service desks. Security gates that are unstaffed or out of sight of staff are useless. Staff members need to be able to see who is passing through gates when alarms sound, and they need to be close enough so that the people who set off the alarms don't just continue walking. Anything more than fifteen feet between gates and desks will probably be a problem.

Some library designers assume that an extra entrance can be left unstaffed, and any problems prevented by the installation of a security gate. But this doesn't work. Or, more bluntly, THIS DOES NOT WORK. When people want you to add extra public entrances to your library, always point out the staffing cost implications, assuring them that providing multiple entrances is probably the single worst decision that can be made in library architecture.*

Because providing desk staff is one of the major costs of operating a library, lending desks need to be placed in ways that allow the staff maximum oversight. In many medium-sized public libraries, there are only three staffed desks—lending, adult reference, and children's reference—and a well-designed building enables these three desks to control all key access points.

---

*Any design feature that allows users to bypass security gates leads to major problems. For example, some designers are in love with the concept of "reading terraces," which unfortunately allow users to pitch items from the terrace into the underbrush for later retrieval. When we point this problem out, some designers respond by using the phrase "secure reading terrace," which is a major oxymoron. Unfortunately, you may need to be prepared for a fight, with your designers trying to bypass the library staff to sell the reading terrace concept to people with no firsthand library experience. If the access to the reading terraces is from outside the secure area of the building, users will have to check out books before taking them out on the terraces, and that solves the problem. Similarly, it's always better to have entrances to restrooms outside the secure area of the building.

In smaller libraries—including not only public libraries but also special libraries, school libraries, and small academic departmental libraries—there may be only one desk that is staffed at all times the library is open, and a major challenge for the architect is placing the desk in such a way that staff members can supervise both the entrance to the library and as much of the inside of the library as possible, while simultaneously providing lending services, reference services, and other assistance.

Some libraries have used sales counters, such as coffee shops, to supervise extra entrances, but coffee shops—particularly in public libraries—have a high rate of business failure, and one can't count on them providing this function forever (or even consistently). If you are considering using a coffee service counter to supervise an exit, you'll need to plan how you'll staff the counter while coffee shop staff members are on breaks, let alone what you'll do when the shop folds.

Lending desks need a substantial amount of public space. Many libraries, for example, set up consolidated waiting lines, and this requires extra floor space. Users also tend to hang around lending desk areas. They stop to say hello to the library staff, and they stand and talk with other users. And all of this takes floor space.

4. Lending Desk Staff Spaces

Because lending desks are work areas, they need space for library staff, book carts, and return book bins.

If books are returned through slots in the lending desk, there will be receiving bins on casters under the desk. Desks lower than the standard forty inches are too low for receiving bins. Often, books are checked in directly from a receiving bin, and this may necessitate two bins for each return slot. As bins fill, staff members pull them out to check materials in, replacing each full bin with an empty bin.

Wherever materials are checked in, each staff workstation will need floor space for a bin full of books to be checked in and one or more carts for books that have just been checked in, in addition to the space required for staff to handle the books.

Most lending areas require shelving for storage of various parts of the collection, including holds, interlibrary loans, high-theft items, and (as noted above) reserve items. There are also such miscellaneous functions as lost and found, storage of frequently needed supplies, and so on.

5. Lending Workrooms

Lending workrooms need to be directly behind lending desks to handle the constant flow of materials. Materials checked in have to be sorted (usually onto book carts) and reshelved. Incoming interlibrary loan materials have to be received, checked in, and users notified. Returned materials that have holds need to be taken out of the flow of materials, set aside, and users notified. Materials needed to fill interlibrary loan requests from other libraries have to be processed after they have been located on library shelves. Supervisory staff members need to have workspaces close to desks for oversight.

The spaces required in lending workrooms can easily change. For example, registration cards can be replaced by online records, including required signatures.

Building programs need to pay close attention to the spaces required in lending workrooms. Features that require space commonly include:

- Desks (or offices) for supervisory staff
- Workstations for checking in returned materials
- System printers for staff computers
- Places where staff can telephone users out of earshot of other users
- Floor space for carts loaded with returned materials
- Shelving for supplies needed on a daily basis
- Shelving for lost and found items
- Shelving for incoming interlibrary loan books and for books on hold
- Shelving for materials set aside for repairs
- Filing cabinets for lending records
- Worktables for unpacking shipments
- Floor space for bins or totes used for outgoing interlibrary loans
- Places to wrap and unwrap interlibrary loans sent by mail or delivery service
- Safes for cash receipts. Small safes are available that bolt to the floor and have slots in the top for the deposit of cash receipts.
- Card files for registration cards
- Coat storage for staff
- Lockers for staff purses. Remember that you need a locker for each worker. (Many young people who work as pages may carry backpacks where they keep wallets. For security, lockers need to be large enough for backpacks. Half-height school hallway lockers work well.)
- Windows to the lending desk, so staff in the workroom can help keep an eye on the desk
- Bulletin boards for staff information
- Sinks for hand washing, which is important to staff members dealing with users who appear to be ill or who turn in surprisingly sticky books

If check-in operations are carried out in a lending workroom, there will be less space needed behind the lending desk but at least a corresponding additional space in the lending workroom.

Many libraries provide separate offices for heads of lending departments because of the large number of people (particularly the pages who shelve books) who need to be hired, supervised, and evaluated.

More information on staff workrooms is provided in chapter 22 on "Staff Workrooms."

6. Seated vs. Standing-Height Lending Desks

Lending desks can be constructed for staff to either sit or stand.

All desks need at least one area at seated height to comply with ADA requirements. Although the ADA permits heights of up to 36 inches, a desk this high is extremely awkward for staff members. Most office desks are about 30 inches high, and something similar may be the most comfortable for your staff.

The ADA also requires at least 27 inches of clearance under desks, so if you opt for a 30-inch-high desk, you will have only 3 inches available for the thickness of the desktop.

Many public libraries also provide seated-height desks because they are more comfortable for children.

If you plan to have staff frequently retrieve materials stored behind the desk, they will probably find it easier to stand rather than sit.

Another problem with seated-height desks is keeping staff busy during the inevitable slow times. Staff who are sitting and waiting for users may just sit and wait. (We've seen a number of libraries with very comfortable seats for checkout clerks, and there can be a great deal of comfortable sitting around between users.)

7. Provisions for Book Return

Many lending desks have slots for book return, with receiving bins under the desk.

Bins are available from a variety of commercial sources. Some have bottoms that sink as the bins fill with books, while others simply have cloth bags to receive the books.

Some libraries provide separate return slots for books and for nonprint materials, usually on the presumption that the weight of a large book falling on a recording may have an evil result.

Often these slots work very well, but there are a couple of potential design problems:

- A slot with a receiving bin needs to be in a full-height counter, 39 or 40 inches high. If you have a slot in a lower counter, there will not be adequate space for a receiving bin beneath it. Designers driven by the need for fearful symmetry in service desks have sometimes balanced one low end to meet the needs of the ADA and children with a matching low end with a book return. *The results were seriously awful.*
- Return slots need to be in places where library users checking out materials and users returning materials are not forced to occupy the same turf.
- The openings at return slots have to be large enough to make the return of most items possible, while small enough to prevent people from reaching through slots to retrieve recently returned items. Having a chute between the slot and the receiving bin helps.
- The chutes that lead returned books from return slots to receiving bins will probably have to bridge over raceways for wires. Be sure there is enough space for the chute to end above the top lip of the bin while still having enough slope for books not to hang up in the chute.

Whether or not you have slots, you will need to be prepared for people simply handing materials across the counter. Your staff will need a convenient and close place to put these materials. (Your staff can always refuse to accept materials and direct users to the return slots, but calling this a less than friendly gesture is an altogether too positive view of the situation.)

A common practice is to separate return slots completely from lending desks. Some libraries have slots just inside entryways, leading either to receiving closets or directly to staff workrooms.

There are a couple of downsides to return slots in remote locations:

- If your library limits quantities on certain types of materials, people may arrive at the library, drop materials in the slot, and pick out new ones, only to discover that they can't borrow them because the old ones haven't been checked in. If staff members have to run to a receiving closet and root through the bins looking for these materials, efficiency of operations can be severely handicapped. (*To be more blunt, it won't work.*) Usually, policies and procedures can be adjusted to take care of problems like this. For example, a library may set operating rules for computerized lending systems at double the number of items that may officially be checked out. If the limit on DVDs, for example, is officially four, the system may be set to allow eight, so that four DVDs recently dropped off but not yet checked in don't prevent a user from borrowing four new DVDs.

- People returning items to slots hidden from the view of the staff may be more likely to include dead squirrels, ice cream cones, half-consumed beer bottles, and other fun stuff. Over the years, a number of serious library fires have been caused by incendiaries in book returns, and any exterior book return slot must lead to a fire-resistant receiving closet with fire suppression devices, alarms, and so on.
- Library staff will have to haul returned items much farther.

8. Off-Desk Workspaces

In most libraries, staffing efficiency requires that work in addition to checking items out takes place at the lending desk.

In many small libraries, the lending desk is the only service desk, and all sorts of library backroom work is carried out at the desk, enabling staff members to simultaneously carry out technical services work, be ready to help users, and keep an eye on the library.

The problems with this are (a) the disorder that accompanies staff projects makes the desk messy, and (b) staff members are frequently dealing with projects the public shouldn't be encouraged to touch.

The solution is to place a separate work counter behind the desk. To be effective, counters of this type have to be placed so staff members standing there are facing users approaching the desk.

Some libraries have counters behind desks that force staff members to face the wall, with their backs to library users. Because these counters take up less space than counters where staff members face library users, architects almost always tend to draw them that way, unaware of the necessity of staff facing users. You will need to be constantly alert to prevent counters from being designed this way.

A work counter behind a standing-height lending desk has to be about the same height as the lending desk to enable staff members to see over the desk and to be seen by library users approaching the desk. Counters also need low barricades to hide the worst of the disarray on the counter from users approaching the lending desk. Eight or nine inches is probably sufficient.

The side of the work counter that faces the main lending desk may provide a good location for a cash drawer. This may make it easier for staff members to reach the drawer from any checkout station, and it will make it impossible for anyone to reach over the desk from the public side and slither a hand into the cash drawer.

9. Visual Barricades on the User Sides of Lending Desks

Lending desks are frequently designed with visual barricades to hide materials stacked on the desk and to prevent users from messing with computer wiring. Sometimes these are partial barricades, with staff members located in strategic gaps, while others run the entire length of the desks. Library supply catalogs are full of desks with front barricades. *We feel strongly that these are bad ideas.*

10. Queuing Space

Desks need space for users to queue up for service. This is common at lending desks, but on busy days, queues can form at reference desks and computer help desks. Users can line up for individual staff members, but many libraries provide consolidated waiting lines.

The advantage of a single queue is that no one "picks the wrong line" and ends up behind a user who is prepared to argue all afternoon over a two-cent late fee.*

Consolidated queues require floor space. They also require some way for users to understand where the line begins and ends. To accomplish this, some libraries have elaborate structures built of metal bars, all reminiscent of devices to encourage cows to return to the correct barn. Unfortunately, structures like this are extremely awkward during low-traffic times, as one can notice in airports. They can also consume a great deal of floor space.

Our experience has been that about all one needs to do is to define the front of the line clearly. Four posts and a couple of five-foot chunks of theater rope may be enough. Sometimes all it takes is a single sign saying "Wait here for service." It may even be possible not to fasten the posts down, although children swinging on the ropes may bring frequent upsets.

---

*We realize that two-cent late fees disappeared with the Harding administration, but it's more fun to say *two-cent late fee* than *two-dollar late fee*.

11. Sorting Rooms

Many libraries maintain sorting rooms where recently returned books are sorted prior to being reshelved.

Although this sounds like a very logical function, in practice such sorting rooms turn out to be more akin to the Black Hole of Calcutta. Inevitably, people reshelving books fall behind on their work, and sorting rooms frequently consist of mounds of materials. Books that fall into categories of materials that are hard to reshelve (such as art books or children's picture books) may be passed over by staff in favor of easy tasks like reshelving mystery stories, leaving the art books and picture books to vanish into layers of bibliographic permacrud, perhaps not emerging for weeks.

In the meantime, if online lending systems inform users that these books are on the shelf, the result is expensive reference staff rooting helplessly around sorting rooms, just in case the missing books are there.

By contrast, public sorting shelves tend to stay neater because failure to keep up is too obvious.

Having been there, we think public sorting shelves (also functioning as "recently returned" shelves) greatly reduce staffing costs and improve the quality of library service.

12. Automated Book-Handling Systems

If you think your library may convert to an automated book-handling system, talk to vendors about space needs.

Sorters can take a lot of space, particularly if you want to be able to switch full and empty bins.

Some libraries have installed book-handling systems with an insufficient number of return slots. It will help you a lot if the structure of your building allows the installation of additional return slots.

Some libraries have installed book-handling systems that transport books between floors. Be sure to work out with your vendor how this will take place, and what you will do if books fall off the transport system. Sending the smallest employee crawling into a tunnel to retrieve books that have fallen off the belt is not a lot of fun. If the entire transport system is on one level and in a single open room, life may be a lot easier.

Librarians with automated book-handling systems joke about "sorter bin envy," but it will help if you have space to extend your sorting system if you turn out to need additional bins.

If you want outside book return slots, you will have to decide whether they will feed directly to the sorter equipment—and how your system will handle the very large quantities of materials that can be returned overnight or during a holiday weekend.

This is only incidental, but we have never seen a serious cost-benefit analysis of automated book-handling systems that did not come from industry sources. Let us know if you've seen one.

13. Drive-Up Book Returns with Receiving Rooms

Most libraries need some provision for the return of materials while the library is closed.

Many libraries have slots leading into rooms with receiving bins.

One main problem with these arrangements is that people put incendiaries into slots and set buildings on fire. The Danforth (Connecticut) library was set on fire in 1996, but it happens elsewhere. A small-town library Fred worked with was nearly burned down when someone shoved a flaming object through a mail slot that served as a book return.

The solution to the problem is to always have book return slots lead to fire-resistant receiving spaces. Losing the contents of the book return closet is a lot less annoying than losing the entire building.

One problem with book return slots is that vehicles come in many different heights. A slot that is at a convenient height for a Hummer won't be at a good height for a Miata. Installing slots at two different heights is possible, but you need to be sure that the lower slot has enough clearance in the receiving room for a receiving bin on casters.

Drive-up book returns typically need one-way driveways, so that drivers can lean out their windows to drop books into the slots.

Drive-up book returns also need fairly generous driveways that allow cars to straighten out and sidle up to the slots. Frequently, driveways are too short, with tight curves leading to short sections of straight wall. As a result, drivers cannot pull up closely enough to the return slots. Instead of reaching out their windows and dropping books into the return slots, drivers have to park beside the book return slots, hop out of their cars, and walk over to the slots to return their books.

You may have arguments with your designers about driveways leading to book returns. The designers may insist that the driveways are just fine, when in reality no one can make them work.

Whether or not you have a drive-up external book return, you'll need a walk-up return. It's possible that one return can serve both purposes, but having pedestrians and cars share the same area is always tricky.

Because of technical problems with drive-up returns, some libraries have considered return slots with three-minute parking spaces beside them.

Many libraries have separate return slots for books and for other materials such as recordings.

Book returns are a problem during holiday weekends because they usually need to be emptied a number of times over a weekend.

Some libraries remove receiving bins during holidays and just put a mattress on the floor, so that staff will not have to stop by the library several times a day to empty the bins. (If the door to the room swings inwards, overflowing books may get in the way of the door swing.)

Depending on design, some book returns can be impressively noisy. If receiving closets are fire-resistant, that may take care of noise transfer as well, but the usual way to control noise is to be sure that the walls of the room extend past the ceiling to the underside of the floor or roof above.

Because of the noise associated with drive-up book returns, we need to be careful where they are located in buildings. Probably the worst places are rooms adjacent to program rooms. Sometimes the falling of books can be heard in the program rooms, and sometimes staff members have to trudge through program rooms when events are taking place, in order to empty book returns.

The easy solution is to always have access to book returns from service corridors and not from public spaces.

Some companies make fire-containing returns with metal chutes leading directly from the exterior slots to enclosed receiving bins. The idea is that this allows the returns to be installed in rooms that are not fire-resistant because the returns themselves can contain fires. However, these returns can make an incredible amount of noise, and it's not fun to watch users and staff leaping convulsively every time a book is returned. If you're thinking of getting one, check with libraries that have them and be sure the return is in a back room of the library rather than in a space occupied by library users or staff members.

The morals of this section are

- Users expect to find after-hours book returns at essentially all libraries.
- Book returns that lead directly into library buildings offer a serious threat of fire.
- Driveways for drive-up book returns have to have curves gentle enough to allow drivers to actually pull up next to the return slots.
- Both pedestrians and drivers need return slots.
- Book returns are inherently noisy, and the receiving bins need to be kept away from user and staff functions.

14. External Book Return Bins

Rather than deal with book return slots, many libraries purchase curbside book return bins.

One of the great advantages of freestanding return bins is that fire cannot spread from the bin to the rest of the library.

As with return slots in buildings, curbside bins require arrangements where bins are on the drivers' sides of cars. This can mean a one-way driveway, which works well, or bins perched on medians in streets, which leads to difficulties with cars stopping in fast lanes and with staff members unloading bins in traffic.

Bins are typically available in more than one height, but even then, drivers complain that they are too high or too low.

Bins are usually available in carbon steel and stainless steel. Our experience is that stainless steel is a lot more expensive up front, but that carbon steel rusts out in a couple of seasons.

Protecting return bins from collisions with cars is always a challenge. Typically, libraries create bollards consisting of six-inch steel pipe filled with concrete. The necessity of bollards is indicated by the amount of colored paint that rubs off on them.

With well-designed bins, the top sections with the return slots can be separated from the base sections with the access doors, allowing the doors to face in whatever direction is best for the library.

> Even bollards can fail to protect return bins. In Fred's library, a backhoe driver crossed the street at right angles and rammed the scoop end of his backhoe between two bollards, thereby destroying a brand-new (and extremely expensive) return bin. The driver then attempted to make a quick getaway, but that's hard to do in a backhoe, and he was spotted by library staff, who noted the company name painted on the backhoe and called his employer. By the time the driver got back to the shop, the employer was ready with serious questions.

15. Exterior Book Pickups

Some libraries install exterior book pickup boxes. Typically, these resemble banks of large post office boxes. Library staff members check out requested items to users and put them in boxes, which are open at the rear for staff access. A keypad next to the array of boxes allows users to enter code numbers. When a user enters a code number, the appropriate box (or more than one box) pops open. And when the user takes the books and closes the box, the access number is canceled.

Libraries that installed these systems assumed that they would be used for after-hours book pickup, but the primary users proved to be people for whom it would be awkward to come into the library, such as parents with children in car seats and elderly couples where one of the two could not be left alone in the car.

Early book pickup boxes were suitable for inside locations only, but modern ones are weatherproof. The main thing that goes wrong is ice forming in the openings between the doors and the frames.

Libraries have told us that wind tends to whistle through exterior pickup boxes, and that the boxes need to be serviced from a hallway or service area rather than from a staff area.

16. Lending Service Windows

Some libraries have drive-up service windows.

We suspect that they are not a great idea. Few users come along, so drivers need to have a way of summoning library staff members, perhaps with a push button connected to a bell. And then they have to wait for a staff member to come to the window.

Some libraries have told us that users tend to treat lending service windows like MacDonald's, not just picking up held items but assuming they can drive up and place a subject request on the order of "I'd like four books on the War of 1812."

17. Additional Lending Desk Spaces

Lending desks are frequently located in high-traffic areas. In a well-designed small public library, the desk faces the entrance and separates the children's and adult departments. Locations of this type mean that lending desks need a substantial amount of extra elbowroom. People moving from the entrance to library departments will pass by the desk, as well as people traveling between departments.

In addition, libraries tend to locate other features next to lending desks because this is a convenient location. For example, you may need:

- **Security gates**
  Magnetic security systems require a space of at least three feet between the security gates and a door. The result is that the gates can extend perhaps six feet past the door. Architects who don't realize this have created libraries where the doors to the lobby have to be locked open in order to prevent proximity to door hardware from setting off alarms. With space between the gates and the doors, some kind of filler panels need to be installed to prevent people from simply walking between the gates and the doors. We've had good luck with wood frames with transparent polycarbonate panels. Even nonmagnetic gates, such as those used with RFID systems, still stick out from the entry door. They require floor space not only for the gates but also to allow users to pass between the gates and the users queued at the lending desk. See chapter 30 on "Security" for a more extensive discussion of security gates.

- **Self-check equipment**
  If your library will have self-check equipment, the best place for it is close to the lending desk. Self-check workstations can take a surprising amount of space, not because the stations are huge but because of the floor space for users using the self-check stations and other users queuing up for their turns. And users may need staff assistance while attempting to use self-check equipment. Regardless of your plans at this time, if your library is a public library, it will be very likely to want self-check equipment eventually. Remember also that self-check equipment requires access to both 110-volt

power and to data conduit. Older adults may not be inspired by self-check equipment, but kids seem to get a huge kick out of operating it.

- **Spaces for public photocopiers**
  Many people come to libraries specifically to copy items that are not part of the libraries' collections. From their point of view, a location right inside the entrance is optimal. Remember that public photocopiers always require small tables where users can put materials they are copying, plus floor space for people waiting to use the machines. Because of this, the standard space allocation for a public photocopier is sixty-five square feet. Copiers never become less complex, and public photocopiers need to be located near friendly library staff, who will routinely be called up to untangle electronic puzzles.

- **Spaces for coin-operated fax machines**
  Faxes take up less space than photocopiers, but the basics are the same. Libraries need to provide space for the machine and for a small table to hold materials people are sending, plus floor space for the person using the machine. Like copiers, public fax machines need to be located near helpful staff. Check to see what your state says about collecting taxes on faxes.

- **New book displays**
  In some libraries, new book displays are part of lending departments. Shelving that is heavily used, such as shelving for new books and book sale books, requires extra space for people to stand. Standard seven-foot-high steel shelving often doesn't work for new book displays because books end up so crammed together that users get in each other's way while looking at new materials. A-frame units with only three or four shelves vertically are available for new books.

- **Used book sale displays**
  Even libraries that have occasional monster book sales may find that a small used book display unit near the lending desk generates a surprising amount of cash over the course of a year. Some libraries have shelving, while others have decorative carts or other types of furniture. If your library will have used book sale shelves by your lending desk, remember that you will need storage space for books used to restock the shelves.

- **Displays of recently returned books**
  Some public libraries put recently returned books out where users can browse through them. These seem to work for a variety of reasons:
  – Public sorting shelves of this kind are a lot better than sorting areas in back rooms. As noted above, sorting rooms tend to be black holes, and books taken there may not emerge for weeks.

- If users understand that every book actually in the library building is either in its regular space on a shelf, on a shelf for recently returned materials, on a cart where staff are checking things in, or in a receiving bin under the desk, they will be much less inclined to insist on poking around the staff areas of the library.
- Shelving for recently returned items is simplest to maintain when it is close to where books are checked in, since it is easier for staff members to rush out with armloads of books. However, displays of recently returned items are probably friendlier for users when they are divided into more than one section and located close to where the appropriate areas of the collection are found.
- Spaces for small displays. The areas around lending desks are one of the great places for displays of books of extremely current interest. For example, when famous authors die, the staff may want to pull their books from the collection and create small displays. Displays of this type are made far easier because modern automation systems allow checking out books to "display." Libraries also use book stack end panels for the display of selected books, with plastic brackets hanging on slat-wall inserts. Books displayed this way may be so close to their usual locations that checkout to "display" is not essential.

- **Shared printers**
  Many lending operations require access to staff printers. For example, users may want printed lists of all the materials they have checked out. Depending on how the library processes overdue notices, some may need to be printed out and sent by mail, especially to users without e-mail. Some small libraries also have system printers for public computer use located on or near their lending desks. These require sufficient space for machinery and access.

- **Registration card files**
  Although the automation of lending functions has led to the elimination of registration card files, many still exist. If registration cards include the signatures of cardholders, libraries can use these as written contracts or to provide a chance to compare signatures. Providing built-in registration card files is almost certainly a bad idea, since your library may eliminate them in the future, but space can be left under or behind lending desks for small freestanding card catalog units. Or if the cards are checked only seldom, card files can be in an adjacent lending workroom.

- **Areas to sort incoming and outgoing interlibrary loan traffic**
  If a library receives interlibrary loan materials in bins, it will need floor space to stack bins while materials are being processed. This will be particularly true in branch systems or in libraries with reciprocal borrowing agreements.

Similarly, if libraries have a lot of outgoing materials, they may need floor space for as many bins as there are delivery routes.

The main point of providing this long list of possibilities is to emphasize that what looks like generous space around a planned lending desk may sometimes be unrealistically small.

B. Reference and Reader Guidance Desks

While in smaller libraries—particularly public libraries—all services may be provided from a single desk, medium-sized and large libraries usually have reference desks.

Public libraries may have multiple reference desks; for example, separate desks for adults, young adults, and children. Depending on local needs, some of these may be staffed only at peak demand times, and this in turn has implications for supervision.

Small academic libraries may have single reference desks, while large libraries have desks in a number of departmental libraries.

In reality, of course, the term *reference desk* is increasingly a misnomer. Reference service has changed in major ways since the advent of library automation, to the point where library professional staff members revel happily when asked the very occasional actual, genuine reference question that lends itself to traditional reference techniques. (One could also argue that many library users have no idea what *reference* means in library jargon, but no one appears to have hit on a successful new word.)

1. Reference Desk Functions

Professional staff members at reference desks provide a wide range of services, including:

- **Traditional reference service**
  Old-fashioned reference questions still continue to be asked, even if there are not enough of them to justify a single-function reference desk.

- **Reader guidance**
  Many public libraries provide reader guidance, helping users find books—particularly fiction—that they will enjoy reading. A few libraries have separate desks for reference and reader guidance, in some cases only a few feet apart.

Sometimes two desks look like serious overkill, but if a public library's adult fiction and nonfiction collections are on separate floors, a separate reader guidance desk on the fiction floor may make sense. Separate reader guidance desks may also be useful if libraries have completely separate staff for the two functions.

- **Computer assistance**
  One of the main functions of reference desks is computer assistance. People who a decade ago might have asked a question about (for example) Afghanistan, now come to the desk and plaintively say, "I just looked up 'Afghanistan' on Google, and I got 17 million hits. Now what do I do?" If you visit libraries with separate reference and computer help desks, you may see the reference desk standing idle while users are lined up in droves at the computer help desks. We are convinced that having separate reference and computer help desks makes very little sense.

- **Supervision**
  As we stress frequently in this book, most reference desks are also responsible for supervising the departments they serve.

2. Reference Desk Heights

The majority of reference desks appear to be seated-height ones, but this can vary with the needs and preferences of the library.

Remember that to meet the requirements of the ADA, you will need one section of the desk no more than 36 inches high, with knee space at least 27 inches high underneath. However, 36 inches is too high for seated staff and users, and too low for standing staff and users, and 30 inches works a lot better.

3. Determining the Number of Service Points at a Reference Desk

When you are planning a reference desk, remember that you may be adding additional functions, and that you may therefore need additional spaces for staff.

In addition, many service desks provide occasional seating for volunteers. At the time of summer reading club registration in public library children's departments, for example, the reference desks may have two or three times the usual number of people.

4. Implications of the "Roving Librarian" Concept

Many libraries have been planning roving librarians, staff members not tied to a desk but rather out on the floor assisting users.

While this appears to be a very successful idea, unless professional librarians are willing to wear colorful vests in the fashion of employees at some big box stores, they can be extremely difficult to find.

> Fred saw a reference desk in a Dutch library that consisted of a high stool, a computer on a tiny shelf, and a post with a little round sign at the top with an "i" for information. (He also waited by the desk for 10 or 15 minutes, hoping to ask the librarian a question, but eventually gave up because he couldn't tell who he or she was, where he or she was, or even *if* he or she was.)

Looking ahead, it seems wise to (a) allow enough floor space for a traditional reference desk, (b) provide a modular desk that can be rearranged or even reduced in size, and (c) be sure that special soffits or lights do not make it impossible to reconfigure the desk. (As we mention endlessly throughout this book, designers want to design, and obtaining this kind of flexibility may require a fight.)

The trend toward roving reference staff can affect the oversight provided by service desks. If you plan to have reference staff on the floor rather than permanently at reference desks, you will need to make sure that the physical presence of the staff at desks is not essential for security.

Information on service desk security appears under the section "Lending Desks," above.

5. Reference Desk Placement

Because reference desks usually have an important secondary function of overseeing library interior space, the strategic placement of reference desks is important.

It's also important that reference desks be immediately visible to people entering a public service department.

In modern libraries, public-use computers tend to require the most staff assistance, and they need to be as close as possible to reference desks. In addition, given some of the engaging materials available on the Internet (with or without filtering), placing public Internet computers where library staff can see the screens is useful. (Obviously this doesn't apply to libraries with separate reference and computer help desks.)

Reference desks also need to be close to reference collections, but in many cases these collections are shrinking, often being replaced by additional computer workstations. This is one of many reasons why it is so important for libraries to have (a) multifunction lighting and (b) access to electrical power and data conduit everywhere.

> If your architects say, "Tell us where you will be putting computers," the only answer is, "Anywhere we want."

Remember the vital importance of always providing two ways staff members can leave *any* service desk. Being cornered by an emotionally challenged person can be scary at best and dangerous at worst.

Ideally, departmental staff workrooms are located close to reference desks. See chapter 22 on "Staff Workrooms."

6. Storage at Reference Desks

Compared with lending desks, reference desks require relatively little storage space.

Many libraries have traditionally had "ready reference" collections of books that reference librarians used almost daily. These were shelved at reference desks rather than in separate reference shelving.

With the growing reliance on electronic reference sources, however, many ready reference collections have come to consist primarily of loose-leaf documents of one sort or another.

Remember that ready reference shelving should be about the same height as the desk, to enable staff to swivel around and have maximum 360-degree oversight over the department.

Some libraries hold materials for readers at reference desks. For example, a librarian in a public library may select books for a schoolteacher and hold them until the teacher arrives at the library and can review the materials with the librarian. If your library provides this type of service, you will need additional storage space at your reference desks.

Other materials stored at reference desks typically need drawers. Frequently these materials consist of standard forms and office supplies (which users constantly ask to borrow).

C. Desks for Entrance and Exit Control

Some large libraries have staffed desks at their entrances that have no function other than security. Typically, a staff member there checks the identification of people entering the library and monitors adjacent security gates for those exiting the building.

Desks of this type are especially common in private academic and research libraries that limit entrance to the library to students and faculty, or that want to identify users.

For a private university, national or state library, or similar limited-access institution, such desks may be essential, but the person who works there may spend a lot of time sitting.

D. Concierge Desks

A few libraries have separate desks that take over the functions of greeting users, providing orientation and information on library programs and events, and similar activities. (Another possible name is *orientation* desks. Some libraries call such desks *information desks*, but we think this blurs the distinction between concierge desks and reference desks.) Concierge desks can soak up other functions. For example, some libraries that have tried to go 100 percent self-check use concierge desks as checkout points for users for whom self-check is not an option.

We have the impression that staff members at concierge desks are often short of things to do, and that these desks may be vulnerable when budgets become tight. The lending desks—which traditionally performed general greeting and orientation functions—take the functions back from the concierge desk staff.

It may be possible to staff concierge desks only during peak hours. We envision problems, however, in attempting to train users to try the concierge desk first and then (if and only if the desk is closed) turn to the lending desk. It may also be hard to get people to understand which questions go to which desk, while staff members who like helping users may try to offer all services at all desks.

Libraries that limit building access to specific people may have staffed entry points that double as concierge desks.

One library Fred is working with is considering combining a concierge desk with a coat check.

> For all but really large libraries, separate concierge desks sound like God's way of telling them they have too much money.

E. Desks for Special Collections

The most common separate desks for special collections have probably been reserve collection desks in academic libraries. Before the growth in electronic reserves, many academic libraries had substantial collections of assigned readings available for very short loan periods, perhaps a couple of hours. Compared with other parts of the collection, materials on reserve received immensely heavy use. The actual materials were stored on closed shelving behind the desk and were brought out on request.

Our impression is that what is left of reserve collections may often be integrated with lending desks.

F. Multifunction Desks

Almost all public service desks in libraries perform multiple functions, but the assortment can vary from desk to desk and from library to library. In larger libraries with multiple desks, duties are occasionally rearranged and regrouped. Most desks are responsible for assisting users and keeping an eye on things, but after that almost anything can happen.

Because of the variations in staff duties, it's sometimes hard to decide what to call a service desk. Some libraries experiment with more accurate names, only to find that users are confused.

> One library changed the sign over the reference desk from "Reference Desk" to "Ask a Librarian." It struck us as a brilliant name, but they later changed it to "Ask a Librarian / Reference Desk."

VII. PUBLIC SERVICE DESKS AND SECURITY

Well-designed and located public service desks can do a great deal to improve security for library users, library staff, and library collections. None of this is accidental, however, and you may need to rely on your background, your staff, and your building consultant to spot proposed designs that will compromise security.

A. Exit Control

All nonemergency exits need to be staffed. Theft control gates work only if a library staff member is nearby.

In small libraries, like school libraries, all-purpose staff service desks can be placed next to the entrance to the library. Unless the library has enough money to staff two desks at all times, a second exit doesn't work, which is one reason why balconies are a seriously bad idea.

In larger libraries, lending desks frequently provide exit control. If the theft control gates are within 10 or 15 feet of the lending desk, staff at the desk can hear the gate alarms and reach the gates in time.

Academic libraries in private universities may limit access to people who are members of the academic community or expected guests. Some of these libraries have a single desk that controls both the library entrance and exit, with one staff member supervising both functions.

One planning problem we frequently encounter is architects' mistaken impression that theft-detection gates don't have to be staffed. We frequently see hidden exits with security gates, although the arrangement doesn't work.

B. Oversight of Library Spaces

A basic function of all public service desks is providing staff oversight of public spaces. Any time a service desk can be relocated to provide improved staff oversight, the entire library is improved.

In a small public library, a single staff service desk can be placed to allow staff to see users entering the building, entering and leaving the public restrooms, entering and leaving the main program room, using public computers, using study rooms, and seated at study tables. If stack aisles are oriented to allow staff members at the service desk to look down the aisles, library staff can see down most of the aisles by just moving a few feet. In a well-designed small library, staff members at the main service desk should be able to see most of the public areas of the building by just looking around, although they may need to step forward and backward a few feet to look down all the book aisles.

Much of this oversight is improved by the use of interior glass partitions. The partitions of the entry foyer need to be glass, as do study room partitions. The walls of meeting rooms and quiet reading rooms can be glass to give staff better oversight. If a children's department is separated from an adult department by a wall, it needs to be a glass wall.

Study room partitions need to be glass from about one foot above the floor to about seven or more feet above the floor. Codes may require a horizontal mullion between the upper and lower halves of glass walls, but that's easy to do.

When libraries have multiple floors open to the public, each floor needs a service desk. That's one reason why large, flat libraries are better than tall, narrow libraries.

If any one floor has more than a single service desk, it helps a great deal if staff members at the two desks can see each other.

As noted above, staff workspaces at service desks need to be arranged so that library staff can supervise the library while they are at work. If there's a staff work counter behind a service desk, it must be set up so that staff working there can look up and see the library. Many libraries have work counters in situations like this that force the staff to turn their backs on the library and face blank walls when they're at work.

C. Security for Library Staff

Public service desks are generally very safe places, but there are many things libraries can do to make their staff members more secure.

- Always design desks so that there are at least two ways out from behind. If some threatening person comes behind the desk, the staff member there has an easy exit.
- If you have a video-based security system, place cameras to record the faces of users (rather than of the staff).
- Consider panic buttons. Panic buttons should be connected to annunciators in a couple of key places, such as administrative offices and main lending desks. Panic buttons can also be linked directly to alarm services (although police departments much prefer telephone calls so they have a better idea of what to expect when they arrive at the library).
- Pay close attention to line-of-sight supervision. If the staff at desks can see staff at other nearby desks, it's much easier to keep an eye on things. Always avoid unnecessary opaque partitions. Blocking sound works just fine with glass partitions.
- Provide enough space to allow the staff at desks to step backwards if someone reaches across.
- Consider enclosing desks with barricades with swinging doors. (Swinging doors can also be a real pain. Be sure doors have mechanisms to allow them to latch open, and be sure they have single swinging panels rather than double panels, since trying to push a book truck through an opening with two swinging panels requires an abnormal number of arms.)
- Make the depth of desks sufficient to prevent people from reaching across to attempt to touch the staff. An extra couple of inches can make a major difference.

VIII. COMMON PROBLEMS IN THE DESIGN OF PUBLIC SERVICE DESKS

Historically, there have been many functional problems with service desks. Some of the most common are listed below.

See also the section above on "Public Service Desks and Security."

A. Monumentality

Some service desks are ungainly and inflexible because they were designed as architectural icons rather than as functional furniture.

Chapter 18 ■ Public Service Desks 549

Circular service desks are frequently very attractive, but there's not much staff space inside. It also takes more work to install storage shelves and drawers.

Small, round service desks look attractive from the front but provide amazingly little interior space for staff to stand and awkward storage space.

One can understand the desire of architects to create something dramatic and memorable with service desks. Functional modern libraries tend to consist of large open spaces that offer disappointingly few opportunities for architectural design, and designing a desk can be really satisfying. As a result, service desks are sometimes built with dramatic illumination, brushed steel fronts, sweeping curves, flickering colored lights, water features, elaborate soffits, and so on. Some of these details are fun, while others are at best engagingly dysfunctional.

Service desks cause particular problems when they are round or semicircular, because essential contents don't fit well into curves. Drawers are almost impossible to install. While the desks are immense from the outside, they have very little space for staff within. If a circulation desk is round, working with essential book bins and book carts may be nearly impossible. (Historic libraries frequently had round lending desks, demonstrating the historic longevity of bad ideas.)

B. Inflexibility

Many service desks have been constructed under the ill-advised presumption that technology, library procedures, and public needs will never change.

A large number of service desks, for example, have matching soffits with inset task lighting. If the soffit matches the configuration of the desk exactly, the desk can never be enlarged, shrunk, or relocated without the expense of tearing out or heavily modifying the soffit. Or having the relocation of the desk apparent to all who approach it.

Typically, soffits over service desks have recessed downlights. Can lights (circular recessed downlights) provide what is probably the worst light one can find in a library, joyously combining uneven illumination, rigidity, unpleasant shadows, and glare. *You don't want can lights. Ever. Serving any possible purpose.*

Moving or relocating soffits can be a particular problem in libraries with sprinkler systems, because individual sprinkler heads may be located on the surfaces of the soffits, forcing alteration of the sprinkler piping if the soffit is altered.

Other desks may have ornamental pendant lights, bright lamps in small glass globes. Some of these are blinding to look at from the side and most project small, harsh circles of light on the desktop. You don't want them either.

One problem with desk design is that cabinetmakers tend to see the project as similar to building kitchen counters rather than modular furniture. If a desk is constructed like kitchen cabinets, any minor modification can require major surgery.

> Soffits with recessed downlights—particularly round can lights—are always nasty. Begin by telling your designers you don't want to see any of them anywhere in your library, but then watch the drawings like a hawk, for soffits and can lights have an evil allure that calls out with siren tones to all who design buildings, and both inevitably appear regardless of your instructions.

1. Modular Desks

Due to changes in library technology and services, service desks are more practical if they are modular, but extremely few desks are designed this way. The main reason appears to be the desire of designers to create striking structures.

Desks are also more flexible if they are installed on top of carpet, so they can be relocated if necessary.

It's possible that freestanding desks might occasionally creep in use, but the libraries with whom we speak have no problems.

If your library has modular service desks, it will be vastly easier to enlarge or shrink them. For example, vast increases in lending may make it necessary to add additional service points. Or wholesale conversion to self-check equipment may make it possible to reduce the size of a lending desk.

As library functions change, service desks sometimes need to be relocated. If a desk is modular, moving it can be easy, but if it's a monument, or it has a matching soffit or special lights, relocating it may cost more than a library can reasonably afford.

Some libraries find that staff space behind service desks is simply too small, and that desks have to be relocated accordingly.

At the worst extreme, a series of service desks may be arranged in a single line (for example, a sweeping curve) and relocation of any unit may be nearly impossible.

> This happened to one library Fred knows. As a result of rigid adherence to the curve, one part of the desk was too small for the staff the day the library opened. There was essentially nothing to do about it without leaving a discordant break in the elegant sweeping line of desks. Or building a long row of brand-new units.

Modular desks can consist of units that simply bolt together. Moving the desks requires unbolting the units, disconnecting the wiring, shoving the desks around, and bolting them back together.

Some libraries have constructed service desks from office system components, with similar gains in flexibility. If not elegance.

For a modular desk to be successful, both ends of every section need to be finished, so no matter how components are rearranged, there are no raw ends exposed.

2. Movable Desks

In addition to using modular desk construction, libraries can ensure flexibility by avoiding architectural features that determine exactly how large a desk can be and where it must be located.

Some features that lead to inflexibility of desk location include:

- Matching soffits. Many service desks having matching soffits above them. If the desk is moved more than a few inches, the desk and soffit no longer line up, and the library is left with the unfortunate choices of (a) abandoning the move, (b) putting up with soffits that are noticeably out of alignment, or (c) having expensive architectural alterations. If a library decides to relocate a soffit, of course, it has to ask itself how long the new soffit will last.
- Special downlights installed to match the location of the desk. As with soffits, the minute the desk is moved the lights no longer match the location of the desk.

In addition to inflexibility, of course, most downlights create unpleasant glare. People who make the mistake of looking up are blinded by concentrated light, and the concentrated sources of light create unpleasant veiling reflections. In addition, harsh downlights cast strong shadows, which aren't a happy thing at any service desk.

C. Fragile Top Surfaces

Most service desks are made of wood with durable tops.

Service desktops, particularly those of lending desks, require the attention of staff and careful discussion. You will want to review their durability, reflectivity, color, ease of adding openings for wiring, and comfort to the touch.

A number of materials are unsuited for service desktops because they are too fragile. This is particularly true of lending desktops, which are subjected to a great deal of friction as books are slid back and forth.

- A common example of insufficiently durable materials is ordinary high-pressure laminates. Unfortunately, laminates of this type are used everywhere, and endless library lending desks have piebald tops where the pattern is partially worn off. If the pattern is wearing off your lending desktop, consider replacing the high-pressure laminate with any one of a number of similar but more durable products, such as solid-core laminate or acrylic polymers, where the color goes through the material rather than just being printed on the surface.
- Wooden desktops are also too fragile. This is particularly true with modern wood, which is less durable than the wood used in some century-old desktops. Because high-pressure laminate and wood are both too fragile for lending desktops, and stronger materials don't come with wood-grain patterns, durable wood-grain surfaces are probably impossible.
- Some libraries have used glass or transparent plastic to protect the surfaces of service desks, and these are almost always a mistake. There are two potential problems. First, many such surfaces are shiny, subjecting the eyes of users and staff to annoying reflections, particularly reflections of overhead light sources. Second, of course, glass breaks, and transparent plastic soon becomes scratched and cloudy and basically ugly.

Some of the most common materials used for successful desktops are acrylic polymers (Corian is a common trade name) and stone. Both are sufficiently durable to withstand the constant friction at lending desks, in part because the color goes all the way through.

- We prefer acrylic polymers because they are warm to the touch, can easily be drilled for grommet holes, and come in an immense variety of colors. And they don't chip.
- Stone is more elegant than acrylic polymers, much more expensive, and much colder to the touch. Some stone is porous and needs to be sealed periodically. And unlike acrylic polymers, it can chip.

Because most libraries add electronic equipment to service desks over the years, it should be possible to add additional grommets (openings for wiring) to the top of the desks. Desktops that are nearly impossible to drill may be a mistake for this reason.

Selecting colors for service desktops is a matter of function as well as aesthetics, so do not simply delegate the decision to a designer. In general, colors with middle values work best. Very dark colors soak up a lot of light, and the contrast between white paper and a dark desktop may lead to eyestrain. White desktops reflect too much light and may therefore lead to eyestrain.

Reference desktops receive slightly less abuse, but they are still subject to vastly more wear than reading tables, where standard laminates are usually sufficiently strong.

D. Persistence of Obsolete Desks Due to Sentiment

If you have a historic library with a painfully obsolete desk, users may insist that it remain in service because they remember it from their childhoods.

Unfortunately, many of the beloved desks in historic libraries are semicircular, with the characteristic total lack of staff space within. Most are also far too small. Many have tops that are made of fragile materials (such as wood), and many are equipped with obsolete features (such as recesses for card tubs).

Sometimes you can expand and remodel a desk like this, but it's probably better to find a politically acceptable way to repurpose it (or even to tuck it behind the furnace).

E. Bad Color Choices

As with surfaces of reading tables, desktops need to be neither white nor black. White tops reflect too much light, blinding users and staff. Black tops cause eyestrain through too much contrast between the desktop and paper. They also soak up a great deal of light, making spaces dark and wasting energy.

Unfortunately, extremely dark or light colors appeal to many designers.

A few service desks have glass tops, sometimes to protect old wooden surfaces. Unfortunately, in addition to being unsuitably fragile, glass surfaces do a great job of reflecting light in unpleasant ways.

F. Fortress Desks

Some service desks have all the warmth and welcome of a castle parapet. Vertical panels form barricades on the front of the desk that hide the staff. Sometimes the barricades have narrow openings through which staff can peer cautiously into the outside world, much as defenders peered through the sawtooth crenellations on the walls of medieval castles. On other desks the barricades are continuous, with staff nearly invisible behind.

Many of the inexpensive desks in library supply catalogs have barricades, and enough desks are designed this way to make a fast review of functional issues worthwhile.

Why you might think a fortress desk is a Good Thing . . .

- The great advantage of fortress desks is that the barricades in front conceal debris piled on desktops. If staff members at a lending desk are checking in magazines or doing other work between users, the desk will look neater if their work is largely concealed.
- Fortress desks with crenellations may help clarify the location of service points. Users will know that they are most likely to be helped where there are openings in the walls.
- The protective panels in fortress desks may keep library users—especially small children—from playing with exposed computer and telephone wires. Most wires of this type are vulnerable because they travel at least a few inches across desktops before vanishing into grommet holes.
- Fortress desks may limit the ability of desk staff to oversee the library. To the extent that staff members are hidden behind barricades, they may not be able to see what's going on.
- Fortress desks may encourage mess. If everything on the desktop is visible, staff members may tend to be neater.
- Fortress desks interfere with a sense of warm greeting for library users. If library staff members appear hidden away, users may feel less welcome.
- Fortress desks with crenellations can exude a kind of medieval feeling, with library staff peering nervously through defensive openings. And to the extent that fortress desks look like bank teller stations, they may alienate users.
- Lending desks that have fortress fronts without crenellations force staff members who are checking books in and out to hand them to users over the top of the barricade rather than simply sliding the books across the desk. This means that every transaction forces staff members to extend heavy objects at arms' length. We assume there are potential health implications.

- If barricades are continuous but countertops are at seated height, users may peer awkwardly over the barricades to see the staff seated below.
- If library technology changes, the more complex construction of fortress desks may lead to more frequent needs for expensive remodeling.

One attractive alternative to barricades is the use of heavy panels of patterned glass directly behind the desktop computer monitors, to hide wiring and keep children from playing with it. Panels of this type are far less intrusive and off-putting than actual barricades, and they lend themselves to easy alteration if desk use changes.

G. Obsolete Features Still Found in Lending Desks

Almost all service desks will change function over the years, and libraries need to plan for changes in usage. Unfortunately, many desks are designed or sold with features that are both inflexible and soon obsolete.

A good example of obsolete design is lending desks with recessed openings for card tubs. For endless decades, libraries kept track of books in use by using "book card"-based lending systems. Each book in the collection had a 3 × 5-inch card in a pocket inside the front or back cover. The card for each book had the identifying information for the specific book, plus space where borrower and date due information could be added. When books were checked out, cards were filed on end in card tubs. When books were returned, the cards were returned to the books and the books reshelved. At any given point in time, therefore, the card tubs contained information on the location of all books that were not in the library.

Other lending systems had single-use "transaction cards" that had much the same information but were discarded when books were returned.

Manual lending systems of this type were a royal pain. Endless pulling of cards ruined the careers of many cuticles. Access to essential information depended on filing order. If each book had a single card, filing order for the cards determined available information. Librarians had easy access to information by title, borrower, or date due—but only one of the three—and there was a lot of manual searching through card tubs—card by card—to solve problems. (In fairness, some research libraries had multiple cards for each book, so the cards could be filed in multiple ways for multifaceted access, but the extra staff time required could be impressive. Other libraries used keysort cards that could be filed by call number but also searched by date due.)

Chapter 18 ■ Public Service Desks 557

Years ago, lending desks often had recesses for the tubs that held the lending records—either book cards or transaction slips. Most libraries converted to digital lending decades ago, but the recesses survive in old lending desks. Desks of this type are still offered in library supply catalogs, and librarians sometimes find to their dismay that designers have included them in libraries without bothering to check with the staff.

Once electronic lending systems actually started working, librarians abandoned card-based systems joyously.

Therefore, while small libraries may still use card tubs, most of the tubs have been made obsolete by automation. Libraries with lending desks that have cutouts for card tubs are then required to rebuild their desks or come up with creative uses for large rectangular recesses in what should be smooth desktops.

> Librarians who are nostalgic for card tubs probably have more cuticles than they really need.

> Actually, very few librarians miss card tubs. In Fred's library, long ago, a little girl leaned over the children's department card tubs and threw up. Since all the information on the location of all the books in use was in the card tubs, the staff couldn't just toss the cards out. So, the staff member with the least seniority ended up hosing off the cards. And then she went home sick.

Unfortunately, library furniture catalogs still show desks with recesses for card tubs. Some architects order this stuff (not knowing what they are doing) while others design lending desks with recesses because they have seen them in catalogs.

We've seen a number of brand-new school libraries with service desks that have openings for nonexistent card tubs.

While this is a handsome service desk, the lighting structure above means that reconfiguring or relocating it will involve major surgery—or leave everything looking unusually awkward. Always shout "No" when designers suggest soffits or other fixed structures over service desks.

H. Bad Lighting

Throughout this book, we have strongly advised libraries not to install light fixtures that provide highly directional, concentrated light.

This type of bad lighting is typically associated with recessed downlights (otherwise known as "can lights").

A favorite design feature for service desks is to build matching soffits over them (a source of major inflexibility) and install can lights in the soffits.

The result is harsh lighting, glare off shiny surfaces, unpleasant shadows, and spotty illumination.

> Although can lights cannot be warded off with garlic, at the start of any library design project, you can tell your designers "no can lights." And then watch very carefully, for can lights have an insidious habit of creeping in when you are least expecting them, not unlike the Spanish Inquisition in *Monty Python*.

Another bad design enthusiasm has been small pendant lights. These frequently have colored glass globes and cast extremely bright light downward. They are often seen over tables and bars in restaurants, where they can make menus possible to read if (and only if) they are laid flat in just the right place on the tabletop. If your library specializes in beer and food and conversation—but not reading—you might explore the idea.

I. Bad Acoustics

Service desks are potentially noisy places for conversations, telephones, computers, and miscellaneous machinery. Lending desks in particular tend to radiate noise.

Unfortunately, lending desks are frequently located in inherently noisy areas. If a lending desk is located in an atrium with a ceramic tile floor and a skylight, the result will be an extraordinary amount of racket. And if the atrium is open to upper floors of the library, the entire building may be permeated with amplified noises of lending.

If your architects develop a design of this type and assure you it will cause no problems, explain politely that they are out of their trees. If they persist, hire an acoustical consulting engineer to review your drawings.

IX. LIBRARY SUPPLY COMPANY SERVICE DESKS

Some standard library supply firms offer components for service desks.

The good point about these is that they encourage flexibility of design. By purchasing a variety of components and bolting them together, the library has the ability to rearrange components, add additional sections, or relocate the entire desk.

However, commercial service desk components have some severe limitations:

- If the tops are made of high-pressure laminate, they will be too fragile to function well for lending. On lending desks in particular, the colors and patterns on the tops will soon wear through. Solid-core laminate and acrylic polymers are strong enough for library use. Unfortunately, many of the desks in library supply catalogs have inexpensive laminate tops, and the grungy results are with us everywhere. The solution is to specify strong materials when you order desks of this sort.
- Some of the components assume long-obsolete library technology. For example, we still see units with cutouts for trays to hold book cards.
- Sometimes individual modules have ornamental ends so that there are no raw ends visible when components are rearranged. However, if these ends stick up above the desktop, the result may be a service desk with low dividers every two or three feet.

X. ENCOURAGING VALEDICTORY REMARKS

If you are a librarian, always remember that librarians know more about library service desks and their functions than architects, campus planners, interior designers, school principals, mayors, library boards, city councils, superintendents of schools, university presidents, and all manner of other people. Plan in advance, make your needs painfully clear, and be totally unmovable.

If you are not a librarian, leave the decisions up to librarians or learn fast.

XI. SNAPPY RULES ON PUBLIC SERVICE DESKS

1. A service desk is a service desk, not a monument.
2. The chance that any service desk will provide the same functions decade after decade is about the same as the chance that your lovely new computer will last you fifty years.
3. Most service desks need occasional rearrangement, relocation, readjustment, and repurposing. Inflexibility of construction is not a virtue. Chant the word *modular* when speaking with your designers.
4. A matching soffit with recessed downlights over a service desk ensures a strong and happy combination of inflexibility and glare. And potentially high cost to eliminate, due to having to relocate sprinkler piping when you remove the soffit.
5. When service desks are being designed, always seek detailed input from the people who use them. All of these people have been employed in libraries. Few (if any) desk designers have been employed in libraries.
6. Almost all service desks in libraries perform multiple functions, one of which is always supervision. An overcomplicated building design that requires separate service desks simply for supervision may lead to fiscal unhappiness.
7. Staff members at service desks should face users entering the space, not be hidden around a corner or behind a partition, and not be working at a counter facing a wall.
8. Lending desktops suffer amazing abrasion. Cute but fragile materials will soon not be cute. Standard high-pressure laminates are cute but fragile. So is wood.
9. A crenellated service desk front that resembles a castle parapet makes the staff members behind it look like they expect users to act like Viking raiders.
10. Roving librarians are a user-friendly idea, but if they're not at their desks, how will users ever recognize them or find them? Or even know they exist? John favors garments emblazoned with scarlet question marks. Fred favors propeller beanies with flashing LEDs.
11. Curved service desks can look massive from the outside but have almost no space inside.
12. A public service desk is no better than the people who staff it. If your employees are unfriendly, no architectural elegance will compensate.
13. You don't want library users behind service desks. Make it clear which areas are "behind."

14. All exterior windows that face any direction except north (including monitor windows, clearstory windows, and skylights) need blinds. Nothing handicaps a service desk faster than an ornamental window high above the floor that admits uncontrolled direct sunlight and blinds the staff at the desk. Readers who are blinded by the sun can move to a different part of the library, but staff members are stuck at the desk.
15. Atriums are rotten places for service desks.
16. If you have a local cabinet firm construct a service desk for your library, remind them to think in terms of modular furniture rather than kitchen cabinets.
17. If you have two service desks on a floor, it's a good thing if the staff at one desk can see the staff at the other desk.

19

Program and Study Rooms

I. INTRODUCTION

The great majority of libraries include one or more special rooms for public programs, meetings, classes, tutoring, and quiet study.

Frequently these rooms serve a wider purpose than the narrow function of the library. Academic libraries have classrooms, seminar rooms, and faculty studies. Public libraries have rooms for both library-sponsored programs and community programs, for children's crafts and stories, for committee and board meetings, and for tutoring. Special libraries have rooms for confidential meetings of organizational staff. School libraries have rooms for study groups.

Most program and study rooms are designed to control noise, either protecting users from the noise of the rest of the library, preventing users of the rooms from disturbing the rest of the library, or providing security for closed meetings. In large meeting rooms, the ability to hear performers or other presentations becomes an important issue. Because of these concerns, the acoustics of program and study rooms is an important consideration.

The heating, ventilating, and air conditioning of program and study rooms is challenging because many rooms alternate between empty and crowded. Many librarians complain that the program and study rooms in their buildings are either too hot or too cold, and either stuffy or drafty. Because of the widely varying demands of these rooms for temperature control and air supply, they cannot be simply piggybacked on the air circulation and controls of large adjacent spaces.

This chapter begins with a review of general planning issues that affect most program and study rooms, and then discusses individual types of rooms and their special needs. Our intent is to avoid duplication of material, but inevitably some concepts are mentioned in both of these sections.

II. GENERAL FEATURES OF TYPICAL MEETING ROOMS

A. Room Configuration

The right floor shape for almost all meeting rooms is a simple rectangle with the front of the room narrower than the sides. This approach provides the best possible viewing of projected material, since viewers to extreme sides of a screen see distorted and frequently dim images. It also provides the best sight lines.

Unfortunately, many meeting rooms are built in odd shapes. Among those we have seen are:

- Banana-shaped meeting rooms, where people at one end cannot see people at the other.
- Meeting rooms with oddly irregular floor plans, which prevent the logical arrangement of seating or tables. For example, there are meeting rooms with abrupt triangular projections or with unexpected curves. None of these improve functions.
- Trapezoid-shaped meeting rooms where rows of chairs get shorter or wider as one progresses from front to rear.
- L-shaped meeting rooms, where a speaker visible to everyone in the room has to stand in one corner of the room, at the bend of the L. Under these circumstances, speakers have to speak in two different directions, and a projection screen at the center has to be viewed at about a 45-degree angle by most of the people in the room.

Most of the odd floor shapes we have seen were a result of gimmicky exterior designs rather than of functional necessity, but occasionally they were the result of complex expansion projects.

If your designers propose anything other than a simple rectangle, it's time to challenge the concept.

B. Determining Meeting Room Capacities

A major problem in planning program and study rooms is determining the number of people each room should be designed to hold.

In situations where individual public school classes will use rooms, standard class sizes are used as a guide. Pessimists will want to provide extra seating on the presumption that in years to come, some schools will find themselves under financial pressures and increase class sizes. Rooms may also need to be able to handle two classes at the same time.

Academic meeting rooms can vary widely in size, providing space for anything from seminar groups to rooms seating hundreds of people. The room size chosen can be driven both by library needs and campus-wide needs.

The size of public library multifunction rooms often depends both on library program needs and the availability of alternate meeting spaces in the community. In a small town, for example, the library may possibly provide the only good group meeting space in the community. Multifunction rooms can also be set up in a number of ways; adults seated at tables take up far more space than children seated on the floor.

Conference rooms are often found in academic libraries, public libraries, and special libraries. Often, they are designed to hold groups of limited size, with the understanding that under unusual circumstances (for example, 100 angry citizens attending a public library board meeting) meetings will have to be relocated to other spaces.

C. Calculating Required Space

This section covers meeting rooms of all types except formal auditoriums. Rooms for serious dramatic or musical performances may require a large amount of support space, and planning the total required square footage for support spaces of this type is beyond the scope of our book.

Calculating the space required for a multifunction meeting room is fairly straightforward. As a first estimate, assume that seating for users in chairs requires about 12 square feet per person, while seating at tables requires at least 25. If all the furniture is removed from a room, an amazing number of children can sit on the floor, perhaps one child for every 6 square feet.

In addition to seating space, you will need to allow space for:

- *Performers.* Meeting rooms often require extra space for performers. This can vary from a few square feet at the front of the room to permanent or portable stages or platforms. Depending on the kinds of performances expected, libraries can provide dressing rooms, green rooms (offstage spaces for performers, with direct access to stages), back passageways allowing performers to cross the stage unseen, storage for scenery and props, sound and light booths, and so on.
- *Furniture storage closets.* Assuming stack chairs on dollies and folding plastic tables (or flip-top tables on casters), your furniture storeroom may be about 10 percent as large as the room itself. But it's important to have your architects calculate closet space needs for you when the room is designed, to be sure that everything can be put away. Furniture storage closets work much better if they are wide rather than deep. You don't want to have to empty an entire closet to get at something tucked in the back. A wide, shallow closet with double (or even more) doors is a lot easier to use.
- *Coat storage.* In the example below, we've assumed coat rods in alcoves at the back of the room, with alcoves 2.5 feet deep and one coat every 3 inches. Other methods of storing coats include hooks along walls and coat racks on casters.
- *Kitchenettes.* Meeting room kitchenettes vary from a counter behind closed doors to full walk-in kitchens.
- *Audiovisual equipment closets.* If members of the public are allowed to set up furniture (or are forced to if the room is free), you will want to keep your AV equipment in a separate closet. The same is true if the meeting room serves as a classroom.
- *Closets for maker space equipment.*

You may also need space for:

- Program equipment storage closets, particularly for children's programs.
- Storage closets for book sale books. If your Friends of the Library group holds sales in the meeting room, you will want the boxes of books to be stacked nearby. It's much easier to move boxes of books one by one to the meeting room between book sales than to move them there all at once from other parts of the library when the sale time arrives.
- Storage closets for groups that use the room on a regular basis and leave their equipment there. Many meeting rooms, particularly those in small-town public libraries, are used routinely by scout groups, clubs, elections, and so on, and we have seen a variety of provisions for storage.

The proper configuration of storage closets may affect room space. Workable storage closets are wide and shallow rather than narrow and deep, and the required double doors may prevent movable furniture from being placed close to walls.

With the possible exception of large, formal auditoriums, most meeting rooms in most libraries are probably too small. In many years of consulting, we have never had libraries complain that their meeting rooms were too large—even when we thought the rooms were amazingly big.

As an example, here is a very preliminary space estimate for a public library meeting room designed to seat 100 adults on stack chairs, provide coat rods for 100 coats, provide a very modest space for performers to stand, and include suitable support spaces. It does not include space for a piano, folding stage sections, extra spaces for simple theatrical performances, storage for club equipment, and so on.

Main meeting room	**1,575 square feet**
100 adults @ 12 sf	1,200
Performer space	150
Coat space for 100 coats @ .75 sf	75
Subtotal	1,425
Circulation space	150*
Total	**1,575 square feet**

Support spaces	**450 square feet**
Furniture storage closet	150
Kitchenette	75
AV equipment storage closet	75
Children's program closet	150
Book sale storage closet	150
Total	**600 square feet**
TOTAL SPACE	**2,175 square feet**

---

*"Circulation space" is extra space for people to move around. For a more detailed discussion, see chapter 8 on "programming."

All of these square footages are estimates, but the important point is that a meeting room for 100 adults requires about 2,200 square feet, or 22 square feet per person.

By contrast, many guides to estimating library space suggest that meeting rooms require about 10 square feet per person. We think the only way to achieve this is to have overcrowded rooms with little or no support space.

Conference rooms require substantially more space per person than do multifunction program rooms, because chairs at tables require more space than chairs in rows. For example, consider a conference room with 10 seats at a conference table, an additional 10 side chairs for observers, and space for serving coffee and snacks.

Conference room	565 square feet
10 people at table @ 25 sf	250
10 side chairs @ 12 sf	120
Coat space for 20 coats @ .75 sf	15
Space at front of room for equipment	50
Kitchenette	15
AV equipment storage closet	15
Subtotal	465
Circulation space	100
TOTAL	**565 square feet**

However, the actual space required for seating at a conference table may be substantially higher than 25 square feet per person, and only a measured drawing of the selected table will provide accurate information. The size of chairs can also make a significant difference in required space. Some pompous boardroom chairs are enormous.

Regardless of formulas, there needs to be enough space—at least three feet of open space—to walk comfortably behind people seated at conference tables without rubbing against walls. In far too many conference rooms, people have too little room to squeeze past occupied chairs.

If the conference room will be lined with side chairs, there needs to be space between the edge of the table and the wall for people seated at the conference table, people seated in side chairs, and people walking between the two rows of chairs. This means eight feet or more of space. If the conference room is designed to be converted from chairs around a table to rows of chairs, there will need to be a substantial extra closet to hold the sections of a modular conference table when the room is set up with rows of chairs, or to hold extra chairs when the room is set up as a conference room. Convertible conference rooms also require chairs of normal proportions rather than immense swivel chairs.

If the role of the conference room is to be an impressive place, that can mean substantially more square footage.

D. Locating Program Rooms in Buildings

Almost all library program rooms—including auditoriums, classrooms, multifunction rooms, and conference rooms—work better when they can be used when the rest of the library is closed. This enables programs to continue after closing time, classes to be scheduled at times when the library is closed, and board meetings to continue when the rest of the library closes.

This kind of flexibility is particularly important in small public libraries with limited hours, but any library that closes at 9:00 p.m. may be forced to end library programs prematurely and to kick out community groups before people are ready to leave if people leaving the meeting room have access to the rest of the library.

If classrooms are buried in the middle of academic libraries, particularly in areas to which the library may someday want to limit access, any attempts by the college or university to schedule classes there can lead to problems.

In all cases, the easy way to separate meeting rooms from the rest of the library is to make them directly accessible from entry foyers. This has become a standard approach to public library design.

Foyers that provide access to meeting rooms also need to provide access to restrooms. (There are additional benefits to locating restrooms off entry foyers, because materials that have not been checked out cannot be taken into restrooms.)

To prevent security problems in these situations, staff members at lending desks should have direct sight lines through the foyer and out the front door of the library, so they can see who is entering the library and entering the restrooms and program rooms.

The floor plan in the chapter 4 sketch shows the most functional relationship between entry foyer, public restrooms, program room, and library in small and medium-sized public library buildings.

One architect Fred worked with insisted that the emergency exit from a public library meeting room should lead to the main library space, from which people could then exit through a different emergency exit. This would have made it impossible to use the meeting room after the library was closed, and it took Fred a month to convince the architect that the design was a bad idea.

E. Furnishings

The comments on furnishings in this section apply in particular to multifunction meeting rooms, conference rooms, seminar rooms, and classrooms. For notes on seating in quiet reading rooms, study rooms, children's craft and story rooms, and multilevel children's reading rooms, please see the relevant parts of this chapter.

1. Seating

- *Stacking Chairs.* By far the best seating for multifunction meeting rooms is provided by stacking chairs. As with all chairs, when the time comes to select stacking chairs, ask manufacturers for samples and have a number of people try them out. Remember that most chairs feel pretty decent when people first sit down, and their failings become apparent only after fifteen minutes or so. All stack chairs need dollies. When selecting stacking chairs, always make sure that there are no sharp places on the frames that will scratch the adjacent chairs in the stack. For example, a tubular frame with a joint at the top may leave extremely visible scratches on the front sides of the chair backs. Stacking chairs are available with either molded plastic seats and backs or upholstered seats and backs, with corresponding tradeoffs between comfort and ease of cleaning. Stacking chairs are also available with plastic mesh seats and backs that provide comfort and unusually light weight.
- *Never buy folding chairs.* They are miserable to set up and take down, and they are extremely hard to store.
- *Conference room chairs.* A wide variety of conference room seating is available, ranging from comfortable swivel chairs that might be used for administrators' desks to high-backed and imposing chairs that suggest corporate boardrooms of a pompous variety. In terms of actual comfort, high backs contribute very little, since most people want support in the lumbar region—the small of the back. So to us, the decision appears to be mainly one of desired message. Remember that pretentious chairs can excite snide blogging by local critics.

If the conference room is planned to be flexible, with a modular table that can be stored, the chairs selected will affect the amount of storage required. Ideally, the chairs will be of modest size.

- *Folding tables.* Many meeting rooms are supplied with folding tables. When specifying tables, remember to require enough to take care of table-intensive situations, such as book sales. The worst kind of tables are the heavy folding tables with metal legs and frames and tops made of laminate-covered chip board. Setting up tables like these is a job for a couple of strong people, who will quickly tire of the metal edges of the frames cutting into their hands and want heavy leather gloves. Similar tables are available with molded plastic tops. These weigh much less than the tables described above, and they don't have sharp edges. If folding tables are six feet long rather than the traditional eight, they will be lighter, and they can be carried vertically through doorways, which are typically 6'8" to 7' high. Standard folding tables used in most meeting rooms are 2'6" from front to back. Narrower ones are available for situations where the members of an audience need a place to write while they all face a speaker or projection screen. Tables of this type can be set up in pairs if the library requires deeper tables.

- *Tables on wheels.* Another option is tables on wheels with tops that flip up vertically for storage. These have the advantage of never having to be picked up. Typically tables on wheels will have locking casters and tops that latch into position. With the tops flipped up for storage, tables of this type usually can be nested together for more compact storage. The great thing is that one small person can easily set up a table, something that is not true of other table types.

- *Conference and seminar room tables.* Large conference tables are expensive and amazingly inflexible. They are extremely heavy and awkward to relocate. If removed from the conference room, they are almost impossible to store.

    For this reason, unless it is important that the conference room be really impressive, we recommend modular tables.

    Modular tables also provide extra flexibility. If the table can be disassembled or folded up and stored in an adjacent closet, a conference room can be temporarily reconfigured as a small meeting room. The closet can hold the extra chairs when the table is in use.

> Fred worked with one library that was forced to hang a conference room tabletop on one wall of its multifunction meeting room because there was literally no other place in the building where it would fit.

A conference room that seats 16 around a table should probably seat about 32 in rows of chairs with the table dismantled and put in a closet. Remember that this kind of flexibility requires practical chairs rather than the monstrous swivel chairs provided in some pompous conference rooms.

- *Furniture storage.* The wide variety of possible meeting room furnishings means that your architects will need to make sure that the furniture storage closet can hold all of the scheduled items. Schematic design drawings should indicate how this storage will work. As with all storage closets, you need to make very clear in your program that no other functions will intrude into the closet. Nothing is more frustrating than finding that your designers added some item of technical equipment to your furniture storage closet, and that it will no longer hold all of your furniture. (This may seem unlikely, but it happens and can cause havoc with meeting rooms.) Closets for furniture storage need to be wide and shallow rather than narrow and deep, so that people setting up furnishings aren't forced to drag half a dozen dollies or stack chairs out of the way to get at a large folding table at the back.

F. Lighting

1. Natural Lighting

Windows in meeting rooms are a mixed blessing because they require blackout shades, and meeting rooms that will be used for projected images may be better off without windows.

We have seen a number of libraries that had windows at the front of their meeting rooms, behind the speakers. Usually this appears to be due to the exterior design of the building, but it creates problems in meeting rooms. Always say "No!" No speaking situation is improved by blinding daylight behind the speaker or behind a projection screen.

2. Artificial Lighting

As with almost all areas in libraries, the best way to light meeting rooms is to bounce the light off the ceiling. This is particularly true in rooms that are intended to be multifunctional, which includes all meeting rooms mentioned here except formal auditoriums, formal conference rooms, and faculty studies.

The ideal level of illumination in meeting rooms varies widely. Some groups (such as stamp collectors' clubs) require fairly bright lighting, while audiences at musical performances may require only low levels of light.

There are two easy ways to provide a variety of light levels. The first is by using three-tube fluorescent fixtures with the center tubes switched separately, or LED fixtures designed to function the same way. This allows either one, two, or three tubes to be illuminated. Suitable illumination levels might include 20, 40, and 60 foot-candles. However, if you plan to have many groups needing very bright light (such as stamp collectors' clubs), you may need higher foot-candle levels.

A second way to provide variable light levels is to use fluorescent lamps with electronic ballasts designed to allow dimming. Dimmers of this type allow light levels to be adjusted, but they do not permit the control range possible with incandescent lamps combined with variable transformers, which can be moved gradually from fully off to fully on. Dimmable fluorescent lights may have to be turned on to full power and then backed off in brightness.

Some rooms benefit from supplementary downlight systems for situations where class members need to take notes while viewing projected material. Downlights can illuminate flat writing surfaces and lecturers' notes while not interfering with projection.

In meeting rooms used for performances or classes, lighting needs to be zoned, with the front or performance end of the room capable of being lighter or darker than the rest of the room.

In planning lighting systems in program and meeting rooms, it's important to avoid situations where pendant uplight fixtures can interfere with projection paths from ceiling-mounted projectors.

One unpleasant (but unfortunately popular) lighting concept is perimeter soffits with inset downlights. Although this design causes fewer problems in meeting rooms than it does in other library spaces, it's still a very bad idea. The use of perimeter soffits with recessed downlights results in odd patterns of light and dark on walls, direct glare from overly concentrated light sources, dark room perimeters, and sometimes low vertical clearances under the soffits. Crown moldings offer a far better way to ornament the junctions between walls and ceilings without screwing up lighting.

If public areas in your library have night-lights that remain on at all times, you may need to have a way to turn them off when programs require darkness. However, modern digital projectors seem to be bright enough to overcome night-lights.

G. Acoustics

Acoustical planning is of major importance in all types of program and study rooms. Unfortunately, we have seen many libraries with problems in this area.

1. Unwanted Sound Transmission

Preventing the unwanted transmission of sound between adjacent program rooms or between program rooms and the rest of the library is important whether the rooms in question are huge meeting rooms, small seminar rooms, or tiny study rooms.

While sound transmission can be merely annoying in most situations, it can be a very serious problem in others. Consider, for example, a medical library that needs to keep conversations between physicians particularly private, or a law library where members of the firm are having a confidential meeting concerning a case.

Some easy ways of limiting sound transmission include:

- Extending partitions between rooms vertically to the bottom of the floor above or the underside of the roof rather than ending them at ceiling level.

> For years, Fred attended monthly meetings in a library building where the suspended ceiling had been installed before the partitions between rooms were installed. When he visited the men's restroom next to the main meeting room, he could see an eighth-inch of light at the top of the partition. He could also hear every word spoken in the meeting room with crystal clarity, giving him uneasy fears of reciprocity.

- Extending partitions to the bottom of the floor or roof above, and only after that installing a suspended ceiling, solves a lot of meeting room problems.
- Providing separately ducted air supplies and returns for all rooms rather than using louvers in the doors. Some libraries have study rooms with air supplies but no returns. Apparently, the designers assumed that air would find its way under the edge of the doors and from there to a central return duct. Air can also be returned through louvers in doors. Unfortunately, louvers in doors transmit sound particularly easily. Louvers in doors are a cheap tract-house-quality substitute for ducted air returns and have no place in a library.

- Avoiding connecting doors between meeting rooms. The small spaces around closed doors, particularly at the bottom, make it easy for sounds to carry between rooms.

> Fred worked with one library that had a door between the boardroom and the multifunction program room. Board meetings conducted at the same time as children's programs were always interesting.

- Limiting sound transmission by using double stud (staggered stud) walls. In walls of this type, drywall in one room is attached to one set of studs, while drywall in the adjacent room is attached to the other set. This prevents vibrations of the drywall in one room being transmitted directly to the drywall in the other room. Wood framed apartment buildings often use this kind of construction between apartments. In libraries, it may be helpful in the walls separating story and craft rooms from adjacent quiet areas. (Fred installed these in a library where the sound of small children bouncing off the wall of a multilevel reading room caused the librarian in the office next door to leap galvanically whenever a small body slammed into the wall a few inches from her desk. After conversion to a double stud wall, it sounded more like a distant pillow fight.)

If you are concerned that the proposed designs for your program rooms will lead to acoustic problems, particularly if your designers do not want to follow the ideas above, consider hiring an acoustic engineer. Few architectural firms have acoustic engineers on staff, and most do not propose to hire them for anything smaller than formal auditoriums, but a number of librarians have insisted on them and have benefited from doing so.

2. The Special Case of Movable Room Dividers

We feel that movable dividers designed to separate large meeting rooms into smaller spaces are almost always a serious mistake.

Dividers of this type are very expensive, but they usually perform poorly, with sounds bleeding through the dividers. Groups using the rooms are usually very much aware of what's happening in the adjacent space.

Large numbers of meeting rooms in new libraries are built with these dividers. Directors tend to speak highly of them, but staff members less emotionally involved in the building projects and more frequently involved in programming often admit that the dividers don't work well.

Dividers are also extremely expensive. Among other things, they require massive steel beams to keep the dividers from sagging in the middle when they are closed.

Some librarians also report that their dividers are difficult to operate. Occasionally staff members even get trapped between sections of movable dividers and have to call for help.

In addition, dividers can be unattractive. Their presence alters the otherwise symmetrical look of meeting rooms. Some dividers stick out into rooms when the dividers are open. Even those that fit into pockets and are hidden by doors affect ceiling designs, interrupting crown moldings or other details.

Dividers frequently complicate projection systems. A digital projector and screen suitable for a large meeting room will probably be in a poor location when the room is divided. One possible outcome is three projectors and three screens—one set for occasions when the entire room is in use, and the two separate sets for occasions when the room is divided.

Dividers can also make it difficult to take room reservations because of the size options. A group that reserves a half-size room, for example, can deny space to a following group that needs a full-size room.

Some librarians complain that it can be almost impossible to locate repair parts for movable dividers.

Our strong recommendation is that you put your money into an extra, small meeting room rather than try to use a movable divider.

> Nothing relieves a boring string quartet more than the happy voices of children playing video games on the other side of the room divider.

3. Room Acoustics

Formal auditoriums require analysis by acoustical engineers and are not covered in this book.

In our opinion, all general-purpose program and study rooms need flat acoustic ceilings.

Although some program rooms are built with washable floors, most are carpeted. In addition to feeling far more welcoming, carpet helps control noise.

Children's program and craft rooms, however, are almost always constructed with tile floors (vinyl or rubber) to allow messes to be cleaned up. To provide places for children to sit during story hours, the libraries purchase area rugs, carpet squares, or pillows. As a result of having hard floor surfaces, story and craft rooms particularly need acoustic ceilings.

H. HVAC

The heating, ventilating, and air conditioning demands of all sorts of meeting rooms are extreme.

Typically, rooms of this type are either empty or packed with people. Since people arrive and depart abruptly, HVAC systems have to be able to respond to changing needs unusually quickly.

The problem, of course, is that people exude large quantities of heat, moisture, and carbon dioxide. A meeting room without a highly responsive HVAC system soon becomes oppressively warm and humid, and excessive CO_2 buildup can make audiences extremely uncomfortable. Modern systems have CO_2 and moisture sensors but they still have to adapt quickly.

Many library employees are unhappy with unresponsive meeting room HVAC systems. They report that rooms are frigid when empty or lightly occupied and quickly become unpleasant when programs take place.

Of all mechanical systems in libraries, HVAC systems are by far the most complex. Be sure to include air-handling needs for meeting rooms in your building program statements.

I. Coat Storage

All meeting rooms larger than study rooms need some kind of way to store coats. Stack chairs are generally too small and aisles between seats are too narrow to accommodate coats draped over the backs of all the chairs. Coats draped on the chairs around a conference table are clumsy and get in the way. On rainy days, wet winter coats can bring the exciting aroma of wet dog to the event.

Without provision for coat storage, children's coats end up piled everywhere on the floor, and adults either pile them on tables or end up wearing them (in rooms that often become too warm when they are filled with people).

1. Coat Hooks or Pegs

One simple method of storing coats is coat hooks or pegs mounted along walls, particularly at the back of the room. To avoid people impaling themselves on hooks, you can specify hooks or pegs with wide faces.

If you have a row of pegs on a wall, consider providing a shelf above for other possessions. (Since people will pile books and other heavy objects on shelves, they need to be unusually strong. Be sure your architects provide for the extra strength by installing blocking in the walls rather than relying on toggle bolts through the drywall.)

You may want pegs at staggered heights, for use by both children and adults.

When you specify hooks or pegs, make sure they are not made of cast zinc. Zinc castings are notoriously breakable. (Fred visited a library with a long row of coat hooks in a children's department. Virtually all had broken off at various lengths, leaving impressively sharp edges at about children's eye level.)

2. Coat Bars

Perhaps a neater way to store coats is on hangers on bars. If the bars are inset in alcoves, it may also help keep rooms looking less cluttered.

In inexpensive house construction, many closets are two feet deep, but coats don't fit in closets that shallow. A minimum depth of 2'6" works a lot better. (Many metal coat rod holders are engineered for two-foot-deep closets. If you use them, you'll need to use wooden blocks to hold the backs of the holders away from the back wall of the closet.)

> Some coat bars come with permanently mounted coat hangers that cannot be removed from the bars. These are about as popular with library users as automated telephone answering gear.

There needs to be a couple of inches of space between the top of hanger bars and any shelves above them.

3. Movable Coat Racks

Coat racks on casters are a standard item in some meeting situations. In many meeting rooms they tend to be too small and too messy, but they have the advantage of being movable, and they can be stored out of sight when not needed.

4. Locations

Because hanging coats are not as decorative as one might hope, some architects find ways to avoid having them on display in meeting rooms. One method is to place coat bars in a short entryway to the meeting room. If you have coat bars in alcoves, you can add doors, making them in essence extremely broad coat closets.

J. Wiring

Most program rooms need a great deal of wiring, and they are likely to need more rather than less as the years pass.

The inexpensive way to provide wiring is to do so during construction. Retrofitting outlets in walls is expensive, and adding outlets for floors that are slab on grade is painfully expensive.

Unfortunately, libraries abound in meeting rooms with inadequate wiring. Just a few years ago, for example, Fred gave a talk in the meeting room of a brand-new library and had to find a fifty-foot extension cord to plug in his projector.

The comments in this section do not apply to formal auditoriums.

1. Electrical Outlets and Circuits

All program rooms, study rooms, and quiet reading rooms need electrical outlets every four or five feet on all the walls.

Rooms also need outlets in a grid in the floor, probably about a 10 × 10-foot grid. Be sure to insist in your printed specifications to your architects that all outlets be completely flush with the floor, so tables and chairs can be positioned anywhere.

The surge in use of laptop computers means that many program and study rooms will need very frequent electrical outlets to prevent users from trailing their laptop cords across walkways.

Conference tabletops need electrical outlets. Many people bring laptops to meetings. Some libraries provide laptops for all of their board members. If they can plug their laptops in on the tabletop, they won't string cords across the walking spaces around the table.

To envision the stress than can be placed on meeting room wiring, imagine a large computer class using laptops, all of which need to be plugged in while keeping the floor free of wires.

Kitchenettes in meeting rooms require a number of separate circuits for times when users bring several heated serving dishes they want to use at the same time. In our experience, most meeting room kitchenettes have far too few circuits, leading to seriously dangerous practices like stringing extension cords down hallways to access extra circuits.

2. Wireless Signals

All modern program and study rooms require strong Wi-Fi signals.

Given the reliability of wireless transmission, you may decide that you do not need a great deal of data conduit in your program and study rooms, but hard-wired connections via Ethernet jacks provide better service. In addition, you will need ways to connect laptops and computers to your ceiling-mounted digital projector.

Whether or not you use laptops in your meeting room, speakers may require strong wireless signals to present their programs.

And who knows what's coming in another 10 or 20 years? Although wireless signals have made some data wiring obsolete, the best time to install data conduit is before the drywall goes up and the floor slab is poured.

K. Audiovisual Equipment

Modern meeting and conference rooms are expected to be compatible with a wide variety of electronic equipment. Among other things, they need projection screens, ceiling-mounted digital projectors, audio amplification systems, strong wireless signals, compatibility with items like whiteboards, and the flexibility to deal with unforeseen technological changes.

The problem with planning audiovisual (AV) equipment for libraries is the tremendous rate of technological obsolescence. A good library building may remain in use for a century or more. Compared to this sturdy longevity, projection and amplification equipment has the life span of a gnat. (Think how recently we were still creating projection rooms with special windows for 16mm projectors.)

So first and foremost, we recommend that you assume frequent updating of equipment.

Here are some miscellaneous observations:

1. Projection Equipment

Properly selecting and locating projection equipment can be challenging. Some architects are very competent at this, and others are not. To verify your design, try to find an AV firm that specializes in audio-video installations.

If you mount your video projector on a drop, things will look neat and tidy, but there's a good chance it will end up in the wrong place with regard to the projection screen when you buy a new projector. If the projector is simply mounted on the ceiling, it will be easier to relocate. (A "drop" is a section of the ceiling that is lowered by an electric motor and provides a platform for a projector. Some require about two feet of clearance above the ceiling, but check with your AV specialists before the construction drawings are finalized.)

To limit damage to projection screens from mishandling (and the predictable failure of the clutch mechanisms that keep screens open), we prefer electrically driven screens with key switches.

Many video projectors come with zoom lenses, but they don't zoom very much.

Be careful that the reflected uplight fixtures that light the room do not interfere with the projection beam of the ceiling-mounted projector.

2. Amplification Equipment

All meeting rooms of any size need sound systems for playing video and audio recordings.

Sound systems are also necessary for amplifying the voices of speakers. We all have mental images of strong-voiced speakers and acute young ears, but programs can also feature the feeble-voiced speaking to the partially deaf.

Be sure your sound system is suitable for both voice and music.

3. Video Recording

You may need to be able to record or broadcast events taking place in meeting rooms. Public library board meetings, classes that have both in-person and remote attendance, and other functions may require this ability.

4. Security

The cost of electronic apparatus in a well-equipped meeting or conference room can be impressive. Depending on anticipated use, there may need to be extra security provisions. For portable equipment, a locking closet may be the best solution.

L. Storage Closets

One of the most frequent errors in program and meeting room design is the failure to provide essential storage closets. Depending on their purposes, program rooms need storage space for furniture, electronic equipment, children's program and craft supplies, book sale books, materials used by cooperating clubs or agencies, materials used by various academic classes, and so on.

As an example of the importance of storage closets in meeting rooms, public library children's departments can be forced to haul program supplies hundreds of feet for each program, when the supplies could simply be left locked in a meeting room closet.

In almost every case, storage spaces need to be separate closets that can be locked individually.

All closets work best if they are broad and shallow rather than narrow and deep. Having to haul out stacks of stuff to get at things at the back of the closet improves no one's mood. Large closets need at least double doors.

The absence of storage closets diminishes the actual capacity of meeting rooms. A room designed to hold sixty people seated in rows theater-style won't be able to do so if tables, AV equipment on carts, and other items are piled around the edges.

Stacks of unused furniture and equipment in meeting rooms also look impressively unprofessional. Librarians may eventually get used to this disarray, much as people eventually fail to note the moving cartons that have been piled in one corner of the living room for a few years, but the first impression outsiders receive is of slovenly disarray.

> Somewhere there is probably a program room with excess storage space, but we have never seen it.

A serious architectural misdemeanor involves using program room storage closets to house irrelevant mechanical and electrical equipment. Include strong words in your program forbidding this practice, and watch your construction drawings for last-minute violations of this necessary requirement.

1. Furniture Storage Closets

All multifunction meeting rooms need furniture storage closets, as do almost all specialized meeting rooms.

Although you can estimate the size of your furniture closet at about 10 percent of actual meeting room space, it's important to have your architect verify this by figuring out the space required for the actual furniture you select. For example, flip top tables on wheels may take up more space than simple folding tables, and extras like portable stage sections require space.

Even conference rooms can benefit from furniture storage closets. For example, if libraries use modular conference tables that can be folded up and stored, conference rooms can be reconfigured as meeting rooms with chairs in rows. But doing so requires space to store the extra chairs when the room is set up conference fashion and space to store the conference table sections when the room is set up with chairs. It also requires smaller chairs (which can be just as comfortable as massive swivel chairs).

2. Audiovisual Storage Closets

Many program rooms—including in particular multifunction program rooms, conference rooms, and classrooms—need space for the secure storage of expensive AV equipment.

They also need space for computer racks to hold projection and amplification equipment.

Separate closets are important here to protect expensive and delicate equipment from being bumped by (for example) furniture, and to allow people using your room to set up their own furniture without mucking about with your equipment.

See also the section on "Closets for 'Maker Space' Equipment" below.

3. Program and Craft Supplies Closets

Probably the most frequent use of public library meeting rooms by departments of the libraries is for children's programs, and almost every public library multifunction room needs closet space for children's program supplies.

Far too many libraries are designed without such closets, forcing children's staff members to waste vast amounts of time hauling materials between children's departments and meeting rooms.

The failure to provide storage closets for children's program supplies in meeting rooms doesn't save space, for the same material will have to be stored somewhere else.

Unlike most other storage closets, children's supply closets need shelving. As with all storage areas, this is one possible place to use obsolete but sturdy shelving when buildings are expanded or replaced. (Think of how much happier you'll be when your old mauve steel shelving is hidden inside a storage closet.)

Children's supply closets also need floor space for such bulky objects as puppet theaters.

In the best of all worlds, a children's program closet will be directly accessible from both the meeting room and the children's craft and story rooms, or from the craft and story room and the children's staff workroom.

4. Book Sale Closets

One of the most aggressive consumers of library space is book sales run by volunteer groups. Librarians always hesitate to cross volunteer groups because support groups are so important, but some groups have taken over vast amounts of floor space for book sale activities, frequently providing more space for individual books than the potential sales prices of the books justify. In some libraries, volunteer groups have actually maintained stack units in which customers can browse for used books.

We think a much more efficient model is to sell used books either in kiosks by lending desks and/or at periodic major book sales in program rooms.

To support the latter, libraries need book sale storage closets directly adjacent to meeting rooms. It's far easier to move boxes of books to the storage closet one at a time between sales, and then pull them all out in one fell swoop when the sale time arrives, than it is to store them far from the meeting room and have to transport them all at one time to the site of the sale. (If you worry about the space it will take to store boxed books by your meeting room, it will cost about the same amount to store them anywhere else in the building.)

Book sale storerooms need to be just large enough to hold books stacked in cartons perhaps five feet high.

5. Computer Storage Closets

One group of important but sometimes underutilized library spaces is computer classrooms. They perform a vital function, but in some libraries they stand idle much of the time.

One approach to avoiding the high cost of little-used computer classrooms is to build them adjacent to groups of public computers, installing sliding glass walls that allow the classroom computers to be used for general purposes when classes are not taking place.

Another possibility is to set up classrooms only when needed. A multifunction meeting room can be set up as a computer classroom with laptop computers. A large number of floor outlets will be needed, but a strong wireless signal should work.

A meeting room designed to serve as a computer classroom will probably need a storage closet for a laptop-charging rack and for a movable teaching station.

6. Closets for Cooperating Groups

Many libraries work with groups that use program spaces on a regular basis and need a place to store equipment and supplies.

In public libraries, groups like the Boy Scouts and Girl Scouts may meet in the library and need space for banners, flags, and program materials. Hobby groups may have equipment that is difficult to transport. If the library serves as a polling place, it may need a closet for voting booths and other equipment.

In academic libraries, equipment needed for specific courses may need to be stored in meeting rooms.

However, the possibility of providing storage for outside groups can be a door that libraries would prefer not to open. Once a group has a storage closet in your meeting room, (a) you'll never get rid of their stuff, even if they never actually use it, and (b) all sorts of other groups will want to store their stuff in your library as well.

7. Closets for "Maker Space" Equipment

At the time this book was written, public libraries were extremely enthusiastic about maker spaces, rooms provided with a variety of equipment for audio and video production work, 3-D printers, and other equipment aimed primarily at young adult users. Complex maker spaces may include small production studies with acoustic separation.

The problem with any spaces designed for young adult purposes is that they stand idle when teenagers are in school.

Some libraries have dealt with this problem by using multifunction meeting rooms for maker spaces, setting up equipment as needed, particularly after school. Given the cost of the equipment, separate storage closets are ideal, although closets for general projection and program equipment can also be used to house maker space equipment.

M. Kitchenettes

A variety of program spaces—particularly the multifunction meeting rooms found in many public libraries—benefit from having small kitchenettes with sinks, refrigerators, and counter space for making coffee.

In small program and conference rooms, these can be no more than simple alcoves (with or without doors), with no actual floor space inside the kitchenette, but larger program rooms often have walk-in kitchens.

If you provide a kitchenette, be sure that the sink has enough clearance to allow a coffee urn to be filled. This means a high gooseneck faucet and perhaps a deeper than normal sink. There's nothing more frustrating for people making coffee than to have to find a janitor's mop sink to fill a coffee urn or have to find a small saucepan to ladle water into the urn.

> No matter how small the meeting or conference room, you don't want a toy sink. Fred worked with a library where the conference room sink was about four inches deep and a foot square. When he asked about problems with the building, the sink was almost the first thing mentioned.

We think that providing stoves or microwaves in public meeting room kitchenettes is generally a bad idea and frequently an extraordinarily bad idea. These greatly increase the chance of users starting fires, and keeping them clean may prove to be less entertaining than one might hope. Sooner or later, someone will heat up something that puts out an unpleasant smell. Depending on local zoning codes, cooktops may require extremely expensive commercial range hoods with fire-suppression systems.

Many libraries keep hospitality gear in their meeting room kitchenettes. For this reason, it's a good idea to provide locks on all cabinet doors and drawers.

If you have a larger walk-in kitchen used for community dining events, you may want a pass-through window for food service.

You will also need to make provisions for trash disposal, both in the kitchenette itself and in the main program room space.

Kitchenettes may also need to meet health codes. On campuses, there may be an agency responsible for kitchen specifications. Public libraries can check with local governments.

Most kitchenettes appear to have an inadequate number of electrical circuits. Even a small kitchenette in a small meeting room in a small library will need five or six separate 20-amp circuits, or users with electrically heated devices like coffee urns, Dutch ovens, and toasters will constantly trip electrical circuit breakers. A large kitchen used for community dinners may need a dozen or more separate circuits. The result of an insufficient number of electrical circuits may be people daisy-chaining cheap extension cords together to access outlets on different circuits. Fire marshals take an extraordinarily dim view of this.

N. Floor Coverings

This section contains brief comments on the use of floor coverings in meeting rooms. For a far more extensive discussion, see chapter 31 on "Walls, Floors, and Ceilings."

1. Carpet

Most modern program and study rooms have carpeted floors. Carpeting soaks up excess noise. It's comfortable to walk on. And it looks less brutally institutional than other floor-covering options.

Traditionally, libraries used broadloom carpet for meeting room floors. However, the improvements in carpet squares in recent years make them a preferred alternative. One of the advantages of carpet squares is the ability to replace one that becomes badly stained through (for example) beverage mishaps.

2. Resilient Flooring

Resilient flooring is smooth flooring that flexes slightly and is more comfortable to stand on.

Some meeting rooms have vinyl or rubber tile floors. Both are less soft underfoot than carpet, but more comfortable than ceramic tile or concrete. They are easy to wash, but they are cold and noisy. And the necessity of occasionally stripping and rewaxing vinyl tile floors means more maintenance than one might like.

With the exception of children's craft rooms, where washability is essential, we don't see many reasons to use VCT (vinyl composite tile) or rubber tile floors.

Some green surfaces may also be workable, including cork and recycled rubber.

3. Concrete

A few harshly modernist libraries have concrete floors. Concrete floors create the welcome aura of (at best) a cheap big box store and (at worst) an old aircraft hangar.

Staining and sealing concrete makes it look a little better. But not much. Staining and sealing don't soak up reverberation or the noise of footfalls. Stain typically doesn't take evenly. And staining and sealing don't make concrete any softer underfoot.

4. Avoiding Stains

One of the easiest ways to avoid permanent stains in carpets is to ban all red and purple beverages.

> The indelible nature of red food coloring is no doubt greatly to the credit of American industry, but you still don't want it in your library.

5. Tarps

If you will be having messy art or craft projects in your meeting room, you may want to protect the floor with tarps. If so, you will want to plan storage space for tarps when they are not in use, as well as storage containers large enough for tarps.

O. Ceiling Height

Meeting rooms need ceilings high enough to allow audiences seated in chairs to see projected images over the heads of the people in front of them. Even in fairly small meeting rooms, this usually means a ceiling height of a minimum of about twelve feet.

Many meeting rooms have built-in raised platforms or folding platform sections to raise performers off the floor so people in the back row can see something over the heads of the people in front of them. This requires even higher ceilings.

The best way to light meeting rooms is with reflected uplight. Because these fixtures must hang down a minimum of two feet from the ceiling, this also adds to ceiling height requirements.

If meeting rooms are set up for video conferencing, they need enough overhead clearance for proper lighting.

Conference rooms seating a dozen or so people around a table can get by with slightly lower ceilings because people frequently sit on both sides of a long table, looking at a projection screen at the end of the room. However, conference rooms of this type are most flexible if they are set up so their large tables can also be stowed and chairs can be arranged in rows. In this case, people using the room may have to see over each other's heads.

Because meeting room ceilings in a library often need to be higher than the ceilings in the rest of the building, a number of libraries have made their meeting rooms separate wings rather than raise all the ceilings on a floor to a far greater height than otherwise needed.

Meeting rooms also benefit from having no occupied spaces above because that results in fewer bearing columns getting in the way of seating and viewing.

When you are working with your architects on plans for a meeting room, a lengthwise cross-section drawing of the meeting room will help you evaluate whether the ceiling is high enough.

P. Accessibility

All meeting rooms should be accessible to users with disabilities.

Making new meeting rooms accessible is easy, but bringing older ones up to code can be difficult.

1. Wheelchairs

Auditoriums with sloped floors need open spaces for wheelchairs. Review specific requirements with your architects.

Other meeting rooms with flat floors just need enough elbowroom to maneuver wheelchairs. Check the clearances in particular in small study rooms, which need to be large enough for the assigned table and for one or more wheelchairs. (This is another argument for having all furnishings movable.)

The major problem in large meeting rooms involves raised stages. If you have a stage, it will need to be accessible. In practice, this means either a ramp from the floor of the room to the stage, a mechanical lift, or access at stage height from some other space in the library.

Ask your architect whether folding stage platforms need to be made accessible. (We think that they should be.)

2. Audio Amplification

Accessibility codes require broadcast gear that functions with individual amplification units.

Most of these require loop antennas linked to the room's PA system. The right time to install a loop of this type is while the room's audio system is being constructed.

Remember that audio amplification is not just for the totally deaf. As with physical access, where libraries cope with users with walkers and strollers, many users simply have failing hearing.

Q. Security

This chapter touches on meeting and study room security in a number of places. To summarize briefly:

- Arrange buildings to permit after-hours access to program rooms and classrooms without allowing people into the library proper.
- To provide staff oversight of multifunction rooms—particularly in public libraries—install internal windows with Venetian blinds between program rooms and service desks.
- Study rooms need to be terrariums, with three glass walls extending from a foot or less above the floor to at least seven feet from the floor. The interiors of *all* study rooms should be visible to staff members seated at service desks. (For some reason, architects tend to resist this. Be insistent.
- Emergency exits from program rooms must lead directly outside the library, not to other areas of the building.
- Provide separate storage closets for furniture and for expensive computer and AV gear. All storage closets should lock.
- All cabinets and drawers in meeting rooms should lock.
- An insufficient number of electrical circuits in kitchenettes is a fire risk as well as a general nuisance.
- Even if codes do not require a second exit from a meeting room, you may still want one because it gives people an extra way out in case of emergencies. If at all possible, emergency exits from meeting rooms should lead outside rather than to another area of the library.
- A wall telephone may provide an extra way to call 911.

III. TYPES OF PROGRAM AND STUDY ROOMS

This section reviews the range of program and study rooms found in typical libraries and comments on their special needs. The section is divided into auditoriums, classrooms, multipurpose rooms and community rooms, conference and seminar rooms, quiet reading rooms, study rooms, children's craft and story rooms, multi-level children's reading rooms, and faculty studies.

Information on general needs common to several types of program and study rooms appears above in section II. Unfortunately, it has proved difficult to eliminate all duplication between sections II and III.

A. Auditoriums

Auditoriums with fixed seating and sloping floors are found primarily in large libraries because of their expense and limited flexibility. Depending on their equipment, auditoriums are used for lectures, musical performances, and dramatic presentations.

In academic libraries, auditoriums may be created primarily to meet wider campus needs. In this case, the auditorium does not reflect library needs as much as a campus shortage of large classroom spaces.

In public libraries, spaces of this type are generally limited to large central buildings of city libraries, but some medium-sized and even small buildings have formal auditoriums with sloped floors.

Unlike many other types of library program and study spaces listed here, auditoriums are fairly inflexible.

Auditoriums have a number of significant advantages when it comes to visibility. By comparison, a performer in a multifunction meeting room can be hard for audience members to see if the heads of other people in the audience get in the way.

Some major planning issues involving auditoriums include:

- Does your library really need a space of this type? Does your library hold enough large classes or formal presentations to justify an expensive space with limited flexibility? Are there other spaces in your city or campus that already meet this specific need?

- If you have a large space of this type, will your parent institution take it over? Having library spaces scheduled by outside agencies can lead to difficult planning and even security problems.
- Do you want a space that will support theatrical performances? Possible support components may include a proscenium arch, curtains, cyclorama, fly loft, lighting and audio equipment, dressing rooms, green room, spaces for set construction and storage, prop storage, and so on. These will require advice from a professional designer of spaces for dramatic performances.
- Do you plan musical performances? Will you have special storage needs, such as space for a piano? Will you need an orchestra pit?
- Is the space designed to serve primarily as a large lecture hall? In this case, support spaces will be far simpler.
- Will you need projection equipment and a screen? This will require professional advice on equipment.
- Acoustic specifications will require professional analysis by an acoustical consulting engineer.
- Where will the auditorium be located within the building? It will need to be usable after regular library hours, which often means that the auditorium must be accessible from the entry foyer or lobby.
- Are you prepared to provide sufficient restrooms? With auditoriums come intermission rushes not found with other types of library program and study spaces. In particular, women's restrooms may need to have far more toilets than men's restrooms.
- Your architect will need to be sure that your facility meets all applicable ADA and state accessibility requirements, both for audience seating and for performer access to the stage. If you have no accessible access to backstage, you will need a ramp in the auditorium. Unfortunately, ramps take up a lot of space. More importantly, although ramps meet the letter of the law, traversing a long ramp in a wheelchair is hard work. For example, the ramp up to a four-foot-high stage will be over fifty feet long.
- If you need lighting that can be brought slowly from total dark to light, you will need incandescent lighting.
- Beware of HID (high intensity discharge—particularly metal halide) lighting, which has characteristics unsuited for auditoriums. Because of restrike time, HID lighting cannot be turned on quickly. It also has inconsistent color. See chapter 25 on "Lighting."

B. Classrooms

Although classes are often held in public libraries, academic and school libraries are probably more likely to construct rooms specifically designed to function as classrooms.

Most educational institutions will have campus standards for classroom design and equipment. Even if these do not apply to the classroom planned for your library, they will be a good source of technical requirements.

Most new classrooms are designed to support a wide range of technology, and this should be incorporated in library classrooms.

One danger of incorporating technology is the rapidity of change. Whatever libraries install now will be obsolete in a decade. This means paying extra attention to details that will be difficult to alter once the classroom has been built. Among the most important are electrical circuits and data conduit. Trying to envision the unexpected future is difficult, but librarians can console themselves in the knowledge that there appear to be few libraries anywhere with too many electrical outlets, too many electrical circuits, or too many communications jacks.

Among the issues affecting classroom design are:

- Who will determine the use of the classroom? For example, if you want a classroom for library instruction classes, will your institution allow you to schedule it to meet your own needs, or will it become part of an institutional pool of classrooms?
- If the classroom is buried in the library, what are the implications for security? What will happen, for example, if the parent institution decides to schedule classes when the library is closed? What will happen if the classroom is accessible through the stacks and you wish to limit stack access? What will happen if the classroom is attached to your rare book room? (The main moral here is, never put classrooms in the back recesses of libraries. Direct access from the entry foyer is always a good thing.)
- How will you protect high-tech gear in your classroom? At the least, classrooms need locking closets.
- What kind of seating will you provide? Writing tablet chairs (chairs with folding writing areas) are probably the most flexible.
- How much seating will you need? The capacities of many classrooms are set by institutional policy, and this will affect the size of any classrooms in your library. The guiding principle, however, should be the special needs of the library. If your library needs a room to seat 20, bowing to university pressure to convert it to a room to seat 60 may result in a classroom that no longer meets your needs.
- Will you need other furnishings, such as folding tables?
- How much flexibility do you need? Ideally, almost nothing in the classroom with the exception of high-tech lecterns will be fastened down.

Although it's always possible to argue with the administration when your classroom is scheduled for what you regard as inappropriate use, things are a lot easier if the design of the building prevents classroom takeovers from causing problems in the library.

Given the uncertainties of classroom use, therefore, we think it's extremely important that any classrooms be accessible when the rest of the library is closed.

C. Multipurpose Rooms and Community Rooms

Many libraries—particularly public libraries—construct multifunction meeting rooms designed to accommodate a wide range of functions and events. Rooms of this type are typically rectangular, with level floors and with ceilings high enough for projected images and sometimes for videoconferencing.

In designing rooms of this kind, maximum flexibility of function is clearly a primary concern.

Many multifunction rooms in public libraries are used both for library-sponsored events and for events sponsored by community groups, and security for library equipment is therefore a major concern.

Many of the planning issues that affect multifunction program rooms appear in section II above, but some special ones are listed here.

1. Seating Capacity

In public libraries, multifunction meeting rooms are usually constructed large enough to house all but the most extraordinary programs. (Every library can remember a program when attendance was triple that of any other program before or since, but most libraries cannot afford to construct space adequate for such extremely unusual events.)

In planning new buildings, however, libraries with currently undersized program rooms can be led astray by the fact that the small size of existing rooms has artificially constrained program attendance, and that past attendance may not be a good indicator of future audience sizes.

Most public library multifunction meeting rooms are designed to serve as community meeting spaces when not needed for library programs, and the likely audience size at community meetings can also influence meeting room size. If a library figures that a 100-person capacity will meet the needs of library programs, there may be good reasons to make the room larger if there are a number of groups in town that need 125-person spaces.

In our experience, errors in planning meeting room capacity are almost always in the direction of planning too small.

The situation is made worse by what we think is a tendency to overestimate how many people can fit comfortably into a multifunction meeting room. See section II-C on "Calculating Required Space," above.

Some state public library standards may specify minimum meeting room sizes, but we haven't seen them. In the absence of standards, make sure that your meeting room is genuinely large enough to meet your needs.

If large community meeting rooms are available near a public library, the library can base the size of its rooms on the space needs of library events only. But making the room so small that the library has to hold many of its programs in other places undermines one of the purposes of programs, which is to bring people into the library. In addition, nearby meeting rooms may cease to be available in the future.

2. Movable Room Dividers

Movable room dividers are frequently recommended for multifunction meeting rooms, but they have a number of very serious problems that lead us to recommend that libraries never use them. See section II-G-2, "The Special Case of Movable Room Dividers," above.

3. Provisions for Performers

Many multifunction meeting rooms need to accommodate a variety of performers. Among the things that can be provided are:

- Floor space. The simplest way to accommodate performers is to have sufficient floor space. Because some performers use a lot of space and others use very little, the lack of a fixed performance space increases the flexibility of the room.
- Ceiling clearance. Be sure your ceiling is high enough to provide adequate vertical clearance for performers, particularly if you have a stage or portable platforms. Remember that both adjustable lighting for performers and suspended uplights will hang down at least two feet below the ceiling.

- Stages. Stages are useful because they elevate performers enough so that they can be seen over the heads of people in the audience. Stages also must be accessible, which means a ramp or lift. Some libraries purchase folding stage sections (platforms about 4 × 8 feet with folding legs, designed to be butted together). However, stage sections are extremely heavy. It will require at least two strong people to set them up and extra space to store them when they are not in use. And you may still need to make them accessible.
- Pianos. If your multifunction room has good acoustics (and it should), it will be in demand for small musical performances. It's a good idea to have enough space for a baby grand piano, in case someone decides to give you one. For security, you can be sure the keyboard cover locks, and you can also buy protective blankets that lock into place. Since people tend to use pianos as tabletops, covers are important. You will probably also want a piano trolley—a carriage with locking casters that will allow you to move the piano easily. Unfortunately, dragging pianos around a lot can throw them out of tune.
- Lecterns. A lectern is a stand that holds notes at a convenient height and provides a structure behind which speakers can position themselves. Many speakers feel naked without a lectern. If you don't have a PA system, lecterns with built-in sound systems are available. Lots of conference centers have lecterns with the name of the center emblazoned on the front where it will be picked up by cameras. Your library can do so too. But you may wish it didn't when the news media photograph the neo-Nazis exercising their legal right to use your library's meeting room.
- Lighting. You may want controllable spotlights. Modern LED fixtures appear to work well.

D. Conference and Seminar Rooms

Many libraries have conference and seminar rooms.

Conference rooms serve a variety of functions. In public libraries, they usually serve as boardrooms. Often these rooms have a table large enough to seat the board of trustees and director, plus side chairs for library department heads, members of the press and public, and the library secretary.

In academic libraries, rooms of this type may serve primarily for seminar groups or for groups that need access to nearby portions of the library's collections.

Conference rooms in special libraries may be used by student groups, planning groups, groups working on projects, and so on. Occasionally these groups may need real privacy, especially in law and medicine.

1. Range of Functions

Planning conference rooms requires a preliminary review of all of the expected functions of the room. As usual, getting things in print helps to clarify what kind of structure and equipment a conference room will need.

The usual expectation is that conference rooms will serve groups that need to sit around a table, including governing boards, library staff, students, and so on. Planning for group use requires a decision on seating capacity. How large a group will be accommodated? Will everyone sit around a single table, or will some people sit in side chairs? Will the side chairs line the walls flanking the table, or will they be in rows at one end of the room? (To us, chairs lining the walls suggests overflow seating, while rows of chairs at one end of the room suggests a distinction between board and audience.)

A major decision in public libraries is whether the conference room will be made available to the general public when it is not being used for library functions. If the room will be open for community use, it will need much better protection for electronic equipment.

2. Location in the Building

A couple of factors affect the location of conference rooms:

- Will the room need to be accessed when the rest of the library is closed?
- Does the room need to be near the library's administrative offices?
- Does the room need to be adjacent to any specific portion of the collection?

Due to the requirements of open meetings acts, public libraries often need to make board meetings accessible to the press and general public. If the board meets in a conference room buried in an administrative area of the library, the building planners will need to decide how the general public will get to the meeting. How will the library prevent users from wandering into other administrative areas once office staff members have left for the day? And how will building-wide security be maintained if the board meeting continues past regular library opening hours?

For all of these reasons, public libraries need to make conference rooms accessible from entry foyers. The downside is that all administrative materials for the meeting will need to be transferred from the administrative offices to the conference room.

One could perhaps assume that the board of trustees will always meet when the library is open, but the life of a building is long. Trustees reserve the right to change their minds, and if a hot topic emerges, a library that seldom has any outsiders attend board meetings may find itself with 100 or more people trying to crowd into the boardroom.

3. Staff Oversight

If conference rooms will be used by non-library staff, there may be a need for staff oversight. As usual, the best way to accomplish this is to have an interior window with a Venetian blind on the conference room side of the window.

4. Ownership

With all conference and seminar rooms, there is always a possibility that a parent institution may decide to take over the room.

If a university or city government takes over a meeting room, the library needs to be able to maintain security while the parent organization is using the room.

The most important point is designing rooms that can be accessed directly from the library foyer, to make sure that users of the room cannot enter the rest of the library when it is closed.

E. Quiet Reading Rooms

Quiet reading rooms are particularly common in academic libraries and public libraries.

Academic reading rooms can be real showplaces, often with special browsing collections, hardwood floors with Persian rugs, and a variety of soft seating.

As public libraries have become busy, crowded places, they have lost their traditional silence. Where once a scholarly hush hovered over the books, accompanied by somber bindings (no overstimulating Mylar dust jacket covers), newspapers on split rods, and sober readers, now there is the constant chatter of staff and visitors, ringing of telephones, beeping of computers, and gurgling of coffee brewers.

In response to the fact that most libraries are no longer quiet places, many public libraries have constructed quiet reading rooms. Typically, these provide isolated housing for reading tables and armchairs, but do not contain computer workstations or other noise generators. Libraries can also ban laptops in rooms like this, but it may be a hard ban to enforce unless the library can block Wi-Fi.*

---

*There are straightforward ways to block Wi-Fi. The principle is that of a Faraday cage. Metallic wallpaper is available, as are paints with a high metal content. Or you can luck out and move into the old x-ray suite and find that the lead lining the walls does a fine job. If you block Wi-Fi, you'll probably block cell phone signals as well.

Here are some design issues and suggestions for quiet reading rooms:

- Quiet reading rooms often offer the opportunity to create elegant spaces. Many quiet reading rooms are low-key showplaces. They may have fireplaces, tables with mounted reading lamps, and area rugs.
- Because of their panache, quiet reading rooms offer major naming opportunities for fundraising campaigns. Having one's name over the door of an elegant reading room is a lot more gratifying that having one's name over the door of a staff restroom.
- Quiet reading rooms in public libraries require visual oversight. Because few of these rooms are staffed, there needs to be provision for staff members at service desks to keep a general eye on what's happening in quiet reading rooms. A typical way is through the use of interior windows.
- Although users of quiet reading rooms frequently are reading current magazines and newspapers, shelving these materials in the rooms leads to problems. Users selecting magazines and newspapers annoy readers who came to the rooms seeking relative silence. It works a lot better to locate magazines and newspapers directly outside the entrances to quiet reading rooms.
- However, browsing collections in academic library reading rooms are common. (Some are full of seldom-read great books.)
- Typical furnishings might include anything from 1 to 4 four-person reading tables and 4 to perhaps 16 armchairs. Smaller tables—such as two-person tables or carrels—can be used as well, but they may look more utilitarian than the library wants.
- When it comes to noise, many quiet reading rooms are almost self-policing. Users seeking solitude glare angrily at those who choose to conduct conversations.
- To emphasize their intent, some libraries label quiet reading rooms "silent reading rooms." We find the name more chastising than we like, but to each his or her own.
- Quiet reading rooms can be alcoves rather than actual rooms. If both ceilings and floors have proper acoustic surfaces, just the interposition of stacks between the alcove and the noisier areas of the library may be enough to block sound. Some quiet reading areas are also separated from noisier areas by freestanding fireplaces or by low partitions. One possible cost advantage of quiet reading alcoves is simplified HVAC. A quiet reading room needs its own thermostat, air supply ducts, and return air ducts. These may not be essential in reading alcoves.
- As with all spaces in libraries, uses may vary over the years. For this reason, if you plan donor recognition through a plaque or lettering, you may want to speak in generalities. For example, "The Johnson Reading Room" may

be a better long-term bet than "The Johnson Reading Room for Eastern European Journals in Nuclear Physics." A simple "The Johnson Room" is even less limiting.

F. Study Rooms

Many libraries have study rooms, which are small rooms for groups of perhaps four to eight people. Study rooms are used for quiet reading, student group projects, small group meetings, tutoring, test taking, gaming (the offspring of *Dungeons and Dragons*), listening to recordings, and other purposes.

In some ways, study rooms are similar to very small conference rooms.

1. Supervision

Oversight of study rooms is particularly important. Librarians in public libraries constantly tell us that they have to be careful who they assign to what study rooms, and they occasionally give study rooms that are extremely difficult to supervise descriptive nicknames like "the sex room."

The main trick in designing study rooms is to regard them as terrariums. People using study rooms need to be visible from all angles, and the users of all study rooms should be completely visible from service desks. If a number of study rooms are in a row, they should be separated by glass walls, so that librarians can see through the entire row like a shotgun house.

Our experience is that architects have a strange aversion to creating study rooms that are easy to supervise, and that libraries abound in study rooms that cause problems. To avoid these problems, you will need to pay very close attention to the proposed design of study rooms in your library. Check the lines of sight from service desks, and then consider how lines of sight will work if you relocate the desks. Insist that you want glass walls rather than windows and get really crabby if your designers don't listen to you. (Codes will require a horizontal mullion in a glass wall. This is fine.)

The last thing your staff should have to do is pace back and forth outside study rooms, peering into each one to make sure that no evil deeds are afoot.

Actually, glass-box study rooms have real advantages for users. Study rooms are small spaces, and if the walls are mostly opaque, the rooms tend to feel oppressively small.

2. Furnishings

For group projects, tutoring, and similar functions, tables can be either in the center of study rooms or pushed up against one wall. Tables against walls allow equipment to be plugged in without wires trailing across floors to encourage tripping.

Built-in counters are a great deal less flexible than movable tables and strike us as a very poor idea.

Rather than purchase large tables for study rooms, we prefer to use one or more standard 3 × 5-foot reading room tables. If a longer table is needed, two reading tables can be pushed together end-to-end.

People using study rooms often group five or six people around a four-person table. For this reason, tables with crossbeams between the legs at the end of the table are a bad idea.

If you have a study room with a solid wall, it helps to have electrical outlets on the wall above tabletop height, allowing users to push a table up against the wall and plug in laptops without having to crawl under the table. It's a good place for a quad box.

3. Locking Doors

You will need to decide whether you want to lock the doors of your study rooms when they are not in use. To meet safety codes, if doors can be locked, there will have to be a dead bolt knob on the inside, and this means users can lock themselves in.

4. Family Computer Rooms

One interesting use of study rooms is to provide a place where a parent with small children can work at a computer while keeping an eye on the children—and containing their noise. It's easy to convert a regular study room to this purpose, and with modern laptops one could improvise the entire arrangement, encouraging parents to pick out books and toys from the children's department, check out a laptop, and then bring kids and toys and laptop to the assigned study room.

This picture of the inside of a children's story and craft room shows good architectural planning. Windows allow staff to keep an eye on the room. And instead of using cast zinc coat hooks, which tend to break, leaving extremely sharp edges, the designers specified steel hooks that can bend but not snap off. (Some librarians prefer craft and story rooms with high windows that allow parents to see in without distracting the children in the room.)

G. Children's Craft and Story Rooms

Children's craft and story rooms in public libraries are probably the most specialized program spaces found in libraries, and for this reason we have included a large amount of special detail.

Although rooms can be constructed for crafts or stories only, many children's librarians like to provide programs that include both activities. Typically, these start with a story—when children can best concentrate—and then progress to a craft.

The use of craft and story rooms is usually limited to events produced by library staff during hours suitable for children, so the rooms do not need to be accessible when the rest of the library building is closed. Some libraries, however, let outside groups use their craft and story rooms, and for this reason locking storage spaces are important.

Providing a separate craft and story room keeps the mess associated with crafts out of the library's multifunction program rooms. Spilled glue, glitter, and gingerbread house frosting fall on washable floors instead of being walked into meeting room carpet.

1. Locations

Most craft and story rooms will not be made available to the general public, and they do not need to be accessible when the library is closed.

Most librarians want craft and story rooms to be directly accessible from children's departments, so that children leaving the rooms after programs find themselves back in the children's department rather than leaving the library. If a craft and story room is at the back of a children's department, children leaving the room will walk through the entire department on their way out.

Some librarians worry about odd adults peering into craft and story rooms. This is another reason for placing these rooms at the back of departments, where non-parents will be far more noticeable.

2. Sizes

Most craft and story rooms are for relatively small groups. Capacities vary with the size of group the children's department staff members are happy with. In our experience, it's usually between 20 and 30 children.

A room for 20 children will need floor space for 20 children to listen to a story, plus enough additional floor space for 20 children doing crafts at tables.

The room will be far more flexible if it's possible to set it up in a variety of ways, including (a) floor space for stories plus tables for crafts, (b) tables put away, with rows of chairs filling the room, and (c) room entirely empty, for children to sit on the floor for stories.

When figuring out the space required for a craft and story room, be sure to find out whether the library intends to have parents attend the programs, since this can require additional floor space.

3. Decor

Some story rooms have been created with elaborately painted backdrops for storytellers. Some of these backdrops are even movable like stage flats.

These can be charming, but they need to be fairly timeless and flexible. A good argument can be made for pinnable walls that lend themselves to frequent redecoration.

Because children rub against the walls and spill craft supplies, craft and story rooms are great places for washable wall coverings like vinyl wallpaper.

4. Floor Coverings

Some story rooms are built with a carpeted area for stories and a larger area with vinyl or rubber tile for crafts.

Other libraries tile the entire room and use portable carpet sections or area rugs for children sitting on the floor. This strikes us as the most flexible option.

With children sitting directly on a tile floor, some libraries install radiant heating in the floor slab.

5. Sinks and Cabinets

Because crafts are messy (especially library crafts, it seems), all craft and story rooms need running water. Usually architects provide what amounts to a kitchen counter with sink and cabinets.

The problem is providing a way for small children to wash their hands. Some installations have a slide-out step by the sink, while others have sinks at two levels. Slide out steps are really clever, but some librarians worry about children falling off or the steps moving when children are standing on them.

Cabinets can be both above and below the countertop. *Everything needs to lock.* As with other built-in furniture, drawers work a lot better with ball-bearing, double-extension suspension.

6. Storage

Children's departments need a surprising amount of space for storage of program supplies, and a closet off the craft and story room is a convenient place. If the closet is large enough, it can also be used for storing furniture, so the craft and story room can be cleared completely, or so tables can be put away and the entire room filled with rows of chairs.

If the library's multifunction meeting room and its craft and story room are on the same floor, it's sometimes possible to have the program supplies storeroom accessible from both program rooms. In other situations, the storeroom can be located between the craft and story room and the departmental offices.

7. Windows

Because of video or puppet presentations in craft and story rooms, it is sometimes necessary to darken the rooms. For this reason, exterior windows can be a problem if they do not have effective blackout shades.

Skylights in craft and story rooms may sound exciting, but they are basically disasters. They reflect sound, the racket of rain falling on skylights can make it difficult to hear storytellers, the glare during the day interferes with programs, the dark ceilings at night are depressing, and sooner or later the skylights leak.

Many librarians are uncertain about first-floor exterior windows leading to craft and story rooms because of the potential of odd people hanging around outside.

In general, librarians who tell stories like story rooms without windows leading to the rest of the library because activities visible through the windows distract the children. In many cases, however, parents inside the library want to be able to see into story rooms to be sure their children are getting along all right. One possible solution is to have a few windows at the right height for parents to see in but too high above the floor for children to see out.

8. Lighting

Because of the variety of activities in craft and story rooms, we think providing lighting options is important.

For general craft work, reflected fluorescent uplighting should work well. Dimmers will allow the general lighting to be darker during stories than during crafts. A simple way to achieve a similar effect is to use three-tube fixtures with the center tube switched separately. If the lights generate about 20, 40, and 60 foot-candles, depending on the number of lamps switched on, 60 foot-candles can be used for craft projects and as little as 20 foot-candles during story times.

The area where the storyteller sits may be a good place for some track lighting with dimmer switches.

As with multifunction meeting rooms, craft and story rooms are not good places for night-lights that cannot be switched off. Fred visited one library where the staff had taped dark paper over the meeting room fixture that stayed on at all times.

9. Acoustics

In general, craft and story rooms are small enough not to need any special acoustic treatments. However, with tile floors, ceilings must be covered with sound-absorbing material.

Fred visited a library with a story room shaped like a high cylinder. The staff told him the room echoed like an empty oil drum until the library retrofitted acoustic wall and ceiling panels. Remember that concave curved walls are usually an acoustic disaster.

10. Other Possible Features You Might Want to Consider

Craft and story rooms lend themselves to a variety of extra features:

- A lightweight curtain between the craft and story sections to allow the librarians to create a cozy story area by pulling the curtain. This also prevents children from being distracted by craft materials set out for them until the curtain is opened and the craft portion of the program begins.
- A built-in puppet theater at one end. This requires a backstage room for the performers, stage, and puppet storage. It also requires duplicate controls for room lighting, controls for stage lighting, and sound system controls. The downside of a theater of this type, of course, is that it is extremely inflexible if the staff lose interest in puppet productions.
- A wall-mounted telephone with an access code for use.
- Restaurant-style reservation buzzers for parents. If you give parents wireless buzzers, they can wander around the library while the program is going on. Five minutes before the end of the program, all the buzzers can go off and recall the parents. And if individual children have meltdowns during the program, their parents can be recalled individually.

11. Children's Restrooms

Many children's librarians want a restroom attached to the craft and story room or just outside the door. It speaks well of children's librarians that small children are so mesmerized by programs that they delay restroom visits until the very last second. Mothers faced with emergencies may appreciate not having to sprint the length of the library holding a small child on the verge of explosion.

12. Public Use of Craft and Story Rooms

Some libraries permit public use of craft and story rooms, either for potentially messy occasions like private birthday parties or for overflow when other meeting rooms in the library are all in use.

If a library lets outside groups use its craft and story room, it will particularly need to have a room with locks on everything, including all storage closets, cabinets, and drawers. It will need to protect permanently mounted equipment. And it will need some way of keeping an eye on things from a service desk.

Allowing private birthday parties to be held in library spaces strikes us as a singularly bad idea, but we're old and crabby. We have also seen the horrible messes they make.

H. Multilevel Children's Reading Rooms

Lots of public libraries have multilevel structures on which children can sit to hear stories. There are right and wrong ways to build these.

Among other things, always remember that your staff may change their minds. Risers that can be easily reconfigured or even bodily ripped out have some significant advantages for long-term occupancy.

All multilevel reading rooms must be accessible to users with disabilities.

Here are some things to *avoid*:

1. Avoid Story Hour Risers Made of Concrete

Flexibility of internal space means libraries occasionally want to rearrange risers or eliminate them entirely. Having to bring in a jackhammer to rearrange a story hour room is no fun.

In addition, concrete platforms are inherently cold and hard.

2. Avoid Wooden Story Hour Risers That Echo

There's nothing like broad steps to encourage jumping, and the resulting hollow thumping will be unwelcome.

One good way to prevent thumping is to do what stage set designers do to keep the ghost of Hamlet's father's footsteps from echoing hollowly as he morosely treads the supposedly stone battlements of Elsinore. Glue Homasote—a compressed paper material that muffles vibrations—to the *undersides* of the plywood platforms of the risers.

Architects are sometimes puzzled by this technique and want to put the Homasote on the tops of the risers, but it's too soft for that purpose. Check your final construction drawings carefully to verify that it's actually underneath.

3. Avoid Bare Wooden Risers

Bare wooden risers are uncomfortable and splintery.

Cheap painted wood looks ratty after a few months of use. Stained and varnished oak is expensive, and the available sizes of wood may limit your options.

4. Avoid Risers in Strange Configurations

The design and layout of story hour risers brings out unfortunate creativity in some designers. When you check your proposed design, watch out for:

- Curved risers. These look cute, but it's extremely difficult to carpet them neatly. Fred's library had a story room with curved risers. The shapes were cute, but attempting to carpet them properly defeated one of the best carpet firms in the area and led to unhappy confrontations.
- Illogical riser heights. Risers should (a) permit all children to see the storyteller and (b) not have height variations that can lead to unpleasant falls. The risers in some story hour rooms are at more or less artistically random heights. Check your construction drawings, and when in serious doubt ask your architect to cobble up a shirt cardboard model.

5. Avoid Story Hour Pits

Even worse than badly designed story hour risers are story hour pits.

Ask the librarian who has fallen into one.

I. Maker Spaces

Maker spaces are rooms or groups of rooms designed to provide access to creative equipment, primarily for teenaged public library users.

The equipment found in maker spaces can include a wide variety of computer-driven devices, 3-D printers, sewing machines, video game systems, and whatever new technology and your imagination can think up.

Many maker spaces also include separate sound-insulated rooms designed to serve as recording or video studios.

Maker spaces became popular earlier in this century and are now found in a wide variety of public library buildings. Some are improvised—basically a variety of equipment set up in a room—while others are purpose-built and sophisticated.

Whether maker spaces are a passing fad or a long-term trend, they still deserve coverage.

J. Faculty Studies

Many university libraries have faculty studies in the stacks.

Typically, these appear to be anything from 50 to 125 square feet. Furnishings may include a desk, shelves, a filing cabinet, and a chair for visitors. Many studies are on the perimeter of stacks, in order to provide daylight for the users.

By and large, faculty studies appear to be a royal pain from the library administration viewpoint.

First, faculty may want access to their studies when the library is closed, and this has to be prevented aggressively. Once faculty start asking for keys to the library, the result would be chaos.

And second, faculty also tend to take books from the shelves and put them in their studies without checking them out, forcing library staff to routinely inspect faculty studies for books not checked out. Libraries with faculty studies have to make clear that the studies can be checked at any time, but it still represents a potentially massive waste of library staff time.

Faculty studies also need windows on the library side as well as the outside window side. The last thing libraries need is (claimed) invisible assaults in faculty studies.

All of this sneaks up on another example of the basic rule: everyone with a key to the library needs to report to the library director.

IV. SPECIAL PROBLEMS AND OPPORTUNITIES WITH PROGRAM AND STUDY ROOMS

A. Loss of Control to Parent Institutions

As noted above, libraries sometimes find that the scheduling and use of their meeting spaces is taken over by their parent institutions.

At times, this can make it difficult for the library to use rooms as originally intended, particularly if scheduling by the parent institution is allowed to override library scheduling.

Outside scheduling can also lead to events being scheduled in meeting rooms when the library is closed, or in rooms located in secure areas of book stacks, with potentially serious implications for security.

Examples of this are everywhere. A classroom at the back of the stacks in a college library is scheduled by the college rather than the library. A public library meeting room is used for city meetings, with the city's schedulers taking precedence over the library's schedulers. The school administration runs out of classrooms and uses the school library for a regular classroom. Or for detention.

If this situation appears to be likely to develop, here are some possible design ideas:

- Make sure that all meeting rooms and classrooms are in locations that can be used when the rest of the library is closed.
- Specify in your building program a room that does not lend itself well to classroom purposes. If your institution will let you.
- Make sure that scheduling is always done by library staff.

B. Donor Recognition Opportunities

Of all spaces in libraries, program and meeting rooms offer some of the best naming opportunities.

This is particular true because the names of meeting rooms are mentioned constantly in library publicity. ("The concert will take place in the library's Helen Grief meeting room.")

Program spaces are also physically attractive. We believe that almost all donors would rather have program rooms named after them than technical services workrooms.

As with all naming opportunities, the most important thing is to work out a price list before you start approaching prospective donors. As with flea markets, once you've sold it too cheaply, there's no backing off from the deal.

C. Meeting Room Issues

If you plan to allow outside groups to use your meeting room, it's important to establish all of your policies before word of the new meeting space gets out in the community. Usually this means before the building is announced.

Most of this applies specifically to public libraries because their activities are not limited by ownership of spaces, but one can envision issues arising in school libraries or on campuses with student groups.

The policies for private use of meeting rooms need to cover an impressive range of issues:

- Will certain types of groups be exempt from rental charges? (We think this is a dangerous area, but if you charge for use of your meeting room by outside groups, some groups will claim that the nature of their undertakings means they should not have to pay.)
- Will rooms be available for private parties, such as children's birthday parties?

> Fred's library did not allow private parties. A mother who complained about this policy said, "I don't want that awful mess in my home!" Fred was tempted to say, "Thanks a lot for wanting to leave your awful mess in the library," but instead he just repeated the policy, trying not to sound totally toneless.

- Will rooms be available for commercial uses, such as promotional and sales events?
- Will you require that private groups using meeting rooms make clear in all of their advertising that the library is not a sponsor of their program?

> In Fred's library, a group put out extensive advertising saying, "Learn about Jesus at The Urbana Free Library," implying library sponsorship. The library was severely criticized and learned to require that groups explain that they were not library-sponsored.

- Must all outside groups have business addresses in the library's service area? Must private users live in the service area?
- How long in advance will the library accept meeting room reservations?
- Will groups bear the cost of major damages, such as spilling red beverages on the carpet (resulting in new carpet, since red dyes are a splendid example of American know-how and never come out)?
- What happens if the library's parent organization tries to preempt a group that has reserved the room?
- Will the library allow buying and selling in its meeting room?
- Will the library allow groups to use meeting rooms when the rest of the library is closed? What kind of extra charge will be made to cover the cost of having staff present to secure the building when the group is through?
- Will groups be allowed to use the library's AV equipment? What will the library do if specific groups predictably demand that library staff drop whatever they're doing to help the groups use the equipment?

> Fred's library had a group that was so demanding that the library eventually had to refuse all use of AV equipment by outside groups.

- May groups charge admission?
- Will the library allow catered meals?
- Will the library require security deposits? If it requires them from only specific groups, is it opening the door to claims of discriminatory treatment?
- Will library staff set up furniture for groups? If so, how will it charge? Or will groups be required to set up their own furniture?

Remember that the use of meeting rooms is controlled by the general time, place, and manner concept. Attempting to accept or refuse groups on the basis of the intellectual content of their undertakings can lead to serious legal unhappiness on the part of the library. Although you may never have to cope with neo-Nazi groups or other unwanted ideologues, you may want to consider what you can do with room design to lessen the likelihood of rioting or the resulting damage.

Our main point is that all meeting rooms, including conference rooms used by boards of trustees, should be accessible from entry foyers, allowing libraries to separate meeting room events from the rest of the library. (Story hour and craft rooms are better off located in children's departments, but that can lead to tangles when outside groups want to use them.)

Fred and John have extremely different opinions on renting out meeting rooms. Fred's library limited the use of its meeting rooms to free public events sponsored by not-for-profit organizations, with no money allowed to change hands. John's library rented out its meeting rooms for a variety of events. Both know they're right.

V. COMMON ERRORS IN THE DESIGN OF PROGRAM AND STUDY ROOMS

As in all areas of library design, planners, owners, and designers have favorite errors. We see them repeatedly. Here are some errors that cause serious problems.

A. Undersized Meeting Rooms

This is a constant problem. Usually the librarians have a much better idea of necessary sizes than anyone else, but they sometimes get voted down.

For example, a large proportion of public libraries appear to have meeting rooms too small to meet their needs.

B. Inadequate Storage Space

Far too many meeting rooms have junk piled around the walls. Often, it's so familiar that the owners of the rooms never step back and say, "Surely we could have better places to stash things."

Outside of (perhaps) a piano (because they are hard to stash and tend to go out of tune when pushed around all the time), multifunction meeting rooms need enough storage closets to allow the rooms to be completely cleared.

Check all drawings starting with the first schematic designs, remembering that few designers are excited about creating storage closets.

C. Study Rooms with Opaque Walls

Requiring staff to patrol the library, peering into study rooms to be sure that excitement is not brewing, is a major waste of library money.

In addition, study rooms with opaque walls are frequently dark holes, unpleasantly cramped spaces, and spooky for users. Glass walls help open things up. Remember that (as we probably say too often) study rooms need to be terrariums, with glass walls on three sides.

Imagine how things will go for your library if someone is assaulted in an overly private study room.

D. Inadequate Wiring

With the possible exceptions of formal auditoriums, program and study rooms need vast numbers of electrical outlets, both along the walls and inset in the floors.

E. Inadequate Kitchenettes

Program and conference room kitchenettes are sometimes equipped with overly shallow sinks, with undersized refrigerators, and with inadequate numbers of electrical circuits.

A sink needs to be deep enough to allow coffee urns to be filled. Watch out for miniature bar sinks, for toy sinks will not improve your mood.

Standard apartment-sized refrigerators are less expensive than under-counter models. They hold a lot more and are available in energy-saving models.

Beware of stoves in meeting room kitchenettes. An awful mess can be left behind and flames in public areas can be a serious mistake. There may also be safety regulations involved.

Be sure you have more electrical circuits than you think you need. What will happen if a group supper involves the simultaneous use of coffee urns, microwave ovens, toasters, Dutch ovens, electric frying pans, and other apparatus? Electrical devices used for food preparation are energy hogs. If people are forced to run extension cords to other areas of the library in order to use electrical devices, everyone (including library users, library administration, and local fire marshals) will be unhappy.

F. No After-Hours Access

The easiest way to increase the flexibility of classrooms, multifunction meeting rooms, and conference rooms—and simultaneously to enhance library security—is to make them accessible when the rest of the library is closed. This can be particularly important in academic libraries, when the institution may overrule the library administration. It's also an issue in public library conference rooms, when library board meetings can continue after the rest of the library is closed.

Be sure your designers include restrooms that are also available to after-hours users and are large enough.

G. Inadequate Acoustics

Program and study rooms require acoustic isolation. The design of far too many rooms fails to block sound effectively.

A few adventurously designed rooms have unpleasant echoes. Flat, acoustic ceilings and carpeted floors are important.

All program and study rooms need to be constructed before their suspended ceilings are installed.

In general, program spaces need live surfaces behind speakers and dead surfaces behind audience members. People listening to programs do not need echoes of speakers' voices bouncing off the walls behind them. The easy way to prevent this problem is to have sound-absorbing surfaces on the back walls of program rooms. (Sound-absorbing surfaces don't have to be acoustic tiles, which are impressively fragile.)

H. Tricky Lighting Control Devices

Beware of complex preset control devices for lighting and other functions. University classrooms can do well with these because only a limited number of users need to be trained, but most meeting rooms in libraries are used by a wide variety of people. You don't want to be forced to have your staff take the time to provide special training or be called in constantly to help people adjust the lighting.

This sounds overly pessimistic, but preset controls are a constant problem. We've heard of libraries ripping them out in frustration, and we've seen them baffle even long-term library staff members.

I. Movable Room Dividers

Movable room dividers are very expensive, they alter the functional configurations of rooms in unfortunate ways (often calling for multiple projectors and screens), they are hard to open and close, they do a very bad job of blocking noise, they are ugly, and they are often difficult to repair.

They are tempting because they promise what sounds like free space. But they are one of the Significant Evils of Library Architecture.

J. Folding Chairs

Folding chairs in meeting rooms are a major pain. They are slow to set up and take down. The racks that hold them never work well (the chairs flop back and forth on the racks, the racks are long and hard to handle, and the racks take a lot of space).

The rule is an easy one: avoid folding chairs at all times.

By contrast, stack chairs are great, and some with mesh seats and backs are both comfortable and amazingly light.

VI. SNAPPY RULES ON PROGRAM AND STUDY ROOMS

1. All program rooms need storage closets for furniture and program supplies. Having to pile materials around the edge of a room is always a mess.
2. Outside of study rooms, quiet reading rooms, and craft and story rooms, most program rooms need to be usable when the rest of the library is closed. This means that program rooms (and the accompanying restrooms) must be directly accessible from the entry foyer.
3. Movable room dividers are expensive, hard to maneuver, do a bad job of acoustical separation, change the shapes of rooms in weird ways, are hard to repair, and prevent large and small groups meeting at the same time. But outside of that they sound like a pretty good idea.
4. Never put a window behind where performers will stand.
5. Acoustic isolation is important. If you can hear everything that's going on in the meeting room when you're in the restroom next door, imagine reciprocity. This means separately ducted air supplies and returns, plus walls that continue past the suspended ceiling to the bottom of the floor above. Movable room dividers fail badly when it comes to acoustics.
6. Meeting rooms need flexible and controllable lighting. Motion detectors are not part of lighting of this kind.

7. Complex lighting and AV control systems with many preset options are acceptable only when you have to train an extremely limited number of people to use them.
8. Some traditional formulas for guesstimating meeting room size are seriously inadequate.
9. Funny-shaped meeting rooms are less amusing than one might hope. Nature loves rectangles.
10. Meeting rooms need a lot more electrical outlets than many architects want to put there.
11. Kitchenettes in meeting rooms need a large number of separate 20-amp electrical circuits, particularly if they are used for serious food service.
12. Very few libraries complain that their meeting rooms are too large.
13. No matter how small the library, each meeting room and study room requires its own thermostat.
14. HVAC systems for meeting rooms need to be able to respond fast. When 60 overheated cub scouts or 100 enthusiastic undergraduates tumble abruptly into your meeting room, the HVAC system needs to cope with a lot of excess heat, carbon dioxide, and moisture. Many systems don't.
15. Unless you have a large and pompous library, conference rooms with large and pompous conference tables and with large and pompous chairs tend to look a little silly.
16. Few public libraries complain that they have too many study rooms, but most of them complain that they have too few.
17. Meeting room storage closets are not for irrelevant equipment, including fire-suppression gear, electrical gear, HVAC equipment, and so on. Make this clear in your building program, watch your construction drawings like a hawk, and tear your designers to shreds if they ignore you.
18. Be careful that parent agencies like universities or city governments don't take over control of your program rooms. And arrange your library spaces so there won't be serious security problems when your parent agencies show that they can override you and take over anyway.
19. Study rooms need to be terrariums—glass boxes that can be supervised from every possible angle and that prevent secret assaults. Many designers will attempt to substitute small windows for your floor-to-ceiling glass walls, or have some study rooms without glass walls facing service desks, or have solid walls between study rooms, and you will need to stop this sort of thing firmly.
20. Having a windowless young adult study room known to your staff as "the sex room" sounds friendly, but your staff will probably not enjoy it.
21. Storage closets, cabinets, and drawers in program and meeting rooms all need to lock.
22. Funny-shaped meeting rooms are less amusing than one might hope.

20

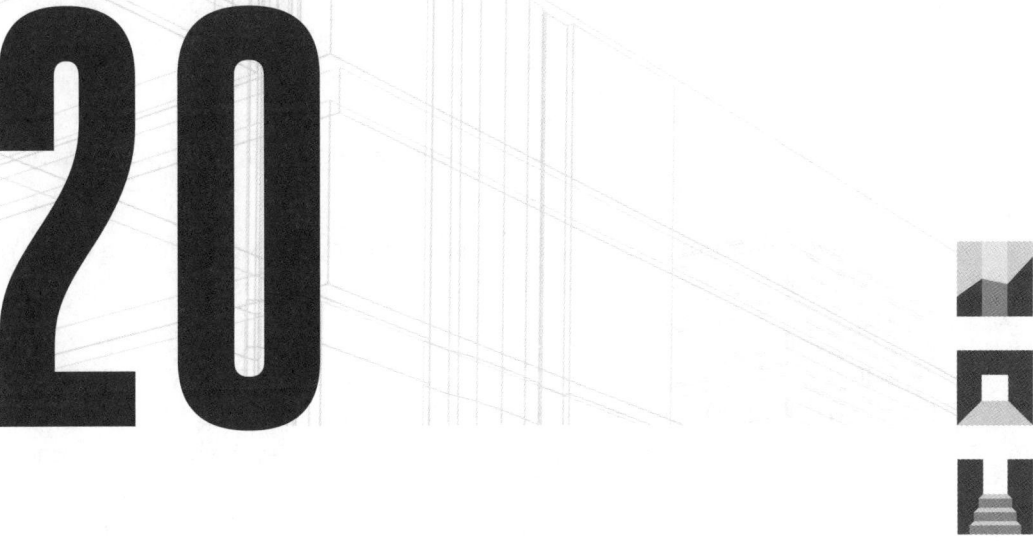

Display and Exhibit Areas

I. INTRODUCTION

A large percentage of libraries appear to have at least modest spaces devoted to displays and exhibits.

Most libraries have some sort of objects on permanent display.

- Perhaps the most common are oil paintings (or reproductions) of founders. America's surviving Carnegie libraries usually have framed portraits of Carnegie (even though he apparently didn't like the idea and charged the libraries for the portraits).
- Many libraries have significant historic objects.
- And they have all sorts of artworks.

And most libraries are set up for temporary displays that are changed every few weeks or months:

- Floor space for traveling exhibits that some libraries book months or even years in advance. Some traveling exhibits are funded by corporate or government grants.
- Display cases, ranging from massive units to hole-in-the-wall display cases in public library children's departments.
- Wall space for art displays.

- Some libraries have historical museum components, with permanent or rotating displays of local artifacts.

As with meeting room use, libraries benefit from policies concerning displays. The problem is when displays become freedom of speech issues.

> Maintaining a suspicions attitude toward displays can be useful. For example, about 50 years ago, a major public library agreed to display the works of a local artist. The artist showed the library a couple of innocuous examples, but when the day came to hang the exhibit, virtually every painting was a vibrant rendering of the male organ. This was in the 1960s, a far more censorious time. Although the library had advertised the exhibit extensively, it panicked and said "No," whereupon the artist took his story of censorship to the press. The library realized it had been had, but the press had a great time taking the library apart without mentioning the actual issues.

> In most cases, accepting an exhibit sight-unseen is more likely to result in something bland rather than something hair-raising. For example, Fred's library once had a display of artistic potholders. The staff members who arranged the exhibit expected creative gauntlets shaped like fish or perhaps alligators or bunnies, but the exhibit turned out to be about 200 identical square potholders of the kind made in Girl Scout camp by weaving elastic loops together. When puzzled library users inquired what this was all about, the staff smiled brightly and said "Potholders!"

Libraries may also reach the point where people with professional museum training may be needed.

All displays have security and insurance implications, especially for the potential loss of valuable (or at least valued) materials.

Displays are pretty straightforward, but there are good and bad ways of doing things. Some are summarized in this chapter.

II. OPEN EXHIBIT AREAS

Many traveling exhibits require only open floor space and effective lighting.

Our experience has been that traveling exhibits come around so seldom that it's better to simply rearrange furniture when the time comes, rather than have an area that's awkwardly open most of the time.

One advantage of the shadowless indirect lighting mentioned in the chapter on lighting is that it is typically compatible with traveling exhibits, making placing exhibits in unplanned areas far easier.

> Fred once cleared out an entire reading room for a display of working models of Leonardo machines that arrived in a semitrailer. It was fine. Library users found different places to sit, and everyone seemed to enjoy seeing the feeling of newness that occurs when old familiar things get moved around. No one made invidious comparisons with the way grocery stores rearrange stock to force customers to look at everything in the store.

III. DISPLAY CASES

Library supply and furniture catalogs often include display cases, and some may meet your needs.

You can also have display cases custom-built. Before you turn your cabinetmakers or architects loose to design your display cases, however, you need to have very carefully written specifications.

As a general rule of thumb, horizontal (tabletop) display cases are commonly used for displays of printed books and drawings, while vertical (wall-mounted) cases are used for artifacts and framed materials.

For some special items, display cases have to be custom-made. For example, Audubon elephant folios need special cases that support the folios at suitably tilted viewing angles.

What features do display cases need?

- Movability. Most display cases work best if they are movable furniture.
- The only cases we've seen that have to be built in are small, brightly lighted "jewel box" cases for children's collections, built into walls at child height.
- Easy access to contents. Although this seems fairly obvious, we've seen a number of architect-designed display cases with major sections of glass that were fixed in place. To set up displays, library staff had to crawl into display cases to reach the areas behind the fixed glass panels.
- Light-colored interiors, usually light, neutral colors like cream. Too many display cases have dark interiors, leading to displays that look like openings into dark cellars. Displays should glow.
- Displays above waist level. Some libraries have been equipped with cases that start at ankle level, but no adult wants to bend double to see a display. (Children's display cases, of course, need to be at child height.)
- Glass in front or on three sides.
- In vertical display cases, easily movable shelves. Shelves need to be ¼-inch plate glass. (We saw one library with ½-inch glass shelves, which most of the staff found too heavy to handle.) One good way of supporting shelves is to use shelf bracket support strips slightly inset into the back of display cases. Keeping the strips inset allows flat artwork to be displayed bridging the support strips when the shelf brackets are removed. Most bracket systems have brackets with a variety of depths, and glass shelves can be made to fit more than one size of bracket.
- Pinnable backs. The inside backs of display cases have to accommodate materials pinned to the backs. Heavy hopsacking fabric over a pinnable board works well.

> One shouldn't have to mention this, but you need to remind your designers that "pinnable" means some kind of surface that accepts push pins and straight pins. Fred inherited an architect-designed display with a back that consisted of 1/16 inch of cork over heavy plywood, resulting in a surface into which push pins could be driven only with a hammer, usually leading them to break. Of a number of ill-advised architect-designed items for the building, it was the first one to be thrown away.

- Bright, low-glare lighting. Lighting for display cases is easy to design so it doesn't shine directly into viewers' eyes. To avoid reflections, things are easier if lights are inside the cases. If a room has a number of display cases,

track-mounted LED floodlights can work well. For horizontal display cases with glass tops, external lighting has to be designed to avoid annoying reflections on the tops of the cases.
  – The best lighting for display cases is fluorescent—or even better LED—since heat buildup is less. Never get talked into incandescent lighting, particularly quartz halogen lighting, which can be miserably hot and quickly burn out in an enclosed display case. And the high heat can't be desirable for the items on display.
- Security. All display cases need to have locks. In addition, libraries that display items that don't belong to them need to carry exhibit floater insurance or get waivers from their exhibitors.
- Horizontal display cases usually resemble glass boxes mounted on top of reading tables. The boxes have four low glass sides (perhaps a foot to eighteen inches high) and flat glass tops. Usually the tops swing open on piano hinges, and they may have movable braces to hold the tops open while displays are being arranged.

IV. WALL SPACES FOR HANGING ARTWORKS

Many libraries have sections of wall set aside for exhibits of artwork.

A variety of systems are available for temporary exhibits. Many resemble old-fashioned picture rail installations, except the artworks are suspended on adjustable rods hanging from the rail rather than by picture wires. The rods have adjustable top and bottom clamps to hold the artworks. (Not all hooks fit all picture rails, so buy everything from the same supplier.)

Artworks for temporary loan are widely available. Talk with local artists, with art galleries that show the work of local artists, with community art leagues, and with university art and architecture departments. Some libraries have annual shows for various groups.

V. PINNABLE SURFACES

Many libraries rely on bulletin boards for temporary displays. The main problem is keeping them occupied. Elementary school teachers complain about the tyranny of bulletin boards, and librarians can too. Nothing is less fun that an administrator telling you that your holiday bulletin board is overdue when you are up to your gills in summer reading programs.

One possibility that comes without bulletin board tyranny is pinnable wall surfaces. Large cloth-covered panels are available to mount on walls. You can stick things anywhere you want, which gives you a lot more space for wild creativity than a bulletin board, and when the pinnable surfaces are empty they look like colored wall sections rather than empty bulletin boards.

One small-town library Fred worked with served as an after-school study center for the children from the K-4 school down the block. The kids came to the library about 3:30 p.m. and worked there for an hour or two until the many working parents came to pick them up. Some days the pinnable walls were covered with "A" papers done in the library.

VI. SECURITY ISSUES

Issues of security are especially important for loaned items that the library does not own. Despite the library's best intents, things can go wrong, ranging from pilferage to fires.

> Damages can come from unexpected quarters. One of Fred's employees decided to put potted plants around the library. Among the plants was one that she placed on top of the exhibit case. When she watered the plant, water dripped onto the exhibit in the case. The exhibitor removed everything that afternoon.

One easy way is to refuse to exhibit anything to which the owner attaches a value. But one can imagine many owners refusing to waive all rights to their display items.

Another possibility is to purchase an exhibit floater policy. Such a policy will probably have a deductible amount and provide coverage limits for items not specifically scheduled (listed individually with agreed-amount valuations). But it may be enough to satisfy people lending material to the library.

VII. PERMANENT WORKS OF ART

Many libraries have permanent works of art. Some may be of great age, commissioned at the time the building was built or donated soon thereafter.

Permanent works of art need labels of some kind, typically explaining the origins of the works and their significance to the library.

> Fred's library had niches with busts of Longfellow and Lincoln flanking the inside of the front entrance. Everyone recognized Lincoln, but essentially no one (not even in a university community) recognized Longfellow. So Fred had labels made. He had one made for Lincoln, but for Longfellow he ordered half a dozen, with additional names such as Kelvin and Marx and Darwin. Every week or so he switched the label under the Longfellow bust. Fred thought this was serious fun, but no one (as in *no one*) shared his opinion. Since he had no other use for the extra labels, Fred tucked them away in the back of a desk drawer. Thirty years later, while he was retiring and cleaning out his desk, he stumbled across the extra labels and found he still had no other use for them.

It's easier to deal with insurance on permanent works of art. First, they belong to the library, so no angry owner will be involved if something goes awry. And second, because they are the permanent property of the library, arranging for insurance is easier.

Occasionally libraries want to deaccession works of art and sell them for cash. In these cases, public relations can be very touchy, just as they are when valuable items in the book collection are cashed in. The main suggestion that occurs to us is to talk things over extensively in private before making any announcements.

VIII. EXTERIOR DISPLAYS

Libraries occasionally have outdoor sculptures.

For a long time there was a vogue for bronze figures, typically life-sized children or adults seated on benches, reading or just enjoying the view. The figures provided a human scale to the exterior of the library, and frequently library users would pose for photos beside them. Entire catalogs of figures were available.

We get the impression that life-size bronze sculptures have probably run their course, but we could be wrong.

Some libraries commission custom sculptures. Fred's library had a tortoise and hare (with intervening books) sculpted on site from a twenty-ton block of limestone. The artist (who grew up locally) was hard at work (and covered with white dust) for about six weeks, which made the whole thing a lot more fun than trucking in one of a number of identical casts by an artist no one knows.

IX. COMBINED LIBRARIES AND MUSEUMS

Some libraries and museums are combined in one building.

There are classic examples such as the Carnegie in Pittsburgh, which includes a public library, a concert hall, and a natural history museum.

For most libraries, combining a library with a museum brings up serious questions of ownership and control. In Fred's one experience, the library board assumed total control of the museum, including ownership of all its collections. Museum employees reported to the director of the library. All went well as a result, but anything less than total library ownership and control would probably have led to problems.

The moral is the same that faces libraries in all sorts of circumstances: Ideally, anything in the library building has to belong to the library, and anyone who works in the library building has to report to the director of the library.

X. POLICIES ON DISPLAYS AND EXHIBITS

All libraries benefit from written policies on displays and exhibits.

Among the things you may want to include are:

- Is ownership of permanent exhibits absolute? Are all permanent exhibits the property of the library? Do the library's governors have the right to keep or dispose of them as they see fit? What level of approval is required for permanent exhibits?
- What will you do when temporary exhibits have unexpected political overtones? If your staff have arranged for an exhibit that turns out to be extremely offensive to some of your users, what will you do?

> This may sound excessively worried, but over the decades, Fred's library had many objections from all ends of the political spectrum—a couple of them totally unanticipated.

- What are the limits on library liability? If a temporary exhibit is damaged, then what? Do traveling exhibits come with insurance, or is the library expected to obtain coverage? Do you want waivers of liability? (And if you insist on waivers, will anyone put anything on display in your library?)
- Do you have any recourse if the charming sculpture installed by the Friends of the Library in 1972 seems embarrassingly treacly in 2017?
- Do you want a policy to never accept permanent works of art?

XI. SNAPPY RULES ON DISPLAY AND EXHIBIT AREAS

1. Beware of open-ended acceptance of temporary displays. Insist on approving all objects. For major displays, approve everything that will appear before announcing the display.
2. Beware of providing permanent exhibit space for things you don't own, because it can lead to turf disputes. If it goes on permanent display, it has to belong to the library.
3. Museums and their technology are a world of their own. For anything major, get technical assistance.
4. Some architects love to design display cases but don't do it very well. When you see an unusual display case in a library, ask the staff who have to maintain it how they like it.
5. Items displayed permanently in the library should be owned by the library. If the library wants to sell a painting, it should have the right to sell the painting, bearing in mind that local folks may take strong exception to the idea.
6. If you take a tour of a library building, and the tour consists entirely of pointing out works of art, you should have questions about priorities.
7. Libraries that want permanent art displays need to organize donor trusts to pick up the costs. And they need to find a way to occasionally say "No" to proposed objects. (Things can get awkward when the husband of the president of the library foundation creates truly ugly art that he wants to see on permanent display in the library.)
8. All sorts of elaborate multipart sculptures hang on wires in library atriums. They can be fun, but budget for dusting.

9. Many artworks on display require explanatory labels. If you have an oil painting of the first president of the university, or a photograph of the board of trustees that created your public library in 1874, you need to point out who they are.
10. The nice thing about local art as opposed to art from catalogs is that people are far less hypercritical when they know the artist personally.
11. Small, brightly lit "jewel box" display cases set into the wall at child height are amazingly popular. If children bring their own displays, all the library staff have to do is unlock the case and dust off the shelves on exhibit-changing day. But custodians sometimes object to having to clean nose grease off the glass every morning.
12. Nobody likes viewing displays below waist level. Children like low display cases because they have low waists.
13. Movable display cases are a lot more useful than fixed display cases. Think "furniture" rather than "building."

21

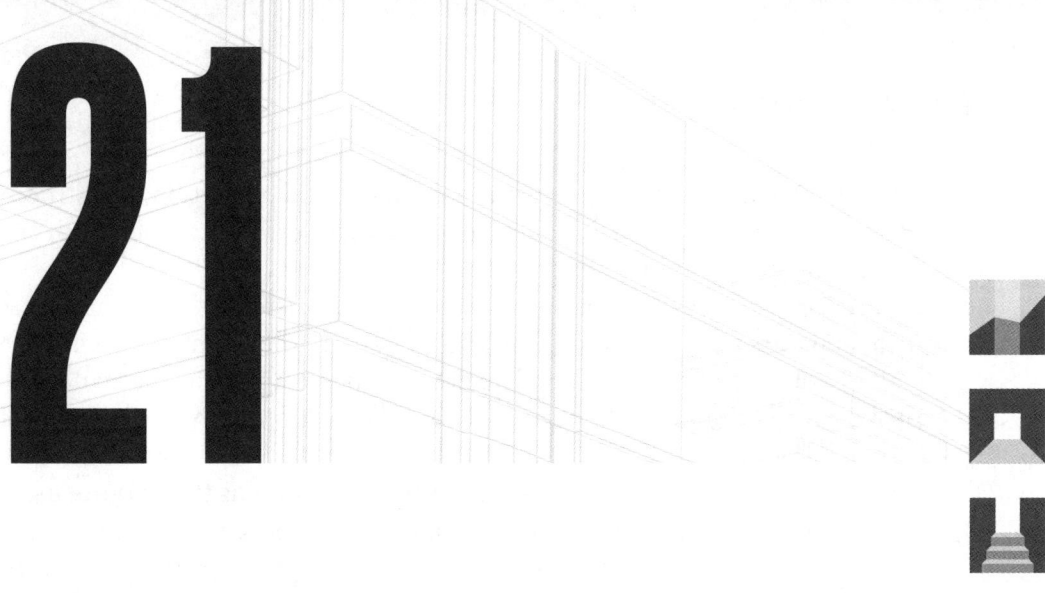

Restrooms

I. INTRODUCTION

With the exception of libraries that consist of a couple of rooms in larger buildings—such as school libraries or law libraries—all libraries need restrooms.

Many librarians wish this were not the case, because restrooms cause problems vastly in excess of the space they occupy.

Although not all problems with restrooms can be eliminated by good design, restrooms in a well-planned building can keep both library users and library staff far happier.

No one who spends years working on library buildings can escape without a fund of stories of Restrooms from Hell. Over the years we have seen:

- Library restrooms where gentlemen at the urinals are all on full display whenever the doors are opened.
- Library restrooms without floor drains. Although this may sound trivial, think about the pleasure of cleaning up major messes using only a bucket and mop.
- Libraries with restrooms for women but not for men.
- Libraries where the only restrooms are accessed through the directors' offices.

- Library restrooms without even rudimentary sound insulation. If restroom users can hear every word spoken in nearby rooms, they are left with the unnerving potential of reciprocity.
- Library restrooms with motion-detector lighting systems that plunge users into total darkness. Fred visited one library where the women's room had a stall out of range of the motion detector. Women trapped in the stall when the lights went out could not turn the lights back on with any amount of arm-waving.
- Library restrooms with motion-detector lighting systems that require users to walk two or three steps into pitch-dark rooms before the lights go on.
- Library restrooms that open directly into inappropriate public areas, such as reading rooms and program rooms.
- Buildings where the restrooms for men have a sufficient number of fixtures, but where women need to stand in line. Concert halls and stadiums provide constant examples of this. (Some male architects ask plaintively why women are so slow. It's easy to explain why women's rooms need to be larger than men's rooms, but a more satisfying response is of course "None of your damn business. Shut up and build larger women's restrooms.")
- Libraries where staff are forced to share restrooms with members of the public because they have no private restrooms of their own.
- Restrooms with diaper-changing tables but no receptacles for dirty diapers.
- Restrooms with insufficient (or even nonexistent) exhaust fans, resulting in nearby spaces that defy both description and occupation.
- Restrooms where users can lock themselves in and enjoy complete privacy while they set wastebaskets on fire, add creative decorations, or do other fun things.
- Staff restrooms that lead directly into staff lunchrooms, with resulting unhappiness for both the staff eating lunch and the staff using the restrooms. (An amazing number of these exist.)
- Restrooms with entry doors that swing inwards but without paper towels to protect freshly washed hands from having to grab handles previously used by the great non-hand-washing masses. (An amazing number of these also exist.)
- Restrooms with stalls so miniaturized that users have to straddle toilets just to close the doors.
- Restroom stalls without coat hooks.
- Restrooms with fancy soap dispensers that break in the first week but are never replaced.
- Restrooms in locations so secret that library staff members spend more time giving directions to the restrooms than in checking out materials, answering reference questions, and providing computer assistance.

All of these problems are easy to prevent by advance planning, but many are difficult or impossible to cure once buildings are constructed. Be sure your building program includes very specific requirements for restrooms, and then review the architectural drawings with a fine-toothed comb. Just because you say you want something doesn't mean you'll get it.

Remember that fixtures and equipment that are just fine in private homes can be disastrously inadequate in public buildings, and that the judgment of laymen may not be helpful. Always consult with your custodians.

The authors of the book of Leviticus were fond of the word *abomination*. It's a good word for describing badly designed library restrooms.

Luckily, there are also really good library restroom stories. Our favorite involves an Illinois public library that began a century ago as a ladies' restroom in a town that had no downtown public restrooms for women. The group that founded it included an anteroom with places to sit and a few things to read, and it just grew.

II. BUILDING CODES

In many cases, state and local building codes will establish base rules for restroom design in public buildings. In addition, the Americans with Disabilities Act has a great deal to say about restroom design.

Codes may specify the minimum number of fixtures, whether lighting must be activated by motion sensors, whether restrooms have floor drains, the presence of nearby mop sinks, and other items.

However, codes provide only minimum legal requirements, and you will want to specify many additional features. For example, toilet stalls can be made more accessible to users with disabilities by exceeding the bare minimums set by the ADA and some state codes.

Some building codes call for greater numbers of toilets and washbasins than libraries generally need. This is sometimes due to libraries being grouped with other types of buildings for the specification of minimum number of fixtures. Because much of the space in libraries can be basically storage of books and other materials rather than user seating, the number of fixtures needed per square foot may be less than codes specify. Library architects are usually very aware of this problem and should be able to help you with interpretations of codes.

One architect friend claims that codes can sometimes be interpreted to lead to the design of library buildings that would consist mostly of restrooms. You can probably have too much of a good thing.

III. FIXTURES AND EQUIPMENT

A. Toilets

All public restrooms need wall-mounted rather than floor-mounted toilets, and most staff restrooms can benefit greatly from them.

Wall-mounted toilets simplify maintenance because there is no joint between the base of the toilet and the floor. With wall-mounted toilets, people cleaning restrooms can simply mop the entire area.

The problem with wall-mounted toilets is the immense weight of some users. A 350-pound person dropping abruptly on a wall-mounted toilet can place tremendous torque on the mounting system. Discuss this with your engineers. Given the extraordinary chubbying up of America, one assumes that plumbing manufacturers will be making stronger mounting brackets.

Although codes may allow you to install flush-tank toilets, you will deeply regret doing so. Flush-tank toilets are extremely high-maintenance devices, and in public restrooms this means serious trouble with cranky flush mechanisms. By contrast, flush valves are amazingly durable and low-maintenance devices that can perform for decades with little attention.

Flush-tank toilets also have removable lids, tempting people to hide things within, or simply to drop and break the lids.

Automatic flush toilets are widely recommended, but not everyone is thrilled with them. When they work, they're great, but if they don't flush properly the result is human misery. If a washbasin operated by electric eye doesn't work properly, you can always move to the next washbasin. But when a toilet operated by electric eye doesn't work properly, it's *too late* when you find out. If you have automatic flush toilets, be sure the valves have manual push buttons.

> Your designers may assure you that modern automatic toilets never cause problems, but we've seen far too many examples to the contrary. In one major library we visited, signs in every restroom advised users to hold their hands over the electric eyes a minimum of twenty seconds in order to flush the toilets.

Flush-valve toilets have a great deal more flushing power than tank toilets do, making it at least somewhat less likely that small children can plug up the entire system by flushing clothes or other objects down the toilets, or that adults can plug everything up by attempting to flush paper towels.

Once you have tank toilets installed, it's extremely difficult to convert to flush-valve toilets, so don't assume you can start with tank toilets and convert later. The water supply pipes leading to flush-valve toilets are substantially larger than those for tank toilets, and they emerge from the wall in different places. To replace tank toilets with flush-valve toilets can mean tearing up large chunks of a building's plumbing system to install larger feed pipes.

Flush-valve toilets require reasonable water pressure. In some very small towns, local water pressure may be inadequate to operate flush-valve toilets. Your architects or engineers can determine whether the water pressure is adequate.

If you have tank toilets and are driven crazy by kids plugging them up, you can purchase replacement tank toilets that have power-assist flushing mechanisms. The mechanisms are impressively noisy, but they offer a way to improve flushing without putting in all-new plumbing.

> We aren't exaggerating the noise of power-assist mechanisms. Fred's library replaced some children's tank toilets with power-assist toilets. In the first couple of days after the new toilets were installed, a mother flushed the toilet while sitting on it herself. Her shriek was audible throughout an entire floor of the library.

> The problems of children plugging up plumbing are also not exaggerated. In Fred's library, a small child flushed his clothes down a toilet, plugging up the library's entire drain system and flooding a freshly recarpeted auditorium. Talk with your designers about drainpipes that discourage clogs.

Wall-mounted toilets require space in the wall behind the toilets to house the brackets that support the toilets. Look for this space when you review your schematic designs and construction drawings. If there's no open space behind the wall, you're not getting wall-mounted toilets.

Toilet seats need to be elongated ones, not the tiny circles found in some older houses, and they need to have open fronts. (Seats with open fronts are also called split seats.)

The main rules for toilets are:

- Always use wall-mounted toilets.
- Always use flush-valve toilets (unless your community has insufficient water pressure).
- Always use elongated toilets with split seats.
- Be sure that stalls are sufficiently large.
- Be sure that automatic flush toilets have supplementary manual controls.
- Be sure you have enough toilets.
- Don't expect to buy library toilets at a discount home supply store.

B. Stall Enclosures

Unless you plan to shoot a World War II barracks comedy, all toilets must have stalls. The minimum size of the handicapped-accessible toilets will be determined by codes, but other stalls are frequently made uncomfortably small.

- Be sure all of the stalls in your restrooms are adequately large. Too many restrooms have one large, accessible stall, accompanied by a number of additional stalls too small for anyone over about six years of age. In some stalls, the door swings barely clear of the front edges of the toilets, and users almost have to straddle toilets in order to close the doors. Stalls not intended to meet accessibility regulations need to be big enough for human beings. In our opinion, this means stalls a minimum of 42 inches wide, with door swings that clear the front edges of toilets by a minimum of 18 inches. Double-check your drawings for adequately large stalls. No matter how often you mention it, a junior engineer assigned to lay out your restrooms may blithely go ahead with tiny stalls. (In defense of designers, some feel that codes require excessively large numbers of toilets, and they end up using undersized stalls to prevent the restrooms from taking over the building. But they need to review the issues with you, not just quietly proceed with tiny stalls.)
- Make sure the stall doors have strong hooks. Nothing is more frustrating than toilet stalls that provide no places to hang coats, but such stalls are

everywhere. Make sure that the doors on the stalls are strong enough to carry the weight of heavy coats and even backpacks. Two hooks are a lot better than one. Imagine a user burdened with a parka, blazer, book bag, and purse, none of which she wants to put on the floor. Hooks made of cast zinc are brittle and frequently break in use, so always specify hooks made of steel or of resilient alloys like brass.

- Talk with your architects about graffiti-resistant surfaces. Some stalls are engineered for use in schools.
- A variety of commercial toilet paper dispensers is available. Most are specifically concerned with ways to prevent stalls from running out of paper during a single day. Other libraries have trouble with the theft of toilet paper, but we hear about this more from overseas libraries than from libraries in the United States. Variations in dispenser design include standard single-roll holders, side-by-side roll holders, drop-down holders where a second roll descends when the first one is used up, and huge-diameter rolls. Single-sheet dispensers are also available. Some units provide both holders for two rolls plus sanitary napkin disposal containers.

C. Urinals

In addition to toilets, all men's rooms require urinals, and they may be specified by the building codes that apply to your library.

Urinals do a great deal to limit mess. Users are much less likely to miss the fixture and splatter on the floor or on the rim of the toilet. And some gentlemen have never been trained to lift toilet seats before urinating from a standing position.

Although old-fashioned urinals were frequently massive devices mounted on the floor, most modern ones are more compact and are wall-mounted.

Urinals in some European restrooms have images of flies imbedded in the enamel, to give users something to aim at, and the practice has now spread to the United States. Not only does this improve neatness, but it also turns a visit to the restroom into a sporting event.

Since flushing urinals uses a substantial amount of water, some buildings have installed waterless urinals. The receiving area in waterless urinals consists of water with a layer of oil intended to allow urine to pass through but to block odors. As urine enters the water below the oil, the overflow goes down the drain. Waterless urinals have mixed reviews. They require a great deal of maintenance, and odors creep through the oil. If people innocently pour liquids (such as coffee) into waterless urinals, this causes serious maintenance problems. There are reports of concentrated urine corroding drainpipes not designed for it. We have no personal experience with waterless urinals, but we'd wait for better reports.

D. Washbasins

The second major component of restrooms is places to wash hands.

All restrooms require washbasins, and all building codes for public buildings should require them.

Unlike toilets, washbasins lend themselves to electric eye activation without the potential for embarrassing problems when mechanisms don't work. In addition, users of public restrooms appreciate being able to wash their hands without having to touch potentially filthy faucet handles.

If you have manual faucets, be sure that they have bat handles that can be operated with a wrist. Round faucet handles are particularly off-putting, since they must be grabbed by the fingertips, the very items we are trying to keep clean.

Getting newly installed electric-eye faucets to operate properly may require expert attention. As part of punch listing, therefore, try out all the restroom faucets in your building and demand that they work without forcing users to hold their hands in extremely specific places. (Almost everyone has had the frustrating experience of moving one's hands back and forth endlessly under a faucet, trying fruitlessly to get it to work.)

Many washbasins are wall-mounted. As with wall-mounted toilets, wall-mounted washbasins will simplify floor cleaning, but they also need to be strong enough to support the weight of people standing on them. Restroom users in libraries have been known to stand on washbasins to lift ceiling tiles and hide personal objects above the ceilings, and the result can be basins broken off walls. One library Fred worked with had a basin broken off the wall almost as soon as it opened.

E. Soap Dispensers

Something as simple as dispensing liquid soap shouldn't require much discussion, but in reality, things often go awry.

Most soap dispensers are wall-mounted boxes. However, one popular modern design for liquid soap dispensers consists of devices mounted on countertops

Sooner or later, almost all restroom soap dispensers stop working. If the original dispensers were mounted in holes in a counter top, most libraries simply add a disposable plastic dispenser to a nearby wall or mirror. (Some libraries remove the nonworking dispensers, leaving round holes in the countertops.)

beside sinks. An arm from the dispenser extends over the sink, and the top of the mounting is a plunger that dispenses liquid soap when pressed.

The main problem with dispensers of liquid soap is that, sooner or later, they all tend to corrode internally and stop working. America's public restrooms are full of sinks with elegant plunger-type dispensers that no longer work, and with fancy stainless wall-mounted dispensers that also no longer work, and both have been supplemented with wall-mounted disposable dispensers, or even with the kind of plastic bottles with plunger tops designed for home use. The old plunger devices sit unused, tempting users to whale away at them without results, or they've been removed, leaving raw holes in the countertops.

What can you do?

- Expect to replace your permanently mounted soap dispensers on a regular basis, hoping that when the time comes you can match the spaces required by your current dispensers. With gadgetry supplied by low bid, this plan may represent the triumph of optimism over experience.

- Use disposable soap dispensers. Most janitorial supply companies can supply these at little or no charge to their customers. Dispensers are mounted on walls or mirrors with double-sided tape and are filled with plastic bags of liquid soap. Because the dispensing tube is part of the bag, the dispenser has no built-in tubes to corrode shut. And if the dispenser breaks, the janitorial firm can give you a new one. One ongoing problem with soap dispensers is dripping liquid soap on the floor. Unfortunately, with separate washbasins it's hard to avoid this because the ADA requires that mirrors virtually touch the top of washbasins, and there's no space between the bottom of mirrors and the tops of sinks for soap dispensers. One solution is to mount disposable soap dispensers directly on the mirrors, where soap will drip on the sink rather than the floor. Soap dispensers operated by electric eye are now available, making it unnecessary for users to touch what may be dirty surfaces. These are attractive devices from the point of view of good public service. Whether or not they have the same clogging problems as older permanent dispensers we don't know.

F. Hand Drying

Many libraries end up deciding between forced-air hand dryers and paper towels, although there are probably no rules saying you have to choose just one.

Users clearly prefer paper towels, but paper towels lead to greater maintenance costs. If your library has paper towel dispensers, you will be faced with:

- Running out of towels in the middle of the day, when custodial staff members may not be around. One partial solution to this is always having two dispensers or having both dispensers and dryers.
- Large quantities of used paper towels. Used paper towels add up quickly. Cute receptacles, such as the neat little bins incorporated in combination towel dispensers and trash bins that are fitted flush into walls, can fill up and overflow in minutes. Unless you want to service restrooms many times a day, you'll need a serious container for paper towels.
- Paper towels on the floor by the door. If your library has restroom doors that open inward, users will (for extraordinarily good reasons) wash their hands and then use a paper towel to open the door, because they don't want to grasp dirty door handles with freshly washed hands. If you are stuck with a library with restroom doors that open inward, you'll need an extra wastebasket right by the door.
- Occasional paper towels flushed down toilets. This appears to be a particular problem in single-user restrooms, which have other bad attributes.

Many libraries install paper towel dispensers that have motion sensors. Each time users wave their hands in front of a dispenser, another section of toweling emerges. One of the great things about these is that they lessen the chance of having to touch what may be a dirty dispenser with freshly washed hands. As with other automatic gadgets, you may want to have two dispensers, in case one is empty or otherwise temporarily out of service. And you'll want to be extremely demanding at punch listing time. Lots of motion-sensor towel dispensers don't work well, and you need to be painfully insistent on perfect performance.

The alternative to paper towels is hand dryers. Users dislike them, but they require less frequent janitorial service.

Dryers can be controlled by push buttons or electric eyes.

Some older hand dryers relied too much on heat and not enough on air movement. The least satisfactory devices combined high heat with limited airflow, burning the hands without drying them.

The trouble with hand dryers is similar to the trouble with electric razors. When razors have blades, people shave until they're through. With electric razors, people shave until they get bored and give up.

One useful innovation that eliminates the boredom factor is high-velocity hand dryers that actually do the job. Of course, they also make an amazing racket, potentially eliminating from libraries the doorless restrooms developed for airports. Another one of the many reasons to have restrooms leading to foyers or other open non-library spaces is to avoid bothering library users with the roar of the dryers.

If at all possible, insist on trying out a working model of your hand dryers before you authorize their installation, judging the model's effectiveness and noise. We see a lot of bad examples in government buildings, perhaps the result of contractors claiming "equivalencies."

G. Mirrors

All restrooms need mirrors.

Most have mirrors directly over the washbasins, but you may benefit from an additional mirror or two.

Check your restroom floor plans carefully to be sure that mirrors are not visible from outside the restrooms when the doors are open. Many restrooms provide an amazing view of the activities within, all reflected in the mirrors over the sinks.

Be sure that the lighting by the mirrors lights the fronts of people's faces as well as the tops of their heads. There are restrooms in which the tops of people's heads are blazingly illuminated while their faces are in deep (but not romantic) shadow. People use mirrors to check their appearances, and they need light to do so.

H. Shelves

Many restrooms have shelves where people can place objects while they are using the restrooms. A common place is above the sinks and below the mirrors, but there may not be space. Shelves can also be located between mirrors.

I. Feminine Hygiene Products

Women's restrooms need coin-operated dispensers for feminine hygiene products. Typically, these can be mounted on a wall in the main area of the restroom, where people will be less tempted to break into them for the paltry amount of change they contain, and where a single dispenser can be equally accessible to all users.

Depending on the effectiveness of your waste plumbing system, you may want containers mounted on the walls of stalls for the disposal of these products. Remember that feminine hygiene products are medical waste, and their handling and disposal is subject to concerns about blood-borne pathogens.

J. Hypodermic Needles

The most common medical waste in restrooms (if you don't count feminine hygiene products) is used insulin syringes. "Sharps" containers for the disposal of syringes are usually bolted to walls somewhere near the sinks, since people taking insulin will probably use sink tops as shelves.

K. Ventilation

Exhaust fans are essential to restroom design. No matter how lovely your restroom decor or how elegant your fixtures, inadequate ventilation will spoil everyone's appreciation.

Most fans are located at the farthest point from the entry door to reduce the chance of any bad smells being detected outside the entrances to the restrooms.

Minimum restroom ventilation requirements are specified by codes, but you may want to exceed the minimum.

L. Mop Basins

To prevent custodians from rinsing out mops in toilets, most codes require a mop basin on any floor that has a toilet.

Mop basins need to be in mop closets. Simply putting mop basins inside restrooms is a really bad idea. They're ugly, and who knows how they'll be abused.

Mop closets are often located near restrooms to consolidate plumbing. However, mop closets that are accessed *through* restrooms are a bad idea because there are problems if the mopper is a different gender from the restroom users. (Don't assume that this will be okay because floors will be mopped only when the library is closed, or because all moppers will be male.)

IV. ACCOMMODATIONS FOR CHILDREN AND INFANTS

A. Children's Restrooms

All larger public libraries need separate restrooms for children, particularly when children's departments and adult departments are on separate floors.

As with adult restrooms, children's restrooms can suffer from vandalism and other problems. Small boys in particular occasionally lock themselves into restrooms and create mayhem.

The best way to prevent vandalism is to never have restrooms with locking doors. Even if a restroom has only one toilet, the toilet can be in a stall, making a locking door to the restroom unnecessary.

Miniature restroom fixtures are available, but we are not taken with them. Most kids manage well with adult-sized fixtures. If they can do it at home, why not at the library as well?

Regardless of fixture size, toilet stalls in children's restrooms must be generously proportioned because they often must simultaneously hold both a child and the parent helping the child.

B. Changing Tables

Virtually all libraries need diaper-changing tables. Although your library may in theory serve only adults, unless you card infants at the door, sooner or later one of them will slither in and promptly need changing. No matter how you feel about all of this, the experience of having a parent change an impressively dirty diaper on top of a reading table will provide positive thoughts about the utility—not to mention pleasantness—of having changing tables in your restrooms.

Both men's and women's restrooms need changing tables. If you assume that only women have infants requiring changing, you will at the very least be branded as a troglodyte.

Changing tables need to be located in both adult and children's restrooms.

Do not make the mistake of placing changing tables in toilet stalls. In some libraries, the changing tables are in the accessible stalls, leading to the very real possibility of users in wheelchairs and users with infants needing to occupy the same turf.

Changing tables can be fixed to a wall, or they can fold down. Commercially available folding tables are designed to be cleaned, but if your architects invent their own fixed tables, be sure the tables are easy to clean.

There needs to be some source of wet wipes or other ways of cleaning off infants.

Be sure you have a receptacle for dirty diapers. It needs to be located right beside the changing table and marked more boldly than you would really think necessary. If the lid is opened by a foot pedal and is equipped with a deodorizer, everyone will be happier. The last thing you need is people flushing disposable diapers down the toilets.

C. Infant Seats

Infant seats are fold-down, wall-mounted seats with restraining straps to keep infants secure while parents are using restrooms. Few parents want to balance infants on their laps while using the toilet, and the options of placing infants on dirty restroom floors or handing them off to strangers are equally icky. Infant seats are inexpensive and take very little space when folded up.

D. Restrooms for Story and Craft Rooms

Many children's librarians note the extreme utility of having at least one small unisex restroom located adjacent to story and craft rooms.

Enchanted by the engaging events in story and craft rooms, children delay mentioning their needs until there are only seconds to spare. For parents, the idea of having to sprint across the entire library carrying a four-year-old time bomb is not a happy one.

E. Restrooms for Users Needing Assistance by People of the Opposite Sex

Many children's departments include "family restrooms." A family restroom provides a place for parents to assist children using the restroom. Family restrooms are particularly important for fathers assisting their small daughters. In restrooms that consist exclusively of stalls, taking a child of the opposite sex to a restroom is relatively simple, but the presence of urinals in men's restrooms sends fathers of little girls into agony. (It doesn't seem to bother little girls, however, who appear at most to be only mildly curious.)

Other assisted-use restrooms are designed for use by adults of opposite sexes who need to assist one another—typically elderly couples.

Unlike other restrooms in libraries, assisted-use restrooms need to be single-person restrooms with locking doors. For this reason, some libraries keep such restrooms locked and ask users to request keys.

V. SIZE AND LOCATION OF RESTROOMS

A. Number of Fixtures

Plumbing codes may dictate the minimum number of toilets for your library. If your state does not have codes specifying minimum numbers of fixtures, you can ask your architects to check the codes of other states.

As we noted at the beginning of this chapter, some plumbing codes can specify more fixtures than your library actually needs. Ask your architect to review code requirements with you and to review the various ways codes can be interpreted.

Regardless of plumbing code requirements, you may wish to provide more toilets for women than for men. This is particularly important if you anticipate major rushes to use restrooms, such as times when large numbers of people are leaving events at the same time.

B. Locations

Most libraries—even very small ones—provide at least two restrooms, one for women and one for men. If you want a single unisex restroom, your architect will determine if that is legal in your area. (It probably will not be.)

Public libraries benefit from restrooms that are accessible from foyers. If a library's meeting rooms and restrooms are both accessible from its entry foyer, the door between the foyer and the rest of the library can be locked and meetings can take place when the rest of the library is closed.

Placing restrooms outside a library's theft control security gates also helps prevent users from taking library materials into restrooms without first checking the materials out. This arrangement can greatly reduce the number of materials left in unusable condition in restrooms.

No restrooms should lead directly to reading rooms, meeting rooms, staff workrooms, staff lunchrooms, and so on. Unfortunately, all of these exist in abundance.

From the point of view of both staff oversight and efficient use of fixtures, it's easier to have fewer and larger restrooms than many small ones.

All entrances to public restrooms should be visible from library staff service points.

When restroom doors are open, baffle walls should prevent views of the insides of the rooms. Far too many restrooms provide passersby with views of all the men at the urinals when the doors open. Views of stall doors are not quite so unwelcome, but they are still inappropriate. If restrooms provide passersby with a view of sinks, the reflections in the mirrors over the sinks may provide views of the urinals and stall doors.

Avoiding restrooms that provide views of this kind is easy, but they unfortunately exist everywhere, including in new and expensive buildings that could have been properly designed. When you are checking over your library designs, always inspect the restroom drawings for inappropriate sight lines.

Some public restrooms in libraries are in such secret locations that no one can find them without assistance. We've even seen some library restrooms that are located in hallways accessed through unmarked doors.

> One library we visited has not only invisible restroom doors but also an agreement with the architect that the library will not install any additional signage. The real blame for this lies with the owners who were foolish enough to give their architect this kind of power after the building is completed.

Library staff members grouse endlessly about giving directions to restrooms. Some of this is unreasonable kvetching, but it helps if restroom locations are reasonably obvious.

When you are evaluating your schematic designs and construction drawings, ask yourself whether users will be able to find the restrooms.

C. Staff Restrooms

Most library staff members strongly dislike sharing toilet facilities with library users, and it is reasonable and proper to provide separate restrooms for library staff members. In the case of a small library, a single unisex staff restroom is probably sufficient, although unisex restrooms may not count toward the minimum number of fixtures specified in some plumbing codes.

One of the most serious but common errors in the creation of staff restrooms is to have them directly accessible from staff lunchrooms. We've seen many libraries where staff members having lunch are actually treated to views of toilets through open restroom doors. It's hard to imagine wanting to eat lunch three feet from a toilet, or wanting to use a toilet three feet from where one's coworkers are eating lunch, but buildings are designed that way all the time. A librarian we know asks of people who design restrooms that way, "What were they *thinking?!*"

D. Implications for Expansion

If you are planning a two-phase library, you will almost certainly want to be sure that the restrooms built for the first phase will be sufficient to serve the expanded building.

If you have to add extra restroom capacity when you expand your building, you may end up trying to cram extra toilets into rooms not designed to hold them or be faced with the far greater cost and loss of flexibility that accompanies having to construct additional restrooms.

Extra restrooms will cost more than larger restrooms, and they can lead to situations where users dash from restroom to restroom trying to find one free.

Extra restrooms are also far more likely to end up in awkward places, like directly off reading rooms.

E. Accommodations for Transgender Users

Increasingly, libraries will want to accommodate transgender users, and this will challenge the traditional rigid division of services into male and female.

Here are some possibilities:

- Have multi-gender restrooms with very private stalls.
- Do the way Europeans have done and regard multi-gender restrooms with ordinary stalls as providing sufficient privacy.
- Retain men's and women's restrooms, but make all toilet accommodations private, including stalls for urinals.
- Create small, single-user, unisex restrooms.
- Create single-user restrooms labeled "men" and "women" and let users select whichever they wish.
- Avoid doors. Provide restrooms that are like airport restrooms.
- One issue with single-user, unisex restrooms is whether to include urinals in all restrooms. Urinals result in far less mess.

In 2017, at the time this book was written, all of these issues appeared to be under review.

VI. SECURITY

A. Staff Oversight

One of the best ways to limit problems with restrooms is to have restroom doors visible from staff workstations.

In public libraries with restrooms and meeting rooms accessible from entry foyers, it's easy for staff to observe people entering and leaving restrooms.

Some libraries that have problems with vandalism in restrooms have restroom doors that are kept locked at all times and unlocked by push buttons at service desks.

It's also possible to have keys at service desks, but keeping an eye on keys can be a real nuisance. Keys usually have to have huge blocks of wood or other objects attached to prevent users from wandering off with them. And who wants to handle potentially dirty wooden blocks all day long?

B. Single-User Restrooms

One major source of security problems in library restrooms is single-user restrooms with doors that lock. If a person can lock himself (or herself, to be

When reviewing proposed floorplans, pay particularly attention to sight lines. In most cases, good sightlines make good libraries, but occasionally they really don't. This photograph was taken by balancing a camera on the romance fiction shelving, where readers can easily be treated to unwanted views of the men's room in action.

perfectly fair, although most problem users are men) in, there's far too much possibility for trouble.

To prevent this, with the exception of staff restrooms, no restroom doors should have locks, and the necessary privacy should be provided by stalls. Providing a stall in a single-user restroom takes somewhat more space, but the reduction in vandalism can be impressive.

Consequently, all public restrooms need baffle walls to prevent people standing outside from viewing the inside of restrooms in action.

C. Doorless Restrooms

Some libraries have doorless restrooms of the style used in airports. While these provide sufficient privacy, they also discourage vandalism because people using them receive no advance warning when someone else enters.

Doorless restrooms let more sound escape, but so do regular restrooms when the doors are open. As long as the restrooms are reached from hallways or foyers, things seem to work well.

D. Video Surveillance

One way to fight vandalism in restrooms is with video surveillance. Although cameras in restrooms are obviously inappropriate, cameras can be located to permit the identification of people leaving restrooms.

E. Restrooms as Tornado Shelters

Libraries in areas prone to tornados frequently include restrooms that can serve as tornado shelters, with concrete walls and ceilings. A small frame-on-slab library is unlikely to withstand a major windstorm, but if the restrooms have concrete walls and ceilings, people can take shelter there.

Restrooms have the advantage of being the only rooms in libraries that are never used for storage. Library staff members are always hunting for places to put stuff, which all libraries have in generous quantities. If any room except a restroom is designed to serve as a tornado shelter, people arriving there may find it full of puppets and used paperbacks and miscellaneous shelving components—and unable to serve as a shelter.

By locating restrooms directly off entry foyers, libraries make their tornado shelters available to people using meeting rooms after regular library hours, as well as to users diving off the street seeking shelter.

Obviously, restrooms designed as shelters cannot have windows and cannot be doorless.

> This sounds like a silly observation, but one library Fred worked with relocated its tornado shelter to the library proper—where it could not be accessed after regular hours—in a room that ended up filled with furniture, all to preserve a translucent glass window that the architect wanted in one of the restrooms.

VII. LIGHTING

A. Motion Sensors

Energy codes may require that your restrooms have lighting operated by motion sensors. If this is the case, you will have to deal with two serious potential problems.

First, motion sensors need to operate the moment the restroom door starts to open and not require users to grope their way into a dark space. This may require a separate detector on the ceiling, not a cheap one combined with a light switch. (If the restroom has cheap detectors, users will reach inside the dark room and attempt to turn on the light switch, usually messing up the setting of the sensor.)

Second, there must be no way that anyone in a stall can fail to be detected and plunged into total darkness. Motion-sensing technology may eventually prevent this, but until then, always provide a dim level of 24/7 night lighting—even if it's just one or two foot-candles—in all public restrooms.

Because restrooms usually have no windows, being in a restroom when the lights go out is a little like being in an unlighted limestone cave. Few non-cavers will appreciate the experience.

Motion sensor lighting is encouraged or required for energy-saving reasons, but to have a complete picture of the situation, you will need to know the effect that constant switching off and on has on the life and efficiency of your electric lamps. The life span and efficiency of fluorescent lamps can be reduced if they are constantly switched off and on, and HID lights *cannot* be constantly switched off and on. The emergence of LED lighting may be the answer.

Some libraries are so antagonized by the functions of motion detectors in restrooms that they quietly replace them with light switches.

B. Manually Switched Lighting

If your restrooms have manual light switches, you will need a way to prevent people leaving restrooms from turning off the lights, leaving other people in the dark without even a slight hope of waving their arms around to bring the lights back on. (This can happen accidentally, or kids can get a kick out of leaving each other trapped in pitch-dark restrooms.)

A standard way to prevent this kind of misery is to use key switches that require a special tool to turn the lights off and on.

C. Light Distribution

People using washbasins need to be able to see their reflections in the mirrors over the basins to check hair, makeup, and so on. If the light provided is harshly vertical, this doesn't work.

There also needs to be at least a minimum amount of light in toilet stalls. The lower the restroom ceiling, the harder this is to achieve from a limited number of light fixtures.

VIII. PLANNING FOR MAINTENANCE

A. Floor Coverings

Although some restrooms have resilient flooring such as vinyl tile, by far the most practical floor covering is ceramic tile.

Unlike ceramic tile, vinyl tile is sufficiently porous to be hard to keep clean in restroom situations, and it can wear quickly in places where users always stand. And moisture may eventually lead vinyl tile to lift and curl and separate.

To work properly in restrooms, ceramic tile needs:

- A surface rough enough to prevent the tile from being slippery when wet. Installing polished stone flooring or terrazzo in a public restroom provides a great opportunity to test your liability insurance coverage.
- Very dark (never pastel) grout. Trying to keep white grout clean is essentially impossible, and it is the bane of cleaning firms everywhere. (Dark grout is, of course, no easier to clean than white grout, but with dark grout the stains don't show.)

We cannot emphasize this point too strongly. If you have white or light-colored grout, you will come to hate white or light-colored grout with true passion.

B. Floor Drains

Regardless of building code requirements, all restrooms need floor drains.

Due to construction errors, some floor drains don't work properly. As part of your punch list process, pour buckets of water on your restroom floors to make sure that water flows toward the drains rather than away from them. If the floor drain in a restroom with a ceramic tile floor installed over concrete doesn't drain properly, both the tile and the concrete beneath will probably need to be replaced. This is another time to be firm with your punch list.

C. Wall Coverings

The best wall covering in restrooms is ceramic tile.

Unlike floor tile, it can be smooth, but dark grout is still important, not only to hide stains but also to prevent creative people—frustrated by the way that glazed ceramic tile rejects ballpoint pen ink and marking pens—from writing messages on the white grout.

The best approach is to install floor-to-ceiling tile. However, some libraries have tile wainscots, with painted drywall above.

D. Graffiti

Restrooms have for generations been favorite places for inventive graffiti.

Glazed ceramic surfaces help, because almost any markings can be washed off. So do stainless steel toilet partitions. Dark grout eliminates the possibility of writing colorful observations on the grout when the tile resists decoration.

Locking single-person restrooms are particularly appealing places because they provide users with the time to write leisurely graffiti.

IX. SNAPPY RULES ON LIBRARY RESTROOMS

1. If your library will have meetings that large numbers of people leave at the same time, you will need more women's toilets than men's toilets.
2. A poorly ventilated restroom is a seriously unlovely object.
3. Floor-mounted toilets are cheaper than wall-mounted toilets, but only if you don't count the cost of maintenance.
4. Always use flush-valve toilets unless your community suffers from low water pressure. You can't start with tank toilets now and switch to flush-valve toilets later, so take the plunge.
5. Always check sight lines into restrooms on your floor plans. One way is to ask if your restrooms would still be sufficiently private if the entry doors were removed.
6. Remember that if people can see the mirrors in the restroom from outside the door, they can probably see everything in the restroom from outside the door.
7. Owners may like hand dryers, but users prefer towels. You can have both.
8. Unless your building successfully bans infants, your restrooms will need changing tables. And receptacles for dirty diapers. (Very few buildings successfully ban infants.)
9. If your washbasins aren't strong enough to bear the weight of adults, sooner or later someone will break one off the wall.
10. Even in tiny libraries, staff do not want to share restrooms with library users. Unless you've spent your life working in libraries, you have no right to regard this as an unreasonable attitude.
11. Restrooms must never open directly into reading rooms, program rooms, or staff lunchrooms. Don't get yourself into a situation where expanding your library will require additional restrooms in unacceptable places.
12. It's easier to control restrooms if the doors are visible from staff workstations. Video cameras recording people entering and leaving restrooms also help.
13. When deciding whether to use automatic fixtures, ask yourself how awkward things will be if a fixture fails to operate as promised.

14. Users with freshly washed hands do not want to grab dirty door handles when they leave restrooms. If your restroom doors do not swing outward, you will need wastebaskets for paper towels right by the exit doors. (If your doors swing inward and you have only hand dryers, your users will speak ill of you.)
15. As part of the punch list process, always make sure that all your restroom gadgets work properly. Check automatic faucets and toilets. Check floor drains. Check soap dispensers. Check hand dryers and automatic towel dispensers. Check exhaust fans. Check that motion detectors don't require people to actually enter the room to turn the lights on, and that lights don't go out too quickly. And never, NEVER pay your holdback until everything works perfectly.
16. If your area is prone to tornados, tornado-proof restrooms are a great idea. Especially in one-story buildings, where people can't take shelter under a strong upper floor. (Unlike other sorts of storm shelters, restrooms are almost never used for storage, and people diving for cover can expect to find the floors clear.)
17. The only suitable restroom floor covering is anti-slip ceramic tile with very dark grout. White grout is impossible to keep clean. Vinyl tile is hard to maintain and tends to come loose. Shiny ceramic tile is excitingly slippery when wet.
18. Cheap fixtures are a lack of joy forever. Fixtures designed for home use are cheap fixtures.
19. Be sure all of your toilet stalls are large enough for actual human beings. Surprisingly, a great many are not.
20. A toilet stall without two sturdy hooks for coats, purses, book bags, jackets, coats, and so on is an abomination.
21. Sooner or later, all soap dispensers and towel dispensers fail. Have a plan.
22. Picturesque, antique restrooms are probably less fun than picturesque, antique stonework.
23. If you are constructing a two-phase building, make your Phase I restrooms large enough to meet Phase II code requirements, or you may end up with extra restrooms added during Phase II construction in seriously unfortunate locations.
24. Wall-mounted toilets allow far easier maintenance. The joint where a floor-mounted toilet meets the floor is always dirty.
25. Faucet handles are probably among the dirtiest objects in public restrooms. Get electric eye-operated faucets or get faucets with bat handles than can be operated by the wrist.
26. Be prepared to accommodate transgendered users.
27. No decent lighting system plunges restroom users into darkness or forces them to grope their way into pitch-dark restrooms.
28. Try to observe recommended fixtures in action before you specify them.

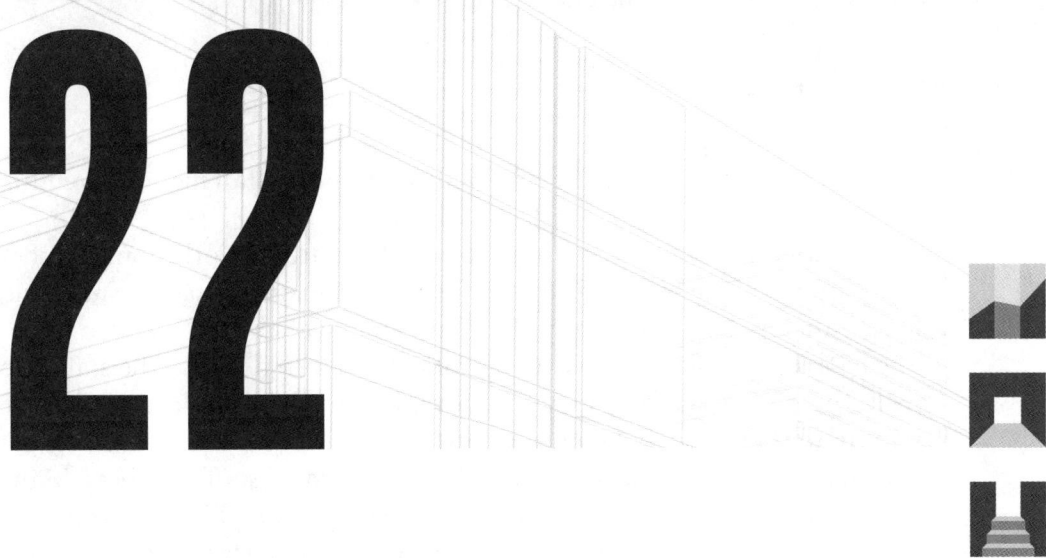

22

Staff Workrooms

I. INTRODUCTION

Most libraries have overcrowded staff workrooms, and many libraries have too few workrooms.

On some occasions this is no doubt the result of librarians who are pack rats, but we suspect that it is more often due to the fact that staff workrooms are almost always inadequate to begin with.

One way to fight this is to make sure that the written building program for your library includes adequate staff workspaces not only for opening day, but also for just as long as you expect the library to continue in use without expansion.

II. GENERAL CONSIDERATIONS FOR STAFF WORKROOMS

Staff workrooms are an essential part of all libraries.

- All libraries larger than broom closets require staff workrooms. Staff need space to spread out work and leave it undisturbed while helping library users. Supervisors need spaces where they can talk with their staff members privately. All sorts of special activities require special equipment and places to

spread it out. And many materials handled by library staff members require secure storage.
- Throughout this book, we've tried to call these areas "workrooms" rather than "offices." The word *office* conjures up an image of spaciousness and luxury that is alien to virtually all library employees.
- The people who know what kind of workspaces they need are the staff who work there. It's easy for remote employers to develop standard workspace sizes (and they probably go with standard because it's easy to do so), but planning workspaces means working with individual staff members. Many library tasks require very specific pieces of equipment, plus elbowroom for the people who operate the equipment, and the actual staff who work there know this best. It doesn't have to be in a private room, but equipment needs to go somewhere.
- Far too many libraries project new shelving to meet decades of growth, but construct workspaces only for current staff. This qualifies as seriously bad planning, but some libraries are adamant.
- Unless there's a need for privacy, go with group work areas. This means that supervisors need private workrooms because they need to have confidential conversations, and bookkeepers need private workrooms because they have financial records, and personnel officers need private workrooms because they have confidential files, and rare book catalogers can't leave rare books just lying around . . . BUT most other staff can be in shared work areas. All sorts of office system furniture is available to facilitate shared workspaces, ranging from traditional cubes to various multifunction units.
- Some businesses have tried putting everyone in group workrooms and then providing spaces that can be used for private conversations. Unfortunately, this makes it painfully clear when an employee is going to get a stern talking to, because everyone sees the supervisor and employee heading off for one of the private conversation spaces. We talked with people who work in environments like this, and they aren't happy.
- Some universities may have standard office sizes based on rank. These don't work with library workspaces, no matter how even-handed they seem. (Imagine a graphic artist with the title of "instructor" trying to fit a scanner and folder and storage for a wide variety of paper sizes into a small workroom.)
- Unless specific furnishings require running water, prefer modular furniture to built-ins. Staff members often want to rearrange their workspaces, and there's no reason they shouldn't. As with all library work areas, this means soft, even, all-purpose lighting and lots (as in LOTS) of electrical outlets at above tabletop height on walls and all over the floor.
- If it weren't for the running water, many workrooms would just be rectangular open spaces.

- Many library workspaces involve storage as well as actual work areas. Storage in the workroom is more convenient than storage down the hall and around the corner and up three steps. Since libraries often pay their staff by the hour, not having people constantly running back and forth to fetch things and put them back is worth money.
- Workrooms benefit from natural light. This is one more reason why upper floors are preferable to basements. (Other reasons include the fact that basements are nearly as expensive as upper floors, basements tend to be damp, and sooner or later many basements end up flooded. As a friend in the insurance business says, "Basements are places you put things you don't want.")
- Workrooms also need controllable natural light. This means (in particular) no skylights, but also movable blinds on all exterior glass surfaces that don't face straight north. (Many architects are enamored of windows that cannot be fitted with blinds, so be prepared to say "No!")
- Many workrooms benefit from interior glass areas facing adjacent areas of the library, both for security of workroom staff and for extra staff oversight of public areas. The time to install interior glass is when you are constructing your building; adding windows later can be extraordinarily expensive. (If you don't need the window right now, keep the blind closed, knowing that you'll rejoice if you need the window later and it's already there.)
- No staff workroom should be a public passageway. (It shouldn't be necessary to say this, but it keeps happening.)
- Interior designers can play a major role in developing good workrooms because so much of the contents are furnishings.
- Many workspaces are impossibly small, especially those with built-in counters. We've seen catalogers forced to balance open books on their laps while working.

III. INDIVIDUAL WORKROOMS

At least some employees will need individual workrooms.

> Fred actually had a corner office in his library, but it sounds better than it was in real life, for it was in a corner of the basement with one high window that led to a light well with a steel grating.

Directors have a lot of individual opinions about ideal workspaces, and a well-written building program will enumerate these.

In our experience, some directors are particularly wary about extra features in their own workrooms. They push strongly for good staff workspaces but are hesitant to request anything for themselves. As a result, programmers need to arrive with a long list of possible features and be sure that directors don't sell themselves (and those who follow them and use the same workrooms) short.

Other single-person workrooms common in libraries include workrooms for deputy directors, department heads, bookkeepers, office managers, personnel managers, and any other staff members who need to be able to have private conversations, particularly staff evaluations, or work with confidential documents.

Individual workrooms can be located in all sorts of places. Some library directors want their workrooms where they can see everyone entering the building—and everyone entering the building can see the directors. Other directors want somewhat more protection, if for no other reason than they have to get some work done once in a while.

Lots of directors' workrooms are reached through secretarial spaces, so that office managers or other workers can greet people who are looking for the director. If the outer rooms have a couple of armchairs and a coffee table, that gives visitors a place to sit while waiting to see the director. Other directors' workrooms are one of two or more workrooms leading off a common lobby, with perhaps office managers and bookkeepers in the other workrooms.

We've seen a few situations where directors' workrooms were passages to other parts of the library, and these arrangements were a terrible mistake.

> In one library Fred worked with, the only restroom in the building was reached by walking through the director's workroom, which people did about every five minutes all day long. When the new library was constructed, the director wanted the most remote room in the entire building. In addition to access through a door in a back corner of the staff workroom, it had a second door leading directly outside.

The best location for workrooms for department heads is probably adjacent to the multi-user staff workrooms of the departments.

IV. ARCHITECTURAL FEATURES OF WORKROOMS

A. Wiring

The main secret of wiring for workrooms is to have lots of electrical outlets on both walls and floors. It's particularly frustrating to find that the office system furniture you have selected blocks access to the only electrical outlet on that wall. (We've seen libraries tackle expensive equipment with saber saws, just to get access to outlets.)

Unless the workroom is intended to be a showplace for an administrator, electrical outlets work a lot better above tabletop height, so that staff members do not have to crawl under furniture in order to plug in pieces of equipment. In addition, some workrooms end up with machinery lined up edge-to-edge all the way around the room, and it's impossible to plug things in without high outlets.

When you're looking at the electrical drawings for your new library, outlets that are 36 inches above the floor should be marked "+ 36."

If you plan data conduit as well as 110-volt service, you can install dual-conduit wire mold that allows both sets of wires in the same enclosure.

B. Natural and Artificial Light

Staff workspaces need bright but low-glare light.

All staff workspaces benefit from the psychological advantages of natural light. Staff members who have windowless basement workrooms hate them.

However, any glass surface that does not face directly north needs an adjustable blind.

We've seen workrooms with skylights. We think that skylights are always a mistake in any sort of library, but designers seem to be less in love with skylights in staff work areas, perhaps because the wider world can't see them. Remember that if skylights are essential, always use a translucent material like Kalwall.

Library staff can be particularly unhappy when condemned to windowless subterranean spaces without natural light. As we continually suggest, basement spaces are no bargain. They cost nearly as much as upper floors, they are unnecessarily depressing, and they tend to flood. *(So don't build basements.)*

One traditional trick for providing natural lighting for workrooms buried in the interior of buildings is "borrowed light." High interior windows in these workrooms result in adjacent rooms with natural light.

Artificial lighting in workrooms needs to be bright but low glare. The kind of allover lighting that works in public reading areas should also be effective in most workrooms. The usual formula is between 70 and 100 percent uplighting, and an absolute minimum of 50 to 60 foot-candles at desktop.

For rooms used for special functions like filming books, extensive light control will be essential, and windows of any kind may cause serious problems.

C. Windows to the Rest of the Library

A window with a Venetian blind between the workroom and the adjacent public area of the library is an important feature, and one that is extremely expensive to retrofit.

Windows between staff workrooms and the public areas of the library provide great opportunities for staff oversight at no additional cost to the library. Staff members who like privacy can just keep the blinds closed. We think that windows of this type are especially important for library directors and supervisors, who may be uneasy about overly private meetings with employees or visitors of the opposite sex.

D. Running Water

With the exception of some private workrooms, all library workrooms need running water and sinks.

The main point is to be sure that sinks are specified in your building program, since retrofitting a sink is a seriously expensive undertaking. As usual, sinks need to be deep enough to allow something relatively serious to be filled. The kind of toy sinks called "bar sinks" may be suitable for playhouses, but they will make workroom occupants unhappy.

Sinks need to be located in fixed counters, but all other work surfaces should be movable furniture to allow long-term flexibility.

E. Temperature Control

To be effective, all workrooms require independent temperature controls. Trying to make a single thermostat (and associated temperature control equipment) do double duty for two separate rooms is an amazingly awful idea, but we occasionally find things set up that way. Inevitably, the people in the workroom without the thermostat will be impressively uncomfortable. (The alternative of a space heater is a great way to start a fire.)

Office system furniture needs adequate clearance between the tops of the partitions and the ceiling above, to allow adequate air circulation.

F. Ventilation

Some workrooms need extra ventilation, particularly graphic arts rooms.

Some preservation equipment also needs extra ventilation.

Ventilation is simple to provide during construction but may be extremely expensive to retrofit. Be sure to specify special ventilation requirements in your building program and check your construction drawings to be sure your architects provided it.

G. Restrooms

It's hard to imagine a library employee who would not rejoice in a private restroom. But many of us who have been directors would be a little hesitant to bring up the idea.

We suspect that most libraries limit themselves to staff restrooms. The main point is that shared staff restrooms should always be accessed from a staff hallway and not from a staff workroom or lunchroom.

H. Clothes Washers and Dryers

Clothes-washing equipment is important in children's department workrooms, where staff otherwise have to haul puppets and similar stuff home with them. Washers and dryers have to be installed up front, because connections are complex (220-volt power for dryers, exhaust vents, water supplies, and drains) and very difficult to install after the fact.

I. Built-In Furnishings

Built-in furnishings violate the core principle of library design—flexibility.

With the exception of counters with sinks, all workstations should be furniture rather than built-ins.

V. WORKROOM FURNISHINGS

This section of the chapter consists of a list of possible furnishings and equipment in staff workrooms.

A. Desks

Many staff members with individual workrooms have desks that serve both as workspaces and as spaces for meeting with people. Some modular office system desks are designed to provide two separate surfaces, a desk (perhaps with storage bins above) and a wide L that provides a surface between visitors and the staff member.

Some directors want very much to have separate furniture for working and for meeting with people. As a result, some directors have installed small, separate conference tables for meeting with visitors. Others have worktables for doing paper work and use their desks for meeting with people.

Most desks have two pedestals, each with a file drawer and a shallower drawer. If the desk has a computer L, the L may replace the drawers on one of the pedestals.

Some desks have shallow pencil drawers between the knee hole and desktop, but these can cramp the available space.

Lots of directors don't want really pompous executive desks in their own workrooms, but sometimes they inherit desks that are uncomfortably grand. It's hard to toss out expensive furniture, and it's also annoying to have to explain to every visitor that your predecessor picked it out. It's even more awkward if the desk is so big you can't circumnavigate it.

Luckily, a huge range of more modest wooden desks is available and suitable for library directors.

For many staff members, high-quality steel desks are a happy choice.

All desks need modesty panels. We see catalog illustrations of minimalist desks that are little more than tables, but we expect that few staff members want to have their legs on display that way. (Modesty appears to be a good option for everyday libraries, and most libraries are everyday libraries.)

Many separate desks are accompanied by credenzas. A credenza is a low cabinet behind a desk. The idea is that the top will provide space for (hopefully) neat storage, while the cabinets and drawers provide extra storage space. Often credenzas are pieces of furniture that match the desk and make a set. We've heard a number of library directors laugh about what they store in their credenzas, sometimes using the term *crud*enza.

B. Modular Office System Workstations

Modular office system workstations are particularly important when a number of staff need to share a workroom. Workstations can be rearranged, and they usually make very efficient use of space. Many have overhead storage bins, shelving, built-in lighting, file drawers, locking desk drawers (for purses), and other features.

Some large staff workrooms have masses of identical modular workstations in rows, a kind of Levittown effect.

The websites of office furniture firms are awash in modular office system workstations. This appears to be an excellent time to work with your interior designer.

C. Workroom Chairs

Desk chairs are highly individual. Never purchase one from a catalog, for you may hate it after fifteen minutes of experimentation.

The main thing with chairs is comfort. It's a shame to spend three hours seated at work, only to find that an ill-conceived chair has led to temporarily frozen knee joints, making it embarrassing when you plan to leap to your feet to greet a visitor and instead lurch to your feet. The wrong chair can also lead to horrible back fatigue. As with all chairs, sitting in them is the only true way to evaluate them.

The best workroom chairs have a lot of adjustments, and some have a maze of levers beneath to allow rearrangement for individual comfort.

Trying to save money on workroom chairs may be extremely shortsighted.

> When Fred arrived as a library director in the mid-1970s, he found a dozen new conference room chairs that had been bought without being tested. They were from a very big-name manufacturer of office furniture, but they were molded plastic bucket seats with no possible adjustments, and they were painful to use. Fred's staff contended the chairs had been carefully selected to keep staff meetings short. One librarian said she hated bucket seats because she had a "different-sized bucket."

D. Space for Visitors

All workrooms for individual staff members need chairs for visitors. Sometimes there are a couple of chairs facing the staff member's desk, while other library staff want several chairs or small conference tables.

The usual problem with conference tables in offices is trying to cram too much table into too little space, forcing people to crawl over each other to get to the corner chair. A small conference table needs at least 25 to 30 square feet per chair. Check your schematic design carefully to be sure that office tables have enough space. There needs to be at least five feet between the edge of the table and the wall.

In some director's workrooms, the conference table doubles as a working surface when visitors aren't present.

Also consider a shared conference room amid a group of staff workrooms. There's nothing better than thanking sales reps, then getting up and going back to your own workroom where they can't follow you.

E. Worktables

Many staff group workrooms have worktables for staff tasks, including packing and unpacking shipments, working on sprawly projects, and similar things. In some workrooms, staff use these tables for occasional meetings by clearing the tabletops.

F. Storage Cabinets

Some administrative offices have storage cabinets, particularly for administrators who tend to store individual projects in separate piles of paper. A lot of administrators make due with standard steel cantilever shelving with separate stacks of papers, but enclosed cabinets are friendly things that lead to long-term neatness.

As administrators, John always had a neat desk and Fred always had stacks of papers. Fred should have had a cabinet for stacks of papers, but he always used open shelving instead. Visitors averted their eyes.

Locking storage cabinets are extremely useful in group workrooms, particularly when high-theft items (such as uncataloged DVDs) are involved.

G. Coat and Purse Storage

Coat storage can range from a hook on the back of the door to a coat tree to a piece of trim on the wall with several coat hooks to a private coat closet. If you opt for the coat tree approach, make sure that there's space for it on your schematic design, and expect to have it tip over once in a while. Remember that cheap coat hooks made of cast zinc usually break, while steel and brass hooks don't.

For accessibility reasons, you may want coat hooks and coat bars at both accessible and standard heights. Long coats on accessible hangers drag on the floor, and standard height hangers are too high to meet accessibility requirements.

In shared workrooms, libraries need to provide a way for staff members to lock up their valuables. Basically, storage needs to be provided for anyone who does not have a personal desk or workstation with locking drawers. If you provide lockers, be sure they're large enough for workers who carry their wallets in backpacks. If they toss their backpacks in the corner of a workroom, sooner or later something will vanish.

H. Shelving

Most staff workspaces need shelving of some kind. Modular office workstations almost always include some shelving, but many offices also include separate shelving. Typically, it's wall-mounted single-faced shelving. Unless the need to show off is great, standard cantilever steel library shelving works very well. If you use the same color of shelving you have in the rest of the building, it's a lot easier to interchange parts.

It's easy to underestimate the need for storage shelving in staff workrooms. Administrators can have large book collections and stacks of papers they want to store flat for easy access. Library supplies need to be stored somewhere, and libraries need to plan spaces for colored paper, printer cartridges, boxes of rubber bands, and other space-consuming stuff. Technical services workrooms need shelving for all sorts of materials in process, as well as wide varieties of supplies.

Copier paper has to be stored somewhere, usually in boxes stacked on the floor. Some libraries keep the stacks of cartons in staff workrooms, while others keep them by a delivery dock. Decide which you prefer and include your decision in your building program.

Some libraries create separate, secure rooms for office supplies and keep careful track of who takes what. Others use an honor system.

I. File Storage

Almost all staff workspaces need filing cabinets. The main choices are between vertical and lateral cabinets, width of drawers (letter or legal, with legal a lot more useful), and number of drawers vertically (five is as high as things usually go). Quality is essential, and that means avoiding discount office supply stores. Cabinets need full suspension hardware and standard library paint colors to allow rearrangement. Ideally, you won't be able to pull out all the drawers at the same time and tip the cabinet over on top of yourself. Locks can be useful, particularly with personnel files. (Key locks are a lot better than plunger locks, since they keep people from locking themselves out accidentally. If you've ever found yourself locked out on the front stoop on Sunday morning in your bathrobe because the front door has a night latch rather than a dead bolt and you have no key in your bathrobe pocket, you'll appreciate why plunger locks on filing cabinets are a threat to civilized world order.)

J. Wall Space

Administrators need open wall space for their diplomas and certificates and (we assume in the case of your library) a wide range of awards.

> All directors have problems with where to put their framed stuff when they retire and have to clear out their offices. Fred used the basement stairs. John—lacking basement space—used a trash can, which may have been an example of rushing to judgment.

K. Open Floor Space

Many individual staff workstations need space for book trucks. You need to make clear to your designers that almost every individual workspace needs floor space for one or more book trucks, and that space for all of the trucks cannot be concentrated at one end of a workroom.

L. Printers

Every workroom needs a printer.

In group workrooms, printers are typically shared, but needs can vary. There are advantages to personal printers in group workrooms, particularly for staff members who load printers with adhesive labels, only to find someone printing a stack of letters onto the labels. Modern printers that require codes to release print orders save supervisors from hitting "print" and racing madly to next-door printers when doing evaluations.

M. Telephones

Every workroom needs at least one telephone. Even if you initially plan lots of sharing, keep your options open for the day when staff get tired of racing across large rooms to answer the only phone. Know what you'll do if the sole phone connection turns out to be in an awkward place.

When we write building programs, we specify a telephone at every workspace, but some libraries delay.

N. Paper Shredders

Library workrooms need paper shredders or easy access to nearby paper shredders. Paper shredders tend to fit neatly under tabletops, but include them in the list of workroom features in your program, and be sure you specify adequate vertical clearance under any furniture.

O. Refrigerators

Some people move dormitory-sized refrigerators into their workrooms. Often these are personal property rather than library-owned.

> The president of the Friends of the Library group in Fred's library hid book sale receipts in the freezer compartment of the little refrigerator he brought from home and tucked under the worktable in his workroom. She contended this was the origin of the expression "cold cash."

P. Bulletin Boards

Every staff workroom needs at least one bulletin board.

Many administrators like to post reminders of projects with deadlines in their personal workrooms. It's easiest to keep track if one can see the reminders when seated at the desk.

All group workrooms need bulletin boards for staff notices, for posting legally required notices, and for posting reminders of projects and due dates. Obviously, locations near entries work best.

Q. Built-In Cabinetry

When in doubt, avoid built-in cabinetry. Moving furniture in or out is a lot cheaper than changing a built-in item. As the snappy rule says, *"Never send architecture to do the work of furniture."*

R. Ventilation

Group workrooms with modular office system workstations require sufficient clearance between the tops of workstation walls and the ceiling to allow for adequate air circulation. If the clearance is too small, individual workstations may be too hot, too cold, or too stuffy. Talk with your HVAC engineers.

S. Secure Storage

Library staff workrooms have lots of materials that need secure storage. Common things are personnel records, fiscal records, and expensive or rare materials. Any plan for staff workstations needs to include information on how security will be maintained.

T. Flexibility

The best way to construct staff workrooms is to use furniture rather than built-ins. Outside of counters with running water, nothing needs to be custom-built or fastened down.

VI. SPACES WITH SHARED EQUIPMENT

Groups of adjacent workrooms can sometimes share equipment. Some libraries have set up shared areas with a counter and sink, photocopier, paper shredder, coffee pot, fax machine, paper cutter, and other equipment for group use.

A good place for shared equipment is a large area connecting a number of staff workrooms.

VII. STAFF CONFERENCE ROOMS

Many libraries have small conference rooms adjacent to administrative offices. Depending on room size and needs, they can be used for library staff meetings, library board committee meetings, meetings with vendors, interviewing job applicants, and so on.

Some public libraries have tried to use staff conference rooms for full board meetings, but it's usually a bad idea. For full board meetings, a conference room needs to be large enough to house the entire board, the library director and the library department heads, members of the press, and members of the general public. Most staff conference rooms are far too small. In addition, staff conference rooms are often tucked into groups of staff offices rather than located with the library's other public meeting rooms, and escorting large numbers of people into staff areas of the library is an awkward undertaking.

Some libraries make their staff conference rooms available for public use on evenings and weekends. This requires extremely careful planning in order to completely separate staff and public functions and be sure that the public has no access to secure areas of the library. If the conference room is buried in the middle of a group of staff offices, making it available to library users is a seriously bad idea.

Unless you are a world-famous private library, avoid the temptation to purchase pompous conference room tables and pompous conference room chairs. (Pompous tables are horribly unwieldly, and pompous chairs are no more comfortable than many ordinary chairs with low backs. Tax-supported libraries that purchase pompous tables and chairs leave themselves open to the jibes of bloggers as well.)

Some useful features for a staff conference room might include:

- Modular conference table with comfortable but reasonable chairs.
- Counter with sink and space for a coffee maker. Sinks need to be real sinks, deep enough to allow a coffee maker to be filled. So-called bar sinks don't work. The counter will need electrical outlets on at least two circuits, to allow a coffee maker and a second power-hungry device to be operated simultaneously. If the counter has cabinets or drawers, all of them should lock. Cabinets should be made of plywood, with no chipboard components. Drawers should have ball-bearing double-extension hardware and key locks.
- Telephone. If the general public will use the conference room, the phone needs to unplug. Speaker phones are useful in conference rooms, but you'll need to be sure they're compatible with your phone system.
- Projection equipment. For staff training and other purposes, you may need a digital projector and a screen. Consider a ceiling-mounted projector and a motor-operated projection screen. New equipment appears every year or so, and by the time this book actually appears there will be endless varieties of new gadgetry. You will need to have places to keep this stuff where you don't stumble over it when circumnavigating the room.
- Coat hooks. A row of hooks on a wall may be the best approach. Be sure to specify hooks made of brass or steel—never cast zinc, which has a tendency to break, leaving sharp edges.

When you are evaluating schematic designs for staff conference rooms, check clearances carefully. Lots of conference rooms are so small that it's almost impossible to squeeze past people seated at the table. Estimated space needs can prove to be inadequate if conference tables are too large.

VIII. SPECIALIZED WORKROOMS

A. Graphic Arts

The amount of space required for graphic arts depends very much on the equipment to be housed. Since it's hard to predict in advance, extra space is a good idea. Large pieces of equipment like plotters can take up a lot of floor space.

It's a good idea to assume you will eventually add extra staff. If your graphic arts space is barely large enough for one person, you are likely to regret the situation.

You may also end up with publicity staff and a graphic arts staff sharing the same workroom. You'll need space for both.

Among the things your graphic arts workroom may need are:

- Computer workstations. Graphic arts are increasingly digital, and most artists will spend most of their time at computers.
- Drafting tables. Although graphic arts work is increasingly digital, people still need to draw and to lay out artwork.
- Flat worktables for assembling projects and laying out materials.
- Printers, especially color laser printers.
- Plotters for printing on wide rolls of paper.
- Paper cutters.
- Paper folders.
- Laminators. (Some laminators are huge. Others exude unpleasant smells, emphasizing the need for good ventilation.)
- Enclosed spray booths with exhaust fans. (Keep the length of exhaust vent as short as possible, for you will need to clean it out now and then, particularly if your graphic artists use spray glue.)
- Wall-sized bulletin boards for large artwork in development, such as temporary murals for special events.
- Storage space for paper, printed posters, artwork, printer cartridges, and other materials on shelves, filing cabinets, map files, and other equipment.
- Excellent, negative ventilation. Aromas from graphic arts should be drawn into the ventilation system rather than blasted out the workroom door whenever it's open. It's not as serious a situation as restrooms, but it's still important. Even if you plan to install a spray booth, specify extra-strong exhaust fans.
- Flexible, low-glare lighting. Graphic arts workrooms need high-quality lighting similar to that under which the artwork will be viewed, especially in terms of CRI (color rendering index) and K (color temperature). In addition, artists may need a variety of light levels. For example, some artists like to work in fairly dim light when they are using computer workstations. As in other areas of libraries, highly direct lighting is almost certainly a bad idea, despite its popularity among designers. See chapter 25 on "Lighting."

It's essential to enumerate the equipment you expect to house to be sure that your graphic arts workroom will be sufficiently large. Some rooms are so small that equipment spills over into adjacent hallways or other workrooms.

Libraries may use a mixture of in-house equipment and farmed-out work for graphic arts, depending on costs and benefits. The real cost of taking artwork to be (for example) folded may be more a matter of the cost of library staff time running to and fro than of the investment in the equipment.

> Fred knows a library where the graphic arts workroom includes a ping-pong table. He has always assumed the table is used for assembling large projects or displays, but there may be a more interesting story.

B. Technical Services

The term *technical services* dates back to the days when academic libraries divided their functions administratively into "public services" and "technical services."

The most common functions performed in technical services are:

- Placing orders for new materials, including standing orders for materials shipped on a regular basis.
- Receiving new materials.
- Cataloging of new materials and (usually) entry into online catalogs.
- Processing new materials, including adding labeling, bar codes, anti-theft devices, Mylar dust jacket covers, special storage containers, and so on.
- Mending, cleaning, and repairing circulating materials.
- Maintaining shelf lists (although paper shelf lists are pretty much a thing of the past).
- Dealing with donated materials.
- Deleting weeded materials from online catalogs.
- Storing materials awaiting processing.
- Providing suitable security for rare and expensive items.
- Transporting processed materials for shelving.
- And other functions, depending on the library.

Each of these activities needs different work and storage spaces and different supplies, and programmers need to work extensively with departmental staff to determine the types of workspaces and equipment needed.

In a very small library, all technical services functions may be performed by a single staff member, but in a large library, technical services can occupy a great deal of space, either in one very large room or a number of smaller spaces.

Some common needs of technical services workrooms include:

- Running water (the only built-in furniture in the department). All sinks need to be deep, with high gooseneck faucets. Sink tops need to be large enough for equipment that needs access to water.
- Flat work surfaces.
- Computer workstations.
- Wall shelving for arriving books, departing books, gift books, supplies, and all manner of other things. In some libraries, every tech services workstation needs a surprising amount of individually assigned shelving in addition to general departmental shelving. When planning technical services, enumerate all of the types of materials that need to be stored, including what kind of space they require.
- Filing cabinets for financial records, order records, and correspondence with vendors.
- Secure storage. This may include locking cabinets, locking filing cabinets, locking closets, or even separate rooms for specialized items. (Rare book rooms and archives may need separate technical services work areas.)
- Worktables for opening shipments and similar jobs.
- Floor space for more book trucks than your designers expect. Be sure your designers provide book truck space at individual workstations, as well as storage areas for groups of book trucks. Some staff members in tech services have desks surrounded by book trucks.
- Bright, low-glare, all-purpose lighting. Architecturally mounted task lighting is unsuitable because it makes it difficult to relocate furniture.
- Vast numbers of electrical outlets, including floor outlets where there's any wild chance you might actually need them.
- A minimum of obstructions, to allow easy rearrangement of furnishings as needs change.
- Depending on staff needs, either wide-open spaces or cubes.
- Separate workrooms for department heads and possibly other staff who deal with private information, such as staff evaluations, negotiations with vendors, and so on. Because of HVAC requirements, separate workrooms are expensive, and libraries need to evaluate the competing needs for privacy and for lower-cost construction and maintenance.
- Floor space for deliveries.
- Heated or chilled containers for shipments from parts of the world that tend to have bugs.

Locations for technical services departments:

- Convenient to delivery doors.
- Not hogging prime space. With a convenient freight elevator, a tech services department on an upper floor can still be essentially right next to a delivery door.
- Convenient to storage facilities, such as storerooms for unprocessed books. (Research libraries are notorious for treasured troves of unprocessed materials, but some small libraries can seriously hold their own.)

C. Children's Departments

Children's departments tend to have amazing quantities of stuff, and their workrooms reflect this. Some things to consider including are:

- Sinks for washing hands (after dealing with oozy children), washing gooey material off books, and so on. Sinks need to be deep and have high, gooseneck faucets to allow containers to be filled. (We have no idea what kind of containers, but we know children's librarians, and the containers will come along.)
    - Remember that retrofitting a sink to a workroom is a very expensive undertaking, so include it in your written building program and make sure it doesn't quietly vanish.
- Washers and dryers for puppets, dress-up clothes, and similar shared materials. If space is an issue, consider stacked washers and dryers designed for apartment use. The main thing is to get the water supply, drain, power supply (often 220 volts, something you otherwise wouldn't have in a workroom), and dryer vent installed when construction is taking place, because you will probably not be able to do so later.
    - In the age of bedbugs, washing puppets and plush toys on a regular basis is a particularly worthwhile undertaking.
- Storage for posters and similar large, flat objects. Some libraries use map cases, while others have vertical slots beneath standing-height work surfaces.
- Space for die-cutting machines and racks for storing dies.
- Space for kits in all sorts of plastic tubs, usually on steel library shelving.
- Extra space for storing things that non-children's librarians might not anticipate.

> Fred's children's department had a plastic wading pool and a hula hoop used for making giant soap bubbles. You can't tuck either one into an everyday storage cabinet.

- Windows with Venetian blinds facing the public areas of the department, to allow staff members to keep an eye on things while they are working. (Our experience is that children's staff are not always thrilled with this idea, but it works well.)
- Space for an accumulation of summer reading club prizes, no two of which were intended to be stored on the same kind of shelf.
- Extra work surfaces. Children's staff members are always making things, and forcing them to do so on public reading tables is not a good thing. (If you work around children with scissors, sooner or later someone will run with them.)
- Storage for seasonal books, such as Christmas books, that may be brought out only at certain times of year.
- Storage for storytelling collections, materials that need to be handy but are not intended to be lent on a regular basis.

> In Fred's home town, the public library was governed by a committee of the school board. Each fall, each grade school teacher was consequently allowed to take one chest of books from the public library for nine months' classroom use. To prevent every children's book purchased in the previous twenty-five years from vanishing, starting in July the children's department staff stored all the books purchased in the last twenty-five years in a back corner of the furnace room, bringing the books back out only after chest-filling time was over. Even if the department had had a good storeroom, the furnace room may have been better, since—like the arrival of the Spanish Inquisition—no one expects all the new children's books to be lurking behind the furnace.

- Craft supplies. It's amazing how much expensive space boxes of toilet paper tubes can occupy.
- Unusual equipment. Filmstrip projectors are probably all gone now, but we can confidently expect other things to turn up.
- Children's departments with more than a couple of staff members need a private workroom for the department head, who will need to evaluate staff and meet with concerned parents. (Never just hand people reconsideration forms, but first take time for polite and sympathetic listening. In 99 percent of the cases, that takes care of things. But you can't do it in the middle of a crowded staff workroom.)

One of the greatest sources of tension between children's librarians and library administrators is storage. Some administrators feel that if children's department storage were not limited, nothing would ever leave the department from generation to generation. Children's librarians in turn hate throwing out useful programming materials. Finding the proper balance can verge on Solomonic.

IX. WORKSPACES IN OTHERWISE PUBLIC AREAS

Many library staff members work at public service desks when they are between requests for help from library users.

If it's a matter of selecting books, this is usually compatible with working at a service desk, but other tasks (such as processing books) may take too much space or involve too much mess.

A standard approach in small libraries is to create a work counter behind the service desk, a place where staff members can work out of the way of library users but simultaneously keep an eye on the library and leave their work when users approach the desk.

To work effectively, work counters need to be arranged so that staff members seated or standing there are facing the public areas of the library rather than having their backs turned to the service desks and to the users approaching the desks. With work counters facing library users, library staff members can work on off-desk tasks while simultaneously keeping an eye on the rest of the library and watching for users needing help. With this kind of arrangement, there needs to be two places for library staff to sit or stand—one behind the main service counter and the second behind the work counter. Both spaces need space for staff chairs, book carts, and so on.

Our experience has been that counters of this type never occur to most architects, who almost always draw work counters facing the wall, so that staff have their backs turned to users and to the spaces they need to supervise. Make clear in your building program how you want things arranged, and even then expect to make your architects redraw things.

Work counters need low front barricades to hide the mess. About eight inches or so is fine.

A work counter of this type needs enough length for open counter space, a computer, printer, and phone.

X. REQUIRED WORKROOM SIZES

Of the making of workrooms there is no end, and the staff who will be working there are your best guide to needs.

As usual, space estimating is great, but the final proof is the architect's schematic drawing. The ability of a workroom to hold the necessary furniture can depend greatly on the general proportions of the room, and a drawing is a great way to test things out. (As we've said endlessly in this book, a schematic design that does not indicate furniture placement is worthless.)

Remember that sketches can also mislead. In Fred's library, an alcove intended for a filing cabinet failed because it turned out to be about half an inch too narrow.

Furniture types can make a big difference in the layout of workroom furniture. For example, vertical filing cabinets and lateral filing cabinets need very different spaces.

Workrooms that are not strictly rectangular will make less efficient use of space. A workroom estimated to need 150 square feet may need 175 or more if the room is L-shaped. And substantially more if the room has the severe misfortune to be triangular or curved.

The absolute minimum size for an individual workroom is 125 to 150 square feet. In our opinion, anything less than 150 square feet is a seriously bad idea.

XI. SNAPPY RULES ON STAFF WORKROOMS

1. Always say *workrooms* or *workspaces* rather than *offices*. The word *office* antagonizes antitax crazies and tight-fisted administrations, and the number of librarians with the sort of luxury corner offices envisioned by their critics can be counted on the fingers of one foot.
2. Beware of universities that have standard workroom sizes based on academic rank. No busy cataloger or graphic artist can work in an "instructor"-level space without overflowing into adjacent areas.
3. Workrooms need windows with Venetian blinds to adjoining workrooms or public spaces. It's a lot easier to close a Venetian blind when you want serious privacy than to install a new window when you seriously need to see out or be seen.

4. Lots of administrators are happiest with separate stacks of loose papers for each project. Our job is to figure out ways to make this possible, not to suggest behavior modification. One approach is to hide the stacks in cabinets with shelves and with doors that close.
5. The great thing about meeting with salespeople in a conference room rather than your workroom is that when the time comes you can just say "Thank you" and get up and leave.
6. We don't have any statistically reliable research data, but our impression is that the great majority of library staff workrooms are far too small, and that a lot are like the steamship stateroom scene in the Marx Brothers' *A Night at the Opera*. ("Is it my imagination, or is it getting crowded in here?")
7. If you plan your new building for thirty years of collection growth but no staff growth, the fact that workers eventually end up sitting on each others' laps shouldn't come as much of a surprise.
8. Library workrooms need more electrical outlets than lots of planners expect, and they need them in places that are easy to reach. Except for dressy workrooms (the kind occupied by administrators, who are expected to look nice for visitors), outlets above countertop height are a friendly gesture to library staff.
9. Every group workroom needs a sink. Not a toy sink like a bar sink, but a seriously sized sink with a high gooseneck faucet.
10. When people are waiting to see the director, where will they sit?
11. Good places for departmental storerooms are spaces right next door to the relevant staff workrooms. A number of public libraries have children's storerooms located between the children's staff workroom and the craft and story room, with convenient access from both directions.
12. If the library director has to pile working papers on chairs originally intended for visitors, that's one warning sign of an undersized workroom.
13. If you want a small conference table in your director's workroom, provide enough space. Too many conference tables in small workrooms require users to crawl over each other to reach the chairs.
14. Outside of counters with sinks, none of the furniture in workrooms needs to be built in. And it shouldn't be. Never send architecture to solve furniture problems.
15. Every workroom needs at least one telephone (or whatever communication device is in use at that time). After that it's a question of how much you expect people to jump up and dash across the room to answer the phone. Put in phone connections in advance for every workstation, just in case the staff grow seriously tired of jumping and dashing.
16. Catalogers faced with built-in work counters have ended up balancing books on their laps when they cataloged them. Beware of cute but tiny built-in workspaces.

17. Every workroom needs a thermostat and individual temperature control. If two separate workrooms share a thermostat, the staff members in the room without the thermostat are likely to be very unhappy for very good reasons.
18. Good shapes for staff workrooms are simple rectangles. Curved walls and diagonal walls cause serious problems, as do L-shaped spaces. All funny-shaped spaces do a bad job of housing furniture. Functional trumps cute.
19. Most workrooms are short of storage space. When in doubt, provide extra floor space for shelving and filing cabinets and for cabinets with doors that close.
20. Departmental staff workrooms need to be immediately adjacent to their departments. (This sounds like an unnecessary remark, but unfortunately it's not.)
21. Be careful when making workrooms passageways to other workrooms, and never make them passageways to public areas.
22. Multi-person workrooms are a lot cheaper per person and a lot more flexible than single-person workrooms. If a staff member does not require privacy or does not deal with materials requiring security, a single-person workroom may be a major waste of money.

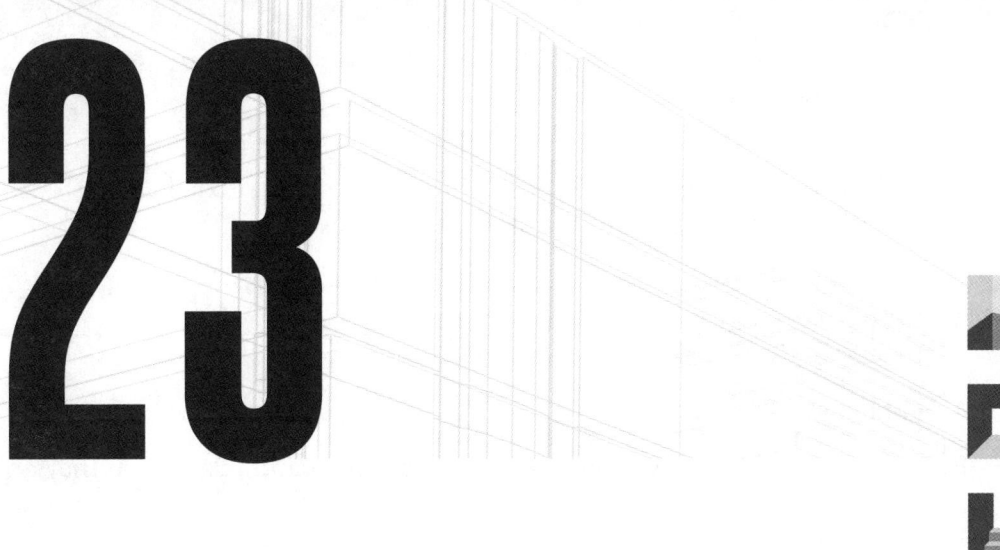

23

Staff Facilities

I. INTRODUCTION

In addition to staff workspaces, all libraries need support spaces for their staff members, including lunchrooms, restrooms, mailboxes, and places to store personal belongings.

Often these spaces are a last thought, and sometimes they are nearly forgotten. Frequently they are small, and sometimes they have major design flaws.

The most common serious mistake is having staff restrooms accessed directly from staff lunchrooms. Clearly, we do not learn from other people's (seriously gross) errors.

> Teachers tell us that they have the same problem with staff restrooms in close proximity to faculty lounges in schools. Which makes us wonder about what (or even if) professional designers are thinking.

There are a few other frequent omissions in staff support spaces:

- Failure to provide enough electrical circuits in staff kitchenettes
- Failure to provide exhaust fans in staff lunchrooms

- Failure to provide garbage disposals in the sinks in staff kitchenettes
- Installation of tiny bar sinks in staff kitchenettes

II. STAFF LUNCHROOMS

A. Functions

Every library needs a place where staff can eat lunch and relax when they are off duty.

At some very small libraries, staff end up eating their lunches at a service desk or a reading table. This can work, but it may be socially awkward if the library does not allow its users to eat in the reading rooms.

Most staff lunchrooms provide a variety of functions. We call them "lunchrooms," but they are places for coffee breaks, places for shared food, places to lie down briefly when feeling bad, places for socializing, and places for retirement parties.

By definition, staff lunchrooms are spaces for staff, not for library users, and library staff members can be extremely protective of their spaces. One serious mistake that library administrators can make is letting people who are not library staff make use of staff lunchrooms.

One of the reasons why staff lunchrooms are important is that libraries tend to have some low-paid staff members—such as book-shelving staff—who cannot afford to eat out, in addition to many staff who prefer to spend their money in other ways. Occasionally there are members of governing bodies who don't understand this and tend to argue, "I go out for lunch every day. Why do we have to provide an expensive lunchroom for the library staff?" Someone needs to take such people gently aside and explain how the other 80 percent lives.

B. Location

In many ways, staff facilities can be put wherever they'll fit, usually somewhere off the beaten path.

Lunchrooms are more pleasant for the staff if they are accessed through staff hallways, where library users can't peer interestedly into staff spaces every time the door opens. The same kind of privacy can be provided with a jog in the entryway, so that when the door opens, staff can't be seen eating their lunches.

Lunchrooms are a lot better off with windows.

Staff restrooms also work well when they are accessible from staff areas of the library, so users don't end up saying, "I don't see why *everyone* can't use that restroom."

The single most important point about staff restrooms is that *STAFF RESTROOMS SHOULD NEVER OPEN DIRECTLY INTO STAFF LUNCHROOMS*. Although this prohibition seems obvious, the country is awash with library staff lunchrooms where people eat their lunch directly next to sanitary fixtures. Since this loony design pattern is well established—or is the result of endless independent invention—librarians working on building plans need to include vigorous prohibitions in building programs and follow up with eagle-eyed oversight as floor plans emerge. Remind your designers that librarians are not unusually subject to gastrocolic reflexes and that close juxtaposition of lunch tables and toilets is not essential.

Many smaller libraries have places in the corners of large workrooms where staff eat lunch. This has some practical advantages, particularly with shared water supplies. The main trick in providing this kind of space for staff lunches is to put the lunch table(s) where library users can't see them. Some libraries have alcoves or doglegs at the back of workrooms to provide a place for staff lunches. Others have used shelving units to block the view.

Staff coat and purse storage can be in a single place in small libraries but is probably best decentralized in larger buildings.

C. Food Preparation and Serving

1. Microwaves, Stoves, and Coffee Makers

Most staff rooms provide microwave ovens. For many libraries, a single microwave is not enough, especially when a number of people are trying to prepare lunch at the same time. Microwaves are cheap; the main planning issue is sufficient counter space and enough electrical circuits.

Some library staff rooms have kitchen stoves, especially if there is a tradition of group eating. Stoves can be great, but there are some major implications:

- The chance of fire is greatly enhanced with stovetop cooking. Open flames are a lot more trouble-prone than microwave ovens.

- While microwaves can be messy, stoves can be Seriously Messy, especially when large numbers of people share them. Someone who is both patient and particular will need to keep the stove clean.
- You may want a range hood with an exhaust fan. These are standard items, but they require exhaust vents.
- Depending on your local building codes, you may need to install a commercial range hood over your stove. Commercial range hoods have fire suppression equipment and are extremely expensive.

Some libraries also have toaster ovens, coffee makers, and other countertop cooking equipment in their staff lunchrooms. Like all other equipment, the main thing these require is counter space, extra electrical circuits, and exhaust fans.

2. Refrigerators

Staff lunchrooms require refrigerators for the storage of lunches. Since food associated with children's programs or with staff social events may also need to be refrigerated, most libraries need at least one full-sized refrigerator in addition to the refrigerators in meeting room kitchenettes.

Ice dispensers set into refrigerator doors may seem like a frippery, but they get around the problem of staff unloading ice cube trays with their bare hands. Microbes on ice cubes will probably not be killed by freezing. Keeping your staff healthy is a nice gesture. For those not motivated by nice, if an ice dispenser in a library with staff health coverage prevents even a week of staff paid sick leave due to illness, it may pay for itself.

Before you decide to provide a stove in a staff room or meeting room kitchenette, check with local building codes. A legally-required range hood can cost 20 times as much as the stove it accompanies. (Parenthetically, ask yourself why you want people messing about with stoves in your library in the first place.)

3. Dishwashers

Dishwashers may sound like silly luxuries, but they have the advantage of being capable of disinfecting dishes.

In many libraries, staff share dishes and tableware, washing everything with bare hands in tepid water. As in the case of handling ice with bare hands, this is a great way to share microbes.

If scalding shared dishes prevents disease transmission, it's both a humane thing to do and (for those of more purely mercenary motives) a way of saving money on paid sick leave costs.

Dishwashers require electric power, water, and drains, and they don't lend themselves to easy retrofitting. Even if you think you don't want one, you may be ahead by roughing in the space where a dishwasher can go if you change your mind.

4. Counters and Sinks

All staff lunchrooms need sinks. Deep sinks with high gooseneck faucets allow staff to fill large containers like coffee urns without having to bail water with a saucepan or go hunting for a mop sink. Single-drainer sinks are probably sufficient for libraries that do not do home-style dishwashing, but review your needs with your staff. (We think home-style dishwashing is a seriously bad idea, as noted above under "Dishwashers," but to each his own.)

Provide garbage disposal units in your staff room sinks. Some staff members are meticulous about putting all food scraps in the garbage, but others just dump foodstuffs in the sink and eventually clog the drain. (The "Staff Room Cloggers" sounds like a folk dance group, but it may not be one.)

> This is not trivial. Library staff rooms abound in signs warning staff that there are no garbage disposal units and asking staff not to put garbage in the sinks. As far as we can tell, these signs are the result of bad experiences.

5. Cabinets and Drawers

All lunchrooms need storage for both permanent and throwaway cooking and eating equipment. Standard kitchen cabinets and drawers work well. A counter long enough to hold a variety of microwaves and other appliances will have plenty of space for under-counter drawers and cabinets.

Be sure that all drawers in base cabinets have ball-bearing double-extension hardware, or you will have staff struggling to drag them open and shove them shut, and either losing objects in the back or dumping the contents of drawers on the floor when they pull the drawers out too far.

You may also want cabinets above countertops, but be careful about clearances. Cabinets that come too close to microwaves and other countertop appliances are a pain.

6. Buffet Shelves

Library staffs frequently bring a wide variety of snacks, especially for staff social events. Putting them on lunch tables leaves no place to eat.

One response to this problem is to install a buffet shelf at a comfortable height for self-service—probably about forty inches above the floor.

As with service counters, buffet shelves need multiple circuits for electrically heated serving equipment.

7. Plumbing Connections and Electrical Circuits

Like kitchens, staff lunchrooms need a lot of plumbing and power.

Sinks, dishwashers, and refrigerators with automatic ice makers need water supplies and drains, limiting your ability to move them around or to add them later.

Some electrical equipment may require 220-volt power supplies, particularly stoves.

A lot of the 110-volt items used in library lunchrooms are power hogs because they use electricity to generate heat. Many of these gadgets may need separate circuits. Imagine a staff holiday dinner with two microwave ovens, a Dutch oven, a toaster, a toaster oven, and a coffee maker in simultaneous use and the resulting need for six separate 20-amp circuits, excluding those for the regular appliances.

As with meeting room kitchenettes, many library staff rooms have far too few separate circuits. Nothing is more fun than blowing circuit breakers and having to figure out which appliances you won't use. Trying to hook up appliances by running extension cords from other rooms in the library is awkward, and if your fire marshal sees you doing it he will be strongly tempted to hyperventilate.

8. Exhaust Fans

It shouldn't be necessary to mention this, but architects have created staff lunchrooms without exhaust fans. Sooner or later, everyone regrets this omission. Mostly sooner.

Some aromas can fill a library quickly. One main culprit is microwave popcorn abandoned to cook while its owners leave the room for just a quick moment and fail to return in time. Another is TV dinners featuring fish.

D. Seating

While round tables are generally anathema in reading areas in libraries, they seem to do well in staff lunchrooms. In part, this is due to the fact that round tables are for conversation and rectangular tables are for work.

Some staff groups play cards on their lunch hours. Folding card tables and chairs take up a modest amount of space and are easy to set up and put away.

All staff lunchrooms need armchairs, places where staff can relax. Some amazingly tacky old armchairs are remarkably popular in staff rooms.

And staff lunchrooms need sofas. Many people use their breaks for catnaps, and the absence of sofas makes this difficult. Just as we try to discourage sofas where our users can sprawl on them, we want to take good care of our sprawling staff.

Estimating quantities of furnishings is tricky. Many library staff stay in the building all day long. This is balanced by staggered lunch hours, where half the staff are on desk service while the other half are at lunch. Some staff members like sitting four to a table, while others are stressed out and want to sit alone. Some staff groups coordinate their lunch hours so they can play games. Libraries will vary, but it seems reasonable that the staff lunchroom should be able to seat a quarter to a third of the staff. However, your experience with your library is a far better guide.

E. Vending Machines

Some library staff lunchrooms provide snack closets on the honor system. This works particularly well when outsiders cannot sneak into the staff room.

Other lunchrooms have vending machines, usually serviced by an outside vendor.

If you are part of a larger organization, your vending machines may come from vendors who have negotiated with the parent institution. Some campuses, for example, have "pouring rights" agreements with soda firms. (Our snide belief is that pouring rights agreements lead to higher prices at the pump, rather than more attractive prices, but we could be wrong.)

Be sure to allocate space for vending machines. Some are monsters.

Remember electrical supplies for vending machinery.

Many vending machines have pictorial plastic fronts with brilliant illumination, apparently intended to make machines visible for miles through night and fog. All of these machines have fluorescent tubes behind their plastic fronts, and you can simply remove the tubes, making visiting your staff lunchroom a far more gracious and welcoming experience.

F. Computer Workstations

Some staff lunchrooms provide one or two computer workstations for use by staff members who have no office computers and want to check their e-mail on breaks.

Workstations of this type take little space. If you allocate thirty square feet per workstation, you should be in good shape.

G. Staff Picture Boards

Many libraries try to provide photos of staff members. Often these are posted on bulletin boards in patterns representing organizational structure.

Keeping picture boards up to date is a lot harder than installing them. It takes a dedicated graphic artist and constant pestering of unphotographed library staff.

H. Bulletin Boards

Many staff rooms provide bulletin boards for photographs of staff members and for notices of staff events.

State laws can also require that a variety of legal notices be posted for staff. Bulletin boards in staff room areas are a good place. Check to see how much space you'll need to meet legal requirements.

I. Secluded Spaces

Many staff rooms provide separate spaces for staff who are feeling ill and wish to lie down. Often these are no more complicated than a separate room with a recliner and a Venetian blind on the window. A couch takes very little more space.

Libraries that want to provide lactation rooms seem to find that the separate spaces can serve this purpose as well.

J. Decor

Staff lunchrooms need to be light, cheerful, welcoming, and comfortable.

Unfortunately, this is not always the case. In 1974, for example, Fred inherited a staff room with one bright orange wall and three battleship gray walls. When the staff immediately painted the gray walls white, the architects were dismayed. The orange wall lasted a few years and then magically turned white as well. (We cannot say too often that no agreement with architects should give them any rights whatsoever regarding the building once construction is completed.)

K. Entertainment

Some staff lunchrooms have television sets. Others have magazine racks or stacks of review copies of forthcoming books.

In large part, this can just happen, but if you want a TV set mounted on a bracket extending from the wall, you may need to plan ahead.

L. Estimating Staff Lunchroom Space Needs

Most staff lunchrooms are small and often pretty makeshift. There's a lot to be said for taking good care of the staff, and that takes planning ahead and reasonable space allocation.

Here are some quick estimates for required space. Remember, however, that a good schematic design (always with a furniture layout) is the real test.

- Counters. Allow space for staff to stand at the counters and for other staff to walk behind them. The total space should be about 7 to 8 times the length of the counter. A 15-foot counter may require 100 to 120 square feet.
- Buffet shelf. About 7 times the length of the shelf. An 8-foot shelf may require 56 square feet.

- Refrigerators and dishwashers. Check the floor space occupied by the machine, then add space for access and for walking around the machine. Many machines also have door swing requirements.
- Tables. For rectangular tables, about 25 square feet per person. For round tables, about 20 square feet in a pinch. But many tables are crammed more closely together.
- Armchairs. About 40 square feet each.
- Sofas. A minimum of about 75 square feet each.
- Bulletin boards and staff photo boards. Bulletin boards don't use any space, but there needs to be space for people to stand while looking at them.
- Staff mailboxes. About 4½ feet per running foot of mailboxes.

As usual, add everything up and then provide some extra "circulation space" to keep people from having to constantly say "excuse me" as they weave their way between furnishings. If your staff room is a simple rectangle, a good place to start is an extra 10 percent.

As with public areas, staff lunchrooms need to be accessible to users with disabilities, which limits crowding furniture together.

III. STAFF RESTROOMS

In all but the very tiniest libraries, staff members should not be expected to share toilets with library users. If library users leave the public toilets in grotty shape, a staff member who is scheduled to be in the library for the next seven hours can't just decide to go home and use the facilities there. (If you are a non-librarian, you are not entitled to argue against staff toilets, although you can always ask librarians how they feel about the issue.)

If your library is a small one and has accessible toilets, you may want to provide only a small restroom for your staff, but it's a lot more considerate not to force a handicapped staff member to use the public toilet that all the other staff get to avoid.

Chapter 21 on "Restrooms" covers many of the basics of good library design. Among the things you will want are:

- Compliance with accessibility codes.
- Wall-mounted flush-valve toilets. (Some designers will suggest that staff restrooms can get along with floor-mounted flush-tank toilets, but they're wrong.)

> For example, one of Fred's head custodians said he spent far more time repairing the staff room flush-tank toilets than the public flush-valve toilets, despite far heavier use of the public toilets and presumably far greater abuse.

- Electric eye-operated washbasin faucets. (Imagine how filthy a washbasin faucet handle can be. Even when it's just librarians using the washbasin. If you can't have an electric eye, get bat-handled faucets that can be operated with a wrist.)
- Ceramic tile floors with dark grout.
- Provision for safe disposal of potential sources of blood-borne pathogens, such as sanitary napkins.
- Provision for the safe disposal of used hypodermic syringes, typically a Sharps container mounted on the wall.
- Dual coat hooks (not made of cast zinc) on the doors.
- Sensor-operated lights that do not force people to grope their way into dark restrooms in order to turn on the lights.
- Effective exhaust fans.

There are also features suitable for staff restrooms that are unsuited for public restrooms:

- Medicine cabinets. (For liability reasons, libraries NEVER medicate their users. Not even with aspirin.)
- Single-user restrooms. (We shouldn't have to worry about staff members indulging in typical restroom vandalism, because we are all out of eighth grade before we can be legally employed.)
- Paper towel dispensers. Everyone hates air dryers. You may need to use them in public restrooms because of problems with paper towel mess, but we hope that won't be a problem in your staff restroom.
- Library supplies, such as extra toilet paper and paper towels, conveniently accessible.

If staff restrooms are single-user restrooms, you may find that unisex restrooms provide for much more efficient use, with staff members simply taking any restroom not in use. Depending on applicable plumbing codes, however, unisex restrooms may not count if you are struggling to meet codes for minimum numbers of toilets or lavatories in your building. Check with your architects. (If it's a code issue requiring a minimum number of toilets for each gender, you can always label single-user staff restrooms M and F and then just ignore the signs once the building has received its occupancy permit.)

As mentioned several times elsewhere in this book, staff restrooms should be accessed from staff corridors and never directly from staff lunchrooms.

IV. STAFF COAT AND PURSE STORAGE

Coat and purse storage is not much of a problem for that rarefied group of staff who are assigned private workrooms with personal keys, but for everyone else it's an issue.

A. Coat Storage

Many private staff workrooms are equipped with coat hooks on the back of the doors, with hooks mounted on wooden supports on the walls, with short coat rods projecting from the walls (with coat hangers), or even with coat closets. (The list attempts to reflect increasing costs, but we may be wrong.)

Shared workspaces can have either individually assigned coat storage or shared storage. With shared storage, the idea is that the entire staff are almost never present at the same time, and the number of coat-storage sites can therefore be smaller than the number of staff members.

In a very small library, all staff coats may be stored in a single place, but libraries with offices and departments may want decentralized storage.

Some coat storage options for shared workspaces include:

- Hooks on wooden beams mounted on walls.
- Coat rods projecting from the walls, with coat hangers.
- Coat trees.
- Hallway lockers of the kind found in school buildings.
- Various combined coat-and-purse storage units, with stacks of purse lockers supporting a coat bar between the stacks (and often a row of purse lockers above the stacks of lockers and connecting the stacks).
- Coat closets. With more than a small staff sharing a closet, you may find that the closet may have to be double-width with double doors. (Remember what a tangle the front hall coat closets are in many homes.)

Along with coat storage goes storage of boots and galoshes dripping with salt-laden slush. You can purchase plastic floor trays. You can make the floor beneath coat-storage areas ceramic tile rather than carpet. And there are probably many other ways.

Most of the methods listed above do not provide protection from theft. If you are concerned about theft, you may have to rely on lockers with padlocks.

You are likely to encounter a couple of common problems with coat storage:

- Accessible-height coat hooks and rods are too low for most coats. You'll probably need both heights. Review this with your architects.
- Cheap coat hooks made of cast zinc tend to break. Steel and brass do not.
- Many coat bars do not extend far enough from the wall, making it particularly hard to store coats on hangers. This can be a problem storing indoor garments, so imagine trying to hang up a jumbo parka. (Standard metal supports for coat rods in home closets have this problem and need to be shimmed out from the back walls of closets.)

B. Purse Storage

Many libraries need to pay special attention to problems with theft from purses. Library users (no doubt feeling the sense of security that accompanies libraries) leave their purses on reading tables while they wander off into the stacks, returning only to find that wallets are surprisingly missing.

While staff areas are usually far more secure than reading tables, thefts nonetheless occur.

One common solution is the provision of purse lockers, small lockers about a foot or fourteen inches square provided in stacks four or five lockers high. Each locker has a hasp for a padlock. Because of the padlocks, you will need a separate locker for every employee. (Actually getting employees to lock up their purses is far harder than purchasing the lockers, so things still vanish now and then.)

A major security problem results from the popularity of backpacks. Many employees will keep wallets in backpacks that are too large to fit into purse lockers. Although they sometimes remove the wallets and lock them up, at other times they just toss the backpacks into a convenient corner.

One solution is to purchase larger lockers. School hallway lockers, for example, are available in half-height versions, with lockers stacked two high.

The library will need to decide whether it wants to provide padlocks or ask employees to bring their own. Providing library padlocks has a couple of advantages. First, all the lockers will actually have padlocks. And second, when staff resign their library positions and leave town, you won't have to use a bolt cutter to remove their padlocks from their lockers.

V. STAFF MAILBOXES

All libraries with more than a couple of employees need a bank of staff mailboxes.

It may be tempting to assume that mailboxes will be replaced by electronic communication, but there's always something that's easier to distribute in hard copy.

A few points are important:

- With the exception of very large buildings, it's easiest to put all the staff mailboxes in one location. Often this turns out to be in or near the staff lunchroom, since this is likely to be the most convenient location for staff members. As with shared lunchrooms, mailboxes in a single location help staff get to know people from other departments of the library.
- Mailboxes need name label holders so that assignments can be altered as staff members come and go. It's probably annoying for staff to find their mailboxes moving mysteriously around in the night, but if the mailboxes get seriously out of alphabetical order, things soon become seriously muddled. Some libraries group mailboxes by department or rank to avoid having to move all the name labels whenever a new person arrives.

The designers for this library provided pigeon holes rather than 10-inch-wide flat openings for staff mail. As a result, everything distributed to staff had to be rolled up first, and large items couldn't be distributed at all. The people who had to use the pigeon holes were not happy.

- Mailboxes need to be large enough to allow the distribution of memos and other materials without having to fold them or roll them up. This means boxes about 10 inches wide and perhaps 14 inches deep. (Some libraries have been equipped with banks of pigeonholes, making distribution of anything larger than flashlight batteries a real pain.)
- Some staff members will use their mailboxes for the storage of personal objects, and libraries need some policies for dealing with this. Sometimes mailboxes get so crowded there's no room left for mail. Sometimes staff store food in their mailboxes, presenting problems similar to old lunches lurking in the backs of staff refrigerators, but offering opportunities for even more rapid deterioration.
- You may need extra mailboxes in addition to those for staff members. For example, public libraries may want mailboxes for board members and for key volunteers, such as Friends of the Library.
- Plan ahead. Having a few mailboxes too many is a lot less annoying than having a few too few.

VI. STAFF BIKE STORAGE AND SHOWERS

In some libraries, everyone bikes to work. In other libraries, the thought that people might bike to work is regarded as reasonably bizarre.

If staff members bike to work, they need a place to stash their bikes. It's better to prepare for this in advance than to be surprised later when everyone is stumbling over staff bikes in an entryway or in the staff lunchroom.

A few libraries provide showers, so that the sweaty staff who bike to work can make themselves sweet before greeting library users.

If this possibility seems to fit your library, LEED points are awarded for staff showers because they encourage biking. (On the other hand, some libraries add showers only because they need LEED points.)

> We don't think many library directors are given to ordering staff members to the showers, but it creates an entertaining image.

VII. SNAPPY RULES ON STAFF FACILITIES

1. A staff lunchroom without a powerful exhaust fan is not as gross as a staff restroom without an exhaust fan, but the general principle is the same. Trust your architects, but always ask to be shown where all the fans are on the plans. (Think fish TV dinners and burnt microwave popcorn.)
2. Staff toilets located directly next to staff lunch areas are depressingly prevalent and are one of the most easily avoided library design idiocies. Toilets next to eating areas are extraordinarily gross for all parties involved, both the lunch eaters and the toilet users. Watch for them carefully on your floor plans, for they spring up like unwanted fungi, just when you thought you had disinfected everything.
3. Sooner or later, staff members will feel ill and want to lie down. They deserve something friendlier than the floor.
4. Check your local building codes before you plan to have a stove in your staff room kitchen. A commercial range hood can cost as much as a modest automobile.
5. Staff lunchrooms are havens for employees stressed out by exuberant participants in story times and library computer labs. No matter how welcoming and warm these staff people may be, they do not want to be on public display while eating lunch.
6. There is no such thing as too many 20-amp circuits in a staff lunchroom. (In both staff lunchrooms and meeting room kitchenettes, designers usually provide far too few separate circuits. No one is sure why, but there it is. Even if your designers are really great folks, they still may not have provided enough circuits.)
7. You do not want any public functions intruding into your staff lunchroom, including receiving bins for book returns.
8. Staff members feel strongly about having staff toilets. If you have never worked in a library, you have no right to suggest that staff use the public toilets instead of having their own facilities.
9. Know what you will do if a staff member needs to use a breast pump. Sending her down to the loading dock is not acceptable.
10. When your staff bike to work, where will they put their bikes? (LEED welcomes bicycles.)
11. One staff member whose hobby is making desserts can turn a library staff room from a Barren Wasteland into a Promised Land.
12. Staff mailboxes need to be large enough for 8½ × 14-inch handouts. Pigeonholes are not acceptable.

13. A staff room sink without a garbage disposal is not a seriously lovely object.
14. Be careful about trying to cram too much furniture into a small staff room. Staff members in wheelchairs deserve to use the room.
15. In case repetition helps, NEVER have a staff toilet directly accessible from a staff lunchroom. It seems to happen in libraries everywhere, and it's an amazingly avoidable screwup.

24

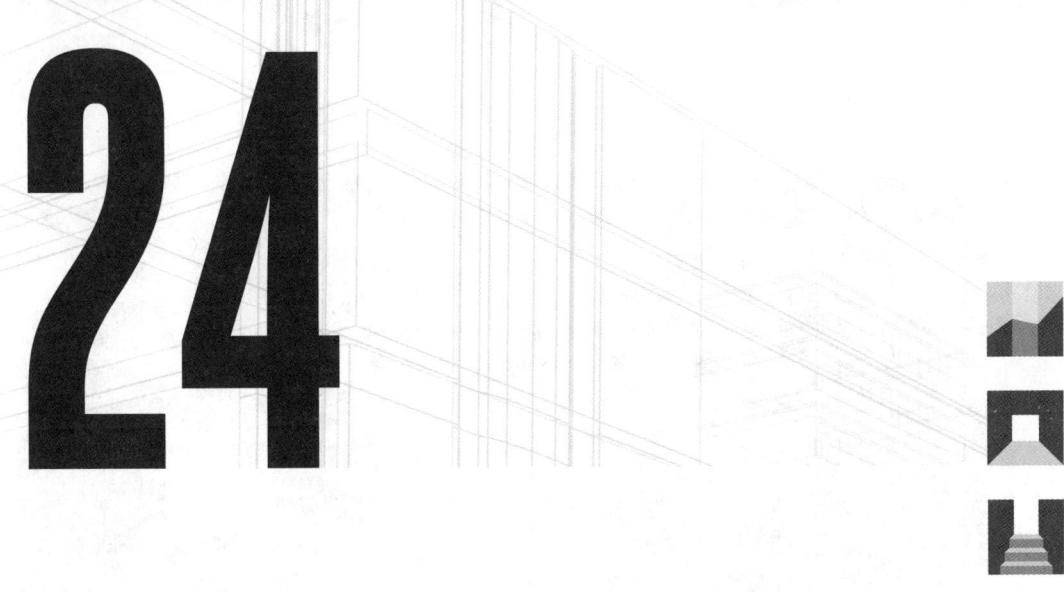

Storerooms

I. INTRODUCTION

Storage sounds like a boring and unexciting topic to those whose jobs don't depend on finding places to put things. For the rest of us, storage is an endlessly compelling topic.

The story of this chapter is a simple one.

- Most libraries have far too little storage space.
- Because of this, library staff members can waste a lot of expensive time hunting for places to put things and hunting for things that have been put somewhere or other.
- In many libraries, storage space is in awkward or inconvenient locations. The same staff members who waste expensive time hunting for places to put things also waste expensive time toting things from where they are stored to where they are used.
- Some storage spaces are badly designed architecturally, making them unnecessarily hard to use.
- Good storage space is always at risk. Library departments steal each other's storage space. Architects cannibalize storage space during the design process. Non-library agencies try to take over storage space.
- Overcrowded storage is sometimes the result of bad housekeeping or pathological hoarding, but it's far more often the result of Not Enough Space.

John once ran a library that converted a former department store to a library. Because the building was larger than the library needed, the library ended up with a 35,000-square-foot storeroom. The great majority of libraries are designed with seriously inadequate storage space, and John was the envy of his fellow directors.

This small room was intended to serve as a workroom for all staff of a public library (including the library director and technical services). It was also intended to serve as a staff lunch room and a storeroom. It failed amazingly, and the library had to wall off one entire end of the building to provide workable space.

- We suspect that most libraries have inadequate storage space because parent organizations don't want to spend the money, and because building designers don't find storage space any fun.
- A few libraries may have too much storage space, tempting them to hang onto things that might really be discarded. But we think they're in the tiny minority. What we see more often is libraries with good stuff stacked everywhere.

It could probably be proved with facts and figures that, just as people feel personally underpaid while everyone around them is overpaid, lots of people think they personally have far too little storage space, while by contrast other people and agencies and departments have more than they really need. But that's probably a standard response to inadequate space for everyone.

Our experience has been that providing enough storage space in library buildings is a real challenge. The storage spaces libraries specify in their building programs often end up smaller or made to do double duty. As a result, librarians need to keep a close eye on things throughout the entire design process.

II. LOCATIONS OF STORAGE SPACES

Storerooms need to be in places that are convenient for library staff members who need to store books, papers, supplies, equipment, and general library miscellanea. The sections that follow review some of the possibilities.

While some storage space is carefully planned, lots of other space is created because it's possible to squirrel things away in corners that are hard to use for other purposes.

A standard place to hide things away is closets under staircases. Since floating staircases with open spaces beneath are threats to life and limb because people crack their heads on the undersides of staircases, one standard solution is to create storage areas beneath staircases, using spaces where there's less than eight or ten feet of clearance to stack stuff. Or better yet, build storage closets under stairs. Often these spaces are hard to use, but they're found in libraries everywhere (and they're a lot better than creased foreheads).

> "Creased" forehead is a major euphemism. Decades ago, for example, there was an architectural design vogue for staircase bannisters that continued past the lower edge of staircases, leaving exposed metal posts hanging down so that people walking under the stairs could cut their heads wide open. Which they did.

The use of otherwise unusable spaces for storage can lead to lots of storerooms in dysfunctional places. Instead of being where library staff need them, storage spaces are tucked into corners of basements or HVAC penthouses, in addition to the old under-the-stairs favorites.

While storage for something used once every couple of years may not require convenient access, we have run into many situations where library staff members waste large amounts of time fetching and carrying from distant storerooms.

The obvious rule is that storage spaces need to be constructed for that purpose—using space that could be used for other purposes.

It's frequently tempting to use basements for storage.

- In modernized Carnegie-era libraries, basements may be of limited use for purposes other than meeting rooms, storage, or restrooms because libraries can't afford to staff two levels. Because basement floors in libraries of that era are frequently only a few feet below grade, they are less prone to flooding than are basements in modern libraries.
- In new libraries built on flat sites, basements will be totally below grade and windowless. (In new libraries, basements cost nearly as much as upper floors, and upper floors have the pleasing advantage of natural light and not flooding, leading one to the very reasonable question of why the library is building a basement in the first place.)

III. ASSIGNED STORAGE SPACES

All library departments need storage space.

Assigned departmental storage space has a number of advantages. It can be convenient to departmental staff workrooms. Because the space belongs to that department alone, its contents can be more easily protected. And the fact that storage areas are protected departmental spaces means that other departments cannot poach space and simply transfer their excess objects to your storage space, hoping that no one will notice.

Some common items requiring assigned storage are:

- Books and other materials, including items that need to be sequestered due to potential theft, items awaiting processing, items in closed stacks, items being considered for withdrawal, and so on. Some academic libraries have truly impressive stocks of unprocessed books. Some academic and public libraries have devices to heat or freeze incoming gift books or books from overseas, in order to preemptively eliminate six-legged wildlife.
- Business records, particularly records stored next to administrative workrooms. Think of personnel and financial records, correspondence, rolls of building plans, and the vast amounts of other paper that need to be kept somewhere.
- Office supplies, not only stuff for graphic arts and other staff workrooms, but also supplies used throughout buildings, such as copier paper. (Some libraries just stack boxes of copier paper in entry areas, letting departments help themselves.)
- Program equipment and supplies, particularly for public library children's departments. Children's departments can have impressive quantities of craft supplies, summer reading club prizes, and similar things. School librarians wake up on Monday morning to discover that twenty new pieces of classroom equipment on carts have appeared magically over the weekend and are now occupying essential floor space in their libraries.
- Furniture, particularly furniture that needs to be stored away when not in use, such as meeting room furniture. Far too many meeting rooms have furniture not used during programs piled around their walls because storage closets are inadequate.
- Book sale books. Friends of the Library groups that hold occasional book sales need places to stash books for the next sale.

> John's library in Williamsburg used off-site, climate-controlled, self-storage for book sale books. To Fred's wonderment, it did not eat up book sale profits.

- Technical services supplies. These can be in storerooms, although many departments seem to prefer open shelving for easy access.
- Custodial supplies that need to be kept locked up, including light bulbs, tools (which tend to vanish if they're not kept under lock and key), cleaning

Desperate needs for storage space lead to unusual solutions. In this library, staff members put a sheet of plywood on top of a staff workroom toilet stall to provide a space for the computer boxes that we are all instructed to save but turn out never to need. After that, staff had to enter the toilet stall at a crouch.

solutions, paint, cleaning supply carts, vacuum cleaners, rug shampoo equipment, lawn mowers, snow blowers, salt for sidewalks, gardening equipment, and so on.

- Attic stock. All new libraries have supplies of ceiling tile, floor tile, carpet squares, broadloom carpet, extra light fixtures, and other items needed to replace things that fail in use. "Attic stock" is important because it's often impossible to match things a few years after the library goes up. Despite the name, "attic stock" is seldom stored in attics.

> Attic stock can take up a lot of space. The director of a library Fred knows says that his main storerooms are completely filled with attic stock.

IV. SHARED STORAGE SPACES

Some libraries have all-purpose storerooms.

- The upside of large, shared storage spaces is flexibility. However, not dividing up areas can lead to exciting storage free-for-alls, with interesting squabbles over who gets what square footage.
- The downside of all-purpose storerooms is the fact that shared spaces are almost always less conveniently located than spaces adjacent to departments.

Some large shared spaces have locked metal cages to define spaces for various purposes. These function in the manner of departmental storerooms.

Because of their central locations, shared storage spaces are typically much less conveniently located and are probably suited only for little-used stuff.

V. MEETING AND PROGRAM ROOM STORAGE SPACES

It should be easy to clear all the furniture out of a meeting or program room and store it in attached closets. Nothing says bad planning more loudly than a program room with unused furniture piled around the walls.

Program rooms usually need separate closets because libraries need to control access. Common closet spaces include:

- Furnishings, including tables, chairs, lecterns, and so on. Furnishings require separate closets because libraries may want users to set up their own furniture but not have access to other stored items. Building programs need to specify the items that will be stored in furniture closets and REQUIRE THAT THE ARCHITECTS MAKE SURE THAT ALL OF THE SPECIFIED FURNITURE WILL ACTUALLY FIT INTO THE ASSIGNED CLOSETS. This is important, because architects occasionally fail to make sure things will fit. During the construction drawings phase of your design, make sure your architects have taken time to calculate things. Once the building is built and the furniture purchased, if things don't fit, it's too late. Remember that when you hold an event that doesn't require any tables or chairs, *ALL* of the furniture needs to fit into the furniture closet. Unfortunately, architects frequently ignore this requirement. Or they put other things into the furniture closet at the last second, leaving no space after all.

> The loud type in this section is due to the many meeting room storerooms that are built too small to hold necessary meeting room furnishings.

- Program equipment and supplies. Many program rooms have associated electronic equipment, ranging from monitors on carts to server racks to places to connect to ceiling-mounted projectors. In some public libraries, meeting rooms are designed to be set up as "maker spaces" from time to time, and storage spaces for all of the associated equipment need to be provided. When it comes to children's departments, it's easy to underestimate the space that program supplies can occupy, particularly if they have large puppet stages and similar objects.
- Book sale books. If your Friends of the Library group holds book sales in your program room, you'll want an attached storeroom for boxed books. Storerooms can be filled a box at a time over the months, but when the time comes for a sale, your friends will want to open closet doors and simply pull the books out. If book sale books are stored in some distant part of the building, setting up a sale will be a serious pain and will probably require hiring a crew to move all of the books at once. Your Friends group will also need a space for receiving, sorting, and boxing books. And they will need easy access to the library dumpster for those occasions when boxes of donated books turn out to be awash in mildew.
- Equipment that belongs to outside groups. Some libraries have permanent relationships with outside groups that require storage space, often separate locking closets for each group. Among those we've seen in public libraries are voting booths and scout equipment. If you are considering letting outside groups use library storage closets, however, remember that you will almost certainly never get the space back, even if you have a great need for it. Saying, "Sorry, but no" up front is probably several thousand times easier than saying, "Sorry, but you'll have to move out" later.
- Kitchenettes. Many program rooms have kitchenettes. Storage is usually provided with cupboards and drawers. All drawers need ball-bearing double-extension hardware, and all drawers *and* cabinets need locks. Cabinets need to be made of furniture-grade plywood with no chipboard components.

The configuration of storage spaces is important. Closets for furniture, equipment, program supplies, and book sale books need to be wide and shallow rather than deep and narrow. Double doors are a lot better than single doors. Furniture closets in particular need doors with steel edges to prevent them from being damaged by people moving furniture in and out.

One of the banes of meeting and program rooms is monster conference tables. If there's no separate conference room, make sure that conference tables are modular, and that there's a place to stash them out of sight. (Unless the scions of the great merchant families of the United States serve on your boards, modest conference tables are just fine.)

Our experience has been that storage closets in meeting rooms—particularly in public libraries—are almost always too few and too small. The result is furniture piled around the edges of rooms because it won't fit in the furniture closet, program supplies awkwardly transferred from other parts of the building for every program, book sale books hauled from remote storage spaces, and electronic equipment in a jumble in undersized closets.

Be very explicit in your building program about storage closets.

- Watch to be sure that storage closets don't magically shrink during the design process.
- Watch to be sure closets that must be separate for security purposes are not merged.
- Watch to be sure that unscheduled items don't migrate into closets, such as mechanical gear that prevents the use of the closets for storage.

A lot can go wrong at the construction drawing stage, and you'll want to keep a wary eye open.

VI. MECHANICAL EQUIPMENT STORAGE SPACES

Libraries need to store all sorts of stuff in addition to books, technical equipment, furnishings, and program supplies.

A. Outdoor Equipment

Public libraries often need space for outdoor equipment, including lawn mowers, snow blowers, salt for sidewalks, gardening equipment, hoses, fertilizer, and so on.

Codes typically require that gasoline-powered equipment and fuel be in spaces that can be accessed directly from out of doors. There may be additional requirements in your jurisdiction. Verify things with your architects.

Ideally, sidewalk salt is stored in closets right next to entries.

Every library needs a place to store ladders. This historic library had no place for ladders and ended up chaining them to a railing next to its historic main entry. The word "unsightly" was developed to cover situations like this.

B. Ladders

Public and academic libraries need to store required ladders and lifts. List these in your building program and then double-check your construction drawings. There's a constant tendency to omit ladder storage from libraries. But ladders have to go somewhere, and parent organizations (such as universities) may have no interest in hauling ladders around to individual buildings.

In Fred's library, the architects lowered the ceiling in an area designed for ladder storage in the last version of the construction drawings, apparently because some junior member of the firm saw no reason for a high ceiling and simply deleted it without talking with the client. Fred spotted the change only when the ceiling grid started to go in. It did not improve his mood.

C. HVAC Equipment

HVAC equipment has necessary supplies that will need to be stored somewhere, typically in the corner of an equipment room. A common item is stacks of disposable air filters. Be sure you enumerate what you'll need to store and mention this in your building program. Your HVAC engineers can help you determine what you'll need to store.

In some very critical situations, such as rare book rooms, libraries may need to keep replacement machinery in stock, so that there are no long delays in obtaining replacement parts.

D. Vehicle Storage

If your library has vehicles, you will probably want garage space. This introduces a whole range of technical requirements and possibilities. Will you have enough elbowroom to load vans and bookmobiles? Will the bookmobile collection be located directly adjacent to the garage space? What provisions will you have to move books into the bookmobile without climbing the entry steps with endless small handfuls of books? Will you want to wash vehicles in your garage? Will you want a concrete floor or some type of poured epoxy finish?

Garage design in public buildings is a huge topic requiring extensive input from your architects and engineers.

VII. DESCRIBING STORAGE SPACES IN BUILDING PROGRAMS

Storage spaces are easy to describe in building programs. Be sure to specify:

- The minimum size of each storage space in total square feet. It's usually wise to estimate generously, since stuff in storage gets bigger in the dark when the closet doors are closed.
- Adjacencies. Administrative records, for example, need to be adjacent to administrative workrooms, not in some other location where they happen to fit. Children's program gear needs to be next to program rooms or next to departmental workrooms. Be sure your designers don't relocate storage spaces because it's easier to do so than to figure out the best way to make everything fit together.
- Configuration. For example, most storage closets are far better wide and shallow than narrow and deep. Double doors are better than single doors.

A rectangular storage closet holds more per square foot than an oddly configured storage closet. Some of the most vicious storage closets in library buildings are located under staircases and accessed from one end.

- Minimum contents. After listing square footages, you may still want to instruct architects to make sure that specified items will fit in the allotted spaces, particularly if the items will vary in size depending on architectural choices. For instance, you can specify that the listed filing cabinets will actually fit into the designed space. Or you can specify that the tables and chairs and other furniture listed for a program room must fit into the allocated storerooms. And specify that it's the architects' responsibility to make sure that things actually fit.
- Irrelevant items. You will want to specify that irrelevant items will not intrude on storage spaces. Then watch construction drawings like a hawk to be sure this doesn't happen. Sometimes designers combine functions, which can be a problem, but sometimes they just cram something extra into the original storage space, which can be a disaster.
- Unalterable dimensions. If you have worked out how filing cabinets and shelving will fit into a storeroom of specific length and width, be sure your designers don't change the dimensions on the assumption that all that matters is total square feet.
- Furnishings. Storage spaces are a great place to use old book-shelving units made surplus by expansion or new construction. They're also great places to use the bright orange or avocado steel shelving your library purchased in 1970.
- Flexibility. If your meeting room furniture storage closet is too tightly configured, you may find it impossible to store slightly different furniture.

Frequently, designers will more or less blow off storage spaces, and you'll need to keep a close eye on things, both at the schematic design phase, when it's tempting to use space for more visible purposes, and at the construction document phase, when architects may feel the need to cram something in somewhere at the last minute and be tempted to cannibalize storage space.

During the programming phase of your project, try to review all the stuff you'll need to store, either chucking it out or making provisions for it. If your storage area will require special equipment (such as locked steel cabinets for high-theft materials), you'll want to list them so your designers can make sure they'll fit.

Pay particular attention to things your parent organization may decide to inflict on you after the fact. This seems to occur on a regular basis with some school libraries, so the programming phase is a good time to watch for new things and to pin the school administration down—if it's not planning extra space just on general principles.

To protect yourself from strange objects taking over your storage space, consider including in the description of each storage space wording something like the following: "This storage closet will be used only for the listed purpose. No additional equipment or functions will be added to the space."

VIII. PROTECTING STORAGE SPACES FROM LOOTERS WHO COVET YOUR SPACE

We've mentioned throughout this book that storage space is almost never adequate and that it can easily be taken from you while your back is turned.

During the design process, architects can cut square footages for storage without mentioning it to you, change the configurations of storerooms so that things no longer fit, relocate storage to less convenient parts of the building, combine individual storerooms (thereby reducing security and convenience), or stick extra objects into storerooms (sometimes making the rooms almost worthless in the process).

- University or high school administrators can come scouting around for storage space and seize upon yours.
- Other school and academic departments can attempt to move their stuff into your storerooms.
- Medical, law, and industrial libraries may find that confidential organization records suddenly appear in their storerooms.
- Storerooms may be combined with non-storage functions to the detriment of storage. If a drive-through book return bin is added to a storeroom, for example, there will be all sorts of safety, access, and noise-control implications.

Protecting necessary storage requires eternal vigilance, including realistically large projections of needed space in building programs, careful oversight during design to be sure that programmed spaces are provided, and making sure that extra things aren't crammed into your storage space when your back is turned. Keep an eye on construction documents, where spaces in the original schematic designs can be suddenly altered.

You can also make sure that your departmental storerooms always look clean and neat but extraordinarily packed to the gills, discouraging people who are scouting around for extra space.

IX. SNAPPY RULES ON STOREROOMS

1. Few libraries have ever built enough storage space on purpose.
2. The minute you plan an important storeroom, someone will scheme to put something else into it.
3. Ladders and lifts and other awkwardly shaped gadgets need to go somewhere. Usually in your building. Be sure your building program and your building plans include the spaces.
4. Describe all of your necessary storage spaces in your building program, and even then be prepared to fight to get them (and retain them).
5. If a gadget runs on gasoline, you'll need a door leading directly from the storeroom to the outside world. Or you may even need a separate building. Ask your designers to double-check applicable codes.
6. If your designers specify light fixtures with 75 different bulbs, imagine the storeroom you'll need to have a stock of each type. (Not to mention the cost of purchasing supplies of 75 different bulbs.)
7. Review your construction drawings with an eagle eye, for it's there that evil forces will suddenly appear to rob you of your storage space. Practice saying, "Get that @#$% out of my storeroom" in the tone of voice even middle-school students don't customarily elicit.
8. Never assume that campus maintenance services will bring their ladders with them when they come to service your library.
9. You'd be impressed by how much storage space a 50-year backlog of uncataloged agricultural monographs in assorted Slavic languages can occupy. Plan for it.
10. Attic stock is vital and can consume an impressive amount of storage space. Don't get caught short-square-footed. (The name *attic stock* sounds cozy and old-fashioned, but few libraries have actual attics that can be used for storage.)
11. Public library children's departments can make good use of any amount of storage space available. One of the tough jobs of library directors is deciding where things are getting out of hand and have to stop.
12. School libraries are prone to having shared equipment abruptly dumped on them. If someone turns up Monday morning with thirty bulky electronic gadgets on tall carts, you need someplace to put them that does not involve your main library room or staff workroom. When your space is first being planned, protecting a space for equipment-yet-to-come may require a stern attitude.
13. Program and meeting rooms need separate storage closets for movable furniture, electronic equipment, book sale books, equipment owned by outside groups, and other kinds of separately owned stuff. It's easy for double doors to closets to completely line one long side of a meeting room.

14. Program room storage closets need to be located adjacent to program rooms, because that's where the stuff in them is used. Dragging stuff from all over the library to a program room every time you have a program is a royal pain. And it's an avoidable pain if you plan first, watch things like a hawk, and stand your ground.
15. Storage closets work infinitely better if they are wide and shallow rather than narrow and deep. A closet with a double door works a lot better than a closet with a single door. Keep a special eye out for proposed designs of closets under staircases.
16. Every floor needs a usable mop basin. The same room that houses the mop basin can sometimes provide space for service carts, vacuum cleaners, carpet shampooers, and other custodial stuff.
17. Few things excite parent organizations and architects much less than storage spaces. Keep an eye on what's proposed, in case your storage spaces slowly head south.
18. If you run a law library, a medical library, or an industrial library, be prepared for the possibility that someone will want to store confidential documents there. It helps to sort things out with the administration in advance, so you don't suddenly find your library storage areas converted to corporate secure storage.
19. A long, narrow storeroom entered from one end is a pain forever.
20. If an outside book return slot leads into a storeroom, make sure that (a) the storeroom is designed to contain a fire, (b) you can get at the receiving bin without moving all sorts of debris out of the way, (c) the noise of falling books does not echo through occupied spaces, and (d) the storeroom is not accessed through a meeting room.
21. Never miss an opportunity to specify lots of locking storage cabinets. Great places are technical services departments, kitchenettes in meeting rooms and staff lunchrooms, and counter areas in children's craft and story rooms.
22. All of the unlikely problems in this list of snappy rules are based on actual real-life occurrences. So beware.

Part VI
Technical Issues

25

Lighting

I. INTRODUCTION

Good lighting is one of the most important necessities of libraries, but unfortunately far too many libraries are poorly lit.

The sad thing about all of this is that lighting libraries is a simple undertaking. Most of the problems occur because people create spaces that are by their nature unnecessarily hard to light, or they install lighting systems that provide unnecessarily ineffective and unpleasant light.

Unfortunately, the emphasis on green buildings has also led to bad lighting, primarily because of unrealistically low limits on wattages and because of inappropriate use of motion detectors.

Because of the frequency of lighting problems in libraries, it's important for librarians to understand how lighting systems work—and don't work. As you are planning your building, you will sometimes feel almost alone as you insist on simple, functional lighting. The more you know about lighting, the less likely you will be to have designers or contractors push you aside and ignore your needs.

Into the twentieth century, libraries were designed with the necessity of relying on natural light. Windows served not to provide a pleasant view of the outside world or to bring in daylight for psychological reasons, but rather to light reading rooms.

The result of the dependence on natural light is seen everywhere in the reading rooms of libraries built before the Second World War. Both the great reading rooms in academic and research libraries and domestic-sized reading rooms in Carnegie-era public libraries all depended on high windows to bring in light. Many of these windows had sills eight or more feet above the floor, to leave space for wall-mounted shelving below, resulting in rooms with daylight but with no view of the world beyond.

Reliance on natural light led, of course, to endless problems with both too little light and too much light. Too little light led to libraries for the elite. In the nineteenth century, for example, great research libraries were criticized for keeping hours of no use to working people, who were not free to read until after dark. By contrast, too much light is frequently with us today. Excessive spans of glass lead to unwanted brightness, with readers blinded by glare and books with spines faded beyond recognition.

Since World War II, and particularly in the last few decades, libraries have relied heavily on artificial light. Artificial light has many advantages. It is consistent in brightness, varying only when we want it to do so. It is also consistent in direction. Instead of being blinded by sunlight at some times and left in the dark at others, we can provide the amount of light we want where we want it and when we want it.

The downside of artificial light, of course, is energy usage. Natural light is essentially free (except for the cost of air conditioning when direct sunlight heats rooms in unwanted ways), while artificial light requires electric current.

This chapter provides a practical review of artificial and natural lighting options in libraries, with recommendations on proven solutions and comments on several lighting concepts that frequently lead to trouble.

II. GENERAL LIGHTING CONCEPTS

A few general concepts are of concern everywhere in lighting, and you will need to be comfortable with them in order to talk about lighting with lighting designers and with architects.

A. A Few Common Lighting Terms

As in many other areas of library building design, familiarity with some of the basic vocabulary in the field is essential. Here are some of the terms and concepts we think you will encounter most frequently in talking with lighting designers and contractors.

- *Ballast.* A ballast is a transformer that provides current for fluorescent and HID lamps by increasing voltage to the point that power can jump the length of the lamp. The most efficient ballasts are electronic. They're always worth using, but some brands burn out faster than others. When it comes to bid time, try to limit acceptable ballast manufacturers to those whose products have good reputations and whose ballasts are stocked at local electric stores. Don't accept unknown manufacturers as "equivalents."
- *Efficacy.* A measure of the efficiency with which lamps convert electrical energy to visible light. The standard measure of lamp efficacy is lumens per watt. There is a wide range in lamp efficacy.
- *Lamp.* In the lighting trade, light bulbs are called "lamps." To avoid confusion, never refer to light fixtures as lamps. Use a more specific term, such as "table lamp," to make clear what you are talking about.
- *Lamp nomenclature.* Most lamps have code numbers that describe the shape of the lamp and its diameter in eighths of an inch. For example, when a fluorescent lamp is labeled T-8, we know that it's a tubular lamp with a one-inch diameter. A G-40 is a globular lamp five inches in diameter.
- *Lumen.* The output of electric lamps is listed in "lumens." For example, a 100-watt incandescent lamp (ordinary light bulb) emits about 1,500 lumens, while a 100-watt high-pressure sodium lamp (the pinky-orange lamps used to light streets) emits about 15,000 lumens.
- *Luminaire.* A combination of a light fixture and the appropriate lamp.
- *Parabolic reflectors.* A parabola is a curve based on a specific mathematical formula. Many lamps and light fixtures employ parabolas as reflectors. If a concentrated source of light is placed at the mathematical focal point of a parabolic reflector, all light emitted from the reflector emerges as a highly directional beam. Many lamps that emit concentrated light in this fashion are identified as PAR lamps, which stands for "parabolic aluminized reflector." PAR lamps frequently behave like automobile headlights—there are no doubt great uses for them, but not in libraries. Some ceiling-mounted fluorescent fixtures use partial parabolic lenses that look like a group of open boxes suspended beneath the fluorescent tubes. These are not the vicious devices that PAR lamps are, but the light they put out is significantly inferior to reflected uplighting.
- *Visible light.* Light is the narrow portion of the electromagnetic spectrum that we can actually see. Violet light has the shortest wavelength and red the longest (hence "ultraviolet" and "infrared" for wavelengths too short or long for people to see).

B. Illumination Levels

The brightness of lighting falling on surfaces is measured in "foot-candles." The derivation of the term can be found in many technical manuals, but what's important to librarians is the level of brightness needed in well-lighted libraries.

The metric equivalent of the foot-candle is the "lux." Ten lux is about one foot-candle.

Foot-candle levels can be as high as 10,000 foot-candles in direct sunlight at noon. By contrast, most people can read regular print very comfortably under high-quality light of about 60 foot-candles.

As far as low levels are concerned, the light of the full moon provides about 0.025 foot-candles. Parking lots are often lit at 1 or 2 foot-candles.

Readers' ability to see is dependent not only on absolute foot-candle levels but also on relative levels. When people enter a building at high noon, their eyes take a few moments to adjust to the difference in light. And when they step back outside, they are momentarily blinded.

The main point here is that readers see best and least painfully when lighting levels are fairly even. Trying to read at a table that is lit by artificial light but has a band of direct sunlight falling across one end is an unpleasant experience. Trying to see books along a wall when the spines are lit at 20 foot-candles but windows every few feet provide hundreds of foot-candles is difficult.

Problems with wide variations in brightness are one of the many reasons to reject with great vigor any suggestion that your library have skylights.

Readers' difficulties in dealing with contrast are the source of the problems that people have with reading tables with white or extremely dark tops. White tops reflect too much light and blind readers. Dark tops contrast too much with white paper, and the result is eyestrain. The reason that so many designers select finishes like natural birch and pale gray laminates for tabletops is not just aesthetics.

One problem libraries encounter in specifying illumination levels is that most commercial specification is in terms of light falling on tabletops, and many light fixtures are designed to direct light entirely downward. In libraries, however, many surfaces that readers need to illuminate are not horizontal. Readers hold books vertically and expect to have workable light falling on the pages. Light on bookshelves needs to illuminate the spines rather than the top edges of the books. Flip bins for CDs and DVDs or children's picture books allow only a narrow gap for light to fall on the front of the recording or book.

For this reason, librarians can't simply specify 60 foot-candles and get workable lighting. Although one can, for example, specify the number of foot-candles falling on vertical surfaces, our experience has been that it's equally important to tell designers exactly how we want our libraries lit.

Always insist that your designers provide you with calculations of foot-candles at tabletop level for all areas of your library. These are generated by computer programs and should be part of the package. "Calcs" provide illumination levels on a grid basis, so the calculations for a room may include a large matrix of numbers. In a well-lighted room, the numbers should be relatively even from edge to edge in all directions. (The placement of shelving can make a huge difference in illumination levels, so be sure your designers' calculation models include the effects of stacks.)

Although you can use various formulas and simple lighting calculators to estimate how much light your chosen light sources will deliver, this is something you really need to leave to professionals. The electrical engineers working on your building are the people you want to provide these calculations.

When you are reviewing calcs, watch in particular for light levels that fall off around the perimeters of rooms. This is a very common problem with some widely used styles of lighting, and you don't want it in your library.

If the calculations show uneven lighting (or dim lighting on perimeters), your designers may say that the figures do not include all fixtures. At this point, they need to rerun the calculations.

Recommended foot-candle levels for a wide variety of circumstances are published by the IESNA—the Illuminating Engineering Society of North America. In recent years, with the growing emphasis on energy conservation, recommended levels have been dropping, making it increasingly important that the lighting system in your library provides even, low-glare illumination. Unfortunately, some of the light levels prescribed by the IESNA are simply inadequate for libraries.

But always remember that calcs don't tell the whole story. Libraries need soft, even light that falls on vertical surfaces as well as horizontal ones. Calcs tell us that the light is bright and uniform, but we need to specify proper fixtures before requesting that calcs be developed.

C. Glare

Glare is unwanted light that blinds us.

Because people live with glare every day, they tend to associate it with adequate lighting, and it's easy to assume that a lack of glare means dim light. But it's just the result of poorly chosen lighting options.

Glare comes in two varieties—direct glare and indirect or reflected glare.

1. Direct Glare

Direct glare is just what it sounds like—a source of light shining directly in someone's eyes. Light may be simply too bright for reading, such as with direct sunlight, but with artificial light glare is more likely to be the result of overly directional lighting.

In addition to windows, typical sources of glare in libraries are ceiling-mounted lights that shine straight downward. The smaller and more concentrated the source, the worse the glare. You know your building has trouble with glare if you realize that an eyeshade would make your life more comfortable.

Direct lighting is a particular problem in libraries because people spend so much time looking upward at books on high shelves. Looking upward at a top shelf, only to find oneself staring into a brilliant light shining downward, is a truly unpleasant experience.

Unfortunately, some of the kinds of artificial lighting most popular with designers create a great deal of direct glare. Of these, the greatest evil (and yet amazingly popular with architects and designers) is the "recessed downlight" or "can light." Can lights are everywhere; look for round six-inch holes in the ceiling. If you don't believe can lights are nasty, just experiment with looking up into them.

Other nasty sources of direct glare are skylights and vertical windows with no blinds, unless the windows face straight north.

> Fred worked for a library where the stacks were full of small skylights. Trying to read spines on tall shelving when a skylight is blazing right behind them is impossible, no matter what designers claim to the contrary.

The best way to avoid direct glare is to illuminate ceilings as evenly as possible, so no areas are brighter than they need to be to provide adequate light.

In addition to being unpleasant, direct glare is usually accompanied by unwanted shadows. Some lighting is so direct that readers cast shadows on their books when they lean over to read, or their hands cast dark shadows on their notes while they write.

To avoid direct glare in your library, start by informing your designers that you will accept no recessed downlights or skylights anywhere, for any purpose whatsoever. And hold them to it, since some designers will agree pleasantly and then use can lights anyway. When John was director of the public library in Decatur, Illinois, the architects called him "No-Can-Lights Moorman." And he had a far better, more user-friendly library as a result.

2. Indirect Glare

Indirect glare consists of unpleasant reflections of concentrated light sources on shiny surfaces. This is frequently called "veiling reflectance," because the images of the lights reflected on the shiny surfaces "veil" the images people are trying to see. Anyone who has tried to read *National Geographic* under recessed downlights and has had to tilt the magazine endlessly to see the pictures knows all about veiling reflectance.

We can fight indirect glare in libraries first by avoiding shiny surfaces. Glass-covered tables, traditionally curved cathode-ray tube monitors, and other highly polished surfaces all reflect images too readily.

When computer monitors were first introduced into libraries, some libraries purchased tables with glass tops over rectangular openings, with monitors set beneath the openings, angling up toward the users. Unfortunately, veiling reflections on the glass tops made it almost impossible to see the monitors under the glass, and black plastic hoods were added to keep room light from falling on the glass. The result was users peering under hoods to see the monitors below. (Computer workstations of this type were also miserable for users with bifocals, who found themselves bending forward to see the monitors beneath the tabletops, then rearing backwards to focus on their notes. The effect was a little like the bobbing toy birds that hook onto the rim of a glass of water, but less entertaining to watch if you are a nice person.)

A second way to fight indirect glare is to avoid concentrated light sources. Veiled reflections on a computer monitor from a nearby skylight are one of the many, many reasons why skylights are a pain in libraries.

D. Color Rendering

A major concern in selecting light sources is the degree to which they portray colors accurately. Daylight and incandescent light both do a great job, but many other kinds of light cause problems. For example, cheap fluorescent lamps can put out such poor-quality light that customers in clothing stores have to carry clothes out into the sunshine just to see what the colors actually are.

The problem is due to the fact that many modern light sources are missing some of the wavelengths that make up white light. If a light source, for example, emits little or no light in the red end of the spectrum, red objects will appear black beneath it. Cheap fluorescent lamps tend to concentrate their light output in the yellow-green area of the spectrum, and red colors correspondingly are inaccurately portrayed.

The ability of light to portray colors accurately is described by "color rendering index," usually abbreviated CRI. CRI ratings usually vary from 0 to 100, but low-pressure sodium light has a CRI of well below 0. High-quality fluorescent light has a CRI of at least 85, and we recommend that you accept nothing lower.

All respectable fluorescent and HID lamps should have boxes indicating CRI. If you can't find information on the CRI of a lamp, never buy it.

We found the push for CFLs (compact fluorescent lamps) ill-advised because CFLs have notoriously bad CRIs. The boxes of CFLs seldom mention color rendering indexes, and the manufacturers' websites steer clear of the subject. People who experiment with CFLs in their homes, particularly when they (for example) put one incandescent lamp in a fixture at one end of a sofa and a CFL in an identical fixture at the other end, note that the CFLs put out the nasty yellow-green light associated with cheap fluorescent tubes decades ago. By the time this book appears, major lighting manufactures may have discontinued CFLs.

While this book was being written, LEDs (light-emitting diodes) were emerging as a major source of lighting. As indicated below, LEDs are tremendously efficient when it comes to energy use. In the past, they have also had a number of serious problems, including bad color rendering, bad color temperatures, and harsh directionality. But improvements have occurred rapidly.

Saving energy is a great idea, but people need to be up front about the implications.

E. Color Temperature

The color temperature of lighting is important to the mood and warmth of libraries.

Color temperature is measured in Kelvin. The higher the number, the bluer the light. For example, daylight has a color temperature of about 6000 K, while candlelight is about 1800 K. Incandescent light varies but averages about 3000 K.

If lighting has a high CRI, people can see colors accurately in a variety of color temperatures. In fact, only when light with two different color temperatures is visible at the same time are people aware of the difference. For example, when people walking in the twilight see lighted interiors, they realize how orange incandescent light is by comparison to daylight. Once they enter buildings and see only incandescent light, it generally ceases to seem warm.

Opinions differ, but we think libraries feel most comfortable when the color of the internal lighting is similar to that provided by incandescent lamps. Many fluorescent lamps are available with color temperatures of 3000 and 3500 K. This is warm enough so that buildings look welcoming when people drive by at twilight and people's complexions look good, but cool enough for reading and for a sense of accurate color.

III. TYPES OF LIGHT SOURCES

To understand artificial lighting and its uses, it's important to review how artificial lighting works.

There are four basic sources of artificial light used in libraries.

- Incandescent (including quartz halogen)
- Fluorescent (including cold cathode fluorescent)
- High-intensity discharge (HID)
- LEDs (light-emitting diodes)

A. Incandescent

Incandescent lamps are the kind we all grew up with, and are basically hot wires in bottles. They've been around for over a century, and they come in a wide variety of shapes, wattages, and colors.

All incandescent lamps have some basic characteristics.

- Easily dimmed. With a regular dimmer switch, it's easy to adjust incandescent lamps to almost any level of brightness.
- High CRI. Because incandescent lamps radiate light in all wavelengths, colors are viewed accurately, as they are with daylight. Most other light sources have problems in this area.
- Warm color. With a color temperature of about 2800 to 3200 Kelvin, incandescent lamps seem warm and welcoming from outside the building.
- Fairly concentrated light. Incandescent lamps are a concentrated source of light. This offers some advantages in fixture design, but most lamps are too bright to look at without shielding or diffusers.
- Standard technology. Because incandescent lamps are widely used in homes, everyone understands them. They can be bought everywhere, and a wide variety of lamps will often fit into a single standard socket.
- Inefficiency. In terms of lumens per watt, incandescent lamps perform poorly. While fluorescent, HID, and LED lamps can put out perhaps 50 to 100 lumens per watt, incandescent lamps provide under 10 lumens per watt.

The extremely low light output per watt from incandescent lamps makes them a generally poor choice in libraries, particularly where energy codes limit the number of watts per square foot. Now that LED lamps are available for track lighting for exhibits, doing without incandescent lamps seems to be a good idea.

- Quartz halogen lamps are a variety of incandescent lamps. The use of a heat-resistant quartz envelope for the lamp and the inclusion of halogens within the lamp allows the lamp to burn hotter (and therefore whiter) without burning out the filament prematurely. Quartz halogen lamps are most commonly encountered in libraries as small-diameter reflector lamps. Unfortunately, the light they put out is painfully concentrated, the lamps burn out quickly, and because the lamps burn hotter they are more dangerous to be near. (The pink light that hovers around the backs of quartz halogen lamps is due to long-wavelength visible light leaking through a layer designed to let heat escape through the backs of the lamps.) Occasionally we encounter grids of quartz halogen reflector bulbs suspended on wires above service desks. Most of the time, most of the lamps are burned out, which is probably A Good Thing. We think that quartz halogen lamps are best used to show off diamonds in shop windows, where extremely intense, white light is important. In libraries quartz halogen lamps are too hot, too glary, and too often burned out. It's easy to say "no" before design work begins. LED spotlights appear to be a fine substitute for quartz halogen lamps.

Small quartz halogen bulbs are popular with designers but have problems in libraries. They are extremely hot and are unpleasant to look at directly. But they have the advantage of often being burned out. (Quartz halogen bulbs are great for illuminating diamonds, but libraries are generally short of diamonds.)

> Quartz halogen lamps are too hot, too glary, and too often burned out. Luckily, energy codes that limit watts per square foot will probably eliminate them in new installations.

B. Fluorescent

Fluorescent lighting has been in use since the late 1930s. High-voltage (and very low-amperage) electric current jumps the length of a tube, creating ultraviolet light that is converted to visible light by phosphors that line the tube.

Modern fluorescent lighting is found everywhere. Among its characteristics are:

- Everyday technology. Fluorescent lights are commonplace and easy to service. All maintenance people are used to working with them.
- Efficient. Fluorescent lighting puts out a lot of light per watt.
- Low intensity. All forms of fluorescent light are less blinding than incandescent, HID, or LED due to larger radiative surfaces. Of all the forms of lighting described here, only fluorescent lamps can be viewed directly without serious discomfort. (In a way, this is also a drawback, since it has led to many fixtures with exposed fluorescent tubes—fine for a big box discount store, perhaps, but not what one expects to see in a library.) Actually, very small-diameter fluorescent lamps such as T-5s can be too bright to view directly, and large-diameter incandescent lamps, such as G-40s with wattages below 150, have a large enough surface to be viewable, so there are exceptions to all sweeping statements.
- Limited dimming possible. Modern fluorescent lights with electronic ballasts can be engineered to dim partially, but they cannot be brought smoothly from dark to bright as incandescent lamps can.
- Color rendering varies. The color quality of fluorescent lighting ranges from poor to fairly excellent. As long as the manufacturer provides CRI information, you can tell what you're getting. (And if the manufacturer does not provide this data, never purchase the lamps.)
- Range of color temperatures available. Fluorescent lamps are available in everything from very cool to quite warm. Many libraries find that about 3500K is about the right color temperature—warm enough so that buildings look welcoming from out of doors in the twilight or dark, but still cool enough so the warmness is not apparent indoors at night.
- Relatively long lamp life. Fluorescent lamps can burn for a couple of years or more in daily use.

- Standard lamp types. Most light fixtures will accept a variety of products. Among the most common are tube fluorescents. Another widely used fluorescent lamp shape is so-called biax fluorescents, slender tubes bent double so both ends can plug into a single double socket.
- Cheap ballasts can be noisy. One of the unpleasant noises in buildings with old fluorescent fixtures is the persistent 60-cycle hum of cheap ballasts. But there are cures for this. When purchasing new fixtures or replacing ballasts, always buy ballasts that are sound rated "A." Modern electronic ballasts are also quiet.
- Mercury. All fluorescent and HID lamps contain mercury, but some modern fluorescent lamps contain so little that they can simply be tossed into the trash. Look for green end caps on lamps.

Fluorescent lamps are the closest we come to nationally standard lighting, and the best ones work extremely well.

- Cold cathode fluorescent lamps have been used in a few libraries because the technology allows an amazing variety of colors and custom shapes. However, the custom-shaped lamps can also cost well over $1,000 apiece. We are familiar with libraries that have chandeliers with great circles of cold cathode lamps that are turned on only for extremely important ceremonial occasions.

C. High Intensity Discharge (HID)

High-intensity discharge (HID) lamps are part of a family of lighting that includes mercury vapor, sodium vapor, and metal halide. HID lighting is very widely used, particularly for outdoor illumination.

- Mercury vapor was the first of this group to be used, and it survives in older fixtures designed for this type of lighting. Mercury vapor lighting is missing most of the red end of the spectrum, and human complexions tend to look liverish (not to mention unpleasantly blotchy) under it. Mercury vapor lighting also tends to lose efficiency as the lamps age, with older lamps putting out much less light but requiring the same amount of energy.
- Sodium vapor lamps have replaced mercury vapor in many new installations. High-pressure sodium light is a pinky-orange color. Like mercury vapor, it is missing portions of the spectrum, and there is something unnatural about the color of the light, but it is used for streetlights everywhere. (Low-pressure sodium lamps put out a dark orange color of light and are little used in the United States.)

- Metal halide lighting is generally white, and this has led to its use in indoor situations where the greater size of fluorescent tubes is unwanted or where there are immense spaces to illuminate. Modern gymnasium lighting, for example, is likely to use metal halide lamps. Uplighting in large, high-ceilinged spaces is usually metal halide. Although metal halide lamps may be slightly less efficient than sodium vapor lamps, it appears that the more complete spectrum emitted by metal halide lamps allows equally good vision with a slightly lower level of illumination.

Here are some of the basic characteristics of HID lighting.

- Efficacy. Like fluorescent lighting, HID lighting is vastly more efficient than traditional incandescent lighting. This has helped make it the standard choice for lighting streets, alleys, parking lots, and other outdoor areas. The pinky-orange color of high-pressure sodium lighting fills American cities.
- Except for metal halide, it is suitable only for exterior use. Both mercury vapor and sodium vapor lamps have color characteristics that make them unsuited for any purpose where reasonable color rendering is needed.
- Highly concentrated light. Because HID lamps are extremely bright, a relatively small lighting fixture can emit a huge amount of light. This makes HID lighting popular for uplighting large spaces.
- Mediocre CRI. No HID lighting has the high-level color rendering index associated with incandescent light or the best fluorescent lamps.
- Color maintenance problems. Even when it appears reasonably white, metal halide lighting has problems with color maintenance. The lamps from a single case may burn in a variety of colors, ranging from white to lavender to blue to even brilliant raspberry pink. The problem is particularly noticeable when metal halide lamps are used for uplighting, and the different colors of light shining on the white walls or ceilings are particularly apparent. Unfortunately, due to its extreme intensity, the best indoor use of metal halide lighting is for uplighting. Ceramic metal halide lamps are engineered to limit problems with color maintenance, but variations from lamp to lamp may still exist.
- Noisy ballasts. HID ballasts often hum noisily, much in the manner of cheap fluorescent ballasts. In some indoor installations, the ballasts are installed in remote places where the hum will not disturb people using the spaces.
- "Catastrophic end of service." This is the delicate way the industry describes the tendency (thankfully rare) for HID lamps to explode, dropping hot shards of glass upon the place beneath.
- Lamps often specific to ballasts. While many fluorescent fixtures will accept a wide variety of tubes of the right dimensions, the fixtures for HID lamps can be extremely limited in the types of lamps they will accept.

- Restrike time. One aspect of HID lighting that makes it inappropriate for many indoor situations is the time it takes to warm up and cool down. When HID lamps are turned on, it can be several minutes before they actually start emitting the full amount of light. When they are turned off, they have to cool down before they can warm up again. For any situation where lights need to be turned off and on during the course of the day, HID lighting is inappropriate. This also explains why libraries with HID lighting need to have light switches where kids can't reach them. In John's library in Decatur, Illinois, the electrical designer used metal halide lamps in the children's program room. When the staff turned the lights out for programs, they had to lead the children out with flashlights afterwards.
- Mercury. Like fluorescent lamps, all HID lamps contain at least some mercury.

D. Light-Emitting Diodes (LEDs)

LEDs were starting to come into common use in library lighting while we were completing this book, so we have to do far more speculating than we like.

Light-emitting diodes are found everywhere. They are durable, and they are efficient to the point where they remain cool in use. LEDs have been used in indicator lamps and digital clocks for years, and as technology improves and prices drop, they are slowly coming into more extensive use.

One thing that has historically limited the use of LEDs for general lighting has been the absence of pleasant white colors. Most LEDs are intensely bright colors, particularly red and green. White LEDs were slow to be developed, and most of the early ones had an extremely unpleasant blue-white color that limited their use. While this book was being written, better white LEDs were being developed and installed.

Another limit to the use of LEDs is their small size. When LEDs are used to create a substantial amount of light, they need to be grouped in large arrays.

LEDs are also quite directional. Individual LEDs function like spotlights, and fixture design needs to convert this highly directional light to gentle ambient light.

In addition to great efficacy, LEDs tend to have a very long life, which should make them an attractive choice for light fixtures that are hard to reach.

For many years, the use of LEDs in libraries was limited primarily to exit lights, lighted push buttons in elevators, and a few other purposes. Before LEDs, exit lights used tubular incandescent lamps that continually burned out. Their replacement by red LEDs spared library maintenance staff members constant lamp replacement. (In addition, standards set by the American Society of Heating, Refrigerating, and Air-Conditioning Engineers (ASHRAE pronounced "ash-rahy") at the time we were writing called for less than 5 watts of power per side of exit signs, and only LEDs make this possible.)

When you are selecting any item with supposedly white LEDs, always ask to see the CRI (color rendering index) and color temperature information. As with fluorescent and HID lighting, you should require a CRI of at least 85. Color temperature should be similar to that of incandescent lighting, roughly 3000K to 3500K.

Fixtures that direct all or most of the light from LEDs straight downward are likely to provide very unpleasant illumination, but fixtures with a large indirect light component are available. Unfortunately, we've seen some LED fixtures with vicious downlight in recent libraries.

When you are considering LED lighting, ask serious questions about maintenance. When individual LEDs in a fixture start to burn out (and they will), how will you maintain the fixtures? Are they designed for individual LED replacement? Or will you have to completely replace the fixture? If you have to replace it, will matching fixtures still be available? If the fixtures have circuit boards, will they be available in the future?

One of the great things about fluorescent lighting is standardization. T-8 tubes are made by many manufacturers and are interchangeable in fixtures. Ballasts are also replaceable and widely made. When LED lighting systems use standardized components maintenance should be easy.

E. Selecting Light Sources

Here are our conclusions about sources of artificial light.

- In our opinion, by far the best source of indoor lighting for libraries is fluorescent. It combines efficiency, standard technology, reasonably priced lamps, the availability of lamps with high CRI, a variety of color temperatures, cool surfaces, availability of silent ballasts, and consistent color maintenance. We expect LEDs may replace fluorescent lighting. But do not compromise on color temperature, color rendering index, or the need for soft ambient lighting.

This library is illuminated with fixtures that bounce 100 percent of the light off white ceiling. Because the ceiling is evenly illuminated, book shelving, user seating, computer workstations, and staff areas can be located wherever needed—and moved around without altering the lighting.

- If at all possible, standardize on a very limited number of lamp types. Until LEDs take over, we see no reason why virtually all of the artificial light in a library cannot be supplied by four-foot T-8 lamps.
- Never select lamps with a CRI of less than 85.
- We personally prefer lamps with a 3500K color temperature, but you may want to view a few installations before you decide. Some people prefer warmer lighting, and many fluorescent lamps with a color temperature of 2700K have been made for home use.
- Once you have selected a lamp type, purchase exactly the same brand and model for all replacements. Never let people buy any old fluorescent lamps for your library. One of the worst lighting effects in any building is the piebald look that comes from the use of fluorescent lamps in a variety of colors.

IV. LIGHTING STRATEGIES

A. Uplighting

Uplighting consists of bouncing light off white ceilings. It's a simple strategy, and strip fluorescent uplight fixtures are widely available. Because the entire

This photo of a waffle-slab ceiling shows two excellent lighting decisions. First, light is bounced off the ceiling rather than supplied by fixtures set in the waffle openings. And second, there is no special lighting for the service desk, making it possible to rearrange or relocate the desk without having to alter the lighting. (Fred thought the "Ask a Librarian" sign was brilliant example of jargon avoidance, but the library later altered it to say "Reference Desk/Ask a Librarian".)

Strip uplighting running perpendicularly to stack aisles avoids dark places in stack aisles.

Uplighting fixtures work best in strips. By lighting the ceiling fairly evenly, they allow almost unlimited reorganization of furnishings (particularly in children's departments like this one, where lower furnishings allow for greater spread of light).

ceiling becomes a source of light, there are few problems with spotty illumination or glare. Well-designed uplighting allows the rearrangement of shelving, reader seating, computer workstations, and staff service desks without altering the lighting.

Many fixtures provide a mix of uplighting and downlighting. Often about three-quarters of the light is directed upward and the remaining light directed downward through perforations in the fixture. Perforations are usually on the sides of the fixtures but not in the flat centers, to hide the presence of dead bugs.

B. Downlighting

Downlight fixtures shine light directly from the ceiling (or other location) straight down on the area to be lighted.

Most of the common types of lighting fixtures are designed to produce downlight. Among these are all of the "troffer" fixtures, light fixtures that are mounted directly in suspended ceiling grids. Troffers are usually two-by-four-foot fluorescent fixtures set flush with the ceiling, although two-by-two troffers are also popular. Troffers tend to have either parabolic grids, through which the fluorescent tubes are visible, or prism lenses. Troffers are relatively inexpensive and easy to install, but they direct most of their light straight downwards. This means that the ceiling of the library is primarily in relative shadow, with the exception of the bright rectangles of light.

Light from fixtures of this type can be extremely spotty. If a stack aisle is located where there happens to be no fixture above, the result is books almost too dark to see. Libraries with ceiling-mounted fixtures over their stacks are constantly moving fixtures or adding extras, and even then they have problems when the ceiling grid doesn't align correctly with the stack aisles. Because ceiling grids are laid out in multiples of two or four feet, and stacks almost never are, the result of troffers over stack aisles is always trouble, with some fixtures centered over aisles and others over the tops of shelves.

This library was originally equipped with two rows of recessed downlights on the sides of the ceiling, leaving the center of the room so dark that a strip of fluorescent lights had to be retrofitted. (The original situation was made worse by the fact that the can lights were metal halide, which led them to overheat and shut down now and then. Because of the restrike time for metal halide lighting, the lights took about fifteen minutes to come back on again, leaving impressively dark areas in a building that was already badly lighted.)

One way to avoid this problem is to run strip fluorescent lights or troffers end-to-end and perpendicular to the aisles in the stacks. No matter how the shelving is moved to alter aisle width, light will still be over each aisle. In a similar way, a few libraries have been built with diagonal strip lights, allowing not only the aisle width to be changed, but also shelving to be rotated ninety degrees.

Fluorescent fixtures can also be ceiling-mounted with wraparound lenses. These are better sources of library light than troffers, because the sides of the lenses provide at least a little illumination on the ceiling. But their brightness creates glare, and they tend to look extremely utilitarian.

Another type of ceiling-mounted fixture is the "direct/indirect" fixture. In fixtures of this type, the fluorescent lamps are hidden behind metal shields and shine upward inside the fixture, where light is reflected from white-painted surfaces. These provide somewhat less glare than other troffer fixtures, but the ceiling is still a dark area punctuated by bright rectangles.

Some direct/indirect fixtures have sections that hang down to project light sideways, where some of it reflects off adjacent ceilings. Other direct/indirect fixtures have perforated baffles where the light from fluorescent tubes is emitted directly but glare is reduced by the solid areas around the perforations.

Can lights (also known as "recessed downlights") are among the most dysfunctional light fixtures possible in libraries. The lighting system visible in the ceiling of the room is spectacularly awful—a mixture of spotty illumination and horrible glare. Put "absolutely no recessed downlights" in your written building program. Fred is entitled to say evil things about this lighting system because this picture was taken in a building he inherited and coped with for many years. In a subsequent remodeling, 100 percent of the can lights—not some weak proportion like 98 percent—went into dumpsters.

By far the worst excrescence in the world of library lighting is the recessed downlight, also known as a "can light" because it is basically a light bulb in a short, concealed tube. Downlights combine the worst of glare, spotty illumination, and harsh shadow, but they are beloved of designers everywhere, whose standard approach is to lard ceilings with hundreds of can lights. We recommend that at the beginning of the design process, you inform your architects and interior designers that you will accept absolutely no can lights for any purpose whatsoever.

People who specify can lights tend to think that the only thing lighting needs to accomplish is to brightly light tabletops. When laying out grids of can lights, they check the cones of illumination to be sure they overlap properly at twenty-nine inches off the floor. But further from the floor, the light from the same can lights is incredibly spotty. The combination of can lights and book stacks is particularly nasty.

> Downlighting is not totally evil, but it comes close enough for all practical purposes.

C. Task Lighting

The basic concept of task lighting is a superficially appealing one. If we put light just where we need it for each task, we won't waste energy, and we'll have plenty of light for reading or other work.

However, the spottiness of task lighting in libraries can mean that users have to hunt for places with enough light to read. People can live with that in their homes, where we can navigate with our eyes closed, but in libraries we need to see everywhere, and spotty illumination is frustrating.

The other functional problem is that a great deal of task lighting is attached to our buildings. This means that we cannot relocate furniture or shelving or service without also relocating lighting. Ceiling or wall-mounted task lighting is a terrible idea, and libraries are full of surviving task lights that at one time illuminated a long-gone desk or table.

One persistent bad idea in library lighting is the installation of soffits with downlights over service desks. If the shape of the soffit matches that of the desk below, the desk can never be reconfigured or relocated without ripping out both the

These photographs demonstrate the foolishness of using architecturally mounted task lighting. The first lights were installed when a service desk was at the back of the skylight, at the rear of the photograph. When the service desk was rotated 90 degrees and moved to the left, the first set of lights no longer served any purpose, and a second set of lights was installed over the new location. The second (vertical) photo shows what happened when the desk was moved again, and the second set of lights was also in the wrong place. The whole mess was solved (as it should have been from the beginning) by adding bright indirect lighting to the room, taking advantage of the existing cove.

soffit and the lights, plus often having to rip out and replace the sprinkler pipes inside the soffit. The whole idea of matching soffits and desks may seem attractive to you when your designer first suggests it, but you will eventually wish your building had greater flexibility in use. Like can lights in general, soffits over service desks are a good thing to ban before design work begins.

To prevent the obsolescence of permanent task lighting, some furniture or equipment comes with its own task lighting attached. This is common, for example, in the office system components used to create cubes, and it's possible to attach lighting units to book shelving.

Lighting units attached to shelving can be centered over aisles on arms extending from shelving units, or they can be strip lights attached directly to the canopy tops of the shelving. The first approach leads to good light on the spines of books, but the second lights primarily the top edges of the books.

The trouble with shelf-mounted lighting is that it has to be connected to electrical outlets in the floor, making it extremely hard to relocate shelving, since we cannot afford to locate floor outlets everywhere we might possibly need them. Some shelving has lighting connected to ceiling electrical outlets by flexible electrical conduit. This provides a serious industrial look.

In rooms with high or dark ceilings, one traditional way of lighting book shelving is with fixtures that extend from the shelving units. Some don't work, so you will need to work with your architects to experiment with sample fixtures and the best way to mount them.

Task lights mounted on shelving are sometimes the only solution in historic rooms with very high, dark ceilings. In rooms like this, chandeliers may provide sufficient allover lighting for users to navigate safely, while table lamps and shelf lights provide the brighter light needed for finding books and for reading.

Our general approach, however, is to tell designers, "No task lighting," and instead rely on uniform, multifunction uplighting.

V. ENERGY-SAVING IDEAS

With increasing concern about buildings that burn too much energy, lighting designers have sought ways to save energy while producing effective lighting. Some of these work well, but others cause trouble.

A. Efficient Lighting

Improvements in lighting technology have made it possible to provide high-quality lighting with less power.

One of the easiest ways to improve efficiency is to get rid of all incandescent lighting. Decades ago, libraries were lit by incandescent lamps, but they can no longer afford them. (This is another reason we object to quartz halogen lamps. In addition to creating unwanted glare, being dangerously hot, and burning out too quickly, they are an extremely inefficient source of light.)

A major way to conserve electricity is to convert your library from T-12 fluorescent lamps with magnetic ballasts to T-8s lamps with electronic ballasts, which often can be done by using the same fixtures. A pair of 40-watt T-12 lamps with a 9-watt magnetic ballast consumes about 89 watts. A pair of 32-watt T-8 lamps puts out about the same amount of light, and an electronic ballast consumes only about 1 watt. The result is a reduction from 89 to 65 watts, a reduction of more than 25 percent.

A second spinoff from efficient lighting is reduced air conditioning costs. For every three watts we save in lighting, we save about an additional watt in air conditioning load.

Years ago, Fred inherited a library with hundreds of 300-watt incandescent lamps in can lights with black linings. By changing lamp types—still incandescent—and painting the insides of the cans white, the library was able to provide good lighting with 75-watt lamps. The reduction of 225 watts per fixture saved another 75 watts in air conditioning load, for a total savings of 300 watts per light fixture. In essence, this was free lighting—although one could argue that replacing an incredibly stupid lighting system with a much less stupid system hardly qualifies as "free."

> The white linings in the cans also made the light less directional. Library users commented on the "new lighting," and everyone was happy except the original designer.

B. Motion Sensor Switches

Many libraries and offices have motion sensor switches. When we enter rooms, the lights automatically turn on, and a few minutes after we leave they switch off again.

Some codes require motion sensor switches in public restrooms. Other codes, such as the International Energy Conservation Code (IECC), may require that all library lighting be activated by motion sensors or timers.

The major problem with motion sensors is that the lights go off when we sit still too long. People in offices always tell stories of suddenly being in the dark.

One thing you can to do limit the downside of motion sensors is to be sure that no room with motion sensors is ever plunged into total darkness. Be sure that a dim light remains on when the motion sensor lights go out.

> Motion sensor switches have been required in library restrooms for a number of years. Fred encountered a library where the restroom motion sensors did not detect motion in some of the stalls. If anyone was in one of these stalls when the lights went out, no amount of frantic arm waving turned the lights back on. Sitting in a stall in a pitch-dark restroom helplessly waving one's arms in the air may lead to some kind of epiphany, but it is not a really good epiphany.

With motion sensor lighting in restrooms, it's also important that the lights come on when the door opens. No one—particularly in a public building—wants to grope his or her way into a dark room in the uncertain expectation that lighting may eventually come on. Accomplishing this may require motion sensors mounted on the ceilings, not the cheap motion sensors embedded in light switches.

In states that have adopted the IECC, libraries may find that even a large reading room is supposed to have motion sensors, with lights in various areas of the room turning off when no one is there. The result is lights flickering off and on in a single room—a singularly dreadful idea. However, codes that require motion sensors for this purpose may also accept timers, which can be set up to keep lights on at all times the library is open.

> We think that everyone having to wave their hands in the air to turn the lights back on may be the origin of the saying, "Many hands make light work."

C. Daylight Sensors

Some libraries are designed with sensors that turn lights off and on as daylight varies. Reading areas located near windows, for example, may not need much artificial light during the day.

By the same token, areas located under skylights do not always need artificial light by day. (Skylights cause so much other trouble, however, that this is interesting rather than useful information.)

While light sensors work when night falls, some librarians tell us that they don't respond fast enough to work well during days when clouds come and go.

For years, librarians have simply turned lights off and on as outside conditions varied, and that continues to be a workable idea.

Here are some things you can do:

- When sensor-based systems are recommended, always visit another library with the kind of system being recommended for yours. If no such library exists, remember the first-kid-on-the-block effect many libraries experienced when purchasing early automation systems. Some designers talk endlessly

about exciting buildings in the planning stages, but they stop talking about the buildings after they're built. When in doubt, always ask to see a working example.
- Get specific information on warranties on sensors, and ask for full parts and labor coverage that lasts for more than a year.
- Expect to have trouble getting daylight sensors to work properly. They tend to be fooled by reflections.

Even without daylight sensors, you can set up light switches so the lamps closest to the windows can be turned off and on separately using traditional light switches. If you have both east and west windows, you'll want to switch the area next to each side separately.

D. Reduced Illumination Levels and Library Security

Some states have laws limiting the number of watts per square foot that can be used for lighting libraries. Typically, these are stringent enough so that only highly efficient lighting (such as high-quality fluorescent, or LEDs) can provide enough light.

We believe that some of these laws have gone farther than current technology permits.

We are particularly concerned about ideas for keeping the public areas of libraries dimly lit. As public buildings with many secluded spaces and (in the case of public libraries) absolutely no limits on users who haven't yet done unacceptable things, libraries can't afford to provide dark corners suitable for lurking.

E. Limits on Efficacy

Efficacy can go only so far. Once 100 percent of electrical energy has been converted to visible light, there is no way to obtain extra light per watt.

VI. COMMON LIGHTING PROBLEMS AND HOW TO AVOID THEM

Although there are many ways of dealing with lighting problems, by far the best way is to stop bad ideas before they are implemented. Be sure people review your building plans carefully before your project is bid and constructed. Be sure to include your custodians and consultant.

A. Lack of Flexibility

If all of us have learned anything about libraries over the years, it is that they are constantly changing. Every few years, new demands alter the way librarians use spaces in their buildings, and within a few years after a library is constructed, staff start rearranging shelving, service desks, study tables, soft seating, computers, and other equipment.

Because libraries are always rearranging things, lighting needs to be all-purpose and flexible. We provide a basic description of such lighting at the end of this chapter on lighting.

Unfortunately, designers are extremely fond of installing special-purpose lighting that assumes nothing will ever move. (Some argue that, although we moved things around constantly in the past, we now have arrived at the perfect solution and don't need to worry about times yet to come.)

The worst source of inflexibility is architecturally mounted task lighting, described in the section above. Another major error is ceiling-mounted lights parallel to shelving aisles in areas where shelving can be relocated.

B. Glare

High-glare lighting is always popular with designers because it brings drama and chiaroscuro. Uneven lighting is exciting. Picking out special features for brilliant illumination while leaving other areas dim is a characteristic of upscale merchandising. Unfortunately, libraries are a lot better off with big box store lighting than exciting lighting.

High-glare lighting is also popular because fixtures can be unobtrusive. Recessed downlights (always nasty in libraries) fit smoothly into ceilings, but they have little else to recommend them. Strip downlights at ceiling level can be an extremely painful source of glare.

LED lighting can be painfully bright because sources can be extremely compact. By and large, you don't want to look straight into an LED lighting fixture unless it provides a great deal of indirect light.

One of the best ways to avoid glare is to *avoid most or all direct lighting.* If you specify fixtures that provide 70 to 100 percent reflected uplight for your library, ban all fixtures that produce only downlight, and control direct daylight, glare should be minimal.

Historic spaces with dark ceilings usually call for low-level ambient light with task lighting for shelving, reading areas, and staff desks. Notice the shelf lighting unit on the right. The modern wing of the same library has a white ceiling that allows reflected uplighting. (Libraries have used low-level general lighting with supplementary shelf and table lights for generations.)

However, avoiding glare this way is difficult. We recommend you say "NO DIRECT LIGHT WHATSOEVER" in your building program and then watch your designers like hawks.

Another source of glare is lighting designed to produce "sparkle." This is not good library lighting.

C. Gloom

A number of architectural decisions result in libraries that are almost impossible to light effectively or attractively.

Probably the worst of these is dark surfaces. A dark ceiling makes it impossible to reflect light off the ceiling, forcing the library to use some kind of harsh, direct lighting. A bright light fixture in a dark ceiling is a lot nastier than a bright light fixture in a white ceiling. Shelving painted dark colors absorbs too much light (in addition to showing accumulated dust to great effect and freezing your color scheme for many decades to come). Tabletops and desk tops in dark colors add to the gloom (and cause eyestrain). Although the occasional dark wall may be fun, dark walls absorb light rather than reflect it.

Soffits that hang down to less than ten feet from the floor are difficult or impossible to light with reflected uplight. The usual approach designers take is to fill soffits with recessed downlights, creating spotty illumination and glare in the process. Soffits that are painted any color except white on their undersides combine the worst features of dark ceilings and low ceilings.

Some older libraries have historic dark ceilings that need to remain their original colors. In this case, the original scheme of dim allover lighting and task lights on tables and shelves may be the only alternative. But it's insane to design new libraries that way.

D. Dark Perimeters

A surprising number of library rooms are too dark around the edges. This problem comes from a number of easily avoidable designs.

Perimeter soffits around the edges of rooms are a popular design detail, but they are almost always too dark underneath. Sometimes the situation is made worse by painting the undersides of the soffits a dark color. Because the soffits are close to the floor, designers tend to install rows of can lights in the soffits. The result is extremely spotty lighting near the bottom of the soffit, odd patterns of light and dark on the walls, and truly nasty direct glare for anyone who makes the mistake of looking upward.

The combination of perimeter soffits with downlights and perimeter shelving is found in many libraries, and it's always an unfortunate idea. Light on the books on the top shelves is irregular, the can lights cast harsh shadows (making it easy for users to block their own light), and looking up at a top shelf often involves staring straight into the glare of a can light, making it nearly impossible to read the spines of the nearby books.

If architectural detail around the perimeter of a room is desired, crown moldings are more attractive than soffits and don't cause illumination problems.

Another cause of dark perimeters is badly spaced light fixtures. If rows of fixtures are spaced six feet apart (for example) in a large room, the space between the last row of fixtures and the wall should be only three feet. This way, no place in the room is more than three feet from a fixture. Frequently, however, designers leave six feet between the last row of fixtures and the wall. Now everywhere in the room except the edges is within three feet of a fixture, but the walls can be up to six feet from the nearest fixture. In some libraries, the situation is even more extreme, with the last rows of fixtures even further from the walls.

We have even seen libraries where no lights were installed over the aisles closest to the walls, and new fixtures had to be awkwardly retrofitted.

E. Architectural Features That Complicate Lighting

A variety of architectural designs lead to lighting problems in libraries. Here are a few to watch out for.

- *Low ceilings.* It's hard to light any library space with a ceiling less than ten feet high, because suspended (pendant) uplight fixtures need to be at least eight feet off the floor and a couple of feet below the ceiling. Low ceilings are particularly characteristic of libraries with balconies, where the ceilings over the balcony spaces and the spaces underneath the balconies are all too low to light.
- *Soffits.* We've mentioned problems with soffits endlessly. Soffits help to interrupt huge, boring expanses of ceiling, but they must not prevent the uniform use of reflected uplighting. Some new libraries feature unruly masses of soffits and promise nothing good for the future. It's a good thing to tell your designers "No soffits" at the start of your project.

- *Dark ceilings.* The moment designers introduce dark ceilings they are forced to use direct lighting, with all the resulting problems with uneven illumination and glare. Librarians sometimes inherit historic dark ceilings, but there's no need to create new ones. If you have a (non-historic) dark ceiling in your library and paint it white, you will be amazed at how the character of the space changes.
- *Atriums.* It's hard to light atriums. Ceiling lights are too far from the floor to maintain unless they can be lowered to the floor. Many atriums have downlights with the subtle look of railroad headlights. (Since atriums also waste space and energy and cause problems with acoustics and user safety, you don't have to fall back on lighting problems alone as a reason to ban them from your building.)
- *Monumental staircases.* Always find out how the lamps in light fixtures over staircases will be changed. If the fixtures are not over landings, even tall ladders may not work, and renting lifts is expensive. (In the old days of incandescent lamps, one could use a long pole with a grabber at the end to change incandescent can lights from below. But most fluorescent lights use lamps that require people to stick their hands into the fixtures to change the lamps.)
- *Skylights.* Skylights are sources of manifest evil in libraries. When it comes to lighting, spaces under skylights are too dark by night and too bright by day. Looking up into skylights (and people have to look up at high shelves) is unpleasant, and the glare may make it impossible to see the shelves. Lighting areas under skylights at night is tricky, because reflected uplight doesn't work. Actually, a lot of library skylights these days are made of translucent, insulated material called Kalwall, which consists of two translucent fiberglass sheets with insulation between them. If you're willing to waste some energy into the night sky, you can bounce light directly off Kalwall. Although we dislike skylights in libraries intensely, if for some reason they are absolutely essential, Kalwall appears to be a very good material. But we still think skylights should be banned from all libraries.

F. Lighting That Is Hard to Maintain

Some forms of lighting are notoriously difficult to maintain.

Among the questions that you (and your custodians) should ask when reviewing designs, one of the most important is how lamps will be changed.

In many libraries and other buildings, some lamps are almost impossible to reach.

When can lights are located high in the air over staircases, it's hard to figure out where to put a ladder or lift when lamps are changed. This campus building is notorious among the university's maintenance staff.

Always insist on very specific answers when you ask your designers how remote devices will be serviced. ("Use a lift" is never a sufficient answer.) The lonely light fixture high above the entrance to this area could not be reached from above, and the design of the doors at the bottom prevented a lift from being brought in. The university upon which this light fixture was inflicted replaced the bulb once by building a several story scaffold, but after seeing the cost they never replaced the bulb again.

Chapter 25 ■ Lighting   751

The attractive arch of light bulbs over this service desk has to be kept turned off because there is no way to reach the bulbs when they burn out without building a scaffolding on top of the desk. (The library tried to place a huge sheet of plywood over the desk to support a stepladder, but apparently it didn't work.) When neatly-spaced light bulbs are used as ornaments, any burnt-out bulb becomes an instant eyesore, spoiling an attractive design.

Fred has been collecting photographs of unreachable light fixtures. Some require the construction of multistory scaffolds each time the lamp needs to be changed (and as a result, the lamps are never replaced once they burn out).

Here are some things you can do.

- Always check with your custodians before approving light fixtures and their placement. (Maintenance people at universities complain that they point out problems in lighting plans, only to find the buildings constructed unchanged and the maintenance staff stuck with trying to change the lamps. But it's still worth fighting for rationality.)
- Begin with the requirement that all lamps can be changed by someone using an eight-foot stepladder. You may have to compromise, but be extremely insistent that your designers provide you with exact maintenance information.

- If your architect nonchalantly tells you that your custodian can "use a lift," insist that the lift and its storage space be included in the project budget. Require that someone verify that the lift can actually fit through the spaces it needs to, and that the furniture, such as shelving, will not have to be moved to make room for the lift.
- If you have high chandeliers that can't be reached with a reasonable stepladder, insist that they be on electric drops so they can be serviced at floor level.
- Avoid fixtures that have to be disassembled in tricky ways before lamps can be changed. This requires close study of cut sheets for proposed fixtures. Fred's library had a fixture in an atrium that required two men standing on lifts to disassemble it in midair before lamps could be changed.

Cold cathode fluorescent lamps are available in decorative curved shapes, but the cost of maintenance can be extraordinary. This library fixture is almost never turned on because the cost of totally replacing burnt out curved fluorescent lamps would probably exceed $20,000.

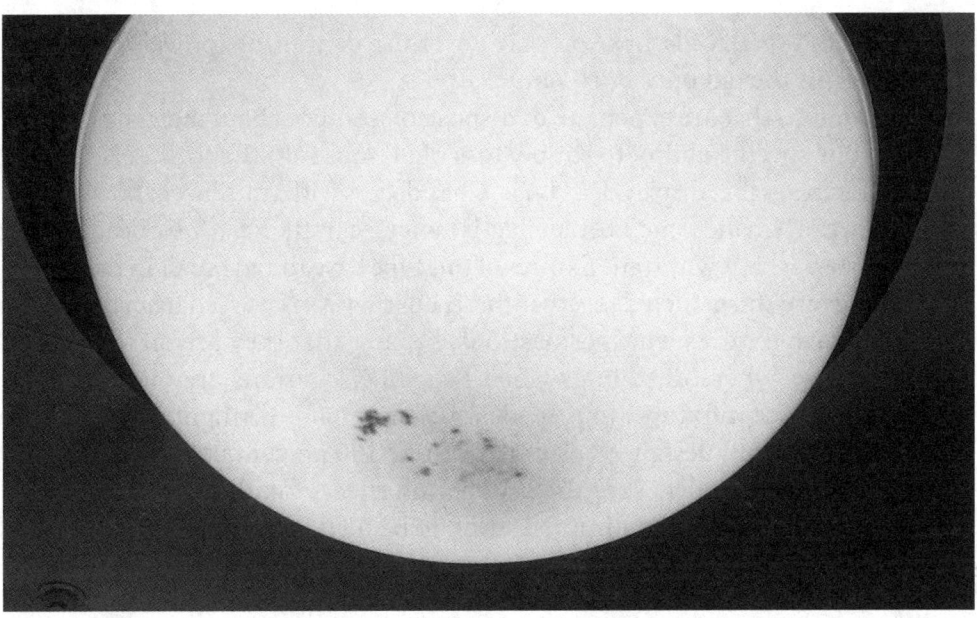

Luckily, fixtures are available with opaque central ornaments to hide the bugs. Unluckily, many designers don't select them. (Campus maintenance staffs have described removing literal bushels of dead bugs from light fixtures.)

- Be particularly careful when your designers are proposing to locate light fixtures over staircases. Find out exactly where the person changing the lamp will stand. Even if your ceilings are reasonably low, the ceiling over a staircase may be impressively high, and there may be no way to reach the light fixtures once the construction scaffolding is removed.
- Stand guard over the brands of electronic ballasts supplied with your light fixtures. Even if you specify (for example) three fixtures with high-quality ballasts available locally, your contractor may ask to substitute something different as an "equivalent." Be sure your architect knows that you will not accept any fixture with a ballast not stocked in your best local-area electric supply firm.
- Avoid multiple lamp types. There's no excuse for having more than half-a-dozen or so different lamp types in a library. The cost and space required to warehouse fifty different lamp types can be depressing.
- Avoid extremely expensive lamps. For all unusual or specialized lighting, ask your designers to provide information on the replacement cost of lamps. Finding out that your clever light fixtures have lamps that cost $1,200 each and come from far overseas gives you a choice of stocking many thousands

of dollars' worth of lamps you may never use or waiting forever to get new ones when the old ones burn out.
- Avoid lamps that are expensive to dispose of. Inquire about mercury content and your specific ability to simply toss old lamps into the trash.
- Avoid fixtures that display dead bugs. Chandeliers with translucent bowls at the bottom can be handsome, but the effect is tempered by the handful of dead bugs in the center. (This is why some fixtures of this type have round finials in the center. The bugs are still gathered together there, but they can't be seen from the floor.) If you have fixtures with perforations, be sure that they are on the side of the fixture, where dead bugs won't show. Perforations are often used in strip fluorescent fixtures to provide an element of downlight. We find this unnecessary, but designers generally dislike 100 percent uplight.
- Require that installers save the instruction sheets for all light fixtures and give them to the library administration to be filed with other building data. Electricians, who deal with this equipment on a daily basis, will not find it puzzling when it needs attention in years to come, but the rest of us may need the instruction sheets.
- As much as possible, locate light switches in staff areas. This prevents users from playing with the lights.

> One of Fred's earliest memories of public libraries is his stretching to reach a long brass switch plate by the public entrance to the main reading room of the Detroit Lakes (Minnesota) Public Library and turning off all the lights one by one. His father reached him just as the last light went out.

G. Buying Lighting

We have found a few helpful ideas when it comes to purchasing lighting.

- Negotiated government discounts. If you run a government-owned library, it's very worthwhile finding out whether your state has an agency that arranges centralized purchasing of items like electric lamps. In Illinois, government agencies were able to buy fluorescent lamps by a major manufacturer at about an 85 percent discount from list price, bringing the cost of a top-of-the-line $12.00 tube down to about $2.00. Depending on the agency, there may be simple requirements for participation, such as a formal motion by your governing agency.

- Lamps from major manufacturers. When you are specifying lighting for a building, stick with products from major manufacturers in the hope you will be able to buy matching lamps when yours burn out.
- Door-to-door lamp salespeople. There are some dubious high-pressure door-to-door salespeople who sell high-priced off-brand lamps, contending that these products are of a quality far superior to everyday lamps. Our experience suggests very much otherwise. Despite the persuasive sales literature, we find this kind of product expensive and of no better quality than standard lighting. We think you are far better off dealing with lamps manufactured by major manufacturers and stocked by large electrical firms. After a few experiences, Fred refused even to speak with lamp salespeople.

H. Pendant Globe Lights and Other Gimmicks

Every age has its own lighting gimmick.

One recent gimmick was pendant lights, cute colored glass shapes hanging from the ceiling. The fixtures glow attractively, but the lamp inside often projected small circles of blazingly bright light straight downward. Unfortunately, no reader benefits from a spot of brilliant light in the middle of an otherwise dimly lit table.

Pendant lights with clear glass shades can be blinding to look at from any direction.

If your designer proposes pendant globe lights, check out an installation before you say "yes." Many can be found in recently decorated restaurants and bars.

One library Fred dealt with ripped out all of its pendant globe lights in terminal annoyance before he had a chance to comment on them.

I. Troublesome Security Lighting

Most modern libraries are designed so that public areas are never completely dark. After all the lights have been shut off for the night, occasional fixtures have a single fluorescent tube that stays illuminated at all times. This allows staff members to negotiate the darkened library on their way out the door at night without tripping over furniture or abandoned skateboards.

Night-lights of this type work well, but they can cause trouble in meeting room or classroom spaces, where you may want to turn off all the lights. Always specify that there be some way to turn off security lights in these rooms.

Among the high-maintenance items in many libraries are the small battery-powered LED emergency lighting units that come on whenever the power fails. Even a medium-sized library can have dozens of them. The units are ingenious. While the power is on, they charge continuously, and the connection to the library's power supply provides constant information on whether the power is on or off.

Battery-powered units of this type are also prone to failure. Every time the fire marshals arrive to check your library, they'll find units that no longer work.

Another (albeit more expensive) option is to use a powerful central battery to power all the night-lights in the building. Units of this type use an inverter, a device that changes the DC of the battery to the AC necessary to operate fluorescent light fixtures. When the time comes to construct your new library, you might inquire about this type of emergency lighting.

J. Historic Lighting Fixtures

Although simple fluorescent strip uplight fixtures can be used effectively in historic buildings, there are situations where something more elaborate is required.

One of the easy solutions is to equip historic fixtures with relatively dim incandescent lamps and provide the actual uplighting from another source.

Earlier we mentioned how the Indianapolis Public Library uses an installation of this kind. The lamps in the great wagon-wheel fixtures were dim enough to avoid glare. The real light came from invisible lamps on top of the fixtures, projecting light upward on the ceiling.

To library users, the feeling was historic, and they don't have to know that the visible lamps are there just to create a pleasant atmosphere reassuring viewers that the light in the room came from understandable place.

Modern uplighting fixtures can also be incorporated in historic rooms with little feeling of inappropriateness, and they may be less obtrusive than the rows of hanging-bowl chandeliers that are sometimes used.

VII. AN EASY FORMULA FOR MULTIFUNCTION LIBRARY LIGHTING

We are convinced that the best way to light general library spaces is with reflected uplighting fixtures hung from the ceiling. This approach allows the endless rearrangement of furniture without expensive changes in light fixtures or wiring. All of the equipment listed is extremely everyday and uncomplicated.

The general specifications include:

- Ceiling height of at least ten feet. Eleven or twelve feet works even better.
- Strip fluorescent or LED uplight fixtures installed end to end, about eight feet above the floor.
- Some fixtures have patterns of small holes on the sides ("perforations" or "perfs") while others are solid metal. We prefer solid metal or perfs, but not slots, on the sides of the fixtures. (Perforations at the bottoms of fixtures display dead bugs, while slots in fixtures let too much blinding light through.)
- LEDs or T-8 fluorescent lamps with electronic ballasts. T-5s are efficient and popular, but they are so bright to look at that you won't want them if your fixtures have perfs. T-5s also appear to have lower CRIs than T-8s do.
- All lamps with a minimum CRI of 85. Some uplight fixtures use biax tubes, small-diameter folded tubes that plug into a socket. Many of these, however, have lower CRIs.
- Color temperature of 3500K.
- One standard type of lamp. Because uplight fixtures shine their light on white ceilings, any variation in color or quality is extremely apparent.
- Fixtures spaced to yield about 60 foot-candles at desktop.
- Fixtures designed to allow at least 50 foot-candles of light to fall on the pages of books held vertically.

VIII. COPING WITH NATURAL LIGHT

Natural light is undependable. It varies from too bright to too dark. And everyone wants it.

When we prepare building programs for new library structures, we always ask the staff what's most important in their workspaces. And they always tell us "windows."

Nothing is sadder than to do a post-occupancy study of a new library building where many of the staff are stuck in windowless basement rooms, along with storage and HVAC.

The importance of natural light is a major argument for avoiding basements in libraries. (Another and even better argument involves water.)

Basements in houses provide inexpensive space, but basements in libraries are almost as expensive as floors above the ground. It's hard to excuse them.

A. Compass Points Matter

In the continental United States at least, the direction of light matters a great deal.

- North light is by far the best light for reading and work. The sun almost never shines directly through north windows.
- West light is the worst. When the sun sets on summer evenings, light through western windows comes blasting in and takes out retinas. Libraries that have west windows without effective blinds find that computers can't be used at busy times in the afternoon and evening. If a library entrance faces west, staff members at a service desk facing the entrance may find that it's almost impossible to work late in the day with the direct sun in their faces.

This library copes with direct sunlight on its east windows by installing awnings that can be removed in the winter, when sunlight comes mostly from the south. (The awnings work because the sun is fairly high in the sky by the time the library opens in the morning. If the windows were on the west side of the building, the setting sun would blast between the bottom edges of the awnings and the window sills, taking out the retinas of people inside.) Awnings this large need to be lashed to removable frames in order to withstand wind.
Photo credit: Benjamin Halpern.

One way to provide natural light is through clearstory windows—windows set vertically in a roof. If the windows face directly north (as these do) the result can be wonderful lighting. If they face other directions, they let in direct sunlight, which tends to be blindingly awful.

- East light on summer mornings can be equally harsh, but libraries are seldom open at dawn. By the time libraries are ready for business, the sun is high enough in the sky for building overhangs or summer awnings to control unwanted light.
- South light is a mixed blessing. In the summer, the sun can be almost directly overhead, and building overhangs can keep the direct sun out of south windows. In the winter, when the sun is lower in the southern sky, some users enjoy sitting in sunny windows to read. But south light that falls directly on service desks or computers is always seriously nasty.

These different qualities of daylight are another reason to have the long dimension of library buildings east-west. If the long walls face north and south, libraries maximize desirable north and south light and minimize problems with east and west light.

Since north entrances are always cold, one approach is to have a sheltered south entrance and concentrate reader seating on the north side of the building.

One can make a very good argument for avoiding west light entirely. If one end of the building must house HVAC gear and garages, why not make it the west end?

This attractive library entrance faces south, which means that the daylight coming through the glass is brutal in the winter. When southern sunlight shines on the service desk inside the door, workers are blinded. Given the complex shape of the windows, adding blinds would be challenging—if not impossible. The library could do as others have done and add dark gray film to the glass to block the sunlight, but that would spoil the appearance of things and make one wonder (as many other libraries have done in similar situations) why the designer provided the glass in the first place.

In this library, a small awning meant the difference between an unassuming door and an attractive friends-of-the-library shop.

B. Controlling Daylight

Building designs are extremely subject to vogues and passing enthusiasms. In the 1960s we had an excess of glass boxes, and we seem to be there again.

Because glass walls are never as well insulated as the best masonry walls, we wonder why glass buildings continue to be constructed given the current emphasis on green architecture.

Some designers assure their clients that with modern glass, west light is no longer a problem. We think that with modern glass, west light can be *less* of a problem, but that you still will hate it if you don't have working blinds.

Libraries with glass walls can save a lot more energy by preventing daylight from falling on the outside of the glass than by blocking the daylight with blinds, particularly dark blinds. By the time daylight enters the building, much of the accompanying heat (solar gain) stays in the building. This is why awnings save more cooling energy than Venetian blinds.

The easy way to control daylight is to control how and where windows are planned.

If you're already stuck with windows facing in bad directions, some possibilities include:

- *Exterior awnings.* These can look very attractive, particularly on eastern windows. By the time library opens on summer mornings, the sun is high enough in the sky so that no light falls through the east windows. Awnings of this size need to be lashed to frameworks to prevent them from blowing away in strong winds. When the sun shifts to the south in the winter, the awnings and their frameworks can be dismantled to let light from the eastern sky enter the library.
- *Vertical Venetian blinds.* Vertical blinds offer an opportunity to angle the slats so that daylight is visible but sun doesn't enter. (Obviously this works only when light is striking the windows at an angle.) One problem with vertical blinds, however, is that they are fragile and frequently damaged by library users or by furniture bumping against them.
- *Perforated vinyl roller blinds.* Blinds of this type have been used very satisfactorily in a number of libraries. While blocking most of the sunshine, they still allow users to see what's outside the building. We recommend that you always use white blinds, which save cooling energy by bouncing some light back out the window and save lighting energy by bouncing interior light rather than absorbing it. By reflecting interior light, white

blinds also improve illumination and make rooms look less dark when the blinds are pulled.
- *Traditional Venetian blinds.* Blinds with horizontal slats do a very effective job of blocking direct sunlight, although enough light leaks around the edges of the slats to prevent the near total blockage of light needed (for example) by some image projection systems. Remember that dark blinds absorb more heat than light blinds do and are somewhat less energy-efficient during cooling seasons. And consider the fun of dusting Venetian blinds.

Unfortunately, some daylight is extremely difficult to control. For example, Fred consulted with a library that has a huge reading room with a cathedral ceiling. At one end of the room, the ridgepole is lowered a few feet, and a chevron of glass connects the higher and lower cathedral ceilings. Unfortunately, the chevron faces west, and because of its configuration it doesn't lend itself to any kind of blinds. During the afternoon, light through the chevron passed slowly over the reading tables and computers, constantly forcing users to relocate until the library covered the glass chevron with a dark film.

> Another library Fred worked with had a cathedral ceiling with small dormer windows set high in the ceiling, also facing west. Because the dormers were set in the middle of slopes, they defied the installation of blinds and were a daily source of unpleasant glare.

Other libraries have rectangular west windows with blinds, topped by arched or triangular windows without blinds. Unfortunately, the western sun can be just as nasty when it comes through an arched window.

Another problem is "monitor" structures, which are raised portions of the roof with vertical glass walls on all sides. Usually these cause nothing but trouble because there is no way to put blinds on the glass sides of the monitors.

When you visit libraries with vertical glass sections set high above the floor, look for signs of nasty glare. Also look for the retrospective installation of dark gray transparent material on the glass of windows that don't face north.

The moral of all this is, never locate a west, south, or east window where you can't install a blind.

This library was equipped with high windows facing west. The resulting afternoon light was blinding. Fitting blinds into windows with sloped tops is difficult, but the library found a good solution by using vertical Venetian blinds. Other libraries with windows set higher in their exterior walls are frequently forced to add dark gray plastic film to the windows, making one wonder why the designers provided the windows in the first place.

One of the problems with historic skylights is figuring out how to provide light at night. This library has added a hanging fluorescent fixture. Others have depended on lamp fixtures mounted on service desks or reading tables. Some libraries have dealt with inconsistent brightness in historic skylights by providing artificial lighting.

Avoid skylights. In this library, as the sun crosses the sky during the day, direct sunlight falls on these service desk computers, making them impossible to use.

Artificial skylights with constant illumination levels work a lot better than skylights that rely on the uncertainty of sunlight. But maintenance can be complex. To change the lights in this skylight, workers span the area between the railings with long planks, place plywood sheets on the planks, and then stand on the assembly to change the lights. (The railings have the kind of horizontal balusters that encourage young visitors to climb up and fall off.)

C. Skylights

Skylights offer a particularly effective example of unwanted light because it is difficult to block light that falls through skylights. Everyday shades and blinds don't work.

In a number of places in this book, we dwell on the fact that skylights and libraries are an extraordinarily bad combination. When it comes to lighting, the areas under skylights are too bright by day and too dark by night. (Skylights also reflect noise and leak, but that's for other chapters.)

Libraries are full of examples of the negative effects of skylights on practical library lighting. For example, we know one library that has a cathedral ceiling over its children's department, with a skylight running along the peak. Since the ridgepole runs from north to south, a band of hot daylight crosses the department each day, as the sun moves from east to west over the building. When the band of light falls on the reference desk, all computer work must cease.

Fred once had an office with this skylight. The area under the skylight was too bright by day and too dark by night. And it leaked, as the plaster damage shows. When the building was expanded, the skylight was joyously removed and roofed over. Although this was a small skylight, its failings are shared on a larger and more unpleasant scale by much larger and more elaborate skylights. Always say "No" when talk of skylights arises.

Another library has skylights over staff desks. Direct sun through the skylights made it impossible for staff members to work, so they installed horizontal rods on the ceiling and draped fabric panels under each skylight.

Another library with a huge skylight has large movable fabric panels running on wire tracks.

Once skylights have been installed in buildings, getting rid of them is expensive. The right time to say "no" (loudly) is when they are first proposed. We write "no skylights" in our building programs. *Writing "absolutely no skylights" is even better.*

One favorite cliché in library design is to connect new and old buildings with large skylights. We know a number of libraries that were initially enthusiastic about this feature but came to hate it. Areas under huge skylights are hard to use. They're noisy, the sun fades the books, and light levels are seldom pleasant for reading. We think it's easy for spaces of this type to end up as noisy concourses, expensive structures to pass through rather than occupy.

The extremely negative effects of skylights can be tempered slightly by using translucent, insulated materials like Kalwall, but even then we find large skylights a major problem.

D. Effects of Unwanted Daylight

Daylight is vastly brighter than any artificial light used for general library illumination.

The contrast between direct sunlight and good artificial light is so great that it can be almost impossible to read under a mixture of the two.

Libraries with shelving that is subject to daily direct sunlight have book spines and labels that have faded to a uniform pale gray.

E. Views of the Outside World

In historic libraries, windows served primarily to illuminate reading areas. In both great university libraries and in small Carnegie-era libraries, windows were set high in the walls, often above wall-mounted shelving.

Many readers today, however, want to be able to see the world go by while they are reading. What, one might ask rhetorically, could be more fun than reading new books while drinking coffee and keeping an eye on the passing throng?

With new buildings, setting windowsills about 24 or 30 inches from the floor is easy. But with expanded historic buildings, it's also easy to have lower windowsills. If the rest of the new windows match the older windows in all other ways, the difference in height of windowsills is not particularly noticeable.

IX. A FINAL WORD ON LIGHTING

Bad lighting is one of the most frequently encountered problems in both old and new library buildings.

Unfortunately, functional library lighting is not exciting to some designers, who want to bring in clouds of glorious daylight, create exciting patterns of darkness and light, and use whatever is the current vogue in novelty lighting fixtures.

Our response is that creating excitement with light in a library is like creating excitement with steps in a nursing home.

X. SNAPPY RULES ON LIBRARY LIGHTING

1. The best way to light a library is to bounce light off a white ceiling.
2. Never compromise on color rendering index (CRI). There's no need to accept anything less than 85.
3. Color temperature is of major importance. People like artificial lighting to be warm-colored—about 3000K to 3500K.
4. Beware of overly expensive lamps (light bulbs). Always inquire about unusual lamps before you approve fixtures. If your lamps cost over $1,000 each to replace (and some curved tube lamps do), they had better be more wonderful than one would believe possible.
5. Unless you suffer from a surfeit of storerooms and maintenance funds, severely limit the number of lamp types and fixtures.
6. Know how you will change your lamps. If your designer says "Use a lift," that is about as helpful as being told to "Use a screwdriver" when you ask how to rebuild the carburetor on your XKE.
7. For situations where lamps will be turned off and on frequently—meeting rooms, some restrooms, and rooms with detectors for natural light—avoid HID lighting, which has a lot of trouble starting and stopping.

8. Avoid direct lighting. The result is always glare and spotty illumination.
9. Any window that can admit direct sunlight needs a blind. "Modern glass" is not a substitute.
10. If your designers insist that you're wrong about modern glass, demand that they show you an installation that works. And test it out in direct sunlight.
11. Avoid incandescent lamps. The worst are quartz halogen lamps, which are unfortunately beloved of some designers. (Luckily, most quartz halogen lamps in most libraries have the life span of gnats and are usually burned out.)
12. Avoid skylights with a passion. Areas under skylights are too dark by night, too bright by day, and noisy. And skylights leak. (Some architects are seriously enamored of skylights, and you will have to be very firm.)
13. Be sure your lighting is bright enough. Anything less than 50 foot-candles of soft, even light is unacceptable, and 60 foot-candles is a lot better.
14. Entryways need to be bright and welcoming, with glowing walls and ceilings even though all most people do is move on through them.
15. Architecturally mounted task lighting is evil. Or at the very least really, really dumb.
16. Perimeter soffits with recessed downlights are beloved of many designers, but they provide rotten light. So do soffits with recessed downlights over service desks.
17. Parabolic lenses in fluorescent light fixtures are designed to direct light straight downward, creating glare and bad light distribution.
18. Can lights (recessed downlights) are inevitably a terrible idea. Tell your designers from the start that you will have none of that.
19. Motion detectors may be called for in codes. Fight them passionately in reading rooms. When you are stuck with them in smaller rooms, insist that they be activated by the motion of doors, not by people entering a room.
20. Motion detectors can be paired with detectors that measure the presence of people in other ways, to reduce the chance of users and staff being plunged into darkness. Talk with your electrical engineers.
21. Avoid tricksy switching of lights in meeting rooms that will be used by people who have not received special training. Most intelligent and well-educated people have not received special training.
22. People who want to read with their books held vertically should be accommodated.
23. Be particularly wary of bits of windows too high above the floor to allow blinds. If they face any direction except due north, you'll end up retrofitting dark gray plastic films and wondering why you wasted money on the windows in the first place.
24. Be very afraid when people start talking about "glorious" light.

25. A favorite (and in our opinion unsatisfactory) location for motion detectors in smaller spaces is in the box where the light switch would be located at the entrance to a room. Unfortunately, these are not activated by the motion of doors and force people to grope their way into dark rooms. Groping your way into a dark room (particularly a restroom) may seem adventurous, but in reality it's no fun at all.
26. Skylights are always evil in libraries. Tiny little skylights are lesser evils than huge skylights, but only because they're smaller. Always tell your designers "No skylights," and then watch them like hawks.
27. The combination of atrium, lending desk, ceramic tile floor, skylight, floating staircase, and open-sided balconies with railings that can be climbed like ladders is not just evil but evil in an almost biblical sense. Unfortunately, the whole idea appeals passionately to some designers, who will need to be sat upon firmly. (Reminding your designers that the whole arrangement is an extremely well-worn cliché may help more than pointing out that it's spectacularly dysfunctional.)
28. With the exception of study rooms, program rooms, and faculty studies, put light switches where library users can't play around with them.
29. Instead of motion detectors for stack aisles, consider pressure switches, which won't let the lights go off just because a user is standing too quietly.
30. In days gone by, high windows in reading rooms served to provide light. These days lots of readers enjoy windows with sills low enough to allow them to see passing traffic while they read.
31. Round lamps on tabletops are cute, but many of them don't provide useful lighting. If you want light for reading, the easiest approach is straight fixtures that run the length of the tabletops. Or experiment first with sample round light.
32. The light at the end of the tunnel is burned out again.

26

Elevators, Staircases, Railings, and Ramps

I. INTRODUCTION

Moving people between floors in a library should be a simple, straightforward undertaking, but it all too often goes awry.

The easiest way to cope with this situation is to build one-story buildings at grade level. Certainly, any building less than 40,000 or so square feet can easily be constructed this way, avoiding the cost of elevators and staircases, avoiding the abuse of users and staff with acrophobia, avoiding people falling on staircases, avoiding users struggling up ramps in the rain, avoiding hiring extra staff to watch extra floors, avoiding the excitement of wondering when the basement will flood, avoiding the high cost of constructing floors strong enough to hold books, and avoiding other bad things.

If a building does have more than one level, the easy thing to do is to avoid converting the connections between the levels into architectural statements. Staircases need to be safe and relatively enclosed, not exciting and soaring monuments. Floating staircases in the middle of atriums are a seriously overworked architectural cliché, but they refuse to go away, terrifying library users on a regular basis.

Some historic library buildings are just plain inaccessible and need to be updated. Unless the building has a single floor that's only a foot or two above grade level, the only solution is an elevator.

Accessibility issues are not just for people who use wheelchairs. Parents who have children in strollers have a terrible time with steps. Lots of people have walkers. Icy steps in the bleak midwinter are a menace to many otherwise highly mobile people. Herding three or four children upstairs is a lot harder than shooing them into an elevator, keeping their fingers out of the door, and pressing "up."

The main points in this chapter concern safety, but there's also some material on maintenance and upkeep.

When architects use the word *conveyance* in cost estimates, they're talking about moving people between floors.

See also chapter 13 on "Remodeling and Expanding Library Buildings."

II. ELEVATORS

If you have a library with more than one floor, or with a floor that is nowhere near grade level, you need a mechanical way to move users from outside the library to the inside, and to move them between floors.

A. Real Elevators

The civilized way to move people between floors is with elevators, and most codes simply require them. However, there are a lot of old multistory library buildings out there that have no elevators and desperately need to be modernized.

A standard way of dealing with two-level, Carnegie-era public libraries is to install an elevator with doors on two sides. One door opens at ground level and the other opens at floor levels in the library—basement, main floor, and sometimes additional floors.

The problem with an elevator like this is that it can compromise collection security. Unless there is a staffed desk at ground level, users can sometimes leave the library without passing by any service desk.

To deal with this problem, larger historic libraries have provided one elevator to lift people from the entry to the main floor. After passing through security gates, library users can then go to one or more elevators that connect all the floors of the library.

Elevators are available in a variety of sizes. If you are installing a brand-new one in a new elevator shaft, ask about accommodation for people in motorized wheelchairs, parents with large strollers, day care groups with only two teachers, people moving furniture, emergency workers moving people on gurneys, and other users requiring open space.

Almost all new elevators that serve up to half-a-dozen floors are based on the operating principle of grease racks. A hydraulic piston lifts the elevator from floor to floor.

Many codes and other rules affect the installation and operation of elevators.

B. Elevator Maintenance and Problems

When you are selecting an elevator, consider:

- If you have a video security system, do you want a camera in the elevator? (Getting security people and elevator people to work happily together may take work, but you can do it.)
- Do your local emergency services have any special requirements? For example, an elevator large enough for a gurney makes things a great deal easier in times of trouble. (Having to tilt seriously ill people on stretchers up on end to fit them into small elevators is not very friendly.)
- How does the elevator respond in case of emergencies? Does it automatically carry passengers to the entry level floor, where the doors open and controls are then limited to emergency personnel? Or do signs simply warn users not to use the elevator in case of emergency? To what degree are your options limited by codes?
- What mechanisms are included to prevent doors from closing on people? What about small children?
- Is your building large enough to require a second elevator?
- If your first floor is above grade level, do you have an elevator to move people between grade level and the main floor? (If you have to move people more than a foot or so vertically, a ramp—particularly an exterior ramp—is an uncivilized idea.)
- If you have a large meeting room that is not on your main floor, what kind of elevators will you need to handle a large number of people leaving at the same time? (Even if viewers arrive one by one, they tend to leave as a mob.)
- Will people who avoid your floating staircases because of their acrophobia appreciate your exciting glass-walled elevators?
- In addition to people with acrophobia, there are also people with claustrophobia who may not enjoy being in small elevator cars.

A few things go wrong with elevators. Luckily, most of them are minor, but some can lead to serious problems,

- Elevators stall between floors. Usually this means a quick rescue trip by the elevator company, but occasionally people trapped inside elevators disintegrate psychologically, and rapid rescue by emergency services is essential. It helps to have a library staff member stand outside the elevator and try to keep the victim calm until help arrives. Not only do people panic when trapped in elevators, but emergency service personnel can also damage elevators when they force their way in to rescue people. As a result, when elevator companies learn of trapped passengers in library elevators, they make a mad dash for the library. The dangers due to stalled elevators are greater when people work alone late at night. When Fred was alone in a building he would use the elevator as a dumbwaiter, sending objects up and down while he used the stairs. Many elevators come with devices that can crank open elevator doors in emergency situations. It helps to keep yours at the lending desk or some other location that is always staffed.
- Sometimes elevator doors close too quickly, pinching users in unacceptable ways. This is usually a matter of installation problems. Getting things adjusted correctly is part of the punch listing process, and you may have to stand your ground until everything is working perfectly.
- Very occasionally, elevator doors can appear to be reacting to invisible stimuli, repeatedly opening and closing when there's no one there. This is a good time to have things adjusted.
- Occasionally, elevator doors open when the car is not aligned properly with the outside floor, and this can lead to serious problems.

> This happened once in Fred's library. A staff member in a wheelchair didn't see the misalignment, rolled into the open elevator door, fell into the elevator car, tipped over, and broke a leg.

- Elevator sumps can be the lowest places in the library. Yours will have a pump and perhaps a backwater valve.
- Despite all sorts of fictional fears, modern elevators don't suddenly plummet down their shafts. Elevators that serve only a few stories are hydraulic, basically multistory grease racks. If the hydraulic systems spring leaks, the cars simply sink slowly. If higher elevators are hoisted by cables, releasing the tension on the cables engages brakes that rub against the guide rails, and the elevators slide down slowly.

- Occasionally, library users vandalize elevators because users feel invisible once the doors are closed. It helps to have video surveillance.
- Some elevators have switches that allow users to stop the elevators between floors. This may lead to problems with teenagers.

> An elevator in Fred's library had a sign beside an indicator light on the fire control panel that said, "When flashing, exit elevator." He felt that this was the kind of behavior the library was actually trying to discourage.

Elevators require maintenance. You will probably want a maintenance contract, especially for those exciting times when someone is caught between floors in a stalled elevator and is starting to hyperventilate. When you are selecting an elevator, always inquire about local maintenance and any extra charges for after-hours calls when people are trapped.

> Elevator companies are eager to be the first to arrive because emergency services can do a great deal of damage to stalled elevators when they fight their way in to rescue panicked people.

Codes will require that your elevator be inspected on a regular basis. Most elevator cars include places where inspection certificates can be displayed, but some building owners keep the original certificates in secure places and post facsimiles or signs announcing where the certificates can be inspected. We assume that this is usually in response to the theft of original certificates from elevator cars.

C. Unfortunate Substitutes for Real Elevators

Many libraries have used unfortunate substitutes for elevators, either to save money (elevators are expensive) or to save space. We know many libraries that are unhappy with their choices.

There are a huge number of products available in this area. Our coverage is extremely brief because we think that while they may be suitable for home use, substitutes for elevators are never suitable for libraries.

A standard substitute used by Carnegie-era libraries is a platform lift, either one sitting on the floor of a room at grade level or one enclosed in a shaft. Some lifts are placed outside buildings, next to entry stoops, and can move people from ground level to the main floor.

Lifts have a number of problems.

- Lifts sometimes serve only the main floor of a library and not the basement, making the building only partially accessible.
- Lifts can require serious effort to open and close doors manually. Library staff may need to run down to the entry foyer, open the lift door for the user in a wheelchair, then run back upstairs to open the upper door.
- Lifts can be so small inside that no one can accompany the person using a wheelchair.
- Fitting a lift into a building may still require the construction of an exterior enclosure for the lift.

We know of some libraries that have installed chair lifts on staircases. These can be platforms that provide a flat space large enough for a wheelchair. The lift maintains a fixed distance from the stairs and simply rides up following the stairs.

Remember that some users use lifts not because they are in wheelchairs but because they cannot bend their legs or have bad balance and are afraid of falling on staircases. Because they will be standing up they may find lifts of this type frightening.

A similar device is a lift that provides a seat running on rails. A person who uses a wheelchair can sit on the platform and ride up, while someone else carries the wheelchair upstairs. Adding to this problem, the person using the chair may have to be lifted onto the platform and then helped off again. Chair lifts are intended for home use and have no place in libraries.

D. Dumbwaiters

Many older library buildings without elevators still have dumbwaiters for moving books from floor to floor. Many of them are operated by hanging loops of rope. Because the hoist mechanisms provide mechanical advantage, one can end up pulling a lot of rope to move a couple of carts of books up a floor.

One of the great pleasures of being teenaged book shelvers is giving your friends rides on the library dumbwaiter. (It sounds like a recipe for trouble, but the rope hoist mechanisms for dumbwaiters can usually be reached from inside the car, reducing the potential for the fun of leaving friends trapped between floors.)

Modern dumbwaiters are electrically powered and far less adventurous.

The advantage of dumbwaiters is that you can ship things from floor to floor without having a staff member accompany them. For example, Fred once installed a dumbwaiter to make it possible for departmental staff members in two different departments to send books to a lending desk on a different floor instead of leaving their departments unstaffed. It was an unusual situation, but the staff in both departments still use the dumbwaiter daily.

III. STAIRCASES

The basics of staircase design are straightforward, and there shouldn't be so many problems.

- The most important thing is that users of staircases should be safe.
- Staircases should have steps of constant dimensions. The depths of the treads and the heights of the risers should be consistent.*
- There should be no funny-shaped treads at corners. Lots of old Carnegie-era libraries have pie-shaped treads on the staircases to their basements, and this is very definitely Not a Good Thing. Lots of libraries have curved staircases, and this is also a bad idea.
- Railings should be in locations and have diameters that are specified by codes. (Some historic libraries have staircases with handrails set lower than current codes require, and walking down them can be unnerving. Our personal opinion is that new or supplementary railings should be installed, but the tensions between function and historic preservation are hard to sort out.)
- Even if your codes allow it, you don't want railings that can be climbed like ladders.
- Staircases should not panic users who are afraid of heights.
- People should not be able to walk under staircases and crack their heads on the underside of the steps. (Or make out under the stairs in the lowest level of the library.)

---

*"Treads" are the flat areas upon which people step. "Risers" are the vertical panels connecting the treads.

- The joints between the treads and the risers should make it instantly clear where the edges of the steps are.
- Extremely long flights of stairs can panic people starting down. They envision tripping and rolling endlessly downstairs, head over heels. It's a lot more friendly to have the stairs make a 180-degree turn (with a rectangular landing and no pie-shaped steps) halfway up. (One library staircase featured on the front of a book on library architecture has a flight of stairs so long that the staff of the library installed a kiddie gate at the top. You can't see the gate on the cover photo.)

All libraries with extra floors need enclosed staircases that serve as emergency exits. Codes are complex and change, so rely on your architects and engineers. In many cases you will be required to have "places of refuge" immediately inside the entrances to exit staircases. Places of refuge provide spaces where people who cannot negotiate exit staircases can wait to be rescued. They include sufficient flat space for wheelchairs and methods of informing emergency personnel that people are waiting for assistance.

Places of refuge are essential because elevators automatically shut off in case of emergency. It's a great deal easier and safer for emergency workers to carry people downstairs than to try to rescue them when they are trapped between floors in stalled elevators.

Safe public staircases are essential, but frequently there are compromises driven by the desire for dramatic appearance. However, if someone falls downstairs in your library, you'll probably be speaking with people specializing in insurance and lawsuits. If the designers of your staircase blew off considerations of comfort and safety in favor of glitzy design, the conversation will be unpleasant.

Unfortunately, all too many libraries have staircases where users get a terrified vise grip on the railings before walking downstairs.

Tripping and falling downstairs is a great deal worse than tripping and falling upstairs, so when in doubt, make things safer for people headed downward.

A. Strangely Configured Staircases

Public buildings are full of staircases that don't just run in a straight, safe line. Some of these are ancient, but others are modern. We keep building them until building codes settle down and ban them.

All staircases are potentially dangerous and therefore bad places for artistic experimentation. In this case, the handrails run diagonally to the run of the staircases, forcing users to either climb without using the rails or to walk crablike up the steps.

Buildings abound in curved staircases. They're ornamental but otherwise seriously nasty. Each tread on a curved staircase is a trapezoid, deeper on one side of the staircase than the other. People climbing curved staircases may find the treads uncomfortably shallow on one side and uncomfortably deep on the other. But where the treads are a comfortable depth, there are no handrails.

Some buildings have diagonal staircases, where the run of the handrail is not perpendicular to the run of the steps. Walking down a staircase designed this way is a pain, since you have to constantly work your way either to left or right or let go of the railings. In some of the worst cases, people using diagonal staircases have to essentially cross their legs at each step.

B. Oddly Shaped Treads

One of the main considerations in staircase design should be avoiding anything that might lead users to trip and fall.

People climbing staircases expect all treads to be completely rectangular and exactly the same. Cute shapes are an anathema. Varied tread widths are an anathema. Pie-shaped treads are an anathema.

Dangerously shaped treads are nothing new. Carnegie-era libraries specialized in basement staircases with pie-shaped treads as they turned corners. Even staff members took tumbles and broke limbs.

People climbing staircases expect the ends of the treads to butt up against flat surfaces. Unfortunately, some designers are bored with this expectation and create treads that stop short of the side wall. Even if users can't slip through the opening between the tread and the side wall, it's still unnerving. And the opening serves no practical purpose whatsoever.

Some libraries have staircases with treads that blend into the side walls with a radius between the tread and the wall. Again, this is a cute design concept rather than a functional one, and users may find it unnerving. If they walk too close to the side wall, they can trip on the up-curved end of the tread. (We are not making this up. Fred tripped on such a tread in the main building of the Seattle Public Library.)

Curved staircases, like this one in a historic building on a university campus, cause a variety of problems. In this case, the treads on the outside of the curve are too deep to use comfortably, while those on the inside of the curve are too shallow for feet. If two people end up on the same side of the staircase—one headed up and the other headed down—someone is forced into an awkward position, particularly if he or she is on the inside of the curve. As a result of all this, everyone climbs the center of the staircase, where the treads are of a rational size and there is an extra handrail.

People using staircases should find it easy to spot the edges of the treads. If you will be installing a ceramic tile or carpeted staircase, you can help by putting contrastingly colored nosings on the edges of the treads. You can also help by making the treads and risers lighter or darker, although that doesn't help people walking downstairs, who need more protection.

The main point is that anything that interferes with depth perception or differentiation of treads and risers is dangerous, whether or not it appeals to the aesthetics of your designers.

C. Floating Staircases

Floating staircases are one of the most prevalent bad design ideas in library architecture.

Some floating staircases have no visible means of support. They're connected to the floor above and the floor below, but they have no supporting columns, not even under landings. They may represent tours de force in structural engineering, but this almost certainly excites the designers more than it does the library users.

> Fred inherited a library with a concrete floating staircase between two floors. From the architects' point of view, it was the showpiece of the building. When the building was expanded, it took a team of workers weeks to demolish the staircase, using jackhammers to dismember the concrete and using saws to cut the rebar.

Other floating staircases have support columns, making them much less complex to construct.

One of the major problems with floating staircases is the space beneath. If the space is open, people of any height can walk beneathe the staircase and crease their foreheads on the lower edges of the staircase. And the space beneath the staircase tends to be filled either (good) with stuff to keep people from hitting their heads or (bad) stuff stuck there because the library has too little storage space.

Other ways to keep people from bashing their heads on the undersides of floating staircases are to put raised platforms under the staircase or to install sets of railings to keep people from wandering under the staircases.

One way to prevent innocent passersby from bashing their heads on the lower edges of floating staircases is to install protective railings.

A tidier way is just to construct a closet under that portion of the staircase that comes within seven or eight feet of the floor.

The combination of atrium and floating staircase is an evil one, but it has strong designer appeal. Never let it happen in your library, although you may be in for a battle to prevent it.

D. Open Risers

One of the most popular design abominations is staircases with open risers.

Back before building codes started forcing sanity, designers created insane staircases. There were staircases consisting of treads extending like planks from walls, with handrails on the wall sides only, providing amazing opportunities to fall off the edge or even (for smaller users) to slip between the treads.

Eventually, codes required railings on both sides. Codes required that the openings between balusters (the vertical posts on railing systems) and between treads be limited to four inches, to make it impossible for infants to slip between or through, but climbers with a fear of heights still get to look nervously between their feet.

The amazing thing is that there is absolutely no need or benefit to staircases with open risers. For the agony of users with fear of heights, there is no compensating exhilaration for those who enjoy looking down from above, for the open risers don't provide much of a view—just enough to upset the climbers with acrophobia.

As with other seriously bad ideas described in this chapter, the first thing to do is to put "There will be no open or transparent risers in staircases anywhere in the building" in your building program. Then follow up by checking the construction drawings and shop drawings, just to be sure that people paid attention to you, because they may say "Yeah, sure" and then just go ahead.

E. Staircases in Atriums

Atriums are multistory openings between floors.

Atriums have some advantages:

- Users standing on the bottom floor can look up and sometimes see where things on other floors are located.
- People can admire the open space.
- And that's about it.

Atriums also cause many problems:

- Atriums tempt designers to include floating staircases, with all of the attendant evils thereof. (That's the reason we mention atriums in this chapter, although you'll find them assaulted in other chapters as well, since they are among the most avoidable stupidities in library design.)
- Atriums transmit noise. If the upper levels of an atrium are not glazed (glassed in), all the noises from the lower level are transmitted to the upper levels. The combination of terrazzo floor, lending operation on the ground level, open walls on the upper floors, and major skylight can turn the space into something resembling a boiler factory.
- Atriums waste energy. Heating and cooling a massive volume of unoccupied space is a remarkably silly idea. Atriums may also complicate temperature control.
- Atriums get in the way. Unless atriums are over entry lobbies, they get in the way on upper floors, and users have to go out of their way to circumnavigate atriums.

- For people with fear of heights, having to walk near an open atrium can be terrifying. If the configuration of the building forces users to walk extremely close to the atrium railing, right at the edge of the drop-off, the designers should be spoken with severely.
- Maintaining light fixtures in atriums can be a major challenge.
- People commit suicide in atriums. Including library atriums.

Staircases in atriums often lead to hidden elevators.

- Traditionally, staircases and elevators are located side by side. People who don't want to climb find the elevator handy, and those who don't want to wait can scamper up the stairs.
- But buildings with monumental staircases in atriums normally have elevators hidden away, sometimes down unmarked side halls. The visitor who has no desire to use the staircase looks around in bafflement, while the staircase tempts him to unwise action by whispering (much like Theda Bara), "Climb me, my fool."

What can you do?

- As usual, the first thing is to say "No atriums" in your building program. But you may have to fight your designer anyway.

If you get overruled and stuck with an atrium:

- Don't let anyone put a floating staircase there.
- Insist that all levels of the atrium above the main floor be glazed.
- Put all light fixtures on electrically powered lifts, so that they can be lowered to the floor for servicing.
- Put the atrium on one side of the building, so users and staff don't have to circumnavigate it on upper floors.

Whenever you have a huge opening with a straight drop of many stories, someone will look downward at the people far below and be tempted to explore the forces of gravity.

F. Staircases with Central Openings

Some traditional staircases are built in multistory shafts with the stairs winding endlessly around the shafts and users able to look downward the entire length of the staircases. We've seen staircases in old hotels or business buildings where one could look down 20 stories or fall 20 stories or at least contemplate the possibility of falling 20 stories.

All of this seems unnecessarily unnerving and completely avoidable. As the familiar exhortation goes, "Just say 'No!'"

G. Glass Walls Adjacent to Staircases

If staircases are enclosed by glass walls, you need some way to prevent people from arriving at the end of a flight of stairs and slamming directly into a wall.

This may sound like an unusual situation, but problems happen all the time. (Fred has seen collisions of this type half-a-dozen times while visiting new library buildings.)

One thing designers do is to put some kind of decals on glass walls that keep people from running into them. If that's insufficient, you may need something more obvious, such as a railing in front of the glass wall.

H. Staircase-Like Structures

Staircase-like structures frequently turn up in libraries. One common place is multilevel structures for story hour spaces in public libraries. There have also been story hour pits, with steps down from the main floor level.

Pits are easily dealt with. Ask any librarian who has accidentally fallen into one. Luckily, one can always fill in pits and be done with them, although it costs money to fill them in.

Story hour structures are very popular, but they require a few cautions:

- Don't make them out of concrete, for if you do you will immediately find that you (a) don't like them and (b) can't afford to bring in jackhammers to remove them.
- If you make story hour structures out of wood with plywood tops, they will echo hollowly when people walk on them. The solution used by some stage set designers is to glue Homasote (a high-density pressed paper product) to the undersides of the plywood platforms, between the supporting timbers. (This really matters in set design. When the Ghost of Hamlet's father walks the battlements of Elsinore, it cuts into the dramatic impact if the battlements echo hollowly.)

- It is nearly impossible to carpet story hour structures that have curved edges. Keep the edges straight or be prepared to have a very unhappy relationship with your carpet firm.
- You will probably want some kind of padding under the carpet, but you'll need institutional-level padding that can be glued in place, not home carpet padding.
- Remember that structures like this are inaccessible to some users with disabilities. Know what you will do to treat these users fairly.
- Kids like to jump. Be prepared for leaping from the highest to the lowest level in a single bound. Parents will be happy with the situation until someone gets hurt, whereupon they will blame the library.

I. Unnecessary Staircases

Even in modern libraries, some designers suggest staircases or ramps merely for architectural interest or to permit some interesting furniture arrangement.

This is another opportunity to stop seriously bad ideas quickly.

J. Staircases and Fires

Building codes are particularly stringent when it comes to staircases, which are far more fire-resistant than the rest of structures. Watch, for example, when new five or six-story buildings are going up, where the staircase and elevator enclosures are constructed first as vertical chunks of masonry, and then the rest of the building is filled in around them.

Codes require fire-resistant staircases. If your building has a dramatic floating staircase, that doesn't count as a safe fire exit.

Special problems occur in ancient buildings like Carnegie-era public libraries, where the upper floors may be served by only one staircase, the staircase is not in a fire-resistant shaft, and it's made of wood. If there are fires in buildings of that vintage, people on upper floors will probably burn to death unnecessarily. This will be a hard event to explain to your community.

Emphasizing their disregard for the safety of small children, the designers of this campus building used railings with horizontal balusters everywhere possible. Many visitors compare the structure to a movie set for *Riot in Cell Block Thirteen*. (Fred actually gets dizzy walking through the building, but he's too old to be a student anyway.)

This (non-library) building has balconies with railings that small children can climb like ladders. And fall off. Regardless of the purpose of the building, unless you plan to card children at the door, they can get in and be injured. (The only reason for horizontal beams in railings is aesthetic, and that's not a good enough reason. Until building codes catch up and ban them, say "No" in your building program.)

IV. RAILINGS

There's not a lot to say about railings, but it's important.

A. Railings That Can Be Climbed

These days, many designers come up with railings that have horizontal bars that can be climbed like ladders. These should be totally banned by building codes, but they're still around.

The problem is that children can easily climb the railings and fall off. And they do.

Some designers will argue that this is not an issue because a specific library is not for children, but unless you plan to card people at the door, children can get in. And fall.

Even if you can successfully eliminate children from your library, adults may also be tempted to climb railings.

The ridiculous thing about all of this is that climbable railings serve absolutely no purpose. It's a matter of cute design trumping functionality and safety.

Your building program should state something like, "There will be no railings that can be climbed like ladders." Then check your construction drawings and shop drawings to be sure that no one is slipping one past you. As far as we can tell, climbable railings are always an enthusiasm of designers and never of owners.

B. Glass Railings

Some designers want railings that are sheets of glass. They are probably safe, but they give people with any touch of acrophobia the willies.

We've heard designers say things to the effect of "Walking through our library will be like floating on air." This is a time to Be Very Afraid. And to tell your designers something to the effect of, "Not a chance!"

> The central Minneapolis Public Library has a narrow walkway with glass railings crossing high above the floor of an atrium. Library users who need to reach the other side and who are usually able to conceal their slight tinges of acrophobia are sorely tried when they cross over. When in doubt, avoid walkways bridging huge atriums, and if you are stuck with them never let them have glass sides.

As with other bad ideas listed in this chapter, the sad thing is that railings of this type are totally unnecessary. There are all kinds of substitutes that are less terrifying.

In many cases, you'll have to stop your designers even after you've shouted "No!" Check the construction drawings and (particularly) shop drawings for signs of unwanted glass, just as you check for horizontal beams on railings.

Chapter 26 ■ Elevators, Staircases, Railings, and Ramps 789

Painted railings tend to look ratty because the paint wears off. Stick with stainless steel.

Door handles are available in a wide range of colors to match building décor. Unfortunately, all colored handles seem to have the finish wear off. Luckily, there is no color to wear off of stainless steel. All handrails and door handles need to be made of stainless steel.

C. Painted Handrails

Lots of buildings have painted handrails. The problem is that the paint swiftly wears out.

If your library has major staircases with painted handrails, you'll have a choice of frequent repainting or constant shabbiness. (We know one library with lemon-yellow painted handrails. In addition to wearing off, lemon-yellow paint looks a nasty green color when it's dirty, and heavily used handrails soon get dirty.)

Most metallic surfaces that are not stainless steel cause equal problems. For instance, brass has to be lacquered if you don't want to polish it daily. Unfortunately, the lacquer soon wears off here and there, leaving the unpleasantly piebald look of mixed lacquered brass (shiny) and brass with lacquer worn off (dingy).

You can run into the same type of problem with colored door handles. Within a few years the color starts wearing off, and the door looks ugly. Unfortunately, colored door handles are in all the hardware catalogs, and they look great on opening day. Ratty-looking colored hand grabs are a constant in contemporary American architecture.

About the only thing that stands up to the constant rubbing that handrails and door handles receive is brushed stainless steel.

The same thing is true of doorknobs and newel posts. The only thing that stands up to library-level use is stainless steel.

If you *must* have painted handrails, emergency exit staircases are a good place to put them.

D. Railings on Narrow Walkways

One thing that can accompany atriums is narrow walkways around the edge.

In some cases, like hotels with large atriums, the walkways usually are wide and the railings are comfortably chest-high. People with a fear of heights can walk around the atriums without being forced to look down.

But in other places the walkways are narrow and the railings less comforting. The New York University (NYU) library, for example, has the reputation of people walking around the atrium while rubbing their shoulders against the outside wall due to the yawning abyss. (As a matter of fact, NYU spent a great deal of money putting up an ornamental screen to provide psychic comfort and prevent the unwanted leaping that had led to suicides in the past.)

So, if you *must* have a big atrium surrounded by walkways, keep the walkways wide and the railings high. (Even better, of course, is to incorporate the phrase "No atriums" into a number of places in your building program, and then be prepared to fight. Designers have an uncanny yearning for atriums.)

E. Railings That Cannot Be Comfortably Grabbed

Too many railings are massive slabs that have to be gripped vise-like between the thumb and fingers. These fail to meet modern building codes, but there are a lot of older examples running around.

Talk with your designers about the legal shapes and widths of handrails. With modern building codes, you're unlikely to get into trouble, but you may still have to cope with yesterday's dumb ideas.

You can make staircases safer and more comfortable for small children by installing a second (and lower) handrail.

F. Railings That People Can Fall Through

Building codes bar them fiercely now, but many railings in days gone by had openings large enough for children (and adults) to fall through. Now the maximum opening is four inches.

If your library has railings—staircase railings or balcony railings—that fail to meet this code, you'll need to do something about it quickly.

G. Low Railings for Children

It's easy to add a second and lower handrail for children. This seems particularly suitable for public libraries and for grade schools.

V. RAMPS

Many libraries have ramps. Older libraries with main floors set above grades may have ramps from the sidewalk up to the main floor or down to a ground floor.

Some libraries have ornamental shifts in floor height in the middle of reading rooms, sometimes with one or two steps stretching the length of the room. These require supplementary ramps.

Some libraries have stages at one end of their meeting rooms. Codes require that stages have ramps for access.

At the time this was written, the maximum legal slope for a ramp was 1:12, or twelve feet of run for every single foot of rise, with a flat area for resting after every 25 feet. Ramps are required to have handrails. (Very short ramps can be steeper.)

A legal sidewalk has a slope of no more than 1:20 and does not require handrails.

Some large auditoriums have sloped floors. If your library will have one, check with your architects about the slope of the floor and make serious decisions if it's greater than 1:12. And provide places where users in wheelchairs can view performances.

Trying to move people between floors by means of ramps is a seriously bad idea. If the top of one floor is ten feet higher than the top of the floor below, the ramp will be 120 feet long, plus 20 additional feet for resting areas. Anyone who thinks this is a good idea should be fitted into a loaner wheelchair and asked to wheel it up a 140-foot ramp. (Fourteen feet from floor to floor is probably an absolute minimum difference in height. It assumes 10-foot ceilings and 4 feet for floor structure and MEP equipment. A ramp connecting floors like this will be nudging 200 feet long.)

The only civilized way to move people between floors is with elevators.

In general, architects have quit designing buildings that require ramps to deal with purely aesthetic features, but there are vast numbers of older buildings that have had to provide ramps. The major use of ramps we see in modern libraries is for access to meeting room stages and similar platforms.

The main point is that ramps are makeshift adaptations, not desirable design features.

VI. SNAPPY RULES ON ELEVATORS, STAIRCASES, RAILINGS, AND RAMPS

1. The rights of people with disabilities overrule the rights of designers to be cute.
2. The fear of heights is not covered by the Americans with Disabilities Act. But it should be. In the meantime, block insanely vertiginous design concepts, of which there are a lot running around.
3. Ramps can be unpleasantly long. For example, if it's eight feet up to the front door, a ramp will be a minimum of over 110 feet long. This is an amazingly uncivilized device, even if you can find a place to put it. And consider how much people will enjoy it in the winter.
4. An open exterior ramp leading to the basement will sooner or later fill with rainwater and flood the basement. Most likely sooner.
5. If your designers suggest a library where you can look straight down at users half-a-dozen floors below, ask them what they think the terminal velocity of a dropped dictionary might be.
6. If you intentionally design a library that is unnecessarily difficult for people with disabilities to use, shame on you. In addition, if you get sued, you'll lose.
7. As with other building codes, the requirements in the Americans with Disabilities Act are legal minimums, not ideals. Don't feel seriously smug about things if your building just barely squeaks through.
8. If you have a Carnegie-era library building with a main floor a number of steps above grade, you'll either have to move to a different building or install an elevator. Historic buildings can be wonderful things, but there's a cost. Exterior ramps are unpleasant at best and an abomination in areas chillier than central Florida.

9. No sane people climbing staircases want to look between their feet and see the floor below.
10. Atriums can provide five minutes of "Wow!" followed by 50 years of major problems. That's a high price to pay for a little bit of "Wow!"
11. The undersides of floating staircases are wonderful places to bump one's head.
12. Steps that serve no necessary purpose whatsoever serve no purpose whatsoever.
13. Long exterior ramps are an assault on library users and staff in nice weather, and are impressively nasty in times of rain or ice.
14. If you have a high atrium surrounded by railings on every level, sooner or later someone will jump off. Universities are particularly prone to this. (While you're sitting at the lending desk at the bottom of the atrium, "splat" is not a comforting sound.)
15. Staircases should not terrify library users, who are nice people and deserve better treatment.
16. Make the edges of the treads on your staircases stand out.
17. If people using your staircases are gripping the railings in a white-knuckled sort of way, find out why.
18. Whether you say "atriums" or "atria," you don't want either one in your library.
19. Tell your architects that atriums with monumental staircases are one of the "most derivative and overworked clichés in architectural design." (We suspect that being accused of imitation bothers some designers more than being accused of dysfunctional designs. So give it a shot.)
20. When it comes to vertiginous drop-offs and glass railings, the thoroughly watched architect gets away with a lot less.
21. Beware of architects pitching soaring spaces and terrifying staircases to groups like governing boards that will never have to actually ascend above the first floor.
22. If you need an elevator, get an elevator. A real elevator.
23. A designer envisions a balcony overlooking a library atrium as an inspirational vantage point. A library manager wonders how long it will be before someone falls off.
24. If you have a 20,000-square-foot, two-story library, you don't need an elevator you need a one story library on a larger site. You need a flatter library on a larger site. (Of course, if your library is an architectural monument, that complicates things.)
25. Libraries that have a choice in the matter keep the doors to their exterior balconies locked at all times.

26. There's no excuse for staircases with funny-shaped treads. (Pie-shaped or curved treads from 1905 are just as dangerous as weirdly artistic treads from 2017.)
27. For some reason, the entire area of atriums, balconies, and artistically lethal staircases is dangerously alluring to designers of libraries. As librarians, it's our duty to make them stop.
28. Staircases and elevators need to be close enough so that people who don't want to use one can look around and see the other. Side-by-side is particularly polite.
29. For people with a serious fear of heights, a glass-walled elevator is not a kindly alternative to a vertiginous staircase.
30. Ramps are excusable only when you have absolutely no other choice. Never build one because it's cute.
31. Railings with horizontal balusters that can be climbed like ladders are an abomination.

27

Electrical Systems

I. INTRODUCTION

MEP (mechanical, electrical, and plumbing) systems are complicated and extremely expensive—accounting for perhaps 40 percent of the cost of a new library building.

In addition to being expensive to install, MEP systems can be extremely expensive to alter. As a result, libraries are often forced to live with ill-advised or dysfunctional systems. The obvious thing to do is to struggle to avoid mistakes in the first place.

This chapter covers some basic points about electrical systems as they apply to libraries, concentrating in particular on a few areas that have caused problems in libraries. The chapter is very much less thorough than some other parts of the book because electrical systems are complicated. This is a time to rely on your electrical engineers, who are heroic.

Electrical systems of particular importance to libraries are covered in separate chapters, and the information there is by and large not covered in this chapter. See in particular the chapters on:

- Lighting
- Meeting rooms
- Staff facilities

Almost all libraries, including brand-new ones, have fewer electrical outlets and circuits than they need.

Many libraries also have too few electrical circuits, particularly in areas where food is prepared and served.

Many electrical requirements are included in electrical codes and are not repeated here, since we assume you will have a legal building. Always remember, however, that codes are minimums, not ideals, and that saying "Our building meets all applicable codes" does not really give you bragging rights.

Electrical power is measured in watts. (Amps times volts equals watts. See the vocabulary list.)

For safety, all electrical circuits have automatic cutoff switches. In days gone by, circuits were equipped with fuses, but the modern thing is circuit breakers, which are resettable switches.

You don't want fuses in your library. If you have them, this would be a really good time to upgrade.

II. NOMENCLATURE

Electrical service is pretty standard, although the details are impressively complex. When your building is being planned and constructed, it's a good thing to know what people are talking about. Here are some basic terms.

- *Ampere.* Typically, in the United States, 110-volt circuits are rated at 20 amps. (People usually say "amp" rather than "ampere.")
- *Circuit breaker.* A device that interrupts the flow of current when the amount of current is too high for the safety of the circuit. Modern circuit breakers are resettable switches.
- *Fuse.* A form of circuit breaker. A fuse has a strip of metal that melts when the amperage in the circuit reaches a specific level. A common problem is the use of fuses that allow unsafe levels of currents in wiring. (In days gone by, people would insert pennies behind fuses in fuse boxes, resulting in a complete loss of protection and occasional fires.) If your library has fuse boxes, today would be a really good time to upgrade.
- *Ground.* Grounded outlets are required by modern building codes. Look for three openings in electrical outlets—two slots and a round opening.
- *Load.* The amount of power drawn from a circuit.

- *Panel room.* A room where the library's main electrical panels are located.
- *Volt.* The standard unit of electrical force. With the exception of HVAC equipment, most electrical outlets in libraries provide 110 volts.
- *Watt.* A measure of electrical power (amps times volts equals watts). A kilowatt hour (the standard unit of electrical usage) is the provision of 1,000 watts of electrical power for one hour.

III. ELECTRICAL CIRCUITS

An electrical circuit is composed of wiring, loads (electrical outlets, lighting, or other energy-consuming equipment), and a safety cutoff for situations when the circuit is overloaded, where something is wrong with the grounding, and so on.

- A circuit is the path followed by current from the power source through whatever device is using power and then back to the power source. The electrical outlets, light fixtures, or other power users on a single path form a circuit. In modern buildings in the United States, circuits for everyday use—lighting, outlets, and so on—are typically 20 amps each. Areas with many pieces of high-amperage equipment—such as kitchenettes—require a number of separate circuits.
- Multiple separate circuits are particularly important in areas where food is prepared or served. Far too many meeting rooms and staff rooms have so few separate circuits that dinners or parties are impossible. Some libraries end up running extension cords from other areas of the library, where other circuits are located. This is an extraordinarily bad idea.
- It's a very good thing to have electric panels with circuit breakers rather than fuses. If your library is old enough to have a fuse box, it's time to think about modernizing your electrical system. With fuse boxes, it's too easy for someone to create a dangerous situation by putting in fuses with amperages too high for the wiring or by putting pennies behind the fuses. (If you have a fuse box, feel the wires coming out of it. If they're warm, turn things off and get help today.)
- Modern 110-volt wiring has three wires, including hot and cold plus ground. Grounded wiring is a lot safer. To check whether your library has grounded wiring, look for the third opening in electrical outlets—two vertical slots and a round hole.
- Ground fault interrupters are devices to prevent situations where faulty pieces of equipment short out through the bodies of people holding the equipment. GFIs are required by codes in areas where people can touch extremely well-grounded items while they are holding faulty equipment. The common use of GFIs is in rooms with plumbing—kitchens and restrooms.

Far too many libraries—even brand new ones—have insufficient electrical wiring. Kitchenettes are notorious for inadequate numbers of circuits, but historic buildings can be short of amperage almost anywhere. Economizing during remodeling or new construction can be a major mistake.

- In many areas of libraries, we keep adding more and more pieces of electrical equipment. Be sure you have enough circuits to cope with future needs. The most common problems seem to occur in food-service areas, but other possibilities are any areas with high-wattage equipment.
- Knob and tube wiring is a system used from the late nineteenth century through the late 1930s. Instead of the modern three wires in a conduit (hot, cold, and ground) knob and tube systems strung individual wires through the walls. Wires were held away from nearby wood by ceramic "knobs," which supported wires above surfaces, and by ceramic "tubes," which allowed wires to pass through beams without touching the beams. Knob and tube wiring has no grounding wire. To put things quickly, you don't want old knob and tube wiring in your library.
- Electrical panel. This is a metal panel with a door in front and rows of circuit breakers inside. In "panel rooms," where the library's main power panels are located, major panels may just have massive switch levers for turning power to groups of panels (or even power to the entire library) off and on.
- For areas like technical services, dual conductor wire mold is available for mounting on the walls above tabletop height. One conductor handles 110-volt

wiring and the other data wiring. The separate passageways in the wire mold keep the 110-volt wiring from messing up data transmission in the other wiring.

IV. ELECTRICAL OUTLETS

One of the most common errors in library design is the provision of too few electrical outlets. While meaning well, your designers are likely to try to save you money by limiting the number of outlets in your building.

The problem is that with the coming of universal laptops and other computers, library staff members and library users are constantly looking for places to plug things in. Batteries don't hold their charges long enough, and they may never do so.

So the basic rule is, provide an extraordinary number of electrical outlets.

Among other things, you will need:

- Electrical outlets on all reading tables. If a table has four chairs it needs four outlets. (Think of students piling into the college library at exam time, with every chair taken and with every student carrying a laptop.)
- Outlets on reading tables should be on top of the tables rather than hidden beneath. Why make library users crawl under tables looking for places to plug in their laptops? If it's an issue of aesthetics, attractive table lamps are available with outlets in their bases.
- Electrical outlets by all soft seating.
- Electrical outlets at all places where computers are scheduled to be located.
- Electrical outlets at all places where self-check equipment will be located.
- Electrical outlets at all places where security gates will be located.
- Electrical outlets all over the place in spaces to be used for group study, especially if furniture is designed to be movable.
- Electrical outlets in places where electronic gadgets may replace reference shelving.
- Electrical outlets at all places where any of the equipment listed above may be located at any time in the future. *WHAT THIS MEANS IS THAT, EXCEPT FOR PERMANENT STACK STRUCTURES, LIBRARIES NEED OUTLETS EVERYWHERE.*
- Outlets spaced sufficiently closely together so that extension cords are never needed. Extension cords are a serious fire hazard. And people trip over them. Make your fire marshal and users happy with lots of outlets. (You can try to ignore unhappy users, but it's hard to ignore unhappy fire marshals.)

> One academic library Fred worked with had so few electrical outlets that the lending desk checked out extension cords to students.

- Outlets on all sections of wall large enough to possibly have something plugged in. This means that a three-foot section of wall between two doors needs an electrical outlet.
- Heavy three-wire extension cords with built-in circuit breakers for situations where you are forced to use extension cords. These are not dime-store items.
- Outlets above tabletop level in staff work areas, to make it unnecessary for staff members to crawl under furniture—or pull furniture away from the wall—in order to plug things in.
- Tamper-resistant (childproof) outlets in all public areas of all public libraries. They are more important in adult areas than in children's areas, because it is in adult areas that busy parents hand their car keys to their children to play with while the parents are using the library. (When children poke the car keys into unprotected outlets, the result is excitement for everyone.) A blue dot on the face of the outlet indicates that it is tamper-resistant. Architects tend to

Where electrical outlets are insufficient, the result can be unattractive power poles, as seen in the center of this picture. (The lighting system visible in the ceiling of the room is spectacularly awful. See the chapter on lighting.)

assume that childproof outlets are needed only in children's departments, but they are WRONG. In addition to saving uproar, childproof outlets add very little cost to construction. (Check your construction drawings to be sure that you're actually getting childproof outlets in ALL public areas. They have a tendency to disappear from drawings, particularly because junior employees in architectural firms assume that childproof outlets have been indicated in adult areas by accident, and simply remove them without asking.)
- Flush outlets in the middle of floors, so that furniture can be located on the boxes until they are needed. A common brand is Walker boxes, which have lids that open to provide access to both 110-volt outlets and data conduit. (If you retrofit floor outlets they'll stick up. And if there's no floor below, you'll pay an astounding price. Considering that you'll need two or three trades to do the work, you may not even be able to find an interested contractor.)
- Outlets not inserted by core drilling through concrete floors, because the outlets are kept in place by flanges resting on the floors, which means they always stick up a quarter of an inch or more.
- No so-called pedestal electrical outlets that stick up like tombstones above the floor. One still sees them, but they are killers, tripping up the unwary mercilessly. Libraries with pedestal outlets end up having to position furniture over them, regardless of whether the furniture blocks the movement of people through the building.
- Grounded electrical outlets. If your outlets don't have three openings (two vertical slots and one round opening), talk to electrical people.
- Checking the correct wiring of electrical outlets is easy to do with a gadget that plugs into outlets, with indicator lights that let you know whether everything is hooked up right. In older buildings, it's a great way to see whether the ground connection in outlets is actually hooked up. Checking outlets for correct wiring can be part of punch listing.

Electrical outlets in the middle of floors need to be sufficiently flush with the floor to allow furniture to be placed on the outlets when they are not in use, and to prevent people from tripping over the outlets.

- A few libraries that have problems with grounding have separately grounded outlets for use with computers. They're colored orange.
- In staff workrooms, consider wall outlets installed above tabletop height. Staff will appreciate not having to crawl under furniture to plug stuff in. The director may need a workroom with outlets concealed for aesthetic reasons, but most other staff members will prefer easy access over hidden outlets.
- Outdoor electrical outlets. You will need a minimum of one on each side of your building and more if the sides of the building exceed fifty feet. Be sure the outlets are on a separate circuit (or separate circuits), so they can all be turned off when outdoor work is not taking place. Never tie outlets into adjacent indoor circuits. Weatherproof outlet covers are available, but being able to shut everything off is a lot better.

Electrical firms will label the back sides of outlet plates with the number of the circuits. Unfortunately, when careful painters repaint the walls, they'll begin by removing all of the plates. The result may be intermixed plates and erroneous information. One approach is to have one of your staff members remove the plates before the painters arrive and use a permanent marker to write the circuit numbers directly on the switch mechanisms.

V. ELECTRICAL SWITCHES

Rooms that house the electrical switching gear for libraries are often called "panel rooms," which take their name from the electrical panels that house groups of circuit breakers. In very small libraries, electrical panels may be located in back rooms that house other functions, such as HVAC equipment or storage.

As with other MEP areas, the points included here deal mainly with errors that libraries encounter.

- One of the first rules of switch placement is to never put light switches where users can mess about with them. (Unless you want users to mess about with the switches, such as the switches in program and meeting rooms, study rooms, and faculty studies.)
- The easy place to put light switches for reading rooms is in a nearby office or staff corridor. Switches also work well behind service desks, but there's always a chance you'll relocate the desk someday and leave the switches alone and vulnerable.
- Key switches are available for use in situations where switches cannot be placed in areas limited to staff and you don't want users playing with the switches. The "key" is usually just a flat strip of steel with a forked end that fits around a block in the switch.

- If you plan to use any of your circuit breakers as switches, be sure they're "switch rated." Or they'll break.

> Using circuit breakers in power panels as light switches is a seriously bad idea anyway. Some cities may require a union electrician to operate the switches located in power panels, and you can't afford that. (Fred worked in a library set up this way, and he suspects that the electricians who shambled out of the basement at closing time were paid more than the department heads.)

- Motion detector switches need to be in places where they can detect motion. The places where the light switches for rooms might be located are often not very workable. You will want to specify that the switches be operated by the motion of the door and NOT force people to grope their way into dark rooms.
- Unfortunately, in many situations in modern buildings, users have to grope their way into dark rooms. Remarks like "The triumph of energy codes over common sense" occur to one.

VI. EMERGENCIES

Things can occasionally go crazy electrically. One of the two feeds on two-phase wiring (not covered in this book) may be lost. Or seriously weird things may start happening.

The best thing to do may be to shut everything off, evacuate the building, and call for help.

> Calling for help can take time. Fred's library once had the power feed to the main electrical panels short out. The fire chief arrived in about thirty seconds. The trucks were there in two minutes. The library staff evacuated the library building in two minutes (thanks to lots of previous rehearsals with the Urbana fire department). And the power company (necessary to disconnect the power supplies) took forty-five minutes to turn up, while everyone stood outside and listened to the crashing and banging of short circuits.

VII. SNAPPY RULES ON ELECTRICAL SYSTEMS

1. The most important place for childproof (tamper-resistant) electrical outlets is in public library adult departments, because that's where parents hand their keys to their children to play with while the parents are occupied.
2. There's no such thing as too many electrical circuits in kitchenettes.
3. Fire marshals fear extension cords with good reason. If you have lots of extension cords, you will in turn learn to fear fire marshals. Have enough electrical outlets, and if you must buy extension cords, always buy heavy-duty three-conductor extension cords with circuit breakers.
4. Any section of wall located between two doors that is large enough for anything that anyone might ever want to plug in needs an electrical outlet.
5. When your architects ask you where you will be placing computers, always answer, "Anywhere we want."
6. Outlets around the walls and on the columns are never enough. Every library needs floor outlets.
7. Floor outlets that stick up are a pain. People trip over them, and they prevent you from putting furniture just where you want it.
8. Wall-mounted computer counters with outlets at the back force users to sit with their backs to the room. Lots of users don't like this much.
9. The easy way to add extra wiring to historic buildings is with wire mold or surface-mounted conduit. It's also the excessively ugly way, and one librarians should be ashamed of.
10. The trickier your electrical gadgetry, the sooner it will fail in use and the more you will need to budget for repairs. Ordinary switches can last for many decades, but automatic ones probably won't.
11. Adding an extra outlet to a slab-on-grade floor is an adventure in spending money. You may even have trouble finding anyone willing to do the work. Specify enough outlets when you are planning your building, and check the construction drawings to be sure the outlets are actually there.

28

Heating, Ventilating, and Air Conditioning Systems

I. INTRODUCTION

Heating, ventilating, and air conditioning (HVAC) systems are extremely complex and constantly changing. HVAC systems are also extremely expensive and represent perhaps 25 percent of the cost of a new library building, so the decisions made about them are of extreme importance. If we tried to be really thorough in covering HVAC systems, this section would be huge, and it would probably be completely out of date by the time the book appeared. And since we are not engineers, we'd probably say some seriously stupid things.

All HVAC systems are complex and require extensive input from engineers. Even if you have a very small library, the planning of HVAC systems will be in the hands of professional engineers, to whom your architects will subcontract the work. Many engineering firms are serious heroes.

HVAC systems have been greatly complicated in recent years by the desire to conserve energy. Your engineers will have to deal with increasingly complex building codes, new energy-saving codes, LEED certification, and the simultaneous need to keep libraries both comfortable and functional for users and safe for books.

The majority of public libraries probably have stand-alone HVAC systems, while many academic libraries are part of campus-wide networks, including centralized heating plants. For academic libraries, HVAC systems are part of campus planning. For public libraries, planning includes making sure that possible building sites have easy access to electric power, natural gas, and other necessary utilities.

Heating, ventilating, and air conditioning systems are so complicated and are changing so rapidly that we have decided to cover only a few basics, in order to prevent the book from being out of date before it rolls off the presses. (And to avoid demonstrating how we can both work with HVAC systems for years and still not know much.)

As librarians, we expect a lot from our HVAC systems. The systems need to:

- Control temperatures, frequently in situations where some areas of the building need to be heated while other areas need to be cooled, or when some areas need immediate and rapid cooling when hordes of users crowd abruptly into small meeting rooms.
- Control humidity. Humidity control is particularly important for preserving books in research collections, but all libraries need to avoid extremes. Public and school libraries may be happy with limiting relative humidity to perhaps something between 30 and 50 percent, but research libraries may need to limit humidity to extremely tight ranges.
- Control the amount of CO_2 (carbon dioxide) in the air. Minor changes in CO_2 levels can make everyone uncomfortable and feeling uncomfortably short of fresh air. Crowded rooms with bad ventilation are probably awash in excess CO_2.
- Clean the air, removing unwanted particles (such as dust and pollen).
- Eliminate odors. Think fish TV dinners in the staff lunchroom, inadequate ventilation in poorly designed restrooms, and seriously unbathed users pretty much anywhere.
- Keep all areas of libraries comfortable while (a) expending as little energy as possible but (b) not compromising on air quality.

II. GENERAL COMPLEXITY

The HVAC system will be by far the most complex and expensive system in your library. A few basic points:

- HVAC systems can be impressively complicated. Experts are essential at every step of the road.
- The HVAC system in your library may cost about 25 percent of total construction cost.

- HVAC equipment can have a fairly short life. While ductwork and radiators can last for many years, the expected life span of HVAC machinery—furnaces, chillers, and so on—can be about 20 years. (Maybe 30 years if you buy high-end equipment and luck out.) This is one reason why remodeling a library or converting an old building to a library may cost a lot more than you expect.
- When your new building is complete, hire an independent HVAC specialist to do the punch list on your equipment. It's far too complicated for anyone to evaluate by simply walking through the building, or just noting that it "feels okay" today.
- As part of transferring control of your HVAC system to your library at the end of construction, the engineers and installers are supposed to provide full operating information and instructions. Try to get everything in print, including copies of all equipment manuals. Anything explained or demonstrated in person needs to be saved as a video.
- When you are visiting libraries, always ask yourself if the air is comfortable and fresh.
- Always know how to shut off your HVAC system. Sometimes you will be in a serious hurry. For instance, at times when dangerous gases are being drawn into your air intakes.

> In Fred's library, a crew digging up a nearby street severed a gas pipe. The escaping gas rose happily into the air and was sucked into the library's air intakes. The staff had to immediately shut down the HAVC system, evacuate the building, and call for help. The moral is that staff need to know how to shut things down.

Heating and cooling systems vary widely in complexity. For very small libraries, they are pretty much like home systems, often with two zones—one for the main part of the library and one for the meeting room. ("Zones" [see below] are areas with separate temperature controls.)

In the days before air conditioning, libraries were usually heated by radiators, using either hot water or steam. (Steam heat is the noisy one. Steam-heated radiators have single feed pipes and clank a lot. Hot water radiators have two pipes and are more acoustically subtle.) Older libraries equipped with radiators sometimes retrofitted air cooling by installing window air conditioners, which are inefficient users of power and are noisy and drip water as it condenses out of the air. But they don't require air ducts.

When old libraries with radiators are modernized, adding air conditioning can be difficult because there is no space to add ductwork.

There are a number of traditional ways of providing different temperatures in different areas of libraries.

Some fairly large libraries have relied on several separate home-sized systems to keep things simple and easy to fix. By contrast, a complex modern system may require expert servicing.

One traditional way of providing heating and cooling was through reheat coils. Air was cooled centrally and then reheated as needed for individual rooms. Humidity was lowered by cooling and then reheating the air, because water condensed out of the air when it was cooled centrally. (Getting rid of air conditioner condensate is important, since in even a modest-sized building the condensate can run like a hose in midsummer.)

Some libraries provide both hot and cold air, mixing them as needed for different areas.

Other libraries control temperatures in part by varying the amount of air entering each area of the building, using so-called VAV (variable air volume) boxes.

III. TEMPERATURE CONTROL AND ZONING

Zoning involves providing separate temperature control for different areas of a library, allowing equipment to provide heat for one area of a library while simultaneously providing cooling for another. It may involve heating the side of a building that faces away from the sun while simultaneously cooling another side that faces the sun. Or it may involve providing a great deal of extra cooling and fresh air when a large number of people abruptly crowd into a meeting room.

- If you use one thermostat for two separate rooms, one of the rooms will be miserable to occupy.
- Some thermostats are set electronically from a central point, and in some cases even from another part of the country. The usual way is to provide access to accredited staff through their computers. Libraries that can't control their own thermostats directly tell us that they're seriously unhappy with this situation.
- If library users can play with thermostats, they will. To prevent this, you can have locking thermostats or set thermostats remotely from your desktop.

Or you can install transparent plastic boxes that enclose thermostats. The boxes have vent holes that allow the thermostats to sense the temperature in the room but prevent passersby from changing settings.
- Staff members also like to play with thermostats. You may want to limit the number of people who have access to your temperature controls.
- In days gone by, some thermostats were operated by compressed air—so-called "pneumatic" thermostats. They're a lot touchier than modern electronic thermostats.
- In tricky situations where you can't control thermostats centrally, use key-operated thermostats. Usually these are used to keep members of the public from playing with them, but sometimes you may have to limit staff access as well.

> In Fred's library, two staff members who shared a workroom had no temperature they both liked. The moment one left the room, the other changed the thermostat setting. Eventually they wore out the pneumatic thermostat. In desperation, Fred had a key-operated thermostat installed and kept the key in his desk. He offered to change the setting whenever asked, but his staff were embarrassed to call him every 20 minutes, and all was well.

Ideal book storage temperatures are cooler than ideal user temperatures, and book storage areas may be kept as much as 20 degrees Fahrenheit cooler than reading rooms. However, libraries worry about the effects on books of moving them quickly to warmer areas, since moisture can condense on cold books as it does on cold beverage glasses. When the temperature differential between book storage areas and reading areas is very large, books may have to be allowed to warm up slowly to prevent condensation.

IV. HUMIDITY CONTROL

Humidity control is particularly important in libraries because books are hygroscopic (absorb water) and are subject to mildew and mold. For archival collections and for academic libraries—particularly for rare book rooms—tight control of humidity levels is essential.

Humidity is measured by the ratio of the amount of water in the air to the amount of water the air can absorb *at that temperature*. This is called "relative humidity." Warm air can hold more water than cold air. For a given amount of water in the air, therefore, lowering the temperature raises the relative humidity. A library that has a desirable relative humidity of 50 percent can approach mildew levels if the temperature is dropped too far.

- Controlling humidity is an essential aspect of HVAC systems.
- Humidification is a lot trickier than dehumidification. If done incorrectly, it can lead to unwanted condensation on interior surfaces. New buildings can be constructed to be compatible with humidification, but if you are considering converting an older building that will require humidification, be sure to check with engineers before buying the building or mentioning your plans in public.

V. DUCTWORK

Most modern HVAC systems need to conduct air from central HVAC equipment to individual spaces in the library.

- If you have slab-on-grade construction, beware of underfloor air ducts. If water collects in your hidden ductwork, it will have to be pumped out. And think of the possibility of Legionnaires' disease, which has an affinity for standing cold water.
- Underfloor air ducts were sometimes installed to avoid having visible ductwork in cathedral ceilings, but they're a high price to pay for cute ceilings.
- Instead of using air ducts, some HVAC systems use plenums, which are open spaces above a ceiling or below a floor through which heating and cooling air flows everywhere rather than being limited by ductwork. The air enters the occupied spaces of the building through grills leading to the plenums.
- Some plenum floors tend to bounce underfoot, which can unnerve library users. Plenum floors that consist of concrete rectangles supported by steel frames don't bounce.
- Wiring that runs loose through plenums needs to be "plenum-rated." This used to be a lot more expensive than regular wire, but things aren't as bad as they used to be.
- If your designers plan to install floor plenums, be sure they're strong enough to carry the weight of books—150 pounds per square foot live load. (The rule is that buildings have to allow you to put books anywhere you want, any time you want.)
- There are standard minimum dimensions for air ducts. If you try to save space by using undersized ducts, you're likely to have the happy sound of rushing air permeating your library.
- One of the major challenges in modernizing old library buildings is finding places in which to install air ducts.

- One bad side effect from overly low ceilings is air ducts enclosed in soffits dangling too close to the floor. Libraries need space above suspended ceilings for properly concealed air ducts.
- Retrofitting modern HVAC systems to historic libraries can be tricky because there may not be any space for air ducts. Before you make final decisions about acquiring or remodeling old buildings, talk extensively with your architects and engineers.

VI. ENERGY CONSERVATION

The entire field of energy conservation in HVAC systems is amazingly complex and constantly changing. It sometimes involves the LEED system (Leadership in Energy and Environmental Design), which is nongovernmental. The LEED system awards points for various building attributes, with levels of compliance resulting in various levels of recognition.

Our main concern is the transitory nature of approaches to energy conservation. Equipment can age more rapidly than one might hope. LEED changes frequently.

- All sorts of energy-saving systems are available.
- When you are comparing various conventional and energy-efficient HVAC systems, be sure to compare the very best conventional systems with the energy-saving systems. Some comparisons load the dice by using obsolete conventional systems for comparison.
- Planners talk in terms of "paybacks" for upgrades to more energy-efficient systems. The idea is that the increased efficiency of a new system will pay for its greater up-front installation cost. The great danger is that the new system can be nearly worn out before you start coming out ahead. Talk with your engineers. Designers tell us that paybacks of over about four years are dangerous from a purely economic point of view.
- If your HVAC design presumes specific policies like lower electric rates at night, what will you do if rates flatten out?
- Libraries are sometimes tempted to save energy by simply opening up buildings when the air is cool outside, saving money and enjoying the pleasant evening air. But the price they pay is unwanted humidity and dust, two things that good HVAC systems control. And open windows are a great way for users to bypass security systems by chucking books out open windows and retrieving them from the shrubbery later. (If you want windows that can be opened, be sure they have key locks, or that you can remove the handles.)
- If you've never spent time in a library without air conditioning and with low reading room ceilings in midsummer with the windows wide open and fans

blowing everywhere, you have no idea how thick the air can feel and how much airborne dirt and crud can accumulate on the seats of chairs and the tops of books.
- Some libraries have installed white roof membranes rather than the usual black membranes or built-up roofs. The idea is that white membranes will reflect sunlight and help keep the building cooler.
- Many old buildings have uninsulated walls and uninsulated windows. If you are considering expanding an old building or converting an old building to a library, consult extensively with your engineers.
- Grants may be available to cover the extra cost of using a more energy-efficient system.

VII. SPECIAL HVAC PROBLEMS

- Screen porches made sense before the days of air conditioning. Although they may still sound romantic today, they cause nothing but trouble in libraries. Most of the year they're too hot or too cold. Dust and rain blow in through the screens, providing an attractive layer of mud on the floor. And screen porches tend to be hard for staff to supervise. Libraries that are equipped with screen porches tend to enclose them, trying to cope with the absence of HVAC ductwork in the process. Say "No!" the first time someone brings up the idea of screen porches, and repeat it as often as needed.
- Having a few windows that can be opened will help if your HVAC system fails and you have an emergency need for fresh air. However, open windows cause all sorts of problems with dust and humidity. They can also throw systems off balance. You never want windows that users can open, and you may have to give staff members stern warnings against "just opening a window."
- Natural gas is colorless and odorless and nonpoisonous. But when mixed with air it can blow up real good. The bad smell is added to warn people of gas leaks before things blow up. (The bad smell is ethyl mercaptan, which can be detected by the human nose in amazingly small quantities, giving lots of warning of leaks before things get dangerous.) Old-fashioned stove gas (coal gas) was in large part carbon monoxide, which was very seriously poisonous. But modern natural gas is primarily methane, which is not lethal but still blows up impressively.
- Always know how to shut off your HVAC system (not to mention your electrical supplies, sprinkler system, and water supplies). If something goes wrong, there's almost never time to call in an outside expert.

VIII. SNAPPY RULES ON HVAC SYSTEMS

1. Study rooms and staff workrooms need individual thermostats. If two rooms share one thermostat, the people in the room without a thermostat will almost certainly be very unhappy.
2. Modern HVAC equipment offers all sorts of tamper-resistant thermostats. You will like these.
3. If you buy a building with propane heating to convert to a library, it helps if you live in the Very Deep South. Natural gas is inexpensive. Propane is very much otherwise. Buildings use propane because there's no natural gas available, not because it has any special virtues of its own.
4. If you have to choose between a site with natural gas and one that requires propane, the propane site needs to have a lot of compensating strengths.
5. If you install an energy-efficient system that takes advantage of lower nighttime costs for electric power, ask what will happen if lower nighttime rates are discontinued.

29

Plumbing Systems

I. INTRODUCTION

This chapter covers some aspects of plumbing systems that are not covered in other chapters. See in particular the chapters on:

- Restrooms
- Meeting rooms
- Staff facilities
- Security (fire sprinkler systems)

By and large, libraries are not huge water users. We use water for restrooms, kitchenettes, technical services, hand-washing, and fire sprinkler systems. We also cope with excess water, particularly runoff from rain.

If we make mistakes, they tend to lie in the direction of too few sources of water and bad preparation for flooding, both from rain and from plumbing run amok.

The majority of public libraries probably have stand-alone plumbing systems, while many academic libraries are part of campus-wide networks. For public libraries, planning includes making sure that possible building sites have easy access to water supplies, sanitary sewers, and storm sewers.

Always know how to shut off all of your plumbing systems in case of emergencies, and train your staff to do this. If your sprinkler system is malfunctioning and flooding the library, you can't wait for outside experts to stop by and fix things.

While libraries can be big energy users due to climate control and lighting, they generally are not significant users of water.

This brief chapter is about miscellaneous library plumbing. It excludes the major areas of restrooms and food preparation, which have separate chapters, and covers half-a-dozen specialized points.

Along with quick reviews of basic points about plumbing, the chapter includes a number of issues that have caused libraries grief in the past.

Plumbing is a complex subject. When it comes to programming and designing your library, you'll mainly want to know the features you want and the features you definitely don't want.

On a daily basis, you mainly need to know what to do until the plumber arrives. This includes knowing how to turn off the entire water supply, how to turn off individual devices (such as faucets and toilets), how to cut the water to your sprinkler system when a sprinkler head fails and water is cascading all over everything, and how to cope with other wet emergencies.*

II. FOOD PREPARATION AND SERVICE AREAS

The chapters on "Program and Study Rooms" and "Staff Facilities" include basic material on areas used for food preparation.

- Areas that are used for food preparation are subject to special requirements. Before planning any area of this type, you or your architects need to sit down with local public health service people to learn the requirements.
- Depending on codes, an area used for preparing and serving food may need a three-drain sink, a grease trap, a hand-washing sink directly behind a service counter, and other plumbing.

---

*Most individual devices like sinks and toilets have small valves below their water inputs. To turn off a flush-valve toilet that won't stop running, turn the attractive pipe cap facing you counterclockwise to remove it (don't scratch it), then use a large, flat-bladed screwdriver to tighten the valve (clockwise) under the cap. (Usually a plumber can rescue you quickly, but sometimes running water means chaos, and you can save the day.)

> One library Fred worked with had no mop sink (although mop sinks are required on any floor that has a toilet). The custodian dealt with the situation by using one of the three drains in the sink in a food preparation area as a mop sink. This eventually led to serious consternation when word got around.

III. STAFF WORKROOM PLUMBING

Most library workrooms need running water. Unfortunately, it is often omitted, forcing library staff to carry water from other parts of the building.

A. Washbasins

Public service departments need washbasins because librarians frequently deal with users who are obviously infected. This is particularly true in public library children's departments, where legions of sneezing kids can send librarians rushing back endlessly to wash their hands one more time, but it happens in all departments.

Any library department that deals with preparing materials for use, repairing them, preparing displays and artwork, and many other functions also needs access to running water.

Retrofitting running water and drains is a lot more difficult than installing them during construction, so postponing them makes no economic sense unless you are sure you won't ever want them.

Washbasins have to be large enough for serious use. Like basins in areas where food is prepared, sinks in workrooms need to be deep. They also need high gooseneck faucets to allow coffee urns and other large containers to be filled. Whether a sink will need one or two drains depends on its long-term use.

The best way to plan is probably to specify that sinks will be provided in all staff workrooms and then to decide which ones aren't really necessary.

B. Washers and Dryers

Some libraries have washing machines and dryers. Public library children's departments that have hand puppets or similar items used by children may want to be able to wash the items in the library instead of having staff take them home to wash in their home washing equipment.

If you think you may need a washer and dryer, you'll find it extremely hard to retrofit, because you will need a water supply, a drain, a dryer vent, and probably a 220-volt power supply for the dryer. Even if you aren't quite sure, the time to install all of these connections (rough them in) is when you are constructing the building. You can always purchase the washer and dryer later (although the cost of providing the necessary connections will probably be far higher than the cost of the washer and dryer).

If space is very tight, apartment-type over-and-under washer and dryer combinations are available, but you may find standard equipment to be less trouble over the years.

IV. CUSTODIAL WORKROOMS

Building codes may require that your library have a mop sink on any floor that has a restroom, but you're a lot better off having one on every floor.

A variety of mop sinks is available—primarily wall-mounted and floor-level sinks—and you and your custodians will need to consult with your architects. The custodians we're worked with like floor-mounted basins because it's easier to empty things into them.

A good way to organize storage space for cleaning equipment—supplies on shelves, floor space for cleaning carts, vacuum cleaners, and rug shampooers—is to store them all in rooms that hold mop sinks.

V. HOSE BIBS

Almost all libraries need external faucets (sometimes called hose bibs or sill cocks) for external access to water.

Hose bibs need to be freeze-proof. A common way to do this is to have the valve for the hose bib inside the library where building heat will keep it from freezing. The external handles for hose bibs have long stems that reach inside the building to engage the actual valve.

Hose bibs also need to be vandal-proof. You don't want people messing with your water system. In some cases, the exterior control handles can simply be removed. Other handles lock.

To help prevent unauthorized use, all of the exterior hose bibs should be controlled by a valve inside the library. The valve (or valves, for a large building) should not affect any water access points inside the building, so that turning off the outside water does not limit any access to water inside the building.

Libraries need to work with their planners and grounds maintenance staff to determine the number of hose bibs needed. A minimum of one on each side of the building is necessary. After that, spacing is a matter of hose length. Hoses longer than about 50 feet are a pain to drag around, which means that hose bibs need to be less than about 75 feet apart, or even closer if water will be needed a long way from the building.

VI. WATER "FEATURES"

A. Indoor Water Features

Water features have been favorite design elements with many architects and interior designers over many years. They include such items as fountains, water walls, reflecting pools, and so on. The main concern of most librarians is the practical effects of interior water features.

Indoor water features have a few appealing aspects:

- Water features can be fun to look at.
- The sound of running water is pleasant.
- Water features provide unexpected fun. Just as with the Spanish Inquisition, no one expects a sudden water feature.

But indoor water features cause many problems:

- Users pitch coins into fountains, blocking the drains and leading to overflows.
- People drop things into fountains. Hopefully their own things, but sometimes the library's things.

> When John was working at a university library, students put fish and frogs into the water features. In a way, it's a friendly gesture, and one that shows an attractive interest in biological studies, but there are probably downsides as well.

- People fall in. Having a user or a mayor take a header into a fountain can spoil a library administrator's day.
- Many librarians with indoor fountains worry about children drowning.
- Fountains can provide pleasant humidity when the air is dry, but they can also add unwanted extra humidity when the air is damp.
- The sound of running water is so persuasive that its sends nearby staff members rushing off to the restroom all day long.
- Most importantly, indoor water features can harbor Legionnaires' disease, which is a deal killer.

There are all sorts of architectural design concepts you do not want in your library. Few of them are more of a pain than indoor water features. No matter how exciting the picture painted by your designers may be, stop the conversation instantly. Rise up firmly and shout, *"We don't want any @#$% indoor water features."*

If you're stuck with an indoor water feature, convert it to a planter.

B. Outdoor Water Features

Many libraries have fountains outside their buildings.

In most cases, these are the ideas of people who are not librarians.

Fountains can be high-maintenance items. They have to be cleaned. In climates with actual winters, fountains have to be drained and covered for winter. While a running fountain can be fun in the summer, a fountain with a tarp over it may not be all that cute in the winter.

Librarians whose buildings have fountains in front tell us they always worry about children falling in.

If you inherit a fountain, you can always cap the pipe, fill the fountain with dirt, and create a handsome flower bed. We know librarians who have done this, and they are pleased with the improvement.

See also the discussion of detention basins later in this chapter.

VII. STORM DRAINS

"Storm sewers" carry away surface runoff and soil moisture. By contrast, "sanitary sewers" carry away all sorts of indoor water from toilets, sinks, showers and bathtubs, dishwashers and clothes washers, and so on.

Not all towns have storm sewer systems. Small drainage ditches between streets and sidewalks are one of the warning signs of the absence of storm drains.

In a town with storm drains, sump pits embedded in basement floors collect water from under the floor slab of the basement and from the bottoms of window wells. As the sump fills with water, a float on the sump pump turns on the pump, which pumps water to the storm sewer outside. To prevent backflow, the highest point in the pipe between the sump pump and the storm sewer needs to be higher than the exterior storm drain gratings. Codes may also require backwater valves in situations like this. If a gully washer leads to more water than the storm sewers can handle, the water backs up to exterior drains rather than to the library basement.

If a library has an open exterior staircase leading down to a basement door, the staircase needs a drain at the bottom. If the drain opening becomes clogged, rainwater coursing down the open staircase simply runs into the basement. The best way to avoid this problem is to have no basement. If you're stuck with a basement, enclosing the steps down to the basement door will help keep water from accumulating right outside the door.

Even worse, if the drain at the foot of the stairs is lower than the storm drain gratings on the street outside, storm water will gush happily from the drain at the foot of the stairs. And into the basement.

Many communities have found that careless construction led to incorrect sewer connections, with sanitary drains leading to storm sewers and storm drains leading to sanitary sewers. Both of these errors lead to serious problems. Correcting them can be expensive and can lead to angry confrontations between landowners and governments.

With crossed connections, during heavy rains, the rainwater fills the sanitary sewer system, increasing the likelihood of toilets backing up. If some sanitary drains dump into the storm system, when the system backs up through your storm drains, the floodwater flowing into your basement will be even less fun.

In general, any space below grade is waiting eagerly to be flooded. Although your library may come pre-equipped with subterranean spaces, you'll be happier without them. In planning libraries, never forget that basements (a) aren't much cheaper per square foot than extra floors, and (b) a heavy rain will not flood an upper floor.

If you construct an open terrace below grade level, you will regret it deeply. The terrace will need storm drains. If the storm drain openings on the terrace are lower than the storm drain openings on the street outside, any water the storm sewers can't handle will back up onto your terrace and flow into your library. If you have backwater valves on your terrace drains to prevent this from happening, sooner or later a valve will clog and water will back up into your library. Standing helplessly while you watch storm water backing up relentlessly into your library is no fun at all (although watching sanitary sewer water backing up is even less fun).

VIII. DETENTION AND RETENTION BASINS

"Detention basins" are areas designed to control the speed of water runoff by detaining the water during rainstorms to help prevent flooding. The general principle is that a detention basin fills quickly with water during a rainstorm. After the rain ends, the water drains away slowly until the basin is empty.

"Retention basins," by contrast, retain part of the water at all times, serving as permanent ponds or lakes.

Detention and retention basins are frequently legally required when a development (such as a new library building or parking lot) decreases the amount of land that can absorb water and thereby increases the rate of runoff.

Since existing structures and paving may be grandfathered in, detention basins may be required only to deal with the reduction in permeable land area that results from a project.

If a library has a tight site with no space for a basin, it may find that it can receive compensating credit for its increased building or parking footprint by using permeable pavers in a parking lot or by adding a green roof.

One of the major downsides of required retention basins is neighborhoods dotted with lakes that harbor Canada geese. While geese are attractive and appealing creatures, they supposedly deposit more poop per pound of goose than cows do per pound of cow. Keeping lawns and parking lots sanitary around retention basins can be a difficult proposition. For this reason, detention basins rather than retention ponds seem more library-friendly.

Retention ponds also provide one more place into which children can fall.

Detention ponds are not maintenance-free. If you have a detention basin, you will need to make sure the device that controls the speed of water exit does not plug up. You will also need to mow the basin when it is dry, and you may need to control plant species.

This is a once-over-extremely-lightly review of detention basins. Depending on where your library is located, it may be subject to a wide variety of rules. Just as your architects and engineers work with local authorities about zoning and building code requirements, they will need to work with them about water runoff control requirements.

You may also need to review with your architects and engineers what will happen when a rain "event" overstresses the capacity of your detention basin. "Hundred-year floods" seem to occur every half-dozen years now, and even the elderly among us will live to see more of them.

Our personal opinion is that limiting water runoff speed is a good thing, but "detained" water is a lot less of a problem than "retained" water. In addition to concerns about child safety, goose poop, and mosquito breeding, retained water is water constantly lying around on your property, and when you have open ponds on your property you may want to think once again about whether you *really* want a basement. (This is just talk. You *don't* want a basement.)

IX. SNAPPY RULES ON PLUMBING SYSTEMS

1. In addition to spreading Legionnaires' disease, indoor "water features" have many other nasty functions. There's no excuse for letting your architects talk you into indoor water features. Shout "NO!" and "NOT A CHANCE!" and "NEVER BRING THIS UP AGAIN!" the second the idea is first mentioned. (If it's still brought up, shout "@#$%&!")
2. Anyone who has dealt with children in a library knows that the word *infectious* does not apply just to laughter. All staff workrooms need washbasins in addition to the customary plentiful hand sanitizers.

3. Libraries are too often equipped with toy washbasins. You don't want any. Washbasins need to be seriously deep and have faucets high enough to allow coffee urns to be filled. (Bar sinks are toy washbasins.)
4. Expanding or retrofitting plumbing is expensive. Don't let people talk you into marginally adequate systems. It makes good sense to rough in plumbing when there is a reasonable chance you may want to add a sink, a washer and dryer, or other feature later.
5. If you have an open exterior staircase leading down to a basement door, sooner or later the drain at the bottom of the steps will plug up and rainwater will flow into your library.
6. Some washbasins may require garbage disposals, particularly in staff lunchrooms. (Imagine a performing group called the "Staff Room Cloggers.")
7. Undesired water is just one of the many reasons that basements are a bad idea in libraries.
8. If you construct an open terrace next to your library below grade level, you will regret it deeply. The terrace will need storm drains. If the storm drain openings on the terrace are lower than the storm drain openings on the street outside, any water the storm sewers can't handle will back up onto your terrace and flow into your library. If you have backwater valves on your terrace drains to prevent this from happening, sooner or later a valve will clog and water will back up into your library. If all the valves work correctly, pressure from the local storm drain system may literally blow one out of one of the drains. You will not enjoy water in your library.
9. If your building site is small and your town requires water detention, explore credits (such as green roofs and permeable pavers) available to offset the new land you plan to occupy.
10. A happy library is a basement-less library.
11. All library employees should know how to turn off water. When the time comes to turn it off, you don't have time to look things up in a leisurely fashion or to wait for outside assistance. Extensive training of staff and labeling of valves helps.
12. A friend of Fred's in the insurance business says, "Basements are places you put things you don't want."

30

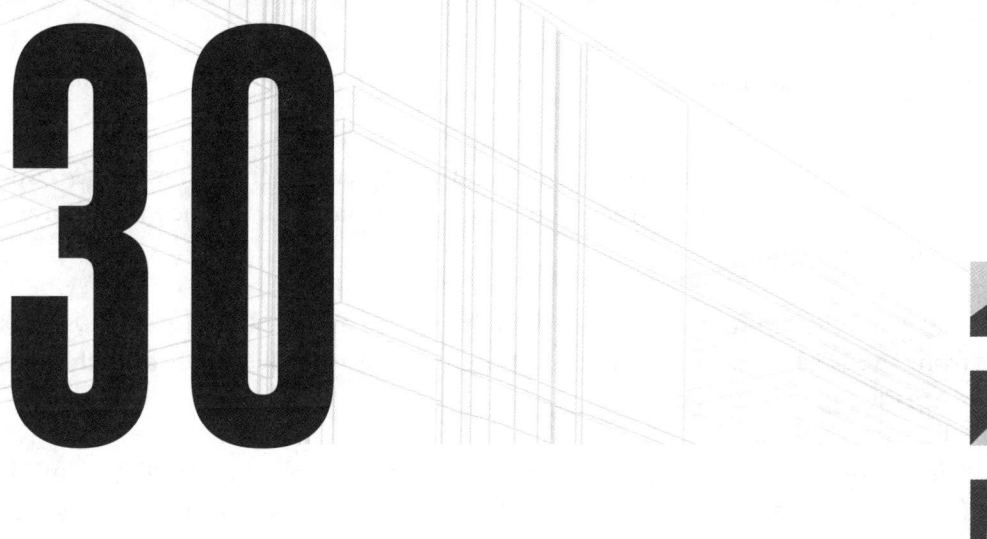

Security

I. INTRODUCTION

All libraries must be concerned with protecting users, staff, collections, and buildings. In that order.

Building codes play a major role in the determination of minimum security equipment, but it's important to remember that codes contain minimum requirements, not ideal requirements. There are a great many options for better or more extensive equipment that libraries should at least consider.

Of the many approaches to security, a surprising number are structural and involve no high-tech gear of any kind. These include site selection, construction materials, and physical arrangement of spaces.

Other approaches involve mechanical or electronic equipment. A wide variety of equipment is available to prevent unauthorized entry or exit, control access to secure areas, limit the theft of library materials, oversee spaces, suppress fires, and protect collections from water. While some equipment is easy to retrofit into most existing library buildings, other equipment involves a certain amount of planning ahead.

We think that the time for a thorough review of all planned security is during the design phases of libraries—and the earlier this takes place, the easier it will be to keep your building secure.

Include your library building consultant in your security discussions, since consultants should have a significant amount of firsthand experience with library security problems.

Make sure that your architects and engineers are aware of your security plans from the beginning, and check with them about improvements and changes since this book was written.

The end of this chapter includes a discussion of insurance as it applies to buildings. The U.S. insurance industry has been a dominant player in the creation of safer buildings. The industry was a prime motivator for the creation of building codes. Knowing what types of construction will lower your insurance rates is a great guide to some of the steps you can take to create a safer building and to reduce some operating costs.

II. SECURITY THROUGH BUILDING DESIGN

While many security systems consist of mechanical or electrical equipment, a large number of opportunities exist for designing library buildings that provide safety for people, collections, and equipment.

Here are a few everyday examples of what one might call "passive" security systems—designing buildings so that they are inherently secure:

A. Fire-Resistant Construction

("Fire *resistive*" is a category of construction type defined by the Insurance Services Office, and is not what we are talking about here.)

One of the easy ways to construct a safer library is to use fire-resistant materials.

In many cases, local building codes will limit the size of a library that can be built with wood frame construction. Some libraries even find that when the time comes to expand, the materials used in the original construction are not legal for a larger building.

You will want to review fire resistance with your architect at one of your first planning meetings. Be sure to discuss the implications of long-term future expansion and of insurance rates.

It is essential that some areas of libraries be unusually fire-resistant. The classic example is book returns that lead directly inside library buildings. Unfortunately, one of the standard causes of library fires is incendiaries in book returns. For instance, a major fire at the Danbury, Connecticut, public library in 1996 was started in a book return. While returns that lead directly into buildings are convenient for staff and help protect books, the receiving areas for returns of this type need to be capable of containing fires. Any fire in a book return is likely to result in the destruction of all the books in the return, but it's a nice thing if that's as far as the damage goes.

> Ill winds blow in various directions. Fred once worked with a library that had a fire in its book return, which consisted of a mail slot in the front door and a cardboard carton to receive the books. The fire department arrived in record time and saved the building. Years later, after a new library had been built on a new site, a board member told Fred that the library would have been better off as an institution if the fire department had been less prompt.

Library furnishings also need to be fire-resistant. The most important requirements involve upholstered furniture. A great deal of soft seating sold in the United States is filled with polyurethane foam that is almost explosively flammable and exudes cyanide gas when it burns. (Remember the Sofa Super Store fire in Charleston, South Carolina, in 2007, in which nine firefighters were killed.)

One good standard you can cite for fire-resistant furniture is CAL 133 (California Technical Bulletin 133), which requires either fire-blocking materials between the foam and the outer upholstery fabric or else foam treated to make it fire-resistant. The CAL 133 standard has been adopted by some other states, but we think it's a good idea for all libraries. However, avoiding flammable foam in the first place is even better.

If you are considering gluing carpet to walls for decorative or acoustic purposes, be sure that the carpet you select meets fire standards for application on vertical surfaces. Carpet attached to walls must meet a higher standard because fires can burn their way vertically up walls, and carpet that is perfectly safe for the floor of your library may be a serious fire hazard on walls.

In many new libraries, any structural wood will be fire-resistant. For example, blocking installed in steel stud walls for later mounting of plaques or other heavy objects may be treated to be fire-resistant.

B. Flood-Resistant Construction

Although major library floods are relatively rare, they occur in the United States almost every year.

Floods are not fun. Wet books are frequently ruined by the time the heavily polluted floodwaters finally recede. Freeze drying is frequently touted in the library literature as a treatment for saturated books, but it's expensive, and the books are never as good as new afterwards. And it doesn't work on coated paper.

One obvious way to protect libraries from floods is to build them on high ground and avoid basements, but for a variety of political, historical, and design reasons, these easy protections are sometimes ignored. It's hard to agree with any of the reasons.

1. Never Build on Floodplains

One of the easiest ways to protect your library from water is to always build on high ground.

Insurance maps showing the locations of floodplains are available for communities throughout the United States. You may even find state regulations that forbid library construction on floodplains.

Even when they avoid floodplains, however, many libraries end up wet when flooding spreads beyond the limits of official floodplains. In recent years, the phrase "hundred-year flood" has become almost a joke, with hundred-year floods seeming to occur in some communities every decade.

Many riverside towns have dike systems to protect low-lying areas, but (as the Mississippi River demonstrated in Louisiana in 2007 and the Cedar River in Iowa in 2008) dikes fail. We think that blissfully counting on the eternal efficacy of dikes is on a par with believing everything one reads on the Internet.

Resist political pressure to build libraries in historic areas that can flood. If your town has a historic riverside section and a modern bluff-top section, you may find yourself under tremendous pressure from local historic organizations to locate your library where floods will sooner or later find it, rather than to locate it safely on high ground.

2. Beware of Basements

We think that the evil allure of basements in libraries is driven primarily by ill-informed stinginess, but it can result in all manner of unpleasant outcomes.

When people construct houses with crawl spaces, the extra cost of basements is relatively modest because (almost) all they have to do is extend the walls and pour a floor. Basements in houses hold all sorts of stuff, and they provide tornado shelters for buildings that are almost always too flimsy to withstand the storms.

But due to the cost of floor construction and sealing basement walls, there's proportionately less saving involved in building basements in libraries than most people believe. When a library has no basement, constructing the main floor is cheap, for it's easy to engineer a concrete slab on grade to carry the weight of books. But when a library adds a basement, the inexpensive main floor slab now must become a massive floor capable of supporting 150 pounds or more per square foot.

Basically, an upper floor is not much more expensive than a basement, and it offers the advantages of natural light and absence of unwanted water.

Basements are bad enough in traditional Carnegie-era buildings where the main floors are half a flight above grade and the basements half a flight below. But in modern buildings with grade-level main floors, basements are completely subterranean. If basement ceilings are high enough to allow good lighting and space is provided above the ceilings for mechanical systems, basement floors in these buildings may be 14 or 15 feet below grade, rather than 5 or 6 feet below grade in Carnegie-era buildings. And any flooding will be worse.

Basements in modern libraries are also windowless, unless you can sneak in a skylight or two along the perimeter of the building. If your library opts for a basement rather than an extra floor, anyone who works in the basement (and there will be more and more of them as the number of staff members grows and the public areas above grade fill with new books and equipment) will be banished forever to windowless gloom.

When we talk with library staff members about what they want in workrooms, the word we hear most often is *daylight*.

There are plenty of examples of modern libraries with basements that flood. Relying on modern construction methods to keep your feet dry is not demonstrably an effective idea.

Sub-basements are of course even more dangerous. The deeper libraries burrow into the earth, the greater the hydrostatic pressure becomes, and the more likely they are to be beneath the water table. One library has constructed a multi-deck underground structure near a lake, and the major question seems to many observers to be not "Will it leak?" but "*When* will it leak?"

Mechanical systems like sump pumps exist for basements, and most of them appear to work most of the time. But even if you have really satisfactory devices, why rely on mechanical gadgets when by building above ground you can have a library with passive systems to keep it dry?

The main point is that basements in libraries cost nearly as much as additional upper floors. The main difference in cost is replacing concrete basement walls with more attractive walls and windows. And you get to save on the cost of waterproofing walls.

From our point of view, there is no good reason for constructing basements in modern libraries. We think libraries should build high, stay dry, and enjoy the view.

C. Single Public Entrances

One of the core principles of good library design is limiting the number of entrances. Every entrance needs to be supervised by a staff member. Book theft detection systems require nearby staff oversight. If a library is open 60 to 70 hours a week, that means a minimum of two full-time people to watch a single door.

Unfortunately, many of the people with whom you will have to work will insist that multiple entrances are essential. City fathers want public libraries with entrances facing both the sidewalks in front of libraries and the parking lots behind them. Architects of community college libraries think it would be great to place the library in the middle of a sprawling building and have entrances from all directions. Campus officials think university libraries are such large buildings that they should have doors on more than one side. School officials want separate entrances from the junior high and the senior high to a shared library.

> All of these may sound imaginary, but we've run into each of these situations. For instance, an Illinois community college was actually constructed the way it's described above, with multiple entrances. The first year it was open, a substantial portion of the collection vanished, and the school had to go through complex restructuring in a partially successful attempt to correct the mess.

The only time multiple entrances are not disasters are where:

- The library is so large it has interior distributor halls with a separate entrance (supervised) to each departmental library.
- The multiple entrances lead to a concourse that has a single entrance to the actual library.

When people pressure you to add extra entrances, always quote the cost of doing so in terms of extra staff, and ask whether they are proposing to pay the additional cost for eternity (or for the life of the library, whichever is less). (Fred has done this several times with town officials, who begin in grumpy disbelief but eventually back down.)

D. Good Sight Lines

One of the easiest ways to provide safer libraries at no extra cost is to take great care with sight lines. Sight lines are direct open visual paths that allow library staff members to see what's going on around the building.

When you review the plans for your library, with furniture locations indicated, always ask yourself how your staff will keep an eye on the library and its users. And also ask whether people will be able to see what they'd rather not see.

1. Beneficial Sight Lines

- *Stack orientation.* For example, if staff members can see down stack aisles when seated at the reference desk, they can keep a much better eye on things than if the aisles are perpendicular to the desk. Although they won't be able to see all the aisles from the desk, they can do so by taking a few steps backward and forward rather than having to walk the length of the library, peering into each aisle.
- *Internal windows.* Another way to maintain good sight lines is through the use of internal windows. Study rooms need glass walls on at least three sides. (A glass wall is a real glass wall, not a tiny window in a solid wall.) If staff

workrooms have windows to the adjacent public areas of the library, staff members working at their desks are more aware of what's going on in the building. If children's departments are walled off for acoustic purposes, the use of glass walls permits better oversight.

2. Evil Sight Lines

The pursuit of better sight lines has also led to some really unfortunate ideas, and some accidental sight lines are real howlers.

- *Hidden corners.* If your library design requires staff to walk the length of a long room just to see what's going on in a back corner or in a small study room, you will spend a great deal of money in frustrated oversight. Study the architect's drawings for problem areas in time for changes to be made. You can always install video surveillance systems to cover hidden corners, but video systems are primarily useful in forensics—finding out what happened after the fact. Few libraries can station someone to stare at monitors by the hour waiting for the very occasional malfeasance. (Very obvious cameras, of course, may intimidate some people by merely being visible.)

Glass walls are a great way to separate noisy areas from quiet areas. In this case, the noise of the children's department in the background is prevented from disturbing people borrowing books. The same principle works with study rooms. (On the other hand, the children's department is far more brightly lighted than the adjacent staff service desk in the lobby, making the lobby seem gloomy.)

- *Radiating book stacks.* Radiating stacks are an eternally appealing but extraordinarily bad concept. The general idea is to arrange shelving units so they radiate out from a central service point like the spokes of a wheel, enabling staff members seated there to look down all the aisles by simply twirling around. The first thing this accomplishes is the waste of expensive space. If aisles are wide enough near the service desk, they can be extraordinarily wide fifty feet away. Some libraries have tried to insert short sections of shelving at the far ends of the radiating aisles, but this leads to confused users—and it still wastes a great deal of space. For more examples of the evil of radiating shelves, see chapter 17 on "Collection Storage."
- *Full-view restrooms.* It always amazes us how many restrooms place users on full display whenever the doors are opened. For example, in many library restrooms (and those in other buildings, to be fair about things), gentlemen standing at the urinals are in plain view whenever the doors are opened. Even when there is no direct view of restroom action, it's often possible to see everything going on reflected in mirrors over the sinks. And we're not sure that users like to be watched while they're standing at sinks anyway.

Single-user restrooms are often laid out so that the toilet is on proud display whenever the door is open. This strikes us as an unsatisfactory idea, particularly because the doors of unoccupied restrooms can stand open.

Staff restrooms are all too frequently placed directly adjacent to staff lunch areas, with the toilets on full display whenever the doors are ajar.

Restrooms should open into hallways, not into library reading rooms or staff lunchrooms. But this is one of the most frequently ignored laws in library design.

It's a good idea to check the proposed floor plans of your library to be sure that the only things visible when restroom doors are open are blank walls.

E. No Places Where People Can Be Trapped

One of the easiest ways to protect library users and staff is to avoid situations where people can be cornered.

- Dead-end book aisles. An obvious example is avoiding dead-end book stack aisles. When faced with overcrowding, libraries are often tempted to eliminate cross aisles and use the space instead for additional shelving. The problem with dead-end aisles is that people can be cornered there. Imagine a fifteen-year-old girl looking for books when an intimidating-looking guy comes along and blocks the exit from the aisle where she is standing. If the aisle

is open at both ends, she can simply leave. But if it is open at one end only, she has to decide whether to scream (and probably feel extremely foolish) or just hope for the best. It's not a pleasant choice.
- Dangerous emergency exits. In large library buildings, most emergency exits are complex. Instead of leading directly out of doors, they lead to exit corridors, some of which can be surprisingly complex. If you have complex exit corridors with multiple one-way doors, it's important to know whether anyone is using them or even trapped there. Motion detectors, alarmed exit doors, and cameras may all help. If you don't have them, you'll need to check daily for lost patrons.
- Service desks where staff members can be trapped. All service desks need two ways out.

F. Windstorm Shelters

Always know where to send library users in case of windstorms.

Some windstorms—such as hurricanes—are fairly predictable. Even if librarians don't know the strength of the hurricane or exactly where it will hit land, they know it's on its way. And architects can plan for predictably nasty weather.

John has had a lot of experience with hurricanes and libraries, and he does not regard them lightly. After surviving a number of them, he emphasizes to his clients the importance of following (or exceeding) all local codes, being prepared for glass damage, and having evacuation plans.

Tornados are a different story. They are amazingly unpredictable, and unlike even the strongest hurricanes, they can wreak virtually total destruction. Although they are concentrated in mid-continental areas, they can occur anywhere.

Even sturdy, modern libraries are vulnerable to tornados and hurricanes. Tornados in particular can rip off roofs and send shards of glass streaking like jet-propelled knives. Given designers' long-term love affair with glass library buildings, one can envision some spectacular results.

Because of the danger to roofs and windows, all library buildings need places of refuge where users and staff can find shelter from tornados and hurricanes.

- In large libraries with more than one floor, staff members need to designate places that have strong floors above them and are protected from possible flying glass. Although the roof may be yanked off the library, a concrete floor sturdy enough to hold library books will probably withstand a storm. Basement hallways are great places of refuge. The current architectural enthusiasm for glass buildings makes us wonder about tornado safety in showplace libraries. For example, where will users of some new libraries where every vertical surface appears to be glass find shelter during a tornado?

- Single-story or wood frame library buildings need to create internal rooms that can withstand the direct hit of a major tornado. Commonly these are restrooms, which in most cases have no windows. One library with which Fred worked was a replacement for one destroyed by a tornado. In the new library, which houses the village hall, library, and an ESDA (Emergency Services and Disaster Agency) office, the restrooms have concrete walls and ceilings. One advantage of using restrooms for windstorm shelters is that they may be the only rooms in a library that will reliably have open floor space when the storm arrives, since library staff members cannot requisition restrooms for storage and fill them with program supplies, excess furniture, and neatly boxed miscellany, thereby making it impossible for panicked people to crowd in. It's hard to imagine a non-restroom storm shelter in a library that will not be filled—sooner or later—with stacked cartons or book sale books.

The trouble with windstorm damage is that everyone is painfully aware of the possibilities for a few years after a nearby storm, but they eventually forget and sometimes don't want to spend the money.

G. Earthquake Preparedness

Libraries need to rely on their architects, engineers, and shelving manufacturers for guidance on preparing for earthquakes. In addition to general building codes, there may be specific codes (as in California) or other requirements. And as with many other codes, requirements may be more demanding after every major earthquake.

One of the major concerns is the stability of book shelving. Cantilever steel shelving units can topple like dominos, and libraries may be required to limit the height of units, to anchor the feet of the units to the floor, or to connect the tops of support posts with steel U-channels that are anchored to walls. (Pictures of toppled shelving units are available and dramatic.)

Connecting the tops of units strikes us as more practical than anchoring the units because of the far greater mechanical advantage, but the connecting steel U-channels will be obvious if the channels are not limited to posts away from the ends of stack ranges.

Individual shelving units may also be required to add gussets to strengthen the connections between the columns and the bases.

Some people suggest that carpeting or other soft materials under shelving will increase the likelihood of tipping by making it easier for shelving units to rock.

Some codes may also require solid walls to resist the tendency of buildings to tip during earthquakes. A main functional question may be whether solid walls interfere with design functions that rely on modular (post and beam) construction.

H. Providing Security by Avoiding Shared Buildings

One source of serious security problems occurs in situations where multiple agencies share buildings.

Libraries are particularly subject to problems in this area because libraries have open spaces rather than individually locked public service spaces like classroom buildings. Once people are inside the library, they have access to almost all the collections, computers, and other equipment.

If non-library staff have keys to the building, almost everyone has keys to the building.

A handy rule of thumb is that no one who does not report to the library director should have keys to the building.

I. Windows

One serious source of theft is windows that can be opened by library users. It's easy to open a window, drop a book into the bushes, and retrieve it later.

Having windows that open may be a good thing in case of HVAC failure, but you want to be sure that only staff members are able to open windows.

Academic libraries have had major thefts by people who lowered bags or baskets of books out of book stack windows.

J. Terraces

Reading terraces always are an attractive concept, but you need to be sure that people cannot use terraces without first checking materials out. As with windows, it's easy to drop books off the edges of terraces for later retrieval.

Architects are frequently enamored by the concept of reading terraces and try to argue that users won't actually drop books off the edges. We often hear stubborn architects use the phrase *secure reading terrace*. But this is a serious oxymoron.

K. Dangerous Architectural Features

A number of ill-considered but popular architectural features have led to injuries to users and staff. It's easy to say "No!" to all of them.

User and staff safety trumps cute design concepts.

1. Atriums

Atriums attract suicides. One major New York City library has had at least three.

We've argued against atriums in many places in this book. Suicides are just one of many good reasons to oppose atriums—although we think it's a sufficient reason.

2. Story Pits

Some libraries have constructed story pits in their children's departments. Sooner or later, someone falls in. Risers for children to sit on work just as well.

3. Oddly Configured Staircases

Staircases are sufficiently dangerous without making the treads odd shapes, without making the treads end before they touch the wall, without moving people diagonally, without having steps that go on forever, without terrifying people with acrophobia, and without lots of other seriously bad ideas.

As we get older, we are more conscious of the possibilities of falling downstairs.

4. Railings That Can Be Climbed Like Ladders

One of the most popular design features in modern architecture is railings with horizontal bars that can be climbed like ladders. People can (and do) fall off. Any sane building code would ban them, but we still see them everywhere.

5. Water Features

Designers are so fond of water inside buildings that the whole concept has a name of its own—"water feature."

We don't know of any deaths in library water features, but librarians are constantly worried because people fall into water features with dismal (or exciting, if you enjoy the news) regularity. And water features harbor Legionnaires' disease.

III. THEFT CONTROL SYSTEMS

For many libraries, one of the primary security problems is preventing users from stealing the collection.

Many of the attempted solutions to problems of book theft have implications for building design.

Much of theft control reflects the general assumption that the theft of library materials is more a matter of opportunity than sophisticated criminal enterprise. For every thief practicing professional sleight of hand as he removes maps from atlases in rare book rooms, there are thousands of university students stealing research materials from book stacks and hundreds of thousands of middle-schoolers filching copies of skateboarding and teenie-bopper rock star magazines.

Librarians have to protect their collections not only against theft, but also against mutilation and hiding. Users cut pictures out of books. They hide items for later use or to keep other users from finding them.

In general, preventing book theft is the easiest problem to solve—or at least combat. However, the most determined thief will get their materials no matter what security system is in place. The theft of audio and video recordings is more difficult to prevent. Mutilation of materials can be almost impossible to prevent if it involves no attempt to remove anything larger than a sheet of paper from the library. And preventing the theft of video games is nearly impossible.

A. Typical High-Risk Materials

From personal experience, most public librarians can predict the types of materials most likely to be stolen. Books on sex, the occult, auto repair, and do-it-yourself anarchy disappear with predictable regularity. Nonprint materials such as recordings of popular music and popular films would vanish almost instantly in many libraries if the materials were ever left lying around loose. And video games vanish almost instantly.

In particular, CDs and DVDs lend themselves to theft because they are in high demand and can easily be concealed in pockets. The side pockets on a man's sport coat, for example, can easily hold several hundred dollars' worth of discs without bulging.

In large academic and research libraries, the regular book stacks are full of materials that would be kept under lock and key in lesser libraries. The managers of rare book rooms in libraries like this are aware of the situation, but the rare book room stacks may be far too small to allow every valuable item to be sequestered.

> One of the engaging variants on theft occurs in competitive academic environments, where students working on assignments hide key volumes from each other. Law school librarians, for instance, have told us about this practice, which in turn may tell us something about lawyers in training.

The carefully controlled clientele of special libraries makes theft a less pressing issue, particularly because physicians and lawyers may have 24/7 access to their libraries.

B. Economic Models

Every library contemplating theft control systems sooner or later faces a cost-benefit analysis, weighing the value of items stolen against the cost of security systems. Often analysis of this type underlies planning discussions, even when it is unvoiced.

The problem with this approach is attempting to set a cost on theft. In addition to the cash value of the stolen item, there are costs for:

- Staff time spent inventorying for theft. (Inventorying requires preliminary shelf reading, and some large libraries can't even afford that.) In some large research libraries, the only staff time spent on missing materials is in response to snags—reports that requested items cannot be located. The fewer problems libraries have with theft, the less time they need to spend verifying what's actually there.

- Staff time wasted hunting for an item and finally coming to the conclusion that it is genuinely gone.
- Difficulty in locating replacements. Most books in most libraries are out of print.
- Dealing with irreplaceable items. Document collections and archives, for example, are full of unique materials. Unless collections have been digitized or duplicated, any small item that makes its way into a convenient briefcase or purse is probably gone forever.
- Staff time ordering and processing replacements. Particularly in the case of out-of-print materials purchased from small vendors, the combined costs for searching, ordering, cataloging, and check issuing can vastly exceed the cost of the item purchased.
- User alienation if high-demand materials are frequently missing or if requests for high-demand materials take forever to fill because the items need to be reordered.

Some libraries have perennial problems locating materials in stacks. Whether this is due to theft, lack of shelf reading, or other problems, the result is a body of users who are unimpressed with the quality of their library.

For all of these reasons, we think that library theft and mutilation problems do not easily lend themselves to a simple economic analysis.

C. Improved Oversight

One way of limiting the theft and mutilation of materials lies in designing library buildings that lend themselves to improved collection oversight.

Here are some basic approaches:

- Concentration on excellent sight lines. The more users are aware of being watched, the less likely they are to remove items from collections.
- Careful positioning of staff points. A reference desk in the middle of a large room provides better staff oversight than one tucked into a corner. Two staff desks placed closely together waste potential oversight opportunities.
- Easily watched tables for people consulting theft-prone materials. Proposed floor plans need to be checked to make sure that tables are visible from service desks. (An associated management problem involves training staff members to insist that users consulting theft-prone materials use designated tables. Users who announce preferences for hidden tables in back corners may be telegraphing felonious intent.)

- Staffed exits. No library exit can be left unwatched unless it is an emergency exit with a very loud alarm and a security camera. Book theft security gates are a tremendous help, but they can easily be defeated when no one is watching.
- Guard stations at exits. Guard stations where briefcases and purses carried by people leaving the building were inspected were common in large libraries before the advent of electronic theft-detection systems, and they may still be in use in some libraries.
- Coin-return lockers for briefcases and purses. Major archives or other collections of rare materials may permit users to bring in absolutely nothing, but in turn provide free yellow pads, pencils, and photocopies. (The problem with people using coin-return lockers as personal storerooms can be solved by emptying lockers nightly.)
- Restrooms outside of theft control gates. Restrooms provide a favorite place for the removal of theft-control devices, particularly plastic anti-theft boxes on CDs and DVDs. They're also a great place for the destructive reading of library materials. By arranging buildings so that nothing can be taken into a restroom before being checked out, libraries can prevent a number of problems.
- Windows that cannot be opened by users. One of the traditional ways of removing items from collections is to pitch them out the windows for later retrieval. Book stacks with windows that open for ventilation offer wonderful opportunities for theft. Users even bring ropes and baskets to lower stolen books into shrubbery below. All libraries planning new construction or remodeling need to specify ways to keep users from opening windows. A standard way is to avoid windows that can be opened, but some libraries like to be able to open windows in case of HVAC failure. Preventing users from opening windows can sometimes be as simple as removing cranks from casement windows. Other windows need key locks. Some libraries that start out with windows that can be opened end up having to bolt their windows shut. If you specify user-proof windows in your building program, be sure that your architect doesn't simply blow off the requirement in the mistaken assumption that the locks serve only to keep intruders out of the library at night.

> Years ago, Fred specified windows that couldn't be opened from inside, to prevent users tossing books out of windows, only to find that in the completed library the architect had provided windows with manual latches. When asked, the architect happily assured everyone that he had ignored the program requirement because custodians could check the library at closing time to be sure that all the

> windows were locked, thereby preventing would-be intruders from slithering into the library in the dark of the night. But he never thought to ask why the library wanted locking windows in the first place.

The main reason to provide a few windows that can be opened is to provide emergency airflow during times of HVAC failure. In any other circumstances, they're just a nuisance. (Opening windows can also screw up the balance of properly functioning ventilation systems.)

Actually, a few libraries may be located in areas where mild and relatively dry climates allow occasional free air conditioning by simply opening windows. Libraries that plan to do this (and we think it's a seriously bad idea) need to figure out how to prevent people from chucking items out the windows. And how to keep dust and dirt from blowing into the building.

All of these security concepts have structural implications. If you want to employ them (or even keep your options open), you will want to be sure that they appear in your building program. You will also need to check proposed floor plans carefully to be sure the requirements have actually been followed.

Few non-librarians have had to cope with the everyday security problems that librarians know all too well. If designers don't understand why librarians need specific features, they may decide to simply omit the features rather than ask.

D. Sequestering Theft-Prone Materials

Placing materials that are valuable or prone to mutilation and theft in closed areas is a traditional way of protecting collections. It's a major function of separate rare book rooms. In smaller libraries (particularly those without electronic theft-control systems), shelving units behind lending desks are frequently provided for materials needing extra protection.

- Sequestering portions of collections requires advance planning in building programs. Even small libraries that need to protect audiovisual collections must calculate the amount of space needed for storing materials.
- For efficient functioning, circulating materials stored behind desks need to be in the containers in which they will be lent. Some libraries try to store CDs and DVDs loose behind lending desks, retrieving them and inserting them in their boxes when users bring the empty boxes to the lending desks.

This is a desperate solution for libraries that have too little space behind desks, but it wastes a great deal of staff time and inflicts extra wear and tear on the recordings. Given the painful fragility of DVDs, rough storage and extra handling are both bad ideas.
- High-demand materials stored behind lending desks need to be close at hand. Fred worked with one public library where lack of space behind the service desk and the inflexible design of the adjacent staff workroom forced the staff to store the DVD collection at the far end of the staff workroom. Every time someone wanted a DVD—and this happened every few minutes—a staff member had to walk a total of nearly 100 feet to retrieve it. Both the inadequate space behind the service desk and the inflexible room behind it were examples of poor original planning.

E. Keeping Unauthorized People out of the Library

For many great university libraries—particularly libraries in private universities—a central approach to security simply involves keeping unauthorized people entirely out of libraries.

The same approach can be taken by special libraries, which can limit access to corporate employees, and by school libraries, which can limit access by nonstudents.

School libraries are generally covered by the increased security necessary after assaults on schoolchildren.

Libraries that limit use by unauthorized people will need space for guard stations controlling access to the building.

They may also want to allow space for access gates using swipe cards or proximity cards carried by students and faculty.

F. Electronic Theft-Prevention Systems

Most medium-sized and large libraries use electronic theft-protection systems.

These systems include targets inserted into each book. When books that have not been properly checked out are carried through exit gates, alarms sound.

Most systems work by disabling targets as a step in the lending operation, which enables users to carry materials through the security gates.

Some libraries, however, use bypass systems. In these libraries, targets are never disabled. Users hand books to staff members, staff members check the books out, users walk through the exit gates, and staff members hand them the books. The system is very much like those used in some airports.

As with library automation systems, the possibility of technical obsolescence is always around. Investing in a very well-established and widely used theft-detection system decreases the chance of it becoming a technological orphan if the manufacturer decides profits are too small and it's time to drop the product.

Theft-detection systems vary widely in price. Opting for anything more complex than a basic magnetic system requires extra study and evaluation.

A major danger with electronic theft-detection systems is false alarms. After enough false alarms, library staff members start waving users through the gates whenever the alarms are activated. For this reason, it seems far better to adjust alarms so that they are slightly insensitive and miss a few items than to have alarms that are activated when they should not be.

1. Space Planning for Electronic Theft-Prevention Systems

If your library is planning to install a theft-prevention system—either when it opens or at a later time—you will need to incorporate space for the associated equipment in your building plans.

All systems use some form of security gates. Be sure that your architect checks with the manufacturer of your equipment concerning space and electrical requirements, including the distances between gates and other parts of your building.

Bypass systems require constructing service counters attached to security gates, so that users can hand books to attendants, walk through the gates, and then collect their books on the far side before leaving the library. The design concept is very much like airport security gates. A bypass system will require extra space for the service counter and accommodations for people entering the library, all plugged into an entryway. The system will also require extra staff if the service counter cannot be combined with the lending desk—a difficult undertaking.

Modern video surveillance systems include alarm inputs that can integrate with theft-detection systems and can be programmed to alert the security staff. These systems also tag the recorded video for easier future access and retrieval.

If you have older video surveillance equipment, you will want lights on top of your exit gates that flash whenever the audio alarm is activated. If the surveillance cameras can pick up the flashing light, you will be able to link specific faces with the alarms. (The beeping sound of the gates is not enough, since most surveillance systems do not include sound, and there will be no way to link a specific person with the alarm.)

2. Magnetic Systems

Magnetic theft-detection systems are widely used and function well.

The only unusual requirement of these systems is that gates need to be about three feet or so away from metal objects, including doors, window walls, and so on. They are especially sensitive to metal parts in loose association, such as panic bar assemblies. Very occasionally, massive steel beams over doors make it impossible to install magnetic detection systems. (Detection gates also need to be several feet away from cathode-ray tubes, but most libraries have converted to flat screen monitors.)

Magnetic detection systems rely on the effects of carrying a strip of Permalloy (a material that is unusually permeable to magnetic flux) through the exit gate. To disable the effect of the strip, small bits of soft iron embedded in the strip are magnetized, frequently by just passing the book over a large magnet. The magnetized bits of iron prevent a Permalloy strip from conducting flux and allow the book to be carried through exit gates without activating the alarm.

Systems of this type are inherently unfriendly to magnetic media, but the manufacturers have workaround equipment. With CDs and DVDs replacing audiocassettes and videocassettes, however, magnetic media are far less central to libraries now than they were a few years ago.

One cost advantage of magnetic theft-control systems is that they are not linked to lending systems. For this reason, not every item in a collection needs to have a detection strip. Libraries can get along well with strips in 100 percent of the high-theft items and in perhaps 10 percent of the rest.

Detection strips without soft iron bits are available, but we think their use is a serious mistake. Books with these strips cannot be disabled and cannot be carried through security gates without setting off alarms. We have seen two uses of such strips:

- Some libraries have installed these strips in books that are never intended to circulate, such as reference works. Unfortunately, many libraries circulate older copies of reference books, or simply convert all reference books to circulating books. Since removing and replacing strips inside book spines can be almost impossible, library staff will have to walk such books through gates for users.
- Some libraries have set up bypass security gates, where users hand their books to an attendant, walk through the gate, and then receive their books back. If libraries of this type use strips that cannot be disabled, they are condemned to use the bypass system forever. And the books they lend will set off alarms in any other library to which they are taken. (This happened in Illinois, where a university library used the bypass system and students constantly set off alarms in a major public library a few blocks away.)

The best-known magnetic theft-detection system is 3-M's "Tattle Tape" system.

3. Resonating Circuit Systems

Resonating circuit systems rely on circuits installed in the book, typically behind the card pocket. To disable the alarm, a bypass card (a sheet of foil between two layers of paper) is inserted in the card pocket. Libraries find a variety of interesting excuses for the bypass cards.

Systems of this type are fairly undemanding as far as equipment placement is concerned.

One problem with systems of this type is that they're easy to circumvent. Once users figure out the purpose of the bypass cards, they can "lose" a card or two and then use the cards to remove items from the library.

The main security system of this type is the Checkpoint system.

4. Radio-Frequency Identification Systems

The current vogue in new theft-detection systems is radio-frequency identification systems (aka RFID systems).

These systems typically combine checkout and security functions. Many are also used in combination with book transport and sorting systems.

Libraries planning to use systems of this type, particularly in combination with book transport systems, will need to plan installations from the very beginning, since the transport systems will have to be fitted into the structure of the library. If the systems begin functioning when books are slipped into return slots—which is one of their strengths—structural planning is even more complex.

Full RFID systems are extremely expensive to install. We are not aware of any published cost-benefit analyses. Nor do we have any information on what will happen to customers if (for example) a company that manufactures the conveyor systems goes out of business. In our bleaker moments, we remember the ill-fated luggage-handling system at the Denver airport.

RFID-based book transport systems have many implications for library building design:

- Systems that include return slots that check items in are often somewhat slow because items need to be fed one at a time. Three or four parents with stacks of picture books can create a major bottleneck. Additional problems can occur if that bottleneck in turn affects the ability of other users to enter or leave the library. The moral is to be sure that there is enough elbowroom around return points, as well as enough space for adding extra return points if they become necessary. And be sure you know what extra return points will cost.
- Any system failure affecting return slots will lead to massive numbers of books being returned manually, and libraries need space to receive them.
- Book-transport systems can literally weave through library structures. There need to be ways to deal with items that jam the conveyor system. If the belt moves from floor to floor through a narrow tunnel, the library may need extraordinarily slender employees to creep into the tunnel and retrieve books that have fallen off the belt.
- In costing out systems, be sure to have accurate information on the cost of maintenance and upkeep once warranties have expired.
- Double-check your proposed system's operating capacity.
  - If your system has a single automatic sorting line, is it possible that use may increase to the point where the line cannot handle the load?
  - How will your book returns handle materials (such as books from other libraries) that do not use RFID tags?
- While magnetic theft-detection strips can be hidden in the spines of books, RFID tags are usually extremely obvious. Libraries have found that it's extremely easy for thieves to simply remove the tags from the books, and sometimes they find handfuls of RFID tags littering the stacks and restrooms.

5. Problem Materials

All theft-detection systems work well with hardbound books, but other materials offer challenges.

Many items offer no good place where targets can be concealed. While a magnetic strip can be inserted inside the spine of a hardbound book and be difficult either to see or remove, what does one do with a DVD or CD?

- Direct mounting of targets. Some libraries, however, have had success mounting theft-detection targets directly on DVDs and CDs. We are always concerned about this approach because (a) the targets are very visible to users, and (b) they may not be compatible with all CD and DVD players. If you can make this approach work, it offers the simplest storage, because recordings can be stored in simple flip bins or even on shelves.
- Plastic security boxes with theft-detection targets. Some libraries use removable plastic boxes that encase DVDs and CDs. Theft-detection targets are built into the boxes. When a recording is checked out, a staff member uses a special key to remove the box. If you are planning to use plastic security boxes of this type, there are a number of space implications:
  - Recordings in security boxes take up more space than recordings without security boxes, and storage capacities of shelving and bins are reduced accordingly.
  - Removing and replacing security boxes takes time and may affect the number of workstations needed at a lending desk. (Be sure to try out sample boxes extensively before settling on a model. Some are extremely difficult to remove.)
  - You will need space under the lending desk to store security boxes as they are removed from recordings.
  - If your restrooms are inside your security gates, users may take recordings to the privacy of toilet stalls and try to break off the security boxes.
- Plastic security boxes that have no targets but are extraordinarily hard to remove without special tools.
- Sequestered storage and selection cards. After experimenting with a variety of approaches for handling recordings, Fred's library settled on sequestering everything behind the lending desk, in a manner similar to that of many video rental stores.
  - Users of DVDs (for example) paged through three-ring binders with double plastic pages into which flattened DVD boxes could be inserted.
  - Each page had a transparent card pocket with a selection card that could be brought to the lending desk and exchanged for the (properly checked out) recording.

- When the selection cards were removed from the plastic pages, stickers behind the cards became visible, advising users that the item was out.
- Cards of items in use were stored in pockets at the end of the storage shelves.
- Selection cards had theft-detection strips (masquerading as bar codes) to prevent people from reserving items informally by taking selection cards home with them.

One major advantage that Fred's library found with this system was that browsers could see what the library owned that was currently checked out.

The space implications for a system like this include storage shelving behind the lending desk for audiovisual collections and table space for selection books.

6. Self-Check Equipment

We don't have numerical data, but we are convinced that self-check equipment plays an increasing role in many libraries. The tradeoffs typically involve efficiency in the use of staff time vs. equipment cost and potential user alienation.

Much self-check equipment interlocks with library security systems, with workstations that desensitize books as users check them out. But stand-alone self-check systems can easily be installed in libraries that do not have theft-detection equipment.

Allocating sufficient space for current and future self-check workstations is important. Vendors can provide advice, but we think that 75 square feet per workstation is about minimal. Spaces for future self-check workstations need both electrical outlets and data connections.

Many libraries with self-check equipment also opt for public shelving for holds and interlibrary loans, with the books wrapped in paper with the borrowers' names written on the spines. If you plan to use this approach, be sure to leave space for the self-pickup shelving.

IV. THEFT OF LIBRARY EQUIPMENT AND OF PERSONAL POSSESSIONS

All libraries are subject to miscellaneous theft. Wallets vanish from users' ignored purses with dependable regularity. People break in and abscond with computers.

Coats vanish. Staff purses are rifled. Students leave their laptops when they use restrooms, and they return to find their laptops gone.

What are some things that may help?

- *Coin-return lockers for patrons.* Perhaps because libraries are such comforting places, users tend to invite theft by putting down their purses and wandering off. If wallets are removed and the purses left in place, it may be hours before the owners realize things are missing. One possible help for the theft of purses, briefcases, and other relatively small personal objects is coin-return lockers—if libraries can talk patrons into using them. The downside of coin-return lockers is patrons who use them for permanent personal storage. Plan to empty them every night.
- *Lockers for staff.* Many staff members without private workrooms simply sling their purses (or backpacks with wallets) down in convenient corners of staff work areas. Inevitably, someone sneaks in and helps him (or her) self. Purse lockers are one option to help prevent theft. They come in stacks of four or five, and each stack occupies the same space as a school hallway locker. Unfortunately, many younger employees carry backpacks in which they keep their wallets. Since the backpacks are too large for purse lockers, employees simply dump the backpacks and assume all will be well. To prevent theft from backpacks, consider purchasing half-height lockers in stacks of two, with enough space to hold backpacks. Lockers work better with hasps for padlocks rather than with built-in key locks. Staff frequently lose keys. Libraries can issue padlocks, keeping a record of the combination for each padlock. And bolt-cutters (always friendly pieces of equipment) can remove padlocks for which no one knows the combinations.

For a single stack of lockers in a staff area, five square feet should be enough space.

- *Coat storage.* Unlike museums, U.S. libraries traditionally make no provision for coat storage for adults. In general, this may not be a problem, because wallets are probably stolen much more frequently than coats.

Many public libraries provide coat hooks for children in children's departments, but assume that adults will want to keep an eye on their coats and will wear them or place them on nearby chairs.

> One of Fred's clients came up with the clever idea of combining a lobby information desk with a coat check room. But it was never built. The big problem with information desks is keeping an employee adequately busy, and because of this, adding one more function may cost nothing more than the space for some coat racks.

- Computer equipment tethers. A number of companies make tethers that allow computer components to be connected to tabletops.

V. ENTRANCE AND EXIT CONTROL EQUIPMENT

Providing proper control over entrances and exits is extremely important. You need to make it easy for your users and staff to go where they need, while at the same time keeping unauthorized people out. You need to make it easy for people to escape from your library during emergencies, but hard for them to leave through unauthorized exits when all is well.

A. Building Codes

Due to a number of horrendous fires, building codes throughout the United States are particularly detailed when it comes to fire safety. Unfortunately, some of the worst tragedies occur in spite of codes.

- For example, 602 people died in the Iroquois Theater fire in Chicago in 1903, due among other things to badly designed exits. The required asbestos safety curtain apparently burned, which makes one wonder about the type of "asbestos" used. In addition, city inspectors had been paid off to allow the theater to open before it was complete. Probably because the theater was in Chicago, no one went to jail.
- The situation in the 1942 Coconut Grove nightclub fire was similar. In this case, some side doors to the club had been welded shut to keep people from sneaking in and out, fire doors opened inward, and the front door was a revolving door, which could handle very few people. The owner went to jail for violating even the loose building codes of the day.

When your building is being designed, your architects will verify that it is in compliance with all applicable safety codes. Fire safety codes are complex, and you don't want to cut corners. Rely on your architects and engineers to make sure that exit doors, fire pull stations, fire alarm buzzers, fire extinguishers, sprinkler systems, and other devices meet codes in terms of type, quantity, and placement.

It's sometimes tempting to evade what appear to be onerous codes, but all librarians have to do is remember some of the worst fires of years gone by.

As an example, one common violation of everyday exit safety codes is the use of double-cylinder locks in library entrances. A double-cylinder lock is opened by key from both sides, with no crash bar (panic bar) to open the door when people try to leave quickly. Fred has run into a number of small-town libraries with these locks. They are appealing because no one can break a pane of glass in the door and reach inside the library to unlock the door. But all one has to do is to imagine someone accidentally locked into the library on the night that a fire breaks out.

> Fred worked with one library where the staff at the service desk inside the building had to hunt for almost five minutes to find the key to unlock the front door. The library was a 100-year-old building on three levels with wooden floors connected by only a wooden interior staircase. The fire exit from the second-story meeting room involved crawling through a window to a semi-flat roof, then scrambling down a vertical steel ladder. Even without worrying about the locked front door, if the elderly ladies of the garden club had been trapped on the second floor with the wooden staircase on fire, how many of them would have managed to crawl through the window and down the ladder?

Many code violations continue unabated in small towns because they have no fire marshals to make safety checks on public and commercial buildings. If you own one of these libraries, it's worthwhile hiring someone to perform a safety check.

In general, evaluating exit code compliance is a job for an expert. If your community has a fire marshal, that's a good place to begin.

B. Modern Panic Hardware

Codes require that all doors used for emergency egress have panic hardware, otherwise known as crash bars. When panicked people flee a library, doors need to open quickly and easily. Any exit doors that require keys to open by people exiting the building are a major threat to life safety.

The problem with exit doors is that users can leave not only in case of fire but also in case of deep personal need to remove portions of the collection without the benefit of checkout formalities.

To combat this, many libraries equip exit door hardware with alarms. If someone uses a panic bar to open a locked door, a loud alarm summons library staff. This is also useful in children's departments, where children can wander out of the library through fire exits.

The problem, of course, is that by the time a staff member arrives, the person who set off the alarm can be long gone.

The solution is to use "delayed egress" panic hardware with built-in time delays. When someone attempts to open a door using panic hardware, the alarm begins immediately, but the door does not open for perhaps fifteen seconds, time for a staff member to find out what's going on. (If the building's fire alarms have been activated, or power has failed, the time-delay function is disabled and the door opens immediately.)

Alarmed exits are frequently set off by accident, particularly in children's departments, where library staff can dash to the exits to keep small children from toddling out into traffic. All staff members need to be able to locate keys quickly to turn off exit alarms.

To get around this problem, some modern delayed-egress systems include a three-second "nuisance alarm" that gives people who press the panic bar time to back off from the door. If people stop pressing the panic bar within three seconds, the system resets itself and the alarm turns off. If people continue pressing the bar, the alarm continues to sound for the full 15 seconds and cannot be turned off without a key.

C. Key Systems

The traditional way to provide access to buildings and rooms within them is through hierarchical keys.

Each individual door usually has its own key.

In addition, master keys can be provided for various groups of doors, as needed by the owners of the building.

It's possible to have a hierarchy of master keys, but the more levels that exist, the greater the chance that a random key made with the same blank will open an inappropriate door.

The loss of master keys can be extraordinarily expensive. If a key opens every door in the library, replacing it will involve modifying every lock in the library and reissuing keys.

Another drawback with keys of all sorts is that there is never a record of who used a door and at what time.

For this reason, the proximity cards described below make good sense for all doors that will be opened by a number of people.

For security, you may wish to have some doors that cannot be opened by any master key. Typically, these might include the library's server rooms and rooms where sensitive records (such as personnel records) are stored.

D. Proximity and Swipe Cards

A variety of modern access-control systems eliminate the expensive problem of lost keys.

In all of these systems, each person authorized to open any doors in the library—even a very limited number of doors on very limited occasions—is issued a swipe card or proximity key. Each card or key has a machine-readable code. Information on the key is transmitted to a central computer that checks whether the individual key is authorized to open that particular door at that particular time. If everything is in order, the door opens.

There are a very large number of advantages to systems of this type.

- Instead of representing a major cost for new locks and keys for an entire building, a lost swipe card or proximity key may cost only a couple of dollars. If staff members aren't sure whether they have their proximity cards, it's cheap and easy for the library to reprogram the system to deny access to the lost card and then issue the staff member a new card.
- Because swipe cards and proximity cards are vastly cheaper than actual keys, staff members may be less worried about admitting they've mislaid them.
- The authorization for each card can be as detailed as you wish. For example, a book shelver's card may normally open only the door to the book-sorting room, but the computer can easily be reprogrammed to allow the same shelver

(for example) to enter the library early on Wednesday mornings to empty the book drops, without being able to get in early on any other morning.
- The small computer that operates the system keeps track of exactly which cards were used on what doors at what times, providing a great deal of additional security information. For example, if a card is lost and disabled, the library can tell if anyone ever tried to use it afterwards. The use of individual doors can be tracked by time and person.
- Proximity and swipe card systems can also be programmed to automatically unlock doors, and more importantly to lock them, in case staff forget to lock a door when the library is closing.

Good candidates for doors with swipe card or proximity card systems are those that need to be kept locked but are used by a number of people. Most of the time these will be doors between public and staff areas of the library.

Doors used by only one or two people—such as doors to private staff workrooms—are generally practical to operate with keys.

If you are considering some kind of swipe card or proximity card system, be sure to investigate it before you construct your building. Some good systems require special door hardware that may be more difficult or expensive to retrofit.

> When Fred's library installed a proximity card system it was under the supervision of the administrative office manager, who got a huge kick (initially, at least) out of watching the computer screen to see who was going through what doors. She said she could follow the progress of people through the building, not unlike the users of the Marauder's Map in the *Harry Potter* books.

VI. INTRUSION ALARMS

Intrusion alarms are everyday items and inexpensive. Every security company knows how to install them, and the systems work.

Intrusion alarms typically guard libraries in two ways.

- *Detecting violations of the perimeter.* If someone opens a door or window that should not be opened, the alarm system is activated.

- *Motion detection.* Once the library is closed, detectors scattered throughout the building detect inappropriate motions and set off the alarm.

If someone has hidden in the building until closing time, when that person begins to move around inside the building the motion detectors pick up his or her presence.

Wireless motion detectors in particular are easy to install. Just stick them up in appropriate places.

Almost all intrusion alarms are linked to emergency services. Sometimes this is a direct link to the police, but often it is a link to the security company, which then in turn telephones the police dispatch center.

When staff are working after regular library hours, only the perimeter of the building (doors and windows) needs to be armed. Any attempt to enter will alert the staff.

When the building is completely empty of staff, both the perimeter and motion detector sensors can be armed to detect anyone entering or moving around in the building.

If you are purchasing an intrusion alarm system, you may want an annunciator that tells which of the many detection units in your building was activated. This will help emergency services go directly to the area where the alarm was activated, and it will help you isolate individual detectors that have a bad habit of sending out false alarms.

The downside of intrusion alarms is false alarms. For example, if a breeze from the HVAC system blows a piece of paper off a desktop, the motion may be picked up by a detector. To minimize these false alarms, detectors are available that combine PIR (passive infrared) detection of heat patterns with microwave detection of actual physical movement. These "dual tech" detectors are not much more expensive than standard detectors but can save a great deal by reducing false alarms and the time required for library staff and police to investigate.

In almost every case, emergency personnel responding to an intrusion alarm when the library is closed will want a member of the library staff to join them while they search the building. Libraries need staff members who (a) live near the library and (b) are not spooked by wandering through the quiet library with the police.

As with all other technical equipment, alarm systems are improved regularly, and selecting places to install detectors requires experience. For these reasons, always consult with at least a couple of good firms before putting out an RFP for an intrusion alarm system.

VII. FIRE PROTECTION SYSTEMS

Fires in libraries are always a threatening possibility. Although it's relatively hard to set shelves packed with books on fire, once they are burning the amount of fuel they supply is impressive.

A wide variety of equipment is available to suppress fires. Although fire suppression systems will protect collections from damage, they are designed first and foremost to preserve human life, and in the process of extinguishing flames they may soak parts of the collection.

Fire protection systems are extensively specified by building codes, and many of the features included in new libraries are not a matter of choice.

Actual fires are different from movie fires. Instead of the drama of roaring flames, they often feature intense, black smoke that obscures everything. Even if exits are extraordinarily well marked, finding one's way through the murk can be extremely difficult.

A. Fire Alarm Systems

Basic components of fire alarm systems include:

- *Detectors.* All libraries need heat and (particularly) smoke detectors with automatic links to emergency services. Your architect will specify detectors in places called for in local building codes. Detectors are particularly important in storage closets and attics, where fires have a particularly good chance of developing unnoticed.
- *Warning horns.* All buildings require audible and visual fire alarms to alert occupants. Alarm units combine electric buzzers with flashing strobe lights. Strobe lights are required by accessibility codes for deaf people who cannot hear alarms. As an alternative to buzzers, recorded spoken announcements are also possible, including instructions about how to exit the building. These are particularly useful because libraries—unlike school classrooms—do not have consistent occupancy, and fire drills for users cannot be held.

- *Annunciators.* All but the very smallest libraries should have annunciators located in their main entries. Annunciators are panels that tell arriving firefighters which detectors have been activated. In a complex building with dozens or even hundreds of spaces, firefighters could spend far too long trying to find out which detector set off the alarm. In the meantime, the fire can quickly spread.
- *Pull stations.* Fire codes will require pull stations that can be used manually by staff or users. Typically, these are located by exits, so people can set off the alarms while leaving the building, rather than possibly heading off into the fire. The problem with pull stations is that many people are afraid to use them, particularly when doing so requires breaking a thin pane of glass or snapping a glass rod. Staff fire drills need to include the breaking of glass.
- *Automatic linkages to fire services.* Depending on local requirements, this linkage may be by way of an alarm company, which will receive your alarm notification and telephone your local emergency services, or it may ring directly in your local fire department.
- *Knox boxes.* Many communities now require that major buildings have small safes built into exterior walls by their main entrances. The safes contain keys to the building, and emergency service personnel in turn carry keys that unlock the safes. Knox boxes eliminate the need for emergency personnel to carry keys to many buildings. Hunting for the right key takes time, and safely keeping track of a large number of keys to secure areas can be a challenge. The whole Knox-box approach is very much like that used by real estate agents who keep keys to houses in small safes attached to front door knobs. All participating agents carry a standard key that fits all boxes.

B. Sprinkler Systems

Librarians have a love/hate relationship with sprinkler systems. They save buildings and lives, but they can make a soggy mess out of collections.

Sprinkler systems are widely specified by building codes. For example, the BOCA Code (now the International Building Code or IBC) has required sprinkler systems in all libraries of 12,000 or more square feet, starting in 1996.

1. Fear of Sprinkler Systems

Librarians by and large fear sprinkler systems, associating them with massive water spillage and the ruin of book collections.

Part of librarians' fear of sprinkler systems is due to misrepresentation in the movies. When sprinkler systems are activated in movies, water immediately begins spraying from every sprinkler head in sight. But actual sprinkler heads are designed to provide water only where fires exist.

The great thing about sprinklers is that they genuinely do save lives. There is no known event in the United States where lives have been lost in a fire in a building that had a properly functioning sprinkler system.

The major frustrations with sprinkler systems occur when sprinkler heads discharge accidentally, dumping hundreds or thousands of gallons of water upon the place beneath them. Although manufacturers tend to say that this almost never happens, Fred knows two libraries in central Illinois that were soaked by faulty sprinkler heads. One was a library where Fred was the consultant, which made him particularly self-conscious about the event.

We have seen several libraries that were carefully planned to be just small enough to slip under code requirements. Although this may seem like a clever idea at the time, it handicaps those who follow behind and who may find that expansion is difficult or almost impossible. A classic example of this is libraries built at just under 12,000 square feet to avoid the necessity of sprinkler systems. Unfortunately, sooner or later they need to expand, and sprinkler systems have to be installed retroactively in spaces that may never have been designed for them.

2. Wet Pipe Systems

Everyday sprinkler systems have pipes permanently filled with water. Sprinkler heads are mounted on the pipes. Each sprinkler head includes a fusible link that melts when heat reaches a specific level. The melted link allows a valve to open. Water rushing from the pipe hits a diffuser that spreads it out into a spray pattern.

Wet pipe sprinkler systems are very widely used.

They have two weaknesses:

- If a sprinkler head is faulty or vandalized, the valve can open, and water goes everywhere. Although sprinkler head failures are not common, they lead to amazing messes.
- After being inside sprinkler pipes for a few years, water contains a combination of mold and corrosion, and it resembles India ink.

3. Dry Pipe Systems

Dry pipe systems are used where there is danger of the water in wet pipe systems freezing.

In dry pipe systems, there is no water in the pipes until one or more sprinkler heads opens. A small air pump creates enough air pressure within the sprinkler pipes to keep water out. When one or more sprinkler heads open, the compressed air in the pipes quickly rushes out through the sprinkler heads, followed by water.

Dry pipe systems have alarms to indicate that the air pressure in pipes is dropping and that the water could be creeping into freezing territory.

A common use of dry pipe systems is when sprinkler pipes must be installed above the ceilings of older buildings. But even some modern buildings are freezing cold above their ceilings. Watch for ceiling tiles that have been removed to let heat into the spaces above.

4. Pre-Action Systems

Pre-action systems provide a fail-safe mechanism to prevent the accidental discharge of water due to the failure of faulty or damaged sprinkler heads.

The sprinkler pipes in a pre-action system are dry at all times until the library's smoke detectors sense smoke in the building. At that time, the sprinkler pipes fill with water, ready for use if sprinkler heads open.

A small air compressor keeps the air in the sprinkler pipes slightly compressed at all times. If one or more sprinkler heads opens when there is no water in the pipes, an alarm indicates that there may be faulty or damaged sprinkler heads.

Occasionally, the smoke detectors for pre-action systems are fooled by something other than the smoke of a fire, and the systems fill with water. For these situations, all pre-action systems have drain valves that allow technicians to drain the system after the detectors have been reset.

> A library Fred worked with liked to hold cooking demonstrations in its community room, and the smoke and fumes kept activating the pre-action sprinkler system, filling the pipes with water. Everything worked in accordance with design, but the library had to call the sprinkler company occasionally to have the system drained.

By requiring that both smoke detectors and sprinkler heads be activated before water is discharged, pre-action systems help to prevent water damage from faulty sprinkler heads.

Pre-action systems are more expensive than the standard wet pipe and dry pipe systems, but they are particularly important with collections that cannot be replaced. In our opinion, they are worth having in all libraries.

5. Types of Sprinkler Heads

Sprinkler heads come in a variety of configurations, depending on whether water is ejected upwards, downwards, or to the side.

For rooms with acoustic ceilings, the most attractive sprinkler heads are concealed by white metal discs that fit relatively flush to the ceiling. When fires occur, the low-melting-point solder that holds the disc to the sprinkler unit melts and the disc falls off, exposing the sprinkler head. The diffuser that directs the sprinkler water in a spray pattern then drops into place. When the temperature becomes slightly higher, the fusable link in the sprinkler opens and water escapes.

We like concealed sprinkler heads not only because they look less mechanical but also because they do not provide an attractive target for vandals.

6. Inert Gas Systems

Some highly secure installations, such as military computers, are protected by systems that fill rooms with oxygen-free gas, stifling fires without the possibility of water damage.

These aren't for libraries, except for protective storage vaults for rare items.

Although these systems sound appealing, they can be used only under highly controlled situations, since people who are in rooms where the system deploys may have only a couple of minutes to leave the room before suffocating. Only spaces with access strictly limited to a few very highly trained personnel can afford to take a chance on quick suffocation.

7. Shutting off Sprinkler Systems

Libraries with sprinkler systems need to train a large number of staff members on how to turn off the systems. If a sprinkler head fails and douses the library with water when there is no fire, the sooner the valves feeding the system are turned off, the less damage is done.

Libraries are at their most vulnerable when they are brand-new and not enough people have yet been trained on shutting off the system.

C. Escape Routes

All libraries need to plan escape routes. The less complex and more familiar these are, the less chance of loss of life there is in the case of fire.

As with other areas of fire safety, escape routes are much controlled by building codes and may need to be posted. Your architects and engineers should help you.

In general, users try to exit buildings using the doors by which they entered. Making it quick and easy for users to retrace their steps helps.

All fire codes require illuminated exit signs that remain illuminated when power fails. Older signs use tubular incandescent lamps, which burn out frequently and are therefore an incredible nuisance. Modern signs all depend upon LEDs. If your library still has incandescent signs, this is a great time to replace them.

Keeping escape routes clear is made difficult by the fact that most fires are accompanied by thick, opaque smoke.

Because the areas clearest of smoke are by the floor, some codes now require additional illuminated exit signs at floor level.

In buildings with more than one floor, codes may require "areas of refuge" in the entry areas of all emergency staircases where the areas do not align with ground level. The idea is that people who are fleeing a fire but cannot deal with stairs can wait in safety to be rescued. Because fire-exit staircases are built to withstand fires better than other spaces in a building, people waiting there are relatively safer. Areas of refuge need equipment that allows people waiting there to alert emergency personnel.

D. Portable Fire Extinguishers

Fire codes require that portable fire extinguishers be located at specified locations in libraries. Depending on code requirements, these extinguishers can be in cabinets or directly hung on wall brackets.

Not all fire extinguishers are suitable for all fires. The standard types of extinguishers include:

- Class A—Burning wood, paper, cloth, plastics, and so on
- Class B—Burning liquids
- Class C—Electrical fires
- Type D—Burning metals

Most libraries will want multi-type extinguishers so that staff members do not have to be trained to identify fires and determine whether or not they can use an extinguisher. In addition, in a public building, a member of the public may decide to step in. Type ABC extinguishers are common in libraries.

All fire extinguishers require periodic maintenance, and they need to be completely serviced if they are used even very briefly.

As a practical note, staff training always has to emphasize first calling emergency services and only then attempting to use portable fire extinguishers to put out the fire. Among other problems, untrained people using fire extinguishers may aim at the visible flames rather than at the burning material.

VIII. HUMIDITY CONTROL

Of all the dangers associated with poor-quality or malfunctioning HVAC systems, one of the greatest threats to libraries and their contents is high humidity.

Relative humidity describes the amount of water in the air compared with the maximum amount of water air can hold *at that temperature.* For any given amount of water in the air, when we lower the temperature, the relative humidity increases. In libraries, somewhere between 30 and 50 percent relative humidity appears to be ideal.

When relative humidity exceeds about 70 percent, mildew and mold can form on books. Mold in particular can be extremely destructive, but mildew is not a great deal of fun either.

The possibility of mold may seem remote, but it can strike even in hallowed halls. In 2008, for example, mold appeared on books in the stacks of a major university's rare book room.

If you have a collection of rare materials, you may want to invest in a recording hygrometer, which keeps a record of changes in relative humidity over time. Or you may want a humidity alarm.

IX. VIDEO SURVEILLANCE SYSTEMS

Libraries increasingly incorporate surveillance cameras in their security systems. Even if people don't notice them, surveillance cameras are everywhere.

Although a library might in theory station a staff member in front of a bank of monitors to watch for problems picked up by surveillance cameras, there would be little benefit. Instead, data recorded by cameras is typically checked after an event takes place. Because surveillance systems link images to times, it is possible to see what happened at a particular place at a particular time.

All modern video surveillance equipment uses solid-state memory. Because images make intensive use of memory, a library with a dozen video cameras may need a terabyte of storage.

Modern surveillance technology uses high-definition cameras that take even more storage space but balance that with great image clarity, which makes it easier to identify people and activities.

Data needs to be retained for about three weeks to give the library and law enforcement employees time to download and preserve relevant images.

Modern surveillance systems use built-in video analytics to identify movement. This allows the recording system to reduce its resolution or recording rates when no movement is detected but to increase both when something happens within the view of the camera. Systems also flag events for easier review and retrieval, reducing the amount of time spent in reviewing data.

In earlier systems, surveillance cameras have motion sensors to allow the system to retain data whenever motion takes place. The system should retain data starting a few seconds before motion is detected by the camera and continuing a few seconds after motion ceases. Some cameras in busy locations may end up retaining data for virtually the entire time the library is open, while others in locations like fire escapes may retain only occasional data.

For reasons of personal privacy, video surveillance systems typically do not include sound recordings. However, the use of audio recording has increased in areas where interactions between staff and users can be uncomfortable or even threatening. To avoid the violation of eavesdropping laws, you will need clearly posted notices stating that audio monitoring is taking place, warning people that they can be subject to accountability for what they say. Check with your security firm about the requirements concerning sound recordings in your state.

A. Equipment Specifications

Video cameras are typically tidy in appearance. Most are under plastic ceiling-mounted domes about six inches in diameter, and they are relatively unobtrusive. However, libraries with video surveillance systems may want to post notices to that effect on entry doors, both to warn people and to provide an extra incentive to good behavior.

Setting a high technical standard is important. Newspapers frequently feature blurred images of people holding up convenience stores, and these can be of little value. The specifications outlined below are typical of those found in high-quality systems. In particular, you never want to compromise on the number of pixels per image, number of images per second, resolution, and light sensitivity.

The quality of surveillance equipment varies widely. If you are purchasing a system for your library, you will want to specify at a minimum:

1. Cameras

- Color images. It's much easier to recognize people with color images than with black-and-white images.
- Sixteen images per second. For comparison, theatrical motion pictures use 24 images per second. Experts tell us that it is hard for people in law enforcement to make good use of data from cameras that record fewer than 16 images per second.
- Motion activation.
- Hot-spot motion detection, with the ability to exclude irrelevant motion within specified areas of a camera's view.
- Minimum image capture rate of one image per second in the absence of detected motion.
- Auto-iris.
- Manual zoom lenses.
- Resolution at a minimum of 750 horizontal lines for standard definition systems.
- Light sensitivity rating of 0.5 lux. This is very dim light, the equivalent of about 0.05 foot-candles or bright moonlight.

- Cameras are also available with built-in infrared illumination to produce usable images in total darkness. Because the image depends on light emitted by the camera, the usability of the image depends on the distance between the subject and the camera.
- Tamper-resistant protective domes.
- Exterior cameras in vandal-resistant domes and outdoor environmental enclosures. Vandal-resistant domes might—for example—resist the impact of a ten-pound hammer.

2. Central units

- Sufficient storage to retain at least three weeks of data.
- Rate of recording adjustable on a camera-by-camera basis.
- Image pixel count of no less than 720 × 486 for all images.
- During alarm state, cameras will record a minimum of 16 images per second. "Alarm state" refers to times where cameras are detecting motion.
- Pre-alarm buffer of 2 seconds at 16 images per second. Because surveillance systems are constantly recording and then eventually discarding non-alarm data, it's always possible to save data from shortly *before* motion is first detected.
- Post-alarm recording of 3 seconds at 16 images per second.
- All images to be matched to clock times. It's extremely important to be able to tie images to specific times.

3. Installation

- Turnkey installation. All work required to install the system and set it in operation should be performed by the vendor, including any necessary architectural modification of the library.
- No surface-mounted wire conduit or exposed wire. As with all systems added to library buildings, no one wants new visible conduit or wire. Exposed wire trailing around is ugly, and conduit is unpleasantly industrial.
- All cable plenum-rated. A plenum is an open space—such as the space under a floor or above a ceiling—that conducts air for an HVAC system. Plenum-rated cable is rated for installation inside plenums.
- Central unit(s) in a rack in the library's main server room (or other specified location). Note our suggestions on server room security.

Due to the large amount of data being transferred, your video surveillance cameras will probably require hard wiring for data transmission.

B. Common Camera Locations

Libraries need to position surveillance cameras in locations where they have had previous problems or where they can anticipate serious problems arising.

For example, libraries may need to record the faces of people threatening staff members at service desks and causing trouble with computer workstations.

Cameras can be placed to record:

- Faces of people at computer workstations. Due to considerations of patron privacy, libraries will probably not want to be able to see screen images of the computers they're using.
- Faces of people speaking to library staff at service desks. If users threaten staff members, libraries need images of the users, not of the staff.
- People exiting restrooms. (No matter how much vandalism takes place inside restrooms, libraries that place cameras inside restrooms are in violation of serious privacy laws that prohibit video surveillance in places where users can expect privacy, such as restrooms, dressing rooms, etc.)
- Elevator cabs. Adding a camera to an elevator will require coordination between a library's elevator company and its security company (who may not want to play nicely together), but if there are problems with vandalism in elevators, it will be worth the extra effort.
- License plates of cars passing through drive-up service lanes. Because of problems with inappropriate things placed in exterior book returns, libraries will almost certainly want to record all use of returns.
- People using walk-up exterior book returns. Recorded for the same reason.
- All possible exits from children's departments. A children's department may need to record images of everyone leaving the department, including use of emergency exits, due to the occasional abduction of children by non-custodial parents.
- Faces of people passing through security gates on the way out of the library. Because of the problems involved with sound recording, it's a good idea to have gates with lights that flash in addition to beeping when theft is detected, so that the record can match the face with the event.

X. MISCELLANEOUS ISSUES IN PATRON AND STAFF SECURITY

A. Panic Buttons

Many libraries provide panic buttons at staff workstations.

Typical panic buttons are concealed beneath desk or countertops. To prevent accidental activation, most consist of small boxes with recessed buttons.

Panic buttons can be linked to the library's emergency service dispatcher, but they also need annunciators at a heavily staffed service point (typically the library's central lending desk) so that staff members and emergency service responders will know not only that someone has pushed a button but also exactly where that person is located.

Police tell us they much prefer phone calls, because they then know what to expect when they arrive at the library.

Even if panic buttons are seldom or never used, they provide a better sense of security for staff members who are occasionally worried.

> In Fred's library, the only time a panic button was pressed was when a little girl crawled under the children's department reference desk and pushed the button. Afterwards, everyone agreed it had been a good test of the system, although there was universal puzzlement when the police arrived, since no one knew which of the many panic buttons had been pressed and there appeared to be no trouble anywhere in the building.

B. Portable Alarm Devices

Staff members can carry alarm devices. Some of these devices can have wireless connections to the library's panic button system, while others just make an incredible racket.

In our experience, the primary staff members who want equipment of this type are pages shelving books, who often end up sharing obscure corners of book stacks with people they would not like to meet in the proverbial dark alley.

Book stacks tend to absorb a lot of the noise from alarm devices that are not connected electronically to a central station, but portable alarm devices are amazingly loud up close and may serve their purpose for that reason alone.

> In Fred's library, the shriek of the lavalier alarm was so earsplitting up close that the creep involved raced from the library like a terrified rabbit. The staff a floor away couldn't hear the alarm, but it still worked well.

C. Public Library Children's Departments

Children's departments in public libraries require special attention to security. Librarians worry about abduction by non-custodial parents, people with a history of child molestation hanging around, and unwatched toddlers wandering out of the building into traffic. Constructing children's libraries in a way that prevents problems is always worthwhile.

Here are some basic principles:

- Children's departments should always be at the end of the line, never a passageway to other parts of the library. If the department is not a passageway, any adult unaccompanied by a child will be particularly evident.

> In the library Fred inherited when he became a library director, the only entrance for users with disabilities was a ramp that led people through the center of the children's department. A number of people who did not need the department's services would linger too long on their way through, to the frequent discomfort of the staff. When the library was expanded, the new children's department was at the end of a hall and through glass doors, and the unwanted lingering essentially ceased—all achieved by better design rather than by security systems.

- Children's departments benefit from walls separating them from the rest of the library. Glass walls provide separation without blocking staff oversight or making visitors feel uncomfortable or insecure about entering an unseen department.

- No item of equipment required by adults, with the exception of parents, should be located within a children's department.
- If children toddle out of the children's department, they should have to pass directly—and conspicuously—by service desks before exiting the building.

> Fred consulted with one library where young children who toddled out of the children's department immediately found themselves next to an exterior automatic door that opened helpfully, encouraging them to wander out into the street immediately outside.

XI. PUBLIC RELATIONS IMPLICATIONS

Each time libraries install new security systems, they worry about negative patron responses. They worry that users will be offended by the implications of distrust.

Our experience, however, has been more that users say "It's about time!" For example, as a graduate student Fred worked in a major metropolitan public library. When the library finally introduced guards who inspected briefcases, users who expressed themselves seemed uniformly pleased.

The main issues appear to be social rather than structural. If staff members are trained to always allow readers to save face, many problems can be averted. It's easy, for example, to apologize when users set off exit alarms, even when the dishonesty of the situation is fairly obvious.

XII. INSURANCE

Insurance developed from groups of shipowners who agreed to jointly cover lost ships belonging to members of the group. If the loss of a ship was a rare experience but devastating to the owner, sharing the risk made tremendous sense.

The same concept applies today. Insurance is for unaffordable losses, not nuisance losses.

A. Basic Insurance Concepts

1. Types of Insurance Coverage

The major risks that libraries insure against are injury to patrons, injury to employees, damage to structures, theft of equipment, and damage to collections.

Liability insurance covers injuries to people and to property that does not belong to the library.

Property insurance covers damage to the library and its contents from fire, windstorm, lightning, theft, flood, earthquake, and other sources.

While liability and property insurance will often be written for the library by a single carrier, the two forms of insurance are always treated separately.

Additional forms of insurance are mentioned very briefly in the section "Insurance Not Relevant to Buildings" later in this chapter.

2. Stress on Covering Major Losses

As with all forms of insurance, the purpose of library insurance is to protect the institution from losses it cannot afford. Although the cost of replacing a stolen laptop or redecorating a small workroom may be frustrating in a year of tight budgets, purchasing insurance to cover small losses is usually a waste of money.

While some libraries purchase insurance directly, nonpublic libraries are usually part of larger organizations that manage risk. In some of these cases, the organization may "self-insure" itself, purchasing insurance coverage only for truly immense losses.

3. Deductibles

Property insurance always has a deductible amount. This amount is paid by the insured before the insurance company steps in to pay the balance. Deductible amounts keep insurance companies from being badgered by endless small claims (which would in turn lead to an increase in premiums). Most agencies that purchase insurance regard this approach as separating affordable and unaffordable losses. For example, if your library carries a $10,000 deductible, the insurance company will pay any insured loss, less the first $10,000.

One of the easiest ways to cut the cost of insurance is to purchase policies with fairly high deductible amounts and thereby limit claims to very serious losses.

By contrast, liability insurance typically has no deductible amounts. If someone falls down the front steps of your library, your insurance company steps in and pays for everything (up to the limits on your policy).

4. Umbrella Policies

Many libraries purchase what are called "umbrella" policies to cover extremely substantial losses in excess of coverage provided in basic policies.

Umbrella policies are typically sold in multiples of $1,000,000. The cost is relatively low because the chance of a loss in excess of the basic policy amount is also low.

> Carrying a multimillion-dollar policy may seem like overkill, but losses of this size do occur. For example, a few years ago an Illinois public library had an $8,000,000 liability settlement but had only a $4,000,000 umbrella policy. The city had to levy an additional $4,000,000 in local taxes to make up the difference.

Unfortunately, there is no real way to know how large an umbrella policy should be, and most libraries appear to just decide informally what feels comfortable.

5. Subrogation

When your library purchases insurance, you authorize your insurance company to act legally on your behalf.

For example, a number of years ago, Fred's library had a serious electrical fire. The library's insurance company paid the entire loss cheerfully, but it turned around and (successfully) sued the local power company *in the name of the library*.

When troubles occur, you should expect to see news articles listing your library as the active party in a lawsuit when it's really the insurance company suing or acting on your behalf. For example, if a child is seriously injured in your library, the news may report that the library is arguing against the settlement the child's family wants. You may feel uncomfortable about this, but that's the way policies are written and the law works.

6. Other Standard Terminology

Although insurance policies can be extremely complex, there are a few basic terms everyone should know.

- *Actual cash value.* Unlike replacement cost, the actual cost value may take depreciation into account.
- *Agreed amount.* A value determined in advance by joint agreement of the underwriter and insured. This is typically done to discourage underinsuring of property.
- *Endorsements.* Extra coverage to a basic policy through the use of endorsements. Typically, these appear as additional sheets of paper stapled to your basic policy and cited in the cover page of the policy.
- *Floater policy.* An all-risk policy covering specifically scheduled items.
- *Insured.* People in the insurance business refer to a customer as "the insured."
- *Loss adjustment.* The process of determining how much your insurance company will pay for your loss is called "adjusting," and the people who do this work are called "adjustors." Some companies use only their own employees as adjustors, while other companies use the services of independent insurance-adjusting firms.
- *Mysterious disappearance.* Sometimes, things just vanish. We can't point to any specific theft incident. All we know is that something is missing. So-called floater policies can cover this kind of loss. They're too expensive for book collections, but you may want to cover objects that appeal to thieves and are continually at risk, such as laptops.
- *Premium.* The cost of the policy.
- *Replacement cost.* The cost to replace an item at today's prices rather than at the original cost, without any deduction for depreciation.
- *Risk.* The type or amount of loss against which policies are issued.
- *Settlement.* Most insurance companies are prepared to make partial payments almost immediately, in order to allow repair work to begin, with final details to be worked out at a later time. Beware of any company that pressures you to accept a final settlement soon after the loss.
- *Underwriter.* The insurance company.

7. Purchasing Insurance

Many libraries are parts of larger institutions and do not purchase their own insurance.

Some independent libraries are members of cooperative groups that purchase insurance jointly for all members of the group.

Libraries that purchase their own insurance need to be sure that they understand how the system works.

Insurance policies can be extremely detailed concerning the risks covered and the values assigned to building and contents. Library staff (or the staff of parent organizations) need to be sure that the amount of coverage provided is appropriate.

Insurance can be purchased either by low bid or by using an independent broker to obtain bids from a number of underwriters. Both approaches have advantages, but as with all bidding situations, you will need a carefully written bid document. This is not a job for a neophyte.

When prices for insurance get high, we recommend that you first explore increasing deductible amounts. The difference between the premiums on $1,000 deductible and $5,000 deductible policies can be significant.

> If insurance companies are eager to insure your library, that's one indication you have built well.

One of the best ways to control insurance costs is to build a library that is an attractive risk to the insurance company. A number of elements will lead to a reduction in insurance cost. They include:

- The age of the building.
- The quality of local fire protection services (Fire Protection Class). PC classes run from PC 1 (the best) to PC 10. PC ratings are based on the technical competence and equipment of fire departments, access to water, and quality of dispatch services. Cities are pleased when their fire departments' PC ratings improve because insurance rates for property within the city drop accordingly. PC ratings are provided by the Insurance Services Office.
- Sprinkler systems. Sprinklered buildings can pay substantially lower rates, due in particular to the reduced likelihood of injuries to occupants.

> Fred tried to argue for even lower rates because his library installed a pre-action sprinkler system, which reduces the danger of flooding due to malfunctioning sprinkler heads, but the company wasn't prepared for fine distinctions, in part because seriously major claims usually involve injuries or loss of life, and wet pipe systems do a great job of preventing injuries. Nevertheless, pre-action systems are great because they limit damages to collections.

- Other security systems. Fire and intrusion alarms linked automatically to central dispatch services lower the likelihood of losses.
- Type of construction. Buildings that are harder to burn are cheaper to insure. The ISO (Insurance Systems Office, not International Standards Organization) lists six levels of construction, listed here from poorest to best. Definitions of the terms are available from the industry.
    1. Frame
    2. Joisted masonry
    3. Masonry non-combustible
    4. Non-combustible
    5. Modified fire resistive
    6. Fire resistive

When you are figuring the actual cost of better construction or new safety equipment, always factor in any potential insurance savings. (Sometimes, of course, there are no savings, so always check with your insurers first.)

B. Fire and Windstorm

Basic property insurance covers losses from fire and windstorm. These are sometimes extended by endorsements to cover risks of loss from earthquake, flood, and other dangers.

Typically, policies exclude losses from war and insurrection. When property is damaged in riots, there can be arguments with underwriters as to whether the policy coverages apply. Given the potential for civil disobedience (consider, for example, angry citizens reacting to the neo-Nazis you were legally unable to bar from your meeting room), you will want to make sure that your policies do not exclude damage resulting from events of this kind.

1. Setting Values

When you meet with an insurance broker to develop coverage for your library, you will need to be prepared to set values on structure and contents. Here are some common ways of doing this.

- *Buildings.* When it comes to buildings, original construction costs are no guide to replacement costs, for the cost of construction can escalate anything from 3 to 8 percent a year. Try to find out what buildings of similar quality are costing to construct per square foot at the time you arrange the policy.
- *Furnishings.* Furnishings can usually be estimated by using formulas that architects use.

- *Collections.* In addition to furnishings, you will need to insure your collection. For ordinary collections that are not filled with valuable objects, a simple formula will probably be sufficient. Remember that the cost of replacing books is not only the purchase price but also the cost of ordering and processing, so be sure that your insurance company recognizes that it is insuring staff time as well as the cost of books and recordings.

2. Coinsurance Clauses

Many people are tempted to underinsure on the premise that their homes or libraries are unlikely to suffer a 100 percent loss. If the building and content are worth (for example) $10,000,000, the library may assume that the loss from any event is unlikely to top $5,000,000, and try to insure for that lower amount.

This is not a smart thing to do. Historically, insurance companies dealt with this kind of planned underinsurance through the concept of "coinsurance," which held that a policy for half the value of the property would lead to a 50 percent payout in case of a loss. In this case, the owners of the property were assumed to be coinsurers, covering half of the loss themselves. To prevent intentional underinsurance, companies may have required, for example, that insurance be for at least 80 percent of replacement cost.

Today, companies and insureds typically take care of this situation through "agreed value" insurance, where both parties agree in advance on what things are worth, jointly signing off on a statement of values (SOV) based on 100 percent replacement cost.

3. Other Property Risks

Other risks for which you might seek insurance on your library and its contents include:

- *Earthquakes.* Earthquake insurance is available as a separate endorsement.
- *Floods.* Flood insurance is not always available through private underwriters. However, separate flood insurance coverage is sold separately by the federal government for properties located on floodplains. The coverage is limited. This is another good reason to plan your library properly and keep well above any possible flood level. (See the section on "Flood Insurance" below.)
- *Sewer backup.* In Fred's library a child flushed his shirt down the toilet, for some obscure reason. The shirt made its way through the sewer pipes to the main sanitary sewer connection, where it stopped, thereby blocking the library's entire sanitary sewer system and flooding the lowest area of

the library—the auditorium—which had (until that precise moment) an attractive new carpet.
- *Valuable objects.* (Personal property floater policies.) If you have expensive objects that you want to protect from all risks (including dropping them on the floor or realizing that they used to be in your workroom but no longer are), you will need to schedule individual items for all-risk coverage. To do this, you will need exact descriptions, including serial numbers on equipment. The costs for this type of coverage are much higher than the costs of general insurance, but it may be worthwhile for items like laptops that are dragged everywhere and can be lost or lifted. Similar policies are available for expensive works of art that require special protection.
- *Exhibits.* In addition to its own valuable objects, a library may need to insure items that belong to other people and are currently on display at the library. One possibility is a general exhibit floater policy that covers unspecified exhibits up to a specified amount.
- *Loss of business income.* Many private businesses purchase this coverage to cover the loss of income when the business is closed due to an insurable loss. Because libraries do not generate much income from sales or fees, typically they do not purchase this kind of coverage. But the loss of income from fines and fees and copying can add up.

Coverage for any nonstandard risk is provided through endorsements, which are typically sheets of paper attached to the back of the basic policy.

4. Theft of Library Property

Property insurance also covers theft, but typically not the kind of theft from which libraries suffer. If someone breaks into your library at night and takes five computers, that is insurable theft. The police will be called in, paperwork will be filed, and everyone will agree on what happened and when.

Most library theft, however, consists of things turning up missing. Sometime in the last six weeks (for example), someone lifted all of a library's James Bond DVDs. But the library doesn't know when or how it actually happened. From the point of view of the insurance industry, this is "mysterious disappearance" and is not covered unless items are individually scheduled.

5. Action in Case of Loss

If you have a loss that you think may involve an insurance claim, you will need to contact your insurance broker immediately.

If the loss involves theft or other criminal activity, you will need to inform law enforcement and file a police report.

In cases of major damage, you will also want to arrange for your own inspection by a qualified engineering firm who represents your library rather than any other agency. You should expect your insurance company to pay for it.

C. Automotive Insurance

Even if your library does not own a vehicle, you will want to be sure that your liability insurance covers any accidents that occur when library staff are operating vehicles while on library business. The term for this coverage is *non-owned auto liability*.

If, for example, one of your employees injures someone while running an errand for the library (even if not requested to do so by library management and while driving his or her own car), the library could be at the least subject to a liability suit.

Automotive coverage of this type should be a standard component of liability policies, but it's important to check.

D. Flood Insurance

Providing flood insurance is a problem for insurance companies because most property owners know whether or not they are in danger.

Insurance works by large numbers of people sharing risks. For insurance to be successful, many people have to buy insurance while only a very small number receive payments. When one person has a loss, the premiums paid by the others are pooled to pay the loss. However, if individual property owners can be fairly certain who will have a loss and who won't, those who are not threatened are not interested in purchasing insurance and there is no business niche for the insurance company.

Property without flood insurance may not be covered for floods caused by other disasters, such as landslides, windstorms, earthquakes, and so on. Windstorm insurance, for example, may cover structural damage due to the windstorm itself but not damage due to flooding caused by the windstorm.

If your library stands comfortably out of floodplains, your insurance agent may be able to provide flood insurance.

Insuring buildings on floodplains is a different story, however, because flooding is predictable rather than a bit of random bad luck.

Because private insurance companies often do not foresee any profitable business in flood insurance for structures on floodplains, the federal government created the National Flood Insurance Program (NFIP) in 1968. NFIP was motivated in part by the tremendous damage caused by category 4 Hurricane Betsy in 1965. At that time, Betsy was the most expensive hurricane in U.S. history.

This federal flood insurance is available in communities that have entered into agreements with the federal government to establish and enforce laws to manage floodplains by reducing the flood risk to new construction. It may also be obtainable through your insurance broker.

Critics feel, however, that NFIP encourages additional construction in areas in danger of flooding, and that property owners hope to collect both on flood insurance and on disaster relief. They also accuse this flood insurance of being a direct federal subsidy, since the program operates at a loss.

Although some flood insurance may be available for your library, we think the best possible advice is to *never build libraries in flood-prone areas.*

We think that sooner or later, people nationwide are going to get thoroughly tired of having to constantly bail out people who insist on constructing and reconstructing buildings in areas prone to flooding, all at government expense. When that time comes, there may be even less assistance available to flooded libraries than there is now, and having built your library far above the raging waters will make even more sense.

E. Liability Insurance

Even before the days of massive personal injury settlements, liability insurance for libraries was important. Now it is absolutely essential.

Liability insurance covers bodily injuries and property damages that are the fault of the library or its employees—or that just take place on library premises.

Although a handful of what appear to be insane settlements occur in liability cases, in most situations settlements are reasonable.

Obviously, you can limit liability claims by keeping your building safe. Look for structural situations that can lead to personal injuries. And when your library is being designed, imagine what can go wrong with the more adventurous features of your new building.

The main secret in dealing with liability situations is to offer any help you can. Call emergency services, but *leave all talking to your insurance company*. The minute you start saying that you're sorry and that you've always known those steps were dangerous, you run the risk of getting your library into a tangle.

F. Builder's Risk Insurance

Builder's risk insurance covers the value of libraries (and all sorts of other buildings) while they are under construction.

Buildings are particularly vulnerable while they are under construction.

- The absence of locking doors and working security systems means that outsiders can wander into partially completed libraries, where they can commit vandalism or fall into unanticipated apertures.
- Partially completed buildings can be far more susceptible to damage because they are not yet fully enclosed or because (for example) rows of roof trusses are not yet held firmly in place by sheathing. In addition, workers using torches are a fairly common source of fires in buildings under construction or repair. The combination of torches and the ancient timber of historic buildings being remodeled or expanded is particularly dangerous. Sprinkler systems may not yet be functional.

As work on a new library building continues, the owner makes regular payments to the contractor for work completed and as a result owns increasingly large portions of the building.

Libraries can purchase their own builder's risk insurance, or they can require in their contracts with construction firms that the firms carry this insurance on the full project.

Builder's risk insurance typically ceases when the building is completed and the owners replace the builder's risk insurance with standard insurance.

G. Insurance Not Relevant to Buildings

Most libraries carry a variety of insurance coverages that have nothing to do with buildings. Some—such as workers' compensation insurance—may be required by law, but others are at the option of the library. The main reason for mentioning them here is because this coverage may be handled by the same firm that provides your other insurance.

- Workers compensation insurance provides coverage for staff members injured on the job or traveling to and from the job. Rates vary with the risk to the worker. Because librarians live in a low-risk environment, the only members of the staff of the average library likely to be expensive to insure are custodians. Insurance rates ("mod rates") are modified each year on the basis of the company's experience with each employer.
- Staff health and life insurance are typically regarded as benefits.
- Directors and officers liability ("D and O liability") covers malfeasance and torts by administrators. Boards and librarians commonly are concerned about accusations of improper hiring and firing, so be sure that your insurance covers alleged civil rights violations.

XIII. SNAPPY RULES ON LIBRARY SECURITY

1. The correct number of entrances to a library is anything up to one.
2. If RFID tags are visible when they're installed in books, users with theft in mind will simply remove the tags.
3. The true cost of a stolen book is vastly more than the value of the book.
4. When you are planning a library building, always ask what additional building codes will come into play when you expand it.
5. Basements cost almost as much as extra floors and can carry a terrible functional price in gloom and moisture. But they carry an evil allure for people who don't know much about commercial grade construction.
6. All entrances need to be staffed, whether or not they have security gates.
7. Never let your library be a passageway to someone else's turf.
8. Anyone who works in a library building must report to the director of the library. Shared facilities are seriously evil.
9. Provide tornado shelters. If your library is destroyed by a tornado, it's hard to explain why you skipped tornado shelters to save a little money.
10. The best tornado shelters are restrooms because no one will store book sale books or puppet stages in them.
11. If it's obvious to library users how your book theft-detection system works, the serious thieves will circumvent it.
12. The lowest-cost theft prevention system is keeping something theft-worthy behind a service desk.
13. Automated book sorting is fun, but there's apparently no serious study of whether it saves money.

14. Meeting rooms need to be accessible from entryways.
15. When you need serious liability insurance coverage, you need serious liability insurance coverage.
16. The way to save money on insurance is to raise the deductible amount rather than cutting the total coverage.
17. Avoid places where staff and users can be trapped. Dead-end book aisles and service desks with only one way out are good examples of bad design. So are exit passages with a series of one-way doors.
18. Public library children's departments must not be passageways to other public areas of a library.
19. Always study your plans for ways to improve staff sight lines. Your architects will not always like this.
20. Group study rooms need to be terrariums, with major glass surfaces on all walls, including those between study rooms.
21. Always show your plans to your building consultants, who have a lot more daily experience with library security than your architects do.

31

Walls, Floors, and Ceilings

I. INTRODUCTION

This chapter is a discussion of special problems with walls, floors, and ceilings in library buildings, not a wide-spectrum review of walls, floors, and ceilings in general. Because of this, the coverage of the topic is incomplete; if we haven't run into specific benefits or problems with certain types of materials or construction, we don't mention them.

Our concern about walls, floors, and ceilings has to do with function, durability, maintenance, and health issues. A whole range of other issues concerns sustainability, and we have not dealt with those in this chapter.

Walls, floors, and ceilings are less permanent that most librarians wish were the case. When you are working with your architect to make choices, be sure that you consider not only these elements' initial cost, but also their ease of maintenance and permanence.

The examples of wall, floor, and ceiling features in this chapter are intended not to be a survey of available products but rather a list of observations on things that we have seen attempted in library buildings and whether they appeared to be successful or disappointing.

II. HEALTH PROBLEMS

Many floor coverings and wall and floor finishes can be sources of health problems, especially during construction.

If you are living in a building while remodeling it, sometimes things can be controlled by keeping an airtight seal between construction areas and occupied parts of the building, but it can be difficult. Moving out during construction brings fewer complications.

Some people react extremely poorly to airborne dust from sanding drywall joints. One of the best employees in Fred's library, for example, had to resign when stray drywall dust sent her to the hospital.

Some cheap plywood used for temporary partitions exudes formaldehyde. (Some of the inexpensive trailers purchased by the federal government [FEMA] after Hurricane Katrina were uninhabitable due to formaldehyde seeping out of cheap plywood. The thousands of people who were sickened by living in the trailers were awarded over $40,000,000 in liability settlements.)

The concept of "sick building syndrome" dates from the 1970s and was named by the World Health Organization in 1986. Among the components may have been a combination of the off-gassing of unhealthy chemicals (such as formaldehyde) present in manufactured building materials and the sealing of buildings more tightly to save energy.

The situation is made far more complex by the lack of research into the toxicity of many industrial products. When it comes to poisons in construction materials, this book will be out of date while it is still at the printer, and for that reason we've limited ourselves to a couple of examples.

- Lead pigments make great paint, but they're all poisonous. They were banned for indoor use in 1978, but they're all over the place in older buildings. For libraries, the main danger appears to be lead pigments chalking off or being made airborne when old finishes are sanded.
- Polyurethane foam, which is used extensively in upholstered furniture, is explosively flammable and emits toxic fumes when it burns. Unfortunately, the chemicals added to make it less dangerously flammable are also nasty.
- Many adhesives contain dangerous organic solvents, such as benzene and toluene, as well as more complex chemicals.
- Asbestos. Until asbestos was banned in the 1970s, it was everywhere. (Like lead, it worked well, except for being poisonous.) Rely on your architects to

arrange suitable testing. We've run into library buildings and buildings being converted to libraries that had asbestos in vinyl asbestos floor tiles (VAT), floor tile mastic (glue), pipe lagging, transite (cement asbestos board) liners in under-slab air ducts, drywall mud, acoustic ceiling tiles, and other unwanted places. Almost every situation requires the evaluation of risks and costs.
- Vinyl. Manufacturing polyvinyl chloride (the basis of vinyl tile) creates serious pollution, but vinyl is everywhere. Who knows what the future will bring?

What can we do when we are planning library buildings?

- Rely on your architects and engineers to help steer you away from toxic chemicals. The kind of information found in project manuals may help protect your library from unpleasant materials that are not technically illegal but are sold over the counter. If you stress to the people specifying materials for your building that you are eager to avoid poisonous materials when possible, they should be able to warn you about the current state of affairs or write specifications that eliminate unhealthy construction products.
- Keep the costs of remediation in mind when planning library expansion and remodeling jobs and when evaluating the conversion of existing buildings to libraries. Before you purchase—or accept as a gift—any building constructed before 1980, get professional advice. Remediation can be surprisingly expensive.
- Be slightly cynical about industry claims concerning the safety of products. (Sometimes you can be seriously cynical.)
- Consider avoiding seriously overstuffed upholstered furniture in order to limit the amount of polyurethane foam in your library.
- If your library will have spray-on foam insulation, look up information on the toxicity of the proposed product.
- After new carpet has been installed, crank up the heat to about 80 degrees for a few days to accelerate off-gassing, then air the building out thoroughly.
- If you will be using solvent-based finishes, arrange for excellent ventilation and consider sealing off the working area from the rest of the library. The psychological effect of strong odors may be a component of staff and public complaints.
- Keep up on changes reported in the press. As we were finishing this book, the federal government was stepping up toxicity testing of common chemicals.
- Know your staff's individual health problems. If your staff will be around a building under construction on a daily basis, try to protect people that you know may be particularly sensitive.

III. WALLS

In most modern libraries, walls are constructed of drywall on steel studs. Most walls are finished with latex paint. It's a combination that lends itself to rapid assembly by skilled workers.

Librarians typically focus on specific problems with walls.

- Walls that block sound transmission.
- Paints that emit minimal odors while drying. It's difficult to move into a freshly painted room when the smell of the paint makes users and staff ill.
- Wall surfaces that are durable and easy to clean.

A. Controlling Sound Transmission

Some libraries have major problems with the transmission of sounds between rooms. Some standard things you can specify are:

- Walls that continue past suspended ceilings to the bottom of the floor or roof above. This is a standard way of keeping sound from migrating between offices or between study rooms.
- In the case of really noisy spaces (such as children's activity rooms), staggered stud walls are possible at only a modest increase in costs. In staggered stud walls, the plate at the bottom of the wall is slightly deeper, and the two sheets of drywall are supported by two sets of studs, eliminating the connection between the two walls that enhances sound transmission.
- Separately ducted air supplies and returns. If air ducts are not separate, they can serve as distressing sound conduits between adjacent rooms.

Since these solutions are all structural, they'll be expensive to retrofit and should be in the basic specifications for your library.

B. Preventing Damage to Drywall and Paint

Probably the most common wall covering in current libraries is drywall with latex paint. Unfortunately, it's also a very delicate product, one easily damaged by minor abrasion. Wooden furniture can easily knock off bits of paint. The sharp ends of rocking-chair rockers can literally cut their way through drywall. Dark paint colors help to make damage extremely obvious, and some dark-colored walls in some libraries are repainted every few months.

If durability is important, semigloss finishes are stronger than flat finishes. Oil-based paint can be tougher than latex.

1. Chair Rails

Chair rails are a fine, traditional solution to the problem of chewed-up walls.

Chair rails are wooden strips mounted horizontally on walls at the correct height to prevent furniture from sliding into walls and damaging the surface.

There's a tendency to designate the height of chair rails without first checking the actual furniture planned for the library. If the backs of the library's armchairs are 32 inches above the floors and chair rails are centered at 38 inches, the chair rails won't do much good. So don't let your architects specify the heights of your chair rails until you've selected your furniture.

Wooden chair rails work far better if they are stained and varnished rather than painted, because painted finishes show far more damage.

Plastic and stainless-steel bumper strips are available that do the same job as chair rails, protecting walls from adjacent furniture, collisions with book trucks, and similar mishaps. Often staff corridors are lined with plastic bumpers.

Chair rails can eliminate a lot of maintenance work. As librarians, we probably don't specify them often enough.

2. Baseboards

Baseboards are another essential architectural feature hallowed by long antiquity of use. (The fact that they are sometimes called "mop boards" accentuates this.)

Today many baseboards are made of vinyl or similar plastics. They are simply called "base" and are found everywhere. Outside of the garage for the library van or restrooms with ceramic tile walls, you may be hard-pressed to find rooms in your library without baseboards.

Vinyl baseboards have the advantage of being inexpensive, quick to glue into place, and easily replaced. While everyone uses simple vinyl baseboards, more ornamental ones are available. (Black vinyl baseboards make fine kick strips on service desks.)

For a more elegant look, you can always specify wooden baseboards, ranging from fairly simple boards with milled upper edges to elaborate combinations of flat wooden planks and ornamental trim pieces. Wooden baseboards need to be back-primed to keep them from warping. They're also a lot harder to maintain than vinyl baseboards.

Baseboards are truly essential.

> Fred once inherited a library without baseboards. The architects apparently felt that baseboards are clunky, and that the crisp, baseboard-free look of library spaces would improve the appearance of the library. But the endlessly chewed-up bottom two or three inches of all the walls proved it to be a seriously stupid idea.

The architectural concept for this part of a library called for no baseboards. The designers may have thought the entire effect would be trim and modern, but it quickly became a battered mess. All sorts of traditional design features (such as baseboards and chair rails and eaves) have been around for a long time for very good reasons, and we abandon them at our risk.

3. Corner Protectors

The protruding corners of walls are amazingly vulnerable to damage from furniture, book trucks, strollers, and other moving objects. Even though drywall corners may have metal L-shaped protective strips buried in the drywall mud, corners are still amazingly easy to damage.

A wide variety of metal and plastic corner protectors are available. We've had the best luck with stainless steel, but durable plastic protectors work well too. Fred suggests that you may want to think twice about corner protectors in some public areas of the library, due to their extremely utilitarian appearance, but he thinks they belong in all staff corridors. John suggests that you need corner protectors wherever you have a corner.

4. Vinyl Wallpaper

Many libraries use vinyl wallpaper as a modestly priced upgrade in wall coverings. Vinyl wallpaper is far easier to wash than painted drywall. One popular place for its use is craft rooms or other places where users may spill things.

Some vinyl wallpaper can be difficult to remove because traditional steaming techniques don't always work with plasticized surfaces. Talk with your architect about paper that can be easily peeled off. You can also use heat-release glue.

IV. FLOORS

A. Bearing Strength

We've talked about bearing strength in floors on a number of occasions in this book, partly because it's a vital concept and because (unfortunately) some designers ignore it.

Library floors—all library floors—must be designed to carry no less than 150 pounds per square foot, live load. The rule is that library buildings have to allow you to put books anywhere you want, any time you want. Outside of factories and warehouses, few buildings need to be as strong as libraries. ("Live load" means the weight of contents. The weight of the building itself is "dead load." Even extraordinarily massive buildings with huge dead loads may not have much leftover strength for heavy live loads. You'll need the opinion of structural engineers.)

Make sure your architects understand that at some future time you may decide to rearrange your library, and that *you need to be able to put shelving anywhere you want.* Where you will put books on opening day is only part of the story. (If you are pushed to say where books will go, the right answer is, "Anywhere we want." It's similar to what you say when designers ask you where you will put computers.)

> In one library Fred worked with, the architect (despite all instructions) specified adequately strong floors only for that part of the building that would house books on opening day. At the ribbon cutting, Fred felt the floor shake oddly when people walked past him. When the library later had a structural engineer look at the floor system, it found it had to reinforce the floors before book shelving areas could be expanded—which was a lot more expensive an undertaking than just doing things right the first time.

Some library loads may require stronger-than-standard library buildings. Fully loaded microfiche storage cabinets can be immensely heavy, as can compact shelving running on rails. In addition, compact shelving requires floors that don't flex, so the shelving won't bend the floors and run downhill. (Floor bending is called "deflection.") If you are planning compact shelving for any location other than slab-on-grade spaces, you'll need to review things with the manufacturer of the shelving and your structural engineers.

B. Floor Surfaces

A wide variety of floor coverings is available. Obviously, we're looking for something that simultaneously (a) is comfortable underfoot, (b) wears like iron, (c) is unusually easy to clean, (d) brings an aura of beauty to our rooms, (e) doesn't make noises when people walk on it, (f) soaks up the sounds that are bouncing around the library, (g) doesn't show dirt, (h) is not slippery when wet, and (i) lends itself to easy replacement of worn-out spots.*

Most library flooring is glued down on top of poured concrete subfloor. Note that poured concrete is typically not as flat as one would wish. Sometimes self-leveling products need to be poured on low spaces before floor coverings are installed.

With the exception of terrazzo, concrete, and ceramic tile, all floor coverings are somewhat resilient and require more than just wet mopping.

---

*If you find a floor covering that meets all of these requirements, please contact the authors.

Also with the exception of terrazzo and concrete, all floor coverings require attic stock. Five or ten years after you install your floor, you may be unable to purchase matching material, and you will be very pleased if you have some extra pieces or rolls lying about the place.

Vinyl base is usually installed after the floor covering.

If you are thinking of anything that is not everyday material, try to view an installation or two of it before deciding.

The following list of floor coverings is based on our years of experience visiting and working on library buildings, so it reflects strong personal experience rather than a survey of all available products. So it's an incomplete list. All of these products are continually changing, so this is just an ultralight oversight. Talk with your architects, but always be a little wary about trendy products and "green" materials without a track record of use in libraries.

1. Broadloom Carpet

"Broadloom" carpet is carpet in rolls, typically 12 or 15 feet wide. The range of quality in broadloom carpet is huge. The best broadloom carpet is amazingly tough, strong, and long-lasting, while the cheapest (and there's a whole lot of that running around) is pretty much total garbage.

The two common varieties of broadloom carpet are loop pile and cut pile. Cut pile carpet resembles the carpet used in homes, while loop pile carpet consists of tight loops. A variety of pile densities may be available, and you are likely to be happier with the densest pile available. By and large, libraries prefer loop pile rather than cut pile because it is more durable.

Expert carpet installers can do an amazing job matching seams in broadloom carpet. Dissimilar carpets can be butted together, although variations in thickness may be apparent at the joints.

Because many poured concrete floors are somewhat irregular, many carpeting jobs include pouring on leveling mixtures that even out the surfaces of floors before carpeting is installed.

Carpeting can be installed on risers, such as those in children's multilevel story rooms, but avoid steps with curved edges.

Broadloom carpet in libraries is installed by gluing it down directly onto concrete. The kind of padding used in homes is unsuited for library use. The seams will split, and the weight of stacks and reading tables will permanently dent the surface of the carpet.

However, one ingenious architect Fred knows was able to pad the carpet behind a lending desk (where staff kill their feet by standing all day long). He did it by limiting the short dimension of the open space to less than twelve feet (the width of broadloom carpet) so he could install a pad while gluing down the back edge so there would be no seam to split where the desk carpet met the adjoining carpet.

Carpet is frequently used on stairs because it is quiet and tends not to be slippery. You may want plastic nosings on your steps to keep the edges from wearing out too quickly and to make the edges of the steps easier to see. You'll also want to be sure that the installers get the carpet glued down perfectly flat, with no irregularities for users to catch their feet on.

Broadloom carpet lends itself to the insertion of ornamental pieces of carpet, such as animal groupings or aerial views of city streets in the carpet of public library children's departments. Check the websites of library supply houses.

Some designers create large patterns using multiple types of broadloom carpet. You may want to evaluate the intersection of these proposed patterns with the furniture layout in your library—including what the effect will be when you move the furniture around. We know of libraries where carpet patterns specified where furniture was to go, and that turned out to be a bad idea, another violation of the law of flexibility. We are also concerned that excessive numbers of seams may lead to the more rapid appearance of problems.

Professionally installed broadloom carpet should be absolutely flat. We've seen bad installation jobs where carpets ended up with bubbles and wrinkles, and you want to reject them instantly.

> One library Fred worked with had carpet so badly wrinkled that it resembled a Shar-Pei dog. Unfortunately, the work was done by somebody's cousin, and the carpet just stayed.

> If you mention a bubble in your new carpet, someone may turn up with a rubber mallet, pound the bubble back down, and say "It's fixed. Please give us the check." Always wait a few days to see if it pops up again. Fred's library once spent six months with popping bubbles before it totally rejected a carpet job and hired another firm to tear out the carpet and put in new.

Because of the wide variations in carpet quality and professionalism of installation, you may want to require in your bid specifications that the carpet vendors provide installation by their own staffs rather than subcontracting the work. In the cheap home carpet market, lots of the installation is done by freelance workers who get the jobs from carpet firms by low bid. If you are installing carpet without the supervision of your architect, you will need to take particular pains to protect your library from substandard work.

2. Carpet Tile (Carpet Squares)

Carpet tiles are typically about 2 × 2-foot or larger sections with adhesive designed to keep corners from lifting but at the same time making it possible to remove and replace individual tiles or to swap tiles around.

One of the great advantages of carpet tile is the ability to replace individual squares in areas where carpet wears out most quickly, such as where people stand at copy machines or in front of service desks.

Modern carpet tiles rely on patterns to conceal the joints between tiles. A standard approach is to use families of tiles with a variety of similar shades to hide places where tiles have been removed and replaced. If all tiles are identical, a new tile will stand out like a sore thumb because it will be noticeably cleaner than all those around it. But if tiles tend in general to vary somewhat in brightness and color, the differences won't stand out as much. (Some maintenance staff members still tend to find the contrast between new and old tiles too extreme and instead bring older tiles out from back portions of rooms and put the new tiles in corners, where they come closer to matching the tiles less trodden upon.)

Original carpet tile products were so unsatisfactory that we used to warn libraries against them, but we think that modern carpet squares are now the best standard floor covering of their type.

3. Vinyl Tile

Vinyl tile remains popular, although it is not a "green" product.

Unlike products designed for home use, commercial vinyl tile requires waxing, stripping, rewaxing, and buffing, so it requires a fair amount of maintenance work.

Vinyl tile includes polyvinyl chloride, which is criticized by some people because manufacturing it leads to toxic by-products.

VCT (vinyl composition tile) is a standard, modestly priced product. Individual tiles are commonly 12 × 12 inches, but some vinyl tile products now come in wood-grained strips.

Despite being discontinued in the late 1970s, VAT (vinyl asbestos tile) is still around in large quantities. A first warning sign is 9 × 9 rather than 12 × 12-inch tiles. As long as VAT is not crumbling, you can probably cover it up with something else, but it's more fun to know that it's not there at all. (With any building constructed before 1980, you always want to have existing vinyl floor tile tested for asbestos.)

4. Rubber Tile

One substitute for vinyl tile is rubber tile, which is a natural product and does not require stripping, waxing, and buffing. It is also a great deal "greener" than vinyl.

Rubber tile is commonly used on staircase treads, particularly on service staircases. Look for rows of raised disks that resemble quarters. This pattern reduces slipperiness; if the staircase is slightly damp, water may settle between the raised quarters and leave the tops of the quarters dry.

Rubber tile is more expensive than vinyl tile but seems to be extremely sturdy and low-maintenance. We've seen it in staff work areas in several libraries, and they seem to be very pleased with its performance.

Rubber tile has a more limited range of colors than vinyl tile.

5. Recycled Tires

Flooring made from recycled rubber tires is a green product and desirable for that reason. It's also fairly comfortable underfoot.

Because rubber flooring is made from old tires, it has a limited range of colors. Various varieties of speckled black are common colors. Our personal feeling is that most of the stuff is pretty ugly.

Architects tell us that rubber flooring can wear out in key traffic areas. One library Fred is working with is having a terrible problem with endless scuff marks on its new rubber flooring.

6. Poured Epoxy

Poured epoxy is an unusually durable and chemical-resistant finish. In libraries, we see it used primarily for back room applications where spilled chemicals may be a problem and in vehicle storage areas.

7. Bare or Stained Concrete

Polished concrete floors are extremely durable, but they are hard on the feet of people who have to stand on them all day. Many are made in various stained colors, but the examples we see tend to have rather irregular colors. A good place to evaluate polished concrete floors is big box stores. While you're there, evaluate the floor for evenness and appearance, especially attractiveness of colors.

To the best of our knowledge, there's no attractive way to add leveling compounds to bare concrete floors, so if your floors are irregular—a frequent problem with poured concrete—you'll have to make good use of the leveling screws on your shelving and on your reading table legs.

This is pretty academic. We haven't seen stained concrete floors in libraries.

8. Terrazzo

Terrazzo is made of marble chips mixed with a grout-like material, cast in place, and then ground smooth when it has set. A wide variety of colors is possible, and patterns are often created by using brass bands to separate mixtures of various colors, much like champlevé work, then grinding the brass down with everything else. Terrazzo is impressively strong and water-resistant. In libraries, it's frequently found in entryways, where slush, snow, and rain can be tracked in and not trickle down to lower levels.

Terrazzo is a very traditional product with a long history of use in high-wear situations, such as school hallways. It's also rock hard and therefore hard on the feet. If your entire library has terrazzo floors, your staff will want to wear sneakers on the job. Our personal experience is that terrazzo seems even harder underfoot than concrete, but that may be just overactive imaginations.

Terrazzo is widely used in entryways, but it is (a) extraordinarily hard and (b) extremely slippery when wet with tracked-in water and slush. The slipperiness of wet terrazzo leads many buildings with terrazzo entryway floors to use rented carpet mats. As a result, the pretty patterns in pictures of terrazzo floors in new buildings are usually obscured in everyday life with carpet mats spread out wherever users can walk.

John has had people slip on wet terrazzo floors, break their hips, and end up suing the library.

9. Bamboo

Bamboo is attractive because it is a green product with a pleasant color. The finished product is made up of many thin strips glued up edge to edge.

Bamboo has many uses in libraries, such as wood end panels for stacks and other kinds of trim. But bamboo is not strong enough for floors in libraries, and we've seen installations that had to be ripped out when they were still fairly new.

10. Hardwood

Hardwood flooring is another extremely traditional product. It can look handsome, but it strikes us as too delicate for almost all library installations. In libraries, we've seen hardwood floors in very formal reading rooms, exhibit areas, stage floors, and similar places.

Hardwood flooring is inherently noisy compared with more commonly used resilient floor coverings such as carpet, cork, vinyl, and linoleum. A library user in spike heels crossing a hardwood floor can't be easily missed.

Hardwood flooring can vary extremely widely in quality. Once again, you'll probably want the advice of an architect and the ability to cite quality standards.

Most hardwood flooring in libraries is tongue-and-groove flooring. We've seen parquet blocks used, but they gave the impression of lifting.

Standard wooden flooring is solid wood. Solid wood flooring lends itself to refinishing, with the top surface occasionally sanded down to provide an undamaged surface. Our experience has been that (a) sanding hardwood floors is a highly skilled undertaking, and (b) you've got perhaps two or three resurfacings before you have to replace the flooring.

The underside of hardwood flooring typically has longitudinal grooves to prevent the flooring strips from cupping or crowning.

Some inexpensive "manufactured" flooring products sold for home use are basically plywood, with a thin top layer of attractive wood glued to layers of less expensive products. These seem flimsy and totally unsuitable for use in libraries.

Oak is the most common wood used in tongue and groove flooring, but hickory, maple, and other woods are available. See also the separate section on bamboo flooring above.

11. Cork Tile

Cork tile is another green product because it's renewable. Cork has been used for flooring for many years, starting before the current emphasis on renewable construction products. Maintenance people tell us that cork is easy to keep up.

12. Ceramic Tile

Ceramic tile is a standard product of tremendous antiquity. It works well in restrooms, foyers, and other places where water can be frequently spilled. Unlike vinyl tile, it does not need to be stripped, waxed, and buffed, but simply wet mopped or (if it's really filthy) scrubbed.

The range of choices of color and surface texture is impressive.

For the safety of library users and staff, ceramic tile needs to have some anti-slip qualities rather than completely smooth top surfaces.

All ceramic tile installations need extremely dark grout. All grout stains permanently, and the grout colors need to be dark enough to hide the stains. Colored grout also has a tendency to fade, so darker is better on installation day. (Maintenance firms tell us that the single hardest thing to keep clean in buildings is white grout.)

Ceramic tile is frequently used on staircases. Although bull-nosed tile is available, we've seen the lead edges chip, and you may want to have metal edges on the treads with inserted plastic strips.

The patterns and colors of ceramic tile change frequently, and in addition, many products are imported. For this reason, attic stock of ceramic tile is important.

13. Walk Off Mats

Many libraries have recessed pans with fitted mats just inside their entrances. The mats have bars with spaces between that let water drain into the bottoms of the pans. When users scuff their way across the mats, salty water ends up in the pans, where the water evaporates. Periodically, the library removes the mats and scrapes up the salt. Some bars on mats have carpet inserts and some have plastic inserts.

14. Rental Floor Mats

Many libraries (and businesses of all sorts) rent rug-surfaced floor mats for use near entries. These are provided by rental services and changed out at arranged intervals.

Even if a library has built-in walk off mats, users will probably track in a great deal of watery slop if the library does not use floor mats as well. In some libraries, potentially slippery areas like terrazzo floors are often completely covered by rental mats.

15. Summary

In many small and medium-sized libraries, the standard flooring materials appear to be carpet tile for reading rooms and staff workrooms and ceramic tile for foyers and restrooms, with rental mats by the entrances to soak up extra water.

V. CEILINGS

For most library purposes, ceilings need to:

- Provide easy access to the tangle of equipment hidden above the ceiling's surface.
- Reflect a high percentage of light for efficient use of reflected uplighting.
- Absorb a high percentage of sound that strikes the ceiling.

The problems come with sloped ceilings (which may not work with acoustic ceiling tile) and with ornamental ceilings (which may not absorb sound or reflect light).

A. Acoustic Tile

For most libraries, the standard ceiling material is suspended acoustic tile.

Suspended acoustic tile has a number of very strong advantages:

- Providing access to the endless variety of MEP stuff hidden above ceilings in modern libraries, including air ducts, plumbing, electrical wiring, data cable, sprinkler piping, and so on. Years ago, some buildings used plaster ceilings with access hatches, and the result was maintenance misery. With an acoustic tile ceiling, almost any section that does not include a light fixture, sprinkler head, or air duct opening can be lifted out of the way. (With access hatches, slender people need to slither through narrow openings and creep around inside the ceilings.)
- Sound absorption. Without acoustic ceilings, many libraries have unpleasant noise transmission and reflection. Especially in the case of sloped ceilings and barrel vaults, surfaces that don't absorb sound can be a serious pain.
- Light reflection. The best way to light libraries is to bounce light off ceilings. Brands of acoustic tile are available that combine high reflectivity with strong sound absorption.
- Generally tidy appearance, particularly with 2 × 2-foot tiles with recessed splines.
- Soffits can easily be created with ceiling tile. (We regard 95 percent of decorative soffits as abominations, but that's another part of the story.)

A couple of major points:

- Impressive acoustic tile is available that absorbs 90 percent of the sound that hits it and reflects 90 percent of the light that strikes it.
- Acoustic ceiling tile can't be painted because that ruins its ability to absorb sound. We've seen libraries with sections of ceilings painted various colors, leading to dark and noisy spaces beneath—always a winning combination.
- Acoustic tile is extremely easily stained by water. Even trivial roof leaks or condensation can lead to major brown splotches on ceilings.
- Because patterns of ceiling tile come and go, and because it's so easily stained, you'll need a substantial attic stock of extra tile.
- Maintenance staff sometimes use secret marks (such as colored map pins) to indicate which acoustic tiles need to be removed for access to mechanical equipment.

B. Drywall

Drywall ceilings are fairly easy to construct, but they reflect sound and limit access to MEP equipment. You don't want them.

Other MEP options are suspending the equipment below ceilings, such as exposed air ducts, placing equipment in spaces beneath the floor (accessed from the floor below), or burying equipment in concrete floor slabs (with the exception of electrical conduit for electrical outlets in the floor, always an extraordinarily bad idea).

C. Wood

Attractive wooden ceilings have been installed in libraries. Unfortunately, especially if they are cathedral ceilings, they tend to be noisy. If your architects are planning a wooden ceiling, you may want the input of an independent acoustical consulting engineer.

Dark wooden ceilings tend to cause lighting problems because they eliminate the ability to bounce light off ceilings, which is one of the best ways of lighting libraries. We've seen modern wooden ceilings where the architects returned to the lighting systems of a century ago—hanging fixtures to supply low levels of ambient light, plus individual light fixtures for all reading tables and shelving units. It's an expensive way to light a library, but if you can't have a brightly lit ceiling, it may be your only option.

D. Summary

Our experience has been that suspended acoustic tile ceilings are the standard of the industry.

VI. SNAPPY RULES ON WALLS, FLOORS, AND CEILINGS

[Walls]

1. Latex paint on drywall has the strength of piecrust. You'll have to find some way to prevent furniture and book trucks from chewing everything up.
2. Chair rails are essential with drywall. Chair rail height is not an aesthetic decision. Decide on heights only after selecting your furniture, or you may end up with chairs that circumnavigate your chair rails and gouge holes in your drywall.

3. Baseboards have been around for centuries because they prevent cleaning gear from damaging the bottoms of walls. Our ancestors knew what they were doing.
4. If your library interior has lots of corners, you'll want lots of corner protectors.
5. It's so hard to match paint colors that when you patch a wall you'll probably need to repaint to the next corner.

(Floors)

1. Regardless of what you'll be doing when you first move in, ALL LIBRARY FLOORS need to be strong enough to bear the weight of shelving.
2. If your entryway has an elegant terrazzo floor, it's possible that no one will ever see it because you'll keep it covered with carpet mats so users don't slip and fall and crack their hips.
3. Never be the first kid on the block to use a new flooring system.
4. Carpet tile is a great product, but it needs pattern to hide the joints.
5. Solid color carpet shows every speck of crud. If your carpet is completely unpatterned, you will receive frequent and unhappy comments from your custodial staff.
6. Carpet patterns that specify the locations of specific items of furniture violate the key principle of flexibility in library design.
7. When the time comes to replace sections of your carpet, it will no longer be in production. That's why people invented attic stock.
8. Library carpet can become impressively dirty. Home-level shampooing machines are cute but fairly helpless. Look for professional cleaning firms with heavy-duty equipment and vacuum extraction of water. And do it twice a year if you can afford it.
9. Ceramic tile and terrazzo can last for generations, but they're rock hard. All comfortable floor coverings have a limited life.
10. Some building owners opt for cheap initial flooring, hoping that budgets will be better at replacement time. Review long-term cost tradeoffs with your architects. (On the other hand, if you pick really trendy colors, you may be glad your carpet wears out quickly.)
11. If your library has a terrazzo floor, all of your staff will insist on wearing tennis shoes.
12. The uglier your carpet, the longer it will last. Fred worked with a library that had avocado carpet that would not die.
13. Attic stock for flooring is essential. Count on the fact that you'll be unable under any circumstances to match your existing carpet or ceramic tile.
14. Ceramic tile always needs very dark grout. Don't let anyone talk you into anything else.

15. Cut pile carpet is generally too delicate for serious library purposes.
16. The quality of carpet varies impressively. The best carpets are tough and last for years, but there are incredible quantities of total slop available.

(Ceilings)

1. Acoustic tile ceilings offer the great combination of enabling reflected uplight, absorbing unwanted sound, and providing easy access to all the MEP gadgetry above the ceilings. Don't sacrifice all this great stuff on an aesthetic whim.
2. If your library has dark ceilings, you'll have to provide individual lights for reading tables and shelves. It's an old-fashioned but expensive approach, with lots of areas where it's too dim to read.
3. *NEVER PAINT AN ACOUSTIC TILE CEILING.*
4. We've warned against ceilings with perimeter soffits in several places in this book, but they're such an abomination we're mentioning them again.

(General)

1. If it comes recommended by LEED but doesn't work, it was a bad recommendation.
2. "Green but dysfunctional" is basically just "dysfunctional."
3. When evaluating flooring systems and wall coverings in other libraries, try to talk with those libraries' heads of maintenance.

Appendix

VOCABULARY

An ancient, traditional, and highly complex craft such as the construction of buildings can develop an immense technical vocabulary. This glossary provides a number of basic terms. It was developed by Fred Schlipf for his class on library buildings.

Knowing the proper names for materials, architectural styles, and structural elements is extremely important when you are dealing with architects and contractors, for it will help avoid misunderstandings and greatly speed communication. (Think of them as "words of power.")

The list is full of Fred's personal opinions on the usability of various items in functional library architecture, and a few of the entries are as much opinion pieces as dispassionate definitions.

Sources for many of the items in the list are given below. Most of the definitions are not verbatim. They have been simplified or altered, and any misinformation that has crept in is therefore Fred's fault. The definition given for a word is for its use in architecture and libraries; many words have additional meanings not listed here.

Words in **boldface** in definitions are themselves defined elsewhere in the list.

SOURCES

AW   Antony White and Bruce Robertson. *Architecture and Ornament: A Visual Guide.* New York: Design, 1990. (Be careful: some usage in this book is British but not American.)

BF   Bannister Fletcher. *A History of Architecture on the Comparative Method.* Many editions. New York: Scribners.

CH   Cyril M. Harris. *Dictionary of Architecture and Construction.* New York: McGraw-Hill, 1975.

FS   Fred Schlipf. (Items with no initials fall into this category.)

JHP   John Fleming, Hugh Honour, and Nicholas Pevsner. *A Dictionary of Architecture.* New York: Penguin, 1998. (Be careful: some usage in this book is British but not American.)

JTF   James T. Frane. *Encyclopedia of Construction Terms.* Carlsbad, CA: Craftsman, 1994.

MR   Frederick S. Merritt and Jonathan T. Ricketts. *Building Design and Construction Handbook.* New York: McGraw-Hill, 2001.

NW   Norval White. *The Architecture Book.* New York: Knopf, 1976.

PL   Philip D. Leighton and David C. Weber. *Planning Academic and Research Library Buildings.* Chicago: American Library Association, 1999.

Definitions without attribution are Fred's.
Thanks to former GSLIS students Wendy Shelburne and Julie Derden for their help in revising this list.

Abatement. Removal of **asbestos**, **lead paint**, or other materials formerly used in buildings but now unacceptable for health reasons.

Abutment. Solid masonry that resists the lateral pressure of an arch, vault, or dome. (BF and NW)

Accessibility codes. Legal rules specifying how buildings must be constructed to be accessible to people with disabilities. You will need to be aware of both federal and state codes.

Acoustic tile. Wall and ceiling tile made of sound-absorbing material. Acoustic tile is seen everywhere in **suspended ceilings**. It is notorious for becoming stained by moisture, but is essential both for acoustic control and for access to mechanical systems above ceilings. Library ceilings need to be white, and the only workable acoustic tile color is white.

Acroterion. Block resting on a pediment to support statuary or an ornament, and/or the ornament itself. (BF and NW) The word comes from the Greek for "high thing."

ADA. See **Americans with Disabilities Act.**

Adaptive reuse. Conversion of an existing structure to another purpose.

Add alternate. An item to be added to the base bid if the owner decides to add the work covered by the alternate. For example, a library may list more elaborate windows as an alternate, and then choose to install them if the base bid price permits. Firms bidding on a job will provide prices for both the base bid and each requested add alternate. (PL and FS) See also **deduct alternate**.

Aggregate. Inert filler material made up of sand, stone, or gravel that is used to strengthen **cement** and form **concrete**. (JTF)

AIA. See **American Institute of Architects.**

Air entrainment. Inclusion of air in concrete mixtures to improve strength.

Alcove. A recess or niche in a wall. (JHP)

American Institute of Architects. The AIA is a national trade association, founded in 1857.

Americans with Disabilities Act. A federal law passed in 1990, based in part on earlier rehabilitation and civil rights legislation. The ADA had immense implications for library buildings, and particularly involved physical access for disabled persons to buildings, book stacks, restrooms, and so on. Your state may have additional accessibility code requirements. Although the ADA was passed over 25 years ago, many libraries still do not conform, and they are occasionally sued. (FS)

Amp. Short for ampere. A unit of quantity of electric current. See also **volt** and **watt**. Amps are equal to watts divided by volts. For example, a 60-watt lamp in a 110-volt system draws about half an amp. Individual circuits are commonly rated at 20 amps. (FS)

Annunciator panel. A panel (usually near the entrance to a library, for the convenience of emergency personnel) that indicates which automatic alarm devices in the building have been activated. (FS)

ANSI. American National Standards Institute. An independent organization of trade associations, technical societies, professional groups, and consumer organizations that establishes and publishes standards. It was formerly the American Standards Association (ASA). (CH) The name is pronounced "ANN-see."

Apron. A raised panel below a windowsill. (JHP)

Apron window. See **awning window.**

Arabesque. Surface decoration, light and fanciful in character, with elaborate continuations of lines. (BF) The American architect Louis Sullivan made extensive use of decoration of this type in terracotta and (as on the Carson, Pirie, Scott building in Chicago) in cast iron.

Arcade. A range of **arches** supported on piers or columns, attached to or detached from the wall. (BF) A line of counterthrusting arches raised on columns or piers. (CH)

Arch. A structure of wedge-shaped blocks over an opening, so disposed as to hold together when supported only from the sides. (BF) The individual wedge-shaped blocks are voussoirs, and the one in the center is the **keystone**. (The implication is that the arch will collapse when the keystone is removed, but in actuality it will collapse when *any* voussoir is removed.) The inside **soffit** is the intrados. The top of the arch is the crown, and the sides are the haunches. Arches have many different names based on their shapes. For example, the typical pointed arch we associate with Gothic cathedrals is called a lancet arch. Page 20 of JHP shows eight shapes and their names. A standard round arch is a segment of a circle. (FS) See also **catenary** and **parabola**.

Architectural awards. See **Awards, architectural.**

Architrave. A word with at least three usages. (1) A **lintel** extending from one column or pier to another. (2) The lowest of the three parts of a classical **entablature**. (3) The molding around a door or window. (JHP)

Art Deco. A decorative jazz age style stimulated by the Paris Exposition International des Arts Decoratifs et Industrielles Modernes of 1925, and widely used in the architecture of the 1930s, including skyscraper designs such as the Chrysler Building in New York. Art Deco design is characterized by strong vertical elements and by sharp angular or zigzag surface forms and ornaments. (CH) There are relatively few Art Deco libraries because the style was popular during the Great Depression, when few new libraries were constructed. One interesting and well-preserved Art Deco library building is the DeKalb (Illinois) Public Library. The Madison building at the U.S. Library of Congress is also Art Deco. (FS)

Art Nouveau. A decorative movement in European architecture heralded in the 1880s and flourishing strongly in the period 1893–1907. Its particular characteristics were a flowing and sinuous naturalistic ornament and avoidance of historical architectural traits. It was called "Jugendstil" in Germany. (BF) In the United States, Art Nouveau design is associated especially with Louis Comfort Tiffany, who produced, among many other things, the stained glass and mosaics in the 1893 Chicago Public Library (now the "Cultural Center"). The greatest Art Nouveau architect was Antoni Gaudi (Spanish, 1852–1926). (FS)

Arts and Crafts Movement. English movement in applied art and indirectly in architecture during the second half of the nineteenth century, emphasizing the importance of craftsmanship and high standards of design for everyday objects. (CH) It was a sort of medieval revival style associated especially with William Morris in the United Kingdom and Gustav Stickley in the United States. A number of extremely attractive Arts and Crafts library buildings have survived, for example the public library in Riverside, Illinois. (FS, JD)

As-built drawings. See **record drawings.**

Asbestos. An incombustible fibrous mineral, once used extensively in construction, particularly to insulate pipes and boilers, and to provide strength in vinyl tile and some ceiling tile, but now recognized as extremely dangerous when loose fibers are inhaled. The cost of asbestos removal in remodeling or conversion projects can be extremely high. See also **abatement** and **VAT**. (FS)

Ashlar. Masonry of smooth, squared stones in regular courses, in contradistinction to rubble work. (BF)

ASHRAE. American Society of Heating, Refrigerating, and Air-Conditioning Engineers. It was formed in 1959 through the merger of the American Society of Heating and Air Conditioning Engineers and the American Society of Refrigerating Engineers. The abbreviation is pronounced "ASH-ray."

Assignable space. Space used to meet the primary functions of a building, as opposed to **nonassignable space**, which consists of space for stairways, elevators, hallways, restrooms, mechanical equipment, chases, janitors' closets, the thicknesses of walls, and so on. (FS)

Atrium. In modern buildings, a covered courtyard within or between buildings, usually on several levels and often acting as a central light well and concourse. (JHP) Architects and librarians tend to differ very strongly on the desirability of atriums. Atriums can provide "wow" spaces, and they sometimes help with orientation if users can see several floors. But atriums cause serious problems in libraries because they interrupt traffic flow on upper floors, transmit noise, waste energy, complicate temperature control, sometimes terrify people with acrophobia, and consume space that could be better used for functional purposes. The New York University library was designed by a leading architect, but its atrium has caused so many problems that architectural screens have been added. Light fixtures over atriums should be on drops to permit maintenance, but they usually aren't. Atriums in entryways with glazed openings on upper floors eliminate many problems, but they still waste energy and are hard to maintain. (FS)

Attic stock. Extra supplies of materials that commonly need to be replaced and may be hard to match when the time comes. Common examples include ceiling tile, floor tile, carpet, and so on. Some new or remodeled libraries underestimate the storage space required for attic stock and find their storerooms almost immediately overcrowded with it. (FS)

Awards, architectural. Architectural awards recognize appearance that appeals to architects rather than functionality, and libraries may wish to take them with a grain of salt when selecting architects.

Awning window, also called **apron window**. A window consisting of a number of top-hinged horizontal sashes one above the other, the bottom edges of which swing outward. (CH)

Backfill. Soil that is replaced in an area that has been excavated previously. (CH) Most construction jobs require backfill around the foundation. The backfill around a new building can compress over the years and need to be added to. (FS)

Balcony. A partial floor overlooking a larger space inside a building, or a small floor with railings projecting from a building. (FS)

Ballast. A transformer that supplies high-voltage power to a lamp, such as a fluorescent or HID lamp, that does not operate on standard 110-volt current. The two common types of ballasts are magnetic and electronic. Most modern fluorescent ballasts are electronic because they conserve energy and reduce flicker. Some inexpensive magnetic ballasts are extremely noisy; see **sound rating**. Some electronic ballasts have a high failure rate; watch out for unfortunate substitutions under the "or equivalent" language of specifications. (FS)

Balloon frame. A system of framing a wooden building, with all exterior **studs** extending the full height of the frame, from the bottom sill to the roof plate. Floor **joists** are attached by nails to the exterior studs. Because multi-floor studs create long chimneys that permit fire to spread easily from floor to floor inside walls, balloon frame walls include fire-stops—short horizontal sections of wood that connect the studs and prevent flames from moving vertically from floor to floor. (CH and FS) Balloon framing has now been replaced by **platform framing**, which does not require long studs or fire-stops.

Baluster. A pillar or column supporting a handrail or coping, a series of such being called a **balustrade**. (BF)

Balustrade. An entire railing system (as along the edge of a balcony) including a top rail and its **balusters**, and sometimes a bottom rail. (CH) Balustrades with horizontal members that can be climbed like ladders are dangerous but unfortunately are not banned. (FS)

Bar. One of the thin strips of wood or metal forming the several divisions of a window sash or a wood panel door, employed to receive the glass. See **muntin**. (CH)

Bar joist. An open-web steel **joist** consisting of a single bar, bent in a zigzag pattern, and welded at its points of contact to upper and lower **chords**. (CH)

Barge. See **rake**.

Bargeboard. See **rake**.

Baroque. Style of European art, architecture, and design from about 1600 to 1730, after the stages of Renaissance learning and experiment had passed and architecture had reached a characteristic, non-Roman expression. (BF) Baroque art and architecture are characterized by complex forms that convey movement, drama, and tension, and by the conspicuous and lavish use of decoration, sculpture, and color. (CH) St. Paul's in London and St. Peter's in Rome are Baroque churches. In France and a bit later in the German-speaking states, the Baroque style was succeeded by the Rococo style early in the eighteenth century.

Barrel vault. A masonry vault of plain, semicircular cross-section, supported by parallel walls or arcades, and adapted to cover longitudinal areas. (CH) Barrel vaults can be very attractive, but they are also inherently noisy. In libraries, barrel vaults need to have acoustic surfaces, which may not appeal to their designers. (FS)

Base bid. The bid for a project exclusive of bids for **add alternates** or **deduct alternates**.

Baseboard. A flat projection from an interior wall or partition at the floor, covering the joint between the floor and the wall and protecting the wall from kicking, bumping, mopping, and so on. It is less commonly called a mop board, scrub board, skirting board, or washboard. In modern buildings, inexpensive baseboards are usually made of flexible plastic. (CH and FS)

Basement. A sub-grade floor. Basements in homes and in old libraries tend to be only partly below grade and have high-set windows, but basements in modern libraries have natural light only if the buildings are built on sloping sites, have window wells, or have atriums leading to upper floors. Basements in modern libraries are set much lower in the ground because main floors tend to be at grade level. The thickness of the floor above and the necessary clearance for library equipment and lighting may place basement floors 14 feet or more below grade, subjecting the walls to substantial hydrostatic pressure. Unlike basements in houses, library basements cost nearly as much as upper floors and are frequently regretted by their owners.

Batter. An inclined face on a wall, commonly seen at the ground-floor level of masonry buildings.

Battlement. A **parapet** with alternating indentations (embrasures) and raised portions (merlons). It is also called a crenellation. (JHP)

Bauhaus. A school of design established in Weimar, Germany, by Walter Gropius in 1919 and shut down by the Nazis in 1933. Several of the school's leaders then moved to America. The term *Bauhaus* became virtually synonymous with modern teaching methods in architecture and the applied arts. Bauhaus structures are typically austere in design. (Some people find them not elegantly austere but depressingly barren.) Bauhaus design ruled modern architecture until the 1970s in the form of the **International Style.** (CH, AW, NW, and FS) It is associated in America with Ludwig Mies van der Rohe, who was responsible for much of the Illinois Institute of Technology campus in Chicago.

Bay. One standard element or unit in a modular building, where a horizontal floor may be divided into rectangular bays with supporting columns at their intersections. Bay size is of particular importance to libraries because of its effect on stack placement. Column spacing needs to be a multiple of aisle spacing in order to avoid columns in the middle of aisles. (FS)

Beam. A horizontal structural member whose prime function is to carry loads, as a **joist**, girder, **rafter**, or **purlin**. (CH)

Bearing wall. A wall that supports a structure above it. (PL) A bearing wall can be either an exterior wall or an interior wall. Structures with bearing walls can be difficult to expand and modernize because it is hard to remove walls to expand or combine spaces. A wall that is not weight-bearing is a **curtain wall**.

Beaux Arts. Historical and eclectic design on a monumental scale, as taught at the École des Beaux Arts in Paris in the nineteenth century. (CH) Beaux Arts buildings tend to feature mixtures of traditional design elements. (In America, at least, Beaux Arts is pronounced "boze arts," with the words run together.) (FS)

Belvedere. A small, enclosed lookout tower on the roof of a house. (JHP) The word basically means "nice view" in Italian.

Bid documents. See **bidding documents.**

Bidding. The fourth of the five steps defined in AIA contract documents (schematic design, design development, construction documents, bidding, and construction administration).

Bidding documents, or **bid documents.** The advertisement or invitation to bid, instructions to bidders, the bid form, and the proposed contract documents, including any addenda issued prior to the receipt of bids.

Big box store. A nickname for stores involving huge open spaces, such as in Kmart, Walmart, and so on. Because of their high ceilings, strong floors, and lack of partitions, big box stores have been successfully remodeled as public libraries.

BIM. See **Building information modeling.**

BOCA Code. Building Officials and Code Administrators Code. Probably the most widely adopted building code in the American Midwest. It has now been supplanted by the **International Building Code.**

Bollard. A thick post used to limit vehicle access to an area. Bollards may be in a series and are sometimes connected by chains. The term is borrowed from the maritime world, where a bollard is a post around which lines are wrapped. Libraries frequently use bollards to prevent curbside book return bins from being damaged by cars or to keep people from driving into pedestrian areas.

BOMA. Building Owners and Managers Association.

Bond. A method of laying bricks, usually referring to a specific pattern of stringers and **headers**, such as **English bond**, **Flemish bond**, **common bond**, and so on. **Bonds** are designed to improve strength by connecting bricks in the same and adjacent layers. Brick walls that are a single brick thick and are not load-bearing sometimes have simulated headers. (FS) See also **bricklaying.**

Bonding. Insurance purchased to protect owners when contractors fail to live up to their sides of construction agreements.

Book matching. A technique for applying veneers where successive sheets are flipped in order to provide bilaterally symmetrical patterns. The term comes from the fact that two sheets of veneer are essentially opened like a book. The major problem with book matching is the tendency of the front and back sides of the veneer to take stains differently, with a resulting zebra stripe effect. Since striping is subjective, you may have trouble enforcing quality. See also **slip matching**. (FS)

Bracket. A projecting member to support a weight. (BF) One of the characteristic details of Italianate architecture in America is elaborate brackets supporting the **eaves**. (FS)

Bricklaying. There are basically six ways a standard brick can be positioned, and each has a name. Those defined here include **header**, **soldier**, and **stretcher**. The three others are sailor (vertical, flat side out), bull header (vertical, narrow end out), and bull stretcher (horizontal, wide side out).

Broadloom. Carpet woven on a loom and provided in rolls, as contrasted with carpet squares.

Brownfield site. A site that has had previous structures built on it. In built-up areas, library additions and new libraries must frequently be constructed on brownfield sites. Doing so requires special attention to buried utilities, buried debris from previous buildings, and buried objects with major EPA implications, such as fuel tanks, all of which can be very expensive to deal with. See also **greenfield site**.

Brutalism. A style of architecture popular in the period from the 1950s to the 1970s, and associated with blocky, irregular shapes and roughly finished, exposed concrete, often with the pattern of the wooden board used for forms visible in the surface of the concrete. Many people find Brutalist architecture basically ugly. (The University of Illinois at Chicago campus is Brutalist. The University of Illinois at Urbana campus had a Brutalist Christian Science center by architect Paul Rudolph. It stood just west of the Armory and appeared in books of significant Illinois architecture. It also leaked like a sieve, was cold in winter, hot in summer, and awkwardly arranged internally. It was eventually demolished. Rudolph also designed the Niagara Falls [New York] Public Library, a sculpturally interesting building that has spaces that are very difficult to use and that leaks vast quantities of water during rainstorms.)

Builder's risk insurance. Insurance purchased by building owners to cover those portions of their buildings for which they have paid the contractors and now own. The rates for builder's risk insurance can be relatively high because buildings are more at risk during construction than after occupancy. (FS)

Building code. A collection of rules and regulations adopted by authorities having appropriate jurisdiction to control the design and construction of buildings, alterations, repair, quality of materials, use, occupancy, and related factors of buildings within their jurisdiction. Building codes may contain minimum architectural, structural, and mechanical standards for sanitation, public health, welfare, and safety, and the provision of light and air. Many governmental units formally adopt existing published codes, always citing the version of the code that they are adopting. See, for example, the **BOCA Code, International Building Code**, and so on. (CH and FS)

Building information modeling (BIM). A computer process now widely used by architects. It yields 3-D representations that include far more data than CADD drawings, including the quantities of materials needed to erect the building. The American Institute of Architects defines BIM as a "model-based technology linked with a database of project information."

Building permit. A license to build, issued by a code-enforcement agency. In almost all U.S. situations, construction cannot begin or continue without a permit.

Building program. See **program.**

Building wrap. Building paper installed under siding to help prevent moisture intrusion. In new construction, the building wrap often goes on a long time before the exterior siding and is often ripped and tattered by wind before it is safely covered up.

Built-up roofing system. A roof covering made of laminations of roofing felt alternating with layers of pitch or asphalt. A built-up roof is topped with a layer of gravel set in pitch or asphalt, or by a cap sheet. Built-up roofs are used on relatively flat roofs. (Pitch and asphalt are incompatible materials, and repairs need to be made by people who can tell the difference between the two.)

Buttress. A mass of masonry built against a wall to resist the pressure of an **arch** or **vault**. (BF) There are many types of buttresses; see the drawings in JHP, page 82. The most famous are flying buttresses, as in Notre Dame Cathedral, Paris, which transfer the thrust of the vaults away from the exterior walls and allow larger windows.

Cabinetwork. High-quality joinery as found in built-in cabinets and shelves, custom-made furniture, and so on. (CH and FS)

Cable tray. A long open-wire tray designed to hold data cabling above a ceiling.

CADD, also spelled **CAD**. Computer-aided design and drafting. The vast majority of architectural plans today are produced by computer. Unfortunately, due to rapid technical changes, records stored on disc may not always be retrievable years later, and libraries need to back them up with printouts on durable paper or Mylar.

Caisson. A watertight structure or chamber, within which work is carried on in building foundations or structures below the water level. Work in caissons may be carried out under high air pressure in order to keep out groundwater, and workers need to take time to decompress when exiting. (CH and FS) The word *caisson* is also used to mean an inset panel like a coffer.

CAL 133. California technical bulletin 133 provides standards for the flammability of upholstered furniture, which can be extremely flammable due to the widespread use of polyurethane foam, a substance that burns very rapidly, emitting hydrogen cyanide gas.

Calcium chloride. See **concrete**.

Calcs. Short for "calculations." Calcs are based on floor plan printouts showing predicted foot-candle levels at various points in a space and are used to judge whether the lighting design will yield desired levels of illumination. Such foot-candle levels are typically calculated for tabletop height and may be quite different, for example, from light levels on the bottom shelves of book stacks or the light level on the pages of a book held open vertically. Calcs can therefore be very deceptive when strong downlighting is employed, since a room that is pitch-dark except for brilliant light on the floor can have impressively high calcs. (FS)

Camber. Slight rise or upward curve of an otherwise horizontal structure. (BF) Horizontal surfaces can be cambered so that they will be flat under expected loads (as in some truck beds) or so that they will drain (as in highways).

Can light. Slang for a round, recessed downlight. Can lights are tremendously popular with designers, particular when inset in soffits, and are among the worst possible lighting choices for libraries. See **recessed downlight**. (FS)

Candlepower. The luminous intensity of a light source, expressed in candelas. (CH)

Cantilever. A horizontal projection (such as a beam) without external bracing and therefore appearing to be self-supporting.

Cantilever shelving. Library shelving that consists of center posts supporting individual shelves that extend from the post. Shelves hook onto slots in the posts to provide maximum flexibility of shelf placement. Steel cantilever shelving is extremely stable and is the most common type of shelving in American libraries. (FS)

Cape. Never trust an architect who wears a cape.

Capital. The crowning feature of a **column** or **pilaster**. (BF)

Carbon monoxide. CO. The primary constituent of coal gas, which was widely used before the advent of natural gas. Coal gas was produced by the partial combustion of coal. Unlike natural gas, which is methane (CH_4), carbon monoxide is poisonous, although both natural gas and coal gas are explosive when mixed with air. Malfunctioning heating equipment can release carbon monoxide, and since carbon monoxide is odorless, detectors are widely used. (The traditional gas odor of carbon monoxide and methane is added for safety.)

Carpet tile. Individual squares of carpet intended to permit the easy repair of damaged areas by replacing single tiles. (FS)

Casement window. A window whose opening lights (sashes) are hinged at the side and open in the manner of a door. (BF)

Catalytic lacquer. Lacquer that contains chemicals that lead the finish to catalyze and to thereafter not be soluble in its original solvent.

Catenary. A shape of curve. A totally flexible, non-stretchable cable draped between two points takes the form of a catenary curve. (FS)

Cavity wall. See **wythe**.

CDs, or **construction documents.** The third of the five steps defined in AIA contract documents (schematic design, design development, construction documents, bidding, and construction oversight).

Cement. Hydraulic cement is a powdered material made by calcining lime and clay. It is mixed with water, sand, and gravel to form **concrete.**

CERT. Construction emergency response team. (FS)

Certificate of occupancy. A permit issued by an agency of local government allowing the use of the building for its planned purpose. (FS)

CFL, or **compact fluorescent lamp.** A fluorescent lamp designed to replace a standard incandescent lamp, using the same socket and current supply, and occupying a comparable physical space. CFLs have electronic ballasts built into their bases. The commonly sold CFLs have narrow fluorescent tubes either in coils or loops. As with all fluorescents, the problem is finding lamps with the warm color that people like in interiors (about 2700 to 3500K) and an acceptably high CRI (see **color rendering index**). The color rendering indexes of CFLs are not impressive; they are always inferior to the best four-foot T-8 lamps, and experience suggests that CFLs are often too dim to match the lumen output of the lamps they supposedly replace. (The packaging on CFLs notoriously does not list CRI, suggesting a universal agreement that the number is nothing to brag about.) Energy savings with the use of CFLs (as with all fluorescents) are greatest in hot climates, where the extra heat output of incandescent lamps puts additional loads on cooling. By contrast, in cold climates, inefficient lighting provides desirable heat and reduces the savings that result from converting to CFLs.

Chair rail. A piece of molding installed at uniform height on a wall and designed to protect the wall from damage due to bumping by chairs. (FS)

Change order. A written order to the contractor, signed by the owner and the architect, issued after the execution of the contract, authorizing a change in the work or an adjustment in the contract sum or the contract time as originally defined in the contract documents. (CH) Change orders can be the result of a variety of circumstances, including errors in drawings, hidden circumstances discovered during construction (such as buried fuel tanks or inaccurate record drawings from previous construction), or owners changing their minds. All construction jobs involve change orders, but it is desirable to keep change orders to a minimum because the prices for change orders are arrived at by means of negotiation rather than bidding, and the costs to the owners are inevitably higher. The inevitability of having at least some change orders is one reason why contingency funds are an essential component of construction budgets. (Some architects have reputations for careless drawings that lead to too many change orders, and it's always legitimate to ask architects about the percentage of construction costs due to change orders on their jobs. If architects' projects consistently have change orders of 5 percent or more due to drawing errors, that's a bad sign. According to popular rumor, contractors may underbid projects by architectural firms that are notorious for sloppy drawings, assuming they'll make it up on change orders.)

Charrette. A group planning process designed to assemble ideas and make decisions quickly. The process is frequently used by architects. The downside of charrettes is that decisions can sometimes be made in haste and regretted at leisure. The term comes from the metaphor of placing ideas on a cart. (FS)

Chase. A recess or multi-floor vertical opening designed to carry pipes, and so on. (FS)

Chicago window. A window consisting of a large fixed pane flanked by narrower, vertical panes, or by narrow double-hung windows. The old Carson Pirie Scott store on State Street in Chicago is loaded with Chicago windows. (The Carson store was designed by Louis Sullivan, with matching additions by Daniel Burnham and by Holabird & Root.)

Chord. A principle member of a **truss** that extends from one end to the other, primarily to resist bending; usually one of a pair of such members. (CH)

Circulation. The traffic pattern through an area or building. It also denotes a scheme providing for the smooth, economical, and functional flow of traffic in a building. (CH) In almost all library spaces, space for circulation is required in addition to the space for furniture in order to provide open pathways between furniture and leave users space to move around. In the area of library building design, there is always danger of confusing *circulation* in the architectural sense with *circulation* in the library materials-lending sense. When speaking with architects, therefore, it's a good idea to refer to materials lending as *lending* rather than as *circulation*. (FS)

Civil engineering. A field of engineering that deals with the design and construction of structures, roads, bridges, dams, and so on. The term *civil* was originally used to distinguish the field from military engineering. The main subdivisions of civil engineering of concern to librarians are construction engineering, geotechnical engineering, and structural engineering.

Classical. The architecture originating in ancient Greece and Rome, the rules and forms of which were largely revived in the Renaissance in Europe and elsewhere. (BF) The usual five **orders** of Classical (and Renaissance) architecture are **Composite**, **Corinthian**, **Doric**, **Ionic**, and Tuscan. All these orders of architecture evolved by degrees, and there are both Greek and Roman versions of some of them. (FS)

Clearstory, also spelled **clear-story**, **clere-story**, or **clerestory.** An upper stage in a building with windows that rise above adjacent roofs. (BF) A vertical wall with windows installed between roofs of different heights. (JFT) Clearstories—particularly north-facing clearstories—offer a way to bring in additional natural light while controlling glare and reducing the likelihood of leakage, both of which are characteristic problems of skylights. Clearstories that face any direction except north, however, will probably require blinds, which may be very difficult to install and adjust at that height. (FS)

CMU. Concrete masonry unit. A cement block. See **concrete masonry unit**. (FS)

Coal gas. Gas manufactured primarily by the partial combustion of coal. It consists primarily of carbon monoxide (CO) and is very poisonous. Coal gas has now been replaced by natural gas, which is explosive but not poisonous. Both gases are odorless; the strong aroma comes from the addition of ethyl mercaptan (C_2H_6S), which is detectable in concentrations of a few parts per billion.

Code. See **building code.**

Coffer. A recessed panel in a ceiling, vault, or dome. (BF)

Cold cathode lighting. A type of electric lamp where the cathodes in the tubes are not separately heated (although they can become very hot in use). In libraries, cold cathode fluorescent lamps are sometimes used when the designer wants tubes curved to specific radii or in specific bright colors. Cold cathode lamps made in this fashion can be very expensive. The most common type of cold cathode lighting is neon light. (FS)

Color rendering index (CRI). A measure of the degree to which a light source renders colors accurately. CRI scores should vary from 1 to 100, with 100 being the most accurate color rendition, but low-pressure sodium light has a CRI of about −44. Typically, 100 is taken to be blackbody radiation, such as the sun or incandescent light. Any non-incandescent lamp should have a CRI figure printed on its packaging, along with lumen output and color temperature; beware of lamps that do not list the CRI. (FS)

Color temperature. A measure of the degree to which light is "warm" or "cool." Color temperature is measured in Kelvin—the higher the number, the cooler or bluer the light. For example, the color temperature of a lamp might be specified as 2700K. (FS)

Columbian Exposition. The 1893 Columbian Exposition in Chicago strongly influenced public building design in subsequent years and is one reason why so many Carnegie libraries—most of which date from about 1900 to 1915—have Classical Revival architecture. (FS)

Column. A vertical support. Decorative columns usually consist of a base, circular shaft, and spreading capital. (BF) The specialized vocabulary associated with columns is huge, with words to designate the number of columns in a group, intercolumniation (the relative spacing of columns), and so on. (FS)

Common bond, also called American bond. A bond in brickwork in which every fifth or sixth course consists of **headers**, the other courses being **stretchers**. (CH)

Compact fluorescent lamp. See **CFL.**

Compaction testing. Testing to be sure that artificially compacted soils meet specifications and can support the loads that will be placed on them.

Composite. A Roman elaboration of the Corinthian order, with carved capitals that have both Corinthian acanthus leaves and Ionic volutes. (FS)

Concept. A pervasive architectural design gimmick selected for a specific building. At their best, concepts lead to a consistent vision. At their worst, they can lead to sweeping ideas that run roughshod over functions and needs. (FS)

Concrete. A mixture of Portland **cement** or any other hydraulic cement, fine **aggregate**, coarse aggregate, and water, with or without admixtures. (MR) Admixtures are ingredients added to change the character of the concrete mixture. Air (as in "air entrainment") is a common admixture that increases strength. Calcium chloride ($CaCl_2$) is an accelerator sometimes used in cold weather conditions. Unfortunately, calcium chloride can lead to severe corrosion problems (including the rebar buried in the concrete) and to surface spalling, and its use should always be proscribed in building specifications. Concrete does not set by drying; when concrete sets, the water in the mixture is chemically incorporated in the final product. For this reason, curing concrete must be protected both from freezing and from the evaporation of moisture. (FS)

Concrete masonry unit (CMU). A cement block, typically with rectangular core openings that can be filled with concrete after the blocks are installed. The standards for concrete masonry units are set by the National Concrete Masonry Association. (FS)

Conditional use permit. A local government permit to allow a certain land use that is otherwise excluded by a local zoning code. (FS)

Conduit. (1) A tube or pipe used to protect electric wiring or to convey fluid. (2) Any channel—either open or closed—that is designed to convey water.

Constructability. The degree to which a proposed structure can be built without major problems, delays, cost overruns, and so on. A constructability review before construction begins may lead to more effective designs.

Construction documents. See **bid documents.**

Construction management firm. A type of company employed in large construction projects. Construction management firms provide **value engineering** and do much of the work general contractors do, including coordinating construction and supervising subcontractors. Because the work of such firms overlaps some of the traditional work of architects and general contractors, construction management firms need to be hired about the same time that architects are hired. A construction management firm that is responsible for constructing a building for an agreed-upon cost is said to work "at risk." (FS)

Construction oversight. The last of the five steps defined in AIA contract documents (schematic design, design development, construction documents, bidding, and construction oversight). Construction oversight involves periodic inspections to make sure that the building is being constructed in accordance with plans and specifications. It is not the same thing as "construction management" or "construction supervision," which mean the daily operation of the project. (Some people use the term *construction administration* rather than *construction oversight*.)

Contextualism. Design emphasis on relating the exteriors of new buildings to those of adjacent structures. Unfortunately, all too often, contextual arguments are far-fetched and become mere silly self-justification. A virtually featureless cube of a building with a few vertical striations, for example, may be claimed to relate to an adjacent Gothic structure because both "express verticality." (FS)

Contingency funds. Line items in construction budgets to cover anticipated extra expenditures. In a typical budget for new construction, contingency funds may be about 5 percent of the construction cost, and in remodeling (where unanticipated circumstances almost always turn up) they may be about 10 percent.

Contractor. One who undertakes responsibility for the performance of construction work, including the provision of labor and materials, in accordance with plans and specifications and under a contract specifying the cost and schedule for completion of the work. (CH)

Convection. A means of transferring heat in air by natural movement, usually a rotary or circular motion caused by warm air rising and cool air falling. (MR) See also **radiation**.

Conveyance. The mechanical movement of people and objects between floors, including elevators, escalators, and so on. It is typically a separate line in cost estimates.

Coping. (1) A protective cap, top, or cover of a wall, parapet, pilaster, or chimney. It may be flat, but is commonly sloping, double-beveled, or curved to shed water so as to protect masonry below from penetration by water from above. A coping is most effective if extended beyond the wall face. (CH) (2) The act of cutting the end of a trim piece (or other member) so that it fits snugly against the face of another trim piece, as in situations where moldings meet at right angles. High-quality trim installation on inside corners is done by coping rather than mitering. (JTF and FS)

Corbel. Successive courses of masonry projecting from the face of a wall to increase its thickness or to form a shelf or ledge. (MR)

Corinthian. The third **order** of Greek architecture. (BF) It is the most ornate of the three, and was popular with the Romans. (CH)

Cornice. In Classical and Renaissance architecture, the crowning or upper portion of the **entablature**. *Cornice* is also used as the term for any crowning projection (BF), as well as for the decorative molding at the top of a wall. (JTF)

Cost-plus-fee agreement. An agreement under which the contractor (in an owner-contractor agreement) or the architect (in an owner-architect agreement) is reimbursed for his direct and indirect costs and, in addition, is paid a fee for his services.

Course. A layer of masonry units running horizontally in a wall. (CH)

Courtyard. An area in the center of a building, open to the air. Courtyards in libraries are frequently charming, but they can be difficult to supervise and frequently lead to poor interior circulation, with users having to detour around the courtyard to get from one area of the building to another. In some buildings, the presence of courtyards results in rooms connected to each other like beads on a string, which is highly undesirable in libraries. (FS)

Cove lighting. Lighting from sources that are out of sight, atop a wall molding, shielded by a ledge or horizontal recess, and that distribute light over the ceiling and upper walls. (CH)

Covenant. See **restrictive covenant.**

Crash bar. See **panic bar.**

Crawl space. An open area between the bottom floor of a building and the surface of the ground beneath.

Crenellation. An opening in the upper part of a parapet. It is furnished with "crenelles" or indentations. (BF) Stereotypical castle walls have crenellations.

CRI. See **color rendering index.**

Cripple. A short stud used to support a lintel, sill, or other structural member. It is also called a **jack stud.**

Cross-section. A section taken at right angles to the longitudinal axis. (CH) Cross-section drawings are designed to show the internal structure of buildings. (JTF)

Crown. Any upper terminal feature in architecture. (CH)

Crown molding. A molding bridging the gap between a wall and ceiling.

Cupola. A spherical roof, placed like an inverted cup over a circular, square, or multi-angular room. (BF) It is also a small, decorative structure shaped like a small house or dome extending upwards from the ridge of a roof. (JTF)

Curtain wall. In modern architecture, a wood or metal frame structure suspended on the face of a building in lieu of a solid, load-bearing wall. (BF) Curtain walls support only themselves rather than the dead weight of the structure. Buildings with modular construction have curtain walls rather than bearing walls. The use of curtain walls makes major remodeling far easier, because walls can be removed without threatening the integrity of the structure. (FS)

Cut sheet. A sheet illustrating a piece of equipment specified for a building. Owners need to receive and approve cut sheets as well as architectural drawings. (FS)

Cylinder lock. A type of door lock with the tumblers enclosed in a cylinder. (JTF)

Damper. A moveable vane or other device inside a duct that controls the amount of airflow. (FS)

DD. Design development. The second step in the AIA definition of architectural services. See **design development**.

Dead bolt. A type of lock in which a bolt slides into a receptacle in the door jamb at the turn of a key or a turn piece. It is also called a deadlock. (JTF) (The bolt connected to the doorknob or lever is called a **latch bolt**). Dead bolts provide very positive locking, and they greatly reduce the chances of being locked out of rooms or homes by accident, but they are more expensive than latch bolts. (FS)

Dead load. The weight of all fixed items in the building, including the structure. (PL) It is also the load on a building structure imposed by the weight of the structure itself. (JTF) See also **live load**.

Decibel. A standard measure of sound intensity, abbreviated dB. An increase of 10 dB represents a tenfold increase in relative sound intensity. Therefore a sound with an intensity of 140 dB has ten trillion times the intensity of one of 10 dB. The inside of a private office is about 40 dB and a conversation about 70 dB. The threshold of pain from loud noises is 130 dB. (FS)

Deduct alternate. It is similar to an **add alternate**, but involves a reduction in the total bid through the deletion of items included in the base bid. Deduct alternates are little used because they are assumed to usually result in higher total prices than the base-bid-plus-add-alternates approach. See also **add alternate**. (FS)

Delivery systems. Organizational methods of constructing buildings.

Design-bid-build. The traditional way buildings are constructed in the United States. The architects' plans are submitted to contracting firms that bid on the project, with the project typically awarded to the lowest responsive, responsible bidder.

Design-build. An approach to construction in which a single firm or group is hired to both design and construct a building, usually for an agreed-upon amount of money, as opposed to design-bid-build. The Harold Washington Library in Chicago was constructed in a design-build competition. (FS)

Design development. The second of the five steps defined in AIA contract documents (schematic design, design development, construction documents, bidding, and construction oversight). It is often referred to as "DD" in documents.

Dimensional lumber. Lumber cut to a particular size and stocked for the building industry. (CH)

Direct-indirect light fixture. A lay-in light fixture that uses curved metal baffles to conceal the lamps from view. Although such fixtures create slightly less glare than standard **troffers**, the effect they create is still rectangles of downlight separated by areas of unlighted ceiling tile. Direct-indirect fixtures are therefore not a substitute for reflected uplights.

Dome. A curved roof structure, more or less hemispherical in shape, covering an area. (FS)

Door nomenclature. In a standard six-panel door, the horizontal members (from top to bottom) include the top rail, frieze rail, lock rail, and bottom rail, while vertical members include a muntin (center) and the hinge stile and lock stile (edges). The areas between the members are panels. (FS)

Doric. The first and least complex **order** of Greek architecture. Every detail of the Doric order has its own technical name, some of which are shared with other orders. Among the useful terms are abacus, annulet, echinus, guttae, metope, regula, tenia, and triglyph—in addition to the more common **acroterion**, **architrave**, **cornice**, **frieze**, **pediment**, stylobate, tympanum, and so on. (FS)

Dormer. A window in a sloping roof. (BF) It is also a projection built out from the slope of a roof that provides additional interior space, light, and ventilation, as in a shed dormer. (JTF and FS) The name derives from the fact that early dormers were bedroom windows. (FS)

Double cylinder lock. A lock requiring a key to open it from either side. Double cylinder locks are clearly incompatible with concerns for life safety, unless the door also has a panic bar. Many older public libraries have double cylinder locks in their front doors, which is a major violation of fire and life-safety codes. (FS)

Double-hung window. A window with two vertically sliding sashes, one above the other, permitting the top or bottom or part of each to be opened. (FS)

Downlight. A direct **luminaire** (recessed, surface-mounted, or suspended) whose light is directed vertically downward. (CH) It is the worst possible commonly used luminaire design for libraries. (FS) See also **recessed downlight.**

Draw. A contractor's request for payment.

Dry pipe sprinkler system. A sprinkler system in which there is no water in the pipes until sprinkler heads are activated. It is used to prevent pipes from freezing in unheated spaces, such as the attics of old buildings to which sprinklers have been retrofitted. Unfortunately, some modern buildings are so poorly designed that sprinkler pipes freeze and dry pipe systems are necessary. Contrast with **pre-action sprinkler systems**. (FS)

Drywall. Interior wall construction or covering using gypsum board. Drywall consists of a sheet of gypsum surfaced with cardboard, which is usually mounted on studs or furring strips. Gypsum is $CaSO_4 \cdot 2H_2O$. Other common names and nicknames for drywall are wallboard, gypboard, sheetrock, rock, gypsum, and so on. The material is ubiquitous in modern construction and is extremely quick to install, but it is much more fragile than traditional plaster. Cheap drywall covered with cheap latex paint has all the structural integrity of piecrust. (FS)

Duct. In electrical systems, a metallic or nonmetallic tube for housing wires or cables. (CH) See also **air duct**.

Dynamic load. Any load that is non-static or moving, such as wind load, solar load, snow load, or dynamic live load. (CH, FS)

Easement. A right of accommodation (for a specific purpose) in land owned by another, such as the right of way or free access to light and air. (CH) A power company easement may give it the right to string power lines over a piece of property. Before property is acquired or improvements begun, it is vital to know about any existing easements. (Some transitional curves are also called "easements," so the possibility of confusion exists.) (FS)

Eave. The lowest part of a roof projecting beyond the face of the wall. (BF)

Eave trough. A northern Midwestern term for gutter. (FS)

EIFS. External insulation finishing system. An exterior finishing system consisting of a skim coat of concrete over fiberglass-reinforced Styrofoam. EIFS was frequently used beginning in the 1990s to resemble stucco. EIFS finishes are controversial because they are fragile and can lead to extremely serious decomposition or mold if water is trapped behind them. They are also hard to repair, and they need to be repainted. Some people pronounce EIFS "*eye*-fiss" or "*ee*-fiss." (FS)

Electrical codes. Published standards for the safe installation of electrical wiring and equipment. In the United States, the National Electrical Code (NEC) is published by the National Fire Protection Association. States and localities can adopt the NEC or establish more stringent requirements. The NEC is published every three years.

Elevation. A drawing showing the vertical elements of a building, either exterior or interior, viewed squarely rather than in perspective. (CH and FS)

Elevator car. The load-carrying unit of an elevator. (CH)

Eminent domain. The power or right of a government to take private property for public use, supposedly with reasonable compensation to the owner. (CH and FS) Eminent domain was very much in the news in 2005 when the U.S. Supreme Court decided that a local government could use eminent domain to take private property on behalf of a private developer. (FS)

English basement. A floor of a residential building, partly below but mostly above ground level, but not having the principal entrance to the building at that level. (CH)

English bond. Brickwork arranged in alternate courses of **stretchers** and **headers**. (BF)

Entablature. The upper part of an order of architecture, comprising **architrave**, **frieze**, and **cornice**, and supported by a colonnade. (BF)

Entasis. The intentional slight convex curving of the vertical profile of a tapered column. It is used to overcome the optical illusion of concavity that characterizes straight-sided columns. (CH) Entasis is sometimes overdone on crudely designed columns, giving them a bulging, squat look. (FS)

Envelope. The imaginary shape of a building indicating its maximum volume; it is used to check the plan and setback (and similar restrictions) with respect to zoning regulations. (CH)

Environmental Protection Agency (EPA). Typical problems with existing buildings or brownfield sites that will involve the EPA include asbestos, lead paint, and buried fuel tanks.

EPA. See **Environmental Protection Agency.**

Equivalent. Some bid documents call for specific items (such as light fixtures, listed by brand and model number) "or equivalent." In public construction, applicable laws may require the possibility of equivalents to avoid work being steered to favorite manufacturers. One of the challenges in construction administration is making sure the items that contractors propose as "equivalent" actually are equivalent and not cheap substitutes. (FS)

Escalation. In construction cost estimates, an allowance for inflation in costs between the time of the estimate and the time the project is bid. (FS)

Façade. The face or elevation of a building. (BF)

FAIA. Fellow of the American Institute of Architects

False ceiling. See **suspended ceiling.**

Fanlight. A semicircular window usually placed over the opening of a door or window. Fanlights are a traditional detail of **Georgian** architecture. (CH, FS) Fanlights installed by themselves rather than above rectangular windows or doors are nontraditional but are popular with some modern designers.

Fascia. A board or plate covering the end of roof rafters. (BF) By extension, it is any applied horizontal strip below the eaves. A fascia is also a flat band between moldings. (FS)

Feasibility study. A detailed investigation and analysis conducted to determine the financial, economic, technical, or other advisability of a proposed project. (CH)

Fenestration. The arrangement and design of windows in a building. (CH)

Ferroconcrete. See **reinforced concrete.**

FF&E. Furniture, fixtures, and equipment.

Final acceptance. The owner's acceptance of a project from the contractor upon certification by the architect that it is complete and in accordance with the contract requirements. (CH)

Fire wall. An interior or exterior wall having sufficiently high fire resistance and structural stability, under conditions of fire, to restrict the fire's spread to adjoining areas of buildings, and possessing a fire rating as required by code. A fire wall usually extends from the lowest floor level to about three feet above the roof, and has all internal openings protected by self-closing fire doors or fire shutters. Strip malls without fire walls above the ceilings of the individual stores have had fires spread throughout the malls by racing through the attics.

Flashing. A thin, impervious material placed in construction (e.g., in mortar joints and through air spaces in masonry) to prevent water penetration and/or provide water drainage, especially between a roof and wall, and over exterior door openings and windows. (CH) One good place to look for flashing is the joint between a chimney and a roof. (FS)

Flemish bond. Brickwork arranged with alternate headers and stretchers in every row. Each header is centered over the stretcher below it.

Floodplain. An area subject to occasional flooding. Building a library on a floodplain is a singularly poor idea.

Floor area ratio. The floor area of a building divided by the size of the lot. Zoning may specify maximum floor area ratios.

Flue. An incombustible and heat-resistant enclosed passage in a chimney to control and carry away products of combustion from a fireplace, furnace, or boiler to the outside air. (CH)

Fluorescent lamp. A low-pressure electric discharge lamp. Ultraviolet light is generated by passing an arc through mercury vapor. Phosphors on the inner surface of the tube in turn convert the UV light to visible light.

Flush. Having the surface or face even or level with the adjacent surface. (CH)

Fluting. The vertical grooves or channels on the shaft of a column. (BF)

Foot-candle. A unit of illumination equal to one lumen per square foot. (CH) Most specifications for level of illumination are in foot-candles. See **calcs**. (FS)

Footing. That portion of the foundation of a structure that transmits loads directly to the soil. (CH) Footings are usually wider than the columns or walls that rest on them, in order to spread loads over wider areas. The necessary dimensions of footings depend on building weight and soil conditions. (FS)

Footprint. The outside perimeter of the building at grade level. (PL)

"Form follows function." (More accurately, "Form ever follows function.") A philosophical attitude toward design made famous by the American architect Louis Sullivan, who suggested that the exterior shape of a building should reflect its intended purpose or function. Sullivan still used exterior ornamentation, but some modernists seized on the phrase as a justification for what many now regard as extraordinarily ugly work. Unfortunately, "form follows function" is widely ignored in some library architecture. See also **functionalism**.

Foundation. That part of a structure that supports the weight of the structure and transmits the load to underlying soil or rock. (MR)

Frieze. The middle division of the Classical **entablature**, between the **architrave** and the **cornice**. (BF) It is also a horizontal band of decorative work. (FS)

Frontage. The length of a lot line or a building site along a street or other public way, or along a body of water forming a boundary. (CH)

Functionalism. A philosophy of architectural design, emerging in the twentieth century, asserting that the form of a building should follow its function, reveal its structure, and express the nature of the material. (CH)

Fusible link. A metal chain link made of a low-melting-point alloy. In the case of fire, the link melts, separating the chain and thereby closing a damper, door, or the like. (CH and FS)

Gable. The vertical triangular portion of the end of a building having a double-sloping roof, from the level of the cornice or eaves to the ridge of the roof. (CH) Even if it's not triangular (as in the case of a gambrel roof) it's still a gable. (FS)

Gambrel roof. A roof with two different slopes on each side. The traditional barn roof is a gambrel roof. (FS)

General contractor. The "prime contractor" who is responsible for most of the work at the construction site, including that performed by the subcontractors. (CH) The general contractor is the contractor who has overall responsibility for the construction project. Subcontractors work under the direct control of the general contractor, who makes up the schedules, coordinates the tasks, and supervises the activities of everyone on the job. (JTF)

Georgian. English Renaissance-style architecture of the period 1702–1830. (BF) It was the prevailing style of the eighteenth century in Great Britain and the American colonies. (CH) American collegiate architecture is frequently Georgian. Look for two or more stories, compact massing, red brick, symmetrical arrangement of windows and doors, small pane windows with white-painted wooden elements, corner **quoins**, hipped roofs with **balustrades**, and massive chimneys at the gable ends. (FS)

Geotechnical engineering. A subfield of civil engineering concerned with how soils and rock support foundations, walls, and other constructed objects. Because a knowledge of local soils is important to foundation design, architects tend to hire for work of this type firms that are located where buildings will be constructed.

GFI. See **ground fault interrupt**.

Glare. Sensation produced when brightnesses within the visual field are sufficiently greater than the luminance to which the eyes are adapted, causing discomfort, loss of visibility, and so on. It includes direct glare and **veiling reflectance**. (FS)

Glazing. (1) Setting glass in an opening. (2) The glass surface of a glazed opening. (CH)

Glu-lam. A structural wooden beam that has been fabricated by bonding several layers of boards together. (JTF) Glulaminated beams can be used in situations calling for wooden structural members that are longer and/or more massive than otherwise available. (FS)

Gothic. The pointed-arch style of medieval architecture prevalent in western Europe from the thirteenth to the fifteenth centuries. (BF) Gothic architecture is characterized by the pointed arch, the rib vault, the development of the exterior flying buttress, and the gradual reduction of the walls to a system of richly decorated fenestration. (CH) The term *Gothic* was applied to this style of architecture only after the end of the Gothic architecture era, and the intent was apparently derogatory.

Gothic Revival. A movement of the late eighteenth and nineteenth centuries, primarily in England, France, and Germany, but also in the United States, which revived the style of Gothic architecture. (based on BF)

Grade beam. Increased thickness in a poured slab to support a wall

Grandfathering. A procedure that allows a **nonconforming** building to remain in use unchanged when codes or regulations are altered. (FS)

Greek Revival. A movement from about 1800 to 1860 in the United States and of similar but perhaps slightly shorter duration in Europe that revived the style of Classical Greek architecture. (AW)

Green Buildings Certification Institute. See **United States Green Buildings Council.**

Greenfield site. A site that has not held previous structures. See also **brownfield site**.

Greenwashing. A snide term for adding trendy "green" details to a project for political points or public relations rather than for actual conservation. As green construction becomes more generally expected, greenwashing is likely to expand. Some critics regard the **LEED** process as partially greenwashing. (FS)

Groin. The ridge, edge, or curved line formed by the intersection of the surfaces of two intersecting vaults in a ceiling. (CH)

Gross space. The total space of a building, as measured from the outside. It includes **assignable space**, **nonassignable space**, and the thickness of the walls. In older masonry buildings, such as Carnegie libraries, the amount of space occupied by walls can be very substantial. (FS)

Ground fault interrupt (GFI). A residual current device (RCD) that detects whether the electrical current is not balanced between the energized conductor and the neutral return conductor, indicating that perhaps someone who is grounded (for example, someone touching plumbing) is allowing some of the current to pass through his body. In these circumstances, GFIs trip and disconnect the power to the devices or outlets involved. GFIs are required by building codes in spaces with water supplies, such as kitchens, bathrooms, rooms with sinks, and so on.

Groundwater. Water present in the soil that applies hydrostatic pressure to basement walls and collects in sumps, heating ducts in concrete slabs, and so on. (FS)

Groundwater level. See **water table.**

Grout. Mortar containing a considerable amount of water so that it has the consistency of a viscous liquid, permitting it to be poured or pumped into joints, spaces, and cracks within masonry walls and floors, between pieces of ceramic clay, slate, and floor tile, and into the joints between preformed roof deck units. (CH) Light-colored grout between ceramic tiles is nearly impossible to keep clean. (FS)

Gutter. A shallow channel of metal or wood set immediately below and along the eaves of a building to catch and carry off rainwater from the roof. (CH) It is sometimes called an **eave trough**.

Gyp board. See **gypsum board.** (FS)

Gypsum board. A wall surface product consisting of a paper-covered sheet of gypsum. (FS) See **drywall**.

Half-timbered building. A structure formed by timber posts, rails, and struts, with the interspaces filled with brick or other material, and sometimes plastered. (BF) The material between the timbers is called **nogging**.

Halogen lamp. A tungsten-filament incandescent lamp filled with a gas containing halogens, enclosed in an envelope of quartz or other material that can withstand high temperatures. (Hence "quartz halogen" lamps.) The presence of halogens allows filaments to burn hotter and whiter without burning out immediately. Halogen lamps have been used in applications where intense light is essential, such as jewelry store display windows. Unfortunate libraries that have been equipped with halogen lamps find that they burn out extremely quickly, are dangerously hot, and often cause unpleasant glare. (The halogens are fluorine, bromine, chlorine, iodine, and astatine.) (FS)

Header. (1) A masonry unit, laid so that its ends are exposed, overlapping two or more adjacent rows of masonry and tying them together. (CH) In brick walls, the headers appear as half-width bricks. See **bricklaying** for additional terms. (2) A structural member spanning the vertical framing of a window or door. It is also called a **lintel**. (FS)

Health Insurance Portability and Accountability Act. See **HIPAA**.

HID. See **high-intensity discharge lamp**.

High-intensity discharge (HID) lamp. Any one of the group including **mercury vapor, metal halide**, and high-pressure **sodium vapor** lamps. High-intensity discharge lamps are widely used, particularly for outdoor lighting. They are characterized by high efficacy, compactness, low CRI, slow **restrike time**, inconsistent color maintenance, noisy ballasts, and occasional "catastrophic end of service" (aka blowing up). (FS)

High-pressure laminate. Formica or another similar material. High-pressure laminates can be inexpensive and are available in a wide range of colors and patterns, but they are too fragile for the tops of lending desks unless colors go all the way through the material ("solid core laminates"). (FS)

Hip. The external angle at the junction of two sloping roofs or sides of a roof. (CH) Contrast with **valley**. A hipped roof has four sloping sides that meet in four hips.

HIPAA. The Health Insurance Portability and Accountability Act is of concern to medical library design because it strictly protects the privacy of patient records. It may affect, for example, the placement of computers on which patient records can be checked. It is usually pronounced "HIP-ah."

Hoistway. A shaftway for the travel of one or more elevators, lifts, or dumbwaiters. (CH)

Hollow wall. See **wythe**.

Hopper light. A window sash that opens inward and is hinged at the bottom. (CH)

HVAC. Heating, ventilating, and air conditioning. (FS)

IAQ. Indoor air quality.

IBC. See **International Building Code.**

I-beam. A rolled or extruded structural metal beam having a cross-section resembling the letter I. (CH) I-beams are used for long spans, such as horizontal structural members in large buildings, or over wide openings, such as double garage door openings. (JTF)

IECC. International Energy Conservation Code, first created by the ICC (International Code Council) in 2000. Like other codes, the IECC can be adopted by various agencies. As in other codes, "International" means "United States."

IESNA. The Illuminating Engineering Society of North America. It was founded in 1906, and it publishes reference material, standards, and recommended practices. (FS)

Improved land. Land that has been provided with water, sewers, sidewalks, and other basic facilities for residential or industrial development. (CH)

Incandescent lamp. A lamp from which light is emitted when a tungsten filament is heated to incandescence by an electric current. (CH) It is basically a hot wire in a bottle. (FS)

Infiltration. The seepage or flow of air into a room or space through cracks around windows, under doors, and so on. (CH)

Insurance. Insurance plays a major role in library construction. Among the types of insurance most relevant during the construction process are liability insurance, builder's risk insurance, and workers compensation insurance. When construction is complete, libraries tend to have insurance on their structures and contents (covering such losses as fire, windstorm, earthquake, etc.), liability insurance, workers comp insurance, umbrella policies, and so on. Flood insurance is purchased separately through a federal program.

Interior finish. The exposed interior surfaces of a building, such as plaster or wood, and applied materials such as wallpaper, paint, or trim. (CH)

International Building Code. A modern building code, replacing the former BOCA code. It is abbreviated IBC. (FS)

International Energy Conservation Code. See **IECC.**

International Style. A functional architecture devoid of regional characteristics, created in western Europe and the United States during the early twentieth century and applied throughout the world. (CH) The style relied strongly on steel frames and glass curtain walls and was particularly favored for skyscrapers. (Somebody referred to the International Style as "ugly Bauhaus," then went on to say that the phrase might be redundant.)

Inverter. An electrical device that converts direct current to alternating current. Operating fluorescent lights on battery power (for example, when night-lights double as emergency lights) requires an inverter. See also **rectifier.** (FS)

Ionic. The second **order** of Greek architecture. It is characterized by capitals with volutes and many other details.

J hook. One of a series of hooks suspended from the bottom of a floor or other support and above a ceiling, used to carry data cabling.

Jack stud. A short stud used to support a lintel or other structural member. It is also called a **cripple**.

Jamb. A vertical or horizontal member framing a door or window. The portion exposed outside the window frame is the reveal. (CH and FS).

Joinery. The craft of woodworking by joining pieces of wood, especially the finish and trim workings of the interior of a structure, such as doors, paneling, sashes, and so on, as distinguished from carpentry, which suggests framing and rough work. (CH)

Joints. A large technical vocabulary exists to describe the ways that materials are connected together. (FS)

Joist. One of a series of parallel horizontal beams of timber, reinforced concrete, or steel used to support floor and ceiling loads. Joists are in turn supported at their ends by larger beams, girders, or bearing walls. (CH)

Keystone. The center, often embellished, stone in an **arch**. It is called a keystone because it locks the other pieces of the arch together, although the other pieces of the arch are also essential. (CH and FS)

Kickplate. A protective plate applied on the lower rail of a door to prevent marking. (CH)

King post. In a truss, a vertical post extending from the ridge to the center of the tie beam below. The king posts support the **ridgepole.** Posts parallel to the king post are **queen posts**; the longitudinal beams these support are called **purlins.** (FS)

Kiosk. A small pavilion for the sale of merchandise such as newspapers or magazines. (CH) Micro branches for public libraries are sometimes called kiosk libraries. (FS)

Knox box. A locked box, similar to a small safe, built into the wall of a building near the entrance. It can be opened by a standard key carried by emergency personnel and contains a key to the entrance of the building. Knox boxes function in the same manner as the key boxes that real estate salespeople attach to the doorknobs of houses listed for sale. (FS)

Labeled. Carrying an identification of a recognized testing laboratory (such as the Underwriters' Laboratories, Inc.) that certifies the results of appropriate fire tests conducted on essentially identical materials or construction, as in a "labeled door," "labeled frame," or "labeled window."

Lacquer. A type of paint that dries by evaporation but does not polymerize, allowing it to be redissolved in its original solvent. See also **precatalyzed lacquer**.

Lagging. Thermal insulation for pipes, preformed to conform to the curved surface. (CH) Old pipe lagging is a major location for asbestos in libraries.

Lamp. A light bulb. The shape of a lamp is usually designated by a letter, preceded by a number indicating the wattage and followed by the diameter in eighths of an inch. For example, a 34T12 lamp is a 34-watt fluorescent tube with a diameter of 1.5 inches. There is obvious potential for confusion because "lamp" can mean either a light bulb or a freestanding light fixture. When dealing with design professionals and contractors, therefore, it's a good idea not to call light fixtures "lamps." (FS)

Landscape architect. A person trained and experienced in the design and development of landscapes and gardens. The term can also refer to a person professionally qualified and licensed. (CH)

Latch bolt. A spring bolt with a beveled surface that allows the door to snap shut. Latch bolts are released by doorknobs or levers. A latch bolt that can be set so that a key is required to open it from the outside is called a night latch, and is the source of endless humorous stories of half-dressed people being locked out of their houses or hotel rooms. Contrast also **dead bolt**. (FS)

Lath. Materials that support plaster. Lath can be nailed to masonry walls or to studs. Lath in older buildings often consists of wooden strips (very rough-sawed, to provide extra tooth for the plaster). Other buildings have **metal lath**, which consists of a metal mesh with about quarter-inch openings and an impressive ability to block wireless transmissions. Plaster can also be installed over drywall.

Lead paint. Paint containing lead pigments, such as red lead (lead tetroxide, Pb_3O_4), white lead (lead carbonate, $PbCO_3$), or lead chromate (chrome yellow, $PbCrO_4$). Lead pigments provide many technical advantages, but they are poisonous and have been banned for many uses since the late 1970s. Buildings constructed before about 1980 may be bad candidates for conversion to libraries because of existing lead paint. (FS)

LED. See **light-emitting diode**.

LEED. Leadership in Energy and Environmental Design. See **United States Green Buildings Council.**

LEED accreditation. A process by which LEED design professionals are accredited.

LEED certification. A certification issued to a building that meets LEED requirements.

Liability insurance. Insurance covering the insured against losses resulting from injury to another person or property. (various sources)

Lien. A right enforceable against specific property to secure payment of a financial obligation. See also **mechanic's lien** and **waiver of lien.**

Lien waiver. See **waiver of lien.**

Life cycle cost. See **occupancy cost.**

Lift. A movable platform that can be raised to (for example) provide access to light fixtures high above a floor. Be very wary when designers assure you that you can "use a lift" for access to awkwardly high items. Among other things, lifts must fit through doorways and other narrow openings. They may also have outrigger legs that are extended for stability once the lifts are in place, and there may not be space in stack aisles for these legs.

Light. A pane of glass installed in a window or a section of a window.

Light-emitting diode. A transistor that emits light. Due to their extremely low power requirements, LEDs are increasingly widely used, especially in situations where lamps are hard to change or where vibration may lead to lamp failure. Until recently, most LEDs used successfully served as indicator lights, not as sources of illumination, but LED lighting is now available and increasingly used in libraries. Watch for LEDs in traffic lights and truck taillights, where they appear as clusters of colored dots. In libraries, the most common use of LEDs for illumination has been in exit signs, but after many years, engineers have finally developed white LEDs that are no longer strongly blue-white and generally unpleasant. When purchasing equipment with white LEDs, always inquire about color temperature and CRI. LED illumination is probably the wave of the future, but it may continue to have color temperature and color rendering problems, and it remains too highly directional. (FS)

Light loss factor. A factor used in calculating the illumination provided by a lighting system after a given period of time and under given conditions. (CH) Light output declines as lamps age and become dirty, fixtures become dirty, reflective ceilings become dirty, and so on. No lighting system can reasonably be expected to maintain the effective light output it has the day it is first installed.

Light well. A shaft within a building, open to the outer air at the top, that is used to admit daylight and air through windows opening onto the shaft. (CH)

Lintel. A horizontal structural member (such as a beam) over an opening that carries the weight of the wall above it. (CH) It is also known as an architrave or **header**. (BF)

Liquidated damages. Provisions in a construction contract to provide financial incentives for the contractor to complete work on time.

Live. Quality of a room having an unusually small amount of sound absorption. (CH)

Live load. The moving or movable load on a structure. It includes the weight of furnishings, people, and equipment, but does not include wind load, solar load or snow load. (CH) Due to the weight of books, live loads in libraries are very substantial, and are far heavier than those in retail buildings, churches, and drive-in garages. (Every university campus appears to be equipped with a popular but false rumor that the library is sinking into the ground because the engineers forgot to include the weight of the books when designing the building.) See also **dead load**.

Load. (1) A force, or system of forces, carried by a structure, or a part of the structure. Loads in buildings include **live loads** (the weight of contents), **dead loads** (the weight of the structure itself), and such **dynamic loads** as wind loads, solar loads, snow loads, etc. (2) The power delivered to a device or piece of electrical equipment. (3) And other meanings. (CH and FS)

Load-bearing wall. A wall capable of supporting an imposed load in addition to its own weight. (CH) And presumed to be doing so. (FS)

Loading dock. An elevated platform at the shipping or delivery door of a building, usually at the same height as the floor of a truck or railroad car to facilitate loading and unloading. (CH)

Loft building. A building containing open, unpartitioned floor space, used for commercial or industrial purposes. (CH) The conversion of former industrial neighborhoods to residential ones frequently involves the use of lofts as large, informal living spaces. (FS)

Louver. An assembly of sloping, overlapping slats. Louvers are used especially in doors and windows, and to control air intake and discharge in mechanical ventilation systems. (CH and FS)

Lumber core. Wood core consisting of narrow strips of lumber glued together. (CH) It is used, for example, in tabletops that are faced with high-pressure laminate (on both sides, to prevent warping). Tabletops, flush doors, and so on can have lumber cores, but they more often have cheaper and less durable cores of chipboard, and other flimsy materials. (FS)

Lumen. A measure of the quantity of light. Lamps are rated (among other ways) in terms of lumen output. (FS)

Luminaire. A complete light fixture, including the **lamp** and (if necessary) **ballast**. (FS)

Luminous-intensity distribution curve. A polar plot representing the light intensity as a function of angle about a light source. (CH) These curves are the little diagrams with concentric curved lines in the literature on luminaires. (FS)

Lux. The metric alternative to the foot-candle. One foot-candle equals about ten lux. (Actually, one foot-candle = 10.764 lux, but people tend not to worry a great deal about this because [a] it's easy to think in ratios of 1:10 and [b] it is hard to measure light levels with an accuracy greater than about ±10 percent.)

Mansard roof. A roof with a steep lower slope and a flatter upper portion on all four sides, named after Mansart. (BF and CH) A true mansard roof slopes inward from the top of the wall. America abounds with grossly ugly fake mansards, which are attached to block buildings and slope down and outwards from the top of the wall, leaving a major overhang where they end. (FS)

Masonry. (1) The art of shaping, arranging, and uniting stone, brick, building blocks, and so on to form walls and other parts of a building. (2) Construction made of such materials. (Pronouncing masonry "masonary" is right up there with pronouncing nuclear "nucular.")

Master plan. A long-term plan including anticipated actions needed and the likely time they will take place.

Matchboards, or **matched lumber.** Lumber with tongue-and-groove edges, such as traditional wooden strip flooring. (FS)

Mechanic's lien. A lien on **real property** created by state statute in favor of persons supplying labor or materials for a building. Lien laws vary widely from state to state, but in most circumstances clear title cannot be obtained until claims on which liens are based have been settled. (CH and FS) See also **lien** and **waiver of lien**.

Medium. The ingredient of a paint that—together with pigment—forms the cured coating after the thinner has evaporated and polymerization has occurred. Typical mediums are oil (linseed oil, alkyd resins, etc.) and latex (various plastics). Traditional lacquers consist of non-polymerizing compounds dissolved in thinner. (FS)

Member. A component of a structure.

Membrane roofing. Roofing for relatively flat roofs consisting of sheets of plastic or synthetic rubber, with joints formed by heat, solvents, and so on. Membrane roofs are popular because leaks in them are easier to locate than in built-up roofs. White membrane roofs are energy-efficient in warm climates where cooling costs more than heating because the roofs reflect rather than absorb solar heat.

MEP. Mechanical, electrical, and plumbing.

Mercury vapor. A **high-intensity discharge** lighting technology characterized by a purplish light of low CRI and by drastic reduction in lumen output during the life of the lamp. As their fixtures wear out, mercury vapor lamps have been replaced by sodium vapor lamps and metal halide lamps for outdoor lighting. (FS)

Metal halide. A **high-intensity discharge** (HID) lighting technology that uses phosphors to increase the color rendering index. Metal halide lighting is much whiter than mercury or sodium vapor lighting, but it can have color maintenance problems, with individual lamps sometimes turning various shades of green, blue, lavender, pink, and so on, limiting their desirability for indoor lighting. As with other forms of HID lighting, metal halide lighting frequently has an extended **restrike time**. (FS)

Metal lath. Metal mesh used as a base for plaster or stucco on walls. (FS)

Methane. CH_4—an extremely simple hydrocarbon and the main constituent of commercial natural gas.

Mezzanine. A low-ceilinged story or extensive balcony, usually constructed between the first and second floors of a building. (BF, CH, and FS)

Millwork. Ready-made products that are manufactured at a wood-planing mill or woodworking plant, and including moldings, doors, door frames, window sashes, stair components, cabinets, and so on. The term normally does not include flooring, ceilings, or siding. (CH)

Miter joint. A joint between two members at an angle to each other. Each member is cut at an angle equal to half the angle of the junction. Usually the members are at right angles to each other. (CH)

Mock-up. A model of an object made in the course of design, built to scale or full size, for purposes of studying construction details, judging appearances, or testing performance. (CH)

Modesty panel. A skirt of a carrel, counter, desk, or table that hides from view most or all of the legs of one sitting behind it. (PL)

Modular construction. Construction in which a selected unit or module is used repeatedly. (CH)

Moldings. Contours given to projecting members. (BF) There are dozens of words to describe various sorts of moldings—far too many to include in this list.

Monitor. A raised section of a ceiling or roof, surrounded by windows. Monitors are a frequent source of difficult glare because they have no shades to block direct sunlight angling in through south, east, or west windows, and they do not lend themselves to the installation of such shades. "Modern glass" does not eliminate the problems caused by monitors. (FS)

Mortar. A plastic mixture of cementious materials with water and a fine aggregate such as sand. Mortar can be troweled in the plastic state and hardens in place. (CH) In other words, it is the stuff they use to lay bricks and concrete blocks. (FS)

Mortise. A hole cut into a timber or piece of other material to receive a **tenon** (for a mortise-and-tenon joint) or some object like a lock. Hence **mortise lock** for a knob and bolt mechanism that is fitted into a door rather than mounted on its surface or is fitted into a round hole that also holds the knob mechanism. (CH and FS)

Mortise lock. A lock set inset in a rectangular opening in the edge of a door. (FS)

Mudjacking, also called **slabjacking.** Lifting sunken concrete floors, patios, and so on by injecting grout under pressure through holes in the floor. Libraries have used mudjacking to level slab-on-grade floors.

Mullion. A vertical member separating windows, doors, or panels set in a series. (BF)

Muntin. A secondary framing member to hold panes within a window, window wall, or glazed door. It is also called a glazing bar, sash bar, and so on. (CH)

NAGPRA. Native American Graves Protection and Repatriation Act. Historic Native American burial sites are strongly protected by law. When purchasing sites for new buildings, libraries need to require from the sellers certification that there are no Native American graves on the sites. (FS)

National Concrete Masonry Association. Association that sets standards for concrete.

Native American Graves Protection and Repatriation Act. See **NAGPRA.**

Natural gas. Gas found in deposits underground, a mixture of methane and more complex molecules. Natural gas used for heating and other purposes in the United States is processed to remove most compounds other than methane. The gas is naturally odorless, and the strong smell is due to the addition of ethyl mercaptan as a safety measure. See also **methane**.

Net assignable space. See **assignable space.** Assignable space plus **nonassignable space** equals **gross space**.

Newel, or **newel post.** A tall and more or less ornamental post at the head or foot of a stair, supporting the handrail. (CH) Due to constant handling, the tops of newel posts can look battered almost immediately, and many modern newel posts have unpleasantly worn finishes. Paint comes off irregularly, as does the protective lacquer on brass. Ask your architects what steps they have taken to prevent this problem. (FS)

NFPA. National Fire Protection Association, which issues widely adopted standards for protection against fires.

Niche. A recess in a wall, usually to contain sculpture or an urn; it is often semicircular in plan, and is surmounted by a half dome. (CH)

Night latch. See **latch bolt.**

NIMBY. Not In My Back Yard. The world is full of people who make heavy use of airports, landfills, electric transmission lines, and so on, but want them out of sight (and sound and smell). Some refer to these people as "nimbies." (FS)

Nogging. See **half-timbered building.**

Nominal. A standard size as opposed to the actual size. "Nominal" 2 × 4s, for example, are actually around 1.5 by 3.5 inches these days. Nominal 2 × 4s were larger in 1950 than in 2000. Some people find the entire concept of nominal sizes offensive and wonder when "nominal 2 × 4s" will eventually shrink to real 1 × 2s. Similarly, 11-inch-deep steel shelves in cantilever shelving systems are called "nominal" 12-inch shelves. (FS)

Nonassignable space. Space in a building that is used for essential purposes that are nevertheless not associated with the main function of the building, including stairs, halls, elevators, restrooms, mechanical and electrical rooms, chases, and so on. (FS)

Nonconforming. Quality of any building that does not comply with the requirements set forth in the applicable codes, rules, or regulations. (CH) Often nonconforming buildings are the result of **grandfathering** existing structures when codes and regulations change.

Norman brick. A brick longer than standard bricks. In America, it is associated in particular with Prairie Revival designs. See also **Roman brick.** (FS)

Nosing, or **nose.** The prominent, usually rounded horizontal edge that extends beyond an upright face below, as the projection of a tread beyond the riser. (CH)

Observation of the work. A function of the architect, who makes periodic visits during the construction phase to familiarize himself with the progress and quality of the work and to determine if the work is proceeding according to the contract documents. (CH)

OC. On center or on centers. The distance between two items as measured from the centerline of one item to the centerline of the next. Standard spacing is commonly expressed this way. (FS)

Occupancy cost. The cost of staffing, service, energy, maintenance, and replacement, including consideration of the residual value of a building, over an amount of time. (PL and FS) Over the life of a library building, occupancy costs are typically much greater than construction costs. For example, if a remodeled building has a large number of separate areas that need to be watched, any savings due to remodeling rather than new construction may quickly be overcome by increased staffing costs.

Occupancy permit. A formal approval of a completed construction project by the appropriate governmental agencies, such as the fire marshal and building inspection department, authorizing the occupancy of the building. (PL) It is also known as a certificate of occupancy. (JD)

Ogee. A molding made up of a convex and a concave curve, somewhat S-shaped.

Open plan. A building plan with a minimum of internal subdivision between spaces designed for different usage. (CH)

Open-web steel joist. See **bar joist.**

Order, also called **order of architecture.** An order in architecture signifies a column, with a base (usually), shaft, and capital, together with the entablature that it supports. The pillars in Classical, Renaissance, Baroque, and Neoclassical buildings typically belong to one of the orders of architecture. (BF)

Organic architecture. A philosophy of architectural design, emerging in the early twentieth century, asserting that in structure and appearance a building should be based on organic forms and should harmonize with its natural environment. (CH)

Orientation. The placement of a structure on a site with regard to local conditions of sunlight, wind, and drainage. (CH)

Ornament. In architecture, every detail of shape, texture, and color that is deliberately exploited or added to attract an observer. (CH)

OSHA. Occupational Safety and Health Administration.

Oubliette. A room that can be entered only through a trapdoor in its ceiling. The oubliette is a traditional and primitive design for prisons. It is seldom found in libraries, but is pleasant to consider as an addition to the complaint department. (FS, etc.)

Outline specifications, also called **outline specs.** A very simplified list of the materials and finishes planned for a building. (FS)

Out-of-plumb. Not truly vertical, according to a plumb line (a weight on the end of a string). (CH and FS)

Out-of-square. Not square. A condition in which a true 90-degree angle should exist but does not. (JTF)

Overhead door. A door, of either the swing-up or roll-up type that, when open, assumes a horizontal position above the door opening. (CH)

Overload. Load, either weight on a structure or current on an electrical circuit, in excess of that for which the structure or circuit was designed. (CH and FS)

Owner. The architect's client and party to the owner-architect agreement. (CH)

Palladian. Architecture following strict Roman forms, as set forth in the publications of the Italian Renaissance architect Andrea Palladio (1508–1580). The term is particularly used in England, where Inigo Jones's Whitehall Palace banqueting house exemplifies the style. (CH and FS)

Pane. A flat sheet of glass, cut to size for glazing a window, door, and so on. Once installed, a pane can also be called a light. (CH)

Panel. An area sunken or raised in walls, ceilings, doors, wainscoting, and so on.

Panic bar, also called **panic hardware.** A door lock release on locked exit doors. When the bar across the inside of the door is pushed, the door latch releases. (CH and FS)

Parabola. A type of curve created when a plane intersects a cone. Parabolic curves are extensively used in reflectors because a light source placed at the mathematical center of the parabola results in a focused beam of light. (FS) See also **arch** and **catenary**.

Parapet. A low wall placed to protect any spot where there is a sudden drop, such as the edge of a bridge or walkway, or the edge of a flat rooftop.

Parquet. Wooden flooring laid in patterns. (FS)

Partition. An internal wall separating two areas. The implication, at least, is that it is not load-bearing. (FS)

Party wall. A wall used jointly by two parties under an easement agreement, erected upon a line dividing two separate parcels of land. A party wall is a common wall. (CH) Party walls can cause special problems when only one of the two buildings that share a party wall is demolished. (FS)

Pedestal. A now-obsolete form of floor-mounted electrical or data outlet that stuck up like a small tombstone and routinely tripped unwary passersby. (FS)

Pediment. In Classical architecture, a triangular piece of wall above the entablature, enclosed by raking cornices. In Renaissance architecture any roof end, whether triangular, broken, or semicircular, is called a pediment. (BF) It is also called a **gable**. A triangular gable shape over a door or window can also be called a pediment.

Pendant light. (1) A light fixture suspended from the ceiling. The light fixtures that provide the reflected uplight that leads to good library illumination are pendant fixtures. (2) In the first decade of the twenty-first century, there was an architectural vogue for small pendant lights with glass globes that directed concentrated light downward. They were cute, but they produced a great deal of glare and little helpful illumination. Some libraries had them removed. (FS)

Penthouse. A small structure on a flat roof, used to house mechanical equipment, or (but not in libraries) a rooftop apartment. (FS)

Performance bond. A bond of the contractor in which a surety guarantees to the owner that the work will be performed in accordance with the contract documents. Owners may require that bidders include performance bonds in their bids. (CH and FS)

Permit. A document issued by a governmental authority, authorizing specific work by the applicant. (CH and FS)

Phosphor. A substance capable of luminescence, such as the fluorescent powder lining fluorescent lamps that emits visible light when it is struck by ultraviolet light. (FS)

Pier. A mass of masonry, as distinct from a column, from which an arch springs, in an arcade or bridge. The wall between doors and windows is also called a pier, (BF) as is a column designed to support a concentrated load. (CH)

Pigment. Non-soluble powder that is used to provide coloring, as opposed to a dye, which is soluble. (FS) A pigment is a finely ground powder that is mixed with a liquid vehicle to make paint, providing color and perhaps also (depending on circumstances) opacity, hardness, durability, or corrosion resistance. The term is also used to describe the powdered coloring matter that is used to color concrete and similar mixtures. (CH) Traditionally, colors were often referred to by the names of the chemical compounds originally used as pigments, such as alizarin, vermilion, Paris green, chrome yellow, and Prussian blue, and these names continue to be used after use of the original pigments has been discontinued. The lead pigments (lead white, chrome yellow, etc.) once widely used in paints are now a major source of trouble because of their poisonous qualities. Other poisonous pigments were based on compounds of such heavy metals as mercury (vermilion) and arsenic (Paris green). Poisonous pigments are particularly dangerous when old finishes are sanded or when children eat pieces of paint-covered plaster. A very few poisonous pigments—such as cadmium reds and yellows—survive as artists' colors. (FS)

Pilaster. An upright rectangular feature in the shape of a pillar, but projecting only about one-third of its breadth from a wall, and the same design as the **order** with which it is used. (BF) Pilasters can be used to provide extra support or they can be strictly ornamental. It is pronounced "pill-ASS-ter," not "PILE-ass-ter."

Pile, also called **piling.** A concrete, steel, or wood column, usually less than two feet in diameter, that is driven or otherwise introduced into the soil, usually to carry a vertical load or provide lateral support. (CH) Many structures are supported on pilings.

Pitch of a roof. The slope of a roof, usually expressed in the ratio of vertical rise to horizontal run. (CH) The pitch is typically indicated on architectural drawings by a small right triangle with the rise and run indicated. A slope with five inches of rise for every foot of run is described as "five over twelve." (FS)

Plan. The representation of the shape of a building showing the general distribution of its parts on the ground. (BF)

Plasterboard. See **drywall.**

Plate. A horizontal board or timber connecting and terminating posts, joists, rafters, and so on. A plate forms the top or bottom of a wood-framed wall. Studs are vertical members between the top and bottom plates, while rafters or joists rest on the top plates. In typical platform framing, a sill plate or mud plate rests directly on top of the foundation. Floor joists rest on the sill plate, subflooring on the joists, and the bottom plates on the subflooring.

Platform frame. A timber framework in which the studs are only one story high. The floor joists of each story rest on the top plates of the story below, or on the foundation sill for the first story. The bearing walls and partitions rest on the subfloor of each story. (CH) Compare with **balloon frame**.

Plenum. The contained space between a hung ceiling and the underside of the floor above that serves as an air passage. (PL) Plenum air supplies and returns are regarded as inferior to ducted supplies and returns, but they are cheaper to install and may require less vertical space. If a single plenum serves more than one room, noises may carry more easily from room to room. Unless underfloor plenums are very inflexible, floors can yield unnervingly underfoot. Footsteps on plenum floors can be noisy. (FS)

Plenum-rated. Material, particularly data cable, that is suited for installation inside plenums. Plenum-rated cable was originally much more expensive than standard cable, but the extra cost is now minimal. (FS)

Pointing. In masonry, the final treatment of the joints by troweling of mortar into them. Joints are finished or "struck" in a variety of styles, designed primarily to protect the masonry from water, but also for appearance. (CH and FS) See also **tuckpointing**.

Polyurethane foam. Widely used in upholstered furniture, polyurethane foam is extraordinarily flammable and produces hydrogen cyanide gas when it burns. Flame retardants can be applied, but they have downsides as well. See **Cal 133**. The continued widespread use of polyurethane foam seems to be another case of manufacturers 10, users 0.

Porte-cochère. A porch roof projecting over a driveway at the entrance to a building, providing shelter for people getting in or out of vehicles. It is pronounced "port co-SHARE." (FS)

Portico. A colonnaded space forming an entrance or vestibule, with a roof supported on at least one side by columns. (BF)

Post and beam construction. Construction using vertical columns (posts) and horizontal beams (lintels) to carry loads over openings. Wooden post and beam construction is frequently seen in old barns. Many modern steel framed buildings use post and beam construction. (JD)

Postmodernism. An eclectic style of architecture that uses elements of various periods, especially those of the Classical tradition, often with ironic intent. (VL) Postmodernism may be "ironic," or it may just be cutesy and quickly dated. (FS) Postmodernist styles partially supplanted the **International Style** in the second half of the twentieth century.

Power pole. A hollow steel column installed between the ceiling (typically a suspended ceiling grid) and floor to provide access to electric current or data conduit. Power poles are used because of the very high cost of adding new and flush electrical and data outlets to existing floors. Power poles are never a first choice—they are easily damaged, inflexible, and frequently unsightly. (FS)

Pre-action sprinkler system. A sprinkler system that cannot deliver water unless smoke or fire alarms have been activated. Pre-action systems are designed to prevent damage from accidental discharge due to sprinkler head failure and so on. (FS)

Pre-catalyzed lacquer. A tough finish coat that is commonly used on wooden library furniture. Unlike regular lacquers, which can be re-dissolved in their original solvents, catalyzed lacquers cure after they are dried. The difference between catalyzed and pre-catalyzed lacquer involves the point in the process at which the catalyzing agent is added to the lacquer. (FS)

Prefabricate. To make units or components prior to their installation at the building site. Usually prefabricated units are made at a mill or plant. (CH and FS)

Prime contractor. Any contractor on a project who has a contract directly with the owner. (CH)

Program, also called **building program.** A detailed list of the spaces required for a building, including their sizes, physical nature, contents, and adjacencies. (FS)

Propane. A basic hydrocarbon (C_3H_8). In the form of an LPG (liquified petroleum gas), propane is commonly used for heating buildings in areas where piped-in natural gas is not available. The complete combustion of propane results in carbon dioxide and water.

Proscenium. The frontispiece of a theater stage. (BF) The term has other meanings when applied to the ancient Greek theater.

Punch list. A list of items of work to be completed or corrected by the contractor before work is deemed to be complete and retainages are paid. (Some people employ the transitive verb "punch" to mean "create a punch list," as in "We're almost through punching the building," a usage that may or may not improve the English language.) There are advantages to having outsiders create punch lists, since people involved directly in the project may be overly tempted to wrap things up quickly and just get it over with. Contractors with punch list items uncompleted may put extreme pressure on owners to pay a larger portion of the retainage than agreed to in construction contracts, and owners need to be firm in insisting that the way to get the money is to finish doing the work. Occasionally, punch list corrections can stretch on for months or even years. (FS)

Purlin. A piece of timber or steel laid horizontally on the principal rafters of a roof to support the common rafters on which the roof covering is laid. (CH) The ends of purlins can be supported by queen posts, just as king posts support the end of the ridgepole. In some cases the ends of the purlins are visible at the gable ends of buildings. (FS)

Qualifications-based selection (QBS). Certain professionals (such as architects) are often hired by the QBS method, which requires that owners rank order architects and then negotiate rates, rather than selecting them on the basis of low bid.

Quarry tile. Unglazed ceramic tile. (CH)

Queen post. A secondary vertical post, parallel to the king post. Queen posts may support **purlins**, which run parallel to ridgepoles.

Quoins. The ornamental or strengthening stones at the corners of buildings. They are usually pronounced "coins." (FS)

Raceway. Any channel to enclose and loosely hold electrical conductors. (CH)

Radiation. The transfer of energy in wave form from a hot body to a colder body independent of any matter between the two bodies. (MR) See also **convection**.

Rafter. One of a series of inclined members to which a roof covering is fixed. (CH)

Rake. (1) A slope or inclination. (2) The sloping edge projecting over the gable of a roof; also called verge or barge. (3) The board or molding along the edge; also called vergeboard, bargeboard, or fly rafter.

Real property. Land, structures, and improvements, including air and mineral rights. As opposed to "personal property," which consists of movable items, such as shelving, books, chairs, tables, bookmobiles, and so on.

Rebar. A steel bar having ribs to provide greater bonding strength when it is used as a reinforcing bar in **reinforced concrete**. (CH)

Receptacle. An electrical outlet; a place to plug in. (FS)

Recessed downlight. Also called **can light.** A cylindrical light fixture inset in a ceiling, and designed to direct light downward. Although recessed downlights are extremely popular with designers, they usually result in terrible glare, spotty illumination, strange patterns of light and dark on walls, and dark ceilings interrupted by brilliant points of light. The result is a combination of brilliant circles of light on the floor and general gloom elsewhere, plus blinding light when one tries to look at top shelves. Instructions to library architects should always include the phrase, "No can lights anywhere for any purpose whatsoever," but owners will still probably have to search construction drawings for unwanted can lights. (FS)

Record drawings. Also called **as-built drawings** or just **as-builts.** Construction drawings that are revised to show significant changes made during the construction process, and usually based on marked-up prints, drawings, and other data furnished by the contractor to the architect. The presumption is that official record drawings will continue to be modified as changes are made to the building after construction is complete, so that there is always a place where an accurate description of the building can be found. However, as-built drawings are frequently wrong, and architects who come later to undertake remodeling or expansion trust existing record drawings at their peril. Using record drawings blindly without checking actual conditions has resulted in serious errors. Record drawings are often supplied on disks, but printouts are also essential because technological changes may make it impossible to print out drawings from disks decades after a building is constructed. (CH, FS, JD)

Rectifier. A device to convert alternating current to direct current, commonly for the operation of electric motors. An **inverter** converts direct current to alternating current.

Reflected ceiling plan. An "X-ray" plan showing how a ceiling would look if you could look downward from above the ceiling, seeing its lower surface from above. Reflected ceiling plans make it possible for all drawings of a building to be oriented the same way. (FS)

Reheat, also called **reheat coil.** A device used to increase the temperature of the air passing through a duct in order to raise the temperature of the area served by the duct to a desired level. (FS)

Reinforced concrete, also called **ferroconcrete.** Concrete in which metal bars or other slender members are embedded in such a manner that the metal and the concrete act together in resisting forces. (CM) (FS) See also **rebar**.

Reinforcing bar. See **rebar**.

"Reinventing the library." When spoken by an architect, a terrifying phrase.

Relative humidity. The amount of moisture in the air relative to the total moisture the air can hold at that temperature. (PL) If the quantity of moisture in a given volume of air does not change, the relative humidity increases when the temperature of the air is decreased. This can lead to major problems (for instance) when night setback thermostats are used in libraries without humidity sensors. High humidity in libraries leads to mildew and mold, while extremely low humidity damages film. Wide swings in relative humidity can damage many hygroscopic (moisture-absorbing) library materials. (FS)

Release of lien. Instrument executed by one supplying labor, materials, or professional services on a project that releases his mechanic's lien against the project property. (CH) See **waiver of lien**.

Renaissance. In architecture, the reintroduction of Classical architecture in Europe in the fifteenth and sixteenth centuries. (BF) The Renaissance style was preceded by the Gothic style in the later Middle Ages and was succeeded by the Baroque style in the early seventeenth century. Renaissance architecture was initially characterized by the use of the classical orders, round arches, and symmetrical composition. (CH)

Rendering. A perspective or elevation drawing of a project or portion thereof with artistic delineation of materials, shades, and shadows. (CH)

Resilience. The capacity of a material to recover its original size and shape after deformation, as in "resilient flooring." (CH)

Restrictive covenant. An agreement between two or more individuals, incorporated within a deed, stipulating how land may be used. The constraints may include the specific uses to which a property can be put, the location and dimensions of fences, the setback of buildings from the street, the size of yards, the type of architecture, limitations on the number, type, and storage of vehicles, and so on. Modern housing subdivisions frequently have restrictive covenants. Covenants cannot be *less* restrictive than applicable zoning. (CH and FS)

Restrike time. The time an HID lamp requires to cool off and then warm up again, once it has been turned off; it is the time delay until full illumination has been reestablished. Because of the long restrike time, the switches for HID lighting in libraries need to be located where they cannot be accidentally used. HID lighting causes particular problems in meeting rooms. (FS)

Retaining wall. A structure whose primary purpose is to provide lateral support for soil or rock. (MR)

Retention basin. A pond created to contain the rush of runoff water from a built-up area.

RFI. Request for information.

RFP. Request for proposals.

RFQ. Request for qualifications.

Ridge, also called **roof peak.** The horizontal line at the junction of the upper edges of two sloping roof surfaces. (CH)

Ridgepole, or **ridgeboard.** A longitudinal member at the apex of a roof that supports the upper ends of the rafters. (CH)

Right-of-way. Any strip or area of land, including surface and overhead or underground space, that is granted by deed or easement for the construction and maintenance of specified linear elements such as power and telephone lines, roads, pipelines, utilities, sewers, and so on. (CH)

Riser. 1. The vertical face of a stair step. (CH) One source of major problems in some staircases is the artistic omission of risers. This can be a safety problem if people slip through, and some users with acrophobia tend to freeze when they can see anything through stairs. As building codes have restricted open risers for safety reasons, designers have retaliated with equally discomfiting transparent risers. It's hard to understand why open or transparent risers remain so popular with designers when they make many people uncomfortable and serve no useful purpose. See also **tread**.

Riser. 2. A platform on a stage. (CH) Libraries that construct wooden risers for such purposes as story time areas need to consult stage design sources for methods of preventing footsteps from thumping loudly and hollowly. One basic technique is to glue a sound-deadening material like Homasote to the *undersides* of the platforms.

Rococo. A style of architecture that was a later development of the Baroque, and was characterized by a profusion of detail and lavish decoration. The Rococo style emerged early in the eighteenth century and flourished for a half-century thereafter. Sometimes the term *rococo* is used generally to describe things that seem excessively ornate, especially if they have lots of Cupids and curlicues. (BF, CH and FS)

Roman brick. Long, thin bricks that were popular in the late nineteenth and early twentieth centuries. They were used by the firm of McKim, Mead and White and later by Frank Lloyd Wright, who used them to emphasize the strong horizontal characteristics of his Prairie-style buildings. They were supposedly based on the proportions of surviving bricks from classical Rome.

Romanesque. A style of architecture based on Roman architecture and prevalent in western Europe from the ninth through the twelfth centuries, from the time of Charlemagne to the coming of Gothic architecture. (BF and AW) The Romanesque style was characterized by massive walls, round arches, and powerful barrel vaults. (CM) Its revival in the United States in the late nineteenth century was associated primarily with H. H. Richardson, who designed several East Coast libraries in the style. (FS)

Roof. A large number of technical terms are used to describe traditional roof construction. See, for example, the list on pages 485–88 of JHP.

Roughing-in. Installing concealed conduit or piping to the point where fixtures will be connected. Sometimes this is done on speculation if an item that may be wanted later would be impossible or expensive to install if conduit did not already exist. Roughing-in is particularly important for in-floor wiring that will be installed in slab-on-grade construction. (FS)

Rustication. A method of forming stonework with rough-hewn surfaces and recessed joints, principally employed in Renaissance buildings. (BF) The term is also used more generally for even, smooth-faced blocks with prominent joints. Rusticated blocks can be extremely large, and their edges are frequently chamfered. Rustication is popular in situations where an impression of stability and permanence is important, such as banks and government buildings. (CH and FS)

Sanitary sewer. A sewer designed to carry away waste requiring treatment, as opposed to rainwater and groundwater, which are carried in **storm sewers**. The incorrect attachment of buildings to sanitary and storm sewers, through reversal of connections, and the resulting introduction of storm water into sanitary sewers, has been a major source of problems in many American cities. (FS)

Sash. Any glazed movable framework of a window. (CH) When the narrator in *The Night before Christmas* "threw up the sash," he was opening the window. Traditionally, the weight of sashes was counterbalanced by using heavy sash weights, which were located inside the wall next to the window and connected to the sash by ropes or chains running over pulleys. (FS)

Schedule. A list on an architectural drawing showing information about the drawing, or listing the sizes and types of items such as doors, windows, wall or ceiling treatments, and so on.

Schematic design. The first of the five steps defined in AIA contract documents (schematic design, design development, construction documents, bidding, and construction oversight). Frequently abbreviated SD.

Schematic design phase. The first phase of the architect's basic services. In this phase, the architect consults with the owner to ascertain the requirements of the project and prepares schematic design studies consisting of drawings and other documents illustrating the scale and relationship of the project components for approval by the owner. The architect also submits to the owner a statement of probable construction costs. (CH) For libraries, which consist in large part of wide-open spaces, it's essential that the architects understand that schematic designs will include furniture layouts.

Sealed. Set of drawings that carry the seal of a licensed architect or engineer. (FS)

Section. A representation of a building cut by an imaginary plane (usually vertical), so as to show the construction. (BF) The term applies to any such section of a solid object. In architecture, sections are usually at right angles to the axes of the structure. (FS)

Sedum. A plant commonly used in green roof installations because it needs minimal attention once established. (FS)

Seismic load. Stress due to earthquakes. (FS)

Setback. The minimum distance between a reference line (usually a property line) and a building, or portion thereof, as required by ordinance or code. (CH) In residential areas, setback lines lead to houses set a uniform minimum distance back from the street. (FS)

Setback line. A line defining the **setback** area. (FS)

Sewer. See **sanitary sewer** and **storm sewer.**

Shaft. The portion of a column between the base and the capital. (BF)

Shop drawings. Drawings prepared by manufacturers or suppliers of special building equipment, provided to the contractor for use in preparing installation of the equipment. (PL) Also drawings supplied by contractors or subcontractors illustrating how construction will take place. Shop drawings are typically approved by the building's architects. Libraries will want to receive photocopies of the drawings with their architects' approval notes.

Sick building syndrome. A problem encountered in new buildings a few years ago when many staff members became ill after they moved in. In many cases, it appears to have been due to the combination of limited air replacement (to save money on heating and cooling) and the outgassing of chemicals like formaldehyde from carpeting and other materials. At least some of the trailers supplied by the federal government to displaced residents of New Orleans after Hurricane Katrina were built with cheap plywood laden with formaldehyde and made their residents ill. (FS)

Side light. A window (light) flanking a door. (FS)

Sight line. A line stretching from a viewer to an observed area. Sight lines in libraries are enhanced by glass walls (for example, in study rooms) and by windows between staff offices and public areas. The failure to provide direct sight lines has led to major occupancy problems in some libraries. (FS)

Signature architecture. Egocentric design intended to showcase the building designer more than to meet the needs of the client. (However, if the client's primary need is to be able to claim a world-famous architect, signature architecture may be just what they wanted.) See also **starchitect.** (FS)

Sill. (1) The horizontal member at the base of a timber-framed wall. (JHP) (2) The lowest horizontal member of a window. (JD)

Skylight. A window (light) in a roof. Although skylights are tremendously popular with designers, the use of skylights in libraries is usually a major mistake. Areas under skylights are too dark by night and too bright by day, and both supplementing and blocking light under skylights is difficult. Skylights reflect and transmit sound in annoying ways. And they tend to leak. In the era of emphasis on green buildings, librarians sometimes find that architects try to guilt them into accepting skylights, but it's possible that skylights can waste more energy than they save through bad insulation and requiring brighter interior lighting of adjacent areas because people's eyes cannot adjust to the extreme contrasts in light levels. (FS)

Slab-on-grade construction. A method of construction in which the concrete floor of a building is cast in place on compacted soil. Slab-on-grade construction offers an inexpensive way to support the massive live loads found in libraries, but it is extremely difficult to alter any in-floor or under-floor utilities after the concrete slab is installed. For this reason (among many others), HVAC ducts under slabs can be a source of very serious trouble. Library buildings with slab-on-grade construction need networks of data and 110-volt conduits buried in the slabs, with flush access points.

Slabjacking. See **mudjacking.**

Slip matching. A method of installing veneer in which successive sheets are applied in the same orientation. Slip matching may be less artistic than **book matching**, but it does not lead to stripes in finishes. (FS)

Slop sink, also called **mop sink**. A deep sink, set low, that is used by janitors for filling and emptying buckets, rinsing out mops, and so on. Building codes often require a mop sink on any floor that has a restroom. (CH and FS)

SMACNA. Sheet Metal and Air Conditioning Contractors of North America.

Snow load. The load that snow can exert on a structure. Innocent Southern structural engineers were noted for designing roofs that collapsed under heavy, wet snows in the author's home town of Fargo, North Dakota. (FS)

Sodium vapor light. A type of **high-intensity discharge** lighting characterized by yellow or pink-yellow light. Sodium vapor light is commonly used for lighting highways, streets, parking lots, and other areas where high efficiency is important and accurate color rendition less important. Sodium lights in the United States are almost all high-pressure sodium. Low-pressure sodium lighting is used overseas; the luminaires are huge, and the light is essentially monochromatic. Sodium vapor lights have replaced mercury vapor lights because they are more efficient and because sodium lamps maintain brightness better over the life of the lamps. (Some research indicates that under very low-light conditions, yellow light provides less visibility than white light, because lack of colors makes it harder to distinguish objects. For this reason, metal halide lights may provide greater visibility per foot-candle and be more efficient in actual practice than they appear when only light intensity is measured.) (FS)

Soffit. The exposed undersurface of any overhead component of a building. (CH) In particular, a soffit is a lowered section of a ceiling. Soffits are commonly seen over kitchen cabinets in homes. Many modern libraries suffer from an excess of soffits. Ornamental soffits with inset recessed downlights are a common source of bad illumination. Perimeter soffits can lead to dark shadows below them. The use of soffits to define the location of furniture—such as service desks—is a major source of inflexibility in library design. If the undersides of soffits are painted any color except white, they lead to poor illumination. In other words, regard all proposed soffits with major caution. Perimeter soffits can be replaced by **crown moldings** with far more attractive effects and no damage to illumination. (FS)

Soil boring. A cylindrical hole drilled into the ground for the purpose of investigating subsurface conditions. (MR) Test borings are taken to determine the ability of soil to bear the weight of a structure, to verify that no buried rubble remains from previous buildings, and so on. (FS)

Soldier course. A course of bricks laid vertically, small end up and narrow side out. For additional terms, see **bricklaying.** (FS)

Solepiece, also called **soleplate.** A horizontal member used to distribute the weight of one or more uprights, such as the timber that serves as the base for the studs in a stud partition. (CH and FS)

Sound rating. Magnetic ballasts that do not have an annoying hum are sound rated A. (FS)

Span. The distance between the supports of an arch, roof, or beam. (FS)

Spanish tile. Clay roofing tile, approximately semi-cylindrical in shape, that is laid in courses with the units having their convex side alternately up and down. (CH)

Sparkle. The reflected highlights provided by small, bright light sources. Although "sparkle" may be desirable in some retail and dining situations, it is an extraordinarily bad idea in libraries, where ease of reading is the essential consideration, and where light sources must never blind users who look upward. (FS)

Specifications. A part of the contract documents contained in the project manual consisting of written descriptions of a technical nature of materials, construction systems, standards, and workmanship. (CH)

Sprinkler system. A system of pipes in a building with heat-activated sprinkler heads for fire suppression. Increasingly, codes require that all but small libraries have sprinkler systems. See also **dry pipe** and **pre-action** systems. (FS)

Sprinklered. Quality of a building or an area of a building that is equipped with an automatic **sprinkler system** for fire suppression. (CH and FS)

Stair. A number of terms are commonly used to describe the parts of a stair, including in particular **riser**, **tread**, **nosing**, **newel**, **baluster**, and handrail. Oddly designed staircases intended to make architectural statements are a major source of trouble in some buildings. (FS)

Starchitect. A mildly snide term applied to world-famous architects, typically those who design seriously dysfunctional buildings with major cost overruns. Some of these architects are sued, but most continue with new and innocent clients. See also **signature architecture**. (FS)

Stile. One of the upright structural members of a frame, as at the outer edge of a door or window **sash**. (CH)

Storm drain. A drain that leads to a storm sewer. Exterior storm drains installed below grade can lead to serious flooding when overloaded storm sewer systems back up through the lowest available storm drain.

Storm sewer. A sewer used for conveying rainwater and groundwater but not sewage or industrial waste. Most cities and campuses try to have two sets of sewers—storm and sanitary—accessible to all structures. Major problems can occur when drains are improperly connected, which has been a common problem in many communities. Storm water entering **sanitary sewer** systems, for example, is a common source of sewage backup in basements during rainstorms. (FS)

Stretcher. A brick laid flat, with the long, narrow side exposed. This is the most common way that bricks are laid. See **bricklaying** for additional terms. (FS)

Structural engineering. A field of civil engineering that is concerned with the design of large buildings, bridges, and so on.

Structural shape. A hot-rolled steel beam of standardized cross-section, temper, size, and alloy, and commonly used for structural purposes. (CH)

Stucco. A plaster medium used for molded surface details, for imitation of stone, and for covering flat exterior wall areas, etc. Modern stucco is applied over metal mesh that has been fastened to the surface of a building, or over rough-surfaced masonry.

Stud. An upright post or support, especially one of a series of vertical structural members that act as the supporting elements in a wall or partition. In modular construction, studs may serve only to support the drywall in partitions. Wooden studs are usually made from dimensional lumber. Steel studs can be made of fairly light-gauge steel and rely on their use with drywall to maintain the strength of the wall. For the housing trade, nominal 2 × 4-inch lumber is sold cut to the correct length for studs in walls with eight-foot ceilings; these 2 × 4s are called "pre-cuts." (CH, JD, and FS)

Subcontractor. A person or organization that has a direct contract with a prime contractor to perform a portion of the work at the building site. (CH)

Sump. A low point in or under a building. (PL)

Sump pump. A pump to remove water from a **sump**. (PL) Most basements, for example, have sumps to collect groundwater and pumps to lift the water so it can be conveyed to adjacent storm sewers before it floods basement floors. (FS)

Surveying. Determination of the location of points and the distances and angles between them. Surveying is widely used to create maps and identify boundaries. Most library construction projects will include a survey to verify building locations, property lines, and so on. Surveyors sometimes leave their names on the landscapes they survey. For example, the great survey of India, which took some thirty-five years to complete, was led by George Everest. (FS)

Suspended ceiling, also called **dropped ceiling.** A nonstructural ceiling suspended below the overhead structural slab or from the structural elements of a building and not bearing on the walls. (CH) Most suspended ceilings today consist of acoustic tiles resting on a metal framework that is hung on wire hangers from joists or from the concrete slab above. The ability to remove most acoustic tiles is essential for the maintenance of the mechanical equipment above the ceiling, including plumbing pipes, sprinkler pipes, wiring, and HVAC ductwork and equipment. **Troffer**-style electric lights rest directly on the metal framework of suspended ceilings. A common source of sound transmission between rooms is the use of room partitions that stop at the suspended ceiling rather than continuing to the bottom of the floor above. (FS)

Sway brace. A diagonal brace used to resist any lateral force, such as wind. (CH) Or earth movement, which can do dramatic things to library stacks. (FS)

Switchgear. Any electrical switching and interrupting devices in combination with their associated control, regulating, metering, and protective devices. (CH)

Task lighting. Lighting designed to provide light in a specific place for a specific purpose, as opposed to general, all-over lighting. Architecturally mounted task lighting has been a major source of functional problems in library buildings. (FS)

Tempered glass. Glass treated to be much stronger than ordinary glass. (FS)

Tenon. The projecting end of a piece of wood or other material, reduced in cross-section so that it may be inserted in a matching cavity (**mortise**) in another piece in order to form a secure joint. (CH and FS)

Tension. The state or condition of being pulled or stretched. (CH) Some nineteenth-century trusses combined iron or steel rods for tension with wooden beams for compression, taking advantage of the different characteristics of the two materials.

Terracotta. Clay baked in molds for use in building construction or decoration. Terracotta is harder than brick and is often glazed. (BF and FS)

Terrazzo. A hard flooring material made of marble or other stone chips set in mortar and then ground and polished. (PL) Precast terrazzo is often used for treads and risers on staircases, and occasionally for countertops. Old, worn terrazzo is characterized by the erosion of the mortar and the protrusion of bits of stone. (FS)

Tie beam. A beam, bar, or rod that ties parts of a building together, and is subject to tensile strain. Tie beams can be made of wood, but they are usually metal, which performs far better under tension. Tie beams are sometimes used to stiffen arches or limit the outward thrust of vaults. (BF and FS)

Tilt-up slab. A method of construction in which vertical concrete members (walls, columns, etc.) are cast flat on site (frequently on floor slabs) and then tilted up to vertical by a crane. Tilt-up construction differs from prefab construction because the components are made on site. The relevant professional association is the TCA, the Tilt-Up Concrete Association.

Tongue and groove. A joint formed by inserting the tongue of one member into the corresponding groove of another. A tongue can be either a continuous ridge along the edge of a board, or a **tenon** at the end. Traditional wooden flooring uses tongue and groove joints. (FS)

Topographic survey. A survey that determines both location (longitude and latitude) and elevation. (FS)

Trades. Occupations requiring specific skills. The building trades include masons, plumbers, electricians, and so on, and are usually defined in terms of trade union agreements.

Transom. The crossbar separating a door from the window (transom window or transom light) above it. (CH and FS)

Tread. The horizontal part of a step. (CH) It is the surface on which people step.

Troffer. A rectangular recessed lighting unit, usually installed so that its opening is flush with the ceiling. (CH) Troffers are very commonly used with suspended ceilings, with the light fixture and ceiling grid system engineered to work together. (FS)

Truss. A structure composed of a combination of members (such as chords, diagonals, and web members), usually in some triangular arrangement so as to constitute a rigid framework. (CH) Trusses have many different names (such as Warren, Howe, or Pratt) depending on how the members are arranged and which ones are under compression and tension. The most commonly seen building trusses today are prefabricated roof trusses, which are used in most homes, and steel bar joists, which are used in many commercial buildings. Trusses are engineered for specific loads and spans, and it is difficult to increase the strength of existing trusses retroactively. Consequently, one of the major problems in converting existing buildings to libraries is that the trusses are not strong enough to support the weight of books. (FS)

Tuckpointing. The repair of brickwork, consisting of the removal and replacement of loose mortar. (FS)

Tudor. English late Gothic architecture of about 1485–1560. Tudor revival styles have been popular in America, as in "stockbroker Tudor" homes. (FS)

UBC Code. Uniform Building Code.

UL. Underwriters' Laboratories, Inc., sponsored by the National Board of Fire Underwriters. UL inspects devices to be sure they are in compliance with the National Electrical Code. (CH)

UL label. Label attached to a building component, piece of equipment, and so on with the authorization of UL, indicating that the product has been tested for fire hazard, electrical hazard, and so on. (CH, vastly simplified) People in the building industry frequently refer to products tested by the UL as simply "labeled."

Unassigned space. See **nonassignable space.**

Uninterruptible power supply (UPS). An electric power system that provides continuity of power to the apparatus or appliances being served, without discernible interruption upon failure of the normal power supply. (CH)

United States Green Buildings Council (USGBC). Organization that is responsible for the LEED (Leadership in Energy and Environmental Design) standards. The USGBC has accredited design professionals since 2001. It also certifies individual buildings. (Starting in 2008, actual certification has been carried out by the Green Buildings Certification Institute.) LEED certification is sometimes required of government buildings, but it can be controversial.

Uplight. Light reflected off ceilings, as opposed to **downlight**, that shines directly downward. (FS)

USGBC. See **United States Green Buildings Council.**

Utilities. The various services required by buildings. Utilities are principally natural gas, water, electric power, and telecommunications. Because of shared planning problems, sanitary and storm sewers may be grouped with utilities by designers. The costs of bringing utilities to a new site or of relocating existing utilities that block construction can be surprisingly high and are easy for inexperienced people to underestimate. The construction of new buildings on brownfield sites can be greatly complicated by existing utilities, which may be extremely expensive to relocate. (FS)

Valley. The trough or gutter formed by the intersection of two inclined planes of a roof. (CH)

Value engineering. A process of design review with the goal of achieving the best and least costly solution meeting an established set of criteria. (PL) Value engineering is far more useful during early stages of the design, when it can help avoid unnecessarily expensive structural concepts. At the end of the design process, there are many fewer opportunities left for value engineering, and it may just lead to the substitution of cheaper windows or flimsy materials that may not save any money in the long run. (FS)

Variance. A written authorization, from the responsible agency, permitting construction in a manner that is not allowed by code or other regulations. (CH)

VAT. Vinyl asbestos tile. VAT was used commonly in buildings until the mid-1970s and is now a frequent source of asbestos removal (abatement) problems during the renovation of public buildings. If a building has 9 × 9-inch vinyl floor tiles (as opposed to 12 × 12-inch tiles), there's a good chance the tiles contain asbestos. See also **VCT**. (FS)

Vault. An arched covering in stone or brick over any building. (BF) For illustrations and names of a wide variety of vaults, see JHP pages 603–4.

VAV box. Variable air volume box. An air-handling device that combines a heating coil with a mechanism to vary the amount of air passing through. (FS)

VCT. Vinyl composite tile. A standard inexpensive floor covering. See also **VAT**. (FS)

Veiling reflectance. Glare produced by the reflections of intense light sources on shiny surfaces. In libraries, veiling reflectance is a common problem resulting from a combination of overly concentrated downlights and the shiny surfaces of computer monitors, glass tabletops, coated book paper, and so on. (FS)

Veneer. (1) A thin sheet of wood used as a facing material. (2) An outside wall facing that provides a decorative, durable surface but is not load-bearing. (CH) A whole vocabulary exists for wood veneers, indicating how they are cut and installed. Common veneer-cutting methods include plain sawing and quarter sawing. Installation methods include **slip matching** and **book matching**. Both cutting and installation need to be specified when ordering veneered surfaces, such as end panels. Wood species, thickness of veneer, regularity of grain ("no wild grain," for example), and durability of finish are also subject to specification. (FS)

Venetian blind. A blind made of thin horizontal slats or louvers, connected in such a way that they overlap each other when closed. Venetian blinds provide a fairly good degree of privacy, but they do not block light sufficiently to black out rooms for some projected images. By contrast, vertical blinds offer the advantages of fitting oddly shaped window openings and being adjustable to admit light while blocking direct sunlight, but they have proved to be very easily damaged in library installations. (FS)

Verge. See **rake**.

Vergeboard. See **rake**.

Vertical circulation. The movement of people and goods between different levels in a building. (FS)

Vinyl. Polyvinyl chloride is very widely used as the basis for vinyl floor tile, but it is believed to have negative environmental impacts. (FS)

Vinyl asbestos tile. See **VAT**.

Vinyl composite tile. See **VCT**.

Visible light. A narrow band in the electromagnetic spectrum that can be detected by human eyes. (Some insects, for example, can see ultraviolet light.)

Visqueen. A brand name of strong plastic sheeting, frequently used generically by workers, like the brand names Kleenex or Xerox. (FS)

VOC. Volatile organic compound. Construction materials that emit large quantities of VOCs can be unhealthy until they have cured.

Volt. A measure of electrical force. Volts equal **watts** divided by **amps**.

VRF. Variable Refrigerant Flow cooling systems

Waffle slab. A poured concrete slab that is reinforced by ribs in two directions, forming a waffle-like pattern as seen from below. (CH and FS) Often these slabs were left exposed as a decorative architectural element, sometimes with can lights (always an extremely bad idea in libraries) tucked into individual openings to provide downlight. Waffle slabs were popular with designers in the late 1960s and early 1970s, particularly as part of Brutalist building design. The desire to expose waffle slabs as aesthetic elements led to the exposure of suspended mechanical systems such as sprinkler piping and air ducts. Waffle slabs also made it possible to lower the profiles of buildings, since the slabs were only a couple of feet thick. (FS)

Wainscot. A decorative or protective facing applied to the lower portion of an interior partition or wall. (CH) Wainscots can be made of wood, ceramic tile, or other materials. (FS)

Waiver of lien. An instrument by which a person or organization who has or may have a right of mechanic's lien against the property of another relinquishes such right. (CH)

Water features. Architectural term for fountains, reflecting pools, and other ornamental constructions. Indoor water features in libraries have led to a variety of problems, some perhaps amusing when passersby take headers into the water features, or when the evocative sound of running water sends staff members constantly running to the restroom. But water features have also harbored Legionnaires' disease. The use of water features in libraries seems particularly ill-advised.

Water hammer. A banging sound or vibration in piping caused by pressures developing during sudden changes in water velocity or sudden stoppages of flow. (MR) Water hammers can physically damage the pipe and cause premature pipe failure. (JTF) Water hammers are prevented by adding air chambers to supply pipes near faucets.

Water table. The level below which the subsoil and rock masses of the earth are fully saturated with water. (CH) It is also called the "groundwater" level. Constructing a library basement below the water table is a perilous undertaking. In spring 2013, a number of libraries in the Chicago area had flooded basements after very heavy rain. While adding a basement to a home is relatively inexpensive, adding a basement to a library is nearly as expensive as adding another floor above grade. Building an extra floor above grade combines the benefits of natural light and freedom from flooding. (FS)

Watt. The standard unit of electrical power. **Amps** times **volts** equals watts. (FS)

Weep holes. Small openings at the bottoms of masonry walls that allow moisture to seep out of internal cavities in the walls. Weep holes are often created in masonry walls by placing pieces of rope in the mortar, and the ends of the cords can often be seen emerging from mortar joints just above the concrete sills of masonry buildings. See also **wythe**.

Wet carrel. A carrel with electrical power and/or electronic connections built in. It is a usage similar to "wet lab." (FS)

White sound, also called **white noise.** Acoustic background that is deliberately created and controlled to mask disturbing sounds. (PL) The most typical example of white sound is the sound of air movement through ductwork and grills. Libraries (and other buildings) can be disconcertingly silent when airflow is shut off.

Wind load. The force that wind exerts on a structure. Structural engineers take wind load into account when designing buildings. (FS)

Window. Window parts have a wide, specialized vocabulary of their own. Some of the most frequently encountered terms are apron, bar, casing, **jamb**, **light**, **mullion**, **muntin**, **pane**, reveal, **sash**, **sill**, stool, and stop.

Wire mold. A surface-mounted electrical conduit. In a totally new building, any wire mold that is not installed over masonry is probably a sign of inadequate wiring design. Data wire and 110-volt wire cannot be run together through a single conduit without interference with data transmission, but divided conduits are available that make shared wiring possible. (FS)

Workers' compensation insurance. Insurance covering the liability of an employer to its employees for compensation and other benefits required by workers' compensation laws with respect to injury, sickness, disease, or death arising from their employment. (CH)

Wythe. A continuous vertical section of a wall that is one masonry unit in thickness. (MR) Insulated masonry walls may consist of two wythes with an air space between them, commonly an inner wall of **concrete masonry units** (cement blocks) and an outer wall of face brick. Part of the airspace will typically have sheets of foam insulation, while the rest of the opening serves to allow any water that infiltrates to drain out at the bottom of the wall through **weep holes**. The inner and outer wythes can be tied together with bricks or with metal ties. This type of wall can be called a cavity wall or hollow wall. (FS)

Zoning. The control by a municipality of the use of land and buildings, the height and bulk of buildings, the density of population, the relation of a lot's building coverage to open space, the size and location of yards and setbacks, allowable signage, and the provision of ancillary facilities such as parking. Zoning, established through the adoption of a municipal ordinance, is a principal instrument for implementing a municipal master plan. (CH and FS)

Index

A

academic libraries
    bad site selection for, 294
    building costs, 415
    compact shelving used in, 485
    construction plaques, 380
    cross aisles in, 498
    exit control, 546
    high-risk materials in, 841
    HVAC systems, 807–808
    lending desks and reserve functions in, 524
    program rooms, seating capacity for, 565
    reference and reader guidance desks, 540
    reserve collection desks, 545
    security, single-staffed desk needing to provide, 526
    special site needs of, 329–330
    tables in, 457
accessibility
    aisle clearance and, 468, 497, 498
    building codes for, 342–344
    conversion of non-library spaces to public libraries, accessibility issues as common problem in, 35, 159
    furnishings evaluated for, 86
    historic entrances and, 405–406
    lending desks compliance with, 528
    lifts and, 776
    in program and study rooms
        audio amplification, 591
        for wheelchairs, 590–591
    ramps, 792–793
    reference desks compliance with, 541
    remodeling and expanding library buildings and, 405–406
    sloped sites and, 302
    tables without aprons, use of, 449
acoustic tile ceilings
    evaluation of, 89
    non-acoustic ceilings as dysfunctional design concept, 123–125
    overview, 901
    for program and study rooms, 577
acoustical engineering, 230
acoustics
    ceilings and, 123–125, 900–902
    in children's craft and story rooms, 607
    evaluation of, 84–85
    problems with
        atriums, 100
        balconies, 129
        ceilings, 73–74, 124
        echoes, 84
        lending desks, 559
        noise, staircases that transmit too much, 110
        overview, 38
        service desks, dysfunctional design of, 559–560
        skylights causing, 96
        staircases that transmit too much noise, 110
        walls, 888
    in program and study rooms
        acoustic ceilings, 577
        audio amplification in, 591
        inadequate acoustics in, 616
        movable room dividers, 575–576
        unwanted sound transmission, 574–575
acrophobia
    atriums and, 100, 131, 734
    avoiding situations causing, 37
    balconies and, 129, 131
    building programs, wording in, 132
    designer staircases and, 103
    dysfunctional design concept, features that induce acrophobia as, 130–132
    evaluation of library buildings for instances triggering, 89–90
    glass railings and, 788
    staircases with open or transparent risers, 107, 783
acrylic polymers used in service desktops, 553
action in case of loss, 879–880

actual cash value defined, 875
ADA (Americans with Disabilities Act), 35, 103, 109, 131–132, 342–344, 528, 541, 631
Adams, Douglas, 114
add alternates, 45, 418
adjacencies for storage spaces, 709
adjacent land, remodeling and expanding library buildings and, 403–404
adjacent transportation, building public libraries near, 328–329
after-hours access in program and study rooms, lack of, 616
agreed amount defined, 875
AIA (American Institute of Architects), 32, 39, 228, 234, 257, 274–275
air conditioning, 158, 810–811. *See also* HVAC systems
airborne dust during construction, 886
ALA (American Library Association), hiring a building consultant with master's degree from a program accredited by, 27
alarms
    audible fire alarms, 859
    intrusion alarms, 857–859
    portable alarm devices, 870–871
    visual fire alarms, 859
Allerton (IL) District Library (design sample)
    floor plan, 58
    general features, 59
    main library room, 59–60
    program room, 59
    rest rooms, 60
ampere defined, 798
amplification equipment for program and study rooms, 582
annunciators, 860
apaceDesign, 58
appearance of building, evaluation of library buildings by walking around and viewing, 80–81
aprons
    defined, 450
    evaluation of, 86
    tables without, 449, 455
archaeological evaluation of potential sites, 318–319
architects
    bidding process, 46–47, 349–356
    building consultants, working with, 27
    building process, role in. *See* subhead: role of architect in the building process
    building programs and, 24, 25
    chain of command, 51
    change orders and, 30, 365
    clients, questions to ask previous, 29–30
    construction administration, 49, 357–358
    construction process. *See* construction process
    contracting with. *See* contracting with architects
    contractor errors, resolving, 365
    conversion of non-library spaces to public libraries, architect's role in, 176
    and design, 28–33
    in design-build projects, 47–48
    design competitions, 279–280
    design concepts, stopping unsatisfactory, 237–238
    designer staircases and, 110
    dysfunctional design, architects claiming donors wanting a, 435
    engineering services and, 230
    examples of dysfunctional design concepts by, 147–148
    fees, 422–423
    final review of written building program, 220
    finished floor plans, architects starting out with, 237
    fundraising assistance
        media, responding to questions from the, 242–243
        with models, 241–242
        public meetings, participation in, 242
        with renderings, 240–241
    hiring
        contracting with architects, 274–277
        evaluating proposals, 262–263
        features, looking for past use of good and bad architectural, 251–252
        final selection, 272–274
        information to request when, 28–29
        interviews, 263–267
        locating architectural firms, 248–249
        overview, 28–33, 247–248
        prior work of architectural firms, researching, 249–252
        proposals from architecture firms, 260
        questions for architect interviews, 268–272
        RFQ (request for qualifications), 252–260
        second-choice firm, usefulness of having a, 273
        team proposals, 261–262
    interviewing
        final selection, 272–274
        information to find out when, 266–267
        litigation or lawsuits, importance of asking about, 267
        overview, 263–264
        purpose of, 266–267
        questions for, 268–272
        recommendations for, 264–265
    project architect. *See* project architect
    psychoanalysis of, 278–279
    role of architect in the building process
        construction documents, creation of, 244–246
        cost estimating, 42–43, 239–240
        design development, 243–244
        existing structures, evaluation of, 232–234
        feasibility studies, 234
        fundraising, assistance with, 240–243
        overview, 228–230
        program review or verification, 230–232

schematic design, 234–239
rules on, 289–292
schematic designs and, 39–40, 222, 234–239, 288
site selection and evaluation of potential sites, 295–297
state law and, 227–228
teams, special problems with, 261–262
unwanted design concepts from, reasons for, 278–279
user seating, architect review of adequate clearances for, 468
what can go wrong when working with
building programs, architects who ignore, 222, 282
costs, owners who are not realistic about, 287
egomaniacs and bullies, architects who are, 288–289
listen to owners, architects who refuse to, 283–284
loss of control to architects, 281–282
owners who are indecisive, 285–286
owners who refuse to pay attention to the process, 284
owners who think they know it all, 287
owners who want to do illegal things, 286
owners with no practical experience with buildings, 284–285
personnel, architectural firms that substitute, 282–283
profits, architects who cut corners to save their own time or increase, 287–288
sloppy work, architects who do, 286
architect's team
interview questions for architects about, 272
interviews, recommendations for, 266–267
special problems with, 261–262
what architect means by, 266
architectural features
dangerous, 839–840
lighting
architectural features that complicate, 748–749
task lighting, architecturally fixed, 117
in staff workrooms
built-in furnishings, 661
clothes washers and dryers, 661
lighting, 659–660
restrooms, 661
sinks, 660
temperature control, 661
ventilation, 661
water, running, 660
windows to the rest of the library, 660
wiring, 659
architectural firms
cost estimating by, 417
donors insisting on particular, 435
personnel, architectural firms that substitute, 282–283

upkeep and maintenance costs, preparation of document projecting, 424
architectural statements, interview questions for architects about, 269
architectural styles in historic exteriors, 401–403
armchairs, 460–461
artificial lighting
advantages of, 718
evaluation of, 83–84
fluorescent, 728–729, 732
HID (high intensity discharge), 729–731
incandescent, 725–728, 741
LEDs (light-emitting diodes), 731–732
for program and study rooms, 572–573
selecting sources for, 732–733
skylights and lighting systems, 97
sources of, 725
for staff workrooms, 660
artificial skylights, 99
as-built (record) drawings
architects not providing, 277
overview, 52–53
asbestos
in conversion of non-library spaces to public libraries, 162
overview, 886–887
in remodeling and expanding library buildings, 394–395
ASHRAE (American Society of Heating, Refrigerating, and Air-Conditioning Engineers), 732
assignable space, estimating, 211
assigned storage spaces, 702–704
atlas cases, 502
atriums
acoustical problems, 100, 783
acrophobia and, 100, 131, 784
defined, 99
as dysfunctional design element, 37, 99–103, 783–784
energy waste and, 101, 783
evaluating, 84
lighting and, 101, 749, 784
mini-atriums, 101
pedestrian bridges and, 100, 131
space required by, 100
staircases in, 783–784
suicides and, 101, 784, 839
throwing items from, temptation of, 100–101
traffic flow and, 101
attic stock, storage of, 704
audible fire alarms, 859
audio amplification in program and study rooms, 591
audio monitoring and surveillance, 866–867
audiovisual equipment for program and study rooms
amplification equipment, 582
overview, 581
projection equipment, 581
security for, 582
video recording capability, 582

audiovisual storage closets, 566, 584
auditoriums, 592–593
authors of this book, methods for contacting, 7
automated book-handling systems, 532–533
automated lending systems, 425
automatic faucets, 636
automatic flush toilets, 632–633
automobile salesroom conversion to public libraries, 174
automotive insurance, 880
awarding contracts to lowest qualified bidder, 356–357
awnings used to control natural light, 758, 761

B

backs to the room, seating without users', 470–471
Bacon, Francis, 25, 183
bad neighbors for libraries, 305–306, 323, 325–326, 331
balconies
    acrophobia and, 129, 131
    balusters too widely spaced, 106
    building codes and, 130
    as dysfunctional design concepts, 129–130
    handrails that can be climbed like ladders, 106
    HVAC (heating, ventilating, and air conditioning) systems and, 129
ballasts
    defined, 719
    in fluorescent lighting, 729
    in HID lighting, 730
balusters too widely spaced on balconies, 106
bamboo floor coverings, 898
bank conversion to public libraries, 167
bare wooden risers, avoiding, 609
barrel-vault ceilings, 73, 124, 901
barricades on service desks, 555–556
baseboards used to prevent damage to drywall and paint, 889–890
basements
    in conversion of non-library spaces to public libraries, 161
    overview, 74–76
    in remodeling and expanding library buildings, 406
    staff workrooms in, 659
    as storage spaces, 702
    subsurface water and, 301
basic configuration of library spaces. *See* physical layout of library buildings
basic rules
    comfortable space for users, providing, 5
    control, maintaining, 5
    flexible, keeping space, 4
    growth, planning for, 5
    lighting, providing bright and low-glare, 4–5
    security, designing for, 4
    simplicity, designing for, 5

beads-on-a-string room arrangement, avoiding, 66, 89, 112
beams, signing steel, 377–378
bearing strength of floors, 891–892
bearing walls
    in conversion of non-library spaces to public libraries, 35, 160–161
    inflexibility of, 125
    in remodeling and expanding library buildings, 395–396
bedbug infestations in soft seating, 463–464
bequests as source for funding, 430–432
betterments, 255
bid documents (construction documents)
    add alternates, 45
    blueprints, 44
    drawings included in, 244–245
    items included in, 244
    overview, 44–45, 46, 244–246
    project manuals, 44–45
    for remodeling work, 244–245
    review by building consultants, 45, 246
    specifications included in, 245–246
bidding
    add alternates included in, 350–351
    advertising for bids, 349–350
    architect, role of, 229
    avoiding, 356
    bid openings, 354–355
    bonding as requirement in
        bid bonding, 352
        overview, 351–352
        payment bonding, 353
        performance bonding, 352–353
        rules on bonding, 353
    deadlines for, 354
    deduct alternates included in, 351
    for design-bid-build projects, 45–47
    errors in, 355
    furniture not included in, 452
    items excluded from general bids, 350
    local contractors and, 356
    overview, 45–47, 349
    pre-bid meetings, 46, 353–354
    prequalification of bidders, 351
    sole source bids, 356
    underbidding, 355
big box store conversion to public libraries, 35, 156, 169–170
bike storage for staff, 695
BIM (building information management) systems, 245
blueprints, 44
BOCA (Building Officials and Code Administrators) code, 341
bond issues as source for funding, 43, 429–430
bonding
    bid bonding, 352
    overview, 351–352

payment bonding, 353
performance bonding, 352–353
rules on bonding, 353
book return slots
    badly positioned, 144
    overview, 528–530
book returns, lending desk provisions for, 528–530
book sales
    displays located near lending desks, 538
    storage of books for, 566, 585, 703, 706
book shelving. *See* shelving
book trucks, floor space in staff workrooms for, 667
bookends, 482
books and traffic flow, 69–71
booths, 466
borrowers' cards, issuing, 522
branches of public libraries, money on hand as source for funding for, 428
brickwork on historic exteriors, 401
briefcases and purses, coin-return lockers for, 843, 852
broadloom carpet, 893–895
brownfield sites, 34, 298, 303–305
budgets
    change orders and, 364
    contingency funds, 364
    interview questions for architects about, 271
    overview, 240–241
buffet shelves for food preparation and serving in staff lunchrooms, 686, 689
builder's risk insurance, 361, 882
Building Blocks for Functional Library Space (American Library Association), 208
building codes
    for balconies, 130
    conversion of non-library spaces to public libraries and compliance issues, 162
    defined, 337–338
    for elevators, 775
    for entrance and exit control, 853–854
    and inflexibility in design concepts, 126
    inspections and occupancy permits, 365–366
    overview, 338, 341
    for railings, 791, 792
    for ramps, 792
    remodeling and expanding library buildings and changes in, 393–394
    for restrooms, 631–632, 643
    rules on, 345–346
    for sprinkler systems, 860
    for staircases, 778, 786–787
building consultants (programmers). *See also* building program
    architects
        evaluation of, 250
        working with, 27, 249
    bid documents, reviewing, 45
    construction documents, review of, 246
    defined, 184

    design decisions, participation in, 183
    design meetings, attending, 236
    egomaniac architects, dealing with, 289
    evaluation of potential sites, 295–297
    fees, 422
    hiring, 26–28, 216–218
    interview questions for architects about, 270
    interviewing architects, having your building consultant present when, 265
    in planning groups, 280
    punch lists and, 385
    references for, questions to ask, 27
    requirements for, 183
    space estimation, 212–214
building costs
    capital costs
        estimating, 416–418
        overview, 416
        projecting building costs prior to design, 416
        published cost figures, use of, 417
    comparison of costs for starting over with a new building and cost of remodeling and expanding library buildings, 393
    components of
        construction, 420
        FF&E (fixtures, furnishings, and equipment), 421–422
        opening day collections for public libraries, 422
        professional fees, 422–423
        site acquisition, 418–419
        site development, 420–421
        utilities, 420
    construction costs, 42–43, 417, 420
    cost estimates. *See* cost estimates
    funding for. *See* funding
    high cost of conversions of non-library spaces to public libraries, 165
    no cost building availability as good reason for conversion of non-library spaces to public libraries, 156
    operating costs, 423–425
    overview, 415
    owners who are not realistic about, 287
    project costs, 42–43, 235, 299, 416, 418
    remodeling and expanding library buildings, 392–393
    rules on, 425–426
    saving money as bad reason for conversion of non-library spaces to public libraries, 156
    technical costs of building on proposed site, determining if you can afford the extra, 297
building engineering, 230
building inspectors
    code inspections, 365–366
    contractor errors, resolving, 365
building permits, fees for, 423
building plans and building program compared, 185

building programs
- advantages of, 181–182
- architects
  - ignoring building program, prevention of instances of, 222, 231
  - interview questions for architects about building programs, 270
  - interviewing architects, watching for signs the firm has reviewed your building program when, 267
  - preparation of building program by, 24, 25
  - review or verification of building programs by, 230–232
  - writing by, 214–216
- building plans compared, 185
- combining numbers to estimate actual amount of space needed, 212–214
- contents of, 198–207
- for conversion of non-library spaces to public libraries, 154–155, 176
- current facilities
  - functional evaluations of, 204
  - structural evaluations of, 204–205
- description of the agency to be served, 201–202
- differences of opinion, as method of sorting out, 187
- executive summaries, 185–186
- existing architecture of location, statement for library to fit in with, 208
- forbidden design options, keeping a list of, 149
- furniture specified in, 450–451
- as grant application requirement, 187, 440, 441
- input on
  - consultants, observations by, 188
  - focus groups, 190, 195–197
  - questions for planning a children's services department in a medium-sized public library (example), 191–195
  - staff and management, interviews with, 188–190
  - surveys, use of, 197–198
- items not included in, 207–208
- items provided in, 184
- lending workrooms, features requiring space in, 527–528
- long-range plans as they relate to space needs, 202
- overview, 24–25, 181–183, 208
- presentations to the community, use of building program for, 185–186
- as proactive statement of need, 186
- problems that occur without use of, 182–183
- purpose of, 184–187
- questions for planning a children's services department in a medium-sized public library (example), 191–195
- for remodeling and expanding library buildings, 392
- rules on, 224–225
- space estimation methods
  - collections, planning space for, 209–211
  - combining numbers to estimate actual amount of space needed, 212–214
  - extra space, 211–212
  - overview, 208
  - quick space estimates using formulas, 223
  - sources of planning numbers, 208–209
- spaces and contents, enumeration of required, 205–207
- staircase design, wording for, 110–111
- standards and restrictions, review of applicable service, 202–204
- storage spaces described in, 709–711
- table of contents, 198–201
- two-phase building programs, 221
- user input before design, providing an opportunity for, 187
- writing
  - by architects, 214–216
  - cutting size of program, 219–220
  - drafts, successive, 218–219
  - final review of written, 220
  - by library building consultants, 214–215
  - methods for, 218–220
  - by owners, 216
  - revisions, 218–219

built-in cabinetry in staff workrooms, 668
built-in furnishings in staff workrooms, 661
built-in soap dispensers leading to maintenance problems, 136
built-in storage for service desks, 516
bulletin boards
- in graphic arts workrooms, 671
- overview, 623–624
- in staff lunchrooms, 688, 690
- in staff workrooms, 668

buried remains of previous building in brownfield sites, 303–304
business records, storage of, 703
bypass theft-prevention systems, 846

C

cabinets
- in children's craft and story rooms, 605
- in staff lunchrooms, 685–686

CAL 133 (California Technical Bulletin 133), 829
call number sequence, shelving placement and, 492–493
can lights (recessed downlights) as dysfunctional design feature, 115, 550, 551, 559, 722, 737–738
canopies, 484
cantilever shelving
- accessories for, 483–484
- advantages of, 478

alternatives to, 487–489
bookends, 482
colors, 479
compact shelving, 485–487, 892
depths, 481–482
dimensions for, 479–482
heights, 479–481
overview, 87, 477–478
specifying, 478–484
widths, 482
capital campaigns, 434
capital costs
    estimating, 416–418
    overview, 416
    projecting building costs prior to design, 416
    published cost figures, use of, 417
carbon dioxide (CO_2) control, 808
card-based lending systems, 556–558
card catalogs, 122
card tubs, 556–558
Carnegie libraries, 301, 343, 393, 441
carpet tile (carpet squares), 895
carpeting
    broadloom carpet, 893–895
    carpet tile (carpet squares), 895
    evaluating, 90
    for program and study rooms, 588
    as punch list items, 385
    walls, carpet attached to, 829
carrels, 453
cash drawers in lending desks, 516
casters
    chairs with, 464
    shelving with, 500
cathedral ceilings, 73, 124, 762, 902
CDs (compact discs), security and, 844–845, 850–851
ceilings
    acoustic problems and, 73–74, 84, 124, 900–902
    acoustic tile ceilings
        evaluation of, 89
        non-acoustic ceilings as dysfunctional design concept, 123–125
        overview, 901
        for program and study rooms, 577
    barrel-vault ceilings, 73, 124, 901
    cathedral ceilings, 73, 124, 762, 902
    damaged ceiling tiles as punch list items, 385
    dark ceilings, 119–120, 749
    drywall, 902
    evaluation of, 89
    lighting and, 748–749
    low ceilings as common problem in conversion of non-library spaces to public libraries, 34, 164
    non-acoustic ceilings as dysfunctional design concept, 123–125
    paddle fans to disperse heat, installation of, 397
    problems with, 748–749, 900–902
    for program and study rooms, 589–590
    rules on, 904
    shed roof ceilings, 124
    sloped ceilings, 124–125, 901
    standards for, 902
    wooden, 902
cell phones, outlets for charging, 456
central openings, staircases with, 784–785
ceramic tile flooring
    overview, 899–900
    in restrooms, 650–651, 691
ceremonies, public. *See* public ceremonies
CFLs (compact fluorescent lamps), 724
chain of command, 51
chair lifts as substitute for elevators, 776
chair rails used to prevent damage to drywall and paint, 889
chairs
    booths, 466
    conference room, 570–571
    evaluating, 86, 87
    novelty seating for children, 467–468
    padded benches, 466
    for program and study rooms, 570–571
    rocking chairs, 138
    side chairs (for seating at tables), 464–466
    soft seating
        armchairs, 460–461
        love seats, 462
        overview, 460
        problems with, 463
        rocking chairs, 462–463
        sofas, 462
    stacking, 570
    for staff lunchrooms, 687
    for staff workrooms, 663–664
    stools, 468
    for visitors in staff workrooms, 664
    window seats, 466–467
change orders
    architects and, 30, 229
    design-bid-build projects, 363–364
    overview, 50–51, 348
changes after construction
    contract mention of, 277
    interview questions for architects about, 272
changing tables, 642
character of existing building, interview questions for architects about, 269
charettes, use of, 236
cheap construction as common problem in conversion of non-library spaces to public libraries, 161
cheap or fragile construction materials, 400
checking in library materials, 521

Index

checking out library materials, 520
Checklist of Library Building Design Considerations (Sannwald), 190
Checkpoint system, 848
chemicals in building materials, illness due to, 886–887
Chicago (IL) Public Library (now Cultural Center), 64, 99
children
    craft and story rooms for
        acoustics, 607
        cabinets in, 605
        decor of, 604–605
        extra features to consider including in, 607
        floor coverings, 605
        lighting, 606–607
        locations for, 604
        overview, 603–604
        public use of, 608
        restrooms, 607, 643
        sinks in, 605
        sizes of, 604
        storage for, 605–606
        windows, 606
    handrails (railings) that can be climbed and, 106, 787–788, 839
    low railings for, 792
    multilevel children's reading rooms
        bare wooden risers, avoiding, 609
        concrete, avoiding story hour risers made of, 608
        curved risers, avoiding, 609
        echo, avoiding story hour risers that, 608–609
        height variations in risers, avoiding illogical, 609
        overview, 608
        story hour pits, avoiding, 609
    novelty seating for, 467–468
    questions for planning a children's services department in a medium-sized public library (example), 191–195
    restrooms for
        changing tables, 642
        children's restrooms, 641–642
        infant seats, 642–643
        story and craft rooms, restrooms for, 643
        users needing assistance by people of the opposite sex, restrooms for, 643
    seated-height lending desks for, 528
    shelving heights, 480
    tables for, 458–460
    tables for very young children, 455
children's departments
    exits, video cameras placed to record at, 869
    glass walls in, 871
    overview, 674–676
    security in, 871–872

chipboard (particleboard), avoiding, 449
churches
    conversion to public libraries, 172–173, 312
    as neighbors, avoiding, 328
circuit breakers
    defined, 798
    electrical switches, used as, 805
    fuse box, use of circuit breakers in place of a, 799
circular rooms, 73
circular staircases, 105
circulation desk, architectural use of term, 524–525
circulation space
    estimating, 211–212
    in staff lunchrooms, 690
civil engineering/engineers, 230, 253
classrooms, 593–595
cleaning the air by removing unwanted particles, 808
clearances, user seating and adequate, 468–469
clearstory windows, natural light and, 759
climbed, handrails that can be, 106, 787–788, 839
closets for program and study rooms
    audiovisual storage closets, 584
    book sale closets, 585, 706
    calculating space for, 566–567
    computer storage closets, 585
    furniture storage closets, 583, 705
    inadequate storage space, 614
    maker space equipment closets, 586, 706
    outside groups, closets for, 586, 706
    overview, 582–583
    program and craft supplies closets, 584, 706
clothes washers and dryers
    for children's departments, 674
    overview, 819–820
    in staff workrooms, 661
coat bars, 578–579
coat hooks or pegs, 578, 670, 691
coat storage
    for patrons, 852–853
    in program and meeting rooms, 566, 578–579
    for staff, 692–693
    in staff conference rooms, 670
    in staff workrooms, 665
Coconut Grove nightclub fire, Boston, Massachusetts (1942), 853
codes
    accessibility codes, 342–344
    building codes. *See* building codes
    energy codes, 341–342
    life-safety codes, 341
    rules on, 345–346
coffee makers for staff lunchrooms, 684
coffee shops in libraries, 526
coin-return lockers for briefcases and purses, 843, 852
coinsurance clauses, 878
cold cathode fluorescent lamps, 729

collection oversight and theft control systems,
    842–844
collection storage
    atlas cases, 502
    dictionary stands, 503
    display shelves
        low-density shelving for intensive
            browsing, 505
        novelty displays for children's books, 505
    flip bins, 501
    high-density storage, 506
    map cases, 503
    microfilm and microfiche cabinets, 503–504
    overview, 475–476
    pamphlet files, 504–505
    planning space for, 209–211
    rules on, 506–508
    shelving
        call number sequence and, 492–493
        cantilever shelving, 87, 477–487
        casters, shelving on, 500
        color of, 87, 479
        conversion of existing non-library
            structures and, 34
        cross aisles, 498
        depth of, 86–87
        earthquake preparedness and, 837–838
        electrical outlets, need for recessed, 492
        end-supported shelves, 487–488
        evaluating, 86–87
        floor strength for book storage, 489
        flow of materials from shelving unit to
            shelving unit, 81, 89
        marking the contents of shelving ranges,
            499–500
        multi-deck shelving supported by shelving
            columns, 499
        non-library shelving, 489
        parallel rows, arranging shelving in,
            490–491
        perimeter shelving, 490
        planning space for, 209–211
        seismic issues, 498–499
        spacing of, 87
        stack aisles, dead-end, 91, 491, 835–836
        stack aisles, lighting for, 493–497
        stack aisles, width of, 86, 476, 497–498
        staff oversight, aisles oriented for best
            practical, 491–492
        tilting shelves, 87
        user seating next to, 469
        wood shelving, 488
    space for, estimating, 506
    spinner racks, 501–502
    temperature control and, 811
    tubs for board books, 505
collections
    cost estimates, 418
    insurance and replacement costs for, 878
    opening day collections for public libraries, as
        component of building costs, 422
college libraries. *See* academic libraries
color
    maintenance problems, colored handrails and
        door handles leading to, 137, 790
    for service desktops, 554
    of shelving, 87, 479
    of tables, 456, 457
color rendering
    fluorescent lighting, 728
    HID lighting, 730
    incandescent lighting, 726
    LED lighting, 732
    selection of light sources and, 733
color temperatures
    fluorescent lighting, 728
    incandescent lighting, 726
    LED lighting, 732
    selection of light sources and, 733
columns
    conversion of existing non-library structures
        and, 35
    upward expansion and, 311
combined libraries and museums, 626
comfortable space for users, providing, 5
commercial service desk components, 560
common problems. *See* problems (common)
compact discs, security and, 844–845, 850–851
compact shelving, 485–487, 892
compass orientation
    of entrances, 61–62
    evaluation of potential sites and
        east-west, longer dimension running, 320
        excess glass and, 320
        northern light for reading, 319
        south or southeast entrances, 319
        west light, 320
    natural light and, 758–760
comprehensive budget, 240–241
computer assistance, providing, 541
computer storage closets, 585
computer workstations
    in graphic arts workrooms, 671
    indirect glare and, 723
    screens that cannot be seen by passersby, need
        for, 127
    seating for, 470–471
    in staff lunchrooms, 688
    tethers to connect computer components to
        tabletops, 853
    video cameras placed to record at, 869
concealed historic remains on proposed site,
    determining if there are any, 297
concierge desks, 544–545
concrete, avoiding story hour risers made of, 608
concrete floors, 589, 897

conference and seminar rooms
    functions of, 598
    location of, 598–599
    overview, 597
    ownership of, 599
    space needed for, 565, 568–569
    staff conference rooms, 669–670
    staff oversight, 599
configuration of library spaces, basic. *See* physical layout of library buildings
connecting old and new buildings with skylights, 98, 766
construction. *See also* construction process (generally)
    administration, 49, 229, 357–358
    architect, role of, 229
    as component of building costs, 420
    cost estimates, 417
    design-build projects, 370–371
    health problems caused by toxic materials use in, 886–887
    librarian's role in, 373–374
    move-out construction, 371–372
    overview, 35–36
    phased construction, 371–372
    post-occupancy inspection, 388
    public ceremonies
        beams, signing steel, 377–378
        construction plaques, 380–381
        cornerstones, laying, 377
        donor receptions, 382
        donor recognition plaques, 382, 383
        groundbreakings, 375–376
        overview, 374–375
        phase 1 completion events, 379
        planning for, 374–375
        reasons for, 374
        ribbon cuttings, 382–384
        topping out, 378–379
        tours of the work in progress, 379–380
    rules on, 388–389
    warranty period, 388
construction costs, 42–43, 417, 420
construction documents (bid documents)
    add alternates, 45
    blueprints, 44
    drawings included in, 244–245
    items included in, 244
    overview, 44–45, 46, 244–246
    project manuals, 44–45
    for remodeling work, 244–245
    review by building consultants, 45, 246
    specifications included in, 245–246
construction drawings and specifications, 244–246, 348–349
construction management firms
    construction coordination meetings and, 359–360
    construction management at risk and, 367–368
    cost estimates and, 420
    fees and, 423
    hiring construction managers, 368–370
    overview, 47, 49, 366–367
    traditional construction management, 367
    value engineering and, 368, 420
construction managers
    construction management at risk and, 367
    hiring, 368–370
    interview questions for, 370
    traditional construction management, 367
    what to look for in, 369–370
construction plaques, 380–381
construction process (generally)
    architects, hiring, 28–33
    as-built (record) drawings, 52–53
    awarding contracts, 356–357
    bid documents (construction documents), 44–45, 46
    bidding, 45–47, 349
    building consultants, hiring, 26–28
    building programs, 24–25
    chain of command, 51
    change orders, 50–51
    construction administration, 49, 357–358
    construction drawings and specifications, 348–349
    conversion of existing non-library structures, 34–36, 51
    design-bid-build projects, 358–366
    design-build projects, 47–48
    design development, 44
    dysfunctional design concepts
        acoustical problems, 38
        atriums, 37
        courtyards, 37
        designer staircases, 37
        downlighting, 38
        electrical outlets, insufficient, 38
        inflexibility, 38
        light fixtures with, 38
        maintenance problems, 38
        non-rectangular interior spaces, 37
        security, bad, 38
        skylights, 37
        water features, 37
        windows with, 37
    expansion, 36, 51
    funds, 42–44
    general contractors, 49
    groundbreaking, 48–49
    lien waivers, 50
    mistakes made during, 51
    motivations for library building projects, 23–24
    moving, 53
    new construction, 35–36
    overview, 49–53, 347–348
    pay requests, 50

phases, remodeling or expansion projects conducted in, 51, 55
project managers, 49, 50
project team, 50
punch lists, 51–52, 384–387
renderings and models, 41–42
ribbon cuttings, 53–54
schematic designs, 39–41
signing off on a project, items to receive before, 52
site selection, 33–34, 36
standard steps in, 348–366
ten-month post occupancy evaluation, 55
type of construction, options for, 33–36
construction site maintenance for design-bid-build projects, 366
consultants
building. *See* building consultants
fundraising consultants, 43–44, 433
contacting the authors, methods for, 7
contingencies (unexpected construction costs), cost estimates for, 418
contracting with architects
changes after construction, mention in contract of, 277
dissolving contracts, mention in contract of, 277
errors by architect, mention in contract of, 275
fees, mention in contract of determining, 276
forms prepared by the American Institute of Architects, 274–275
items to include in contract, 275–277
low bid, selecting architects by, 274
low bid is greater than architect's estimate, mention in contract of what happens if, 277
not delivering everything promised, mention in contract of, 277
overview, 32–33
ownership of plans, mention in contract of, 277
payment schedule, mention in contract of, 276
project architect, mention in contract of, 276
reimbursable expenses, mention in contract of, 276
schematic design, mention in contract of, 275
contrast, reading tables and, 720
control, maintaining, 5
conversion of non-library spaces to public libraries
accessibility, 35
architect's role in, 176, 232–234
bad reasons for, 156–157
bearing walls, 35
book shelving, 34
building codes and, 233
building program for, 154–155, 176
cable and wiring, 34
ceiling height, 34
column spacing, 35
common problems
accessibility issues, 159
air conditioning, obsolete or nonexistent, 158
asbestos, 162
basements, 161
bearing walls, 160–161
ceilings, low, 164
cheap construction, 161
code compliance issues, 162
electrical wiring and outlets, insufficient, 164
expansion space, lack of, 159
"extra floor, buildings designed for adding an," 163–164
floor strength, insufficient, 158
high cost of conversions, 165
historic structures, converting, 162–163
lead paint, 162
lighting, unworkable, 164
locations, 157–158
parking issues, 160
partitions and floors, unwanted, 157
pollutants, 162
utilities, lack of, 159
windows, poor natural light and insufficient, 157
cost estimate for, 176
dysfunctional design concepts and, 149
environmental issues, 35, 233
exteriors, 35
floor strength and, 34, 232–233
good reasons for, 155–156
humidity control, 35
local zoning and, 233
meeting rooms, 35
MEP systems and, 233
open spaces, 35
overview, 34–36, 51, 153–154, 175–177
physical stability of structure and, 232
planning for, 154–155
reasons for, 155–157
requirements for, 34–35, 175–177
restrooms, 34
rules for, 177–178
types of buildings for conversion
automobile salesrooms, 174
banks, 167
big box stores, 169–170
churches, 172–173
department stores, 167–168
government buildings, abandoned, 174–175
historic retail spaces, 170–172
houses, 173–174
schools, 165–166
strip malls, 168–169
water infiltration and, 233
windows, 35
conveyance defined, 772

Coogan, Julie, 58
cork tile floors, 899
corner bracket defined, 450
corner protectors used to prevent damage to drywall and paint, 891
cornerstones, laying, 377
corporate grants as source for funding, 441
cost estimates
    from architects, 42–43
    for conversion of non-library spaces to public libraries, 176
    as grant application requirement, 440, 441
    list of items requiring, 417–418
    overview, 239–240, 417–418
    for remodeling and expanding library buildings, 393
costs, building. *See* building costs
counters
    in staff conference rooms, 670
    in staff lunchrooms, 685, 689
courthouse square buildings conversion to public libraries, 170–172
courtyards as dysfunctional design concept, 37, 111–112
covenants
    defined, 337
    overview, 340
    rules on, 345–346
crash bars for entrance and exit control, 854–855
credentials, interview questions for architects about, 272
credenzas, 663
CRI (color rendering index), 724
crooked or skewed items as punch list items, 386
cross aisles and shelving placement, 498
curbside bins, 535–536
"The Curse of Carnegie: Can Modern Public Libraries Find True Happiness in Historic Buildings: 21 Useful Aphorisms" (Public Library Association 2006 conference program), 3
curtain to block off story area in children's craft and story rooms, 607
curved risers, avoiding, 609
curved staircases as dysfunctional design concept, 105, 779, 780
curved walls, 61, 74, 114–115, 126
custodial supplies, storage of, 703–704
custodial workrooms, plumbing systems for, 820
custom computer tables, 455
cut pile carpet, 893
cut sheet, 45, 362

D

Danbury (CT) Library, 533, 829
dark ceilings, 119–120, 749
dark perimeters, lighting and, 747–748
"The Dark Side of Library Architecture: The Persistence of Dysfunctional Designs" (Schlipf), 5, 95

daylight. *See* natural light
daylight sensors, 743–744
DD. *See* design development
dead bugs, light fixtures filled with, 38, 84, 753, 754
dead-end stack aisles, 91, 835–836
dead load, 891
decor
    in children's craft and story rooms, 604–605
    in staff lunchrooms, 689
deduct alternates, 418
deductibles, insurance, 873–874
delayed-egress panic hardware, 855
deliveries and trash removal, parking and driveways for, 308
department stores conversion to public libraries, 167–168
departmental libraries in universities, money on hand as source for funding for, 428
depth of shelving
    cantilever shelving, 481–482
    overview, 86–87
description of the agency to be served in building program, 201–202
design awards, practical function of buildings *versus*, 81
design-bid-build projects
    bidding process for, 349–356
    change orders, 363–364
    code inspections and occupancy permits, 365–366
    construction administration, 49
    construction coordination meetings, 359–360
    construction site maintenance, 366
    drawings and specifications, verifying construction matches, 361
    draws, lien waivers, and holdbacks, 360–361
    equivalencies, resolving claims of, 361–362
    overview, 347, 358
    resolving contractor errors, 365
    shop drawings, 362–363
design-build projects, 47–48, 370–371
design competitions, architects and, 279–280
design development, 44, 243–244
design features that lead to particular maintenance problems, 132–139
design process
    and architects, 28–33
    charettes, use of, 236
    construction documents, creation of, 244–246
    cost estimating, 239
    design development, 44, 243–244
    finished floor plans, architects starting out with, 237
    meetings, 238
    outline specifications, 238
    overview, 227–228
    planning groups, 280–281
    rules on, 289–292
    shop drawings, 246

designer staircases
- acrophobia and, 103
- architects and, 110
- balusters too widely spaced, 106
- building programs, wording for staircase design in, 110–111
- circular staircases, 105
- curved staircases, 105
- as dysfunctional design element, 37, 103–111
- elevators, staircases too far from, 110
- floating staircases, 104–105, 131
- handrails not perpendicular to run of staircase, 105–106
- handrails that can be climbed like ladders, 106
- handrails that can't be grabbed, 109–110
- with light fixtures that aren't reachable, 108–109
- noise, staircases that transmit too much, 110
- oddly shaped treads, 105
- open or transparent risers, 107, 131
- overly long staircases, 108
- overview, 37
- slippery treads, 107
- space and energy, staircases that waste, 110
- transparent treads, 107
- treads curve upward into the walls, 108
- treads with drop-offs at the ends, 108

desks in staff workrooms, 662–663
detail, writing a building program in, 25
detention basins, 300–301, 421, 824–825
diagonal staircases, 779
diaper-changing tables, 642
dictionary stands, 503
differences of opinion, building program as method of sorting out, 187
direct glare, 722–723
direct/indirect light fixtures, 737
directional signage, 67–69, 70
directors and officers liability (D and O liability), 883
discomfort for patrons and staff as disadvantage of phased construction, 407–408
dishwashers in staff lunchrooms, 685, 690
display and exhibit areas
- bulletin boards, 623–624
- for combined libraries and museums, 626
- display cases, 621–623
- exterior displays, 625–626
- open exhibit areas, 621
- overview, 619–620
- permanent works of art, 625
- pinnable surfaces, 623–624
- policies on displays and exhibits, 626–627
- rules on, 627–628
- security issues, 624
- wall spaces for hanging artworks, 623

display cases, 621–623
display shelves
- low-density shelving for intensive browsing, 505
- novelty displays for children's books, 505

disposable soap dispensers, 638
dissolving contracts, mention in contract of, 277
divider shelves, 484
dividers, room, 575–576
donor receptions, 382
donor recognition
- inscribed paving bricks for, 437
- letters, 382, 383
- naming opportunities, 436–437
- overview, 436–437
- in program and study rooms, 611–612
- public ceremonies for
    - beams, signing steel, 377–378
    - construction plaques, 380–381
    - cornerstones, laying, 377
    - donor receptions, 382
    - donor recognition plaques, 382, 383
    - groundbreakings, 49, 375–376
    - overview, 374–375
    - phase 1 completion events, 379
    - planning for, 374–375
    - reasons for, 374
    - ribbon cuttings, 382–384
    - topping out, 378–379
    - tours of the work in progress, 379–380
- reading room, plaque or lettering in, 600–601

donors
- lead gifts from, 434–435
- making the ask to, 435–436
- problems with, 435

door handles
- painted, 137, 790
- stainless steel, 789, 790

door-to-door lamp sales people, 755
doorless restrooms, 648
double-cylinder locks in library entrances, 854
double stud (staggered stud) walls used to limit sound transmission, 575
downlighting, 38, 115–116, 735–738
drawings
- construction drawings and specifications, 244–246, 348–349
- elevation drawings, 41
- shop drawings, 52, 246, 347, 357, 362–363

draws, approval of, 229, 358, 360–361
drive-through services
- bank service windows converted to book pickup windows, 167
- drive-up book returns with receiving rooms, 533–535
- lending service windows, 536–537
- turning space for, 308
- video cameras placed to record at, 869

driveways. *See* parking and driveways
dry pipe sprinkler systems, 862
dryers, clothes. *See* washers and dryers
drywall
- ceilings, 902
- damage to, preventing, 888–891

dual conductor wire mold, 800–801
ductwork, 812–813
dumbwaiters used to move books from floor to floor, 776–777
dust during construction, airborne, 886
DVDs, security and, 844–845, 850–851
dysfunctional design
    acoustical problems, 38
    acrophobia, features that affecting people with, 130–132
    atriums, 37, 99–103
    balconies, 129–130
    ceilings, non-acoustic, 123–125
    courtyards, 37, 111–112
    designer staircases, 37, 103–111
    downlighting, 38
    electrical outlets, insufficient, 38
    entrances, multiple public, 120–122
    esoteric glass, use of, 142–144
    examples of dysfunctional design created by internationally famous architects, 147–148
    expansion, buildings not equipped for, 139–140
    furniture problems, architectural solutions to, 122–123
    inflexibility, 38, 125–126, 127
    light fixtures, 38
    lighting, 115–120
    maintenance problems, features that lead to particular, 38, 132–139
    monitors, 141–142
    nature of librarians as reason for, 4
    non-rectangular interior spaces, 37, 113–115
    phased construction, as disadvantage of, 408
    in program and study rooms
        acoustics, inadequate, 616
        after-hours access, lack of, 616
        folding chairs, use of, 617
        kitchenettes, inadequate, 615
        lighting control devices, difficult to use, 616
        movable room dividers, use of, 617
        opaque walls, study rooms with, 615
        storage space, inadequate, 614
        undersized rooms, 614
        wiring, inadequate, 615
    reading terraces, 146–147
    repetition of, 93, 95
    rules on, 150–151
    screen porches, 140–141
    security, bad, 38
    of service desks
        bad acoustics, 559–560
        bad lighting, 559
        color choices, 554
        fortress desks, 555–556
        fragile top surfaces, 553–554
        functionality, lack of, 548–550
        inflexibility, 550–552
        obsolete features, 556–558
        overview, 144–146
        sentiment, persistence of obsolete desks due to, 554
    sight lines, bad, 126–128
    skylights, 37, 72, 96–99
    soffits, excessive use of, 128–129
    sources of, 95, 148–149
    staff members, design problems and, 80
    water features, 37, 112–113
    windows, 37

E

e-mail notifications for holds and interlibrary loans, 522–523
earthquakes
    preparedness through building design, 837–838
    property insurance, 878
    shelving placement and, 498–499
easements, 320
east light, 759
echoes, 84, 608–609
efficacy defined, 719
efficient lighting, 741–742
egomaniacs and bullies, architects who are, 288–289
EIFS (external insulation finishing systems), 88, 94, 136–137
electrical circuits
    circuit breakers, use of, 799
    dual conductor wire mold, 800–801
    fuses, use of, 799
    future needs, having enough circuits for, 800
    GFIs (ground fault interrupters) for, 799
    grounded wiring for, 799
    overview, 799–801
    in panel rooms, 800
    in program and study rooms, 580
    in staff lunchrooms, 686, 799
electrical fixtures as punch list items, 385
electrical outlets
    conversion of non-library spaces to public libraries and, 164
    flush outlets, 803
    grounded, 803–804
    insufficient amount of, 38, 164
    locations for, 801–802
    movable seating and, 470
    need for recessed, 492
    outdoor, 804
    overview, 801–804
    pedestal outlets, 803
    and poured slab floors, 125, 164
    in program and study rooms, 579–580
    as punch list items, 385
    in staff work areas, 802
    in staff workrooms, 804
    in tables, 456

tables with 110-volt electrical outlets, using, 449
tamper-resistant (childproof) outlets, 802–803
wiring of, checking for correct, 803
electrical switches
　circuit breakers used as, 805
　key switches, 804
　motion detector switches, 805
　overview, 804–805
　placement of, 804
　as punch list items, 385
electrical systems
　emergencies, 805
　overview, 797–798
　rules on, 806
　terminology, 798–799
electrical wiring
　conversion of existing non-library structures and, 34
　conversion of non-library spaces to public libraries and, 164
　dysfunctional design and, 125
　evaluation of, 85
　in program and study rooms, 579–580, 615
　remodeling and expanding library buildings and, 397–398
　in staff workrooms, 659
　wire management troughs on tables, 458
electronic equipment, service desks need to accommodate, 515–516, 517
electronic theft-prevention systems
　bypass systems, 846
　false alarms, 846
　magnetic systems, 847–848
　overview, 845–846
　problem materials for, 850–851
　resonating circuit systems, 848
　RFID (radio-frequency identification) systems, 848–849
　self-check equipment and, 851
　space planning for, 846–847
elevation drawings, 41
elevators
　hidden, 784
　inspection of, 775
　lifts as substitute for, 776
　maintenance, 773–775
　overview, 772–773
　problems with, common, 774–775
　rules on, 793–795
　security and, 772
　selecting, items to consider when, 773
　staircases too far from, 110
　stalled, 774
　substitutes for real, 775–776
　trapped passengers, 774
　video cameras placed to record at, 869
emergencies
　electrical systems and, 805

lighting and, 756
emergency exits
　complex, 836
　enclosed staircases as, 778
end panels
　marking the contents of shelving ranges on, 499–500
　overview, 483–484
end-supported shelves, 487–488
endorsements defined, 875
energy codes, 341–342
energy conservation
　HVAC systems, 813–814
　lighting, 741–744
energy waste
　atriums and, 101
　skylights and, 98
engineering services
　architects and, 230
　fees for, 423
　potential sites, evaluation of, 295–297
entertainment in staff lunchrooms, 689
entrance and exit control
　building codes and, 853–854
　escape routes, 864
　key systems, 855–856
　lending desk supervision of entrances, 522
　multiple public entrances as dysfunctional design concept, 120–122
　overview, 853
　panic hardware (crash bars), 854–855
　proximity keys, 856–857
　security and, 91, 832–833
　service desks and, 544, 546
　swipe cards, 856–857
　thefts and unstaffed exits, 843
entrances
　compass orientation of entrances, 61–62
　evaluation of, 82
　location of, 62
　and parking lots, 160
　single-entrance rule, 62–63, 832–833
　south entrances, 61
entry foyers
　program room access through, 569–570
　rental floor mats in, 900
　terrazzo used in, 898
　walk off mats in, 900
environmental issues
　brownfield sites, 34, 298, 303–305
　conversion of existing non-library structures and, 35
　protection from the elements, evaluation for, 90
　sick building syndrome, 886–887
EPA (Environmental Protection Agency), 305
equivalencies, resolving claims of, 361–362
errors in design
　architect, mention in contract of errors by, 275
　interview questions for architects about, 271

escalation, cost estimates for, 418
escape routes, 864
esoteric glass, use of, 142–144
Euclid Ohio vs. Ambler Realty, 339
evaluation. *See also* evaluation of library buildings by walking around; evaluation of potential sites
    of current facilities
        building program used for evaluation of, 25
        functional evaluations of, 204
        structural evaluations of, 204–205
    of proposed service desks
        schematic designs, evaluating, 518–519
        trial models of desks, 519–520
    ten-month post occupancy evaluation, 55
evaluation of library buildings by walking around
    acoustics, 84–85
    acrophobia, avoiding situations causing, 89–90
    appearance of building, 80–81
    ceilings, 89
    electrical wiring, 85
    entrances, 82
    expandability, 92
    flexibility of space and elements, 88
    floor coverings, 90
    fragile construction materials, 88
    furnishings, 86–87
    HVAC (heating, ventilating, and air conditioning), 85–86
    lighting
        artificial light, 83–84
        natural light, 82–83
    ornamental spaces, 90
    protection from the elements, 90
    reasons for, 79
    rooms, functional arrangement of, 89
    security, 91–92
    shelving, 86–87
    staff members, design problems and, 80
    staff service points, 82
    storage, 87–88
    user seating, 86–87
    water features, 92
    welcome, sense of, 81
evaluation of potential sites
    archeology
        general archaeological issues, 318
        NAGPRA (Native American Graves Preservation and Repatriation Act), 318–319
    bad neighbors, examples of, 305–306
    brownfield sites, 303–305
    compass orientation
        east-west, longer dimension running, 320
        excess glass and, 320
        northern light for reading, 319
        south or southeast entrances, 319
        west light, 320
    easements, 320

floodplains, 301–302
historic buildings and neighborhoods
    assistance with, sources of, 317–318
    groups involved with, 316–317
    legal issues, 316–317
    overview, 315–316
land ownership, 320–321
overview, 294–295
professional assistance in, 295–297
site configuration, 302
site topography, 302–303
size of site
    expansion space, 309–315
    footprint of building, 307
    overview, 306
    parking and driveways, 307–308
    plantings and landscapings, 309
    setbacks, 308–309
    surface water detention, 309
soil conditions, 297–298
subsurface water, 301
surface water runoff detention and retention, 300–301
utilities, 298–300
executive summaries in building program, 185–186
exhaust fans in staff lunchrooms, 687
exhibit areas. *See* display and exhibit areas
exhibits, insuring, 879
existing architecture of location, statement in building program for library to fit in with, 208
exit control. *See* entrance and exit control
expansion of library buildings. *See* remodeling and expanding library buildings
experts on historic architecture assisting with historic buildings and neighborhoods, 317
extended construction time as disadvantage of phased construction, 407
extension cords, use of, 801–802
exterior book pickups, 536
exterior displays, 625–626
exterior glass, use of, 142–144
external book return bins, 535–536
external configuration of library buildings
    compass orientation of entrances, 61–62
    curved walls, 61
    number of entrances, 62–63
    rectangular structures, 61
    south entrances, 61
    structural shapes, 61
    where to put entrance, 62
external faucets (hose bibs), 820–821
"extra floor, buildings designed for adding an" as common problem in conversion of non-library spaces to public libraries, 163–164

F

facilities for staff. *See* staff facilities
faculty studies, 610–611

false alarms
    electronic theft-prevention systems, 846
    intrusion alarms, 858
family computer rooms, study rooms as, 602
family restrooms, 643
faulty fixtures and equipment as punch list items, 386
fax machines located near lending desks, public, 538
fear of heights. *See* acrophobia
feasibility studies during building process, 234
feminine hygiene products in restrooms, 640, 691
FF&E (furniture, fixtures, and equipment), 418, 421–422
file storage in staff workrooms, 666
finished floor plans, architects starting out with, 237
fire alarm systems, 859–860
fire and windstorm insurance, 877–878. *See also* property insurance
fire-containing book returns, 534–535
fire extinguishers, portable, 864–865
fire protection systems
    escape routes, 864
    fire alarm systems, 859–860
    fire extinguishers, portable, 864–865
    overview, 859
    sprinkler systems, 860–864
fire-resistant construction
    overview, 828–829
    of staircases, 786
fire services, automatic linkage of your fire alarm system and, 860
501(c)(3) foundations, 43, 438–439
flammability of soft seating, 463
flexibility
    evaluation of, 88
    in lighting, 745
    overview, 4
    in staff workrooms, 669
    of storage spaces, 710
flip bins, 483, 501
floater policy defined, 875
floating staircases, 104–105, 131, 781–782
flood insurance, 878, 880–881
flood-resistant construction
    basements, avoiding construction of, 831–832
    floodplains, never building on, 301–302, 830
    overview, 830
    as passive security system, 830–832
floor coverings
    bamboo, 898
    carpeting
        broadloom carpet, 893–895
        carpet tile (carpet squares), 895
        evaluating, 90
        for program and study rooms, 588
        as punch list items, 385
        walls, carpet attached to, 829
    ceramic tile flooring
        overview, 899–900
        in restrooms, 650–651, 691
    children's craft and story rooms, 605
    concrete, 589, 897
    cork tile, 899
    evaluation of, 90
    hardwood, 898–899
    poured epoxy, 897
    problems with, 892–900
    for program and study rooms
        carpet, 588
        concrete, 589
        resilient flooring, 588
        stains, avoiding, 589
        tarps used to protect floors, 589
    recycled tires, 896–897
    rental floor mats, 900
    restrooms, 650–651
    rubber tile, 896
    rules on, 903–904
    standards for, 900
    terrazzo, 897–898
    types of, 892–900
    vinyl tile, 896
    walk off mats, 900
floor drains in restrooms, 651
floor-mounted toilets, 632
floors
    conversion of existing non-library structures and, 34
    glass floors for upper level walkways, 499
    moving people between, 771–772. *See also* elevators; handrails (railings); ramps; staircases
    problems with
        bearing strength, 158, 313, 489, 891–892
        floor coverings, 892–900
    rules on, 903, 904
    technical services workrooms, floor space for, 673
    upward expansion and, 311
fluorescent lighting, 573, 728–729, 732
flush electrical outlets, 803
flush-tank toilets, 135, 632–633
flush-valve toilets, 632–633
focus groups, use of, 190, 195–197
folding chairs in program and study rooms, 617
folding tables for use in program and study rooms, 571
food preparation and serving in staff lunchrooms
    buffet shelves, 686, 689
    cabinets and drawers, 685–686
    counters, 685, 689
    dishwashers, 685, 690
    electrical circuits for, 686, 799
    exhaust fans, 687
    garbage disposals, 685
    microwaves, stoves, and coffee makers, 683–684
    plumbing for, 686, 818
    refrigerators, 684, 690
    sinks, 685

foot-candles (unit of measurement), 720–721
footings, upward expansion and, 311
footprint of building, 307
formaldehyde in building materials, 886
forms prepared by the American Institute of Architects, 274–275
formulas, quick space estimates using, 223
fortress desks, 555–556
fragile construction materials, evaluation of, 88
fragile top surfaces of service desks, 553–554
freeze-drying books as rescue method, 75
Friends of the Library, 435–436
fritted glass, 82–83
functional needs driving structural spaces, 66
funding
    overview, 42–44, 427–428
    primary sources of, 43–44
    problems, sources of, 427–428
    resources on, list of, 443–444
    rules on, 442–443
    sources for
        bequests, 430–432
        bond issues, 429–430
        501(c)(3) foundations, 438–439
        fundraising. *See* fundraising
        grants, 439–442
        money on hand, 428
        mortgages, 432
        referendums, 429–430
        savings set aside from operating funds, 429
        special appropriations, 442
fundraising
    architect assistance with
        media, responding to questions from the, 242–243
        with models, 241–242
        public meetings, participation in, 242
        with renderings, 240–241
    capital campaigns, 434
    consultants, use of, 433
    donor recognition, 436–437
    fees for, 423
    501(c)(3) foundations, 438–439
    inscribed paving bricks, use of, 437
    lead gifts, 434–435
    making the ask, 435–436
    overview, 432–433
    private fundraising, 43–44
    record keeping for, 436
    smaller donations, recognizing, 437–438
fundraising consultants, 43–44
furnishings
    architectural solutions to furniture problems, avoiding, 122–123
    built to order, 452–453
    chairs. *See* chairs
    evaluation of, 86–87
    fire-resistant, 829
    insurance and replacement costs for, 877
    inventories of existing, 452
    laptop security provisions, 458
    ordering, 452–453
    for program and study rooms, 570–572
    samples of, 453
    schematic design, furniture layout included in, 235, 239
    selecting new, 452–453
    shelving. *See* shelving
    for staff workrooms, 662–669
    storage of, 566, 583, 703, 705
    for storage spaces, 710
    for study rooms, 602
    tables. *See* tables
    user seating. *See* user seating
furniture firm booths at library conferences, visiting, 449
furniture storage closets, 566, 583, 705
fuses, 798, 799

G

game tables, 455
garage space, 709
garbage disposals in staff lunchrooms, 685
general contractors
    construction coordination meetings and, 359–360
    construction site maintenance and, 366
    in design-bid-build projects, 45
    in design-build projects, 45
    punch list items and, 384–387
geotechnical engineering/engineers, 230, 253, 258, 269, 296
GFIs (ground fault interrupters), 799
gimmicks, lighting, 755
glare
    avoiding, 745–747
    direct glare, 722–723
    indirect glare, 723
    overview, 722
    from skylights, 96–97
glass desktops used in service desks, 553
glass floors for upper level walkways, 499
glass handrails, 788
glass walls
    natural light and, 761
    service desks and, 513–514, 547
    staircases, adjacent to, 785
    in study rooms, 64, 126, 601
gloom, 747
government buildings, conversion of abandoned, 174–175
government construction projects and equivalencies, 361–362
government discounts, lighting and, 754
government grants as source for funding, 439–442

government sites, shared, 322–324
graffiti in restrooms, 651–652
grants
    building program as required documentation for applications for, 187
    as source for funding, 439–442
graphic arts workroom, 670–672
greeting library users, 522
Gressco (company), 467
ground defined, 798
groundbreakings, 48–49, 375–376
grounded electrical outlets, 803–804
grounded wiring for electrical circuits, 799
group work areas, 656
growth, planning for, 5
guard stations at exits, 843
Guggenheim Museum, 147

H

hand dryers, 639
hand drying in restrooms, 638–639
handrails (railings)
    children, low railings for, 792
    climbed, handrails that can be, 106, 787–788, 839
    colored handrails and door handles leading to maintenance problems, 137, 790
    comfortably grabbed, railings that can't be, 109–110, 791
    fall through, railings that people can, 792
    glass railings, 788
    on narrow walkways, 790–791
    overview, 777
    painted, 137, 790
    rules on, 793–795
    stainless steel, 789, 790
    staircase, handrails not perpendicular to run of, 105–106
hard to reach light bulbs leading to maintenance problems, 84, 108–109, 133–134, 749–754
hardwood floors, 898–899
Harold Washington Library, 371
health problems caused by toxic materials in library building, 886–887
heating, 810–811. *See also* HVAC (heating, ventilating, and air conditioning) systems
heights, fear of. *See* acrophobia
HID (high intensity discharge) lighting, 729–731
hidden corners and sight lines, 834
hidden elevators, 784
high-density storage, 506
high humidity as threat to library and its contents, 865–866
high-pressure laminates used in service desktops, 553
high-tech presentations by architects, 265
high-theft materials
    lending desk storage of, 523–524
    theft control systems and, 840–841

higher bids as disadvantage of phased construction, 408
highways, building public libraries near, 328
HIPAA (Health Insurance Privacy and Portability Act), 127
hiring
    architects
        contracting with architects, 274–277
        evaluating proposals, 262–263
        features, looking for past use of good and bad architectural, 251–252
        final selection, 272–274
        interviews, 263–267
        locating architectural firms, 248–249
        overview, 28–33, 247–248
        prior work of architectural firms, researching, 249–252
        proposals from architecture firms, 260
        questions for architect interviews, 268–272
        RFQ (request for qualifications), 252–260
        second-choice firm, usefulness of having a, 273
        team proposals, 261–262
    building consultants, 26–28, 216–218
    construction managers, 368–370
historic buildings and neighborhoods
    assistance with, sources of, 317–318
    conversion of historic structures to public libraries, 162–163
    evaluation of, 315–318
    groups involved with, 316–317
    legal issues, 316–317
    overview, 296, 315–316
    retail space conversion to public libraries, 170–172
historic exteriors
    architectural styles, 401–403
    brickwork, 401
    matching, 401–403
    stonework, 401
    windows, 401
historic lighting fixtures, 756
historic (traditional) libraries
    overview, 324
    remodeling and expanding. *See* remodeling and expanding library buildings
The Hitchhiker's Guide to the Galaxy (Adams), 114
holdbacks, 360–361
holds for borrowers, 522–523
Homasote used to muffle vibrations, use of, 609
homeless shelters, building public libraries near, 325–326
hooks in toilet stalls, 634–635
horizontal display cases, 623
hose bibs (external faucets), 820–821
house conversion to public library, 173–174

982 Index

humidity control
    conversion of existing non-library structures and, 35
    high humidity as threat to library and its contents, 865–866
    overview, 808, 811–812
hurricanes, shelter from, 836–837
HVAC (heating, ventilating, and air conditioning) systems
    balconies and, 129
    carbon dioxide (CO_2) control, 808
    cleaning the air by removing unwanted particles, 808
    complexity of, 808–810
    as component of operating costs, 424
    conversion of non-library spaces to public libraries and, 158
    drawings and specifications, verifying that construction matches, 361
    ductwork, 812–813
    energy conservation, 813–814
    equipment storage, 709
    evaluation of, 85–86
    humidity control, 808, 811–812, 865–866
    life span of, 809
    obsolete or nonexistent air conditioning, 158
    odors, elimination of, 808
    overview, 807–808
    phased construction, HVAC equipment warranty problems as disadvantage of, 408–409
    problems, 814
    program and study rooms, 577
    as punch list items, 386
    remodeling and expanding library buildings and, 396–397
    requirements of, 808
    rules on, 815
    shutting off, 809, 814
    temperature control, 808, 810–811
    thermostats, 810–811
    transfer of control of, 809
    two-phase construction and, 372
    zoning, 810–811
hypodermic needle disposal in restrooms, 640

I

IBC (International Building Code), 337, 341, 394
IECC (International Energy Conservation Code), 742, 743
IESNA (Illuminating Engineering Society of North America), 721
illumination levels, 720–721
incandescent lighting, 725–728, 741
index tables, 454
Indianapolis (IN) Public Library, 120, 756
indirect glare, 723
individual staff workrooms, 657–658
inert gas sprinkler systems, 863

infants
    changing tables for, 642
    restrooms equipped for, 642–643
    seating for, 460
inscribed paving bricks, use of, 437
inspection of elevators, 775
insurance
    automotive insurance, 880
    builder's risk insurance, 882
    buildings, insurance not relevant to, 882–883
    deductibles, 873–874
    directors and officers liability (D and O liability), 883
    earthquake, 878
    flood, 878, 880–881
    liability, 881–882
    major losses, covering, 873
    overview, 872
    property, 877–880
    purchasing, 875–877
    reductions in cost of, 876–877
    sprinkler systems and, 876
    staff health and life, 883
    subrogation, 874
    terminology, 875
    types of insurance coverage, 873
    umbrella policies, 874
    workers compensation, 883
insured defined, 875
interior designers
    existing furniture, taking an inventory of, 452
    fees, 422
    interview questions for architects about, 269
interlibrary loans, 522–523, 539–540
internal layout and room shapes
    beads-on-a-string room arrangement, avoiding, 66, 89, 112
    functional needs driving structural spaces, 66
    labyrinths, avoiding, 63
    "Main Streets," use of, 65, 512
    sight lines, maintaining, 64
    strangely-shaped spaces, avoiding, 65
    T-shaped space, using, 66
intrusion alarms, 857–859
inventorying for theft, 841
Iroquois Theater fire, Chicago, Illinois (1903), 853
issues of standing, 318
Ivanhoe (Scott), 305

J

jewel-box display cases, 622
jobbers, 422

K

Kalwall, 749
Kelvin (unit of measurement), 725
Kerr, Jean, 148

key locks for file cabinets, 666
key switches, 804
key systems for entrance and exit control, 855–856
kitchenettes in program and study rooms, 566, 586–588, 615, 706, 818
knob and tube wiring, 397, 800
Knox boxes, 860

L

L-shaped rooms, 65
labyrinths in internal layout, avoiding, 63
ladders, storage space for, 708
lamp defined, 719
lamp nomenclature defined, 719
land
    adjacent, buying and keeping, 314
    evaluation of potential sites, land ownership and, 320–321
landscaping as component of building costs, 421
large building as reason for phased construction, 409
latex paint on drywall leading to maintenance problems, 138–139
LCSA (Library Services and Construction Act of 1964), 43
lead gifts, 434–435
lead paint
    in conversion of non-library spaces to public libraries, 162
    in remodeling and expanding library buildings, 394–395
LED (light-emitting diode) lighting
    color rendering and, 724
    as component of operating costs, 424
    energy codes and, 342
    evaluation of, 83
    overview, 134, 731–732
    for program and meeting rooms, 573
LEED (Leadership in Energy and Environmental Design), 235, 344–345, 813
LEED rating
    schematic design and, 235
    staff showers, points for, 695
leg clearance for tables, 455
legal issues
    bidding process for design-bid-build projects involving attorneys, 46
    historic buildings and neighborhoods, 316–317
    litigation or lawsuits, interview questions for architects about, 267, 271
    owners who want to do illegal things, 286
    referendums and bond issues, legal advice on, 430
legs, requirements for table, 456
lending desks
    additional lending desk spaces, 537–540
    automated book-handling systems and, 532–533
    bad acoustics and, 559
    book returns, provisions for, 528–530
    drive-up book returns with receiving rooms and, 533–535
    drive-up service windows and, 536–537
    dysfunction in design of, 145
    exterior book pickups and, 536
    external book return bins and, 535–536
    features located next to
        book sale displays, 538
        fax machines, public, 538
        interlibrary loan traffic, areas to sort, 539–540
        new book displays, 538
        photocopiers, public, 538
        printers, 539
        recently returned books, displays of, 538–539
        registration card files, 539
        security gates, 537
        self-check equipment, 537–538
        small displays of books of current interest, 539
    functions of, 520–524
    lending workrooms, 527–528
    obsolete features, 556–558
    off-desk workspaces, 530–531
    overview, 520
    placement of, 525–526
    queuing space, 531
    seated-height, 528
    sorting rooms and, 532
    staff space, 526
    standing-height, 528
    terminology for, 524–525
    visual barricades on the user sides of, 531
lending operations and physical layout of library buildings, 71
lending workrooms, 527–528
"Let There Be at Least Halfway Decent Light: How Library Illumination Systems Work—And Don't Work" (Public Library Association 2002 conference program), 3
liability insurance, 881–882
librarians
    role in construction process, 373–374
    service desks, knowledge of, 560
library book jobbers, 422
library building consultants. *See* building consultants
"Library Buildings: Planning and Programming" (Moorman), 6
library directors, individual workroom for, 657–658
library foundations, 427
library furniture. *See* furnishings
Library Services and Construction Act of 1964 (LCSA), 43
library spaces, basic configuration of. *See* physical layout of library buildings

library supply company service desks, 560
lien waivers, 50, 358, 360
life-safety codes, 341
lifts as substitute for elevators, 776
light fixtures. *See also* lighting
    dead bugs, light fixtures filled with, 38, 84, 753, 754
    direct/indirect fixtures, 737
    dysfunctional design concepts, 38
    evaluation of, 83–84
    hard to reach or unreachable, 108–109, 133–134, 749–754
    historic lighting fixtures, 756
    for stack aisles, 493–497
    troffers, 735–736
lighting. *See also* light fixtures
    artificial lighting
        advantages of, 718
        evaluation of, 83–84
        fluorescent, 728–729, 732
        HID (high intensity discharge), 729–731
        incandescent, 725–728, 741
        LED. *See* LED lighting
        for program and study rooms, 572–573
        selecting sources for, 732–733
        skylights and lighting systems, 97
        sources of, 725
        for staff workrooms, 660
    atriums and, 101
    bad lighting
        architecturally fixed task lighting, 117
        dark ceilings, 119–120
        downlighting, 115–116
        metal halide lighting, 118–119
        overview, 115
        quartz halogen lighting, 116
    for children's craft and story rooms, 606–607
    color rendering, 724
    color temperature, 725
    in conversion of non-library spaces to public libraries, 164
    daylight sensors, 743–744
    for display cases, 622–623
    downlighting, 735–738
    dysfunctional design concepts for, 115–120
    efficient lighting, 741–742
    emergency lighting, 756
    energy-saving ideas for, 741–744
    evaluation of
        artificial light, 83–84
        natural light, 82–83
    glare
        avoiding, 745–747
        direct glare, 722–723
        indirect glare, 723
        overview, 722
    in graphic arts workrooms, 671
    illumination levels, 720–721
    LED lighting. *See* LED lighting
    motion sensor switches, 386, 742–743
    movable seating and, 470
    multifunction library lighting, specifications for, 756–757
    natural light
        awnings used to control, 758, 761
        clearstory windows and, 759
        compass orientation and, 758–760
        controlling, 761–764
        dependence on, 717–718
        east light, 759
        evaluation of, 82–83
        northern light, 758
        overview, 757–758
        perforated vinyl roller blinds used to control, 761–762
        for program and study rooms, 572
        skylights and, 765–766
        south light, 759, 760
        for staff workrooms, 657, 659–660
        traditional blinds used to control, 762
        unwanted light, effects of, 766
        vertical blinds used to control, 761, 763
        western light, 758
    in non-rectangular interior spaces, 114
    overview, 717–718
    preset control devices, difficulty with, 616
    problems (common)
        architectural features that complicate lighting, 748–749
        buying lighting, 754–755
        dark perimeters, 747–748
        flexibility, lack of, 745
        gimmicks, 755
        glare, 745–747
        gloom, 747
        historic lighting fixtures, 756
        maintain, lighting that is hard to, 749–754
        pendant lights, 755
        security lighting, 755–756
    for program and study rooms
        artificial lighting, 572–573
        lighting control devices, 616
        natural lighting, 572
    providing bright and low-glare, 4–5
    for restrooms
        distribution of light, 650
        manually switched lighting, 650
        motion sensors, 649–650
    rules on, 767–769
    security, reduced illumination levels and, 744
    skylights and, 97
    specifications, 756–757
    stack lighting, 83, 493–497
    for staff workrooms, 659–660
    strategies for, 733–741
    table lamps, 458, 459

task lighting, 738–741
terminology, 718–719
uplighting, 733–735, 756–757
lips, 483
litigation or lawsuits, interview questions for architects about, 267, 271
live load, 891
load defined, 798
local activist groups assisting with historic buildings and neighborhoods, 317–318
local planning agencies assisting with historic buildings and neighborhoods, 317
location
    for children's craft and story rooms, 604
    as common problem in conversion of non-library spaces to public libraries, 157–158
    for conference and seminar rooms, 598–599
    for electrical outlets, 801–802
    for electrical switches, 804
    as good reason for conversion of non-library spaces to public libraries, 155
    for lending desks, 525–526
    for program and study rooms, 569–570
    for reference and reader guidance desks, 542–543
    for restrooms, 644–645
    for service desks, 512–514
    for staff lunchrooms, 682–683
    for storage spaces, 701–702
    for technical services workrooms, 674
    for user seating
        backs to the room, seating without users', 470–471
        clearances, adequate, 468–469
        movable seating, 470
        shelving, seating next to, 469
        windows, seating by, 469
    for video cameras, 869
lockers for staff, 693, 852
locking doors for study rooms, 602
long flights of stairs, 778
long-range plans as they relate to space needs in building program, 202
loop pile carpet, 893
loss adjustment defined, 875
loss of business income insurance, 879
loss of control to architects, 281–282
louvers in doors, 574
love seats, 462
low bid
    is greater than architect's estimate, mention in contract of what happens if, 277
    selecting architects by, 274
low ceilings, lighting problems and, 748
LSTA (Library Services and Technology Act of 1996), 43
lumen defined, 719
luminaire defined, 719
lux (unit of measurement), 720

M

machine tables for computers, 455
magnetic theft-prevention systems, 847–848
mailboxes for staff, 690, 694–695
"Main Streets" in internal layout, use of, 65, 512
maintenance
    of elevators, 773–775
    problems
        built-in soap dispensers leading to, 136
        colored handrails and door handles leading to, 137
        dysfunctional design features that lead to particular, 132–139
        EIFS leading to, 136–137
        features that lead to particular, 132–139
        flush-tank toilets leading to, 135
        latex paint on drywall leading to, 138–139
        light fixtures that are difficult to reach leading to, 84, 108–109, 133–134, 749–754
        overview, 38
        white grout in ceramic tile leading to, 134–135
    of restrooms
        floor coverings, 650–651
        floor drains, 651
        graffiti, 651–652
        wall coverings, 651
major losses, insurance covering, 873
maker spaces
    overview, 610
    storage for, 586, 706
making the ask, 435–436
manual light switches
    in restrooms, 650
    in stack aisles, 495
manufacturers, lighting purchased from, 755
map cases, 503
Masonic Order, cornerstones laid by members of the, 377
master keys, 855–856
matching funds as grant application requirement, 440
mechanical assist compact shelving, 485–486
mechanical equipment storage spaces
    HVAC equipment, 709
    ladders, 708
    outdoor equipment, 707
    vehicle storage, 709
meeting rooms. *See* program and study rooms
meetings
    building consultants (programmers) attending, 236
    design-bid-build projects, construction coordination meetings for, 359–360
    minutes taken during, 238, 283
    planning groups, 280–281
    pre-bid meetings, 46, 353–354

MEP (mechanical, electrical, and plumbing), 156, 230, 361, 797. *See also* electrical systems; HVAC (heating, ventilating, and air conditioning) systems; plumbing systems
Merchandise Mart, 453
mercury in fluorescent lighting, 729, 731
mercury vapor lighting, 729
metal halide lighting, 118–119, 730
microfilm and microfiche cabinets, 503–504
microwaves in staff lunchrooms, 683–684
middle schools, building public libraries near, 327
mildew, humidity and, 865
mini-atriums, 101
Minneapolis (MN) Public Library, 788
mirrors in restrooms, 639–640
Misselhorn, Mark, 58
mistakes made during construction process
    change orders and, 363
    credit issued instead of undoing mistake, 51
    resolving contractor errors, 365
models. *See* renderings and models
modern glass, sunlight and, 320
modesty panels for desks, 663
modular workstations
    for service desks, 517, 551–552
    in staff workrooms, 663
mold, humidity and, 865
moldings and trim as punch list items, 385
money
    building costs. *See* building costs
    funding. *See* funding
money on hand as source for funding, 428
monitors, 11, 72, 77, 99, 141–142, 762
monumental staircases, lighting problems and, 749
mop basins, 641, 819, 820
mortgages as source for funding, 432
motion detection alarms, 857–858
motion sensor lights
    energy codes and, 342
    overview, 742–743, 805
    in restrooms, 649–650
    in stack aisles, 495
motivations for library building projects, 23–24
movable coat racks, 579
movable room dividers
    for multipurpose rooms and community rooms, 596
    for program and study rooms, 575–576, 617
movable seating, 470
movable service desks, 552
move-out construction, 371–372
moving
    additional moves as disadvantage of phased construction, 409
    overview, 53
multi-deck shelving supported by shelving columns, 499
multi-gender restrooms, 646, 691

multifunction desks, 545
multifunction library lighting, specifications for, 756–757
multilevel buildings, moving people between floors in, 771–772. *See also* elevators; handrails (railings); ramps; staircases
multilevel children's reading rooms
    bare wooden risers, avoiding, 609
    concrete, avoiding story hour risers made of, 608
    curved risers, avoiding, 609
    echo, avoiding story hour risers that, 608–609
    height variations in risers, avoiding illogical, 609
    overview, 608
    story hour pits, avoiding, 609
multiple public entrances as dysfunctional design concept, 120–122
multipurpose rooms and community rooms
    movable room dividers and, 596
    overview, 595
    performers, provisions for, 596–597
    seating capacity, 595–596
museums, combined libraries and, 626
mysterious disappearance, 875, 879

N

naming opportunities for donors, 436–437
narrow walkways, handrails (railings) on, 790–791
National Opinion Research Center, 197
National Register of Historic Places, evaluation of potential sites and, 316–317, 318
natural gas, heating with, 814
natural light
    awnings used to control, 758, 761
    clearstory windows and, 759
    compass orientation and, 758–760
    controlling, 761–764
    dependence on, 717–718
    east light, 759
    evaluation of, 82–83
    northern light, 319, 758
    overview, 757–758
    perforated vinyl roller blinds used to control, 761–762
    for program and study rooms, 572
    skylights and, 765–766
    south light, 759, 760
    for staff workrooms, 657, 659–660
    traditional blinds used to control, 762
    unwanted light, effects of, 766
    vertical blinds used to control, 761, 763
    western light, 758
neighbors for libraries, bad, 305–306, 323, 325–326, 331
Neo Con, 453
new book displays located near lending desks, 538

new construction. *See* construction
New York University Library, 790–791
NFIP (National Flood Insurance Program), 881
non-library shelving, 489
non-library spaces, conversion of. *See* conversion of non-library spaces to public libraries
non-owned auto liability, 880
non-rectangular interior spaces
    dysfunctional design concepts, 113–115
    lighting in, 114
    overview, 37
non-rectangular sites, evaluation of, 302
northern light, 319, 758
novelty seating for children, 467–468

O

obsolete features in desks, 556–558
occupancy permits, 366
oddly-shaped treads, 105, 108, 779–781
odors, elimination of, 808
off-desk workspaces for lending operation, 530–531
office supplies, storage of, 703
offices. *See* staff workrooms
old and new buildings connected with skylights, 98, 766
on-site parking, 308
opaque walls in program and study rooms, 615
open exhibit areas, 621
open floor space in staff workrooms, 667
open or transparent risers, 107, 131, 782–783
open windows and HVAC systems, 814
opening day collections for public libraries as component of building costs, 422
operating costs, 423–425
operating manuals, 52
orientation (concierge) desks, 544–545
ornamental items (fountains, statuary, etc.) as component of building costs, 421
O'Rourke, P. J., 9
outdoor electrical outlets, 804
outdoor equipment, storage for, 707
outdoor sculptures, 625–626
outlet boxes, 85
outline specifications, 238
outside groups
    closets for, 586, 706
    using meeting rooms, 612–614
outward expansion, 310
overly long staircases, 108
oversight of library spaces. *See* security
oversized books, 210, 480
overstuffed furniture, 87
owners
    architects who refuse to listen to owners, 283–284
    changing their mind during construction process, 364
    contractor errors, resolving, 365
    meetings, representation in, 284–285
    with no practical experience with buildings, 284–285
    representation in planning groups, 280
    who are indecisive, 285–286
    who refuse to pay attention to the process, 284
    who think they know it all, 287
    who want to do illegal things, 286

P

padded benches, 466
paddle fans to disperse heat, installation of, 397
paint
    damage to, preventing, 888–891
    punch list item, painting as, 385
painted handrails (railings), 137, 790
pamphlet files, 504–505
panel rooms, 799, 800
panic buttons at staff workstations, 548, 870
panic hardware (crash bars) for entrance and exit control, 854–855
paper shredders, 667
paper towel dispensers, 638–639, 691
parabolic reflectors, 719
parallel rows, arranging shelving in, 490–491
parent institutions, loss of control of program and study rooms to, 611
parking and driveways
    as component of building costs, 420
    conversion of non-library spaces to public libraries
        parking issues as common problem in, 160
        parking lot as good reason for, 155
    for deliveries and trash removal, 308
    drive-through services, 308
    drive-up book returns, 533–534
    historic (traditional) libraries and, 324
    on-site parking, 308
    size of site and, 307–308
passive security systems (through building design)
    architectural features, dangerous, 839–840
    earthquake preparedness, 837–838
    entrances, single public, 832–833
    fire-resistant construction, 828–829
    flood-resistant construction, 830–832
    shared buildings, avoiding, 838
    sight lines, 833–835
    terraces, avoiding, 839
    trapped, avoiding situations where people can be, 835–836
    windows that can be opened by users, avoiding, 838
    windstorm shelters, 836–837
pay-as-you-go construction as reason for phased construction, 409
pay requests, 50

paybacks, 813
payment schedule, mention in contract of, 276
pedestal outlets, 803
pedestrian bridges, atriums and, 100, 131
pendant lights, 559, 755
perforated vinyl roller blinds used to control natural light, 761–762
performers
    calculating space in program rooms for, 566
    ceiling height in multipurpose rooms and community rooms for, 596
    floor space in multipurpose rooms and community rooms for, 596
    lecterns in multipurpose rooms and community rooms for, 597
    lighting in multipurpose rooms and community rooms for, 597
    pianos in multipurpose rooms and community rooms for, 597
    stages in multipurpose rooms and community rooms for, 597
perimeter alarms, 857–858
perimeter shelving, 490
permanent exhibits. *See* display and exhibit areas
permanent works of art, 625
personal possessions, theft of, 851–853
phase 1 completion events, 379
phased construction
    additional moves as disadvantage of, 409
    advantages of, 407
    disadvantages of, 407–409
    discomfort for patrons and staff as disadvantage of, 407–408
    dysfunctional design as disadvantage of, 408
    extended construction time as disadvantage of, 407
    higher bids as disadvantage of, 408
    HVAC equipment warranty problems as disadvantage of, 408–409
    lack of space for staging construction as disadvantage of, 407
    large building as reason for, 409
    overview, 51, 55, 371–372, 407
    pay-as-you-go construction as reason for, 409
    reasons for, 409
    space availability as reason for, 409
    timing as reason for, 409
photocopiers, public, 538
photographs of buildings, asking architects in interviews about professional, 265
physical construction of building on proposed site, determining possibility of, 295–296
physical layout of library buildings (generally)
    Allerton (IL) District Library (sample plan)
        floor plan, 58
        general features, 59
        main library room, 59–60
        program room, 59
        rest rooms, 60
    basements, 74–76
    books and traffic flow, 69–71
    ceiling shapes, 73–74
    curved walls, 74
    directional signage, 67–69, 70
    external configuration
        compass orientation of entrances, 61–62
        curved walls, 61
        number of entrances, 62–63
        rectangular structures, 61
        south entrances, 61
        structural shapes, 61
        where to put entrance, 62
    internal layout and room shapes
        beads-on-a-string room arrangement, avoiding, 66, 89, 112
        functional needs driving structural spaces, 66
        labyrinths, avoiding, 63
        "Main Streets," use of, 65, 512
        sight lines, maintaining, 64
        strangely-shaped spaces, avoiding, 65
        T-shaped space, using, 66
    lending operations, 71
    overview, 57
    rules for, 76–78
    sorting rooms, 71
    traffic flow, 67–71
    window placement, 71–73
physical stability of structure, remodeling and expanding library buildings and, 393
picture boards in staff lunchrooms, 688, 690
pinnable backs for display cases, 622
pinnable surfaces for displays, 623–624
places of refuge, 778, 864
planning groups, 280–281
platform lifts as substitute for elevators, 776
Please Don't Eat the Daisies (Kerr), 148
plenum floors, 812
plumbing systems. *See also* restrooms
    for custodial workrooms, 820
    detention basins, 824–825
    for food preparation and service areas, 686, 818
    hose bibs (external faucets), 820–821
    overview, 817–818
    retention basins, 824–825
    rules on, 825–826
    for staff workrooms
        washbasins, 819
        washers and dryers, 819–820
    storm drains, 823–824
    for water features, 821–822
policies on displays and exhibits, 626–627
political necessity as good reason for conversion of non-library spaces to public libraries, 156

politicians assisting with historic buildings and neighborhoods, 318
pollutants
    in brownfield sites, 304, 305
    in conversion of non-library spaces to public libraries, 162
    health problems and, 886–887
    neighbors, polluting, 306
    in remodeling and expanding library buildings problems, 394–395
portable alarm devices, 870–871
post-occupancy inspection, 388
poured epoxy floors, 897
power-driven compact shelving, 486
pre-action sprinkler systems, 862–863
premium defined, 875
prequalification of bidders for design-bid-build projects, 47
presentations to the community, use of building program for, 185–186
preset lighting control devices, difficulty with, 616
pressure sensor lights in stack aisles, 496
prevailing wage laws, 356–357
printers
    lending desks, located near, 539
    in staff workrooms, 667
privacy panels on carrels, 458
problems (common)
    with ceilings, 900–902
    in conversion of non-library spaces to public libraries
        accessibility issues, 159
        air conditioning, obsolete or nonexistent, 158
        asbestos, 162
        basements, 161
        bearing walls, 160–161
        ceilings, low, 164
        cheap construction, 161
        code compliance issues, 162
        electrical wiring and outlets, insufficient, 164
        expansion space, lack of, 159
        "extra floor, buildings designed for adding an," 163–164
        floor strength, insufficient, 158
        high cost of conversions, 165
        historic structures, converting, 162–163
        lead paint, 162
        lighting, unworkable, 164
        locations, 157–158
        parking issues, 160
        partitions and floors, unwanted, 157
        pollutants, 162
        utilities, lack of, 159
        windows, poor natural light and insufficient, 157
    electronic theft-prevention systems, problem materials for, 850–851
    with elevators, 774–775
    with floors
        bearing strength, 891–892
        floor coverings, 892–900
    with HVAC systems, 814
    with lighting
        architectural features that complicate lighting, 748–749
        buying lighting, 754–755
        dark perimeters, 747–748
        flexibility, lack of, 745
        gimmicks, 755
        glare, 745–747
        gloom, 747
        historic lighting fixtures, 756
        maintain, lighting that is hard to, 749–754
        pendant lights, 755
        security lighting, 755–756
    maintenance
        built-in soap dispensers leading to, 136
        colored handrails and door handles leading to, 137
        dysfunctional design features that lead to particular, 132–139
        EIFS leading to, 136–137
        features that lead to particular, 132–139
        flush-tank toilets leading to, 135
        latex paint on drywall leading to, 138–139
        light fixtures that are difficult to reach leading to, 84, 108–109, 133–134, 749–754
        overview, 38
        white grout in ceramic tile leading to, 134–135
    in remodeling and expanding library buildings
        accessibility, 405–406
        adjacent land, 403–404
        asbestos, building containing, 394–395
        basements, 406
        bearing walls, 395–396
        building codes, changed, 393–394
        cheap or fragile construction materials, 400
        electrical wiring, 397–398
        historic exteriors, matching, 401–403
        HVAC, 396–397
        lead-based paint, building containing, 394–395
        new code categories resulting from expansion, 394
        pollutants, building containing, 394–395
        poor functional locations, 400
        windows, 398–399
    with walls
        damage to drywall and paint, preventing, 888–891
        sound transmission, controlling, 888
professional assistance in evaluation of potential sites, 295–297

990 Index

professional fees as component of building costs, 422–423
program and craft supplies closets, 584, 706
program and study rooms
    auditoriums, 592–593
    children's craft and story rooms
        acoustics, 607
        cabinets in, 605
        decor of, 604–605
        extra features to consider including in, 607
        floor coverings, 605
        lighting, 606–607
        locations for, 604
        overview, 603–604
        public use of, 608
        restrooms, 607
        sinks in, 605
        sizes of, 604
        storage for, 605–606
        windows, 606
    classrooms, 593–595
    conference and seminar rooms
        functions of, 598
        location of, 598–599
        overview, 597
        ownership of, 599
        staff oversight, 599
    conversion of existing non-library structures and, 35
    design dysfunction in
        acoustics, inadequate, 616
        after-hours access, lack of, 616
        folding chairs, use of, 617
        kitchenettes, inadequate, 615
        lighting control devices, difficult to use, 616
        movable room dividers, use of, 617
        opaque walls, study rooms with, 615
        storage space, inadequate, 614
        undersized rooms, 614
        wiring, inadequate, 615
    faculty studies, 610–611
    general features
        accessibility, 590–591
        acoustics, 574–577
        audiovisual equipment, 581–582
        calculating space required for room, 565–569
        ceiling height, 589–590
        chairs, 570–571
        coat storage, 578–579
        configuration of room, 564
        floor coverings, 588–589
        furnishings, 570–572
        HVAC, 577
        kitchenettes, 586–588, 706
        lighting, 572–573
        locating program rooms in buildings, 569–570
        number of people each room is designed to hold, 565
        security, 591
        storage closets, 582–586, 705–707
        tables, 571
        wiring, 579–580
    maker spaces, 610
    multilevel children's reading rooms
        bare wooden risers, avoiding, 609
        concrete, avoiding story hour risers made of, 608
        curved risers, avoiding, 609
        echo, avoiding story hour risers that, 608–609
        height variations in risers, avoiding illogical, 609
        overview, 608
        story hour pits, avoiding, 609
    multipurpose rooms and community rooms
        movable room dividers and, 596
        overview, 595
        performers, provisions for, 596–597
        seating capacity, 595–596
    overview, 563–564
    quiet reading rooms, 599–601
    rules on, 617–618
    special problems and opportunities with
        donor recognition, 611–612
        outside groups using meeting rooms, 612–614
        parent institutions, loss of control to, 611
    storage spaces for, 705–707
    study rooms
        as family computer rooms, 602
        furnishings for, 602
        locking doors for, 602
        overview, 601
        supervision of, 601
    two-phase building programs, 221
    types of, 592–611
programmers (building consultants). *See also* building program
    architects
        evaluation of, 250
        working with, 27, 249
    bid documents, reviewing, 45
    construction documents, review of, 246
    defined, 184
    design decisions, participation in, 183
    design meetings, attending, 236
    egomaniac architects, dealing with, 289
    evaluation of potential sites, 295–297
    fees, 422
    hiring, 26–28, 216–218
    interview questions for architects about, 270
    interviewing architects, having your building consultant present when, 265
    in planning groups, 280

punch lists and, 385
references for, questions to ask, 27
requirements for, 183
space estimation, 212–214
programming. *See* building programs
project architect, 30–31, 33, 253, 268, 270, 276
project costs, 42–43, 235, 299, 416, 418
project managers, 49, 50
project manuals, 44–45
projection equipment
    for program and study rooms, 581
    in staff conference rooms, 670
propane, buildings heated by, 159
property insurance
    action in case of loss, 879–880
    coinsurance clauses, 878
    earthquakes, 878
    exhibits, 879
    fire and windstorm, 877–878
    floods, 878
    loss of business income, 879
    overview, 877
    setting values on structure and contents, 877–878
    sewer backup, 878–879
    theft of library property, 879
    valuable objects, 879
proximity keys, 856–857
public ceremonies
    beams, signing steel, 377–378
    construction plaques, 380–381
    cornerstones, laying, 377
    donor receptions, 382
    donor recognition plaques, 382, 383
    groundbreakings, 375–376
    overview, 374–375
    phase 1 completion events, 379
    planning for, 374–375
    reasons for, 374
    ribbon cuttings, 382–384
    topping out, 378–379
    tours of the work in progress, 379–380
public libraries
    construction plaques, 380
    conversion of non-library spaces to. *See* conversion of non-library spaces to public libraries
    footprint of building, 307
    on-site parking, 308
    reference and reader guidance desks, 540
    referendums and bond issues as source for funding, 429
    site selection and
        adjacent transportation, building public libraries near, 328–329
        churches, building public libraries near, 328
        government sites, 322–324
        homeless shelters, building public libraries near, 325–326
        new sites, expansion options as factor in choosing, 312
        overview, 321
        retail sites, 321–322
        "River Cit"" sites, 324
        schools, building public libraries near, 327
        secure locations, 326–327
    upward expansion and, 311
    zoning, 339–340
Public Library Association, 3
public relations, security and, 872
public service desks. *See* service desks
public sorting (recently returned) shelves, 532, 538–539
pull stations, 860
punch lists
    electrical outlets, checking for correct wiring of, 803
    HVAC systems, 809
    list of items to include in, 384–386
    overview, 51–52, 348, 384–387
puppet theater in children's craft and story rooms, including a, 607
purse storage for staff, 693, 852
push button lights in stack aisles, 495
push surveys, 198

Q

quartz halogen lighting, 116, 726–728, 741
questionnaires used for input on library buildings, 197–198
queuing space near lending desks, 531
quiet reading rooms, 599–601

R

radiating book stacks and sight lines, 835
radiators, 809–810
radio-frequency identification (RFID) systems, 848–849
rail defined, 450
railings. *See* handrails (railings)
railroads, building public libraries near, 328–329
ramps
    overview, 792–793
    rules on, 793–795
reader guidance desks. *See* reference and reader guidance desks
reading terraces, 10, 78, 92, 146–147, 839
receiving bins, 528, 533–534
recently returned books, displays near lending desk of, 538–539
recessed downlights (can lights) as dysfunctional design feature, 115, 550, 551, 559, 722, 737–738
recognition of participants. *See* donor recognition

record (as-built) drawings
  architects not providing, 277
  overview, 52–53
rectangular tables
  with dividers, 454
  for four users, 454
  overview, 449
recycled tire floors, 896–897
reference and reader guidance desks
  chairs for users at, 518
  computer assistance, providing, 541
  dysfunction in design of, 145
  functions of, 540–541
  heights, 541
  overview, 540
  placement of, 542–543
  reader guidance, providing, 540–541
  roving librarians and, 542
  service points at, determining number of, 541
  storage at, 543–544
  supervision, providing, 541
referendums as source for funding, 429–430
refrigerators
  in staff lunchrooms, 684, 690
  in staff workrooms, 667–668
refuge, areas of, 778, 864
registration card files located near lending desks, 539
reheat coils, 810
reimbursable expenses, mention in contract of, 276
relative humidity, 811–812, 865
relocating utilities, 298–300, 421
"Remodeling and Expanding Carnegie-Era Library Buildings" (Schlipf), 5
remodeling and expanding library buildings
  architect's role in, 232–234
  building codes and, 233
  building program for, written, 392
  comparison of costs for starting over with a new building and cost of, 393
  construction documents for, 244–245
  costs of, 392–393
  dysfunctional design concept, buildings not equipped for expansion as, 139–140
  EPA problems and, 233
  estimated cost for, 393
  evaluation of existing structure by an architect, 232–234
  evaluation of library buildings by walking around, 92
  expansion space
    critics of need for expansion, 312–313
    estimating site acreage, rules of thumb for, 315
    evaluation of potential sites and, 309–315
    floors, need for strong, 313
    land, buying and keeping adjacent, 314
    outward expansion, 310
  remodeling and expanding library buildings, lack of expansion space for, 403–404
    upward expansion, 311
  floor strength and, 232–233
  local zoning and, 233
  MEP systems and, 233
  overview, 391–392
  phasing expansion projects
    advantages of, 407
    disadvantages of, 407–409
    overview, 407
    reasons for, 409
  physical stability of structure and, 232, 393
  problems with
    accessibility, 405–406
    adjacent land, 403–404
    asbestos, building containing, 394–395
    basements, 406
    bearing walls, 395–396
    building codes, changed, 393–394
    cheap or fragile construction materials, 400
    electrical wiring, 397–398
    historic exteriors, matching, 401–403
    HVAC, 396–397
    lead-based paint, building containing, 394–395
    new code categories resulting from expansion, 394
    pollutants, building containing, 394–395
    poor functional locations, 400
    windows, 398–399
  restrooms and, 126, 645–646
  rules on, 410–411
  schematic design for, 393
  water infiltration and, 233
remote locations, book return slots in, 529, 533
renderings and models
  architect's interview, beware of renderings presented during, 266
  models defined, 41
  overview, 41–42
  renderings defined, 41
  representation, accuracy in, 42
  software for, 41–42
  study models, 42
renovating existing non-library structures. *See* conversion of non-library spaces to public libraries
rental floor mats, 900
repair and upkeep as component of operating costs, 424
repetition of dysfunctional design concepts, 93, 95
replacement cost defined, 875
research libraries
  high-risk materials in, 841
  tables in, 457
reservation buzzer system in children's craft and story rooms, including a, 607

resonating circuit theft-prevention systems, 848
restrooms
    building codes and, 631–632
    built-in soap dispensers leading to maintenance problems, 136
    for children and infants
        changing tables, 642
        children's restrooms, 641–642
        infant seats, 642–643
        story and craft rooms, restrooms for, 607, 643
        users needing assistance by people of the opposite sex, restrooms for, 643
    conversion of existing non-library structures and, 34
    dysfunctional design in, 629–630
    evaluating, 91
    exits, video cameras placed to record at, 869
    expansion and, 126
    fixtures and equipment in
        feminine hygiene products, 640
        hand drying, 638–639
        hypodermic needles, 640
        mirrors, 639–640
        mop basins, 641
        number of, 643–644
        as punch list items, 386
        shelves, 640
        soap dispensers, 636–638
        stall enclosures, 634–635
        toilets, 632–634
        urinals, 635–636
        ventilation, 640–641, 691
        washbasins, 636
    flush-tank toilets leading to maintenance problems, 135
    lighting
        distribution of light, 650
        manually switched lighting, 650
        motion sensors, 649–650, 691, 742–743
    maintenance
        floor coverings, 650–651
        floor drains, 651
        graffiti, 651–652
        wall coverings, 651
    multi-gender restrooms, 646, 691
    overview, 629–631
    rules on, 652–653
    security
        doorless restrooms, 648
        single-user restrooms, 647–648
        staff oversight, 646–647
        tornado shelters, restrooms as, 648–649
        video surveillance, 648
    sight lines and, 127, 644, 835
    size and location of
        expansion, implications for, 645–646
        locations, 644–645
        number of fixtures, 643–644
        staff restrooms, 645
        transgender users, accommodations for, 646
    for staff, 661, 683, 690–691
    theft and, 843
    two-phase building programs and, 221
    unisex restrooms, 646, 691
retail sites, public libraries site selection and, 321–322
retention basins
    as component of building costs, 421
    overview, 824–825
return book bins, 526
RFID (radio-frequency identification) systems, 848–849
RFP (request for proposal), 53
RFQ (request for qualifications)
    accreditation, requesting, 257
    biographical information on the people who will be doing the work, 253
    change orders, does firm have excessive number of, 255–256
    client requests, determining if firm is responsive to, 254–255
    completed projects, requesting list of, 256–257
    construction managers, hiring, 368–369
    consulting professionals in the team, requesting list of outside, 258
    day on which interviews will take place, 259
    evaluating, 262–263
    function, whether artistic design trumps, 255
    how much work of this type the firm has done, 253
    library work done by firm, 252–253
    list of people who will make up team, requesting, 257
    number of firms you plan to interview included in, 259
    overview, 252
    project architect, requesting information on the, 258
    proposals
        directions on where to send copies of, 258
        specific day and time due for, 258–259
    questions to ask in, 256–260
    satisfaction of previous clients, 253
    sources for additional information included in, 260
    whether the buildings the firm designs actually work, 254
    who will be doing the work, 256
    who will do construction oversight, 256
ribbon cuttings, 53–54, 382–384
risk defined, 875
"River City" sites, public libraries site selection and, 324
rocking chairs, 138, 462–463

room dividers, 575–576
room shapes, internal layout and. *See* internal layout and room shapes
rough surfaces as punch list items, 385
round tables, 449, 454
roving librarians, reference and reader guidance desks and, 542
rubber tile floors, 896
rules
    on architects, 289–292
    basic rules
        comfortable space for users, providing, 5
        control, maintaining, 5
        flexible, keeping space, 4
        growth, planning for, 5
        lighting, providing bright and low-glare, 4–5
        security, designing for, 4
        simplicity, designing for, 5
    on building codes, 345–346
    on building costs, 425–426
    on building program, 224–225
    on ceilings, 904
    on codes, 345–346
    on collection storage, 506–508
    on construction, 388–389
    on conversion of non-library spaces to public libraries, 177–178
    on covenants, 345–346
    on display and exhibit areas, 627–628
    on dysfunctional design, 150–151
    on electrical systems, 806
    on elevators, 793–795
    entire list of rules for good and evil in library architecture, 9–20
    on floor coverings, 903–904
    on floors, 903, 904
    on funding, 442–443
    on handrails (railings), 793–795
    on HVAC systems, 815
    on lighting, 767–769
    on physical layout of library buildings, 76–78
    on plumbing systems, 825–826
    on program and study rooms, 617–618
    on ramps, 793–795
    on remodeling and expanding library buildings, 410–411
    on restrooms, 652–653
    on security, 883–884
    on service desks, 511–512, 561–562
    on staff facilities, 696–697
    on staff workrooms, 677–679
    on staircases, 793–795
    on storage spaces, 712–713
    on toilets, 634
    on user seating, 471–474
    on walls, 902–903, 904
    on zoning, 345–346

S

San Francisco (CA) Public Library, 63, 101
sanctuaries, conversion of church, 172–173
sanitary sewers, 823
Sannwald, William W., 190
savings set aside from operating funds as source for funding, 429
SBC (Standard Building Code), 337
schematic designs
    architects and, 39–40, 222, 234–239, 288
    contract mention of, 275
    evolution of, 40
    furniture layout included in, 57, 235, 239
    as grant application requirement, 440, 441
    items included in, 39
    LEED rating and, 235
    overview, 39–41, 234–239
    for remodeling and expanding library buildings, 393
    reviewing, 40
    for service desks, 518–519
    for staff conference rooms, 670
    for staff workrooms, 677
    table comparing designed square footage in each area of the building floor plan with the square footage in the building program, inclusion of, 222
school libraries
    bad site selection for, 294
    building costs, 415
    construction plaques, 380
    exit control, 546
    expansion and need for strong floors, 313
    money on hand as source for funding, 428
    referendums and bond issues as source for funding, 429
    security, single-staffed desk needing to provide, 526
    special site needs of, 330–331
schools
    building public libraries near, 327
    conversion to public library, 165–166
Scott, Walter, 305
screen porches as dysfunctional design concept, 140–141, 814
sculptures, outdoor, 625–626
SD. *See* schematic design
seated-height lending desks, 528
seating. *See* user seating
Seattle (WA) Public Library, 108, 500, 780
secluded spaces in staff lunchrooms, 689
second-choice firm, when hiring architects having a, 273
secure storage
    for staff workrooms, 668
    for technical services workrooms, 673
security
    for audiovisual equipment for program and

study rooms, 582
  bad sight lines and, 126–128
  in children's departments, 871–872
  dead-end stack aisles, preventing arrangement of, 491
  designing for, 4
  for display and exhibit areas, 624
  dysfunctional design, 38
  electronic theft-prevention systems
    bypass systems, 846
    false alarms, 846
    magnetic systems, 847–848
    overview, 845–846
    problem materials for, 850–851
    resonating circuit systems, 848
    RFID (radio-frequency identification) systems, 848–849
    self-check equipment and, 851
    space planning for, 846–847
  elevators and, 772
  entrance and exit control
    building codes and, 853–854
    desks for, 544
    key systems, 855–856
    overview, 853
    panic hardware (crash bars), 854–855
    proximity keys, 856–857
    swipe cards, 856–857
  evaluation of, 91–92
  fire protection systems
    escape routes, 864
    fire alarm systems, 859–860
    fire extinguishers, portable, 864–865
    overview, 859
    sprinkler systems, 860–864
  high-theft items, lending desks storing, 523–524
  humidity control, 865–866
  insurance
    automotive, 880
    builder's risk, 882
    buildings, insurance not relevant to, 882–883
    deductibles, 873–874
    flood, 880–881
    liability, 881–882
    major losses, covering, 873
    overview, 872
    property, 877–880
    purchasing, 875–877
    reductions in cost of, 876–877
    subrogation, 874
    terminology, 875
    types of insurance coverage, 873
    umbrella policies, 874
  intrusion alarms, 857–859
  laptop security provisions, 458
  lending desk placement and, 525–526
  library equipment, theft of, 851–853
  overview, 4, 827–828
  panic buttons at staff workstations, 548, 870
  personal possessions, theft of, 851–853
  portable alarm devices, 870–871
  privacy panels on carrels, 458
  program and study rooms, 591
  public libraries site selection, secure locations and, 326–327
  public relations and, 872
  reading terraces and, 146–147
  reduced illumination levels and, 744
  restrooms
    doorless restrooms, 648
    single-user restrooms, 647–648
    staff oversight, 646–647
    tornado shelters, restrooms as, 648–649
    video surveillance, 648
  rules on, 883–884
  self-check workstations and, 521
  service desks
    exit control, 546
    glass walls, use of, 547
    oversight of library spaces, 547
    overview, 145, 514
    staff members, security for, 548
  sight lines and, 64
  theft control systems
    collection oversight, improved, 842–844
    cost-benefit analysis of, 841–842
    electronic theft-prevention systems, 845–851
    high-risk materials, 840–841
    overview, 840
    sequestering theft-prone materials, 844–845
    unauthorized people, limiting use of library by, 845
  through building design (passive security systems)
    architectural features, dangerous, 839–840
    earthquake preparedness, 837–838
    entrances, single public, 832–833
    fire-resistant construction, 828–829
    flood-resistant construction, 830–832
    shared buildings, avoiding, 838
    sight lines, 833–835
    terraces, avoiding, 839
    trapped, avoiding situations where people can be, 835–836
    windows that can be opened by users, avoiding, 838
    windstorm shelters, 836–837
  video surveillance systems
    audio monitoring, 866–867
    equipment specifications, 867–868
    locations for video cameras, 869
    overview, 866–867

security boxes, 524
security gates, 518–519, 522, 525, 537, 869
security lighting, 755–756
seismic issues
    preparedness through building design, 837–838
    property insurance, 878
    shelving placement and, 498–499
self-check equipment
    electronic theft-prevention systems and, 851
    lending desks, located near, 537–538
    overview, 520–521
seminar rooms. *See* conference and seminar rooms
service desks
    barricades on, 555–556
    commercial service desk components, 560
    concierge desks, 544–545
    dysfunctional design of
        bad acoustics, 559–560
        bad lighting, 559
        color choices, 145, 554
        fortress desks, 555–556
        fragile top surfaces, 144, 553–554
        functionality, lack of, 548–550
        inflexibility, 550–552
        list of common dysfunctional features, 144–146
        obsolete features, 556–558
        sentiment, persistence of obsolete desks due to, 554
    entrance and exit control, desks for, 544
    evaluation of proposed
        schematic designs, evaluating, 518–519
        trial models of desks, 519–520
    functions of, 510–512, 514–517
    lending desks
        additional lending desk spaces, 537–540
        automated book-handling systems, 532–533
        bad acoustics, 559
        book returns, provisions for, 528–530
        drive-up book returns with receiving rooms, 533–535
        drive-up service windows, 536–537
        exterior book pickups, 536
        external book return bins, 535–536
        functions of, 520–524
        lending workrooms, 527–528
        obsolete features, 556–558
        off-desk workspaces, 530–531
        overview, 520
        placement of, 525–526
        queuing space, 531
        seated-height, 528
        sorting rooms, 532
        staff space, 526
        standing-height, 528
        terminology for, 524–525
        visual barricades on the user sides of, 531
    librarian's knowledge of, 560
    library supply company service desks, 560
    modular, 551–552
    movable, 552
    multifunction desks, 545
    overview, 509–510
    placement of, 512–514
    reference and reader guidance desks
        computer assistance, providing, 541
        functions of, 540–541
        heights, 541
        overview, 540
        placement of, 542–543
        reader guidance, providing, 540–541
        roving librarians and, 542
        service points at, determining number of, 541
        storage at, 543–544
        supervision, providing, 541
    requirements for, 514–517
    rules on, 511–512, 561–562
    security issues
        exit control, 546
        glass walls, use of, 547
        oversight of library spaces, 547
        staff members, security for, 548, 836
    special collections desks, 545
    types of, 520–546
    video cameras placed to record at, 869
    work counters behind, 530–531, 547, 676
settlement defined, 875
"The Seven Deadly Sins of Library Architecture" (Public Library Association 1998 conference program), 3
sewer backup insurance, 878–879
sewer systems, 823–824
shape of proposed site, evaluating, 296
shared buildings, avoiding, 838
shared equipment, spaces in staff workrooms for, 669
shared storage spaces, 705
Sharps containers for hypodermic needles in restrooms, 640, 691
shed roof ceilings, 124
shelf-mounted lighting, 740–741
shelving
    call number sequence and, 492–493
    cantilever shelving
        accessories for, 483–484
        advantages of, 478
        alternatives to, 487–489
        bookends, 482
        colors, 479
        compact shelving, 485–487, 892
        depths, 481–482
        dimensions for, 479–482
        heights, 479–481
        overview, 87, 477–478

specifying, 478–484
widths, 482
casters, shelving on, 500
collections, planning space for, 209–211
color of, 87, 479
conversion of existing non-library structures and, 34
cross aisles, 498
depth of, 86–87
display shelves
low-density shelving for intensive browsing, 505
novelty displays for children's books, 505
earthquake preparedness and, 837–838
electrical outlets, need for recessed, 492
end-supported shelves, 487–488
evaluating, 86–87
floor strength for book storage, 489
flow of materials from shelving unit to shelving unit, 81, 89
marking the contents of shelving ranges, 499–500
multi-deck shelving supported by shelving columns, 499
non-library shelving, 489
parallel rows, arranging shelving in, 490–491
perimeter shelving, 490
in restrooms, 640
seismic issues, 498–499
spacing of, 87
stack aisles
dead-end, 91, 491, 835–836
lighting for, 493–497
width of, 86, 476, 497–498
staff oversight, aisles oriented for best practical, 491–492
in staff workrooms, 665–666
for technical services workrooms, 673
tilting shelves, 87
user seating next to, 469
wood shelving, 488
shop drawings, 52, 246, 347, 357, 362–363
showers for staff, 695
shutting off
HVAC systems, 809, 814
sprinkler systems, 863–864
sick building syndrome, 886–887
side chairs (for seating at tables), 464–466
sidewalks as component of building costs, 421
sight lines
bad sight lines, 126–128, 834–835
beneficial, 833–834
hidden corners, 834
maintaining, 64
as passive security system, 833–835
radiating book stacks, 835
restrooms and, 127, 644, 835
from service desks, evaluating, 518

stack orientation, 833
theft and, 842
windows, internal, 833–834
signage, directional, 67–69, 70, 81
signing off on a project, items to receive before, 52
simplicity, designing for, 5
single-user restrooms, 647–648, 691
single-user tables, 453
sinks
in children's craft and story rooms, 605
in children's departments, 674
in restrooms, 636, 691
in staff conference rooms, 670
in staff lunchrooms, 685
in staff workrooms, 660, 819
site acquisition
as component of building costs, 418–419
cost estimates for, 418
site configuration and evaluation of potential sites, 302
site development as component of building costs, 420–421
site selection
bad sites, examples of, 293–294
dysfunctional design concepts and, 148
evaluation of potential sites
archeology, 318–319
bad neighbors, examples of, 305–306
brownfield sites, 303–305
buildable, confirming site is, 419
compass orientation, 319–320
easements, 320
entrances, compass orientation of, 419
floodplains, 301–302
historic buildings and neighborhoods, 315–318
land ownership, 320–321
overview, 294–295
professional assistance in, 295–297
site configuration, 302
site topography, 302–303
size of site, 306–315, 419
soil conditions, 297–298
subsurface water, 301
surface water runoff detention and retention, 300–301
utilities, 298–300
zoning and, 419
expansion options as factor in choosing site, 312
overview, 33–34, 36, 293–294
rules on, 333–335
special site needs of libraries
academic libraries, 329–330
public libraries, 321–329
school libraries, 330–331
special libraries, 331–332
site topography and evaluation of potential sites, 302–303

size of site
    expansion space, 309–315
    footprint of building, 307
    overview, 306
    parking and driveways, 307–308
    plantings and landscapings, 309
    setbacks, 308–309
    surface water detention, 309
skylights
    acoustical problems caused by, 96
    artificial skylights, 99
    connecting old and new buildings with, 98, 766
    covering, 397
    as dysfunctional design element, 37, 72, 96–99
    energy wasted by use of, 98
    evaluating, 82
    glare from, 96–97
    lighting and, 97, 749, 765–766
    in staff workrooms, 659
slab-on-grade construction
    ductwork and, 812
    floor strength and, 158
    overview, 75
    shelving and, 475
slippery treads, 107
slope-top tables, 459–460
sloped ceilings, 124–125, 901
sloped sites, evaluation of, 302–303
sloppy work, architects who do, 286
small displays of books of current interest located near lending desks, 539
smoke detectors, 859
snappy rules for good and evil in library architecture. *See* rules
soap dispensers in restrooms, 636–638
sodium vapor lamps, 729
sofas, 462
soffits
    defined, 128
    excessive use of soffits as dysfunctional design concept, 128–129, 551
    lighting problems and, 748
    perimeter, 747–748
    service desks and, 550, 552
soft openings, 54
soft seating
    armchairs, 460–461
    evaluating, 86, 87
    love seats, 462
    overview, 460
    problems with, 463
    rocking chairs, 462–463
    sofas, 462
soil conditions and evaluation of potential sites, 297–298
sorting rooms, 71, 532
sound. *See* acoustics
south light, 759, 760
south or southeast entrances, 61, 319

space availability as reason for phased construction, 409
space estimation
    for collection storage, 209–211, 506
    combining numbers to estimate actual amount of space needed, 212–214
    extra space, 211–212
    overview, 208
    quick space estimates using formulas, 223
    sources of planning numbers, 208–209
space needs, site selection and, 295
spaces and contents, in building program enumeration of required, 205–207
spacing
    for light fixtures, 748
    of shelving, 87
    for user seating, 451
special appropriations as source for funding, 442
special collections desks, 545
special libraries
    bad site selection for, 294
    building costs, 415
    expansion and need for strong floors, 313
    money on hand as source for funding, 428
    security, single-staffed desk needing to provide, 526
    special site needs of, 331–332
specialized staff workrooms
    children's departments, 674–676
    graphic arts, 670–672
    technical services, 672–674
specification books, 349
specifications, construction drawings and, 244–246, 348–349
speeches during ribbon cuttings, 54
spinner racks, 501–502
splat defined, 450
sprinkler heads, 863
sprinkler systems
    building codes and, 860
    dry pipe systems, 862
    evaluation of, 91
    expansion of building and, 394
    fear of sprinkler systems and ruined book collections, 860–861
    fire protection systems, 860–864
    inert gas systems, 863
    insurance and, 876
    overview, 860
    pre-action systems, 862–863
    shutting off, 863–864
    sprinkler heads, 863
    wet pipe systems, 861
square tables for two users, 454
stack aisles
    dead-end, 91, 491, 835–836
    lighting for, 83, 493–497
    width of, 86, 476, 497–498
stack orientation and sight lines, 833

stacking chairs for use in program and study rooms, 570
staff and management
    fire extinguishers, training on use of, 865
    health and life insurance, 883
    interviews with, 188–190
    inventorying for theft by, 841
    oversight by
        conference and seminar rooms, 599
        restroom security, 646–647
        shelving placement and, 491–492
    parking for, 160
    in planning groups, 280
    salaries as component of operating costs, 423–424
    service desks and, 514–515, 548
    theft, staff time spent on, 841–842
    workarounds, staff members' use of, 188–189
staff facilities
    bike storage, 695
    coat storage, 692–693
    conference rooms, 669–670
    lockers, 693, 852
    lunchrooms. *See* staff lunchrooms
    mailboxes, 690, 694–695
    omissions in, 681–682
    overview, 681–682
    purse storage, 693, 852
    restrooms, 661, 683, 690–691
    rules on, 696–697
    showers, 695
    valuables, place to lock up, 693
    workrooms. *See* staff workrooms
staff lunchrooms
    bulletin boards, 688, 690
    circulation space, 690
    computer workstations, 688
    decor, 689
    entertainment, 689
    food preparation and serving
        buffet shelves, 686, 689
        cabinets and drawers, 685–686
        counters, 685, 689
        dishwashers, 685, 690
        electrical circuits for, 686
        exhaust fans, 687
        garbage disposals, 685
        microwaves, stoves, and coffee makers, 683–684
        plumbing connections for, 686
        refrigerators, 684, 690
        sinks, 685
    functions of, 682
    location for, 682–683
    picture boards, 688, 690
    restrooms and, 683
    seating, 687, 690
    secluded spaces, 689
    space needs for, 689–690
    tables, 687, 690
    vending machines, 687–688
staff workrooms
    architectural features
        built-in furnishings, 661
        clothes washers and dryers, 661
        lighting, 659–660
        restrooms, 661, 683
        sinks, 660
        temperature control, 661
        ventilation, 661
        water, running, 660
        windows to the rest of the library, 660
        wiring, 659
    electrical outlets in, 804
    furnishings
        built-in cabinetry, 668
        bulletin boards, 668
        chairs, 663–664
        coat and purse storage, 665, 692–693
        desks, 662–663
        file storage, 666
        flexibility in, 669
        modular office system workstations, 663
        open floor space, 667
        paper shredders, 667
        printers, 667
        refrigerators, 667–668
        secure storage, 668
        shelving, 665–666
        storage cabinets, 665
        telephones, 667
        valuables, place to lock up, 665, 693
        ventilation, 668
        visitors, space for, 664
        wall space, 666
        worktables, 664
    general needs for, 655–657
    group work areas, 656
    individual workrooms, 657–658
    interior glass walls in, 657
    lending workrooms, 527–528
    natural light in, 657
    overview, 655–657
    plumbing systems for
        washbasins, 819
        washers and dryers, 819–820
    in public areas, 676
    rules on, 677–679
    shared equipment, spaces for, 669
    size requirements for, 677
    specialized workrooms
        children's departments, 674–676
        graphic arts, 670–672
        technical services, 672–674
    staff conference rooms, 669–670
    two-phase building programs, 221
stainless steel handrails (railings), 789, 790
staircase-like structures, 785–786

staircases
- acrophobia and, 103
- architects and, 110
- in atriums, 783–784
- balusters too widely spaced, 106
- broadloom carpet used on, 894
- building programs, wording for staircase design in, 110–111
- with central openings, 784–785
- circular staircases, 105
- curved staircases, 105, 779, 780
- diagonal, 779
- dysfunctional design, 37, 103–111
- elevators, staircases too far from, 110
- enclosed staircases as emergency exits, 778
- fires and, 786–787
- floating staircases, 104–105, 131, 781–782
- glass walls adjacent to, 785
- handrails
  - climbable, 106
  - grabbed, that can't be, 109–110
  - not perpendicular to run of staircase, 105–106
- with light fixtures that aren't reachable, 108–109
- long flights of stairs, 778
- noise, staircases that transmit too much, 110
- northwest exterior flight of steps, dysfunctional design of, 62
- open or transparent risers, 107, 131, 782–783
- overly long staircases, 108
- overview, 37, 777–778
- rules on, 793–795
- space and energy, staircases that waste, 110
- staircase-like structures, 785–786
- under storage spaces, 701
- strangely configured, 778–779, 839
- treads
  - curving upward into the walls, 108
  - with drop-offs at the ends, 108
  - oddly-shaped, 105, 779–781
  - slippery, 107
  - transparent, 107
- unnecessary, 786

stall enclosures for restrooms, 634–635
stalled elevators, 774
standing-height lending desks, 528
stangely-shaped tables, 449
state historic preservation agencies assisting with historic buildings and neighborhoods, 317
state law and architects, 227–228
steel beams, signing, 377–378
steel cantilever shelving. See cantilever shelving
stone used in service desktops, 553
stonework in historic exteriors, 401
stools, 468
storage cabinets in staff workrooms, 665
storage spaces
- adjacencies, 709
- assigned, 702–704
- basements as, 702
- building programs, describing storage spaces in, 709–711
- for children's craft and story rooms, 605–606
- for children's departments, 674–675
- closets for program and study rooms
  - audiovisual storage closets, 584
  - book sale closets, 585, 706
  - calculating space for, 566–567
  - computer storage closets, 585
  - furniture storage closets, 583, 705
  - inadequate storage space, 614
  - maker space equipment closets, 586, 706
  - outside groups, closets for, 586, 706
  - overview, 582–583
  - program and craft supplies closets, 584, 706
- configuration of, 709–710
- dimensions, 710
- evaluation of, 87–88
- flexibility of, 710
- furnishings for, 710
- irrelevant items not intruding on, 710
- items requiring assigned storage, 703–704
- items retrieved from, lending desk staff and, 522–523
- locations of, 701–702
- for mechanical equipment
  - HVAC equipment, 709
  - ladders, 708
  - outdoor equipment, 707
  - vehicle storage, 709
- overview, 699–701
- protecting, 711
- at reference and reader guidance desks, 543–544
- rules on, 712–713
- secure storage
  - for staff workrooms, 668
  - for technical services workrooms, 673
- shared, 705
- size for, 709
- specified items fitting into allotted spaces, verifying, 710
- staircases, under, 701
- two-phase building programs and, 221

storerooms. See storage space
storm drains, 823–824
storm sewers, 823–824
story hour pits, 609, 785–786, 839
stoves for staff lunchrooms, 683–684
strangely configured staircases, 778–779
strangely-shaped spaces in internal layout, avoiding, 65
stretchers defined, 450
strip mall conversion to public library, 168–169
structural shapes, 61
study models, 42
study rooms
- as family computer rooms, 602
- furnishings for, 602

locking doors for, 602
overview, 601
supervision of, 601
style defined, 450
sub-basements, 832
subrogation, 874
subsurface water, 301
suicides, atriums and, 101, 784, 839
supervision
    of reference and reader guidance desks, 541
    of study rooms, 601
surface water runoff detention and retention, 300–301
surveys
    building program use of, 197–198
    fees for, 423
swinging doors used to define staff areas, 515, 548
swipe cards, 856–857
switching as energy saving method, 342

T

T-shaped space in internal layout, using, 66
table lamps, 458, 459
table of contents in building program, 198–201
tables
    with 110-volt electrical outlets, using, 449
    age of users, adaptations based on, 458–460
    aprons, tables without, 449, 455
    carrels, 453
    color of, 456, 457, 720
    conference and seminar room, 571–572
    configurations for, 453–455
    custom computer tables, 455
    electrical outlets in, 456
    evaluating, 86
    folding, 571
    game tables, 455
    index tables, 454
    leg clearance, 455
    legs, requirements for, 456
    machine tables for computers, 455
    options for, 458
    privacy panels on carrels, 458
    program and study rooms, 571, 707
    rectangular tables, 449, 454
    requirements for, 455–457
    round tables, 449, 454
    single-user tables, 453
    slope-top tables, 459–460
    square tables for two users, 454
    staff lunchrooms, 687, 690
    stangely-shaped, 449
    tops, requirements for, 455–456
    for very young children, 455
    on wheels, 571
    wire management troughs on, 458
tamper-resistant (childproof) outlets, 802–803
tarps used to protect floors in program and study rooms, 589
task lighting, 117, 738–741

Tattle Tape (3M), 848
technical equipment, space for, 122–123
technical services, storage of supplies for, 704
technical services workrooms, 672–674
telephone calls answered at lending desk, 523
telephones
    in staff conference rooms, 670
    in staff workrooms, 667
    wall-mounted telephone with access code in children's craft and story rooms, including a, 607
temperature control, 661, 808, 810–811
temporary exhibits. *See* display and exhibit areas
ten-month post occupancy evaluation, 55
terminology
    for electrical systems, 798–799
    for insurance, 875
    for lending desks, 524–525
    for lighting, 718–719
    for user seating, 450
terraces, reading, 10, 78, 92, 146–147, 839
terracotta, architectural, 400
terrazzo floors, 897–898
theft control systems
    collection oversight, improved, 842–844
    cost-benefit analysis of, 841–842
    electronic theft-prevention systems, 845–851
    high-risk materials, 840–841
    overview, 840
    sequestering theft-prone materials, 844–845
    sight lines and, 842
    unauthorized people, limiting use of library by, 845
theft of library property, insurance for, 879
thermostats, 810–811
tilting shelves, 87, 483
timing as reason for phased construction, 409
toilet paper dispensers in restrooms, 635
toilets in restrooms, 632–634
top rail defined, 450
topping out, 378–379
tornados, shelter from, 648–649, 836–837
tours of the work in progress, 379–380
toxicity of building materials, 886–887
traditional reference service, 540
traffic flow
    atriums and, 101
    overview, 67–71
transgender users, restroom accommodations for, 646
transparent plastic used in service desktops, 553
transportation, building public libraries near, 328–329
trapped, avoiding situations where people can be, 835–836
trash removal and deliveries, parking and driveways for, 308
treads
    curving upward into the walls, 108
    design of, 777

treads (*continued*)
    with drop-offs at the ends, 108
    oddly-shaped, 105, 108, 779–781
    rubber tile used on, 896
    slippery, 107
    transparent, 107
trial models of desks, 519–520
triangular rooms, 65
trim and moldings as punch list items, 385
troffers, 735–736
tubs for board books, 505
two-phase building programs, 221
two-phase construction, 51, 371–372, 645
two-position chairs, 464

U

umbrella policies, 874
unassignable space, estimating, 211–212
unauthorized people, limiting use of library by, 845
underfloor air ducts, 812
undersized rooms as program and study rooms, 614
underwriter defined, 875
"(Un)desidrata: 27 Snappy Rules for Good and Evil in Library Architecture" (Public Library Association 2000 conference program), 3
unexpected conditions during construction process, change orders and, 363
unisex restrooms, 646, 691
United States Green Buildings Council, 344
university libraries. *See* academic libraries
University of Chicago, 330
University of Illinois, 106, 109, 313
unprocessed books, storage of, 703
unreachable or hard to reach light fixtures, 133–134, 749–754
uplighting, 733–735, 756–757
upward expansion, 311
urinals in restrooms, 635–636
user input before design, building program providing an opportunity for, 187
user seating
    best options for, 449
    chairs. *See* chairs
    evaluating, 86
    examples of bad decisions on, 448
    furniture firm booths at library conferences, visiting, 449
    overview, 447–450
    placement of
        backs to the room, seating without users', 470–471
        clearances, adequate, 468–469
        movable seating, 470
        shelving, seating next to, 469
        windows, seating by, 469
    for program and study rooms, 570–572
    quantities and types of, 450–451
    rules on, 471–474
    spacing for, 451
    in staff lunchrooms, 687, 690
    tables. *See* tables
    terminology, 450
utilities
    as component of building costs, 420, 421
    in conversion of non-library spaces to public libraries
        lack of utilities as common problem in, 159
        utility hookups as good reason for, 156
    evaluation of potential sites and, 298–300

V

vacant landmark structure availability as bad reason for conversion of non-library spaces to public libraries, 157
valuable objects, insurance for, 879
valuables, place for staff to lock up, 665, 693
value engineering, 47
VAT (vinyl asbestos tile), 395, 896
VCT (vinyl composition tile), 896
vehicle storage, 709
veiling reflectance, 723
vending machines in staff lunchrooms, 687–688
ventilation. *See also* HVAC (heating, ventilating, and air conditioning) systems
    in graphic arts workrooms, 671
    in restrooms, 640–641
    in staff workrooms, 661, 668
vertical blinds used to control natural light, 761, 763
vertical display cases, 622
video cameras for surveillance systems, 867–868
video recording capability for program and study rooms, 582
video surveillance systems
    audio monitoring, 866–867
    equipment specifications
        central units, 868
        installation of equipment, 868
        overview, 867
        video cameras, 867–868
    locations for video cameras, 869
    overview, 866–867
    for restrooms, 648
vinyl tile floors, 395, 896
vinyl wallpaper used to prevent damage to drywall and paint, 891
visible light defined, 719
visitors, space in staff workrooms for, 664
visual barricades on the user sides of lending desks, 531
visual fire alarms, 859
volt defined, 799

W

waivers of lien, 229
walk off mats, 900
walk-up exterior book returns, 869
wall coverings in restrooms, 651
wall-mounted telephone with access code in children's craft and story rooms, including a, 607
wall-mounted toilets, 632, 634, 691
wall-mounted washbasins, 636
wall space
    for hanging artworks, 623
    in staff workrooms, 666
wallpaper used to prevent damage to drywall and paint, vinyl, 891
walls
    bearing walls
        in conversion of non-library spaces to public libraries, 35, 160–161
        inflexibility of, 125
        in remodeling and expanding library buildings problems, 395–396
    curved walls, 61, 74
    double stud (staggered stud) walls used to limit sound transmission, 575
    glass walls
        natural light and, 761
        service desks and, 513–514, 547
        staircases, adjacent to, 785
        in study rooms, 64, 126, 601
    location of, early tweaking of, 373–374
    placement of items in walls, marking, 373
    problems with
        damage to drywall and paint, preventing, 888–891
        overview, 888
        sound transmission, controlling, 888
    rules on, 902–903, 904
    unnecessary walls, avoiding, 63
warning horns, 859
warranty period, 388
washbasins. *See* sinks
washers and dryers
    for children's departments, 674
    overview, 819–820
    in staff workrooms, 661
water features
    defined, 112
    as dysfunctional design concept, 112–113, 840
    evaluation of, 92
    overview, 37
    and plumbing systems, 821–822
waterless urinals, 635–636
watt defined, 799
welcome, experiencing a sense of, 81
western light, 758
wet pipe sprinkler systems, 861
wheelchair users. *See* accessibility

Wheeler, Joseph, 321
white grout in ceramic tile leading to maintenance problems, 134–135
window seats, 466–467
windows
    in children's craft and story rooms, 606
    for children's departments, 675
    in conversion of non-library spaces to public libraries, 35, 157
    crooked windows as punch list items, 386
    dysfunctional design concepts and, 37
    historic exteriors and, 401
    internal windows and sight lines, 833–834
    open windows and HVAC systems, 814
    outside world, readers having views of the, 766–767
    placement of, 71–73
    in remodeling and expanding library buildings, 398–399
    small-pane windows replaced with double-pane, 397
    in staff workrooms, 660
    theft and, 838, 843–844
    user seating by, 469
windstorm shelters, 836–837
wire management troughs on tables, 458
wireless signals for program and study rooms, 580
wiring, electrical. *See* electrical wiring
wood shelving, 488
wooden ceilings, 902
wooden desktops used in service desks, 553
work counters, 530–531
workarounds, staff members' use of, 188–189
workers compensation insurance, 883
workspaces, staff. *See* staff workrooms

Y

Yeats, W. B., 95

Z

zoning
    code regulations and zoning allowing building on proposed site, evaluation of, 296
    defined, 337
    overview, 338–339
    remodeling and expanding library buildings, changes in zoning and, 404
    rules on, 345–346